MORALIA IN JOB

MORALS ON THE BOOK OF JOB

BY

SAINT GREGORY THE GREAT

THE FIRST POPE OF THAT NAME

TRANSLATED

WITH NOTES.

IN THREE VOLUMES.

VOL. I. – PARTS I. AND II.

BOOKS I–X.

EX FONTIBUS COMPANY

2012

Visit us

DATE OF THIS PUBLICATION: 2015-02-20

CONTACT@EXFONTIBUS.COM

EXFONTIBUSCOMPANY@GMAIL.COM

HTTP://WWW.EXFONTIBUS.COM

HTTP://WWW.FACEBOOK.COM/EXFONT

THE

MORALIA IN JOB

OF

ST. GREGORY THE POPE,

OR

AN EXPOSITION ON THE BOOK OF BLESSED JOB.

FIRST VOLUME—BOOKS I–X.

CONTENTS.

THE

MORALIA IN JOB

OF

ST. GREGORY THE POPE,

OR

AN EXPOSITION ON THE BOOK OF BLESSED JOB.

THE EPISTLE

Wherein he explains the time, occasion, division, plan, and the method of discourse and of interpretation pursued in his work.

To the Most Devout and Holy Brother, my fellow Bishop Leander[*], Gregory, the servant of God's servants.

WHEN I knew you long since at Constantinople, my most **I.**
blessed brother, at the time that I was kept there by the affairs[†]

[*] Leander, who is honoured as a Saint and Doctor in Spain, was a native of Carthagena; his father Severianus was brother in law to Theodoric king of the Ostrogoths. He early devoted himself to a monastic life, and after a long continuance in it he was made Bishop of Seville, where he maintained the Faith against the Arianism which then prevailed, and received Herminigild, who reigned there under his father Liuvigild, into the Church. He went on an embassy to the Emperor Tiberius as presently stated, after which he returned to Spain, but was banished by Liuvigild, who, however, on his deathbed, appointed him tutor to his son Recared, whom he converted from Arianism, and with his assistance established the Catholic Faith amongst the Wisigoths and the Suevi. He took part (and perhaps presided, see Baronius An. 589.x.ix. and xliv. Boll. Act. Sanct. Ap. xiii. p. 277) in the third Council of Toledo, in which the Goths were united to the Catholic Church, A.D. 589. He died in 595. He wrote a rule for Virgins to his sister Florentina, which is extant in Holstein's Codex Regularum, a Homily of his, on the conversion of the Goths, accompanies the acts of the Synod of Toledo, and the Mozarabic Missal is said by some to be founded on one arranged by him; his other works are lost. See Cave, Hist. Lit. an. 585. also the Isidoriana of Arevalus in his edition of St. Isidore, Rome 1797. There are three epistles of St. Gregory to Leander. Lib. i. Ep. 43. Lib. V. Ep. 49, and Lib. Ix. 121. accompanying the Pallium. His brother Fulgentius, Bp. of Carthagena and Eceja, Bolland. Jan. xiv. p. 971. and his sister Florentina, Ap. xiv. and Jun xx, who devoted herself to a life of Virginity, are locally honoured as Saints. He was succeeded in the See of Seville (then called *Hispalis*,) by his younger brother St. Isidore.

[†] *Responsa*, these were all matters concerning the Roman See, that were brought

of the Apostolical See, and that you had been brought thither by an embassage, with which you were charged, on counts touching the faith of the Wisigoths*, I then detailed in your ears all that displeased me in myself, since for late and long I declined the grace of conversion, and after that I had been inspired with an heavenly affection I thought it better to be still shrouded in the secular habit. For though I had now disclosed to me what I should seek of the love of things eternal, yet long-established custom had so cast its chains upon me, that I could not change my outward habit: and while my purpose [*animus*] still compelled me to engage in the service of this world as it were in semblance only, many influences began to spring up against

---

under the notice of the Emperor, and the person intrusted with them was entitled Apocrisiarius. He was the Pope's Ambassador at the Imperial Court with varying powers. He was one of the Cardinal Deacons, for which reason St. Gregory on being appointed to this office, was ordained Deacon, vide Du Cange in voce Apocrisiarius; also Bingham Antiq. b. iii. c. xiii. s. 6. where the office is correctly described. Vide Baronius Ann. tom. x. p. 378. (an. 583. xii. xiii.) Gibbon speaks of St. Gregory's services at the Imperial Court thus; "As soon as he had received the character of Deacon, Gregory was sent to reside at the Imperial Court, and he boldly assumed in the name of St. Peter a tone of independent dignity which would have been criminal and dangerous in the most illustrious layman of the Empire." See his History c. xlv. London 1813. t. viii. p. 164. also p. 143.

* Herminigild was deposed by Liuvigild, chiefly, it seems, for embracing the Catholic Faith. The contemporary writers however, both St. Gregory of Tours and St. Isidore, consider him to have acted wrongly toward his father. Baronius indeed says that Leander went on an embassy to ask help for him from the Emperor, which he obtained, but the Greek officers betrayed his cause. An ancient Roman Breviary however says he went to Constantinople to attend a Council, 'Pro confirmandis capitulis Sanctæ Trinitatis,' to confirm the articles on the Holy Trinity. This he may have done previously, the fifth General Council being A.D. 553. Herminigild was unsuccessful, and obliged to leave his kingdom.

He found means however to return into Spain, and maintained himself by the help of the Greeks against his father, and it is at this time that his conduct in attempting a surprise is severely blamed by St. Gregory of Tours, Hist. Franc. vi. 43. He was at last overpowered, and taken prisoner. St. Gregory of Rome, Dial. iii. 31. says, that he was then urged by his father to communicate with an Arian Bishop, and, after resisting alike promises and threats, was put to death. He also mentions a supernatural light surrounding his body. These circumstances are not noticed by St. Isidore or St. Gregory of Tours. Liuvigild however very soon after acknowledged privately the true faith, and recalled Leander, and placed his son and successor Recared under his direction. Herminigild is honoured as a Martyr by the Latin Church, April 13. See Isidoriana caps. xviii. and lxxxix. S. Isid. Hist. Goth. c. 49. The account of Mariana is more circumstantial, but seems partly imaginary.

me from caring for this same world, so that the tie which kept me to it was now no longer in semblance only, but what is more serious, in my own mind. At length being anxious to avoid all these inconveniences, I sought the haven of the monastery, and having left all that is of the world, as at that time I vainly believed, I came out naked from the shipwreck of human life. For as the vessel that is negligently moored, is very often (when the storm waxes violent) tossed by the water out of its shelter on the safest shore, so under the cloak of the Ecclesiastical office, I found myself* plunged on a sudden in a sea of secular matters, and because I had not held fast the tranquillity of the monastery when in possession, I learnt by losing it, how closely it should have been held. For whereas the virtue of obedience was set against my own inclination to make me take the charge of ministering at the holy Altar, I was led to undertake that upon the grounds of the Church requiring it [*sub Ecclesiae colore*], which, if it might be done with impunity, I should get quit of by† a second time withdrawing myself; and subsequently notwithstanding my unwillingness

---

* He was sent to Constantinople as Apocrisiarius immediately upon his ordination, Bar. an. 583. The Benedictive Biographer places the event earlier, in 578. or 579. life. l. i. c. 5. op. t. iv. p. 211.

† There is an allusion to this in the 'Pastoral Rule' which begins thus, "You blame me, most dear brother, with kind and lowly purpose, that I would have escaped the burthens of the Pastoral charge by keeping myself concealed, which lest any should take to be light, I set forth in the writing of this present work all that reflection has impressed on me concerning their weightiness." In speaking again of the responsibility of the office he says, "It is hence that the very Mediator between God and man shunned to take a kingdom upon earth, Who, surpassing the knowledge and faculties even of spirits above, rules in the heavens before the world began. For who could have exercised authority over man so entirely without blame as He Who would only be governing those, whom He had Himself formed? But because He had for this reason come in the flesh that He might not only redeem man by His Passion, but also instruct him by His conversation, to give an example to those that follow Him, He refused to be made King, but voluntarily consented to the stock of the Cross. He eschewed the proffered glory of exaltation, He sought the woe of an ignominious death, &c." ch. iii. [Lastly, Battifol, in his 'St. Gregory the Great,' p. 22, records that "a rather ordinary inscription," composed "by Gregory himself," appears on the portrait of him at his own Monastery of St. Andrew of the *Clivus Scauri*. It is a prayer to Christ: Christe potens Domine nostri largitor honoris / Indultum officium solita pietate guberna; that is, "O Christ, mighty Lord, giver of our honor"—that is, the post of bishop—"with Thy customary goodness, guide and govern the office bestowed upon us."]

and reluctance, at the very time when the ministry of the Altar was a heavy weight, the further burden of the Pastoral charge was fastened on me, which I now find so much the more difficulty in bearing, as I feel myself to be unequal to it, and as I cannot take breath in any comfortable assurance in myself. For because, now that the end of the world is at hand*, the times are disturbed by reason of the multiplied evils thereof, and we ourselves, who are supposed to be devoted to the inner mysteries, are thus become involved in outward cares; just as it happened then also when I was brought to the ministry of the Altar, this was brought about for me without my knowledge, viz. that I should receive the mighty charge of the Holy Order, to the end that I might be quartered under less restraint [*licentious excubarem*] in an earthly palace, whither indeed I was fol-

---

* 'Amidst the arms of the Lombards and under the despotism of the Greeks, we again enquire into the fate of Rome, which had reached about the closer of the sixth century the lowest period of her depression.' Gibbon, Decline and Fall, Lond. 1813. t. viii. p. 158, see also p. 159, 169. and S. Greg. Orat. ad Pleb. Rom. t. i. p. 1660. Ben. Bar. Ann. A.D. 590. xvii. xxii. xxiv. On the end of the world being at hand, St. Gregory thus delivers himself in Homily on St. Luke xxi. 25. &c. "Of all which (viz. the signs described by our Lord,) some we see already accomplished, others we dread to be upon us nigh at hand. For we see already that nation rises up against nation and that the push and press of them has settled upon the lands worse in our own times than we read in records. That earthquakes overwhelm countless cities, ye know how often we have heard from other parts of the world. We endure pestilences without pause, but signs in the sun and moon, and stars, we do not at all as yet see manifestly; but that even these things are not far off, we collect from the mere change of the atmosphere already, though before Italy was given up to be smitten by the sword of a Gentile foe, we beheld[a] fiery ranks in the heavens, the very blood itself of the human race, which was afterwards spilt, streaming. Further the confounding of the waves and of the sea has not as yet sprung up in new sort, &c." Hom. i. in Ev. §. i. see also sects. 3. 5. "But because I being unworthy and weak have taken upon me the old and much battered vessel, for the waves make a way in on all sides, and the rotten planks shattered by a daily and vehement tempest tell of shipwreck, I beseech you by Almighty God, to stretch the hand of your prayers in this my peril, since you may implore mercy even so much the more earnestly, in proportion as you also stand the further removed from the agitated state of calamity which we undergo in this land." Ep. iv. 6. 1. written soon after he had succeeded to the Pontificate. [[a] This was probably the appearance of the Aurora Borealis, which Speed describes as 'fiery dragons.' Hist. p. 300. and Matthew of Westminster as 'appearances of lances and fiery spears.' Matth. of West. p. 101. Speed speaks also of a shower of blood, and *blood crosses falling on men's garments*.]

lowed by many of my brethren from the monastery, who were attached to me by a kindred affection [*germana*]. Which happened, I perceive, by Divine dispensation, in order that by their example, as by an anchored cable, I might ever be kept fast to the tranquil shore of prayer, whenever I should be tossed by the ceaseless waves of secular affairs. For to their society I fled as to the bosom of the safest port from the rolling swell, and from the waves of earthly occupation; and though that office which withdrew me from the monastery had with the point of its employments stabbed me to death as to my former tranquillity of life, yet in their society, by means of the appeals of diligent reading, I was animated with the yearnings of daily renewed compunction. It was then that it seemed good to those same brethren, you too adding your influence, as you yourself remember, to oblige me by the importunity of their requests to set forth the book of blessed Job; and as far as the Truth should inspire me with powers, to lay open to them those mysteries of such depth; and they made this too an additional burden which their petition laid upon me, that I would not only unravel the words of the history in allegorical senses, but that I would go on to give to the allegorical senses the turn of a moral exercise, with the addition of somewhat yet harder, that I would crown [or 'fortify,' *cingerem*] the several meanings with testimonies*, and that the testimonies, which I brought forward, should they chance to appear involved, should be disentangled by the aid of additional explanation.

II. At first however, when in this obscure work, which hitherto had been thoroughly treated by none before us, I learnt the extent and character of the task to which I was forced, being overcome and wearied with the mere burthen of hearing of it, I confess that I sank under it. Yet immediately, when, in a strait between my alarms and my devout aspirations, I lifted up the eyes of my mind to the Bestower of all gifts [James 1, 17], waiving my scruples, I fixed my thoughts on this, that what an affection flowing from the hearts of my brethren enjoined upon me, could not certainly be impossible, I despaired, indeed, of being a match for these things, but, stronger for my very despair of myself, I forthwith raised my hopes to Him, by Whom the tongue of the dumb is opened, Who *maketh the lips of*

* i.e. the texts of Holy Scripture, see Vinc. Ler. Common. c. xxv.

babes to speak eloquently, [Wisd. 10, 21], Who has marked the undistinguished and brute brayings of an ass with the intelligible measures of human speech. What wonder, then, that a simple man should receive understanding from Him, Who whenever He willeth, utters His truth by the mouths of the very beasts of burthen? Armed then with the strength which this thought supplied, I roused mine own drought to explore so deep a well; and though the life of those, to whom I was compelled to give my interpretation, was far above me, yet I thought it no harm if the leaden pipe should supply streams of water for the service of men. Whereupon, without further delay, I delivered the former parts of the book, in presence*, to the same brethren assembled before me; and because I found my time to be then somewhat more free, in treating of the latter portion I used dictation; and when longer intervals of time were at my disposal, many things being added, a small number omitted, and some few left as they were, all that had been taken down in my presence as I spoke, I arranged in books with amendments. For when I was giving the last part by dictation, I in like manner carefully considered the style in which I had spoken the first part, so that my business was both with regard to those parts, which I had given orally, by going through them with a careful correction, to bring them up to somewhat like dictation, and with regard to what I had dictated, that it should not greatly differ from the style of colloquial delivery; so that the one being drawn out, and the other contracted, that which unlike modes produced might be formed into a not inconsistent whole. Though it must be added that the third portion of this work I have so left for the most part as I gave it by word of mouth, because the brethren, drawing me away to other things, would not have this to be corrected with any great degree of exactness. Pursuing my object of obeying their instructions, which I must confess were sufficiently numerous, now by the work of exposition, now by the flights of contemplation, and now by moral instruction, I have completed this work extending through thirty-five books [*volumina*], and six tomes [*codicibus*], and hence I shall be often found therein to put rather in the back-ground the order of exposition, and to employ myself at

* The work was begun while St. Gregory was at Constantinople, A.D. 583. and it was being completed in the first year of his Pontificate, A.D. 590. Bar. t. x. an. 583. s. xxxvi.

greater length upon the wide field of contemplation and of moral instruction. But yet whosoever is speaking concerning God, must be careful to search out thoroughly whatsoever furnishes moral instruction to his hearers; and should account that to be the right method of ordering his discourse, if, when opportunity for edification requires it, he turn aside for a useful purpose from what he had begun to speak of; for he that treats of sacred writ should follow the way of a river, for if a river, as it flows along its channel, meets with open valleys on its side, into these it immediately turns the course of its current, and when they are copiously supplied, presently it pours itself back into its bed. Thus unquestionably, thus should it be with everyone that treats of the Divine Word, that if, in discussing: any subject, he chance to find at hand any occasion of seasonable edification, he should, as it were, force the streams of discourse towards the adjacent valley, and, when he has poured forth enough upon its level of instruction, fall back into the channel of discourse which he had proposed to himself.

III. But be it known that there are some parts, which we go through in a historical exposition, some we trace out in allegory upon an investigation of the typical meaning, some we open in the lessons of moral teaching alone, allegorically conveyed, while there are some few which, with more particular care, we search out in all these ways together, exploring them in a threefold method. For first, we lay the historical foundations; next, by pursuing the typical sense, we erect a fabric of the mind to be a strong hold of faith; and moreover as the last step, by the grace of moral instruction, we, as it were, clothe the edifice with an overcast of colouring. Or at least how are the declarations of truth to be accounted of, but as food* for the refreshment of the mind? These being handled with the alternate application of various methods, we serve up the viands of discourse† in such sort as to prevent all disgust in the reader, thus invited as our guest, who, upon consideration of the various things presented to him, is to take that which he determines to be the choicest. Yet it sometimes happens that we neglect to interpret the plain words of the historical account, that we may not be too

* See S. Chrys. Hom. iv. on St. John, init.

† 'Ferculum oris.' A. reads 'ori,' 'viands for the palate.'

long in coming to the hidden senses, and sometimes they cannot be understood according to the letter, because when taken superficially, they convey no sort of instruction to the reader, but only engender error; for here, for instance, it is said, *Under Whom they are bent who bear the world*[*]. [Job 9, 13]. Now in the case of one so great, who can be ignorant that he never so follows the vain fictions of the poets, as to fancy the weight of the world to be supported by the labour of the giants. Again, under the pressure of calamities he exclaims, *So that my soul chooseth strangling, and death rather than life.* [Job 7, 15] Now who that is in his right senses could believe that a man of so high praise, who in a word, we know, received from the Judge of that which is within[†] the reward of the virtue of patience, settled amidst his afflictions to finish his life by strangling? And sometimes even the very literal words forbid its being supposed that perchance they ought to be understood according to the letter. Thus he says, *Let the day perish wherein I was born, and the night in which it was said, There is a man child conceived.* [Job 3, 3] And a little while afterwards he subjoins, *Let darkness seize it, and let it be involved in bitterness*[‡]. [ver. 5] And in cursing the same night he adds, *Lo! let that night be solitary*. Assuredly this day of his birth, which rolled itself out in the mere current of time, could never stand fast. In what way then did he wish it might be involved in darkness? For having gone by, it no longer was, neither yet, if it had existence in the nature of things, could it ever feel *bitterness;* it is evident therefore that the words cannot possibly be spoken of a day without feeling, when the wish expressed is that it be struck with a feeling of bitterness; and if the night of his conception had gone by, blended with the other nights, after what fashion would he have it become solitary, which as it could not be arrested from the flight of time, so neither could it be separated from union with the other nights. Again he says, *How long wilt Thou not depart from me, nor let me alone, till I swallow down my spittle*. [Job 7, 19] Yet he had said a little above, *The things which my soul refused to touch are as my sorrowful meat.* [Job 6, 7] Now who does not know that spittle is more easily swallowed than food? it is wholly inconceivable then in what connection he, who tells of his taking

---

[*] E.V. *The proud helpers do stoop under Him.*

[†] Interno. Some editions read, 'the Eternal Judge.'

[‡] E.V. *Let the shadow of death stain it.*

food, declares that he cannot swallow his spittle. Again he says, *I have sinned; what shall I do unto thee, O Thou preserver of men?* [Job 7, 20] Or more unequivocally, *Wouldest Thou destroy me by the iniquities of my youth.* [Job 13, 26] And yet in another answer he subjoins, *My heart shall not reproach me so long as I live.* [Job 27, 6] How then does his heart not condemn him so long as he lives, who by a public avowal testifies that he has been a sinner, for faultiness of practice and acquittal of conscience can never meet together. Yet doubtless whereas the literal words when set against each other cannot be made to agree, they point out some other meaning in themselves which we are to seek for, as if with a kind of utterance they said, 'Whereas ye see our superficial form to be destructive to us, look for what may be found within us that is in place and consistent with itself.'

IV.

But sometimes, he who neglects to interpret the historical form of words according to the letter, keeps that light of truth concealed which is presented to him, and in laboriously seeking to find in them a further interior meaning, he loses that which he might easily obtain on the outside. Thus the Saint says, *if I have withheld the poor from their desire, or have caused the eyes of the widow to fail; or have eaten my morsel myself alone, and the fatherless hath not eaten thereof; . . . if I have seen any perish for want of clothing, or any poor without covering; if his loins have not blessed me, and if he were not warmed with the fleece of my sheep;* [Job 31, 16–20] where it is to be observed, that if these words be violently strained to an allegorical signification, we make void all his acts of mercy. For as the word of God, by the mysteries which it contains, exercises the understanding of the wise, so usually by what presents itself on the outside, it nurses the simple-minded. It presenteth in open day that wherewith the little ones may be fed; it keepeth in secret that whereby men of a loftier range may be held in suspense of admiration. It is, as it were, a kind of river, if I may so liken it, which is both shallow [*planus*] and deep, wherein both the lamb may find a footing, and the elephant float at large. Therefore as the fitness of each passage requires, the line of interpretation is studiously varied accordingly, in that the true sense of the word of God is found out with so much the greater fidelity, in proportion as it shifts its course through the different kinds of examples as each case may require.

V. This exposition being such as I have described, I have transmitted to your Blessedness for your inspection, not as being due for its worth's sake, but because I remember that I promised it on your making the request. In which whatsoever your Holiness may discover that is languid or unpolished, let it be most readily excused in proportion as the circumstance is known that it was said in a state of sickness; for when the body is worn down with sickness, the mind being also affected, our exertions to express ourselves likewise become faint*. For many a year's circuit has gone by since I have been afflicted with frequent pains in the bowels, and the powers of my stomach being broken down, makes me at all times and seasons weakly; and under the influence of fevers, slow, but in constant succession, I draw my breath with difficulty; and when in the midst of these sufferings I ponder with earnest heed, that according to the testimony of Scripture, *He scourgeth every son whom He receiveth;* [Heb. 12, 6] the more I am weighed down by the severity of present afflictions, from my anticipations for eternity, I gather strength to breathe with so much the better assurance. And perchance it was this that Divine Providence designed, that I a stricken one, should set forth Job stricken, and that by these scourges I should the more perfectly enter into the feelings of one that was scourged. Yet it will be evident to all that consider the thing aright, that bodily ailment hinders the pursuits wherein I labour, and that with no slight power of opposition in this respect†, that, when the powers of the flesh are not strong enough to discharge the office of speech, the mind cannot adequately convey its meaning. For what is the office of the body saving to be the organ of the mind; and though the musician be ever so skilled in playing [*cantandi*], he cannot put his art in practice unless outward aids accord with himself for that purpose, for we know that the melody [*canticum*] which the hand of the proficient bids, is not rightly given back by instruments that are out of order; nor does the wind express his art, if the pipe, gaping with crevices, gives a grating sound. How much more affected in quality then is a thing like this exposition of mine, wherein the grace of delivery is so dissipated by

* His letters add severe attacks of gout to the infirmities mentioned here. See l. xi. ep. 32. &c.

† 'Adversitate.' This sense should be borne in mind when the Church prays against 'adversity.'

the broken condition of the instrument, that no contrivance of skill can avail to recover it! But I beg that in going through the statements of this work, you would not seek the foliage of eloquence therein: for by the sacred oracles the vanity of a barren wordiness is purposely debarred those that treat thereof, in that it is forbidden to plant a grove in the temple of God. And doubtless we are all of us aware, that as often as the overrank crop shows stalks that abound in leaves, the grains of the ears are least filled and swelling. And hence that art of speaking itself, which is conveyed by rules of worldly training, I have despised to observe; for as the tenor of this Epistle also will tell, I do not escape the collisions of metacism*, nor do I avoid the confusion of barbarisms, and I slight the observing of situations and arrangements, and the cases of prepositions; for I account it very far from meet to submit the words of the divine Oracle to the rules of Donatus†. For neither are these observed by any of the translators thereof, in the authoritative [*auctoritate*] text of Holy Writ. Now as my exposition takes its origin from thence, it is plainly meet that this production, like a kind of offspring, should wear the likeness of its mother‡. Now it is the new Translation that I comment on; but when a case to be proved requires it, I take now the new and now the old for testimony, that as the Apostolic See, over which I preside by ordinance of God, uses both, the labours of my undertaking may have the support of both.

---

* i.e. either the collision of ms, or the letter m at the end of a word, followed by a vowel at the beginning of another. Vide Du Cange, in voc.

† Donatus was a great grammarian of the fourth century, the preceptor of St. Jerome, who highly commends him. His work on grammar was in such general use as to be calle a 'Donatus' as we speak of a 'Virgil,' or a 'Horace,' or an 'Ainsworth.' Vide Biogr. Univ. Paris, 1814. t. xi.

‡ There was a great number of Versions of both the Old and New Testament in the Latin tongue, from the Greek. Of these there was one generally received, and the which became by prescription the Authorized Version in the Latin Church; this long disputed precedence with St. Jerome's Version, which in the New Testament was only a correction of the Text, and in the Old a New Translation from the Hebrew: in the course of time, but not without great opposition, this Version superseded the 'Old' or 'Italic' Translation. Vide Du Pin. Bibl. Writers, t. i. c. vii. s. 1 and 2. t. ii. c. iv. s. 1.

THE FIRST PART.

THE PREFACE

Wherein he in few words goes through the particulars, which are to be laid open in the course of the entire work.

1. IT is often a question with many persons, who should be held for the writer of the Book of the Blessed Job; and some indeed conjecture that Moses was the author of this work, others, some one of the Prophets. For because it is related in the Book of Genesis [Gen. 36, 33] that Jobab sprung from the stock of Esau, and that he succeeded Bale [Bela E.V.] the son of Beor upon the throne, they have inferred that this Blessed Job lived long before the times of Moses, evidently from ignorance of the manner of Holy Writ, which in the earlier parts is wont to touch slightly upon events that are not to follow till long afterwards, when the object is to proceed without delay to particularize other events with greater exactness. Whence it happens, that in that case likewise it is mentioned of Jobab, that he was *before there arose kings in Israel.* Therefore we clearly see that He never could have lived before the Law, who is marked out as having lived during the time of the Judges of Israel; which being little attended to by some, they suppose that Moses was the writer of his acts, as placing him long before, [*ut vide licet*] so that in effect the self-same person who was able to deliver the precepts of the Law for our instruction; should be supposed also to have commended to us examples of virtue derived from the life of a man that was a Gentile. But some, as has been said, suppose some one of the Prophets to have been the Author of this work, maintaining that no man could have knowledge of those words of God, which have such deep mystery, save he whose mind was raised to things above by the spirit of Prophecy. i.

2. But who was the writer, it is very superfluous to enquire; since at any rate the Holy Spirit is confidently believed to have been the Author. He then Himself wrote them, Who dictated the things that should be written. He did Himself write them Who both was present as the Inspirer in that Saint's work, and by the mouth of the writer has consigned to us his acts as patterns for our imitation. If we were reading the words of some great man with his Epistle in our

hand, yet were to enquire by what pen they were written, doubtless it would be an absurdity, to know the Author of the Epistle and understand his meaning, and notwithstanding to be curious to know with what sort of pen the words were marked upon the page. When then we .understand the matter, and are persuaded that the Holy Spirit was its Author, in stirring a question about the author, what else do we than in reading a letter enquire about the pen?

3. Yet we may with greater probability suppose that the same blessed Job, who bore the strife of the spiritual conflict, did likewise relate the circumstances of his victory when achieved; nor should it influence us that it is said in the same book, 'Job said,' or, 'Job bore this or that;' for it is the manner of Holy Scripture for the persons who are writing so to speak of themselves in it, as though they were speaking of others. Whence it is that Moses says, *Now the man Moses was very meek above all the men which were upon the face of the earth*. [Numb. 12, 3] Hence John says, *that Disciple whom Jesus loved*; [John 19, 26] hence Luke says, *that two of them were walking by the way, Cleophas and another*; [Luke 24, 13] which other indeed, while he was so carefully silent about him, he showed to have been no other than himself, as some assert. The writers then of Holy Writ because they are moved by the impulse of the Holy Spirit, do therein so bear witness of themselves as though of other persons. Thus the Holy Spirit by the mouth of Moses spake of Moses, the Holy Spirit speaking by John spoke of John. Paul too intimates that he did not speak from the dictates of his own mind, by saying, *Since ye seek a proof of Christ speaking in me*. [2 Cor. 13, 3] It is hence that the Angel who is described to have appeared to Moses, is now mentioned as an Angel, now as the Lord; an Angel in truth, in respect of that which was subservient to the external delivery; and the Lord, because He was the Director within, Who supplied the effectual power of speaking. Therefore as the speaker is inwardly directed, by virtue of his obedience to instructions, he receives the name of Angel, by virtue of his inspiration, that of Lord. Hence David exclaims, *Give ear, O my people, to my law; incline your ears to the words of my mouth*. [Ps. 78, 1] For it was neither David's law, nor David's people, but he, assuming the character of Him from whom He spoke, speaks with His authority with Whose inspiration he was filled. This we perceive to be daily practised in the Church, if we regard the thing attentively; for the reader standing in the midst of the people exclaims, *I am the God of*

Abraham, the God of Isaac, and the God of Jacob. [Exod. 3, 61] Yet that he is himself God, he says not certainly with truth, nor yet by saying what he does is the line of truth deviated from; for by his voice he first proclaims the sovereignty of Him, Whose minister he is in the office of reading. Therefore the writers of Holy Writ, because when full of the Holy Spirit they are lifted above their own nature, are as it were put out of themselves, and in this manner they deliver sentiments about themselves, as though about other persons. In this way Blessed Job also, being under the influence of the Holy Spirit, might have written his own acts, which were, for that matter, gifts of inspiration from above, as though they were not his own; for in so far as it was a human being, who spoke things which were of God, all that he spake belonged to Another, and in so far as the Holy Spirit spake of what is proper to a human being, it was Another that gave utterance to the things that belonged to him.

4. But we should now leave these points behind us, and hasten forward to consider the particulars of the Sacred History. **ii.**
Every man, even from this, that he is a man, ought to understand the Author of his being, to Whose will he must submit the more completely, in the same proportion that he reflects that of himself he is nothing; yet we, when created I by Him, neglected to take God into our thoughts. Precepts were had recourse to: precepts likewise we have refused to obey. Examples are added; these very examples too we decline to follow, which we see were set forth to us by those under the Law; for because God did openly address Himself to particular persons who were placed under the Law, we regard ourselves as unconcerned with those particular precepts, to whom they were not specially addressed; wherefore to confound our shamelessness, a Gentile is handed down to be our example, that as he that is set under the Law disdains to pay obedience to the Law, he may at least be roused by comparing himself with him, who without the Law lived as by law, The Law then was given to one gone astray; but when even under the Law he still strays, he has the testimony of those brought before him, who are without the pale of the Law, that forasmuch as we would not keep to the order of our creation [*conditionis*], we might be admonished of our duty by precepts, and because we scorned to obey the precepts, we might be shamed by examples, not, as we have said, the examples of those who had the re-

straint of the Law, but of those who had no law to restrain them from sin.

5. The Divine Providence has compassed us about, and cut off all excuse; all opening to man's equivocating arts is every way closed; a Gentile, one without the Law, is brought forward to confound the iniquity of those that are under the Law; which is well and summarily shown by the Prophet, when He says, *Be thou ashamed, O Zidon, says the sea*; [Isai. 23, 4] for in Sidon we have a figure of the stedfastness of those settled upon the foundation of the Law, and in the sea of the life of the Gentiles; accordingly, *Be thou ashamed, O Zidon, says the sea*, because the life of those under the Law is convicted by the life of Gentiles, and the conduct of men in a state of religion is put to confusion by the conduct of those living in the world, so long as the first do not, even under vows, observe what they hear enjoined in precepts: the latter by their manner of life keep those ways whereunto they are not in any wise bound by legal enactments. Now for the authority this book has received, we have the weighty testimony of the sacred page itself, where the Prophet Ezekiel says, that those men alone should have deliverance granted to them., viz. Noah, Daniel, and Job; nor is it without propriety, that in the midst of Hebrew, lives, that of a righteous Gentile is placed in that authority which commands the reverence of men; because as our Redeemer came to redeem both Jews and Gentiles, so He was willing to be prophesied of by the lips both of Jews and Gentiles, that He might be named by either people [*utrumque populum*], Who was at a future time to suffer for both.

6. This man then, with all the surpassing powers whereby he was sustained, was known to his own conscience and to God; but had he not been stricken he would never have been the least known to us. For his virtue had its exercise indeed even in peaceful times, but it was by strokes that the report of; his virtue was stirred up to fragrance: and he, who in repose kept within himself all that he was, when disturbed did scatter; abroad the odour of his fortitude, for all to know. For as unguents, unless they be stirred, are never smelt far off, and as aromatic scents spread not their fragrance except they be burned, so the Saints in their tribulations make known all the sweetness that they have of their virtues. Whence it is well said in the Gospel, *If ye have faith as a grain of mustard seed, ye shall say unto this mountain, Remove hence to yonder place, and it shall remove*. [Matt. 17,

20] For unless a grain of mustard seed be bruised, the extent of its virtue is never acknowledged. For without bruising it is insipid [*lene*], but if it is bruised it becomes hot, and if gives out all those pungent properties that were concealed in it. Thus every good man, so long as he is not smitten, is regarded as insipid [*lenis*], and of slight account. But if ever the grinding of persecution crush him, instantly he gives forth all the warmth of his savour, and all that before appeared to be weak or contemptible, is turned into godly fervour, and that which in peaceful times he had been glad to keep from view within his own bosom, he is driven by the force of tribulations to make known; so that the Prophet says with justice, *Yet the Lord hath commanded His lovingkindness in the day time, and in the night He hath declared it*; [Ps 42, 9] for the lovingkindness of the Lord is commanded in the day time, because the season of rest is perceived by the sense of it [*cognoscendo*], but 'in the night it is declared,' because the gift which is received in tranquillity is made manifest in tribulation.

7. But we ought to search out more particularly why so **iii.**
many strokes fell to the lot of him who maintained without blame such strict guard of the several virtues: for he had humility, as he himself even testifies, *If I did despise to be judged in the cause of my manservant or of my maidservant, when they contended with me.* [Job 31, 13] He showed hospitality, as himself describes, when he says; *the stranger did not lodge in the street: but I opened my doors to the traveller.* [Job 31, 32] He maintained a vigorous exercise of discipline, as his own words show; *The princes refrained talking, and laid their fingers on their mouth.* [Job 29, 9] With that vigour he yet retained mildness, according to his own confession, where he says, *I sat chief, and dwelt as a king in the army, yet as one that comforteth the mourners.* In almsdeeds he cherished a bountiful spirit, as he himself intimates by saying, *If I have eaten my morsel myself alone, and the fatherless hath not eaten thereof.* [Job 31, 17] Whereas then he performed all the precepts of the several virtues, one thing was wanting to him, viz. that when stricken even he should learn to render thanks: it was known that he knew how to serve God when surrounded by blessings, but it was meet that a most searching severity should put it to the test, whether even under the lash he would yet remain constant to his God, for chastisement is the test, whether when let to rest a man really loves. Him the adversary sought indeed to obtain that he

might prove deficient [*deficeret*] in godliness, but obtained that he might prove a proficient [*proficeret*] therein. The Lord in loving-kindness permitted that to be done, which the devil in his wickedness required; for when the enemy had got leave to have him with the purpose of destroying him, by his temptations he effected that his merits were augmented. For it is written, *In all this Job sinned not with his lips*. [Job 1, 22] Yet doubtless there are certain words of his rejoinders, which sound harshly to readers of little experience, for the sayings of the Saints these are unable to understand in the pious sense in which they are spoken, and because they are unskilled to make their own the feelings of the afflicted Saint, therefore it is impossible for them to interpret aright the expressions of grief, for it is a sympathy that lowers itself to his state of suffering, that knows how to estimate aright the meaning of the sufferer.

8. And so they conclude that blessed Job was a defaulter in his speech, without sufficiently considering, that if they convict the blessed Job's replies, they at the same time bear witness that God's sentence concerning him was untrue. For the Lord says to the devil, *Hast thou considered My servant Job, that there is none like him in all the earth, a perfect and an upright man, one that feareth God, and escheweth evil?* [Job 1, 8] To Whom the devil presently replies, *Doth Job fear God for nought? Has not Thou made an hedge about him, and about his house? But put forth Thine hand now, and touch him, and see if he hath not blessed Thee to Thy face*. [v. 9, 10] The enemy then put forth his strength upon the blessed Job, but in doing this he entered the lists against God, and in this way blessed Job became the intermediate subject of the contest between God and the devil. Whoever then maintains that the holy man, when in the midst of the strokes, committed sin by the words which he uttered, what else doth he than reproach God, Who had pledged Himself [*proposuerat*] for him, with having been the loser? For the same God was pleased to take upon Himself the cause of the Saint under his trial, Who both extolled him before his afflictions, and on thus extolling allowed him to undergo the trial of those scourges. If then Job is said to have gone wrong, his advocate is made out to have been foiled: though the gifts vouchsafed him alone testify, that he did not transgress at all: for who does not know that what is due to faults is not reward but chastisement? He then who merited to receive back double what he had lost, proved by this compensation that there was nought of evil, but only

virtue in all that he said, and to this declaration too it is further added, that he is himself the intercessor in behalf of his guilty friends. For one that is involved in great sins, can never, when burthened with his own, discharge another's score; he then is shown to be clear in his own case, who could obtain for others their clearance from guilt. If however it be displeasing to any, that he is himself the relator of his own goodness, let them know that in the midst of so many losses of his substance, amidst so many wounds of the body, amidst so many deaths of his children, with the friends, who had come to comfort him, breaking out into reproaches, he was urged to despair of his life, and he whom such repeated calamities had sorely smitten, was further stricken by the insulting language of the reproachers; for these, that had come to comfort him, while they upbraided him with his unrighteousness as it seemed to them, were driving him quite to give up all hope of himself; whereas then he recalls his good deeds to mind, it is not that he lifts himself up in self applause, but sets anew [*reformat*] his mind to hope, when as it were sunk down amid those reproaches and those strokes. For the mind is smitten with a heavy weapon of despair, when it is both hard pressed with the tribulations of wrath from above, and galled by the reproaches of men's tongues without. Blessed Job therefore, thus pierced with the darts of so many woes, when he now feared to be brought down by their reproaches, recalled himself to a state of confidence, by the assurance derived from his past life. He then did not thereby fall into the sin of presumption, because he resisted an inward impulse to despair by the outward expression of his own eulogies, to the end that while he recounted the good things which he had done he might be saved from despairing of the good that he had sought.

9. But now let us follow out the actual course of his trial. **iv.**
The enemy, full of rage, and striving to conquer the firm breast of that holy man, set up against him the engines of temptation, spoiled his substance, slew his children, smote his body, instigated his wife, and while he brought his friends to console him, urged, them to the harshest upbraiding. One friend too was more cruel in his reproaches, he reserved with the last and bitterest invective, that by the frequency of the stroke, if not otherwise, the heart might be reached by that which was ever being repeated with a fresh wound. For because he saw that he had power in the world, he

thought to move him by the loss of his substance, and finding him unshaken, he smote him by the death of his children. But seeing that from that wound which made him childless he even gained strength to the greater magnifying of God's praise, he asked leave to smite the health of his body. Seeing moreover that by the pain of the body he could not compass the affecting [*passionem*] of the mind, he instigated his wife, for he saw that the city which he desired to storm was too strong; therefore by bringing upon him so many external plagues, he led an army as it were on the outside against him, but, when he kindled the feelings of his wife into words of mischievous persuasion, it was as though he corrupted the hearts of the citizens within; For so from external wars we are instructed how to think of those within. For an enraged enemy, that holds a city encircled by his surrounding armies, upon perceiving its fortifications to remain unshaken, betakes himself to other methods [*argumenta*] of attack, with this object, that he may corrupt the hearts of some of the citizens also within; so that, when he has led on the assailants from without, he may also have cooperators within, and that when the heat of the battle increases outside, the city being left without succour by the treachery of those within, of whose faith no doubt is felt, may become his prey.

10. And thus a battering ram having been planted on the outside, as it were, he smote the walls of this city with blows many in number, as the several times that he brought tidings of calamities; while on the inside, he, as it were, corrupted the hearts of the citizens, when he set himself to undermine the strong bulwarks of this city by the persuasions of the wife. In this manner he brought to bear, from without, an hostile assault, from within, baneful counsels, that he might capture the city the sooner, in proportion as he troubled it both from within and from without. But because there are times when words are more poignant than wounds, he armed himself, as we have said, with the tongues of his friends. Those indeed that were of graver years, might perchance give the less pain by their words. The younger is made to take their place, to deal that holy bosom a wound so much the sharper, the meaner was the arm that be impelled to strike blows against it. Behold the enemy mad to strike down his indomitable strength, how many the darts of temptation that he devised, see, what numberless beleaguering engines he

set about him! See how many weapons of assault he let fly, but in all his mind continued undaunted, the city stood unshaken.

11. It is the aim of enemies, when they come up face to face, V.
to send off some in secret, who may be so much the more free to strike a blow in the flank of the hostile force, in proportion as he that is fighting is more eagerly intent upon the enemy advancing in front. Job, therefore, being caught in the warfare of this conflict, received the losses which befel him like foes in his front; he took the words of his comforters like enemies on his flank, and in all turning round the shield of his stedfastness, he stood defended at all points, and ever on the watch, parried on all sides the swords directed against him. By his silence he marks his unconcern for the loss of his substance; the flesh, dead in his children, he bewails with composure; the flesh in his own person stricken, he endures with fortitude; the flesh in his wife suggesting mischievous persuasions, he instructeth with wisdom. In addition to all this his friends start forth into the bitterness of upbraiding, and coming to appease his grief, increase its force. Thus all the engines of temptation are turned by this holy man to the augmentation of his virtues; for by the wounds his patience is tried, and by the words his wisdom is exercised. Every where he meets the enemy with an undaunted mien, for the scourges he overcame by resolution, and the words by reasoning. But his friends, who came indeed to administer consolation, but who deviate from their purpose even to using terms of reproach, must be thought to have erred more from ignorance than wickedness. For we must never imagine that so great a man had evil minded friends, but, while they fail to discern the cause of his scourges, they slide into a fault.

12. For of scourges there are sundry kinds; for there is the scourge whereby the sinner is stricken that he may suffer punishment without withdrawal [*retractione*], another whereby he is smitten, that he may be corrected; another wherewith sometimes a man is smitten, not for the correction of past misdeeds, but for the prevention of future; another which is very often inflicted, whereby neither a past transgression is corrected, nor a future one prevented, but which has this end, that when unexpected deliverance follows the stroke, the power of the Deliverer being known may be the more ardently beloved, and that while the innocent person is bruised

by the blow, his patience may serve to increase the gain of his merits; for sometimes the sinner is stricken that he may be punished, without withdrawal, as it is said to Judaea when doomed to destruction, *I have wounded thee with the wound of an enemy, with the chastisement of a cruel one*; [Jerem. 30, 14] and again, *Why criest thou for thine affliction? thy sorrow is incurable.* [v. 15] Sometimes the sinner is stricken that he may be amended, as it is said to one in the Gospel, *Behold, thou art made whole, sin no more, lest a worse thing come unto thee*; [John 5, 14] for the words of his deliverer indicate that it was past sins which were exacting all the violence of the pain which he had endured. In some cases the person is smitten, not for the obliteration of a past offence, but for the avoidance of a future one, which the Apostle Paul openly testifies of himself, saying, *And lest I shall be exalted above measure through the abundance of the revelations, there was given to me a thorn in the flesh, the messenger of Satan to buffet me*. [2 Cor. 12, 7] For he who says, not 'that he was exalted,' but, 'lest he should be exalted,' clearly shows that by that stroke it is held in check that it may not take place, and that it is not a fault that has taken place now clearing away. But sometimes the person is stricken neither for past not yet for future transgression, but that the alone mightiness of the Divine power may be set forth in the cutting short of the striking; whence when it was said unto the Lord concerning the blind man in the Gospel, *Who did sin, this man, or his parents, that he was born blind?* the Lord answered, saying, *Neither hath this man sinned, nor his parents, but that the works of God should be made manifest in him*: [John 9, 2. 3.] in which manifestation what else is done, saving that by that scourge the excellence of his merits is increased, and while there is no past transgression wiped away, the patience may engender a mighty fortitude. For which reason the same blessed Job is first extolled by the voice of the Judge, and is then given up into the hand of the Tempter, and whereas God, in recompensing him after the scourge, speaks to him in a more familiar manner, it is plainly shown how much greater he became by the stroke; so then the friends of blessed Job, while they were unable to distinguish the different kinds of strokes, believed him to be stricken for his guiltiness, and while they endeavoured to vindicate the justice of God in smiting him, they were driven to reprove blessed Job of unrighteousness; not knowing in fact that for this reason he was stricken, viz. that the stroke might redound to the praise of God's glory, and not that by those strokes he might be brought to amend the evil, which he had never done; and hence they are the sooner restored to pardon, because they sinned from ignorance rather than from an evil disposition; and their pride the Divine Justice puts down with so much the stronger hand, as It refuses to renew them in Its favour, saving by means of him whom they had despised. For a high mind is effectually struck down when it is bowed beneath the very person over whom it has exalted itself.

vi.

13. But amongst these marvellous works of Divine Providence it yields us satisfaction to mark, how, for the enlightening the night of this present life, each star in its turn appears in the face of Heaven, until that towards the end of the night the Redeemer of mankind ariseth like the true Morning Star; for the space of night, being enlightened by the stars as they set and rise in their courses, is passed with the heavens in exceeding beauty. Thus in order that the ray of stars, darting forth at its appointed time, and changed in succession, might reach the darkness of our night, Abel comes to show us innocency; Enoch, to teach purity of practice; Noah, to win admittance for lessons of endurance in hope and in work; Abraham, to manifest obedience; Isaac, to show an example of chastity in wedded life; Jacob, to introduce patience in labour; Joseph, for the repaying evil with the favour of a good turn; Moses, for the showing forth of mildness; Joshua, to form us to confidence against difficulties; Job, to show patience amid afflictions. Lo what lustrous stars see we in the sky, that the foot of practice may never stumble as we walk this our night's journey; since for so many Saints as God's Providence set forth to man's cognizance, He, as it were, sent just so many stars into the sky, over the darkness of erring man, till the true Morning Star should rise, Who, being the herald to us of the eternal morning, should outshine the other stars by the radiance of His Divinity.

14. And all the elect, whilst by their holy living serving as His forerunners, gave promise of Him by prophesying both in deeds and words. For there never was any Saint who did not appear as His herald in figure; for it was meet that all should display that goodness in themselves whereby both all became good, and which they knew to be for the good of all, and therefore that blessing ought also to be promised without pause which was vouchsafed both to be received without price [*sine aestimatione*] and to be kept without end, that all

generations might together tell what the end of all should bring to light, in the redemption of which all were partakers. And therefore it behoved that blessed Job also, who uttered those high mysteries of His Incarnation, should by his life be a sign of Him, Whom by voice he proclaimed, and by all that he underwent should show forth what were to be His sufferings; and should so much the more truly foretel the mysteries [*sacramenta*] of His Passion, as he prophesied then not merely with his lips but also by suffering. But because our Redeemer has shown Himself to be one with the Holy Church, which He has taken to Himself; for of Him it is said, *Who is the Head of us all*; [Eph. 4, 15] and of the Church it is written, *the Body of Christ, Which is the Church*, [Col. 1, 24] whosoever in his own person betokens Him, at one time designates Him in respect of the Head, at another of the Body, so as to have not only the voice of the Head, but also of the Body; and hence the Prophet Isaiah, in giving utterance to the words of the same Lord, says, *He hath put upon me a mitre like unto a Bridegroom, and hath decked me with jewels as a Bride*. [Isa. 61, 10 Vulg.] Therefore because the same person that in the Head is the Bridegroom, is in the Body the Bride, it follows that when, at times, anything is spoken from the Head, there must be a turning down by degrees or even at once to the voice of the Body, and again when anything is said that is of the Body, there must be presently a rising to the voice of the Head. Accordingly the blessed Job conveys a type of the Redeemer, Who is to come together with His own Body: and his wife who bids him curse, marks the life of the carnal, who having place within the Holy Church with unamended morals, as by their faith they are brought near to the godly, press them the more sorely by their lives, since while they cannot be shunned as being of the faithful, they are endured by the faithful as the greater harm by how much nearer home [*deterius quanto et interius*].

15. But his friends, who, while acting as his counsellors, at the same time inveigh against him, are an express image of heretics, who under show of giving counsel, are busied in leading astray; and hence they address the blessed Job as though in behalf of the Lord, but yet the Lord does not commend them, that is, because all heretics, while they try to defend, only offend God. Whence they are plainly told, and that by the same holy man *I desire to reason with God; first showing that ye are forgers of lies, ye are followers of corrupt doctrines*. [Job 13, 3. 4.] According to which it appears that these by their erroneous no-

tions stood a type of heretics, whom the holy man charges with adhering to a creed [*cultui*] of corrupt doctrines. But every heretic, in this, that he is seen to defend God, is a gainsayer of His troth, according to the testimony of the Psalmist, who says, *That Thou mightest still the enemy and the defender* [Ps. 8, 2. E.V. *avenger*], for he is an *enemy and defender*, who so preaches God as thereby to be fighting against Him.

16. Now that blessed Job maintains the semblance of the **vii.**
Redeemer to come, his very name is a proof. For Job is, if interpreted, 'grieving;' by which same grief we have set forth, either our Mediator's Passion, or the travails of Holy Church, which is harassed by the manifold toils of this present life. Moreover by the word which stands for their name his friends mark out the quality of their conduct. For Eliphas is called in the Latin tongue, 'contempt of the Lord,' and what else do heretics, than in entertaining false notions of God contemn Him by their proud conceits. Baldad is by interpretation 'Oldness alone.' And well are all heretics styled, 'Oldness alone,' in the things which they speak concerning God, forasmuch as it is with no right purpose but with a longing for temporal honour that they desire to appear as preachers. For they are moved to speak not by the zeal of the new man, but by the evil principles of the old life. 'Sophar' too is rendered in the Latin language 'dissipation of the prospect,' or, 'one dissipating the prospect.' For the minds of the faithful lift themselves to the contemplation of things above; but as the words of heretics aim to prevent them in their contemplation of light objects, they do their best to 'dissipate the prospect.' Thus in the three names of Job's friends, we have set forth three cases [*casus*] of the ruin of heretical minds. For unless they held God in contempt, they would never entertain false notions concerning Him; and unless they drew along with them a heart of oldness, they would: never err in the understanding of the new life; and unless they marred the contemplations of good things [or, of good men], the Supreme judgments would never condemn them with so strict a scrutiny for the guiltiness of their words. By holding God in contempt, then, they keep themselves in oldness, and by being kept in oldness, they injure the contemplation of right objects by their erring discourses.

THE FIRST PART.

viii. 17. Now because it sometimes happens that heretics being penetrated with the bountiful streams of Divine grace return to the unity of Holy Church, this is well represented in the very reconcilement of his friends. Yet blessed Job is bidden to intercede for them, because the sacrifices of heretics can never be acceptable to God, unless they be offered in their behalf by the hands of the universal Church, that by her merits they may obtain the recovery of salvation, whom they did strike before by assailing her with the darts of their words; and hence seven sacrifices are recorded to have been offered for them, for whereas in confessing they receive the Spirit of sevenfold grace, they do as it were obtain expiation by seven offerings. It is hence that in the Apocalypse of John the whole Church is represented by the number of seven Churches [Rev. 1, 12]. Hence it is said of wisdom by Solomon, *Wisdom hath builded her house; she hath hewn, out her seven pillars.* [Prov. 9, 1] And thus by the very number of the sacrifices those reconciled heretics set forth what they were before, in that these are not united to the perfection of sevenfold grace, except by returning.

18. But they are well described as having offered for themselves bulls and rams. For in the bull is figured the neck of pride, and in the ram, the leading of the flocks that follow. What then is it to slaughter bulls and rams in their behalf, but to put an end to their proud leading, so that they may think humbly of themselves, and not seduce the hearts of the innocent to follow after them. For they had started away from the unity of the Church with a swelling neck, and were drawing after them the weak folk like flocks following behind. Therefore let them come to blessed Job; i.e. return to the Church; and present bulls and rams to be slaughtered for a sevenfold sacrifice, and that they may be united to the universal Church, let them with the interposition of humility kill all the swelling humour wherewith their proud leadership savoured them.

ix. 19. Now by Heliu, who speaks indeed with a right sense, yet runs down [*derivatur*] into foolish words of pride, is set forth a representation of every proud person. For there are many within the pale of Holy Church, that are too proud to put forward in a right manner the right sentiments, which they profess, and hence he is both rebuked with the words of God's upbraiding, and yet no sacrifices offered in his behalf, in that he is a believer indeed, yet high-minded. By the truth of his belief he is within, but by the obstacle which his pride presents he is not acceptable. Him [read *Hunc ergo*, as old ed. and Mss.] therefore rebuke reproves, but sacrifice does not restore him, because he is indeed in the faith that he ought to be in, yet the Supreme Justice, charging him with things over and above what need to be, keeps him at a distance. Hence Heliu is well rendered in the Latin tongue, 'That my God,' or, 'God, the Lord.' For proud men within Holy Church, though they keep away from God by living proudly, yet acknowledge Him by believing truly. For what is it for him to say by his name, 'That my God,' but to show forth Him Whom he believed with a public avowal? Or what is it to say, 'God the Lord,' but to accept Him both as God by virtue of His Divinity, and to hold Him For Man by His Incarnation?

20. It is well that after the losses of his substance, after the death of his children, after the tortures of his wounds, after the strife and conflict of words, he is raised up again with a double reward, clearly, in that Holy Church, even while yet in this present life, receives a double recompense for the toils she undergoes, since having taken in the Gentiles to the full, at the end of the world she converts to herself the souls of the Jews likewise. For it is on this account written, *Until the fulness of the Gentiles be come in. And so all Israel shall be saved*. [Rom. 11, 25. 26.] And she will afterwards receive a double recompense, in that, when the toils of this present time are over, she rises not alone to the joy of souls, but to a blessed estate of bodies. And hence the Prophet rightly says, *therefore in their land they shall possess the double*. [Isa. 61, 7] For 'in the Land of the Living' the Saints possess the double, because we know they are gladdened with blessedness both of mind and body. Hence John in the Apocalypse, because it was before the resurrection of bodies that he saw the souls of the Saints crying, beheld how that they had given them a stole to each, saying, *And white robes were given, one* [*singulae*] *to every one of them, and it was said, that they should rest yet for a little season until their fellow-servants also and their brethren, that should be killed as they were, should be fulfilled*. [Rev. 6, 11] For before the Resurrection they are said to have received a stole to each, for that as yet they are gifted with blessedness of mind alone; and therefore they will receive each one two, whenever, together with the perfect bliss of souls, they shall be clothed also with incorruptibility of bodies. **x.**

THE FIRST PART.

21. Now it is very properly that the affliction indeed of blessed Job is told, but the length of time that he was under the affliction is kept back, for we see the tribulation of Holy Church in this life, but know nothing for how long she is here to undergo bruising and delay; and hence it is spoken by the mouth of Truth, *It is not for you to know the times or the seasons which the Father hath put in His own power.* [Acts 1, 7] Herein then, that the suffering of blessed Job is told us, we are taught what we are made acquainted withal by experience; and herein, that the length of time that he continued in his suffering is withheld, we are taught what it is we must remain ignorant of.

We have drawn out these words of preface to some length, that by briefly running over it we might in a manner give a view of the whole. Now then that by long discoursing we have been brought to the commencement of our discourse, we must first settle the root of the historical meaning, that we may afterwards let our minds take their fill of the fruits of the allegorical senses.

BOOK I.

The first verses of the first chapter of the Book of Job are explained first historically, then in an allegorical, and lastly in a moral sense.

1. *There was a man in the land of Uz, whose name was Job.* [Job 1, i.
1] It is for this reason that we are told where the holy man dwelt, that the meritoriousness of his virtue might be expressed; for who knows not that Uz is a land of the Gentiles? and the Gentile world came under the dominion of wickedness, in the same proportion that its eyes were shut to the knowledge of its Creator. Let us be told then where he dwelt, that this circumstance may be reckoned to his praise, that he was good among bad men; for it is no very great praise to be good in company with the good, but to be good with the bad; for as it is a greater offence not to be good among good men, so it is immeasurably high testimony for any one to have shown himself good even among the wicked. Hence it is that the same blessed Job bears witness to himself, saying, *I am a brother to dragons, and a companion to owls.* [Job 30, 29] Hence it was that Peter extolled Lot with high commendation, because he found him to be good among a reprobate people; saying, *And delivered just Lot, vexed with the filthy conversation of the wicked; for he was righteous in seeing and hearing* [so Vulg.], *dwelling with them who vexed his righteous soul from day to day with their unlawful deeds.* [2 Pet. 2, 7.8.] Now he evidently could not have been vexed unless he had both heard and witnessed the wicked deeds of his neighbours, and yet he is called righteous both in seeing and in hearing, because their wicked lives affected the ears and eyes of the Saint not with a pleasant sensation, but with the pain of a blow. Hence it is that Paul says to his disciples, *In the midst of a crooked and perverse nation, among whom ye shine like lights in the world.* [Phil. 2, 15] Hence it is said to the Angel of the Church of Pergamos, *I know thy works, and where thou dwellest, even where Satan's seat is; and thou holdest fast My name, and hast not denied My faith.* [Rev. 2, 13] Hence the Holy Church is commended by the voice of the Spouse, where He says to her in the Song of love, *As the lily among the thorns, so is my love among the daughters.* [Cant. 2, 2] Well then is the blessed Job described, (by the mention of a gentile land,) as having dwelt among the wicked, that according to the testimony borne by the Spouse, be might be shown to have grown up a lily among thorns, for which reason it is well subjoined immediately after, *And that man was simple* [so Vulg.] *and upright.*

THE FIRST PART.

ii. 2. For there are some in such wise simple as not to know what uprightness is, but these walk wide of the innocence of real simplicity, in proportion as they are far from mounting up to the virtue of uprightness; for while they know not how to take heed to their steps by following uprightness, they can never remain innocent by walking in simplicity. Hence it is that Paul warns his disciples, and says, *But yet I would have you wise unto that which is good, and simple concerning evil.* [Rom. 16, 19] Hence again he says, *Brethren, be not children in understanding, howbeit in malice be ye children.* [1 Cor. 14, 20] Hence Truth enjoins Her disciples by Her own lips, saying, *Be ye wise as serpents and harmless as doves.* [Mat. 10, 16] For in giving them admonition, He needfully joined the two together, so that both the simplicity of the dove might be instructed by the craftiness of the serpent, and again the craftiness of the serpent might be attempered by the simplicity of the dove. Hence it is that the Holy Spirit has manifested His presence to mankind, not in the form of a dove only, but also in the form of fire. For by the dove simplicity is indicated, and by fire, zeal. Therefore He is manifested in a dove, and in fire, because all they, who are full of Him, yield themselves to the mildness of simplicity, in such sort as yet to kindle with a zeal of uprightness against the offences of sinners. It follows, *And one ,that feared God and eschewed evil.*

iii. 3. To fear God is never to pass over any good thing, that ought to be done. Whence it is said by Solomon, *Whoso fears God, neglects nothing* [Eccl. 7, 18, (Vulg.) 19.]; but because there are some, who practise some good actions, yet in such wise that they are by no means withheld from certain evil practices; after he is said to have been *one that feared God*, it is still rightly reported of him that he also *eschewed evil*; for it is written, *Depart from evil, and do good* [Ps. 37, 27]; for indeed those good actions are not acceptable to God, which are stained in His sight by the admixture of evil deeds; and hence it is said by Solomon, *He who offendeth in one point, spoileth many good deeds* [Eccl. 9, 18]. Hence James bears witness, saying, *For whosoever shall keep the whole law, and yet offend in one point, he is guilty of all.* [James 2, 10] Hence Paul says, *A little leaven leaveneth the whole lump* [1 Cor. 5, 6]. So then that it might be shown us how spotless the blessed Job stood forth in his good actions, it is wisely done that we have it pointed out how far he was removed from evil deeds.

4. But it is the custom of narrators, when a wrestling match is woven into the story, first to describe the limbs of the combatants, how broad and strong the chest, how sound, how full their muscles swelled, how the belly below neither clogged by its weight, nor weakened by its shrunken size, that when they have first shown the limbs to be fit for the combat, they may then at length describe their bold and mighty strokes. Thus because our athlete was about to combat the devil, the writer of the sacred story, recounting as it were before the exhibition in the arena the spiritual merits in this athlete, describes the members of the soul [*mentis*], saying, *And that man was perfect and upright, and one that feared God, and eschewed evil*; that when the powerful setting of the limbs is known, from this very strength we may already prognosticate also the victory to follow. Next comes,

5. Ver. 2. *And there were born unto him seven sons and three daughters.* The heart of the parent is often enticed into avarice by a numerous offspring, for he is the more inflamed with ambition for laying up an inheritance, in proportion as he abounds in the number to inherit it. In order then that it might be shown what holiness of mind blessed Job possessed, he is both called righteous, and is said to have been the father of a numerous offspring. And the same man in the beginning of his book is declared devout in offering sacrifices, and besides he afterwards with his own mouth records himself as ready in giving alms. Let us then consider with what resolution he showed himself to be endowed, whom no feelings of affection for so many heirs could ever dispose to be greedy of an inheritance for them. It proceeds; **iv.**

5. Ver. 3. *His substance also was seven thousand sheep, and three thousand camels, and five hundred yoke of oxen, and five hundred she asses, and a very great household.* We know that the greater the loss, the greater the grief with which it affects the mind; to show then how great was his virtue, we are told that it was very much, that he lost with patience; for never without pain do we part with aught, saving that which we hold without fondness; therefore while the greatness of his substance is described, yet soon after he is reported as resigned to the loss of it; thus parting with it without regret, it is plain that he had kept it without regard. It is also to be noted that in the first instance the riches of his heart are described, **vi.**

and afterwards the wealth of the body; for an abundant store is wont to make the mind so much the more slack to the fear of God, as it obliges it to be occupied with a diversity of cares; for inasmuch as it is dissipated by a multitude of objects, it is prevented standing fast in that which is within. Which was pointed out by Truth Itself in setting forth the Parable of the sower; *He also that received seed among the thorns, is he that heareth the word, and the care of this world, and the deceitfulness of riches, choke the word, and he becometh unfruitful.* [Matt. 13, 22] See how the blessed Job is both said to have great possessions, and a little after is related to be devoutly assiduous in the divine sacrifices.

7. Let us then consider how great was the holiness of that man who though thus busied disengaged himself for such assiduous attendance upon God. Nor had the power of that precept as yet shone out, which bids us leave all things; yet blessed Job already kept the intent of it in his heart, in that he surely had left his substance in intention, which he kept without taking delight in it.

8. *So that this man was the greatest of all the men of the East.* [Job 1, 3] Who does not know that the men of the East are very wealthy, accordingly 'he was the greatest of all the men of the East;' as though it were expressly said that he was even richer than the rich.

9. Ver. 4. *And his sons went and feasted in their houses, every one his day; and sent and called for their three sisters to eat and to drink with them.*

vii. Greater wealth usually becomes the cause of greater discord between brethren. O, inestimable praise of a father's training! the father is both declared rich, and the sons at peace together, and while the wealth to be divided among them was there, an undivided affection yet filled the hearts of all.

10. Ver. 5. *And it was so, when the days of their feasting were gone about, that Job sent, and sanctified them, and rose up early in the morning, and offered burnt-offerings according to the number of them all.*

viii. When it is said, *sent and sanctified them*, it is openly shown what strictness he practised with those when present, for whom when absent he was not wanting in concern. But this circumstance demands our discreet consideration, that, when the days of feasting were past, he has recourse to the purification of a holocaust for each day severally; for the holy man knew that there can scarcely be feasting without offence; he knew that the revelry of feasts must be cleansed away by much purification of sacrifices, and whatever stains the sons had contracted in their own persons at their feasts, the father wiped out by the offering of a sacrifice; for there are certain evils which it is either scarcely possible, or it may be said wholly impossible, to banish from feasting. Thus almost always voluptuousness is the accompaniment of entertainments; for when the body is relaxed in the delight of refreshment, the heart yields itself to the admission of an empty joy. Whence it is written, *The people sat down to eat and drink, and rose up to play*. [Exod. 32, 6]

11. Almost always talkativeness is an attendant upon feasts, and when the belly is replenished, the tongue is unloosed; whence the rich man in hell is well described as thirsting for water, in these words, *Father Abraham, have mercy on me, and send Lazarus, that he may dip the tip of his finger in water, and cool my tongue, for I am tormented in this flame*. [Luke 16, 24] He is first said to have fared sumptuously every lay, and then it is recorded that he craved a drop of water upon his tongue; for as we have said, because at feasts talking is wont to give itself full vent, the fault is indicated by the punishment, in that he, whom the Truth had said *fared sumptuously every day*, was described as most on fire in his tongue. They that attune the harmony of stringed instruments arrange it with such exceeding skill, that frequently, when one chord is touched, a very different one, placed with many lying between, is made to vibrate, and when this last is sounded, the former, which is attempered to the same tune [*cantu*], rings without the others being struck. According to which Holy Scripture very often so deals with the several virtues, and vices too, that while by express mention it conveys one thing, it does by its silence bring before us another, for nothing is recorded against the rich man relating to talkativeness, but while the punishment is described as in the tongue, we are shown, which among others was his greatest offence in his feasting.

12. But whereas the seven brethren are described as making feasts, each one in his day, and whereas, when the days of feasting were over, Job is related to have offered seven sacrifices; the account plainly indicates that, in offering a sacrifice on the eighth day, the blessed Job was celebrating the mystery of the Resurrection. For the day, which is now named 'The Lord's day,' is the third from the death of our Redeemer, but in the order of creation it is the eighth, which is also the first in the work of creation, but because, on com-

ing round again, it follows the seventh, it is properly reckoned the eighth; whereas then it is said that he offered sacrifices on the eighth day, it is shown that he was full of the Spirit of sevenfold grace, and served the Lord for the hope of resurrection. Hence that Psalm is entitled 'for the Octave,' wherein joy for the resurrection is proclaimed, but, that the sons of blessed Job had been forearmed by the discipline of such perfect training, that they neither offended by word nor deed at their feasts, is plainly shown, in that it is subjoined,

ix. 13. *For Job said, It may be that my sons have sinned, and cursed God in their hearts.* For he had taught them to be perfect in deed and in word, about whose thought alone the father entertained fears. Now that we should not judge rashly of other men's hearts, we perceive in the words of this Saint, who does not say, 'that they *have* cursed God in their hearts,' but *it may be that they have cursed God in, their hearts.* Whence it is well said by Paul, *Therefore judge nothing before the time, until the Lord come, Who both will bring to light the hidden things of darkness, and will make manifest the counsels of the hearts*; [1 Cor. 4, 5] for whoever deviates from the right line in thought, sins in darkness; we then should be the more backward boldly to condemn the hearts of others, in proportion as we know that we cannot by our own sight throw light into the darkness of another man's thought. But here [al. this] we should consider with discrimination, with what severity that father was likely [*potuit*] to correct the deeds of his children, who set himself with so much solicitude to purify their hearts. What do those rulers of the Faithful say to this, who know nothing even of the very overt acts of their disciples? What are they thinking of in excuse for themselves, who mind not in those committed to them even the wounds of evil actions? But that his perseverance too in this holy work may be demonstrated, it is well added,

x. 14. *Thus did Job all the days; for it is written, But he that shall endure unto the end, the same shall be saved.* In the sacrifice then, the holiness of his conduct is shown, and in the entire number of the days of the sacrifice, perseverance in that holy conduct. These particulars we have gone through cursorily in following out the history. Now the order of interpretation requires that beginning afresh we should at this point open the secrets of its allegories.

15. Ver. 1. *There was a man in the land of Uz, whose name was Job.* We believe from the history that these things took place, but let us here turn to see in what way they were allegorically fulfilled; for, as we have said, Job is interpreted, 'a mourner,' and Uz 'a counsellor.' Whom else then does the blessed Job express by his name, saving Him, of Whom the Prophet speaks, saying, *Surely He hath borne our griefs?* [Isa. 53, 4] He dwells in the land of Uz, in that He rules the hearts of a people of wise counsels; for Paul says, that Christ is *the Wisdom of God and the Power of God* [1 Cor. 1, 24]; and this same Wisdom Herself by the lips of Solomon declareth, *I Wisdom dwell with Prudence, and am in the midst of witty inventions.* [Prov. 8, 12] So Job is an inhabitant of the land of Uz, because Wisdom, Which underwent the pain of the Passion in our behalf, has made an habitation for Herself in those hearts, which are instinct with the counsels of life. **xi.**

16. *And that man was perfect and upright.* In uprightness, justice is signified, and in simplicity, mercy [or 'meekness,' *mansuetudo*]. We in following out the straight line of justice, generally leave mercy behind; and in aiming to observe mercy, we deviate from the straight line of justice. Yet the Incarnate Lord maintained simplicity with uprightness; for He neither in showing mercy parted with the strictness of Justice, nor again in the exactitude of justice did He part with the virtue of mercifulness. Hence when certain persons, having brought an adulteress before Him, would have tempted Him, in order that He might step into the fault either of unmercifulness or of injustice, He answered both alternatives by saying, *He that is without sin among you, let him first cast a stone at her.* [John 8, 7] *He that is without sin among you*, gives us the simplicity of mercy, *let him first cast a stone at her*, gives us the jealous sense of justice. Whence too the Prophet says to him, *And in Thy Majesty ride prosperously, because of truth, and meekness, and righteousness.* [Ps. 45, 4] For in executing truth, He kept mercy united with justice, so that He neither lost the jealous sense of rectitude in the preponderance of mercy's scale, nor again unsettled the preponderance of mercy by that jealousy of rectitude. **xii.**

17. *And one that feared God, and eschewed evil.* It is written of Him, *and the Spirit of the fear of the Lord hath filled Him*; for the Incarnate Lord showed forth in His own person whatsoever He **xiii.**

hath inspired us withal, that what He delivered by precept, He might recommend by example. So then according to our human nature our Redeemer feared God, for to redeem proud man, He took for man's sake an humble mind. And His acting likewise is fitly designated hereby, in that the blessed Job is said to eschew evil. For He Himself eschewed evil, not evil which He came in contact with in the doing, but which upon meeting with it, He rejected; for He forsook the old life after man's method, which He found at His birth, and He stamped upon the character of His followers that new life, which He brought down with Him.

xiv. 18. Ver. 2. *And there were born to him seven sons and three daughters*. What is conveyed to us in the number of seven, saving the sum of perfection? for to say nothing of the arguments of human reasoning which maintain that it is therefore perfect, because it consists of the first even number, and of the first uneven; of the first that is capable of division, and of the first which is incapable of it; we know most certainly that holy Scripture is wont to put the number seven for perfection, whence also it tells us that on the seventh day the Lord rested from His works; and it is hence too ,that the seventh day was given to man for a rest; i.e. for a 'Sabbath.' Hence it is that the year of jubilee, wherein we have a full rest set forth, is accomplished in seven weeks, being completed by the addition of the unit of our uniting together.

19. *Thus there were born to him seven sons*; namely, the Apostles manfully issuing forth to preach; who in putting in practice the precepts of perfection, as it were maintained in their manner of life the courage of the superior sex. For hence it is that twelve of them were chosen, who should be replenished with the perfection of the sevenfold grace of the Spirit. As from the number seven we rise to twelve; for seven multiplied in its component parts is extended to twelve; for whether four be taken by three or three by four, seven is changed into twelve, and hence, forasmuch as the holy Apostles were sent to proclaim the holy Trinity in the four quarters of the globe, they were chosen twelve in number, that by their very number they might set forth that perfection, which they proclaimed both by their lips and in their lives.

20. *And three daughters*. What do we understand by the daughters but the weaker multitudes of the faithful, who, though they never

adhere with a virtuous resolution to perfection of life, yet cleave with constancy to the belief of the Trinity which has been taught them. Thus by 'the seven sons' is represented the order of the Preachers, and by 'the three daughters' the multitude of the hearers. By 'the three daughters' may also be signified the three orders of the faithful, for after mention of the sons the daughters are named, in that succeeding next to the distinguished courage of the Apostles came three divisions of the faithful, in the state of life in the Church; viz. of Pastors, of those following continence, and of the married. And hence the prophet Ezekiel declares that he heard three men named that were set free; viz. Noah, and Daniel, and Job [Ezek. 14, 14f]; for what is signified by Noah who guided the Ark in the waters, but the order or rulers, who, while they govern the people for the fashioning of their lives, are the directors of holy Church amidst the waves of temptation? What is represented by Daniel, whose marvellous abstinence we have described to us, but the life of the continent, who, while they give up everything that is of the world, rule with elevated mind over Babylon which lies beneath them? What is signified by Job but the life of the good that are married, who, while they do deeds of mercy by the good things of the world which they possess, do as it were advance to their heavenly country by the paths of earth? Therefore because after the holy Apostles there came these three divisions of the faithful, after the sons rightly follows the mention of the three daughters that were born to him. It proceeds:

Ver. 3. His substance also was three thousand sheep and three thousand camels.

21. That believing hearers have been gathered from various manners of life, a truth which is first declared generally by the mention of the daughters, the same is afterwards brought before us in detail by the specification of the animals. For what does he set forth in the seven thousand sheep, but some men's perfect innocency, which comes from the pastures of the Law to the perfect estate of grace? what again is signified by the three thousand camels, but the crooked defectiveness of the Gentiles coming to the fulness of faith. Now in Holy Scripture, sometimes the Lord Himself is expressed by the title of a camel, and sometimes the Gentile people. For the Lord is signified by the name of a camel, as when it is said by that very Lord to the Jews that set themselves against Him, *who strain* **XV.**

at a gnat, and swallow a camel. [Mat. 23, 24] For a gnat wounds while it whispers, but a camel of free will bends to receive its load. Thus the Jews strained at a gnat, in that they sought that a seditious robber should be let go, but they swallowed a camel, in that Him, Who had come down of His own accord to take upon Him the burthens of our mortal nature, they strove to overwhelm by their clamours. Again, the Gentile state is signified by the naming of a camel; and hence Rebecca on going to Isaac is brought on a camel's back, in that the Church, which hastens from the Gentile state to Christ, is found in the crooked and defective behaviour of the old life; and she, when she saw Isaac, descended, in that when the Gentile world knew the Lord, it abandoned its sins, and descending from the height of self-elation sought the lowly walks of humility; and she too in bashfulness covers herself with a veil, in that she is confounded in His presence for her past life. And hence it is said by the Apostle to these same Gentiles, *What fruit had ye then in those things whereof ye are now ashamed?* [Rom. 6, 21] Whereas then by the sheep we understand the Hebrews coming to the faith from the pastures of the Law, nothing hinders but that we understand by the camels the Gentile people, crooked in their ways and laden with idolatrous ceremonials. For because they devised them gods of their own selves whom they should worship, there had grown up as it were out of themselves a load upon their back which they should carry.

22. Furthermore in that they are common animals, it is possible that by camels is represented the life of the Samaritans. For camels chew the cud, but do not divide the hoof. So likewise the Samaritans do as it were chew the cud, in that they receive in part the words of the Law, but do not divide the hoof as it were, forasmuch as they despise it in part. And they bear a grievous burthen upon the mind's pack, in that they weary themselves in whatsoever they do without any hope of eternity. For they are strangers to faith in the Resurrection, and what can be more grievous or more burthensome than to endure the tribulation of this passing state of existence, and yet never, for relief of mind, to look forward to the joy of our reward; but forasmuch as the Lord, when He appeared in the flesh, both filled the Hebrew people with the grace of perfection, and brought some of the Samaritans to the knowledge of the faith by showing marvellous works, it might well be said of the shadow

which was to express the reality, that he possessed both seven thousand sheep, and three thousand camels. It goes on;

And five hundred yoke of oxen, and five hundred she asses.

23. We have said above that by the number fifty, which is completed by seven weeks and the addition of an unit, rest is signified, and by the number 'ten' the sum of perfection is set forth. Now forasmuch as the perfection of rest is promised to the faithful, by multiplying fifty ten times, we in this, way arrive at five hundred. But in sacred Writ, the title of 'oxen' sometimes represents the dulness of the foolish sort, and sometimes the life of well doers. For because the stupidity of the fool is represented by the title of an ox, Solomon says rightly, *he goeth after her straightway, as an ox goeth to the slaughter*. [Prov. 7, 22] Again, that the life of every labourer is forth by the title of oxen, the Precepts of the Law are a testimony, which enjoined through Moses; *Thou shalt not muzzle the ox when he treadeth out the corn*. [Deut. 25, 4] And this again is declared in plain words; *the labourer is worthy of his hire*. [Luke 10, 7] By the title of asses, too, we have represented sometimes the inertness of fools, sometimes the unrestrained indulgence of the wanton, sometimes the simplemindedness of the Gentiles; for the inertness of fools is imaged by the designation of asses, as where it is said through Moses, *Thou shalt not plough with an ox and an ass together*. [Deut. 22, 10] As though he said, 'do not associate fools and wise men together in preaching, lest by means of him who has no power to accomplish the work, you hinder him who has abundant power.' The unrestrained indulgence of the wanton is likewise set forth by the appellation of asses, as the prophet testifies, where he says, *whose flesh is as the flesh if asses*. [Ezek. 23, 20] Again, by the title of asses is shown the simplicity of the Gentiles. Hence when the Lord went up toward Jerusalem, He is related to have sat upon a young ass, for what is it for Him to come to Jerusalem sitting upon an ass, except taking possession of the simple hearts of the Gentiles to conduct them to the vision of peace, by ruling and ordering them? And this is shown by one passage, and that a very easy one; in that both the workmen of Judaea are represented by oxen, and the Gentile peoples by an ass, when it is said by the Prophet, *The ox knoweth his owner, and the ass his master's crib*. [Isa. 1, 3] For who appears as the ox, saving the Jewish people, whose neck was worn by the yoke of the Law? and who was

xvi.

the ass but the Gentile world, which was found like a brute animal of every deceiver, and was overlaid with whatever deceit he pleased, without resisting by any exercise of reason? Thus the ox knoweth his owner, and the ass his master's crib, in that both the Hebrews found out the God Whom they worshipped but as yet knew Him not, and the Gentile world received the food of the Law, which it had none of. That therefore which is spoken above in the designation of the sheep and of the camels, is here repeated below in the oxen and the asses.

24. Now even before the coming of the Redeemer Judaea possessed oxen, in that she sent out labourers to preach, to whom it is said by the voice of Truth, *Woe unto you, Scribes and Pharisees, hypocrites! for ye compass sea and land to make one proselyte; and when he is made, ye make him twofold more the child of hell than yourselves*. [Mat. 23, 15] These were weighed down with the heavy yoke of the Law, because they were burthened with the ordinances of the external letter, to whom it is spoken by the voice of Truth, *Come unto Me, all ye that labour and are heavy laden, and I will refresh you. Take My yoke upon you, and learn of Me, for I am meek and lowly in heart*. [Mat. 11, 28. 29.] That in the Gospel, therefore, rest is promised to those that labour well, is the same thing as that five hundred yoke of oxen are made mention of in this place; for whereunto does their way lead, who submit their necks to the dominion of our Redeemer, excepting to rest? And hence we are told of five hundred she asses, forasmuch as the Gentile folk that are called, so long as they desire to attain to rest, gladly bear all the burthens of the commandments; and hence, that this rest should be sought of the Gentiles, Jacob in addressing his sons did mean to signify by the voice of prophecy, saying, *Issachar is a strong ass, crouching down between the boundaries* [Vulg. *Terminus,* E.V. burthens]: *And he saw that rest was good, and the land that it was pleasant, and bowed the shoulder to bear*. [Gen. 49, 14. 15.] For to crouch down between the boundaries is to rest forestalling the end of the world, and to seek nought of those things, which are now going forward amongst men, but to long after the things that shall be at the last; and the strong ass sees the rest and the pleasant land, when the simple Gentile world lifts itself up to the strong effort of good works, and that because it is on its way to the land of life eternal; and it bows the shoulder to bear, in that having beheld the rest above, it submits itself in doing its work even to severe precepts,

and whatever littleness of mind represents as hard to bear, the hope of the reward makes this appear to it light and easy. So because both Judaea and the Gentile world are gathered to eternal rest as a portion of the elect, he is rightly related to have possessed five hundred yoke of oxen, and five hundred she asses. The account goes on;

And a very great household.

xvii.

25. What means it that the number of the animals is first described, while the household is not mentioned till the end, but that the foolish things of the world are first gathered in to the knowledge of the faith, that afterwards the crafty things of the world may also be called? as Paul bears witness, who says; *For ye see your calling, brethren, how that not many wise men after the flesh, not many noble, not many mighty are called; But God hath chosen the foolish things of the world to confound the wise.* [1 Cor. 1, 26. 27.] For the first beginnings [*principia*] of holy Church are reputed to have been without knowledge of letters, plainly for this reason, that in His preachers the Redeemer might manifest to all, that it was not their discourse, but their cause, which had influence with the numbers [*populos*] that believed unto life. It proceeds;

So that this man was the greatest of all the men if the East.

xviii.

26. That our Redeemer is styled *The East* is declared by the testimony of the Prophet, where he says, *And lo! the Man whose name is The East*. [Zech. 6, 12 Vulg. *Orients,* E.V. *the Branch*] And thus all that live in this Orient by faith, are rightly called men of the East. Now because all men are only men, whereas 'The East' Himself is both God and Man, it is rightly said, *He was the greatest of all the men of the East.* As though it were said in plain words, 'He surpassed all those that are born to God in faith.' Because it is not by adoption, as others are, but by the Divine Nature that He is exalted, Who though He appeared like to others in His human Nature, yet in His Divine Nature continued above all men without fellow.

Ver.4. And his sons went and feasted in their houses.

xix.

27. The sons went to feast at their houses, when the Apostles as preachers, in the different regions of the world, served the banquet of virtue to hearers as it were to eaters. And hence it is

said to those very sons concerning the hungering multitude, *Give ye them to eat*. [Mat. 14, 16] And again; *And I will not send them away fasting, lest they faint by the way* [Mat. 15, 32]; that is, let them by your preaching receive the word of consolation, that they may not by continuing to fast to the food of truth, sink under the labours of this life. Hence again it is said to the same sons, *Labour not for the meat which perisheth, but for that meat which endureth unto everlasting life*. [John 6, 27] And how these feasts were set forth is added, whereas it is forthwith subjoined,

Everyone in his day.

XX. 28. If without any doubt the darkness of ignorance is the night of the soul, the understanding is not improperly styled the day. And hence Paul says, *One man esteemeth one day above another; another esteemeth every day alike*. [Rom. 14, 5] As, if he had said in plain words; 'One man understands some things so as that some are left out, and another acquaints himself with all things that are possible to be understood, in such sort as they may be seen. Thus each son sets forth a feast in his day, in that every holy preacher, according to the measure of the enlightening of his understanding, feeds the minds of his hearers with the entertainments of Truth. Paul made a feast in his own day, when he said, *But she is happier if she so abide according to my judgment*. [1 Cor. 7, 40] He bade each to take account of his own day; when he said, *Let every man be fully persuaded in his own mind*. [Rom. 14, 5] It goes on;

And sent and called for their three sisters to eat and to drink with them.

XXI. 29. The sons call their sisters to the feast, in that the holy Apostles proclaim to hearers that are weak the joys of the refreshment above, and inasmuch as they see their souls to be starved of the food of truth, they feed them with the feast of God's Word. And it is well said, to eat and to drink with them. For holy Scripture is sometimes meat to us, and sometimes drink. It is meat in the harder parts, in that it is in a certain sense broken in pieces by being explained, and swallowed after chewing; and it is drink in the plainer parts, in that it is imbibed just as it is found. The Prophet discerned holy Scripture to be meat, which was to be broken in pieces in the explaining, when he said, *The young children ask, and no man breaketh it unto them* [Lam. 4, 4], i.e. the weak ones sought that the stronger declarations of holy Scripture might be crumbled for them by explanation, but he could no where be found who should have explained them. The Prophet saw that holy Writ was drink, when he said, *Ho, everyone that thirsteth come ye to the waters*. [Isa. 55, 1] Had not the plain commandments been drink, Truth would never have cried out with His own lips; *If any man thirst, let him come unto Me and drink*. [John 5, 37] The Prophet saw that there was, as it were, a lack of meat and drink in Judaea, when he declared, *And their honourable men are famished, and their multitude dried up with thirst*. Isa. 5, 13] For it belongs to the few to attain a knowledge of the mighty and hidden meanings, but to the multitude it is given to understand the plain sense of the history. And therefore he declares that the honourable men of Judaea had perished not by thirst, but hunger, in that those who seemed to stand first, by giving themselves wholly to the outward sense, had not wherewithal to feed themselves from the inward parts by sifting their meaning, but forasmuch as when loftier minds fall away from the inward sense, the understanding of the little ones even in the outward meaning is dried up; it is rightly added in this place, *And the multitude dried up with thirst*. As if he said in plainer words, 'whereas the common sort give over taking pains in their own lives, they now no longer seek even the streams of history.' And they bear witness that they understood both the deep and the plain things contained in divine Writ, who in complaining to the Judge that rejects them, say, *We have eaten and drunk in Thy presence* [Luke 13, 26]; and this they subjoin in plain terms by explaining it; *And thou hast taught in our streets*. Therefore because the sacred oracles are broken in the more obscure parts, by the explanation thereof, but in the plainer parts are drunk in just as they are found, it may be truly said, *And they sent and called for their three sisters, to eat and to drink with them*. As though it were said in plain terms, they drew every weak one to themselves by the mildness of their persuasions, that both by setting forward great truths contemplatively, they might feed their minds, and by delivering little things historically, they might give them nourishment. The account proceeds:

Ver. 5. And it was so, when the days of their feasting [V. *thus*] *were gone about, that Job sent and sanctified them, and rose up early in the morning, and offered burnt offerings according to the number of them all.*

THE FIRST PART.

xxii. 30. 'The days of feasting are gone,' when the ministrations of preaching are brought to an end; and when the feasts were ended, Job offered an holocaust for his sons, in that our Redeemer besought the Father in behalf of the Apostles, when they returned from preaching. Now it is rightly said, that he 'sent and sanctified,' in that when He bestowed the Holy Spirit Which proceeds from Himself, upon the hearts of His disciples, He cleansed them from whatsoever might be in them of offence, and it is rightly delivered that he rose up early to offer sacrifices; forasmuch as through this His offering up the prayer of His Intercessions in our behalf, he dispelled the night of error, and illumined the darkness of man's mind; that the soul might not be polluted in secret by any defilements of sin contracted from the very grace of preaching; that it might never attribute to itself aught that it does; that it might not, by attributing them to itself, lose all the things it had done. Hence it is well added,

For Job said, It may be that my sons have sinned, and blessed God in their hearts.

xxiii. 31. For this blessing God, which means cursing, is the taking glory to one's self from a gift of His hand. Hence the Lord did well to wash the feet of the holy Apostles after their preaching, doubtless with this view, that He might show plainly, both that very frequently in doing good the dust of sin is contracted, and that the steps of the speakers are often defiled by the same means whereby the hearts of their hearers are purified. For it often happens that some in giving words of exhortation, however poorly, are inwardly lifted up, because they are the channel, by which the grace of purification comes down; and while by the word they wash away the deeds of other men, they as it were contract the dust of an ill thought from a good course. What then was it to wash the disciples' feet after their preaching, but after the gloriousness of preaching to wipe off the dust of our thoughts, and to cleanse the heart's goings from inward pride? Nor does it hinder the universal knowledge which our Mediator has, that it is said, *It may be*; for knowing all things, but in His mode of speech taking upon Him our ignorance, and, in taking the same, giving us a lesson, He sometimes speaks as it were with our doubts; as where He says, *Nevertheless, when the Son of Man cometh shall He find faith on the earth?* [Luke 18, 8]

When the feasting then was over, Job offered a sacrifice for his sons, saying, *It may be that my sons have sinned, and cursed God in their heart*; in that our Saviour, after He had cleansed His preachers from the evils that beset them even in the midst of the good things which they had done, kept them from temptations. It goes on,

Thus did Job continually.

xxiv.

32. Job does not cease 'to offer sacrifice continually,' in that our Redeemer offers a holocaust for us without ceasing, Who without intermission exhibits to the Father His Incarnation in our behalf. For His very Incarnation is itself the offering for our purification, and while He shows Himself as Man, He is the Intercession that washes out man's misdeeds, and in the mystery of His Humanity He offers a perpetual Sacrifice, even because those things too are eternal which He purifies.

33. Now because in the very opening of our exposition we so made the Lord to be set forth in the person of blessed Job, that we said that both the Head and the Body, i.e. both Christ and His Church, were represented by him; therefore since we have shown how our Head may be taken to be represented, let us now point out, how His Body, which we are, is set forth; that as we have heard from the history somewhat to admire, and learnt from the Head somewhat to believe, we may now deduce from the Body somewhat to maintain in our lives. For we should transform within ourselves that we read, that when the mind is moved by hearing, the life may concur to the execution of that which it has heard.

There was a man in the land of Uz, whose name was Job.

xxv.

34. If 'Job' signifies 'grieving' and 'Uz' 'a Counsellor,' every elect person is not improperly represented by either name; in that be certainly abides in a mind of wise counsel, who hastens grieving from things present to things eternal. For there are some that take no heed to their life, and whilst they are seeking transitory objects, and either do not understand those that are eternal, or understanding despise them, they neither feel grief nor know how to entertain counsel, and when they are taking no account of the things above which they have lost, they think, unhappy wretches, that they are in the midst of good things. For these never raise the eyes of their mind to the light of truth which they were created for, they

never bend the keenness of desire to the contemplation of their eternal country, but forsaking themselves amidst those things in which they are cast away, instead of their country they love the exile which is their lot, and rejoice in the darkness which they undergo as if in the brightness of the light. But, on the contrary, when the minds of the elect perceive that all things transitory are nought, they seek out which be the things for which they were created, and whereas nothing suffices to the satisfying them out of God, thought itself, being wearied in them by the effort of the search, finds rest in the hope and contemplation of its Creator, longs to have a place among the citizens above; and each one of them, while yet in the body an inhabitant of the world, in mind already soars beyond the world, bewails the weariness of exile which he endures, and with the ceaseless incitements of love urges himself on to the country on high. When then he sees grieving how that that which he lost is eternal, he finds the salutary counsel, to look down upon this temporal scene which he is passing through, and the more the knowledge of that counsel increases, which bids him forsake perishable things, the more is grief augmented that he cannot yet attain to lasting objects. Hence Solomon well says, *He that increaseth knowledge increaseth sorrow* [Eccles. 1, 18]; for he that already knows the high state which he does not as yet enjoy, is the more grieved for the low condition, in which he is yet held.

35. Job therefore is well said to dwell in the land of Uz, in that the mind of every elect person is kept going grieving in the counsels of knowledge. We must also observe what absence of grief of mind there is in precipitancy of action. For they that live without counsel, who give themselves over precipitately to the issue of events, are meanwhile harassed by no grief of reflection. For he that discreetly settles his mind in the counsels of life, heedfully takes account of himself, exercising circumspection in his every doing, and lest from that which he is doing a sudden and adverse issue should seize him, he first feels at it, gently applying to it the foot of reflection; he takes thought that fear may not withhold him from those things which ought to be done, nor precipitance hurry him into those which ought to be deferred; that evil things may not get the better of him through his desires by an open assault, nor good things work his downfall insidiously by vain glory. Thus Job dwells in the land of Uz, in that the more the mind of the elect strives to live by following counsel,

so much the more is it worn with the grief of so narrow a way. It goes on;

And that man sincere [*simplex,* E.V. *perfect*] *and upright, one that feared God, and eschewed evil.*

xxvi.

36. Whoso longs for the eternal country, lives without doubt *sincere and upright*; I mean, *perfect* in practice, and *right* in faith, sincere in the good that he does in this lower state, right in the high truths which he minds in his inner self. For there are some who in the good actions that they do are not sincere, whereas they look to them not for a reward within but to win favour without. Hence it is well said by a certain wise man, *Woe to the sinner that goeth two ways* [Ecclus. 2, 12]; for the sinner goes two ways, when at the same time that what he sets forth in deed is of God, what he aims at in thought is of the world.

37. Now it is well said, *one that feared God and eschewed evil*; in that the holy Church of the elect enters indeed upon its paths of simplicity and of uprightness in [al. from] fear, but finishes them in charity, and it is hers then entirely 'to depart from evil,' when she has begun now from the love of God to feel unwillingness to sin. But whilst she still does good deeds from fear, she has not entirely departed from evil; because she sins even herein, that she would sin if she could have done it without punishment. So then when Job is said to fear God, it is rightly related that he also 'departs from evil,' in that whereas charity follows upon fear, that offence which is left behind in the mind is even trodden under foot in the purpose of the heart. And forasmuch as each particular vice is stifled by fear, whilst the several virtues spring from charity, it is rightly added,

And there were born unto him seven sons and three daughters.

xxvii.

38. For there are seven sons born to us, when by the conception of good intent the seven virtues of the holy Spirit spring up in us. Thus the Prophet particularizes this inward offspring, when the Spirit renders the mind fruitful, in these words; *And the Spirit of the Lord shall rest upon Him, the spirit of wisdom and understanding, the spirit of counsel and might, the spirit of knowledge and piety, and the spirit of the fear of the Lord shall fill him.* [Isa. 11, 2] So when by the coming of the Holy Spirit there is engendered in each of us, 'wisdom, understanding, counsel, might, knowledge, piety, and

the fear of the Lord,' something like a lasting posterity is begotten in the mind, which preserves the stock of our nobility that is above unto life, for so much the longer as it allies it with the love of eternity. Yet surely the seven sons have in us three sisters, forasmuch as all that manly work which these virtuous affections [*virtutum sensus*] do, they unite with faith, hope, and charity. For the seven sons never attain the perfection of the number ten, unless all that they do be done in faith, hope, and charity. But because this store of antecedent virtues is followed by a manifold concern for good works, it is rightly added,

Ver.3. His substance also was seven thousand sheep and three thousand camels.

xxviii. 39. For, saving the historical truth, we are at liberty to follow in a spiritual way that which our ears receive in a carnal shape. Thus we possess seven thousand sheep, when we feed the innocent thoughts within our breast, in a perfect purity of heart, with the food of truth which we have sought after.

40. And we shall have three thousand camels likewise in our possession, if all that is high and crooked in us be subdued to the order [*rationi*] of faith, and when of our own free will, and in our longing after humility, it is made to bow down itself under a knowledge of the Trinity. For we possess camels, whensoever we put down in humility all the high notions that we entertain. Surely we are in possession of camels, when we bend our thoughts to sympathy with a brother's weakness, that bearing our burthens by turns, we may by lowering ourselves thereto know how to compassionate the weakness of another man. By camels, too, which do not cleave the hoof, but chew the cud, may be understood the good stewardships of earthly things, which, in that they have something of the world, and something of God, must needs be represented by a common animal. For though earthly stewardship may be subservient to our eternal welfare, yet we cannot acquit ourselves of it without inward disquietude. Therefore because both at the present time the mind is disturbed thereby, and also a reward laid up for ever, like a common animal, it both has something of the Law, and something it has not. For it does not cleave the hoof, in that the soul does not wholly sever itself from all earthly doings, but yet it ruminates, in that by the right dispensation of temporal things, it gains a hope of heavenly

blessings with an assured confidence. Thus earthly stewardships agree with the law in the head, disagree therewith in the foot; forasmuch as while the objects which they desire to obtain by living righteously are of heaven, the concerns with which they are busied by their performances are of this world. When then we submit these earthly stewardships to the knowledge of the Trinity, we have camels in possession, as it were, by faith. The account goes on;

And five hundred yoke of oxen, and five hundred she asses.

xxix.

41. There are yokes of oxen for us in our possession, when the virtues in harmony plough up the hardness of our mind. We also possess five hundred she asses, when we restrain wanton inclinations, and when whatever of a carnal nature seeks to rise up in us, we curb in the spiritual mastery of the heart. Or indeed to possess she asses is to govern the simple thoughts within us, which, while they have no power to run in a more refined intelligence, by how much more lowly they walk, bear with so much the more meekness their brother's burthens. For there are some who not understanding deep things constrain themselves the more humbly to the outward works of duty. Well then do we understand the simple thoughts by she asses, which are an animal slow indeed, yet devoted to carrying burthens, in that very often when made acquainted with our own ignorance, we bear the more lightly the burthens of others; and whereas we are not elevated as by any special height of wisdom, our mind bends itself in patience to submit to the dulness of another's soul. Now it is well done, whether it be the yokes of oxen or the she asses, that they are mentioned as five hundred, in that, whether in the case that through prudence we are wise, or in the case that we remain in humble ignorance, so long as we are in search of the rest of eternal peace, we are as it were kept within the number of the Jubilee. It goes on;

And a very great household,

xxx.

42. We possess a very great household, when we restrain our host of thoughts under the mastery of the mind, that they may not by their very number get the better of the soul, nor in disordered array tread under the authority which belongs to our faculty of discernment. And the multitude of our thoughts is well marked out by the designation of a very great household. For we

know that when the mistress is away the tongues of the handmaids wax clamorous, that they cease from silence, neglect the duties of their allotted task, and disarrange the whole ordered method of their life. But if the mistress suddenly appear, in a moment their noisy tongues are still, they renew the duties of their several tasks, and return to their own work as though they had never left it. Thus if reason for a moment leave the house of the mind, as if the mistress were absent, the den of our thoughts redoubles itself, like a bevy of talkative maids. But so soon as reason has returned to the mind, the confused tumult quiets itself at once, and the maids as it were betake themselves in silence to the task enjoined, whilst the thoughts forthwith submit themselves to their appropriate occasions for usefulness. We possess, then, a great household, when with righteous authority we rule our innumerable thoughts by a discerning use of reason; and assuredly when we do this wisely, we are aiming to unite ourselves to the Angels by that very exercise of discernment: and hence it is rightly subjoined;

So that this man was the greatest of all the men of the east.

xxxi. 43. For we are then rendered great amongst all them of the east, when the cloud of carnal corruption being kept down by the rays of our discernment, we are, as far as the possibility of the thing admits, made the associates of those Spirits, which abide in the eastern light: and hence Paul says, *Our conversation is in heaven* [Phil. 3, 20]. For he that follows after temporal things, which are subject to decay, seeks the west [*occasum*], but whoso fixes his desires upon things above, proves that he dwells in the east. He then is great not among them of the west but among them of the east, who aims to excel not amid wicked men's scenes of action, who seek low and fleeting things, but amongst the choirs of the citizens above. It proceeds;

Ver. 4. And his sons went and feasted in their houses, every one his day.

xxxii. 44. 'The sons feast in their houses,' when the several virtues feed the mind after their proper sort; and it is well said, *Everyone his day*, for each son's day is the shining of each virtue. Briefly to unfold then these same gifts of sevenfold grace, wisdom has one day, understanding another day, counsel another, fortitude another, knowledge another, piety another, fear another, for it is not the same thing to be wise that it is to understand; for many indeed are wise [*sapiunt*] in the things of eternity, but cannot in any sort understand them. Wisdom therefore gives a feast in its day in that it refreshes the mind with the hope and assurance of eternal things. Understanding spreads a feast in its day, forasmuch as, in that it penetrates the truths heard, refreshing the heart, it lights up its darkness. Counsel gives a feast in its day, in that while it stays us from acting precipitately, it makes the mind to be full of reason. Fortitude gives a feast in its day, in that whereas it has no fear of adversity, it sets the viands of confidence before the alarmed soul. Knowledge prepares a feast in her day, in that in the mind's belly, she overcomes the emptiness of ignorance. Piety sets forth a feast in its day, in that it satisfies the bowels of the heart with deeds of mercy. Fear makes a feast in its day, in that whereas it keeps down the mind, that it may not pride itself in the present things, it strengthens it with the meat of hope for the future.

45. But I see that this point requires searching into in this feasting of the sons, viz. that by turns they feed one another. For each particular virtue is to the last degree destitute, unless one virtue lends its support to another. For wisdom is less worth if it lacks understanding, and understanding is wholly useless if it be not based upon wisdom, in that whilst it penetrates the higher mysteries without the counterpoise of wisdom, its own lightness is only lifting it up to meet with the heavier fall. Counsel is worthless, when the strength of fortitude is lacking thereto, since what it finds out by turning the thing over, from want of strength it never carries on so far as to the perfecting in deed; and fortitude is very much broken down, if it be not supported by counsel, since the greater the power which it perceives itself to have, so much the more miserably does this virtue rush headlong into ruin, without the governance of reason. Knowledge is nought if it hath not its use for piety; for whereas it neglects to put in practice the good that it knows, it binds itself the more closely to the Judgment: and piety is very useless, if it lacks the discernment of knowledge, in that while there is no knowledge to enlighten it, it knows not the way to show mercy. And assuredly unless it has these virtues with it, fear itself rises up to the doing of no good action, forasmuch as while it is agitated about everything, its own alarms renders it inactive and void of all good works. Since then by reciprocal ministrations virtue is refreshed by virtue, it is

truly said that the sons feast with one another by turns; and as one aids to relieve another, it is as if the numerous offspring to be fed were to prepare a banquet each his day. It follows;

And sent and called for their three sisters, to eat and to drink with them.

xxxiii. 46. When our virtues invite faith, hope, and charity into everything they do, they do, as sons employed in labour, call their three sisters to a feast; that faith, hope, and charity may rejoice in the good work, which each virtue provides; and they as it were gain strength from that meat, whilst they are rendered more confident by good works, and whereas after meat they long to imbibe the dew of contemplation, they are as it were from the cup inebriated.

47. But what is there that we do, in this life, without some stain of defilement, howsoever slight? For sometimes by the very good things we do we draw near to the worse part, since while they beget much in the mind, they at the same time engender a certain security, and when the mind enjoys security, it unlooses itself in sloth; and sometimes they defile us with some self-elation, and set us so much the lower with God, as they make us bigger in our own eyes. Hence it is well added,

Ver. 5. And it was so, when the days of their feasting were gone about, that Job sent and sanctified them.

xxxiv. 47. For, when the round of the days of feasting is gone about, to send to his sons and to sanctify them, is after the perception [*sensum*] of the virtues to direct the inward intention, and to purify all that we do with the exact sifting of a reexamination, lest things be counted good which are evil, or at least such as are truly good be thought enough when they are imperfect. For thus it very often happens that the mind is taken in, so that it is deceived either in the quality of what is evil or the quantity of what is good. But these senses of the virtues are much better ascertained by prayers than by examinings. For the things which we endeavour to search out more completely in ourselves, we oftener obtain a true insight into by praying than by investigating. For when the mind is lifted up on high by the kind of machine of compunction, all that may have been presented to it concerning itself, it surveys the more surely by passing judgment upon it beneath its feet. Hence it is well subjoined,

And rose up early in the morning and offered burnt offerings, according to the number of them all.

xxxv.

48. For we rise up early in the morning, when being penetrated with the light of compunction we leave the night of our human state, and open the eyes of the mind to the beams of the true light, and we offer a burnt offering for each son, when we offer up the sacrifice of prayer for each virtue, lest wisdom may uplift; or understanding, while it runs nimbly, deviate from the right path; or counsel, while it multiplies itself, grow into confusion; that fortitude, while it gives confidence, may not lead to precipitation, lest knowledge, while it knows and yet has no love, may swell the mind; lest piety, while it bends itself out of the right line, may become distorted; and lest fear, while it is unduly alarmed, may plunge one into the pit of despair. When then we pour out our prayers to the Lord in behalf of each several virtue, that it be free from alloy, what else do we but according to the number of our sons offer a burnt offering [*holocaustum*] for each? for an holocaust is rendered 'the whole burnt.' Therefore to pay a 'holocaust' is to light up the whole soul with the fire of compunction, that the heart may burn on the altar of love, and consume the defilements of our thoughts, like the sins of our own offspring.

49. But none know how to do this saving those, who, before their thoughts proceed to deeds, restrain with anxious circumspection the inward motions of their hearts. None know how to do this saving they who have learnt to fortify their soul with a manly guard. Hence Ishbosheth is rightly said to have perished by a sudden death, whom holy Scripture at the same time testifies to have had not a man for his doorkeeper but a woman, in these words; *And the sons of Rimmon the Beerothite, Rechab and Baanah, went and came about the heat of the day to the house of Ishbosheth, who lay on a bed at noon; and they came thither into the midst of the house:, and the portress of the house was fallen asleep, winnowing wheat. And they came privily into the house fetching ears of wheat, and they smote him in the groin.* [2 Sam. 4, 5–7. Vulg.] The portress winnows the wheat, when the wardkeeping of the mind distinguishes and separates the virtues from the vices; but if she falls asleep, she lets in conspirators to her master's destruction, in that

when the cautiousness of discernment is at an end, a way is set open for evil spirits to slay the soul. They enter in and carry off the ears, in that they at once bear off the germs of good thoughts; and they smite in the groin, in that they cut off the virtue of the soul by the delights of the flesh. For to smite in the groin is to pierce the life of the mind with the delights of the flesh. But this Ishbosheth would never have perished by such a death, if he had not set a woman at the entrance to his house, i.e. set an easy guard at the way of access to the mind. For a strong and manly activity should be set over the doors of the heart, such as is never surprised by sleep of neglect, and never deceived by the errors of ignorance; and hence he is rightly named Ishbosheth, who is exposed by a female guard to the swords of his enemies, for Ishbosheth is rendered 'a man of confusion.' And he is 'a man of confusion,' who is not provided with a strong guard over his mind, in that while he reckons himself to be practising virtues, vices stealing in kill him [al. 'kill his soul'] unawares. The entrance to the mind then must be fortified with the whole sum of virtue, lest at any time enemies with insidious intent penetrate into it by the opening of heedless thought. Hence Solomon says, *Keep thy heart with all diligence, for out of it are the issues of life* [Prov. 4, 23]. It is meet then that we form a most careful estimate of the virtues that we practise, beginning with the original intent, lest the acts which they put forth, even though they be right, may proceed from a bad origin: and hence it is rightly subjoined in this place;

For Job said, It may be that my sons have sinned, and cursed God in their hearts.

xxxvi. 50. Our sons curse God in their hearts, when our righteous deeds proceed from unrighteous thoughts; when they put forth good things in public, but in secret devise mischief. Thus they curse God, when our minds reckon that they get from themselves that which they are. They curse God when they can understand that it is from Him that they have received their powers, and yet seek their own praise for His gifts. But be it known that our old enemy proceeds against our good actions in three ways, with this view, namely, that the thing which is done aright before the eyes of men, may be spoiled in the sight of the Judge within. For sometimes in a good work he pollutes the intention, that all that follows in the doing may come forth impure and unclean, because it is hereby made to rise troubled from its source. But sometimes he has no power to spoil the intention of a good deed, but he presents himself in the action itself as it were in the pathway; that whereas the person goes forth the more secure in the purpose of his heart, evil being secretly there laid, he may as it were be slain from ambush. And sometimes he neither corrupts the intention, nor overthrows it in the way, but he ensnares the good deed at the end of the action; and in proportion as he feigns himself to have gone further off, whether from the house of the heart or from the path of the deed, with the greater craftiness he watches to catch the end of the good action; and the more he has put a man off his guard by seeming to retire, so much the more incurably does he at times pierce him with an unexpected wound.

51. For he defiles the intention in a good work, in that when he sees men's hearts ready to be deceived, he presents to their ambition the breath of passing applause, that wherein they do aright, they may swerve by crookedness in the intention to make the lowest things their aim; and hence under the image of Judaea, it is well said by the Prophet of every soul that is caught in the snare of mal-intention, *Her adversaries are the chief* [Lament. 1, 5]. As though it were said in plain words, 'when a good work is taken in hand with no good intent, the spirits that are against us have dominion over her from the commencement of the conception, and the more completely possess themselves of her, even that they hold her under their power by the very beginning.'

52. But when they are unable to corrupt the intention, they conceal snares which they set in the way, that the heart, lifting itself up in that which is done well, may be impelled from one side to do evil; so that what at the outset it had set before itself in one way, it may go through in act far otherwise than it had begun. For often whilst human praise falls to the lot of a good deed, it alters the mind of the doer, and though not sought after, yet when offered it pleases; and whereas the mind of the well-doer is melted by the delight thereof, it is set loose from all vigorousness of the inward intention. Often when our sense of justice has begun to act aright, anger joins it from the side; and whereas it troubles the mind out of measure, by the quickness of our sense of uprightness, it wounds all the healthiness of our inward tranquillity. It often happens that sadness, attaching itself from the side, as it were, becomes the attendant of seriousness

of mind, and that every deed which the mind commences with a good intention, this quality overcasts with a veil of sadness, and we are sometimes the slower in driving it away even in that it waits as it were in solemn attendance on the depressed mind. Often immoderate joy attaches itself to a good deed, and while it calls upon the mind for more mirth than is meet, it discards all the weight of gravity from our good action. For because the Psalmist had seen that even those that set out well are met by snares on the way, being filled with the prophetic spirit, he rightly delivered it; *In this way that I walked they hid it snare for me* [Ps. 142, 3]. Which Jeremiah well and subtilly insinuates, who, while busied with telling of outward events, points out what things were done inwardly in ourselves, *There came certain from Shechem, from Shiloh, and from Samaria, even fourscore men, having their beards shaven, and their clothes rent, and having cut themselves, with offerings and incense in their hand, to bring them to the house of the Lord. And Ishmael the son of Nethaniah went forth from Mizpah to meet them, weeping all along as he went; and it came to pass, as he met them, he said unto them, Come unto Gedaliah the son of Ahikam. And it was so, when they came into the midst of the city, that Ishmael the son of Nethaniah slew them.* [Jer. 41, 5–7] For those shave their beard, who remove from them confidence in their own powers. They rend their clothes, that spare not themselves in tearing in pieces outward appearance. They come to offer up in the house of the Lord frankincense and gifts, who engage to set forth prayer in union with works in sacrifice to God. But if in the very path of holy devotion they skill not to keep a wary eye on every side, Ishmael the son of Nethaniah goes forth to meet them; in that assuredly every evil spirit, after the example of its chief, even Satan, begotten in the erring principle of pride, presents itself as a snare to deceive. And it is likewise well said concerning him; *weeping all along as he went*; forasmuch as in order that he may cut off devout souls by smiting them, he hides himself as it were under the guise of virtue, and whereas he feigns to agree with those that really mourn, being thus with greater security admitted to the interior of the heart, he destroys whatsoever of virtue is there hidden within. And most often he engages to guide to higher things; and hence he is related to have said, *Come unto Gedaliah the son of Ahikam*; and while he promises greater things he robs us even of the very little that we have; and hence it is rightly said, *And it was so, when they came into the midst of the city, that Ishmael the son of Nethaniah slew them.* So then he slays in the midst of the city the men that are come to offer gifts to God, in that those souls which are devoted to works of God, unless they watch over themselves with great circumspection, lose their life on the very way, through the enemy intercepting them unawares, as they go bearing the sacrifice of devotion; and from the hands of this enemy there is no escape, unless they speedily hasten back to repentance. Hence it is fitly added there, *But ten men were found among them, that said unto Ishmael, Slay us not for we have treasures in the field, of wheat, of barley, and of oil, and of honey. So he slew them not.* [Jer. 41, 8] For the treasure in the field is hope in repentance, which, in that it is not discernible, is kept buried closely in the earth of the heart. They then that had treasures in the field were saved, in that they who after the fault of their unwariness return to the lamentation of repentance, do not likewise perish when taken captive.

53. But when our old adversary neither deals a blow at the outset of the intention, nor intercepts us in the path of the execution, he sets the more mischievous snares at the end, which he so much the more wickedly besets, as he sees that it is all that is left to him to make a prey of. Now the Prophet had seen these snares set at the end of his course, when he said, *They will mark my heel.* [Ps. 56, 6] For because the end of the body is in the heel, what is signified thereby but the end of an action? Whether then it be evil spirits, or all wicked men that follow in the steps of their pride, they 'mark the heel' when they aim at spoiling the end of a good action; and hence it is said to that serpent, *it shall mark thy head, and thou shalt mark his heel.* [Gen. 3, 15. Vulg. thus] For to mark the serpent's head is to keep an eye upon the beginnings of his suggestions, and with the hand of needful consideration wholly to eradicate them from the avenues of the heart; yet when he is caught at the commencement, he busies himself to smite the heel, in that though he does not strike the intention with his suggestion at the first, he strives to ensnare at the end. Now if the heart be once corrupted in the intention, the middle and the end of the action that follows is held in secure possession by the cunning adversary, since he sees that that whole tree bears fruit to himself, which he has poisoned at the root with his baleful tooth. Therefore because we have to watch with the greatest care, that the mind even in the service of good works be not polluted by a wicked intention, it is rightly said, *It may be that my sons have*

sinned, and cursed God in their hearts. As if it were said in plain words, 'That is no good work which is performed outwardly, unless the sacrifice of innocency be inwardly offered for it upon the altar of the heart in the presence of God.' The stream of our work then is to be looked through, all we can, if it flows out pure from the well-spring of thought. With all care must the eye of the heart be guarded from the dust of wickedness, lest that which in action it shows upright to man, be within set awry by the fault of a crooked intention.

54. We must take heed, then, that our good works be not too few, take heed too that they be not unexamined, lest by doing too few works we be found barren, or by leaving them unexamined we be found foolish; for each several virtue is not really such, if it be not blended with other virtues; and hence it is well said to Moses, *Take unto thee sweet spices, stacte, and onycha, and galbanum, of good scent, with pure frankincense; of each shall there be a like weight. And thou shalt make it a perfume, a confection after the art of the apothecary, well tempered together, and pure.* [Exod. 30, 34. 35.] For we make a perfume compounded of spices, when we yield a smell upon the altar of good works with the multitude of our virtues; and this is 'tempered together and pure,' in that the more we join virtue to virtue, the purer is the incense of good works we set forth. Hence it is well added, *And thou shalt beat them all very small, and put of it before the Tabernacle of the Testimony.* We 'beat all the spices very small,' when we pound our good deeds as it were in the mortar of the heart, by an inward sifting, and go over them minutely, to see if they be really and truly good: and thus to reduce the spices to a powder, is to rub fine our virtues by consideration, and to call them back to the utmost exactitude of a secret reviewal; and observe that it is said of that powder, *and thou shalt put of it before the Tabernacle of the Testimony*: for this reason, in that our good works are then truly pleasing in the sight of our Judge, when the mind bruises them small by a more particular reexamination, and as it were makes a powder of the spices, that the good that is done be not coarse [*grossum*] and hard, lest if the close hand of reexamination do not bruise it fine, it scatter not from itself the more refined odour. For it is hence that the virtue of the Spouse is commended by the voice of the Bridegroom, where it is said, *Who is this, that cometh out of the wilderness like a rod of smoke of the perfume of myrrh and frankincense, with all powders of the merchant?* [Cant. 3, 6] For holy Church rises up like a rod of smoke from spices, in that by

the virtues of her life she duly advances to the uprightness of inward incense, nor lets herself run out into dissipated thought, but restrains herself in the recesses of the heart in the rod of severity: and while she never ceases to reconsider and go over anew the things that she does, she has in the deed myrrh and frankincense, but in the thought she has powder. Hence it is that it is said again to Moses of those who offer a victim, *And he shall flay the burnt offering, and cut it into his pieces*. [Lev. 1, 6] For we strip the skin of the victim, when we remove from the eyes of the mind the overcast of virtue; and we 'cut it in his pieces,' when we minutely dissect its interior, and contemplate it piecemeal. We must therefore be careful, that when we overcome our evil habits, we are not overthrown by our good ones running riot, lest they chance to run out loosely, lest being unheeded they be taken captive, lest from error they forsake the path, lest broken down by weariness they lose the meed of past labours. For the mind ought in all things to keep a wary eye about it, aye and in this very forethought of circumspection to be persevering; and hence it is rightly added,

Thus did Job all the days.

xxxvii.

55. For vain is the good that we do, if it be given over before the end of life, in that it is vain too for him to run fast, who fails before he reaches the goal. For it is hence that it is said of the reprobate, *Woe unto you that have lost patience*. [Ecclus. 2, 14] Hence Truth says to His elect, *Ye are they that have continued with life in My temptations* [Luke 22, 28]. Hence Joseph, who is described to have remained righteous among his brethren until the very end, is the only one related to have had 'a coat reaching to the ancles.' [Gen. 37, 23. Vulg.] For what is a coat that reaches to the ancles but action finished? For it is as if the extended coat covered the ancle of the body, when well doing covers us in God's sight even to the end of life. Hence it is that it is enjoined by Moses to offer upon the altar the tail of the sacrifice, namely, that every good action that we begin we may also complete with perseverance to the end. Therefore what is begun well is to be done every day, that whereas evil is driven away by our opposition, the very victory that goodness gains may be held fast in the hand of constancy.

56. These things then we have delivered under a threefold sense, that by setting a variety of viands before the delicate [*fastidienti*] sense

of the soul, we may offer it something to choose by preference. But this we most earnestly entreat, that he that lifts up his mind to the spiritual signification, do not desist from his reverence for the history.

BOOK II.

From the sixth verse of the first chapter to the end, he follows out the exposition according to the threefold interpretation.

Historical 1. Holy Writ is set before the eyes of the mind like a kind of mirror, that we may see our inward face in it; for therein we learn the deformities, therein we learn the beauties that we possess; there we are made sensible what progress we are making, there too how far we are from proficiency. It relates the deeds of the Saints [al. 'of the strong'], and stirs the hearts of the weak to follow their example, and while it commemorates their victorious deeds, it strengthens our feebleness against the assaults of our vices; and its words have this effect, that the mind is so much the less dismayed amidst conflicts as it sees the triumphs of so many brave men set before it. Sometimes however it not only informs us of their excellencies, but also makes known their mischances, that both in the victory of brave men we may see what we ought to seize on by imitation, and again in their falls what we ought to stand in fear of. For, observe how Job is described as rendered greater by temptation, but David by temptation brought to the ground, that both the virtue of our predecessors may cherish our hopes, and the downfall of our predecessors may brace us to the cautiousness of humility, so that whilst we are uplifted by the former to joy, by the latter we may be kept down through fears, and that the hearer's mind, being from the one source imbued with the confidence of hope, and from the other with the humility arising from fear, may neither swell with rash pride, in that it is kept down by alarm, nor be so kept down by fear as to despair, in that it finds support for confident hope in a precedent of virtue. **i.**

Ver. 6. Now there was a day when the sons of God came to present themselves before the Lord, and Satan came also among them.

2. It is interesting to observe the method followed by Holy Writ in delineating, at the commencement of its relations, the qualities and the issues of the particular cases. For one while by the position of the place, now by the posture of the body, now by the temperature of the air, and now by the character of the time, it marks out what it has coming after concerning the action which is to follow; as by the position of the place Divine Scripture sets forth the merits of the circumstances that follow, and the results of the case, **ii.**

as where it relates of Israel that they could not hear the words of God in the mount [Ex. 19, 17], but received the commandments on the plain; doubtless betokening the subsequent weakness of the people who could not mount up to the top, but enfeebled themselves by living carelessly in the lowest things. By the posture of the body it tells of future events, as where in the Acts of the Apostles, Stephen discloses that he saw Jesus, *Who sitteth at the right hand of the Power of God* [Acts 7, 55, 56], in a standing posture; for standing is the posture of one in the act of rendering aid, and rightly is He discerned standing, Who gives succour in the press of the conflict. By the temperature of the air, the subsequent event is shown, as when the Evangelist was telling that none out of Judaea were at that time to prove believers in our Lord's preaching, he prefaced it by saying, *and it was winter*, for it is written, *Because iniquity shall abound, the love of many shall wax cold.* [John 10, 22. Mat. 24, 12.] Therefore he took care to particularize the winter season, to indicate that the frost of wickedness was in the hearers' hearts. Hence it is that it is beforehand remarked of Peter, when on the point of denying our Lord, that *it was cold, and Peter stood with them, and warmed himself.* [John 18, 18] For he was now inwardly unenlivened by the warmth of Divine love, but to the love of this present life he was warming up, as though his weakness were set boiling by the persecutors' coals. By the character of the time moreover the issue of the transaction is set forth, as it is related of Judas, who was never to be restored to pardon, that he went out at night to the treachery of his betrayal, where upon his going out, the Evangelist says, *And it was night*. [John 13, 30] Hence too it is declared to the wicked rich man, *This night shall thy soul be required of thee*; for that soul which is conveyed to darkness, is not recorded as required in the day time, but in the night. Hence it is that Solomon who received the gift of wisdom, but was not to persevere, is said to have received her in dreams and in the night. Hence it is that the Angels visit Abraham at midday, but when proposing to punish Sodom, they are recorded to have come thither at eventide. Therefore, because the trial of blessed Job is carried on to victory, it is related to have begun by day, it being said,

Now there was a day, when the sons of God came to present themselves before the Lord, and Satan came also among them.

3. Now who are called the sons of God, saving the elect Angels? and as we know of them that they wait on the eyes of His Majesty, it is a worthy subject of inquiry, whence they come to present themselves before God. For it is of these that it is said by the voice of Truth, *Their angels do always behold the face of My Father, Which is in heaven?* [Mat. 18. 10] Of these the Prophet says, *thousand thousands ministered unto Him, and ten thousand times ten thousand stood before Him.* [Dan. 7, 10] If then they ever behold and ever stand nigh, we must carefully and attentively consider whence they are come, who never go from Him; but since Paul says of them, *Are they not all ministering spirits, sent forth to minister to them that shall be heirs of salvation?* [Heb. 1, 14] in this, that we learn that they are sent, we discover whence they are come. But see, we add question to question, and as it were while we strive to unloose the loop, we are only fastening a knot. For how can they either always be in presence, or always behold the face of the Father, of they are sent upon external ministration for our salvation? Which will however be the sooner believed, if we think of how great subtlety is the angelical nature. For they never so go forth apart from the vision of God, as to be deprived of the joys of interior contemplation; for if when they went forth they lost the vision of the Creator, they could neither have raised up the fallen, nor announced the truth to those in ignorance; and that fount of light, which by departing they were themselves deprived of, they could in no wise proffer to the blind. Herein then is the nature of Angels distinguished from the present condition of our own nature, that we are both circumscribed by space, and straitened by the blindness of ignorance; but the spirits of Angels are indeed bounded by space, yet their knowledge extends far above us beyond comparison; for they expand by external and internal knowing, since they contemplate the very source of knowledge itself. For of those things which are capable of being known, what is there that they know not, who know Him, to Whom all things are known? So that their knowledge when compared with ours is vastly extended, yet in comparison with the Divine knowledge it is little. In like manner as their very spirits in comparison indeed with our bodies are spirits, but being compared with the Supreme and Incomprehensible Spirit, they are Body. Therefore they are both sent from Him, and stand by Him too, since both in that they are circumscribed, they go forth, and in this, that they are also entirely present, they

never go away. Thus they at the same time always behold the Father's face, and yet come to us; because they both go forth to us in a spiritual presence, and yet keep themselves there, whence they had gone out, by virtue of interior contemplation; it may then be said, *The sons of God came to present themselves before the Lord;* inasmuch as they come back thither by a return of the spirit, whence they never depart by any withdrawal of the mind.

And Satan came also among them.

iv. 4. It is a very necessary enquiry, how Satan could be present among the elect Angels, he who had a long time before been damned and banished from their number, as his pride required. Yet he is well described as having been present among them; for though he lost his blessed estate, yet he did not part with a nature like to theirs, and though his deserts sink him, he is lifted up by the properties of his subtle nature. And so he is said to have come before God among the sons of God, for Almighty God, with that eye with which He regards all spiritual things, beholds Satan also in the rank of a more subtle nature, as Scripture testifies, when it says, *The eyes of the Lord are in every place, beholding the evil and the good*; [Prov. 15, 3] but this, viz. that Satan is said to have come before the presence of God, comes under a grave question with us; for it is written, *Blessed are the pure in heart, for they shall see God.* [Matt. 5, 8] But Satan, who can never be of a pure heart, how could he have presented himself to see the Lord?

5. But it is to be observed, that he is said to have come before the Lord, but not that he saw the Lord. For he came to be seen, and not to see. He was in the Lord's sight, but the Lord was not in his sight; as when a blind man stands in the sun, he is himself bathed indeed in the rays of light, yet he sees nothing of the light, by which he is brightened. In like manner then Satan also appeared in the Lord's sight among the Angels. For the Power of God, which by a look penetrates all objects, beheld the impure spirit, who saw not Him. For because even those very things which flee from God's face cannot be hidden, in that all things are naked to the view of the Most High, Satan being absent came to Him, Who was present.

Ver. 7. And the Lord said unto Satan, Whence comest thou?

6. How is it that it is never said to the elect Angels, when they come, 'Whence come ye?' while Satan is questioned whence he comes? For assuredly we never ask, but what we do not know; but God's not knowing is His condemning. Whence at the last He will say to some, *I know you not whence ye are; depart from me, ye that work iniquity*. [Luke 13, 27] In the same way that a man of truth, who disdains to sin by a falsehood, is said not to know how to lie, not in being ignorant if he had the will to lie, but in disdaining to tell a falsehood, from love of truth. What then is it to say to Satan, *Whence comest thou?* but to condemn his ways, as though unknown. The light of truth then knows nought of the darkness, which it reproves; and the paths of Satan, which as a judge it condemns, it is meet that it should inquire after as though in ignorance of them. Hence it is that it is said to Adam in his sin by his Creator's voice, *Adam, where art thou?* [Gen. 3, 9] For Divine Power was not ignorant to what hiding place His servant had fled after his offence, but for that He saw that he, having fallen in his sin, was now as it were hidden under sin from the eyes of Truth, in that He approves not the darkness of his error, He knows not, as it were, where the sinner is, and both calls him, and asks him, saying, *Adam, where art thou?* hereby, that He calls him, He gives a token that He recalls him to repentance; hereby, that He questions him, He plainly intimates that He knows not sinners, that justly deserve to be damned. Accordingly the Lord never calls Satan, but yet He questions him, saying, *Whence comest thou?* without doubt because God never recalls the rebel spirit to repentance, but in not knowing his paths of pride, He condemns him; therefore while Satan is examined [*discutitur*] concerning his way, the elect Angels have not to be questioned whence they come, since their ways are known to God in so much as they are done of His own moving, and whilst they are subservient to His will alone, they can never be unknown to Him, in so far as, by His approving eye, it is Himself from Whom and before Whom they are done. It follows,

Then Satan answered the Lord, and said, From going to and fro in the earth, and from walking up and down in it.

7. The toilsomeness of labour is wont to be represented by the round of circuitous motion. Accordingly Satan went toiling round about the earth, for he scorned to abide at peace in the height of heaven; and whereas he intimates that he did not fly, but that he **vi.**

walked, he shows the weight of sin, by which he is kept down below. *Walking* then *up and down*, he went to and fro in the earth, for tumbling down from that his soaring in spiritual mightiness, and oppressed by the weight of his own wickedness, he came forth to his round of labour. For it is for no other reason that it is said of his members also by the Psalmist, *The wicked walk on every side*; for while they seek not things within, they weary themselves with toiling at things without. It follows ;

Ver. 8. And the Lord said unto Satan, Hast thou considered My servant Job, that there is none like him in the earth, a perfect and upright man, one that feareth God, and escheweth evil?

vii. 8. This point, viz., that blessed Job is by the voice of God called *a perfect and an upright man, one that feareth God, and escheweth evil*, having explained above minutely and particularly, we forbear to rehearse what we have said, lest while we go over points that have been already examined, we should be slow in coming to those which have not. This then requires our discreet consideration, how it is either that the Lord is said to speak to Satan, or that Satan is said to answer the Lord, for we must make out what this speaking means. For neither by the Lord Who is the supreme and unbounded Spirit, nor by Satan, who is invested with no fleshly nature, is the breath of air inhaled by the bellows of the lungs, after the manner of human beings, so that by the organ of the throat it should be given back in the articulation of the voice; but when the Incomprehensible Nature speaks to an invisible nature, it behoves that our imagination rising above the properties of our corporeal speech should be lifted to the sublime and unknown methods of interior speech. For we, that we may express outwardly the things which we are inwardly sensible of, deliver these through the organ of the throat, by the sounds of the voice, since to the eyes of others we stand as it were behind the partition of the body, within the secret dwelling place of the mind; but when we desire to make ourselves manifest, we go forth as though through the door of the tongue, that we may show what kind of persons we are within. But it is not so with a spiritual nature, which is not a twofold compound of mind and body. But again we must understand that even when incorporeal nature itself is said to speak, its speech is by no means characterized by one and the same form. For it is after one method that God speaks to the Angels, and after another that the Angels speak to God; in one manner that God speaks to the souls of Saints, in another that the souls of Saints speak to God; in one way God speaks to the devil, ill another the devil speaks to God.

9. For because no corporeal obstacle is in the way of a spiritual being, God speaks to the holy Angels in the very act of His revealing to their hearts His inscrutable secrets, that whatsoever they ought to do they may read it in the simple contemplation of truth, and that the very delights of contemplation should be like a kind of vocal precepts, for that is as it were spoken to them as hearers which is inspired into them as beholders. Whence when God was imparting to their hearts His visitation of vengeance upon the pride of man, He said, *Come, let us go down, and there confound their language.* [Gen. 11, 7] He says to those who are close about Him, *Come,* doubtless because this very circumstance of never decreasing from the contemplation of God, is to be always increasing in the contemplation of Him, and never to depart from Him in heart, is as it were to be always coming to Him by a kind of steady motion. To them He also says, *Let us go down, and there confound their language.* The Angels ascend in that they behold their Creator; the Angels descend in that by a strict examination they put down that which exalts itself in unlawful measure. So then for God to say, *Let us go down, and confound their speech*, is to exhibit to them in Himself that which would be rightly done, and by the power of interior vision to inspire into their minds, by secret influences, the judgments which are fit to be set forth.

10. It is after another manner that the Angels speak to God, as in the Revelation of John also they say, *Worthy is the Lamb that was slain to receive power, and riches, and wisdom*; for the voice of the Angels in the praises of God is the very admiration itself of inward contemplation. To be struck dumb at the marvels of Divine goodness is to utter a voice, for the emotion of the heart excited with a feeling of awe is a mighty utterance of voice to the ears of a Spirit that is not circumscribed. This voice unfolds itself as it were in distinct words, while it moulds itself in the innumerable modes of admiration. God then speaks to the Angels when His inner will is revealed to them as the object of their perception; but the Angels speak to the Lord when by means of this, which they contemplate above themselves, they rise to emotions of admiration.

11. In one way God speaks to the souls of Saints, in another the souls of Saints speak to God; whence too it is again said in the Apocalypse of John, *I saw under the altar the souls of them that were slain for the word if God, and for the testimony which. they held: and they cried with a loud voice, saying, How long, O Lord, holy and true, dost Thou not judge and avenge our blood on them that dwell on the earth?* [Rev. 6, 9. 10.] Where in the same place it is added, *And white robes were given unto every one of them, and it was said unto them that they should rest for a little season, until their fellowservants also and their brethren that should be killed as they were should be fulfilled*; [Rev. 6, 11] for what else is it for souls to utter the prayer for vengeance, but to long for the day of final Judgment, and the resurrection of their lifeless bodies? For their great cry is their great longing; for everyone cries the less, the less he desires; and he utters the louder voice in the ears of an uncircumscribed Spirit in proportion as he more entirely pours himself out in desire of Him, and so the words of souls are their very desires. For if the desire were not speech, the Prophet would not say, *Thine ear hath heard the desire of their heart;* [Ps. 10, 17] but as the mind which beseeches is usually affected one way and the mind which is besought another, and yet the souls of the Saints so cleave to God in the bosom of their inmost secresy, that in cleaving they find rest, how are those said to beseech, who it appears are in no degree at variance with His interior will? How are they said to beseech, who, we are assured, are not ignorant, either of God's will or of those things which shall be? Yet whilst fixed on Himself they are said to beseech anything of Him, not in desiring aught that is at variance with the will of Him, Whom they behold, but in proportion as they cleave to Him with the greater ardour of mind, they also obtain from Him to beseech that of Him, which they know it is His will to do; so that they drink from Him that which they thirst after from Him. And in a manner to us incomprehensible as yet, what they hunger for in begging, they are filled withal in foreknowing; and so they would be at variance with their Creator's will, if they did not pray for that which they see to be His will, and they would cleave less closely to Him, if when He is willing to give, they knocked with less lively longing. These receive the answer spoken from God, *Rest yet for a little season, till your fellowservants and your brethren be fulfilled.* To say to those longing souls, *rest yet for a little season*, is to breathe upon them amid their burning desires, by the very foreknowledge,

the soothings of consolation; so that both the voice of the souls is that desire which through love they entertain, and God's address in answer is this, that He reassures them in their desires with the certainty of retribution. For Him then to answer that they should await the gathering of their brethren to their number, is to infuse into their minds the delays of a glad awaiting, that while they long after the resurrection of the flesh, they may be further gladdened by the accession of their brethren who remain to be gathered to them.

12. It is in one way that God speaks to the devil, and in another that the devil speaks to God. For God's speaking to the devil is His rebuking his ways and dealings with the visitation of a secret scrutiny, as it is here said, *Whence comest thou?* But the devil's answering Him, is his being unable to conceal anything from His Omnipotent Majesty; whence he says, *From going to and fro in the earth, and from walking up and down in it.* For it is as it were for him to say what he had been doing, that he knows that he cannot hide his doings from the eyes of That Being. But we must understand that, as we learn in this place, God has four ways of speaking to the devil, and the devil has three ways of speaking to God, God speaks to the devil in four modes, for He both reprehends his unjust ways, and urges against him the righteousness of His Saints, and lets him by permission try their innocence, and sometimes stops him that he dare not tempt them. Thus he rebukes his unjust ways, as has been just now said, *Whence comest thou?* He urges against him the righteousness of His own elect, as He says, *Hast thou considered My servant Job, that there is none like him in all the earth?* [Job 1, 8] He allows him by permission to put their innocence to the test, as when He says, *All that he hath is in thy power.* [ver. 12] And again He prevents him from tempting, when He says, *But upon himself put not forth thy hand.* But the devil speaks to God in three ways, either when he communicates to Him his dealing, or when he calumniates the innocence of the elect with false charges, or when he demands the same innocence to put it to trial. For he communicates his ways who says, *From going to and fro in the earth, and from walking up and down in it.* [ver. 7] He calumniates the innocence of the elect, when he says, *Doth Job fear God for nought? Hast not Thou made an hedge about him, and about all his house, and about all that he hath on every side?* [ver. 9, 10] He demands the same innocence to be subjected to trial, when he says, *But put forth Thine hand now and touch all that he hath and he will curse Thee to Thy*

face. But God's saying, *Whence comest thou?* is His rebuking by virtue of His own goodness that one's paths of wickedness. His saying, *Hast thou considered My servant Job, that there is none like him in all the earth?* is His making the elect, by justifying them, such as a rebel angel might envy. God's saying, *All that he hath is in thy power*, is, for the probation of the Saints, His letting loose upon them that assault of the wicked one, by the secret exercise of His power. God's saying, *Only upon himself put not forth thine hand,* is His restraining him from an excessive assault of temptation, even in giving him permission. But the devil's saying, *From going to and fro in the earth, and from walking up and down in it,* signifies His inability to conceal from His unseen eyes the cunning of his wickedness. The devil's saying, *Doth Job fear God for nought?* is his complaining against the just within the hiding places of his own thoughts, his envying their gains, and from envy searching out flaws for their condemnation. The devil's saying, *Put forth Thine hand now and touch all that he hath*, is his panting with the fever of wickedness to afflict the just. For in that through envy he longs to tempt the just, he seeks as it were by entreaty to put them to the test. Now then, as we have briefly described the methods of inward speaking, let us return to the thread of interpretation, which has been slightly interrupted.

Ver. 8. Have thou considered My servant Job, that there is none like him in the earth, a perfect and an upright man, one that feareth God, and escheweth evil?

13. The point has been already discussed in the foregoing discourse, that the devil proposed a contest not with Job but with God, blessed Job being set between them as the subject of the contest; and if we say that Job amid the blows erred in his speech, we assert what it is impious to imagine, that God was the loser in His pledge. For, lo, here also it is to be remarked, that the devil did not first beg the blessed Job of the Lord, but the Lord commended him to the contempt of the devil; and unless He had known that he would continue in his uprightness, He would not assuredly have undertaken for him. Nor would He give him up to perish in the temptation, against whom, before the temptation was sent, those firebrands of envy were kindled in the tempter's mind from God's own commendations.

14. But the old adversary, when he fails to discover any evil of which he might accuse us, seeks to turn our very good points into evil, and being beaten upon works, looks through our words for a subject of accusation; and when he finds not in our words either ground of accusation, he strives to blacken the purpose of the heart, as though our good deeds did not come of a good mind, and ought not on that account to be reckoned good in the eyes of the Judge. For because he sees the fruit of the tree to be green even in the heat, he seeks as it were to set a worm at its root. For he says,

Ver. 9, 10. Doth Job fear God for nought? Hast Thou, not made an hedge about him, and about his house, and about all that he hath on every side? Thou hast blessed the work of his hands, and his substance is increased in, the land.

15. As if he said in plain terms, 'What wonder is it, if he who has received so many blessings upon earth should behave without offence in return for them? He would then be really innocent, if he continued good in adversity; but why is he to be called great, whose every work has its recompense attending upon him, in all this abundance of good things?' For the crafty adversary, when he bethinks himself that the holy man had acted well in prosperity, hastens by means of adversity to prove him guilty before the Judge. Whence it is well said by the voice of the Angel in the Apocalypse, *The accuser of our brethren is cast down, which accused them before God day and night.* [Rev. 12, 10] Now holy Scripture is often used to set the day for prosperity, and the night for adversity. Accordingly he ceases not to accuse us by day and by night; forasmuch as he strives to show us to be chargeable one while in prosperity, another while in adversity. In the day he accuses us, when he slanders us that we abuse our good fortune; in the night he accuses us, when he shows that we do not exercise patience in adversity; and therefore because no strokes had as yet touched blessed Job, he was as it were still wholly without that whereof he might be able to accuse him by night, but because in prosperity he had thriven in a great holiness, he pretended that it was in return for his good fortune that he had done well, lying in the crafty assertion, that he did not keep his substance for the profit [*usum*] of the Lord, but that he served the Lord for the profit [*usum*] of his substance. For there are some who, to enjoy God, deal with this life like stewards, and there are some who to enjoy this life

would make use of God by the bye. When then he describes the gifts of Divine bounty, he thinks to make light of the acts of the resolute doer, that he might impeach [*addicat*] the heart of him as though on the score of secret thoughts, whose life he was unable to reprove on the score of works; falsely asserting that whatever outward innocence of life there might be, was in compliance not with the love of God, but with his longing after temporal prosperity. And so knowing nothing of the powers of blessed Job, and yet being well aware that everyone is most truly tried by adversity, he demands him for trial, that he who throughout the day of prosperity had walked with unfailing foot, at least in the night of adversity might stumble, and by the offence of impatience might be laid low before the eyes of his commender. Whence he adds,

Ver. 11. But put forth Thine hand now, and touch all that he hath, and he will curse Thee to Thy face.

x. 16. When Satan has a desire to tempt the holy man, and yet tells the Lord that He must put forth His hand against him, it is very deserving of notice that even he, who is so especially lifted up against the Maker of all things, never claims to himself the power to strike; for the devil knows well that he is unable to do anything of himself, for neither in that he is a spirit does he subsist by himself. Hence it is that in the Gospel, the legion, which was to be cast out of the man, exclaimed, *If Thou cast us out, suffer us to go away into the herd of swine*; [Mat. 8, 31] for what wonder is it if he, who could not by his own power enter into the swine, had no power without the Creator's hand to touch the holy man's house?

17. But we must know that the will of Satan is always evil, but his power is never unjust, for his will he derives from himself, but his power he derives from God. For what he himself unrighteously desires to do, God does not allow to be done except with justice. Whence it is well said in the book of Kings, *the evil spirit of God came upon Saul*. [1 Sam. 18, 10] You see that one and the same spirit is both called the Lord's spirit and an evil Spirit; the Lord's, that is, by the concession of just power, but evil, by the desire of an unjust will, so that he is not to be dreaded, who has no power but by permission; and, therefore, that Power is the only worthy object of fear, which when It has allowed the enemy to vent his rage, makes even his unjust will serve the purpose of a just judgment. But he

requires that His hand should be *put forth a little*; they being external things, of which he seeks the hurt. For Satan even does not consider himself to accomplish much, unless he inflicts a wound in the soul, that by so smiting he may bring one back from that country, from which he lies far removed, laid prostrate by the weapon of his own pride.

18. But why is it that he says, *if he have not blessed Thee to Thy face?* [so Vulg.] We look, it means, toward that we love, but that we would be quit of, we turn away our face from it. What then is the face of God, unless the regard of His favour is set before us to be understood? Accordingly he says, *But put forth Thine hand a little* [Vulg. *paullullum,* E.V. *now*], *and touch all that he hath, and he will curse Thee to Thy face.* As if he had said in plain words, 'Withdraw the things which Thou hast given him, for if he lose Thy gifts, he will no longer seek the regard of Thy favour, when his temporal good things are taken away. For if he no longer has the things in which he takes delight, he will despise Thy favour even to cursing Thee.' By which crafty address The Truth Whom he challenges is in no wise overcome; but that is permitted the enemy to his own undoing, which may be reckoned to the faithful servant for the increase of his reward; for which cause it is immediately subjoined,

Ver. 12. Behold, all that he hath is in thy power; only upon himself put not forth thine hand.

19. We should mark in the Lord's words the dispensations of heavenly pity, how He lets go our enemy, and keeps him in; how He looses, and yet bridles him. He allows him some things for temptation, but withholds him from others. *All that he hath is in thy hand, only upon himself put not forth thine hand.* His substance He delivers over, but still He protects his person, which notwithstanding after a while He designs to give over to the tempter; yet He does not loose the enemy to everything at once, lest he should crush His own subject [*civem*] by striking him on every side. For whenever many evils betide the elect, by the wonderful graciousness of the Creator they are dealt out by seasons, that what by coming all together would destroy, may when divided be borne up against. Hence Paul says, *God is faithful, Who will not suffer you to be tempted above that ye are able, but will with the temptation also make a way to escape, that ye may be able to bear it.* [1 Cor. 10, 13] Hence David says, *Examine me, O Lord,* xi.

and prove me. [Ps. 26, 2] As if he said in plain words, 'first examine my powers, and then, as I am able to bear, let me undergo temptation.' But this that is said, *Behold, all that he hath is in thy power, only upon himself put not forth thine hand,* is also capable of another sense, viz. that the Lord knew well, indeed, that His soldier was brave, yet chose to divide for him his contests with the enemy, that, though victory should in every case be sure to that staunch warrior, yet that from one conflict first the enemy might return to the Lord defeated, and that then he might grant him another encounter to be again worsted, so that his faithful follower might come forth the more incomparable conqueror, in proportion as the vanquished foe had repaired his forces again for fresh wars with him. It follows,

So Satan went forth from the presence of the Lord.

xii. 20. What is this, that Satan is said *to go forth from the presence of the Lord?* For how is it possible to *go forth* from Him, Who is every where present? Whence it is that He says, *Do not I fill heaven and earth?* [Jer. 23, 24] Hence it is written concerning His Spirit, *For the Spirit of the Lord filleth the world*. [Wisd. 1, 7] Hence it is that His Wisdom says, *I alone compassed the circuit of heaven*. [Ecclus. 24, 5] Hence it is that the Lord says again, *The heaven is My throne, and the earth is My footstool*. [Isa. 66, 1] And again it is written of Him, *He meteth out heaven with the span, and comprehended the dust of the earth in a measure*, [Is. 40, 12. Vulg.] for He abides both within and without the seat, whereon He rules. By His 'meting out heaven with a span, and comprehending the earth in a measure,' He is shown to be Himself on every side beyond the circuit of all things which He has created. For that which is enclosed within is from without held in by that which encloseth it. By the throne, therefore, whereon He is seated, it is meant that He is within and above; by the 'measure,' wherewith , 'He comprehends,' He is represented to be beyond and beneath; for whereas the same Being abides within all things, without all things, above all things, beneath all things, He is both above by virtue of His Dominion, and beneath by virtue of His Upholding; without, by His Immensity, and within, by His Subtlety; ruling from on high, holding together from below; encompassing without, penetrating within; not abiding by one part above, by another beneath, or by one part without, and by another part within, but One and the Same, and wholly every where, upholding in ruling, ruling in upholding; penetrating in encompassing, encompassing in penetrating; whence He ruleth from above, thence upholding from beneath, and whence He enfoldeth from without, thence filling up within; ruling on high without disquietude, upholding below without effort; within, penetrating without attenuation, without, encompassing without expansion. So that He is both lower and higher, without place; He is wider without breadth; He is more subtle without rarity.

21. Whither then is there any 'going forth' from Him, Who being through the bulk of a body no where present, is through a Substance unlimited no where absent? Still, so long as Satan, kept down by the power of His Majesty, was unable to execute the longing of his wickedness, he, as it were, stood in the presence of the Lord, but he 'went forth' from the presence of the Lord, because, being freed from above from the pressure of an inward withholding, he went to the execution of his desire. He went forth from the presence of the Lord, forasmuch as his evil will, long bound by the fetters of a severe control, did at length proceed to fulfilment. For, as has been said, whilst that which he desired he had no power to fulfil, in a manner, he ;stood in the presence of the Lord,' because the Supreme Providence restrained him from the execution of his wickedness, but 'he went forth from His presence,' because in receiving the power to tempt, he arrived at the goal, at which his wickedness aimed. It goes on:

Ver. 13, 14, 15, And there was a day when his sons and his daughters were eating and drinking wine in their eldest brother's house: And there came a messenger unto Job, and said, The oxen were plowing, and the asses feeding beside them: And the Sabeans fell upon them, and took them away; yea, they have slain the servants with the edge of the sword; and I only am escaped alone to tell thee.

22. We ought to observe what times are suited for temptations; for the devil chose that as the time for tempting, when he found the sons of the blessed Job engaged in feasting; for the adversary does not only cast about what to do, but also when to do it. Then though he had gotten the power, yet he sought a fitting season to work his overthrow, to this end, that by God's disposal it might be recorded for our benefit, that the delight of full enjoyment is the forerunner of woe. But we should observe the craft with which the losses that were inflicted by him are themselves related; xiii.

for it is not said, 'the oxen have been carried off by the Sabeans,' but 'the oxen, which have been carried away, were ploughing,' with the view doubtless that by mention of the profit of their labour, his cause for sorrow should be increased; for the same reason also [LXX. αι ψηλει–αι ονοι] among the Greeks it is not only asses, but asses with young, that are reported to have been taken away, that while such insignificant animals might less hurt the mind of the hearer from their value, they might from their productiveness inflict the sorer wound; and as misfortunes afflict the mind the more in proportion as, being many in number, they are also suddenly announced, the measure of his woes was enlarged even through the junctures at which the tidings arrived. For it follows,

Ver. 16, While he was yet speaking, there came also another, and said, The fire of God is fallen from heaven, and hath burned up the sheep, and the servants, and consumed them; and I only am escaped alone to tell thee.

23. Lest the loss of his property might not stir up sufficient grief at the hearing, he urges his feelings to exceed by the very words of the messengers. For it is to be remarked how craftily it is said, *the fire of God*, as though it were said, 'thou art suffering the visitation of Him, Whom thou desiredst to appease by so many sacrifices: thou art undergoing the wrath of Him, in Whose service thou didst daily weary thyself!' For in signifying that God, Whom he had served, had brought upon him his misfortunes, he mentions a sore point on which he may break forth; to the end that he might recall to mind his past services, and reckoning that he had served in vain, might be lifted up against the injustice of the Author. For the godly mind, when it finds itself to meet with crosses from the hands of man, finds repose in the consolations of Divine favour; and when it sees the storms of trial gather strength without, then seeking the covert of trust in the Lord, it takes refuge within the haven of the conscience. But that the cunning adversary might at one and the same moment crush the bold heart of the holy man, both by strokes from man and by despair in God, he both brought tidings at first that the Sabeans had made an irruption, and announced immediately afterwards that the fire of God had fallen from heaven, that he might as it were shut up every avenue of consolation, whereas he shows even Him to be against him, Who might have solaced his spirit amidst his adversities; so that considering himself in his trials to be on every side forsaken,

and on every side in a strait, he might burst into reviling with so much the more hardihood as he did it in the greater desperation. It goes on;

Ver. 17. While he was yet speaking, there came also another, and said, The Chaldeans made out three bands, and fell upon the camels, and have carried them away, yea, and slain the servants with the edge of the sword; and I only am escaped alone to tell thee.

24. Lo again, lest anything should be wanting to his grief for the adversity that came of man, he brings tidings that bands of the Chaldeans had broken in, and lest the calamity that came from above should strike him with too little force, he shows that wrath is repeated in the heavens. For it follows; **xv.**

Ver. 18, 19. While he was yet speaking, there came also another, and said, Thy sons and thy daughters were eating and drinking wine in their eldest brother's house: And, behold, there came a great wind from the wilderness, and smote the four corners of the house, and it fell upon the young men, and they are dead; and I only am escaped alone to tell thee.

25. He who is not laid low by one wound is in consequence stricken twice and thrice, that at one time or another he may be struck to the very core. Thus the blow from the Sabeans had been reported, the Divine visitation by fire from heaven had been reported, tidings are brought of the plundering of the camels, by man again, and of the slaughter of his servants, and the fury of God's displeasure is repeated, in that a fierce wind is shown to have smitten the comers of the house, and to have overwhelmed his children. For because it is certain that without the Sovereign dictate the elements can never be put in motion, it is covertly implied that He, Who let them be stirred, did Himself stir up the elements against him, though, when Satan has once received the power from the Lord, he is able even to put the elements into commotion to serve his wicked designs. Nor should it disturb us, if a spirit cast down from on high should have the power to stir the air into storms, seeing that we know doubtless that to those even who are sentenced to the mines fire and water render service to supply their need. So then he obtained that tidings should be brought of misfortunes; he obtained that they should be many in number; he obtained that they should come suddenly. Now the first time that he brought bad tidings he

inflicted a wound upon his yet peaceful breast, as upon sound members; but when he went on smiting the stricken soul, he dealt wound upon wound, that he might urge him to words of impatience.

26. But we should observe with what craftiness the ancient foe busied himself to break down the patience of the holy man, not so much by the loss of his substance as by the very order of the announcements. He, taking pains to announce first the slight disasters, and afterwards the greater ones, last of all brought him intelligence of the death of his sons, lest the father should account the losses of his property of slight importance, if he heard of them when now childless, and lest it should the less disturb him to part with his goods, after he had learnt the death of his children, considering that the inheritance were no more, if he first removed out of the way those who were reserved to inherit it. So beginning from the least, he announced the worst intelligence last; that while worse disasters were made known to him in succession, every wound might find room for pain within his breast. Take notice of the craft with which so many a weight of ill is announced, both separately and at the same time suddenly, that his grief being increased both of a sudden and in point after point, might not contain itself within the hearer's breast, and that it might so much the more inflame him to utter blasphemy, as the fire, kindled within him by those sudden and multiplied tidings, raged in a narrower space.

27. Nor do I think that this ought to be lightly passed over, that the sons when they perish were feasting in the house of their elder brother. For it has been declared above that feasts can scarcely be gone through without transgression. To speak then of our own concerns and not of theirs, the lesson we ought to learn is, that what the younger ones do for pleasure's sake is checked by the control of the elder, but when the elder are themselves followers of pleasure, then, we may be sure, the reins of license are let loose for the younger; for who would keep himself under the control of authority, when even the very persons, who receive the right of control, freely give themselves to their pleasures? And so while they are feasting in the house of their elder brother, they perish, for then the enemy gets more effective power against us, when he marks that even those very persons, who are advanced for the keeping of discipline, are abandoned to joviality. For he is so much the more free and forward to strike, as he sees that they too, who might intercede for our faults, are tak-

en up with pleasure. But far be it from us to suspect that the sons of so great a man were by devotedness to feasts given up to the gorging of the belly. But still we know for certain that though a man, by the observance of self control, may not pass the bounds of necessity in eating, yet the animated earnestness of the mind is dulled amidst feasting, and that mind is less apt to reflect in what a conflict of temptations it is placed, which throws off restraint in a sense of security. In the eldest brother's day then he overwhelmed the sons, for the old foe in compassing the death of the younger, seeks an inlet for their ruin through the carelessness of the elder ones. But as we have marked with what piercing darts the tidings struck him, let us hear how our man of valour stands fast amid the blows. It proceeds;

Ver. 20. Then Job arose, and rent his mantle, and shaved his head, and fell down upon the ground, and worshipped.

xvi.

28. There are some who account it a high degree of philosophical fortitude, if, when corrected by severe discipline, they are insensible to the strokes, and to the pains of those stripes. And there are some who feel to such excess the infliction of the blows, that under the influence of immediate grief, they even fall into excesses of the tongue. But whoever strives to maintain true philosophy, must go between either extreme, for the weightiness of true virtue consists not in dulness of heart, as also those limbs are very unhealthy from numbness which cannot feel any pain even when cut. Again, he deserts his guard over virtue, who feels the pain of chastisement beyond what is necessary; for while the heart is affected with excessive sorrow, it is stirred up to the extent of impatient reviling, and he who ought to have amended his misdeeds by means of the stripes, does his part that his wickedness should be increased by the correction. Agreeably to which, against the insensibility in the chastised, the words of the Prophet are, *Thou hast stricken them, but they have not grieved; Thou hast consumed them, but they have refused to receive correction*. [Jer. 5, 3] Against the faintheartedness of the chastened the Psalmist hath it, *They will never stand fast in adversity*; [Ps. 140, 10. Vulg.] for they would 'stand fast in adversity,' if they bore calamities with patience, but so soon as they sink in spirit, when pressed with blows, they as it were lose the firmness of their footing, amidst the miseries inflicted on them.

29. Thus because blessed Job observed the rule of the true philosophy, he kept himself from either extreme with the evenness of a marvellous skill, that he might not by being insensible to the pain contemn the strokes, nor again, by feeling the pain immoderately, be hurried madly against the visitation of the Striker. For when all his substance was lost, all his children gone, *he rose up, and rent his mantle, and shaved his head, and fell down upon the ground, and worshipped*. In that *he rent his mantle*, in that *he shaved his head and fell down upon the ground*, he shows, we see, that he has felt the pain of the scourge; but in that it is added that *he worshipped*, it is plainly shown that even in the midst of pain, he did not break forth against the decree of the Smiter. He was not altogether unmoved, lest by his very insensibility he should show a contempt of God; nor was he completely in commotion, lest by excess of grief he should commit sin. But because there are two commandments of love, i.e. the love of God, and of our neighbour; that he might discharge the love of our neighbour, he paid the debt of mourning to his sons; that he might not forego the love of God, he performed the office of prayer amidst his groans. There are some that use to love God in prosperity, but in adversity to abate their love of Him from whom the stroke comes. But blessed Job, by that sign which he outwardly showed in his distress, proved that he acknowledged the correction of his Father, but herein, that he continued humbly worshipping, he showed that even under pain he did not give over the love of that Father. Therefore that he might not show pride by his insensibility, he fell down at the stroke, but that he might not estrange himself from the Striker, he so fell down as to worship. But it was the practice of ancient times for everyone, who kept up the appearance of his person by encouraging the growth of his hair, to cut it off in seasons of mourning; and, on the other hand that he who in peaceful times kept his hair cut, should in evidencing his distress cherish its growth. Thus blessed Job is shown to have preserved his hair in the season of rest, when he is related to have shaven his head for the purpose of mourning, that whereas the hand of the Most High was fallen upon him in all the circumstances of his condition, the altered mien of penance might even by his own act overcloud him. But such an one, spoiled of his substance, bereft of his children, that rent his mantle, that shaved his head, that fell down upon the ground, let us hear what he says!

Ver. 21. Naked came I out of my mother's womb, and naked shall I return thither.

xvii.

30. Oh! upon how elevated a seat of the counsels of the heart does he sit enthroned, who now lies prostrate on the earth with his clothes rent! For because by the judgment of the Lord he had lost all that he had, for the preserving his patience he brought to mind that time, when he had not as yet those things which he had lost, that, whilst he considers that at one time he had them not, he may moderate his concern for having lost them; for it is a high consolation in the loss of what we have, to recall to mind those times, when it was not our fortune to possess the things which we have lost. But as the earth has produced all of us, we not unjustly call her our mother. As it is written, *An heavy yoke is upon the sons of Adam, from the day that they go out of their mother's womb, till the day that they return to the mother of all things.* [Ecclus. 40, 1]

Blessed Job then, that he might mourn with patience for what he had lost here, marks attentively in what condition he had come hither. But for the furtherance of preserving patience, with still more discretion he considers, how he will go hence, and exclaims, *Naked came out of my mother's womb, and naked shall I return thither.* As though he said, 'Naked did the earth bear me, when I came upon this scene, naked it will receive me back, when I depart hence. I then who have lost what I had indeed given me, but what must yet have been abandoned, what have I parted with that was my own?' But because comfort is not only to be derived from the consideration of our creation [*conditionis 'conditoris.'*], but also from the justice of the Creator, he rightly adds,

The Lord gave, and the Lord hath taken away; as it hath pleased the Lord, so is it done. [*so V. and lxx.*]

xviii.

31. The holy man, under trial from the adversary, had lost everything, yet knowing that Satan had no power against him to tempt him, saving by the Lord's permission, he does not say, 'the Lord hath given, the devil hath taken away,' but *the Lord gave, the Lord hath taken away.* For perchance it would have been a thing to grieve for, if what his Creator had given him, his enemy had taken from him: but when no other hath taken it away, saving He Who Himself gave it, He hath only recalled what was His own, and

hath not taken away what was ours. For if we have from Him all that we make use of in our present life, what cause for grief that by His own decree we are made to surrender, of Whose bounty we have a loan? Nor is he at any time an unfair creditor, who while he is not bound to any set time of restitution, exacts, whenever he will, what he lends out. Whereupon it is well added, *As it hath pleased the Lord, so is it done*; for since in this life we undergo things which we would not, it is needful for us to turn the bias of our will to Him, Who can will nought that is unjust. For there is great comfort in what is disagreeable to us, in that it comes to us by His disposal, to Whom nought but justice is pleasing. If then we be assured that what is just is the Lord's pleasure, and if we can suffer nothing but what is the Lord's pleasure, then all is just that we undergo, and it is great injustice, if we murmur at a just suffering.

32. But since we have heard how the intrepid speaker put forward the vindication of his cause against the adversary, now let us hear how in the end of his speech he extols the Judge with benedictions. It follows, *Blessed be the Name of the Lord*. See how he concluded all that he felt alight with a blessing on the Lord, that the adversary might both perceive hence, and for his punishment under defeat take shame to himself, that he himself even though created in bliss had proved a rebel to that Lord, to Whom a mortal even under His scourge utters the hymn of glory.

But be it observed, that our enemy strikes us with as many darts as he afflicts us with temptations; for it is in a field of battle that we stand every day, every day we receive the weapons of his temptations. But we ourselves too send our javelins against him, if, when pierced with woes, we answer humbly. Thus blessed Job, when stricken with the loss of his substance and with the death of his children, forasmuch as he turned the force of his anguish into praise of his Creator, exclaiming, *The Lord gave, and the Lord hath taken away; as it hath pleased the Lord, so is it done; blessed be the Name of the Lord:* by his humility, struck down the enemy in his pride, and by his patience, laid low the cruel one. Let us never imagine that our combatant received wounds, and yet inflicted none. For whatever words of patience he gave forth to the praise of God, when he was stricken, he as it were hurled so many darts into the breast of his adversary, and inflicted much sorer wounds than he underwent; for by his affliction he lost the things of earth, but by bearing his affliction with humility, he multiplied his heavenly blessings. It follows,

Ver.22. In all this Job sinned not, nor charged God foolishly.

33. Since, when we are laid hold of by distressing trials, we may even in the silent working of our thoughts, without word of mouth, be guilty of sin; the testimony both of the lips and of the heart is given to blessed Job. For it is first said, *he sinned not*, and then it is afterwards added, *nor charged God foolishly*: for he, who uttered nothing foolishly, kept offence from his tongue, and whereas the words, he sinned not, come before, it appears that he excluded the sin of murmuring even from his thought, so that he neither sinned nor spake foolishly, since he neither swelled with indignation in his silent consciousness, nor gave a loose to his tongue in reviling. For he does 'charge God foolishly,' who, when the strokes of divine chastisement are fallen upon him, strives to justify himself. For if he venture in pride to assert his innocence, what else does he, but impugn the justice of the chastiser? Let it suffice for us to have run through the words of the history thus far: let us now turn the discourse of our exposition to investigate the mysteries of allegory. And herein, that it is written,

Ver.6. Now there was a day when the sons of God came to present themselves before the Lord, and Satan came also among them.

Allegorical **XX.**

34. It is first to be made out, wherefore anything is said to be done on a particular day before the Lord, whereas with Him the progress of time is never marked by the variation of day and night. For neither does that light, which without coming enlighteneth whatsoever it chooseth, and without going forsaketh those things which it rejects, admit any imperfection of mutability; for, while it abideth unchangeable in itself, it orders all things that are subject to change, and has in such sort created all transient beings in itself, that in it they are incapable of transition, nor is there inwardly in His sight any lapse of time, which with us, without Him, has its course. Whence it comes to pass that those revolutions of the world remain fixed in His eternity, which, having no fixedness out of Him issue into existence [*emanant*]. Why then in relation to Him is it said, *one day*, in that His one day is His eternity? Which same the Psalmist perceived to be closed by no ending, and

to open with no beginning, where he says, *One day in Thy courts is better than a thousand*. [Ps. 84, 10. Vulg.]

35. But as Holy Scripture speaks to those who are brought forth in time, it is meet that it should use words significant of time, in order that it may lift us up by so condescending, and that while it relates something that belongs to eternity after the manner of time, it may gradually transfer to the eternal world those who are habituated to the things of time, and that that eternity, which is unknown, while it amuses [*blanditur*] us with words that are known, may successfully impart itself to our minds. And what wonder is it, if in Holy Writ God is not overhasty to disclose the unchangeableness of His Nature to the mind of man, since after He had celebrated the triumph [*solemnitate*] of His Resurrection, it was by certain progressive steps that He made known the incorruptibility of the Body which He resumed again. For we have learnt from the testimony of Luke, that He first sent Angels to some, that were seeking for Him in the tomb; and again to the disciples who were talking of Him by the way, He Himself appeared, yet not so as to be known by them, Who indeed after the delay of an exhortation did show Himself to be known of them in the breaking of bread; but at last, entering suddenly, He not only presented Himself to be known by sight, but to be handled also. For because the disciples still carried about with them faint hearts, in coming to the knowledge of this marvellous mystery they were to be nourished by such a method of its dispensation, that by little and little in seeking they might find some portion, that finding they might gain growth, and growing they might hold the faster the truths which they had learnt. Inasmuch then as we are not led to the eternal world at once, but by a progression of cases and of words as though by so many steps, this or that is said to be done on a certain day before Him within, Who views even time itself also out of time.

36. Or forasmuch as Satan too was there, was it the aim of Holy Scripture, when it says that this was done on a certain day, to point out that in the light God beheld the darkness? For we are unable to embrace light and darkness in one and the same view, in that when the eye is fixed upon darkness, the light is put to flight, and when the eye is directed to the glittering rays of light, the shades of darkness disappear. But to that Power, Which in unchangeableness beholds all things changeable, Satan was present as in the day, in that It em-

braces undimmed the darkness of the apostate Angel. We, as we have said, cannot survey at one view both the objects which we choose in approval, and those which we condemn in disapproval; for while the mind is directed to the one subject, it is withdrawn from the other, and when it is brought back to this latter it is taken off from that, to which it had attached itself.

37. But forasmuch as God without changing beholds all things at the same instant, and without extension embraces all, i.e. both the good that He aids, and the evil that He judges; both that which thus aiding He rewards, and that which so judging He condemns; He is not Himself different in the things which He sets in different order. Accordingly Satan is said to have come before Him *on a day*, in that the light of His eternity is proof against the overclouding of any change; and herein, that the darkness is made present to Him, he is said to have presented himself among the sons of God, because in fact the impure spirit is penetrated by the self-same Power of Righteousness, wherewith the hearts of pure spirits are replenished; and that being is pierced through with the same ray of light, which is so shed abroad in them as that they shine.

38. He came among the sons of God, in that, though they serve God in rendering aid to the elect, he does this, in putting them to trial. He presented himself among the sons of God, in that, although they dispense the succours of mercy to all that labour in this present life, this one unwittingly serves the ends of His secret justice, while he strives to accomplish the ministry of their condemnation. Whence it is justly said by the Prophet in the books of Kings, *I saw the Lord sitting upon His throne, and all the host of Heaven standing by Him, on His right hand and on His left. And it was said, Wherewith shall I deceive Ahab, that he may go up and fall at Ramoth Gilead; And one said on this manner, and another said on that manner. And there came forth one and stood before the Lord, and said, I will deceive him. And it was said, Wherewith? and he said, I will go forth, and I will be a lying spirit in the mouth of all his prophets*. [1 Kings 22, 19. &c]

For what is the throne of the Lord, unless we understand the Angelic Powers, in whose minds enthroned on high He disposeth all things below? And what is the host of heaven, unless the multitude of ministering Angels is set forth? Why then is it, that the host of heaven is said to stand on His right hand and on His left? For God, Who is in such sort within all things, that He is also without all, is neither bounded on the right hand nor on the left. However, the right hand of God is the elect portion of the Angels, and the left hand of God signifies the reprobate portion of Angels. For not alone do the good serve God by the aid which they render, but likewise the wicked by the trials which they inflict; not only they who lift upward them that are turning back from transgression, but they who press down those who refuse to turn back. Nor because it is called the host of heaven, are we hindered from understanding therein the reprobate portion of the Angels, for whatsoever birds we know to be poised in the air, we call them 'the birds of heaven.' And it is of these same spirits that Paul says, *Against spiritual wickedness in high places*. [Ephes. 6, 12] And describing their head, he says, *According to the prince of the power of the air*. [Ephes. 2, 2] On the right hand and on the left hand of God, then, stands the Angelic Host, forasmuch as both the will of the elect spirits harmonizes with Divine mercy, and the mind of the reprobate, in serving their own evil ends, obeys the judgment of His strict decrees. Hence too it is said, that a spirit of falsehood immediately leaped forth in the midst, to deceive king Ahab, as his deserts called for. For it is not right to imagine that a good spirit would ever have served the ends of deceit, so as to say, *I will go forth, and I will be a, lying spirit in the mouth of all his prophets*. But because king Ahab by his previous sins had made himself worthy to be cursed with such deception, in order that he who had many times willingly fallen into sin, might for once unwillingly be caught for his punishment, leave is given by a secret justice to the evil spirits, that those whom with willing minds they strangle in the noose of sin, they may drag to the punishment of that sin even against their will. What then it is there to describe the Host of heaven as having stood on the right hand and on the left hand of God, the same it is here to declare Satan to have presented himself among the sons of God. So on the right hand of God there stood Angels, for that the sons of God are named; so on His left hand angels are standing, because Satan presented himself among them.

39. But as we have determined to search out the hidden senses of the allegory, we not unfitly take it to mean, that the Lord beheld Satan in the day, in that He restrained his ways in the Incarnation of His Wisdom; as though it were not to have seen him, to have for so long borne with his wickedness in the ruin of the human race. Whence it is straightway said to him by the voice of God,

Ver. 7. *Whence comest thou?*

40. In the day Satan is demanded of his ways, for that in the light of revealed Wisdom the snares of the hidden foe are discovered. Because, then, the devil is rebuked by the Incarnate Lord, and restrained from his baneful license, it is well subjoined, *And the Lord said unto Satan, Whence comest thou?* For He then by arraigning attainted the ways of Satan, when by the Advent of the Mediator restraining the wickedness of his persuasions, He rebuked the same. And it is not without reason that the sons of God are related to have stood in the presence of the Lord on this day, forasmuch as it is by the light of Wisdom illuminating them that all the elect are gathered to the calling of their eternal country. Who, though Incarnate Wisdom came to assemble them in actual deed, were yet by virtue of His foreknowledge already inwardly present to His Divinity. But since the old enemy, at the coming of the Redeemer, is questioned of his ways, let us hear what he says. **xxi.**

Ver. 7. *From going to and fro in the earth, and from walking up and down in it.*

41. For from the time of Adam till the coming of the Lord, he drew after him all the nations of the Gentiles; he went *to and fro in the earth, and walked up and down in it*, in that he stamped the foot-prints of his wickedness throughout the hearts of the Gentiles. For when he fell from on high he gained lawful possession of the minds of men, because he fastened them as willing captives in the chains of his iniquity; and he wandered the more at large in the world, in proportion as there was no one found who was in all things free from that his guilt. And his having gone to and fro in the world as with power, is his having found no man who could thoroughly resist him. But now let Satan return back, i.e. let the Divine power withhold him from the execution of his wickedness, since He has now appeared in the flesh, Who had no part in the infection of sin from the infirmity of the flesh. He came in humility for the proud enemy himself to wonder at, that he who had set at nought all the mightiness of His Divinity, might stand in awe even of the very infirmities of His Humanity. Wherefore also this very weakness of His human nature is immediately set forth against him with wonderful significance as an object to confound him; whereas it is said, **xxii.**

Ver. 8. Hast thou considered My servant Job, that there is none like him in the earth?

xxiii. 42. That Job means by interpretation, 'Grieving,' we have already said a little above. And He is truly called 'Grieving' in figure, Who is declared by the testimony of the Prophet 'to bear our griefs.' [Isa. 53, 4] Who has not His like on the earth; for every man is only man, but He is both God and Man. He has not His like on earth, because though every son by adoption attains to the receiving of the Divine nature, yet none ever receives so much, as to be, by nature, God. He was even rightly styled a servant, because He did not disdain to take the form of a servant. Nor did His taking the humility of the flesh injure His sovereignty, for in order that He might both take upon Him that which He was to save, yet not undergo alteration in that which He had, He neither lessened the Divine by the Human, nor swallowed up the Human in the Divine; for although Paul hath it, *Who being in the form of God thought it not robbery to be equal with God; but emptied Himself, and took upon Him the form of a servant;* [Phil. 2, 6. 7.] yet to Him it is 'emptying Himself,' of the greatness of His Invisible Being to manifest Himself as Visible; so that the form of a servant should be the covering of That Which without limitation enters into all things by virtue of Godhead. Again, God's saying to Satan in figure, *Hast Thou considered My servant Job*, is His exhibiting in his despite the Only-Begotten Son as an object of wonder in the form of a servant. For in that He made Him known in the flesh as of so great virtue, He as it were pointed out to the adversary in his pride what it would grieve him to contemplate; but now that He had brought before him a perfect object for him to admire, it remains that in order to strike down his pride he should further go on to enumerate its excellencies. It goes on,

Ver. 8. A perfect and an upright man, one that feareth God, and escheweth evil.

xxiv. 43. For there came among men the Mediator between God and Man, the Man Christ Jesus, for the giving an example of living, *perfect* [*simplex*]; in respect of His rigour towards the evil spirits, *upright*; for the exterminating pride, *fearing God*; and for the wiping off impurity of life in His Elect, *departing from evil*. For it is said of Him by Isaiah in a special manner, *And shall make him of* *quick understanding in the fear of the Lord*. [Is. 11, 3] And He did in a special manner *depart from evil*, who refused to imitate the actions which He found among men, since, as Peter bears witness, *He did no sin, neither was guile found in His mouth*. [1 Pet. 2, 22] It follows;

Ver. 9, 10. Then Satan answered the Lord, and said, Doth Job fear God for nought? Hast not Thou made an hedge about him, and about his house, and about all that he hath on every side? Thou hast blessed the work of his hands, and his substance is increased in the land.

The old enemy knew that the Redeemer of mankind was come to be the conqueror of himself; and hence it is said by the man possessed in the Gospel, *What have we to do with Thee, Jesus, Thou Son of God? Art Thou come hither to torment us before the time?* [Mat. 8, 29] Yet before, when he perceived Him to be subject to passion, and saw that He might suffer all the mortal accidents of humanity, all that he imagined concerning His Divinity became doubtful to him from his exceeding pride. For savouring of nothing else but pride, whilst he beheld Him in humility, he doubted of His being God; and hence he has recourse to proof by temptation, saying, *If Thou be the Son of God, command that these stones be made bread*. [Matt. 4, 3] In this way, because he saw that He was subject to passion, he did not believe Him to be God by birth, but to be kept by the grace of God. And for the same reason too he is in this place said to allege,

Ver. 10. Hast not Thou made an hedge about him, and about his house, and about all that he hath on every side? Thou hast blessed the work of his hands, and his substance is increased in the land.

44. For he urges that both himself and his house are hedged about by God; because he could not find an entrance to His conscience by tempting him, He declares his substance to be hedged about, in that he dares not to attack His elect servants. He complains that *God had blessed the work of his hands, and that his substance was increased in the land*, for this reason, that he pines at beholding that faith in Him enlarges its bounds, in man's coming to the knowledge of Him by the preaching of the Apostles. For His substance is said to be increasing, all the time that by the labours of the preachers the number of the faithful daily waxes larger. Satan's saying this to God, is his seeing these things with an envious eye. Sa- **xxv.**

tan's saying this to God, is his grieving at these things with a pining spirit. It proceeds:

Ver. 11. But put forth Thine hand a little, and touch all that he hath, and he will curse Thee to Thy face.

45. For He, Whom he thought in time of tranquillity to be under the keeping of God's grace, he imagined might be led to sin by means of suffering; as though he had plainly said, 'One, Who for the miracles which He works is accounted God, being put to the test by afflictions, is discovered to be a sinner, and nothing better,' So the Lord said to Satan,

Ver. 12. Behold, all that he hath is in thy power; only upon himself put not forth thine hand.

xxvii. 46. Whereas we are examining Holy Scripture under its figurative import, by the hand of Satan is to be understood not his power, but the extent of his tempting. All, then, that he hath is given into the hand of the Tempter, and he is only forbidden *to put forth his hand upon him*, which nevertheless, when his substance is gone, is permitted him; for that first Judaea, which was His possession, was taken from Him in unbelief, and that afterwards His flesh was nailed to the stock of the Cross, He then Who first underwent the opposition of Judaea, and afterwards came even to the Cross, in a manner first lost that He had, and then in His own Person endured the wickedness of the adversary.

So Satan went forth from the presence of the Lord.

xxviii. 47. Just as it was said above, *Satan went forth from the presence of the Lord*, in that he attained the objects of his desire; for he was in a certain sense in His presence, all the time that on account of Him, he failed to accomplish all that he mischievously thirsted after.

Ver. 13, And there was a day, when his sons and his daughters were eating and drinking wine in their eldest brother's house.

xxix. 48. We have said that the sons and daughters of blessed Job were a representation either of the order of the Apostles, or of the whole multitude of the faithful. Now the Lord Incarnate first chose a few out of Judaea unto faith, and afterwards He gathered to Himself the multitude of the Gentile people. But who was the eldest son of the Lord, unless the Jewish people is to be understood, which had been a long time born to Him by the teaching of the Law which He gave? and who the younger son but the Gentile people, which at the very end of the world was gathered together? And therefore whereas, when Satan was unwittingly contributing to the welfare of the human race, and having corrupted the hearts of those persecutors was demanding warrant for the Passion of the Lord, the Holy Apostles were as yet ignorant that the Gentile world were to be gathered to God, and preached to Judaea alone the mysteries of the Faith. When Satan is said to have gone out from the Lord, the sons and daughters are described to be feasting in the house of their elder brother. For it had been commanded them, *Go not into the way of the Gentiles.* [Mat. 10, 5] Now after the Death and Resurrection of our Lord, they turned to preaching to the Gentiles, for which reason too in their Acts we find them saying, *It was necessary that the word of God should first have been spoken to you, but since ye put it from you, and judge yourselves unworthy of everlasting life, lo, we turn to the Gentiles.* [Acts 13, 46] And thus these children of the bridegroom, of whom it is declared, and that by the voice of the same Bridegroom, *The children of the bridechamber shall not fast as long as the bridegroom is with them*, [Matt. 9, 15] are feasting in the house of their elder brother, for this reason, that the Apostles still continued to be fed with the sweets of Holy Scripture in the gathering of the single people of the Jews.

Ver. 14, 15. And there came a messenger unto Job, and said, The oxen were ploughing, and the asses feeding beside them; And the Sabeans fell upon them, and took all away; yea, they have slain the servants with the edge of the sword, and I only am escaped alone to tell thee.

49. What else do we take the oxen to mean in figure, but well-doers; what the asses, but certain men of simple ways? **XXX.** These are properly described to be feeding beside the oxen, because simple souls, even when they are incapable of comprehending deep mysteries, are near to the great, inasmuch as they account the excellencies of their brethren to be their own also by force of charity; and while envy of the knowledges [*sensibus*] of others is a thing unknown, they are never divided at pasture. The asses then take their food in company with the oxen, in that duller minds, when joined with the

wise, are fed by their understanding. Now the Sabeans mean by interpretation 'captivators;' and who are signified by the name of 'captivators,' but the impure spirits who lead all men captive to infidelity, whom they make subject to themselves? These too strike the youths [*pueros*] with the sword, in that they inflict grievous wounds, with the darts of temptation, upon those whom the constancy of manhood does not yet maintain in freedom and hardiness. These indeed enter fairly upon well-doing, but while still in the delicate state of a first beginning, they are prostrated beneath the unclean spirits that take captive; these are stricken with the sword of the enemy, in that he pierces them with despair of life eternal.

50. But what is this, that the messenger comes with these words, *and I only am escaped alone?* Who is this messenger, who, when the rest are destroyed, 'escapes alone,' but the prophetic word, which, whilst all the evils happen, which it foretold, alone returns as it were unharmed to the Lord? For when it is known to speak the truth concerning the fate of the lost, it is in a certain sense shown to live among the dead. It is hence that the servant is sent to bring down Rebecca, on the occasion of Isaac's marrying; doubtless because the intervening Prophecy does service in espousing the Church to the Lord. So when the Sabeans made their assault, one servant alone escaped to give the tidings, because by means of malignant spirits leading captive weak minds, that declaration of Prophecy was confirmed, which, in foretelling the same captivity, says, *Therefore My people are gone into captivity, because they have no knowledge*. [Is. 5, 13] The prophecy therefore is in a manner preserved safe, when the captivity, which it foretold, is brought to light. It proceeds,

Ver. 16. While he was yet speaking, there came also another, and said, The fire of God is fallen from Heaven, and hath burned up the sheep, and the servants, and consumed them; and I only am escaped alone to tell thee.

51. All, who held the office of preaching in the Synagogue, were rightly named, 'the heavens,' plainly because they were supposed to be imbued with heavenly wisdom; and for this reason, when Moses was urging the Priests and the people to take heed of his words of admonition, he exclaimed, *Give ear, O ye Heavens, and I will speak; and hear, O earth, the words of my mouth*; [Deut. 32, 1] evidently signifying by the Heavens the order of rulers, and by the earth the people under them. There is then in this place no unfitness in interpreting the

Heavens to mean either the Priests or the Pharisees, or the Doctors of the Law, who, to the eyes of men, while they attended on heavenly duties, seemed as it were to shed light from on high. Now because they were greatly stirred up in opposition to our Redeemer, it was as though 'fire fell from heaven;' whilst from those very men, who were accounted teachers of the truth, the flames of envy burst out, to the deceiving of the ignorant people. For we know from the testimony of the Gospel, that through envy at the truths which He taught they sought an opportunity for His betrayal, but that from fear of the people they dared not make known what they went about. Hence too it is therein written, that in order to dissuade the people they say, *Have any of the rulers or of the Pharisees believed on Him? but this people, who knoweth not the Law, are cursed*. [John 7, 48. 49.] But what do we understand by the sheep and the servants, save all inoffensive, but still as yet fainthearted persons, who, while they feared to undergo the persecution of the Pharisees and the Rulers, were devoured by the fires of infidelity. So let it be said; *The fire of God is fallen from Heaven, and hath burned up the sheep and the servants*; i.e. the flame of envy hath come down from the hearts of the rulers, and burnt up all that there was of good springing up in the people; for while the wicked rulers are claiming honour to themselves in opposition to the Truth, the hearts of their followers are turned from every right way. And here too it is well added, *And I only am escaped alone to tell thee*; for whereas the predicted case of wickedness is fulfilled, that word of prophecy escapes the extinction of falsehood, wherein it is said, *yea, the fire of thine enemies shall devour them* [Is. 26, 11]; as though it were plainly expressed, 'not only are the wicked afterwards tormented by fire sent in vengeance, but even now they are consumed therewith through envy;' in that they who are hereafter to be visited with the punishment of just retribution, inflict upon themselves here the tortures of envy. And thus the servant flies and returns alone, and announces that the sheep and the servants have been destroyed by fire, when Prophecy in forsaking the Jewish people shows that she has declared the truth, saying, *Jealousy has taken hold of a people without knowledge*; as though it said in plain words, 'when the people would not make out the words of the Prophets, but gave their belief to the words of the envious, the fire of jealousy consumed them, seeing that they were burnt in the fire of other men's envy.' It goes on,

Ver. 17. Whilst he was yet speaking, there came also another, and said, The Chaldeans made out three bands, and fell upon the camels, and have carried them away, yea, and slain the servants with the edge of the sword, and I only am escaped alone to tell thee.

xxxii. 52. Knowing that the Chaldeans are to be interpreted 'fierce ones,' who else are represented by the name of Chaldeans but the stirrers of that of the persecution, who burst out even in open cries of malice, saying, *Crucify Him! Crucify Him!* [Luke 23, 21.] These *made themselves into three bands*, when the Pharisees, Herodians, and Sadducees came severally to put questions. [Mk. 15, 13. 15.] Assuredly they were vanquished by the mouth of Wisdom, but forasmuch as we must suppose that they drew some foolish ones after them, having made themselves into bands, they carried away the camels; for each set of them poisoned the hearts of the foolish according to the evil notions, with which it was itself embued; and while by their persuasions they drag them to destruction, it was as if they led captive the crooked [*tortuosas*] minds of the weaker sort. Thus when the Lord preached in Samaria, there were many of the Samaritans that were joined to the heritage of that our Redeemer. But did not they, who, on the ground of the seven husbands of one woman that were dead, tempted the Lord against the hope of resurrection, do their best to bring back the believing Samaritans from their faith, who plainly knew nothing of the hope of a resurrection? Who, while they receive some things out of the Law, and disregard others, do as it were, after the manner of camels, ruminate indeed like a clean animal, but like an unclean animal do not cleave the hoof. Though camels which ruminate, yet do not cleave the hoof, are likewise a representation of those in Judaea, who had admitted the historical fact after the letter, but could not spiritually discern the proper force thereof. Upon these the Chaldeans seize in three bands, in that the Pharisees, Herodians, and Sadducees, by their evil persuasions, turn them aside from all right understanding. And at the same time they smite the servants with the sword; for though there were those among the people who were now capable of exercising reason, yet these they met not with force of reasoning, but with authoritativeness of power; and while they desire to be imitated as rulers by their subjects, notwithstanding if their followers can understand somewhat, yet they drag them to destruction by the prerogative of assumed authority. And it is fitly that one servant escapes from them to bring the tidings, in that when the Pharisees, Herodians, and Sadducees do wickedly, that word of Prophecy, whilst forsaking them, is established sure, which says, *And they that handle the Law knew me not.* [Jer. 2, 8] The account proceeds,

Ver. 18, 19. While he was yet speaking, there came also another, and said, Thy sons and thy daughters were eating and drinking wine in their eldest brother's house: And, behold, there came a great wind from the wilderness, and smote the four corners of the house, and it fell upon thy children, and they are dead.

xxxiii.

53. We have said a little above that by the sons and the daughters we understand the Apostles that preached, and the people under them; who are said to be feasting in their eldest brother's house, for that it was in the lot of the Jewish people still that they were fed with the sweets of the sacred truths preached. *And, behold, there came a great wind from the wilderness.* The wilderness is the heart of unbelievers, which being forsaken by the Lord is without an inhabitant to tend it. And what is the great wind, but strong temptation? Accordingly there came a great wind from the wilderness; for at the Passion of our Redeemer there came from the hearts of the Jews strong temptation against His faithful followers. The wilderness may likewise not unaptly be taken for the forsaken multitude of impure spirits, from whom came a wind and smote the house, in that they were the source whence the temptations proceeded, and overturned the hearts of the persecutors.

54. But this house wherein the sons were feasting was builded on four corners. Now we know the three orders of Rulers in the Synagogue, viz. the Priests, the Scribes, and the Elders of the people; to whom if we add the Pharisees likewise, we shall have found the four corners in this house. There came then a wind from the wilderness., and smote the four corners of the house; in that temptation burst forth from the unclean spirits and stirred up the minds of the four orders to the wickedness of persecution. That house fell and overwhelmed His children, forasmuch as when Judaea fell into the cruelty of persecuting our Lord, it overwhelmed the faith of the Apostles with fears of despair. For they had only to see their Master laid hold of, and, lo, they fled every way, denying Him. And though the Hand within did by foreknowledge hold their spirits in life, yet

meanwhile carnal fear cut them off from the life of faith. They then who forsook their Master, when Judaea raged against Him, were as if killed by the house being overthrown, when its corners were smitten. But what do we think became of the flock of the faithful at that time, when, as we know, the very rams took to flight? Now in the midst of these events one escaped to bring tidings, in that the word of Prophecy, which had given warning of these things, approves itself to have been confirmed in saying of the persecuting people, *My beloved one hath done many crimes in Mine house* [Jer. 11. 15. Vulg.]; of the preachers, who though good yet fled at the Passion, *My neighbours stood afar off*; [Ps. 38, 12] saying again of the whole number, who were greatly afraid, *Smite the shepherd, and the sheep shall be scattered.* [Zech. 13, 7] It proceeds;

Ver. 20. Then Job arose, and rent his mantle.

xxxiv. 55. When his sons were destroyed in the ruin of the house, Job arose, because when Judaea was lost in unbelief, and when the Preachers were fallen in the death of fear, the Redeemer of mankind raised Himself from the death of His carnal nature; He showed in what judgment He abandoned His persecutors to themselves. For His rising is the showing with what severity He forsakes sinners, just as His lying down is the patient endurance of ills inflicted. He rises then, when He executes the decrees of justice against the reprobate. And hence He is rightly described to have rent his mantle. For what stood as the mantle of the Lord, but the Synagogue, which by the preaching of the Prophets clung to the expectation of His Incarnation? For in the same way that He is now clothed with those by whom He is loved, as Paul is witness, who says, *That He might present it to Himself a glorious church, not having spot nor wrinkle* [Eph. 5, 27]; (for that which is described as having neither spot or wrinkle is surely made appear as a spiritual robe [*vestis rationalis*]; and at once clean in practice, and stretched in hope;) so when Judaea believed Him as yet to be made Incarnate, it was no less a garment through its clinging to Him.

56. But because He was looked for before He came, and coming, taught new truths, and teaching, wrought wonders, and working wonders, underwent wrongs, *He rent His mantle*, which He had put on Him, seeing that in Judaea some he withdrew from unbelief, whilst some He left therein. What then is the rent mantle but Ju-

daea divided in contrary opinions? For, if His mantle had not been rent, the Evangelist would not have said that, at the preaching of our Lord, there arose strife among the people; *For some said, He is a good man; others said, Nay, but He deceiveth the people*. [John 7, 12] For that mantle of His was rent, in that being divided in opinions it lost the unity of concord. It proceeds; *And shaved his head, and fell down upon the ground, and worshipped.*

xxxv.

57. What is signified by the hair that was shorn but the minuteness [*subtilitas*] of Sacraments? what by the head but the High Priesthood? Hence too it is said to the prophet Ezekiel, *And thou, son of man, take thee a sharp knife, take thee a barber's razor, and cause it to pass upon thine head, and upon thy beard*; [Ezek. 5, 1] clearly that by the Prophet's act the judgment of the Redeemer might be set out, Who when He came in the flesh 'shaved the head,' in that he took clean away from the Jewish Priesthood the Sacraments of His commandments; 'and shaved the beard,' in that in forsaking the kingdom of Israel, He cut off the glory of its excellency. And what is here expressed by the earth, but sinful man? For to the first man that sinned the words were spoken; *Dust thou art, and unto dust shalt thou return*. [Gen. 3, 19] By the name of the earth then is signified the sinful Gentile world; for whilst Judaea thought herself righteous, it appears how damnable she thought the Gentile world, as Paul is witness, who says, *We who are Jews by nature, and not sinners of the Gentiles*. [Gal. 2, 15] Therefore our Mediator, as it were, *shaved His head, and fell down upon the earth*, seeing that in forsaking Judaea, whilst He took away His Sacraments from her Priesthood, He came to the knowledge of the Gentiles. For He 'shaved the hair from His Head,' because He took away from that His first Priesthood the Sacraments of the Law. And He fell upon the earth, because He gave Himself to sinners for their salvation; and while He gave up those who appeared to themselves righteous, He took to Himself those, who both knew and confessed that they were unrighteous. And hence He Himself declares in the Gospel, *For judgment I am come into this world, that they that see not might see, and that they which see might be made blind*. [John 9, 39] And hence the pillar of the cloud, which went before the people in the wilderness, shone with a radiant flame of fire not in the day but in the night; for this reason, that our Redeemer, in giving guidance to those that followed Him by the exam-

ple of life and conduct, yielded no light to such as trusted in their own righteousness, but all those who acknowledged the darkness of their sins, He shone with the fire of His love. Nor, because Job is said to fall on the earth, let us account this to be an unworthy representation of our Redeemer. For it is written, *The Lord sent a Word into Jacob, and it hath fallen* [E.V. *lighted*] *upon Israel.* [Is. 9, 8] For *Jacob* means one that overthrows another, and *Israel*, one that sees God. And what is signified by Jacob but the Jewish people, and by Israel but the Gentile world? For in that very One Whom Jacob aimed to overthrow by the death of the flesh, the Gentile world, by the eyes of faith, beheld God. And thus the Word, that was sent to Jacob, lighted upon Israel; for Him whom the Jewish people rejected when He came to them, the Gentile world at once owned and found. For concerning the Holy Spirit it is written, *The Spirit of God fell upon them*. [Acts 11, 15]

58. And for this reason either the Word of God or the Holy Spirit is said to fall in Holy Scripture, to describe the suddenness of His coming. For whatever rushes down or falls, comes to the bottom directly. And therefore it is as if the Mediator had fallen upon the earth, that without any previous signs He unexpectedly came to the Gentiles. And it is well said, that *He fell down upon the earth and worshipped*, in that whilst He Himself undertook the low estate of the flesh, He poured into the hearts of believers the breathings of humility. For He did this, in that He taught the doing of it, in the same way that it is said of His Holy Spirit, *But the Spirit itself maketh request* [Vulg. *postulat*] *for us with groanings which cannot be uttered*. [Rom. 8, 26] Not that He petitions, Who is of perfect equality, but He is said to make request for no other reason than that He causes those to make request whose hearts He has filled: though our Redeemer, moreover, manifested this in His own Person, Who even besought the Father when He was drawing nigh to His Passion. For what wonder if, in the form of a servant, He submitted Himself to the Father by pouring out His supplications to Him, when in the same He even underwent the violence of sinners, to the very extremity of death. It proceeds:

Ver.21. Naked came I out of my mother's womb, and naked shall I return thither.

59. The mother of our Redeemer, after the flesh, was the Synagogue, from whom He came forth to us, made manifest by a Body. But she kept Him to herself veiled under the covering of the letter, seeing that she neglected to open the eyes of the understanding to the spiritual import thereof. Because in Him, thus veiling Himself with the flesh of an human Body, she would not see God, she as it were refused to behold Him naked in His Divinity. But He 'came naked out of His mother's womb,' because when He issued from the flesh of the Synagogue, He came openly manifest to the Gentiles; which is excellently represented by Joseph's leaving His cloak and fleeing. For when the adulterous woman would have used him to no good end, he, leaving his cloak, fled out of the house; because when the Synagogue, believing Him to be simply man, would have bound Him as it were in an adulterous embrace, He too left the covering of the letter to its eyes, and manifested Himself to the Gentiles without disguise for the acknowledgment of the Power of His Divinity. And hence Paul said, *But even to this day, when Moses is read, the vail is upon their hearts* [2 Cor. 3, 15]; for this reason, that the adulteress kept the cloak in her own hands, but Him, Whom she wickedly laid hold of, she let go naked. He then Who coming from the Synagogue plainly disclosed Himself to the faith of the Gentiles, 'came naked out of His mother's womb,' But does He wholly give her up? Where then is that which the Prophet declares, *For though thy people Israel be as the sand of the sea, yet a remnant of them shall return?* [Is. 10, 22] where that which is written, *Until the fulness of the Gentiles be come in; and so all Israel shall be saved?* [Rom. 11, 25. 26.] The time will be, then, when He will show Himself clearly to the Synagogue also. Yes, the time will doubtless come in the end of the world, when He will make Himself known, even as He is God, to the remnant of His People. Whence it is likewise justly said in this place, *and naked shall I return thither.* For he 'returns naked to His mother's womb,' when, at the end of the world, He, Who being made Man in time is the object of scorn, is revealed to the eyes of His Synagogue as God before all worlds. It proceeds; -

Ver. 21. The Lord gave, and the Lord hath taken away; as it hath pleased the Lord, so is it come to pass; blessed be the Name of the Lord.

xxxvii.

60. Our Redeemer, in that He is God, gives all things with the Father; but in that He is Man, He receives at the

hands of the Father, as one among all. Therefore let Him say of Judaea, so long as she believed in the mystery of His Incarnation to come, *the Lord hath given*. Let Him say of her, when she slighted the looked for coming of His Incarnation, *the Lord hath taken away*. For she was 'given,' when in the persons of a certain number she believed what was to be; but she was 'taken away,' as the just desert of her blindness, when she scorned to hold in veneration the truths believed by those.

61. But let Him instruct all that believe in Him, that when under scourges they may know how to bless God, in the words that are added, *As it hath pleased the Lord, so is it done* [not in E.V.]; *blessed be the Name of the Lord*. Whence likewise, as the Gospel is witness, when He is described to be drawing near to His Passion, He is said to have taken bread and given thanks. And so He gives thanks Who is bearing the stripes of the sins of others. And He, Who did nothing worthy of strokes, blesses humbly under the infliction of them, doubtless that He might show from hence what each man ought to do in the chastisement of his own transgressions, if He thus bears with patience the chastisement of the transgressions of others, that He might show hence what the servant should do under correction, if He being equal gives thanks to the Father under the rod. It proceeds;

Ver. 22. In all this Job sinned not, nor charged God foolishly.

62. 'That he neither sinned, nor charged God foolishly,' Peter, as we have said, above testifies of Him in plain terms, saying, *Who did no sin, neither was guile found in His mouth*. [1 Pet. 2, 22] For guile in the mouth is so much the more senseless folly with God, the more that in the eyes of men it passes for crafty wisdom, as Paul bears witness, saying, *The wisdom of this world is foolishness with God*. [1 Cor. 3, 19] Forasmuch then as there was no guile in His mouth, verily He said nothing foolishly. The Priests and the Rulers believed that He charged God foolishly, when, being questioned at the time of His Passion, He testified that He was the Son of God. And hence they question, saying, *What further need have we of witnesses? Behold now we have heard His blasphemy*. [Mat. 26, 65] But He did not charge God foolishly, in that speaking the words of truth, even in dying He brought before the unbelievers that concerning Himself, which He soon after manifested to all the redeemed by rising again.

Moral 63. We have briefly gone through these particulars, regarded under the view of representing our Head. Now, as they tend to the edification of His Body, let us explain them to be considered in a moral aspect; that we may learn how that, which is described to have been done in outward deed, is acted inwardly in our mind. Now when the sons of God present themselves before God, Satan also presents himself among them, in that it very often happens that that old enemy craftily blends and unites himself with those good thoughts, which are sown in our hearts through the instrumentality of the coming of the Holy Spirit, to disorder all that is rightly conceived, and tear in pieces what is once wrongly disordered. But He, Who created us, does not forsake us in our temptation. For our enemy, who hid himself in ambush against us, He makes easy to be discovered by us, through the illumination of His light. Wherefore He says to him immediately, *Whence comest thou?*

64. For His interrogating the crafty foe is the discovering to us his ambush, that where we see him steal into the heart, we may watch against him with resolution and with caution. **xxxix.**

Ver. 7. Then Satan answered the Lord, and said, From going to and fro in the earth, and from walking up and down in it.

65. Satan's *going to and fro in the earth* is his exploring the hearts of the carnal, and seeking diligently whence he may find grounds of accusation against them. He 'goeth round about the earth,' for he comes about the hearts of men, that he may carry off all that is good in them, that he may lodge evil in their minds, that he may heap up on that he has lodged, that he may perfect that he has heaped, that he may gain as his fellows in punishment those whom he has perfected in sin. And observe that he does not say that he has been flying through the earth, but that he has been *walking up and down in it*; for, in truth, he is never quick to leave whomsoever he tempts; but there where he finds a soft heart, he plants the foot of his wretched persuasion, so that by resting thereon, he may stamp the prints of evil practice, and by a like wickedness to his own may render reprobate all whom he is able; but in despite of him blessed Job is commended in these words; **xl.**

Ver. 8. Hast thou considered My servant Job, that there is none like him in the earth, a perfect and an upright man, one that feareth God, and escheweth evil?

xli. 66. To him, whom Divine Inspiration makes strong to meet the enemy, God gives praise as it were in the ears of Satan; for His giving him praise is the first vouchsafing virtues, and afterwards preserving them when vouchsafed. But the old enemy is the more enraged against the righteous, the more he perceives that they are hedged around by the favour of God's protection. And hence he rejoins, and says;

Ver. 10. Doth Job fear God for nought? Hast not Thou made an hedge about him, and about his house, and about all that he hath on every side? Thou hast blessed the work of his hands, and his substance is increased in the land.

xlii. 67. As though he plainly said; 'Wherefore dost Thou extol him whom Thou stablishest with Thy protection? for man would deserve Thy praises, while Thou despisest me, if he withstood me by his own proper strength.' Hence also he immediately demands on man's head with evil intent, what man's Defender concedes though with a merciful design. For it is added,

Ver. 11. But put forth Thine hand now, and touch all that he hath; and he will curse Thee to Thy face.

xliii. 68. For when we yield plentifully the fruits of virtue, and when we are flourishing in uninterrupted prosperity, the mind is somewhat inclined to be lifted up, so as to imagine that all the excellency that she hath comes to her from herself. This same excellency, then, our old enemy with evil intent desires to lay hands on, whilst God no otherwise than in mercy allows it to be tried; that while the mind, under the force of temptation, is shaken in the good wherein it exulted, learning the powerlessness of its own frail condition, it may become the more strongly established in the hope of God's aid; and it is brought to pass by a marvellous dispensation of His Mercy, that from the same source, whence the enemy tempts the soul to destroy it, the merciful Creator gives it instruction that it may live; and hence it is rightly added,

Ver. 12. Behold, all that he hath is in thy power; only upon himself put not forth thine hand.

69. As if He said in plain words; 'I give thee so to try the good that is in each one of Mine Elect by temptation from without, that thou mayest acquaint thine own self that I keep him holding on to Me by the inward root of the mind; and hence it is rightly added, **xliv.**

So Satan went out from the presence of the Lord.

70. For in that he is not suffered to prevail so far as to withdraw the heart, being thus shut out from the interior, he roams without. Who, even if he very often work confusion in the virtues of the soul, herein does it without, in that, through God's withholding him, he never wounds the hearts of the good to their utter ruin. For he is permitted so far to rage against them as may be necessary, in order that they, thus instructed by temptation, may be stablished, that they may never attribute to their own strength the good which they do, nor neglect themselves in the sloth of security, loosing themselves from the bracings of fear, but that in keeping guard over their attainments they may watch with so much the greater prudence, as they see themselves to be ever confronting the enemy in the fight of temptations. **xlv.**

Ver. 13, 14, 15. And there was a day when his sons and his daughters were eating and drinking wine in their eldest brother's house: And there came a messenger unto Job, and said, The oxen were plowing, and the asses feeding beside them: and the Sabeans fell upon them; yea, they have slain the servants with the edge of the sword; and I only am escaped alone to tell thee.

71. In the hearts of the Elect wisdom is first engendered, before all the graces that follow; and she comes forth as it were a first born offspring by the gift of the Holy Spirit. Now this wisdom is our faith, as the Prophet testifies, saying, *If ye will not believe, surely ye shall not understand* [E.V. *be established*]. [Is. 7, 9] For then we are truly wise to understand, when we yield the assent of our belief to all that our Creator says. Thus the sons are feasting in their eldest brother's house, when the other virtues are feasted in faith. But if this latter be not first produced in our hearts, all besides cannot be good, though it may seem to be good. The sons feast in their eldest brother's house, so long as our virtues are replenished **xlvi.**

with the good of holy writ, in the dwelling place of faith; for it is written, *without faith it is impossible to please God* [Heb. 11, 6]; and so our virtues taste the true feasts of life, when they begin to be sustained with the mysteries [*sacramentis*] of faith. The sons feast in their eldest brother's house, in that except the other virtues, filling themselves with the feast of wisdom; do wisely all that they seek to do, they can never be virtues.

72. But observe, while the good that we do is fed with the rich fare of wisdom and of faith, our enemy carries off the *oxen* that *are plowing, and the asses feeding beside them, and kills the servants with the sword*. What are the *oxen plowing*, except we understand our serious thoughts, which while they wear [*conficiunt*] the heart with diligent tillage, yield abundant fruits of increase? and what do we take to be *the asses feeding beside them*, but the simple emotions of the heart, which, whilst carefully withheld from straying in double ways, we feed in the free pasture of purity? But oftentimes the crafty enemy, spying out the serious thoughts of our heart, corrupts them under the cloak of that beguiling pleasure which he insinuates; and when he sees the simple emotions of the heart, he displays the subtleties and refinements of discoveries, that while we aim at praise for subtlety, we may part with the simplicity of a pure mind; and though he has not the power to draw us to a deed of sin, nevertheless by secret theft [*subripiens*] he spoils the thoughts of good things through his temptations, that while he is seen to trouble the good that is in their mind, he may seem as though he had completely made spoil of it. By the oxen ploughing may also be understood the intents of charity, whereby we endeavour to render service to others, when we desire to cleave the hardness of a brother's heart by preaching; and by the asses also, for that they never resist with a mad rage those that are loading them, may be signified the meekness of patience, and oftentimes our old enemy, seeing us anxious to benefit others by our words, plunges the mind into a certain sleepy state of inactivity, that we are not disposed to do good to others, even though our own concerns leave us at liberty. Accordingly he carries away the oxen that are ploughing, when, by insinuating sloth that causes negligence, he breaks the force of those inward purposes, which were directed to produce the fruit of a brother's welfare, and although the hearts of the Elect keep watch within the depths of their own thoughts, and, getting the better of it, take thought of the mischief, which they re-

ceive at the hands of the tempter; yet by this very circumstance, that he should prevail over the thoughts of good things though but for a moment, the malicious enemy exults in having gotten some booty.

73. Now oftentimes, when he sees the mind in a readiness to endure, he contrives to find out what it loves the best, and there sets his traps of offence; that the more the object is beloved, our patience may be the sooner disquieted by means of it. And indeed the hearts of the Elect ever return heedfully to themselves, and chastise themselves sorely, even for the slighest impulse to go wrong, and whilst by being moved they learn how they should have stood fast, they are sometimes the more firmly established for being shaken. But the ancient enemy, when he puts out our purposes of patience, though but for a moment, exults that he has, as it were, carried off the asses from the field of the heart. Now in the things which we determine to do we carefully consider, with the watchfulness of reason, what is proper, and to what cases. But too often the enemy, by rushing upon us with the sudden impulse of temptation, and coming unawares before the mind's looking out, slays as it were with the sword the very servants that are keeping watch, yet one escapes to tell that the rest [*alia*] is lost; for in whatsoever the mind is affected by the enemy, the discernment of reason ever returns to it, and she doth in a certain sense show that she hath escaped alone, which doth resolutely consider with herself all that she has undergone. So then all the rest perish, and one alone returns home, when the motions of the heart are in the time of temptation put to rout, and then discernment comes back to the conscience; that whatever the mind, which has been caught by a sudden onset, calculates that she has lost, she may recover, when bowed down with heartfelt contrition.

Ver. 16. While he was yet speaking, there came also another, and said, The fire of God is fallen from heaven, and hath burned up the sheep and the servants, and consumed them; and I only am escaped alone to tell thee.

xlvii.

74. What is signified by sheep but the innocency of our thoughts? what is signified by sheep, but cleanness of heart in the good? Now we have said a little above that we speak of the aerial 'heaven,' whence too we name the birds of heaven. And we know that the impure spirits, that fell from the ethereal heaven, roam abroad in the mid space between this heaven and earth. These are the more envious that the hearts of men should mount up to the

realms of heaven, that they see themselves to have been cast down from thence by the impurity of their pride. Forasmuch then as the glances of jealousy burst forth from the powers of the air against the purity of our thoughts, 'fire fell from heaven upon the sheep;' for oftentimes they inflame the pure thoughts of our minds with the fires of lust, and they do as it were consume the sheep with fire, when they disorder the chaste feelings of the mind with the temptations of sensuality. This is called the fire of God, for it owes its birth, though not to the making, yet to the permission of God. And because by a sudden onset they sometimes overwhelm the very cautions of the mind, they slay with the sword as it were the servants that are their keepers. Yet one escapes in safety, so long as persevering discernment reviews with exactness all that the mind suffers, and this alone escapes the peril of death; for even when the thoughts are put to rout, discretion does not give over to make known its losses to the mind, and as it were to call upon her lord to lament.

Ver. 17. While he was yet speaking there came also another, and said, The Chaldeans made out three bands, and fell upon the camels, and have carried them away, yea, and slain the servants with the edge of the sword; and I only am escaped alone to tell thee.

75. By the camels, which have a clean mark, in that they ruminate, and an unclean, in that they do not cleave the hoof, are meant, as we have already said above, the godly stewardships of temporal things, in which in proportion as the charge is more extensive, the more doth the enemy multiply his plots against us. For every man who is set over the management of temporal affairs, is the more largely open to the darts of the hidden foe. For some things he aims to do with an eye to the future, and often whilst, thus cautious, he forecasts future events with exactness, he incautiously neglects to regard present evils. Often while his eye is on the present, he is asleep to the anticipation of coming events. Often in doing some things slothfully, he neglects what should be done with energy. Often in showing himself overactive in the execution, by the very restlessness of his mode of acting he hurts the more the interests of his charge. Again, sometimes he strives to put restraint upon his lips, but is prevented keeping silence by the requirements of his business. Sometimes, whilst he restrains himself with excessive rigour, he is silent even when he ought to speak. Sometimes, while he gives him-

self more liberty to communicate necessary things, he says at the same time what he should never have given utterance to. And for the most part he is embarrassed with such vast complications of thoughts, that he is scarce able to bear the mere things, which with foresight he ponders in his mind, and while he produces nothing in deed, he is grievously overburdened [*insudat*] with the great weight upon his breast. For as that is hard to bear which he is subject to within his own bosom, even while unemployed and at rest from work without, he is yet wearied. For very frequently the mind as it were views coming events, and every energy is strung to meet them; a vehement heat of contention is conceived, sleep is put to flight, night is turned into day, and while the bed holds our limbs which are outwardly at rest, the cause is inwardly pleaded with vehement clamours in the court of our own heart. And it very often happens that nothing comes to pass of the things foreseen, and that all that thinking of the heart, which had so long been strung up in preparation to the highest degree of intensity, proves vain, and is stilled in a moment. And the mind is so much the longer detained from necessary concerns, as it thinks on trifles to a wider extent. Forasmuch therefore as the evil spirits one while deal a blow against the charges of our stewardship by a slothful or a headlong mode of action, at another time throw them into disorder by a backward or an unchecked use of speech, and are almost always burthening them with excessive loads of care, the Chaldeans in three bands carry off the camels. For it is as it were to make three bands against the camels, to spread confusion amidst the business of earthly stewardship, now by unwarranted deed, now by overmuch speech, now by unregulated thought, so that while the mind is striving to direct itself effectually to outward ministrations, it should be cut off from the consideration of itself, and know nothing of the injuries which it sustains in itself, in the same proportion that it exerts itself in the affairs of others with a zeal above what is befitting. But when a right mind undertakes any charge of stewardship, it considers what is due to self and what to neighbours, and neither by excess of concern for others overlooks its own interests, nor by attention to its own welfare, puts behind the affairs of others. But yet it very often happens that while the mind is discreetly intent upon both, while it keeps itself clear for the utmost precautions, both as regards itself and the things which have been entrusted to it, still being thrown into confusion by some unexpected point in any case that arises, it is so hurried away headlong, that all its precautions are overwhelmed thereby in a moment. And hence the Chaldeans strike with the sword the servants that were the keepers of the camels. Yet one returns; for amidst all this the rational thought of discretion meets the eyes of our mind, and the soul, taking heed to herself, is led to comprehend what she has lost within by the sudden onset of temptation. It follows;

Ver. 18, 19. While he was yet speaking, there came also another, and said, Thy sons and thy daughters were eating and drinking wine in their eldest brother's house: And, behold, there came a great wind from the wilderness, and smote the four corners of the house, and it fell upon the young men, and they are dead; and I only am escaped alone to tell thee.

xlix. 76. As we have before said, 'the wilderness' is the deserted multitude of impure spirits, which when it forsook the felicity of its Creator, as it were lost the hand of the cultivator. And from the same there came a strong wind, and overthrew the house; in that strong temptation seizes us from the unclean spirits, and overturns the conscience from its settled frame of tranquillity. But this house stands by four corners for this reason, that the firm fabric of our mind is upheld by Prudence, Temperance, Fortitude, Justice. This house is grounded on four corners, in that the whole structure of good practice is raised in these four virtues. And hence do four rivers of Paradise water the earth. For while the heart is watered with these four virtues, it is cooled from all the heat of carnal desires. Yet sometimes when idleness steals on the mind, prudence waxes cold; for when it is weary and turns slothful, it neglects to forecast coming events. Sometimes while some delight is stealing on the mind, our temperance decays. For in whatever degree we are led to take delight in the things of this life, we are the less temperate to forbear in things forbidden. Sometimes fear works its way into the heart and confounds the powers of our fortitude, and we prove the less able to encounter adversity, the more excessively we love some things that we dread to part with. And sometimes self-love invades the mind, makes it swerve by a secret declension from the straight line of justice: and in the degree that it refuses to refer itself wholly to its Maker, it goes contrary to the claims of justice. Thus 'a strong wind smites the four corners of the house,' in that strong temptation, by hidden impulses, shakes the four virtues; and the corners being smitten, the house is as it were uprooted; in that when the virtues are beaten, the conscience is brought to trouble.

77. Now it is within these *four corners of the house* that the sons are feasting, because it is within the depths of the mind, which is carried up to the topmost height of perfection in these four virtues especially, that the others like a kind of offspring of the heart take their food together. For the gift of the Spirit, which, in the mind It works on, forms first of all Prudence, Temperance, Fortitude, Justice, in order that the same mind may be perfectly fashioned to resist every species of assault, doth afterwards give it a temper in the seven virtues, so as against folly to bestow Wisdom, against dulness, Understanding, against rashness, Counsel, against fear, Courage, against ignorance, Knowledge, against hardness of heart, Piety, against pride, Fear.

78. But sometimes, whilst the mind is sustained with the plenitude and richness of a gift so large, if it enjoys uninterrupted security in these things, it forgets from what source it has them, and imagines that it derives that from itself, which it sees to be never wanting to it. Hence it is that this same grace sometimes withdraws itself for our good, and shows the presumptuous mind how weak it is in itself. For then we really learn whence our good qualities proceed, when, by seemingly losing them, we are made sensible that they can never be preserved by our own efforts. And so for the purpose of tutoring us in lessons of humility, it very often happens that, when the crisis of temptation is upon us, such extreme folly comes down upon our wisdom, that the mind being dismayed, knows nothing how to meet the evils that are threatened, or how to make ready against temptation. But by this very folly, the heart is wisely instructed; forasmuch as from whatever cause it turns to folly for a moment, it is afterwards rendered by the same the more really, as it is the more humbly, wise; and by these very means, whereby wisdom seems as if lost, it is held in more secure possession. Sometimes when the mind lifts itself up in pride on the grounds of seeing high things, it is dulled with a remarkable obtuseness in the lowest and meanest subjects; that he, who with rapid flight penetrated into the highest things, should in a moment see the very lowest closed to his understanding. But this very dulness preserves to us, at the very time that it withdraws from us, our power of understanding. For whereas it abases the heart for a moment, it strengthens it in a more genuine way to understand the loftiest subjects. Sometimes while we are

congratulating ourselves that we do everything with grave deliberation, some piece of chance takes us in the nick, and we are carried off with a sudden precipitancy; and we, who believed ourselves always to have lived by method, are in a moment laid waste with an inward confusion. Yet by the discipline of this very confusion we learn not to attribute our counsels to our own powers; and we hold to gravity with the more matured endeavours, that we return to the same as if once lost. Sometimes while the mind resolutely defies adversity, when adverse events rise up, she is struck with violent alarm. But when agitated thereby, she learns to Whom to attribute it, that on any occasion she stood firm; and she afterwards holds fast her fortitude the more resolutely, as she sees it now gone as it were out of her hand the moment that terror came upon her. Sometimes whilst we are congratulating ourselves that we know great things, we are stunned with a blindness of instantaneous ignorance. But in so far as the eye of the mind is for a moment closed by ignorance, it is afterwards the more really opened to admit knowledge, in that in fact being instructed by the stroke of its blindness, it may know also from whom it has its very knowing. Sometimes while ordering all things in a religious spirit, when we congratulate ourselves that we have in abundant measure the bowels of pious tenderness, we are struck with a sudden fit of hardness of heart. But when thus as it were hardened, we learn to Whom to ascribe the good dispositions of piety which we have; and the piety, which has been in a manner extinguished, is recovered with more reality, seeing that it is loved with fuller affection as having been lost. Sometimes while the mind is overjoyed that it is bowed under the fear of God, it suddenly waxes stiff under the temptations of pride. Yet immediately conceiving great fears that it should have no fear, it speedily turns back again to humility, which it recovers upon a firmer footing, in proportion as it has felt the weight of this virtue by seeming to let it go.

79. When the house, then, is overthrown, the sons perish; because when the conscience is disturbed under temptation, the virtues that are engendered in the heart, for any advantage from ourselves knowing them, are speedily and in the space of a moment overwhelmed. Now these sons live inwardly by the Spirit, though they perish outwardly in the flesh; because, forsooth, although our virtues in the time of temptation be disordered in a moment, and fall from the safety of their seat, yet by perseverance in endeavour they hold

on unimpaired in the root of the mind. With these the three sisters likewise are slain, for in the heart, sometimes Charity is ruffled by afflictions, Hope shaken by fear, Faith beaten down by questionings. For oftentimes we grow dull in the love of our Creator, while we are chastened with the rod beyond what we think suitable for us. Often while the mind fears more than need be, it weakens the confidence of its hopes. Often while the intellect is exercised with endless questionings, faith being staggered grows faint, as though it would fail. But yet the daughters live, who die when the house is struck. For notwithstanding that in the seat of the conscience the disorder by itself tells that Faith, Hope, and Charity, are almost slain, yet they are kept alive in the sight of God, by perseverance in a right purpose of mind; and hence a servant escapes alone to tell these things, in that discretion of mind remains unhurt even amid temptations. And the servant is the cause that Job recovers his sons by weeping, whilst the mind, being grieved at what discretion reports, keeps by penitence the powers which it had in a manner begun to part with. By a marvellous dispensation of Providence are we thus dealt with, so that our conscience is at times struck with the smitings of guilt. For a person would count himself possessed of great powers indeed, if he never at any time within the depth of his mind felt the failure of them [see S. Macarius, Hom. xv.]. But when the mind is shaken by the assaults of temptation, and is as it were more than enough disheartened, there is shown to it the defence of humility against the arts of its enemy, and from the very occasion, whence it fears to sink powerless, it receives strength to stand firm. But the person tempted not only learns from Whom he has his strength, but is made to understand with what great watchfulness he must preserve it. For oftentimes one, whom the conflict of temptation had not force to overcome, has been brought down in a worse way by his own self-security. For when anyone awearied relaxes himself at his ease, he abandons his mind without restraint to the corrupter. But if, by the dispensations of mercy from above, the stroke of temptation falls upon him, not so as to overwhelm him with a sudden violence, but to instruct him by a measured approach, then he is awakened to foresee the snares, so that with a cautious mind he girds himself to face the enemy in fight. And hence it is rightly subjoined,

Ver. 20. Then Job arose.

THE FIRST PART.

l. 80. For sitting betokens one at ease, but rising, one in a conflict. His rising, then, when he heard the evil tidings, is setting the mind more resolutely for conflicts, after the experience of temptations, by which very temptations even the power of discernment is the gainer, in that it learns the more perfectly to distinguish good from evil. And therefore it is well added,

And rent his mantle.

li. 81. We 'rend our mantle,' whenever we review with a discriminating eye our past deeds; for unless with God our deeds were as a cloak that covered us, it would never have been declared by the voice of an Angel, *Blessed is he that watcheth, and keepeth his garments, lest he walk naked, and they see his shame* [Rev. 16, 15]; for 'our shame' is then 'seen,' when our life, appearing worthy of condemnation in the eyes of the righteous in judgment, has not the covering of after good practice. But because, as often as we are tempted with guilt, we are prompted to mourning, and being stirred by our own lamentations, open the eyes of the mind to the more perfect perception of the light of righteousness, we as it were rend our mantle in grief, in that in consequence of our weeping discretion being strengthened, we chastise all that we do with greater strictness, and with wrathful hand. Then all our high-mindedness comes down, then all our overcunningness is dropped from our thoughts; and hence it is added,

And shaved his head, and fell down upon the ground, and worshipped.

lii. 82. For what do we understand in a moral sense by hair, but the wandering thoughts of the mind? and hence it is elsewhere said to the Church, *Thy lips are like a thread of scarlet; and thy speech is comely*; [Cant. 4, 3] for a thread [*vitta* Vulg.] binds the hairs of the head. So the *lips* of the Spouse are *like a thread*, in that by the exhortations of Holy Church all dissipated thoughts in the minds of her hearers are put in bands, that they may not roam at large, and be spread abroad amongst forbidden objects, and thus spread abroad, lie heavy on the eyes of the mind, but may as it were gather themselves to one direction, in that the thread of holy preaching binds them. Which also is well represented to be *of scarlet*; for the preaching of the Saints glows only with charity. And what is signified by the head, but that very mind, which is principal in every action?

Whence it is elsewhere said, *And let thy head lack no ointment* [Eccl. 9, 8]; for *ointment* upon the head is charity in the heart; and there is lack of ointment upon the head, when there is a withdrawal of charity from the heart. The shaving of the head then is the cutting off all superfluous thoughts from the mind. And he shaveth his head and falls upon the earth, who, restraining thoughts of self-presumption, humbly acknowledges how weak he is in himself.

83. For it is hard for a man to do great things, and not to harbour confident thoughts in his own mind on the score of his great doings. For from this very fact, that we are living in strenuous opposition to our vices, presumptuous imaginations are engendered in the heart; and while the mind valorously beats down the evil habits without her, she is very often inwardly swoln within herself; and now she accounts herself to have some special merits, nor ever imagines that she sins in the conceits of self-esteem. But in the eyes of the severe Judge she is so much the worse delinquent, as the sin committed, in proportion as it is the more concealed, is well nigh incorrigible; and the pit is opened the wider to devour, the more proudly the life we lead glories in itself. Hence, as we have often said before, it is brought to pass by the merciful dispensations of our Creator, that the soul that places confidence in itself is struck down by a providential temptation; that being brought low it may find out what it is, and may lay aside the haughtiness of self-presumption. For as soon as the mind feels the blow of temptation, all the presumption and swelling of our thoughts abates.

84. For when the mind is lifted up in pride, it breaks out as it were into usurpation. And it has for the attendants of its tyrannical power, its own imaginations that flatter it. But if an enemy assaults the tyrant, the favour of those attendants is speedily at an end. For when the adversary finds entrance the attendants fly, and fall away from him in fear, whom in time of peace they extolled with cunning flattery. But, when the attendants are withdrawn, he remains alone in the face of the enemy; for when high thoughts are gone, the troubled mind sees itself only and the temptation, and thus upon healing of evil tidings, the head is shaved, whensoever under the violent assault of temptation the mind is bared of the thoughts of self-assurance. For what does it mean that the Nazarites let their hair grow long, saving that by a life of special continency proud thoughts gain ground? And what does it signify, that, the act of devotion

over, the Nazarite is commanded to shave his head, and cast the hair into the sacrificial fire, but that we then reach the height of perfection, when we so overcome our external evil habits, as to discard from the mind even thoughts that are superfluous? To consume these in the sacrificial fire is, plainly, to set them on fire with the flame of divine love; that the whole heart should glow with the love of God, and burning up every superfluous thought, should as it were consume the hair of the Nazarite in completing his devotion. And observe that he fell upon the earth and worshipped; for he sets forth to God the true worship, who in humility sees that he is dust, who attributes no goodness to himself, who owns that the good that he does is from the mercy of the Creator; and hence he says well and fitly,

Ver. 21. Naked came I out of my mother's womb, and naked shall I return thither.

liii. 85. As if the mind when tempted and taken in the powerlessness of its weak condition were to say, 'Naked I was by grace first begotten in the faith, and naked I shall be saved by the same grace in being taken up into heaven [*in assumptione*].' For it is a great consolation to a troubled mind, when, smitten with the assaults of sin, it sees itself as it were stripped of all virtue, to fly to the hope of Mercy alone, and prevent itself being stripped naked in proportion as it humbly thinks itself to be naked and bare of virtue, and though it be perchance bereaved of some virtue in the hour of temptation, yet acknowledging its own weakness, it is the better clad with humility itself, and is stronger as it is laid low than as it was standing, in that it ceases to ascribe to itself without the aid of God whatever it has. And hence it also at once owns with humility the hand of Him Who is both Giver and Judge, saying,

The Lord gave, and the Lord hath taken away.

liv. 86. Observe how he grew great by the discipline of temptations, who both in the possession of the virtue acknowledges the bounty of the Giver, and in the disorderment of his fortitude, the power of the Withdrawer; which fortitude nevertheless is not withdrawn, but is confounded and loses heart, that the assaulted mind, while it dreads every instant to lose the quality as it seems, being alway made humble, may never lose it.

As it hath pleased the Lord, so is it done; Blessed be the Name of the Lord.

87. In this circumstance, viz. that we are assaulted with inward trouble, it is meet that we refer the thing to the judgment of our Creator, that our heart may resound the louder the praises of its Maker, from the very cause that makes it, on being smitten, the more thoroughly to consider the impotency of its frail condition. Now it is justly said, **lv.**

Ver. 22. In all this Job sinned not, nor charged God foolishly:

88. In that the mind in grief ought to watch with wariness and diligence, lest, when the temptation prompts it within, it break forth inwardly into the utterance of forbidden words, and murmur at the trial; and lest the fire, which burns it like gold, by the excesses of a lawless tongue, may turn it to the ashes of mere chaff. **lvi.**

89. Now nothing hinders that all that we have said concerning virtues, be understood of those gifts of the Holy Spirit which are vouchsafed in [vid. chap. 91.] manifestation of virtue, for to one is given the gift of Prophecy, to another different kinds of tongues, to another the gifts of healing. But forasmuch as these gifts are not always present in the mind in the same degree, it is clearly shown that it is for our good that they are sometimes withdrawn, lest the mind should be lifted up in pride. For if the Spirit of Prophecy had always been with the Prophets, plainly the Prophet Elisha would never have said, *Let her alone, for her soul is vexed within her, and the Lord hath hid it from me, and hath not told me.* [2 Kings 4, 27] If the Spirit of Prophecy had been always present to the Prophets, the Prophet Amos when asked would never have said, *I am* [so Vulg.] *no Prophet*; where he also adds, *neither a Prophet's son, but I am an herdsman and a gatherer of sycamore fruit.* [Amos 7, 14.] How then was he no Prophet, who foretold so many true things concerning the future? or in what way was he a Prophet, if he at the time disowned the truth concerning himself? Why, because, at the moment that he was called in question [*requisitus*], he felt that the Spirit of Prophecy was not with him, he bore true testimony concerning himself, in saying; *I am not a Prophet.* Yet he added afterwards, *Now therefore hear thou the word of the Lord. Therefore thus said the Lord, Thy wife shall be an harlot in the city, and thy sons and thy daughters shall fall by the sword, and thy land*

shall be divided by line; and thou shalt die in a polluted land. [ver. 16, 17.] By these words of the Prophet it is plainly shown, that while he was bearing that testimony about himself he was filled, and on the instant rewarded with the Spirit of Prophecy, because he humbly acknowledged himself to be no Prophet. And if the Spirit of Prophecy had always continued with the Prophets, the Prophet Nathan would never have allowed King David, when he consulted him about the building of the Temple, what a little while after he was to refuse him.

90. And hence, how justly is it written in the Gospel, *Upon Whom thou shalt see the Spirit descending, and remaining on Him, the same is He Which baptizeth with the Holy Ghost.* For the Spirit descends into all the faithful, but remains in the Mediator alone, in a special manner. For He has never left the Human Nature of Him, from Whose Divine Nature He proceedeth. He remains therefore in Him, Who only can both do all things and at all times. Now the faithful, who receive Him, since they cannot always retain the gifts of miracles, as they desire, testify that they have received Him as it were in a passing manifestation. But whereas on the other hand it is said by the mouth of Truth concerning the same Spirit to the Disciples, *For He dwelleth with you, and shall be in you*, [John 14, 17] how is it, that this same abiding of the Holy Spirit is by the voice of God declared to be the sign of the Mediator, where it is said, *Upon Whom thou shalt see the Spirit descending, and abiding on Him?* If then according to the words of the Master He abideth in the disciples also, how will it be any longer a special sign, that He abides in the Mediator? Now this we shall learn the sooner, if we discriminate between the gifts of the same Spirit.

91. Now there are some of His gifts, without which life is never attained; and there are others whereby holiness of life is made known for the good of other men. For meekness, humility, faith, hope, charity, are gifts that come from Him, and they are such as man can never reach to life without. And the gift of Prophecy, healing, different kinds of tongues, the interpretation of tongues [*sermonum*], are His gifts; yet such as show forth the presence of His power for the improvement of all beholders. In the case of these gifts then, without which we can never attain to life, the Holy Spirit for ever abides, whether in His preachers, or in all the Elect; but in those gifts whereof the object is not the preservation of our own life,

but of the lives of others through the manifestation of Him, He by no means always abides in the Preachers. For He is indeed always ruling their hearts to the end of good living, yet does not always exhibit the signs of miraculous powers by them, but sometimes, for all manifestation of miracles, He withdraws Himself from them, in order that those powers, which belong to Him, may be had with greater humility, in the same degree that being in possession they cannot be retained.

92. But the Mediator of God and men, the Man Christ Jesus, in all things hath Him both always and continually present. For the same Spirit even in Substance proceeds from Him. And thus, though He abides in the holy Preachers, He is justly said to abide in the Mediator in a special manner, for that in them He abides of grace for a particular object, but in Him He abides substantially for all ends. For as our body is cognizant of the sense of touch only, but the head of the body has the use of all the five senses at once, so that it sees, hears, tastes, smells, and touches; so the members of the Supreme Head shine forth in some of the powers, but the Head Itself blazes forth in all of them. The Spirit then abides in Him in another sort, from Whom He never departs by reason of His Nature. Now those of His gifts, by which life is attained, can never without danger be lost, but the gifts, whereby holiness of life is made evident, are very often withdrawn, as we have said, without detriment. So then the first are to be kept for our own edification, the latter to be sought for the improvement of others. In the case of the one let the fear alarm us, lest they perish, but in the other, when they are withdrawn for a season, let humility be our consolation, for that they may chance to lift up the mind to entertain pride. Accordingly when the power of miracles which had been vouchsafed is withdrawn, let us exclaim as is right, *The Lord gave, and the Lord hath taken away; blessed be the Name of the Lord*. For then, and only then, we really show that we have held in a right spirit all that we had given us, when we bear with patience the momentary withdrawal thereof.

THE FIRST PART.

BOOK III.

The whole of the second chapter of the Book of Job is explained after the manner of the former Books, historically, allegorically, and morally.

i. Historical

1. BLESSED Job, though aimed at for death in his temptation, gained growth unto life by the stroke. And our old enemy grieved to find that he had only multiplied his excellences by the very means, by which he had thought to do away with them, but whereas he sees that he has been worsted in the first struggle, he prepares himself for fresh assaults of temptations, and still has the boldness to augur evil of that holy man; for one that is evil can never believe goodness to exist, though proved by his experience. Now those circumstances, which were promised in the first infliction, are again subjoined, when it is said,

Ver. 1, 2, 3. Again there was a day when the sons of God came to present themselves before the Lord, and Satan came also among them to present himself before the Lord. And the Lord said unto Satan, Whence comest thou? And Satan answered the Lord, and said, From going to and fro in the earth, and from walking up and down in it. And the Lord said unto Satan, Hast thou considered my servant Job, that there is none like him in the earth, a perfect and an upright man, one that feareth God, and escheweth evil?

Because we have discussed these particulars very fully above, we the rather pass them over in silence, lest, whilst we often repeat points once gone into, we delay too long in coming to such as are untouched; although what is said to Satan by the Lord's voice, *Whence comest thou?* I cannot consider to be addressed to him just as it was before; for whereas he returns defeated from that contest upon which he had been let loose, and yet is asked 'whence he comes,' when it is known from whence he comes, what else is this but that the impotency of his pride is chidden? As though the voice of God openly said, 'See, thou art overcome by a single man, and him too beset with the infirmities of the flesh; thou, that strivest to set thyself up against Me, the Maker of all things!' Hence when the Lord immediately went on to declare the excellences of Job, as He did before, it is together with the triumphs of his victory that He enumerates this, and adds,

And still he holdeth fast his integrity.

2. As if He said explicitly, 'Thou indeed hast wrought thy malice, but he has not lost his innocence; and thou art forced to serve to his advancement by the very means whence thou thoughtest to lessen his advancement. For that inward innocency, which he honourably maintained when at rest, he has more honourably preserved under the rod. It follows; ii.

Although thou movedst Me against him, to destroy him without cause.

3. Whereas God is a just and a true God, it is important to enquire how and in what sense He shows that He had afflicted Job without cause. For because He is just, He could not afflict him without cause, and again, because He is true, He could not have spoken other than what He did. So then that both particulars may concur in Him that is just and true, so that He should both speak truth, and not act unjustly, let us know, that blessed Job was both in one sense smitten *without cause*, and again in another sense, that he was smitten not without cause. For as He that is just and true, says the thing of Himself, let us prove both that what He said was true, and that what He did was righteous. For it was necessary that the holy man, who was known to God alone and to his own conscience, should make known to all as a pattern for their imitation with what preeminent virtue he was enriched. For he could not visibly give to others examples of virtue, if he remained himself without temptation. Accordingly it was brought to pass, both that the very force of the infliction should exhibit his stores of virtue for the imitation of all men, and that the strokes inflicted upon him should bring to light what in time of tranquillity lay hidden. Now by means of the same blows the virtue of patience gained increase, and the gloriousness of his reward was augmented by the pains of the scourge. Thus, that we may uphold the truth of God in word, and His equity in deed, the blessed Job is at one and the same time not afflicted without cause, seeing that his merits are increased, and yet he *is* afflicted *without cause*, in that he is not punished for any offence committed by him. For that man is stricken without cause, who has no fault to be cut away; and he is not stricken without cause, the merit of whose virtue is made to accumulate. iii.

4. But what is meant when it is said, *Thou movedst Me against him?* Is 'the Truth' then inflamed by the words of Satan, so that at his instigation He falls to torturing His servants? Who could imagine

those things of God which he even accounts unworthy of a good man? But because we ourselves never strike unless when moved, the stroke of God itself is called the 'moving' Him. And the voice of God condescends to our speech, that His doings may in one way or another be reached by man's understanding. For that Power which without compulsion created all things, and which without oversight rules all things, and without labour sustains all, and governs without being busied, corrects also without emotion. And by stripes He forms the minds of men to whatsoever He will, in such sort still that He never passeth into the darkness of change from the light of His Unchangeable Being. It follows;

Ver. 4, 5. And Satan answered the Lord, and said, Skin for skin, yea, all that a man hath will he give for his life. But put forth thine hand now, and touch his bone and his flesh, and he will curse Thee to Thy face.

iv. 5. The old enemy derives from outward things the charge which he urges against the blessed man's soul. For he affirms that 'skin is given for skin;' as it often happens that when we see a blow directed against the face, we put our hands before our eyelids to guard the eyes from the stroke, and we present our bodies to be wounded, lest they be wounded in a tenderer part. Satan then, who knew that such things are customarily done, exclaims, *Skin for skin, and all that a man hath will he give in exchange for his life.* As if he said in plain words, 'It is for this reason that Job bears with composure so many strokes falling without, because he fears lest he should be smitten himself, and so it is care of the flesh that makes him unmoved by hurt done to the feelings of the flesh; for while he fears for his own person, he feels the less the hurt of what belongs to him.

And hence he immediately requires his flesh to be smitten, in these words;

But put forth Thine hand now, and touch his bone and his flesh, and he will curse Thee to Thy face.

He had said above, *Touch all that he hath, and he will curse Thee to Thy face.* [Job 1, 11] Now, as if forgetting his former proposal, being beaten upon one point, he demands another. And this is justly allowed him by God's dispensation, that the audacious disputer, by being over and over again overcome, may be made to keep silence. It proceeds;

Ver. 6. And the Lord said unto Satan, Behold, he is in thine hand; but save his life.

6. Here again, the safeguard of protection goes along with the permission to smite, and the dispensation of God both while guarding, forsakes his elect servant, and while forsaking, guards him. A portion of him He gives over, a portion He protects. For if he had left Job wholly in the hand of so dire a foe, what could have become of a mere man? And so with the very justice of the permission there is mixed a certain measure of pity, that in one and the same contest, both His lowly servant might rise by oppression, and the towering enemy be brought down by the permission. Thus the holy man is given over to the adversary's hand, but yet in his inmost soul he is held fast by the hand of his Helper. For he was of the number of those sheep, concerning whom Truth itself said in the Gospel, *Neither shall any man pluck them out of My hand.* [John 10, 28] And yet it is said to the enemy, when he demands him, *Behold, he is in thine hand*. The same man then is at the same time in the hand of God, and in the hand of the devil. For by saying, *he is in thine hand*, and straightway adding, *but save his life*, the pitiful Helper openly showed that His hand was upon him whom He yielded up, and that in giving He did not give him, whom, while He cast him forth, He at the same time hid from the darts of his adversary. **V.**

7. But how is that it is said to Satan, *but save his life* [*animam*]? For how does he keep safe, who is ever longing to break in upon things under safe keeping? But Satan's *saving* is spoken of his not daring to break in, just as, conversely, we petition The Father in prayer, saying, *Lead us not into temptation*; [Matt. 6, 13] for neither does the Lord *lead us into temptation*, Who is ever mercifully shielding His servants there from. Yet it is as it were for Him 'to lead us into temptation,' not to protect us from the allurements of temptation. And He then as it were 'leads us not into the snare of temptation,' when He does not let us be tempted beyond what we are able to bear. In like manner then as God is said to 'lead us into temptation,' if He suffers our adversary to lead us thereinto, so our adversary is said to 'save our soul [*animum,* same as above],' when he is stayed from overcoming it by his temptations.

Ver. 7. So Satan went forth from the presence of the Lord.

THE FIRST PART.

How 'Satan goes forth from the presence of the Lord,' is shown by the remarks which have been already [some Mss. add 'often'] made above. It goes on;

And smote Job with sore boils, from the sole of his foot unto his crown.

vi. 8. Strokes are to be estimated in two ways, viz. to consider either of what kind, or how great. For being many they are often made right by their quality, and being heavy by their quantity, i.e. when, if they be many, they be not heavy, and if they be heavy, they be not many; in order to show, then, how by the sharpness of the stroke the adversary flamed against the holy man, not only in the badness of the kind, but also in the heaviness of the amount: to prove the quality, it is said, *And smote Job with sore boils*; and to teach the quantity, from the sole of his foot unto his crown. Plainly, that nothing might be void of glory in his soul, in whose body there is no part void of pain. It goes on;

Ver. 8. And he took him a potsherd to scrape himself withal; and he sat down among the ashes.

vii. 9. What is a potsherd made from, excepting mud? and what is the humour of the body, but mud? Accordingly he is said 'to scrape the humour with a potsherd,' as if it were plainly said, 'he wiped away mud with mud.' For the holy man reflected, whence that which he carried about him had been taken, and with the broken piece of a vessel of clay he scraped his broken vessel of clay. By which act we have it openly shown us, in what manner he subdued under him that body of his when sound, which even when stricken he tended with such slight regard; how softly he dealt with his flesh in its sound state, who applied neither clothing, nor fingers, but only a potsherd to its very wounds. And thus he scraped the humour with a potsherd, that seeing himself in the very broken piece, he might even by the cleansing of the wound be taking a remedy for his soul.

10. But because it often happens that the mind is swelled by the circumstances that surround the body, and by the way men behave toward us the frailty of the body is removed from before the eyes of the mind, (as there are some of those that are of the world, who while they are buoyed up with temporal honours, whilst they rule in elevated stations, whilst they see the obedience of multitudes yielded

to them at will, neglect to consider their own frailty, and altogether forget, nor ever take heed, how speedily that vessel of clay which they bear, is liable to be shattered,) so blessed Job, that he might take thought of his own frailty from the things about him, and increase the intensity of his self-contempt in his own eyes, is described to have seated himself not anywhere on the earth, which at most in every place is found clean, but upon a dunghill. He set his body *on a dunghill*, that the mind might to its great profit consider thoroughly what was that substance of the flesh, which was *taken from the ground*. [Gen. 3, 23] He set his body on a dunghill, that even from the stench of the place he might apprehend how rapidly the body returneth to stench.

11. But see, while blessed Job is undergoing such losses in his substance, and grieving over the death of so many children whereby he is smitten, while he is suffering such numberless wounds, while he scrapes the running humour with a potsherd, whilst, running down in a state of corruption, he sat himself upon a dunghill, it is good to consider how it is that Almighty God, as though in unconcern, afflicts so grievously those, whom He looks upon as so dear to Him for all eternity. But, now, while I view the wounds and the torments of blessed Job, I suddenly call back my mind's eye to John, and I reflect not without the greatest astonishment, that he, being filled with the Spirit of prophecy within his mother's womb, and who, if I may say so, before his birth, was born again, he that was the *friend of the Bridegroom*, [John 3, 29] he than whom *none hath arisen greater among those born of women*, [Matt. 11, 11] he that was so great a Prophet, that he was even *more than a Prophet*, he is cast into prison by wicked men, and beheaded, for the dancing of a damsel, and a man of such severe virtue dies for the merriment of the vile! Do we imagine there was aught in his life which that most contemptible death was to wipe off? When, then, did he sin even in meat, whose food was but locusts and wild honey? How did he offend even by the quality of his clothing, the covering of whose body was of camel's hair? How could he transgress in his behaviour, who never went out from the desert? How did the guilt of a talkative tongue defile him, who was parted far from mankind? When did even a fault of silence attach to him, who so vehemently charged those that came to him? *O generation, of vipers, who hath warned you to flee from the wrath to come?* [Matt. 3, 7] How is it then, that Job is distinguished above other men by

the testimony of God, and yet by his plagues is brought down even to a dunghill? How is it that John is commended by the voice of God, and yet for the words of a drunkard suffers death as the prize of dancing? How is it, that Almighty God so utterly disregards in this present state of being those whom He chose so exaltedly before the worlds, saving this, which is plain to the religious sense of the faithful, that it is for this reason He thus presses them below, because He sees how to recompense them on high? And He casts them down without to the level of things contemptible, because He leads them on within to the height of things incomprehensible. From hence then let everyone collect what those will have to suffer There, that are condemned by Him, if here He thus torments those whom He loves, or how they shall be smitten, who are destined to be convicted at the Judgment, if their life is sunk so low, who are commended by witness of the Judge Himself. It proceeds;

Ver. 9. Then said his wife unto him, Dost thou still retain thine integrity? curse God, and die.

viii. 12. The old adversary is wont to tempt mankind in two ways; viz. so as either to break the hearts of the stedfast by tribulation, or to melt them by persuasion. Against blessed Job then he strenuously exerted himself in both; for first upon the householder he brought loss of substance; the father he bereaved by the death of his children; the man that was in health he smote with putrid sores. But forasmuch as him, that was outwardly corrupt, he saw still to hold on sound within, and because he grudged him, whom he had stripped naked outwardly, to be inwardly enriched by the setting forth of his Maker's praise, in his cunning he reflects and considers, that the champion of God is only raised up against him by the very means whereby he is pressed down, and being defeated he betakes himself to subtle appliances of temptations. For he has recourse again to his arts of ancient contrivance, and because he knows by what means Adam is prone to be deceived, he has recourse to Eve. For he saw that blessed Job amidst the repeated loss of his goods, the countless wounds of his strokes, stood unconquered, as it were, in a kind of fortress of virtues. For he had set his mind on high, and therefore the machinations of the enemy were unable to force an entrance on it. The adversary then seeks by what steps he may mount up to this well-fenced fortress. Now the woman is close to the man and joined to him. Therefore he fixed his hold on the heart of the woman, and as it were found in it a ladder whereby he might be able to mount up to the heart of the man. He seized the mind of the wife, which was the ladder to the husband. But he could do nothing by this artifice. For the holy man minded that the woman was set under and not over him, and by speaking aright, he instructed her, whom the serpent set on to speak wrongly. For it was meet that manly reproof should hold in that looser mind; since indeed he knew even by the first fall of man, that the woman was unskilled to teach aright. And hence it is well said by Paul, *I permit not a woman to teach*. [1 Tim. 2, 12] Doubtless for that, when she once taught, she cast us off from an eternity of wisdom. And so the old enemy was beaten by [*perdidit ab*] Adam on a dunghill, he that conquered Adam in Paradise; and whereas he inflamed the wife, whom he took to his aid, to utter words of mispersuasion, he sent her to the school of holy instruction; and she that had been set on that she might destroy, was instructed that she should not ruin herself. Yes, the enemy is so stricken by those resolute men of our part, that his very own weapons are seized out of his hand. For by the same means, whereby he reckons to increase the pain of the wound, he is helping them to arms of virtue to use against himself.

13. Now from the words of his wife, thus persuading him amiss, we ought to mark with attention, that the old enemy goes about to bend the upright state of our mind, not only by means of himself, but by means of those that are attached to us. For when he cannot undermine our heart by his own persuading, then indeed he creeps to the thing by the tongues of those that belong to us. For hence it is written; *Beware of thine own children, and take heed to thyself from thy servants*. [Ecclus. 32, 22. Vulg.] Hence it is said by the Prophet; *Take ye heed every one of his neighbour, and trust ye not in any brother*. [Jer. 9, 4] Hence it, is again written; *And a man's foes shall be they of his own household*. [Matt. 10, 36] For when the crafty adversary sees himself driven back from the hearts of the good, he seeks out those that they very much love, and he speaks sweetly to them by the words of such as are beloved by them above others, that whilst the force of love penetrates the heart, the sword of his persuading may easily force a way in to the defences of inward uprightness. Thus after the losses of his goods, after the death of his children, after the wounding and

rending of his limbs, the old foe put in motion the tongue of his wife.

14. And observe the time when he aimed to corrupt the mind of the man with poisoned talk. For it was after the wounds that the words were brought in by him; doubtless that, as the force of the pain waxed greater, the froward dictates of his persuasions might easily prevail. But if we minutely consider the order itself of his temptation, we see with what craft he worketh his cruelty. For he first directed against him the losses of his goods, which should be at once, as they were, out of the province of nature, and without the body. He withdrew from him his children, a thing now no longer indeed without the province of nature, but still in some degree beyond his own body. Lastly, he smote even his body. But because, by these wounds of the flesh, he could not attain to wound the soul, he sought out the tongue of the woman that was joined to him. For because it sorely grieved him to be overcome in open fight, he flung a javelin from the mouth of the wife, as if from a place of ambush: as she said, *Dost thou still retain thine integrity? Bless God and die*. Mark how in trying him, he took away everything, and again in trying him, left him his wife, and showed craftiness in stripping him of everything, but infinitely greater cunning, in keeping the woman as his abettor, to say, *Dost thou still retain thine integrity?* Eve repeats her own words. For what is it to say, 'give over thine integrity,' but 'disregard obedience by eating the forbidden thing?' And what is it to say, *Bless* [see Book I, 31.] *God and die*, but 'live by mounting above the commandment, above what thou wast created to be?' But our Adam lay low upon a dunghill in strength, who once stood up in Paradise in weakness. For thereupon he replied to the words of his evil counsellor, saying,

Ver. 10. Thou speakest as one of the foolish women speaketh. What? shall we receive good at the hand of God, and shall we not receive evil?

ix. 15. See the enemy is every where broken, every where overcome, in all his appliances of temptation he has been brought to the ground, in that he has even lost that accustomed consolation which he derived from the woman. Amid these circumstances it is good to contemplate the holy man, without, void of goods, within, filled with God. When Paul viewed in himself the riches of internal wisdom, yet saw himself outwardly a corruptible body, he says, *We have this treasure in earthen vessels.* [2 Cor. 4, 7] You see, the earthen vessel in blessed Job felt those gaping sores without, but this treasure remained entire within. For without he cracked in his wounds, but the treasure of wisdom unfailingly springing up within issued forth in words of holy instruction, saying, *If we have received good at the hand of the Lord, shall we not receive evil?* meaning by the *good*, either the temporal or the eternal gifts of God, and by the evil, denoting the strokes of the present time, of which the Lord says by the Prophet, *I am the Lord, and there is none else. I form the light, and create darkness; I make peace, and create evil.* [Is. 45, 6. 7.] Not that evil, which does not subsist by its own nature, is created by the Lord, but the Lord shows Himself as creating evil, when He turns into a scourge the things that have been created good for us, upon our doing evil, that the very same things should at the same time both by the pain which they inflict be to transgressors evil, and yet good by the nature whereby they have their being. And hence poison is to man indeed death, but life to the serpent. For we by the love of things present have been led away from the love of our Creator; and whereas the froward mind submitted itself to fondness for the creature, it parted from the Creator's communion, and so it was to be smitten by its Maker by means of the things which it had erringly preferred to its Maker, that by the same means whereby man in his pride was not afraid to commit sin, he might find a punishment to his correction, and might the sooner recover himself to all that he had lost, the more he perceived that the things which he aimed at were full of pain. And hence it is rightly said, *I form the light, and create darkness.* For when the darkness of pain is created by strokes without, the light of the mind is kindled by instruction within. *I make peace, and create evil.* For peace with God is restored to us then, when the things which, though rightly created, are not rightly coveted, are turned into such sort of scourges as are evil to us. For we are become at variance with God by sin. Therefore it is meet that we should be brought back to peace with Him by the scourge, that whereas every being created good turns to pain for us, the mind of the chastened man may be renewed in a humbled state to peace with the Creator. These scourges, then, blessed Job names *evil*, because he considers with what violence they smite the good estate of health and tranquillity.

THE FIRST PART.

16. But this we ought especially to regard in his words, viz. with what a skilful turn of reflection he gathers himself up to meet the persuading of his wife, saying, *If we have received good at the hand of the Lord, shall we not receive evil?* For it is a mighty solace of our tribulation, if, when we suffer afflictions, we recall to remembrance our Maker's gifts to us. Nor does that break down our force, which falls upon us in the smart, if that quickly comes to mind, which lifts us up in the gift. For it is hence written, *In the day of prosperity be not unmindful of affliction, and in the day of affliction, be not unmindful of prosperity*. [Ecclus. 11, 25] For whosoever receives God's gifts, but in the season of gifts has no fear of strokes, is brought to a fall by joy in his elation of mind. And whoever is bruised with scourges, yet, in the season of the scourges, neglects to take comfort to himself from the gifts, which it has been his lot to receive, is thrown down from the stedfastness of his mind by despair on every hand. Thus then both must be united, that each may always have the other's support, so that both remembrance of the gift may moderate the pain of the stroke, and misgiving and dread of the stroke may bite down the joyousness of the gift. And thus the holy man, to soothe the depression of his mind amidst his wounds, in the pains of the strokes weighs the sweetness of the gifts, saying, *If we have received good at the hand of the Lord, shall we not receive evil?* And he does well in saying first, *Thou hast spoken like one of the foolish women*. For because it is the sense of a bad woman, and not her sex, that is in fault, he never says, 'Thou hast spoken like one of the women,' but 'of the foolish women,' clearly that it might be shown, that whatsoever is of ill sense cometh of superadded folly, and not of nature so formed. The account goes on;

In all this did not Job sin with his lips.

x. 17. We sin with our lips in two ways; either when we say unjust things, or withhold the just. For if it were not sometimes a sin also to be silent, the Prophet would never say, *Woe is me, that I held my peace*. [Is. 6, 5. Vulg.] Blessed Job, then, in all that he did, sinned no wise with his lips; in that he neither spake proudly against the smiter, nor withheld the right answer to the adviser. Neither by speech, therefore, nor by silence did he offend, who both gave thanks to the Father that smote him, and administered wisdom of instruction to the ill-advising wife. For because he knew what he owed to God, what to his neighbour, viz. resignation to his Creator, wisdom to his wife, therefore he both instructed her by his uttering reproof, and magnified Him by giving thanks. But which is there of us, who, if he were to receive any single wound of such severe infliction, would not at once be laid low in the interior? See, that when outwardly prostrated by the wounds of the flesh, he abides inwardly erect in the fences of the mind, and beneath him he sees every dart fly past wherewith the raging enemy transfixes him outwardly with unsparing hand; watchfully he catches the javelins, now cast, in wounds, against him in front, and now, in words, as it were from the side. And our champion encompassed with the rage of the besetting fight, at all points presents his shield of patience, meets the darts coming in on every hand, and on all virtue's sides wheels round the guarded mind to front the assailing blows.

18. But the more valiantly our old enemy is overcome, the more hotly is he provoked to further arts of malice. For whereas the wife when chidden was silent, he forthwith set on others to rise up in insults till they must be chidden. For as he essayed to make his blows felt, by the often repeated tidings of the losses of his substance, so he now busies himself to penetrate that firm heart by dealing reiterated strokes with the insults of the lips. It proceeds;

Ver. 11. Now when Job's three friends heard of all this evil that was come upon him, they came everyone from his own place; Eliphaz the Temanite, and Bildad the Shuhite, and Zophar the Naamathite: for they had made an appointment together to come to mourn with him and to comfort him.

19. We have it proved to us how great a love they entertained both for each other, and for the smitten man, in that they came by agreement to administer consolation to him when afflicted. Though even by this circumstance, viz. that Scripture bears witness they were the friends of so great a man, it is made appear that they were men of a good spirit and right intention; though this very intention of mind, when they break forth into words, upon indiscretion arising, becomes clouded in the sight of the strict Judge. It goes on; **xi.**

Ver. 12. And when they lifted up their eyes afar off, and knew him not, they lifted up their voice, and wept; and they rent everyone his mantle, and sprinkled dust upon their heads toward heaven.

THE FIRST PART.

xii. 20. Because the scourge had altered the appearance of the stricken man, his friends 'lift up their voice and weep,' 'rend their garments,' 'sprinkle dust upon their heads;' that seeing him altered to whom they had come, their voluntary grief might likewise alter the very appearance even of the comforters also. For the order in consolation is, that when we would stay one that is afflicted from his grief, we first essay to accord with his sorrow by grieving. For he can never comfort the mourner who does not suit himself to his grief, since from the very circumstance that his own feelings are at variance with the mourner's distress, he is rendered the less welcome to him, from whom he is parted by the character of his feelings; the mind therefore must first be softened down, that it may accord with the distressed, and by according attach itself, and by attaching itself draw him. For iron is not joined to iron, if both be not melted by the burning effect of fire, and a hard substance does not adhere to a soft, unless its hardness be first made soft by tempering, so as in a manner to become the very thing, to which our object is that it should hold. Thus we neither lift up the fallen, if we do not bend from the straightness of our standing posture. For, whereas the uprightness of him that standeth disagreeth with the posture of one lying, he never can lift him to whom he cares not to lower himself; and so the friends of blessed Job, that they might stay him under affliction from his grief, were of necessity solicitous to grieve with him, and when they beheld his wounded body, they set themselves to rend their own garments, and when they saw him altered, they betook themselves to defiling their heads with dust, that the afflicted man might the more readily give ear to their words, that he recognised in them somewhat of his own in the way of affliction.

21. But herein be it known, that he who desires to comfort the afflicted, must needs set a measure to the grief, to which he submits, lest he should not only fail of soothing the mourner, but, by the intemperance of his grief, should sink the mind of the afflicted to the heaviness of despair. For our grief ought to be so blended with the grief of the distressed, that by qualifying it may lighten it, and not by increasing weigh it down. And hence perhaps we ought to gather, that the friends of blessed Job in administering consolation gave themselves up to grief more than was needed, in that while they mark the stroke, but are strangers to the mind of him that was smitten, they betake themselves to unmeasured lamentation, as if the

smitten man who was of such high fortitude, under the scourge of his body, had fallen in mind too. It proceeds;

Ver. 13. So they sat down with him upon the ground seven days and seven nights, and none spake a word unto him; for they saw that his grief was very great.

xiii.

22. Whether they sat with the afflicted Job for seven days and seven nights together, or possibly for seven days and as many nights kept by him in assiduous and frequent visiting, we cannot tell. For we are often said to be doing anything for so many days, though we may not be continually busied therein all those days. And often holy Scripture is wont to put the whole for a part, in like manner as it does a part for the whole. Thus it speaks of a part for the whole, as where, in describing Jacob's household, it says, *All the souls of the house of Jacob which came into Egypt were threescore and ten*. [Gen. 46, 27] Where indeed, while it makes mention of souls, it clearly takes in the bodies also of the comers. Again it puts in the whole for a part, as where at the tomb Mary complains, saying, *They have taken away my Lord, and I know not where they have laid Him*. [John 20, 2] For it was the Body of the Lord only that she had come to seek, and yet she bewails the Lord as though His whole Person had been altogether taken away [*tultum*]; and so in this place too it is doubtful whether the whole is put for a part.

23. Yet this circumstance, viz. that they were a long while silent, and yet in speaking after all were condemned, must not be passed over carelessly. For there are some men who both begin to speak with precipitation, and follow out that unchecked beginning with still less check. While there are some who are indeed backward to begin to speak, but having once begun know not how to set limits to their words. Accordingly the friends of blessed Job, upon seeing his grief, were for long silent, yet, whilst slow to begin, they spoke with indiscretion, because they would not spare him in his grief. They held their tongue that it might not begin over-hastily, but once begun they never ruled it, that it might not let itself out from imparting consolation so far as to offer insults. And they indeed had come with a good intention to give comfort; yet that which the pious mind offered to God pure, their hasty speech defiled. For it is written, *If thou offerest rightly, but dividest not rightly, thou has sinned*. [Gen. 4, 7. lxx.] For it is rightly offered, when the thing that is done is done

with a right intention. But it is not 'rightly divided,' unless that which is done with a pious mind be made out with exact discrimination. For to 'divide the offering aright' is to weigh all our good aims, carefully discriminating them; and whoso puts by doing this, even when we offer aright, is guilty of sin.

24. And so it often happens, that in what we do with a good aim, by not exercising careful discrimination therein, we know nothing what end it will be judged withal [*quo judicetur fine*], and sometimes that becomes ground of accusation, which is accounted an occasion of virtue. But whoever considers the doings of blessed Job's friends, cannot but see with what a pious intention they came to him. For let us consider, what great love it showed to have come together by agreement to the stricken man; what a preeminent degree of long-suffering it proved to be with the afflicted, without speaking, seven days and nights; what humility, to sit upon the earth so many days and nights; what compassion, to sprinkle their heads with dust! But yet when they began to speak, by the same means, whereby they reckoned to win the price of a reward, it was their lot to meet with the arraignment of rebuke; for to the unwary even that which is begun for the object of recompense alone, oftentimes turns to an issue in sin. Observe! By hasty speech they lost that good which it cost them so much labour to purchase. And unless the grace of God had bidden them to offer sacrifice for their guilt, they might have been justly punished by the Lord, on the very grounds whereon they reckoned themselves exceeding well-pleasing to Him. By the same proceeding they displease the Judge, whereby, as if in that Judge's defence, they please themselves through want of self-control. Now it is for this reason that we speak thus, that we may recall to the recollection of our readers, for each one to consider heedfully with himself, with what dread visitations the Lord punishes the actions which are done with an evil design, if those which are begun with a good aim, but mixed with the heedlessness of indiscretion, are chastised with such severe rebuke. For who would not believe that he had secured himself ground of recompense, either if in God's defence he had said aught against his neighbour, or at all events if in sorrow for a neighbour he had kept silence seven days and nights? And yet the friends of blessed Job by doing this were brought into sin for their pains, because while the good aim of comforting which they were about was known to them, yet they did not know with

what a balance of discretion it was to be done. Whence it appears that we must not only regard what it is that we do, but also with what discretion we put it in execution. First indeed, that we may never do evil in any manner, and next, that we may not do our good deeds without caution; and it is in fact to perform these good deeds with carefulness, that the Prophet admonishes us when he says, *Cursed be he that doeth the work of the Lord negligently*. [Jer. 48, 10. Vulg.] But let these things stand us in stead to this end, that before the exact and incomprehensible scrutiny of the Awful Judge shall be, we may not only fear for all that we have done amiss, but if there be in us aught of the kind, for the very things that we have done well; for oftentimes that is found out to be sin at His Judgment, which before the Judgment passes for virtue, and from the same source, whence we look for the merciful recompense of our works, there comes upon us the chastisement of righteous vengeance.

Allegorical

25. We have run through these particulars thus briefly considered according to the letter of the history, now let us turn our discourse to the mystical sense of the allegory. But as, when, at the beginning of this work, we were treating of the union betwixt the Head and the Body, we premised with earnest emphasis how close the bond of love was between them, forasmuch us both the Lord in fact still suffers many things by His Body, which is all of us, and His Body, i.e. the Church, already glories in its Head, viz. the Lord, in heaven; so now we ought in such sort to set forth the sufferings of that Head, that it may be made appear how much He undergoes in His Body also. For if the torments that we endure did not reach our Head, He would never cry out to His persecutor even from heaven in behalf of His afflicted Members, *Saul, Saul, why persecutest thou Me?* [Acts 9, 4] If our agony were not His pain, Paul, when afflicted after his conversion, would never have said, *I fill up that which is behind of the afflictions of Christ in my flesh*. [Col. 1, 24] And yet being already elevated by the resurrection of his Head, he says, *And hath raised us up together, and made us sit together in heavenly places*; [Eph. 2, 6] in this way, namely, that the torments of persecution had enchained him on earth, yet while sunk down with the weight of his pains, lo, he was already seated in heaven, through the glory of his Head. Therefore because we know that in all things the Head and the Body are one, we in such wise begin with the smiting

of the Head that we may afterwards come to the strokes of the Body. But this, viz. that it is said, "that on a day Satan came to present himself before the Lord;" that he is interrogated 'whence he comes?' that the blessed Job is distinguished by his Creator's high proclaim; forasmuch as we have already made it out more than once, we forbear to explain again. For if the mind is a long time involved in points that have been examined, it is hindered in coming to those which have not been, and so we now put the beginning of the allegory there, where, after often repeated words, we find something new added. So then He says,

Ver. 3. Though thou movedst Me against him, to destroy him without cause.

xiv. 26. If blessed Job bears the likeness of our Redeemer in His Passion, how is it that the Lord says to Satan, *Thou movedst Me against him?* Truly the Mediator between God and man, the Man Christ Jesus, came to bear the scourges of our mortal nature, that He might put away the sins of our disobedience; but forasmuch as He is of one and the self-same nature with the Father, how does the Father declare that He was moved by Satan against Him, when it is acknowledged that no inequality of power, no diversity of will, interrupts the harmony between the Father and the Son? Yet He, that is equal to the Father by the Divine Nature, came for our sakes to be under stripes in a fleshly nature. Which stripes He would never have undergone, if he had not taken the form of accursed man in the work of their redemption. And unless the first man had transgressed, the second would never have come to the ignominies of the Passion. When then the first man was moved by Satan from the Lord, then the Lord was moved against the second Man. And so Satan then moved the Lord to the affliction of this latter, when the sin of disobedience brought down the first man from the height of uprightness. For if he had not drawn the first Adam by wilful sin into the death of the soul, the second Adam, being without sin, would never have come into the voluntary death of the flesh, and therefore it is with justice said to him of our Redeemer too, *Thou movedst Me against him to afflict* [E.V. *destroy*] *him without cause.* As though it were said in plainer words; 'Whereas this Man dies not on His own account, but on account of that other, thou didst then move Me to the afflicting of This one, when thou didst withdraw that other from Me by thy cunning persuasions.' And of Him it is rightly added, *without cause.* For 'he was destroyed without cause,' who was at once weighed to the earth by the avenging of sin, and not defiled by the pollution of sin. He 'was destroyed without cause,' Who, being made incarnate, had no sins of His own, and yet being without offence took upon Himself the punishment of the carnal. For it is hence that speaking by the Prophet He says, *Then I restored that which I took not away.* For that other that was created for Paradise would in his pride have usurped the semblance of the Divine power, yet the Mediator, Who was without guilt, discharged the guilt of that pride. It is hence that a Wise Man says to the Father; *Forasmuch then as Thou art righteous Thyself, Thou orderest all things righteously; Thou condemnest Him too that deserveth not to be punished.* [Wisd. 12, 15. Vulg.]

27. But we must consider how He is righteous and ordereth all things righteously, if He condemns Him that deserveth not to be punished. For our Mediator deserved not to be punished for Himself, because He never was guilty of any defilement of sin. But if He had not Himself undertaken a death not due to Him, He would never have freed us from one that was justly due to us. And so whereas 'The Father is righteous,' in punishing a righteous man, 'He ordereth all things righteously,' in that by these means He justifies all things, viz. that for the sake of sinners He condemns Him Who is without sin; that all the Elect [*electa omnia*] might rise up to the height of righteousness, in proportion as He Who is above all underwent the penalties of our unrighteousness. What then is in that place called 'being condemned without deserving,' is here spoken of as being 'afflicted without cause.' Yet though in respect of Himself He was 'afflicted without cause,' in respect of our deeds it was not 'without cause.' For the rust of sin could not be cleared away, but by the fire of torment, He then came without sin, Who should submit Himself voluntarily to torment, that the chastisements due to our wickedness might justly loose the parties thereto obnoxious, in that they had unjustly kept Him, Who was free of them. Thus it was both without cause, and not without cause, that He was afflicted, Who had indeed no crimes in Himself, but Who cleansed with His blood the stain of our guilt.

Ver. 4, 5. And Satan answered the Lord, and said, Skin for skin; yea, all that a man hath will he give for his life. But put forth Thine hand now, and touch his bone and his flesh, and he will curse Thee to Thy face.

xv. 28. When the evil spirit sees our Redeemer shine forth by miracles, he cries out, *We know Who Thou art, the Holy One of God.* [Luke 4, 34] And in saying this, he dreads, whilst he owns, the Son of God. Yet being a stranger to the power of heavenly pity, there are seasons when, beholding Him subject to suffering, he supposes Him to be mere man. Now he had learnt that there were many in the pastoral station, cloked under the guise of sanctity, who, being very far removed from the bowels of charity, held for very little other men's ills. And thus as though judging of Him by other men, because after much had been taken from Him, he did not see him subdued, he so flamed against Him even to His very flesh, in applying the touch of suffering, as to say, *Skin for skin; yea, all that a man hath will he give for his life. But put forth Thine hand now, and touch his bone and his flesh, and he will curse Thee to Thy face.* As though he said in plain terms, 'He does not care to be moved by the things that are without Him, but it will then be really known what He is, if He shall experience in Himself what may make Him grieve.' This Satan expressed in his own person not by words, but by wishes, when he desired to have it brought to pass; in his members he brought it on both by words and wishes at once. For it is himself that speaks, when, according to the words of the Prophet, his followers say, *Let us put the wood in his bread, and let us raze him out from the land of the living.* [Jer. 11, 19. Vulg.] For 'to put the wood into the bread,' is to apply the trunk of the cross to His body in affixing Him thereto; and they think themselves able to 'raze out' His life from the land of the living, Whom while they perceive Him to be mortal mould, they imagine to be put an end to by death.

Ver. 6. And the Lord said unto Satan, Behold, he is in thine hand, but save his life.

xvi. 29. What fool even would believe that the Creator of all things was given up into 'the hands of Satan?' Yet who that is instructed by the Truth can be ignorant that of that very Satan all they are members who are joined unto him by living frowardly? Thus Pilate showed himself a member of him, who, even to the extremity of putting Him to death, knew not the Lord when He came for our Redemption. The chief priests proved themselves to be his body, who strove to drive the world's Redeemer from the world, by persecuting Him even to the cross. When then the Lord for our salvation gave Himself up to the hands of Satan's members, what else did He, but let loose that Satan's hand to rage against Himself, that by the very act whereby He Himself outwardly fell low, He might set us free both outwardly and inwardly. If therefore the hand of Satan is taken for his power, He after the flesh bore the hand of him, whose power over the body He endured even to the spitting, the buffetting, the stripes, the cross, the lance; and hence when He cometh to His Passion He says to Pilate, i.e. to the body of Satan, *Thou couldest have no power at all against Me except it were given thee from above*; [John 19, 11] and yet this power, which He had given to him against Himself without, He compelled to serve the end of His own interest within. For Pilate, or Satan who was that Pilate's head, was held under the power of that One over Whom he had received power; in that being far above He had Himself ordained that which now condescending to an inferior condition He was undergoing from the persecutor, that though it arose from the evil mind of unbelievers, yet that very cruelty itself might also serve to the weal of all the Elect, and therefore He pitifully ordained all that within, which He suffered Himself to undergo thus foully without. And it is hence that it is said of Him at the supper, *Jesus knowing that the Father had given all things into His hands, and that He was come from God, and went to God; He riseth from supper, and laid aside His garments*. [John 13, 3] Behold how, when He was about to come into the hands of those that persecuted Him, He knew that those very persecutors even had been given into His own hand. For He, Who knew that He had received all things, plainly held those very persons by whom He was held, that He should Himself inflict on Himself, for the purposes of mercy, whatsoever their permitted wickedness should cruelly devise against Him. Let it then be said to him, *Behold, he is in thine hand*, in that when ravening thereafter he received permission to smite His flesh, yet unwittingly he rendered service to the Power of that Being.

30. Now he is ordered to 'save the life of the soul,' not that he is forbidden to tempt it, but that he is convicted of being unable to overcome it. For never, as we that are mere men are oftentimes

shaken by the assault of temptation, was the soul of your Redeemer disordered by its urgency. For though our enemy, being permitted, took Him up into an high mountain, though he promised that he would give Him the kingdoms of the earth, and though he showed Him stones as to be turned into bread, yet he had no power to shake by temptation the mind of the Mediator betwixt God and man. For He so condescended to take all this upon Himself externally, that His mind, being still inwardly established in His Divine Nature, should remain unshaken. And if He is at any time said to be troubled and to have groaned in the spirit, He did Himself in His Divine nature ordain how much He should in His Human nature be troubled, unchangeably ruling over all things, yet showing Himself subject to change in the satisfying of human frailty; and thus remaining at rest in Himself, He ordained whatsoever He did even with a troubled spirit for the setting forth of that human nature which He had taken upon Himself.

31. But as, when we love aright, there is nothing among created things that we love better than the life of our soul, and like as we say that we love those as our soul toward whom we strive to express the weight of our love, it may be that by the life of His Soul [*per animam*], is represented the life [*vita*] of the Elect. And while Satan is let loose to smite the Redeemer's flesh, he is debarred the soul, forasmuch as at the same time that he obtains His Body to inflict upon it the Passion, he loses the Elect from the claims of his power. And while That One's flesh suffers death by the Cross, the mind of these is stablished against assaults. Let it then be said, *Behold, he is in thine hand; but save his life*. As if he had heard in plain words, 'Take permission against His Body, and lose thy right of wicked dominion over His Elect, whom foreknowing in Himself before the world began He holdeth for His own.'

Ver. 7. So went Satan forth from the presence of the Lord, and smote Job with sore boils, from the sole of his foot unto his crown.

xvii. 32. No one entereth into this life of the Elect, that has not undergone the contradictions of this enemy. And they all have proved themselves the members of our Redeemer, who, from the first beginning of the world, whilst living righteously, have suffered wrongs. Did not Abel prove himself His member, who not only in propitiating God by his sacrifice, but also by dying without a word, was a figure of Him, of whom it is written, *He is brought as a lamb to the slaughter, and as a sheep before her shearers is dumb, so He openeth not His mouth.* [Is. 53, 7] Thus from the very beginning of the world he strove to vanquish the Body of our Redeemer; and thus He inflicted wounds 'from the sole of the foot to His crown,' in that beginning with mere men, he came to the very Head of the Church in his raging efforts. And it is well said;

Ver. 8. And he took him a potsherd to scrape the humour withal.

33. For what is the potsherd in the hand of the Lord, but the flesh which He took of the clay of our nature? For the potsherd receives firmness by fire. And the Flesh of our Lord was rendered stronger by His Passion, in so far as dying by infirmity, He arose from death void of infirmity. And hence too it is rightly delivered by the Prophet, *My strength is dried up like a potsherd.* [Ps. 22, 15] For His 'strength was dried up like a potsherd,' Who strengthened the infirmity of the flesh which He took upon Him by the fire of His Passion. But what is to be understood by *humour* [*saniem*] saving sin? For it is the custom to denote the sins of the flesh by *flesh* and *blood*. And hence it is said by the Psalmist, *Deliver me from blood.* [Ps. 51, 16] Humour then is the corruption of the blood. And so what do we understand by humour but the sins of the flesh, rendered worse by length of time? Thus the wound turns to humour when sin, being neglected, is aggravated by habit. And so the Mediator between God and man, the Man Christ Jesus, in giving up His Body into the hands of those that persecuted Him, scraped the humour with a potsherd, forasmuch as He put away sin by the flesh; for He came, as it is written, *in the likeness of sinful flesh, that He might condemn sin of sin.* [Rom. 8, 3. Vulg.] And whilst He presented the purity of His own Flesh to the enemy, He cleansed away the defilements of ours. And by means of that flesh whereby the enemy held us captive, He made atonement for us whom He set free. For that which was made an instrument of sin by us, was by our Mediator converted for us into the *instrument of righteousness*. And so 'the humour is scraped with a potsherd,' when sin is overcome by the flesh. It is rightly subjoined;

And he sat down upon a dunghill.

34. Not in the court in which the law resounds, not in the building which lifts its top on high, but on a dunghill he takes **xix.**

his seat, which is because the Redeemer of man on coming to take the flesh, as Paul testifies, *hath chosen the weak things of the world to confound the mighty*. [1 Cor. 1, 27] Does not He, as it were, sit down upon a dunghill, the buildings being ruined, Who, the Jews in their pride being left desolate, rests in that Gentile world, which He had for so long time rejected? He is found outside the dwelling all in His sores, Who herein, that He bore with Judaea, which set itself against Him, suffered the pain of His Passion amid the scorn of His own people; as John bears witness, who says, *He came unto His own, but His own received Him not*. [John 1, 11] And how He rests Himself upon a dunghill, let this same Truth say for Himself; for He declared, *Likewise I say unto you, there is joy in the presence of the angels of God over one sinner that repenteth, more than over ninety and nine just persons which need no repentance*. [Luke 15, 7. and 10.] See, He sits upon a dunghill in grief, Who, after sins have been committed, is willing to take possession of penitent hearts. Are not the hearts of penitent sinners like a kind of dunghill, in that while they review their misdoings with bewailing, they are, as it were, heaping dung before their eyes in abusing themselves? So when Job was smitten he did not seek a mountain, but sat down upon a dunghill, in that when our Redeemer came to His Passion, He left the high minds of the proud, and rested in the lowliness of the heavy laden. And this, while yet before His Incarnation, He indicated, when He said by the Prophet, *But to this man will I look, even to him, that is poor, and of a contrite spirit, and trembleth at My word*. [Is. 66, 2]

35. But who can think what numberless outrages He underwent at the hands of men, Who showed to men such unnumbered mercies? Who can think how great those are which He even yet undergoes, yea now that He reigns from above over the hearts of the faithful? For it is He that endures daily all wherein His Elect are racked and rent by the hands of the reprobate. And though the Head of this Body, which same are we, already lifts itself free above all things, yet He still feels in His Body, which He keeps here below, the wounds dealt it by reprobate sinners. But why do we speak thus of unbelievers, when within the very Church itself we see multitudes of carnal men, who fight against the life of our Redeemer by their wicked ways. For there are some, who set upon Him with evil deeds, because they cannot with swords, forasmuch as when they see that what they go after is lacking to them in the Church, they become

enemies to the just, and not only settle themselves into wicked practices, but are also busy to bend the uprightness of good men to a crooked course. For they neglect to lift their eyes to the things of eternity, and in littleness of mind they yield themselves up to the lust of temporal things, and they fall the deeper from eternal blessings, in proportion as they look upon temporal blessings as the only ones. The simplicity of the righteous is displeasing to these, and when they find opportunity for disturbing them, they press them to lay hold of their own duplicity. Hence also this is in just accordance, which is added,

Ver. 9. Then said his wife unto him, Dost thou still retain thine integrity? curse God, and die.

36. For of what did that mispersuading woman bear the likeness, but of all the carnal that are settled in the bosom of Holy Church, who in proportion as by the words of the Faith they profess they are within the pale, press harder on all the good by their ill-regulated conduct. For they would perchance have done less mischief, if Holy Church had not admitted in and welcomed to the bed of faith those, whom, by receiving in a profession of faith, she doubtless puts it almost out of her power to eschew. It is hence that in the press of the crowd one woman touched our Redeemer, whereupon the same our Redeemer at once says, *Who touched Me?* And when the disciples answered Him, *The multitude throng Thee and press Thee, and sayest Thou, Who touched Me?* He therefore subjoined, *Somebody hath touched Me, for I perceive that virtue is gone out of Me.* XX.

37. Thus many press the Lord, but one alone touches Him; in that all carnal men in the Church press Him, from Whom they are far removed, while they alone touch Him, who are really united to Him in humility. Therefore the crowd presses Him, in that the multitude of the carnally minded, as it is within the pale, so is it the more hardly borne with. It 'presses,' but it does not 'touch,' in that it is at once troublesome by its presence, and absent by its way of life. For sometimes they pursue us with bad discourse, and sometimes with evil practices alone, for so at one time they persuade to what they practise, and at another, though they use no persuasions, yet they cease not to afford examples of wickedness. They, then, that entice us to do evil either by word or by example, are surely our persecu-

tors, to whom we owe the conflicts of temptation, which we have to conquer at least in the heart.

38. But we should know that carnal men in the Church set themselves to prompt wickedness at one time from a principle of fear, and at another of audacity, and when they themselves go wrong either from littleness of mind or pride of heart, they study to infuse these qualities, as if out of love, into the hearts of the righteous. So Peter, before the Death and Resurrection of our Lord, retained a carnal mind. It was with a carnal mind that the son of Zeruiah held to his leader David, whom he was joined to. Yet the one was led into sin by fear, the other by pride. For the first, when he heard of his Master's Death, said, *Be it far from Thee, Lord; this shall not be unto Thee*. [Matt. 16, 22] But the latter, not enduring the wrongs offered to his leader, says, *Shall not Shimei be put to death for this, because he cursed the Lord's anointed?* [2 Sam. 19, 21] But to the first it is immediately replied, *Get thee behind Me, Satan*. [Matt. 16, 23] And the other with his brother immediately heard the words; *What have I to do with you, ye sons of Zeruiah, that ye are this day turned into a Satan* [So Vulg. E.V. *Adversaries*] *unto me?* [2 Sam. 19, 22] So that evil prompters are taken for apostate angels in express designation, who, as if in love, draw men to unlawful deeds by their enticing words. But they are much the worse, who give into this sin not from fear but from pride, of whom the wife of blessed Job bore the figure in a special manner, in that she sought to prompt high thoughts to her husband, saying, *Dost thou still retain thine integrity? Curse God, and die*. She blames the simplicity in her husband, that in contempt of all things transitory, with a pure heart, he longs after the eternal only. As though she said, 'Why dost thou in thy simplicity seek after the things of eternity, and in resignation groan under the weight of present ills? Transgress [*Excedens*], and contemn eternity, and even by dying escape from present woes.' But when any of the Elect encounter evil within coming from carnal men, what a model [*formam*] of uprightness they exhibit in themselves, let us learn from the words of him, wounded and yet whole, seated yet erect, who says,

Ver. 10. Thou speakest as one of the foolish women speaketh. What? shall we receive good at the hand of the Lord, and shall we not receive evil?

xxi. 39. Holy men, when fastened upon by the war of afflictions, when at one and the same moment they are exposed to this party dealing them blows and to that urging persuasions, present to the one sort the shield of patience, at the other they launch the darts of instruction, and lift themselves up to either mode of warfare with a wonderful skill in virtue, so that they should at the same time both instruct with wisdom the froward counsels within, and contemn with courage the adverse events without; that by their instructions they may amend the one sort, and by their endurance put down the other. For the assailing foes they contemn by bearing them, and the crippled citizens they recover to a state of soundness, by sympathizing with them. Those they resist, that they may not draw off others also; they alarm themselves for these, lest they should wholly lose the life of righteousness.

40. Let us view the soldier of God's camp fighting against either sort, He says, *Without were fightings, within were fears.* [2 Cor. 7, 5] He reckons up the wars, which he underwent eventually, in these words, *In perils of waters, in perils of robbers, in perils by mine own countrymen, in perils by the heathen, in perils in the city, in perils ,in the wilderness, in perils in the sea, in perils among false brethren.* [2 Cor. 11, 26] Now in this war, what were those darts which he sent against the foe, let him add, *In weariness and painfulness, in watchings often, in hunger and thirst, in fastings often, in cold and nakedness.* [ib. 27] And let him say, when caught amidst such numerous assaults, with what a watchful defence he at the same time guarded the camp too. For he forthwith proceeds, *Beside those things that are without, that which cometh upon me daily, the care of all the churches.* [ib. 28] See how bravely he takes upon himself those fights, how mercifully he spends himself in defending his neighbours. He describes the ills which he suffers, he subjoins the good that he imparts. So let us consider how toilsome it must be, at one and the same time to undergo troubles without, and to defend the weak within. Without, fightings are his lot, in that he is torn with stripes and bound with chains; within he suffers alarm, in that he dreads lest his sufferings do a mischief, not to himself but to his disciples. And hence he writes to those same disciples, saying, *That no man should be moved by these afflictions; for yourselves know that we are appointed thereunto.* [1 Thess. 3, 3] For in suffering himself he feared for the fate of others, lest while the disciples perceive him to be afflicted for the faith with stripes, they be backward to confess themselves to be of the faithful. Oh! bowels of boundless love! All that he suffers himself, he disregards, and is

concerned lest the disciples should suffer ought of evil prompting within the heart. He slights the wounds of the body in himself, and heals the wounds of the soul in others. For the righteous have this proper to themselves, that in the midst of the pain of their own woe, they never give over the care of others' weal, and when in suffering afflictions they grieve for themselves, still by giving needful instruction they provide for others, and are like some great physicians, that being smitten are brought into a state of sickness. They themselves suffer from the lacerations of the wound, yet they proffer the salves of saving health to others. But it is very far less toilsome, either to instruct when you are not suffering, or to suffer when you are not giving instruction. Hence holy men skilfully apply their energies to both objects, and when they chance to be stricken with afflictions, they so meet the wars from without, that they take anxious thought that their neighbour's interior be not rent and torn. Thus holy men stand up courageously in the line, and on the one hand smite with the javelin the breasts advanced against them, and on the other cover with the shield their feeble comrades in the rear. And thus with a rapid glance they look out on either side, that they may at the same time pierce their daring foes in front, and shield from wounds their trembling friends behind. Therefore, because holy men then are skilled so to meet adversities without, that they are at the same time able to correct froward counsels within, it may be well said, *Thou speakest as one of the foolish women speaketh.* For as it is said to the Elect, *Act like men, and He shall comfort your heart*; [Ps. 31, 24. Vulg.] so the minds of carnal men, which serve God with a yielding purpose, are not undeservedly called 'women.'

41. *What? shall we receive good at the hand of God, and shall we not receive evil?* As though he said, 'If we are bent upon eternal blessings, what wonder if we meet with temporal evils?' Now these blessings Paul had his eye fixed on with earnest interest, when he submitted with a composed mind to the ills that fell upon him, saying, *For I reckon that the sufferings of this present time are not worthy to be compared with the glory which shall be revealed in us*. [Rom. 8, 18]

In all this did not Job sin with his lips. When holy men undergo persecution both within and without, they not only never transgress in injurious expressions against God, but they never launch words of reviling against their very adversaries themselves; which Peter, the leader of the good, rightly warns us of when he says, *But let none of you suffer as a murderer, or as a thief, or as an* [So Vulg.] *evil speaker*. [1 Pet. 4, 15] For the evil speaker's way of suffering is, in the season of his suffering, to break loose in abuse at least of his persecutor. But forasmuch as the Body of our Redeemer, viz. Holy Church, so bears the burthen of her sorrows, that she never transgresses the bounds of humility by words, it is rightly said of this sorrower;

In all this did not Job sin with his lips.

Ver. 11. Now when Job's three friends heard of all this evil that was come upon him, they came everyone from his own place; Eliphaz the Temanite, and Bildad the Shuhite, and Zophar the Naamathite.

42. In the Preface to this work we said that the friends of blessed Job, though they come together to him with a good purpose, yet do for this reason bear the likeness of heretics, in that they fall away into sin by speaking without discretion; and hence it is said to them by blessed Job, *Surely I would speak to the Almighty, I desire to reason with God; but ye are forgers of lies, and followers of corrupt doctrines*. [Job 13, 3. 4.] Thus Holy Church, which is set in the midst of tribulation all this time of her pilgrimage, whilst she suffers wounds, and mourns over the downfall of her members, has other enemies of Christ besides to bear with, under Christ's name. For to the increasing of her grief, heretics also meet together in dispute and strife, and they pierce her with unreasonable words like as with a kind of dart.

43. And it is well said, *they came every one from his own place*. For 'the place' of heretics is very pride itself. For except they first swelled with pride in their hearts, they would never enter the lists of false assertion. For the place of the wicked is pride, just as reversely humility is 'the place' of the good. Whereof Solomon says, *If the spirit of the ruler rise up against thee, leave not thy place*. [Eccles. 10, 4] As though he said in plain words, 'If thou perceivest the spirit of the Tempter to prevail against thee in aught, quit not the lowliness of penitence;' and that it was the abasement of penitence that he called 'our place,' he shows by the words that follow, saying, *for healing* [ib. Vulg.] *pacifieth great offences*. For what else is the humility of mourning, save the remedy of sin. Heretics therefore come each from 'his place,' in that it is from pride that they are urged to attack Holy Church.

THE FIRST PART.

44. And their froward conduct, moreover, is collected from an interpretation of their names. For they are named 'Eliphaz,' 'Baldad,' 'Sophar;' and as we have said above Eliphaz is, by interpretation, rendered, 'contempt of God.' For if they did not condemn God, they would never entertain wrong notions concerning Him. And Baldad is rendered 'oldness alone.' For while they shrink from being fairly defeated, and seek to be victorious with froward purpose, they pay no regard to the conversation of the new life, and all that they give heed to is 'of oldness alone.' And Sophar, 'dissipating prospect;' for they that are set in Holy Church humbly contemplate with true faith the mysteries of their Redeemer, but when heretics come to them with false statements, they 'dissipate the prospect,' in that they turn aside from the aim of right contemplation the minds of those, whom they draw over to themselves.

45. Now the places from whence they come are described in fitting accordance with the practices of heretics. For there is a Themanite, and a Suhite, and a Naamathite named. Now *Thema* is by interpretation 'the south;' *Suhi*, 'speaking;' *Naama*, 'comeliness.' But who does not know that the south is a hot wind; so heretics, as they are over ardent to be wise, study to have heated wits beyond what needs. For sloth goes with the torpor of cold, whilst reversely the restlessness of unrestrained curiosity accords with unabated teeming heat, and so because they long to feel the heat of wisdom beyond what they ought, they are said to come from 'the south.' Paul busied himself to cool the minds of the faithful to this heat of unrestrained wiseness, when he said, *Not to be overwise beyond what he ought to be wise, but to be wise unto sobriety*. [Rom. 12, 3. Vulg.] It is hence that David smites at the *valleys of salt*, [2 Sam. 8, 13] viz. in that our Redeemer, by the piercing of His severity, extinguishes the foolishness of unrestrained wit in all that entertain wrong notions regarding Him. And *Suhi* is rendered 'talking,' for they desire to be warm-witted, not that they may live well, but that they may talk high; thus they are said to come from *Thema* and *Suhi*, i.e. from 'heat,' and 'talkativeness,' for herein, viz. that they show themselves as studious of Scripture, they teem with words of talkativeness, but not with bowels of love. And *Naama* is interpreted 'comeliness,' for because they aim not to be, but to appear learned, by words of deep learning they put on the guise of well living, and by their teeming wit in talk, exhibit in themselves a form of 'comeliness,' that by the

comeliness of the lips they may more easily recommend evil counsels, in proportion as they commonly hide from our senses the foulness of their lives. But neither are the very names of the places set down in undistinguished order in the relation. For *Thema* is set first, then *Suhi*, and next *Naama* in that first an excessive warmth of wit sets them on fire, next smartness of speech lifts them up, and then, finally, dissimulation presents them comely to the eyes of men.

For they had made an appointment together to come and mourn with him and to comfort him.

xxiii.

46. Heretics 'make an appointment together,' when they hold in common certain false opinions contrary to the Church, and in the points wherein they are at variance with the truth agree together in falsehood. But all they that give us instruction concerning eternity, what else are they doing, save amid the tribulations of our pilgrimage administering consolation to us? And forasmuch as heretics desire to impart to Holy Church their own opinions, they come to her as though to comfort her. Nor is it strange if they who set forth a figure of enemies, are called friends, when it is said to the very traitor, *Friend, wherefore art thou come?* [Mat. 26, 50] and the rich man that is consumed in the fire of hell, is called *son* by Abraham. [Luke 16, 25] For though the wicked refuse to be amended by us, yet it is meet that we style them friends, not of their wickedness, but by virtue of our own lovingkindness.

Ver. 12. And when they lifted up their eyes afar off, and knew him not, they lifted up their voice, and wept.

xxiv.

47. All heretics, in contemplating the deeds of Holy Church, lift up their eyes, in that they are themselves down below, and when they look at her works, the objects, which they are gazing at, are set high above them. Yet they do not know her in her sorrow, for she herself covets to 'receive evil things' here, that so being purified she may attain to the reward of an eternal recompence, and for the most part she dreads prosperity, and joys in the hard lessons of her training. Therefore heretics, who aim at present things as something great, know her not amidst her wounds. For that, which they see in her, they recognise not in the reading of their own hearts. While she then is gaining ground even by her adversities, they themselves stick fast in their stupefaction, because they

know not by experiment the things they see. And they rent everyone his mantle, and sprinkled dust upon their heads toward heaven.

XXV. 48. Like as we take the garments of the Church for the whole number of the faithful; (and it is hence that the Prophet says, *Thou shalt clothe thee with them all as with an ornament*; [Is. 49, 18]) so the garments of heretics are all they that attaching themselves with one accord to them are implicated in their errors. But heretics have this point proper to themselves, that they cannot remain stationary for long in that stage wherein they leave the Church, but they are day by day precipitated into further extremes, and by hatching worse opinions they split into manifold divisions, and are in most cases parted the wider from one another by their contention and disorderment. Thus because all those, whom they attach to their ill faith [*perfidiae*], are further torn by them in endless splitting, it may well be said that the friends who come rend their garments [*rumpunt*], but when the garments are rent, the body is shown through; for it oftentimes happens, that when the followers are rent and torn, the wickedness of their imaginings is disclosed, for discord to lay open the artifices, which their great guilt in agreeing together had heretofore kept close.

49. But now, they 'sprinkle dust upon their heads to heaven.' What is represented by *dust*, saving earthly senses; what by the head, saving that which is our leading principle, viz. the mind? What is set forth by 'heaven,' but the law of heavenly revelation? So, to 'sprinkle dust upon the head to heaven,' is to corrupt the mind with an earthly perception, and to put earthly senses upon heavenly words. Now they generally canvas the words of God more than they take them in, and for this reason they sprinkle dust upon their heads, forasmuch as they strain themselves in the precepts of God, following an earthly sense, beyond the powers of their mind.

Ver. 13. So they sat down with him upon the ground seven days and seven nights.

XXVI. 50. In the day we make out the objects that we look at, but in the night, either from the blindness we discern nothing, or from the uncertainty we are bewildered. Accordingly by 'day' we have 'understanding' represented, and by 'night,' 'ignorance.' And by the number seven the sum of completeness is expressed; and hence in seven days, and no more, the whole of this transitory period is accomplished. How then is it that the friends of blessed Job are said to sit with him seven days and seven nights, saving that heretics, whether in those things wherein they admit the true light, or in those wherein they are under the darkness of ignorance, as it were feign to let themselves down to Holy Church in her weakness, while under colour of caresses, they are preparing their snares to catch her withal? and though, whether in the things which they do understand, or in those which they are unable to understand, through the swelling of a bloated self-elation, they account themselves great in their own eyes, yet sometimes in semblance they bend to Holy Church, and while they make soft their words, they insinuate their venom, 'To sit upon the earth,' then, is to exhibit somewhat of the figure of humility, that whilst their exterior appears humble, they may recommend the proud doctrines which they teach.

51. But it is possible that by 'the earth' may be also represented the Incarnation of our Mediator. And hence it is said to Israel, *An altar of earth shalt thou then make unto Me*. [Ex. 20, 24] For to make an *altar of earth* for the Lord is to trust in the Incarnation of our Mediator. For then our gift is received by God, when our humility has placed upon His Altar, i.e. upon the belief of our Lord's Incarnation, all the works that it performs. Thus we place our offered gift upon an altar of earth, if our actions be firmly based upon faith in the Lord's Incarnation. But there are some heretics, who do not deny that the Incarnation of the Mediator took place, but either think otherwise concerning His Divinity than is true, or in the character of the Incarnation itself are at variance with us. They then that with us declare the true Incarnation of our Redeemer, as it were sit alike with Job upon the earth, and they are described as sitting upon the ground seven days and seven nights; forasmuch as whether in this very thing that they understand somewhat of the fulness of truth, or in this that they are thoroughly blinded by the darkness of their foolish minds, they cannot yet deny the mystery of the Incarnation. And so to sit upon the earth with blessed Job, is to believe in the true Flesh of our Redeemer in unison with Holy Church.

52. Now sometimes heretics wreak their animosity against us in punishments as well, sometimes they pursue us with words only. Sometimes they provoke us when quiet, but sometimes, seeing us

hold our peace, they remain quiet, and they are friendly to the dumb, but hostile to them that open their lips, and hence forasmuch as blessed Job had not as yet said aught to them in converse, it is rightly added, *And none spake a word unto him.* For we find our adversaries hold their peace, so long as we forbear by preaching to beget sons of the true faith. But if we begin to speak aright, we immediately feel the weight of their reviling by their reply; forthwith they start into hostility, and burst out into a voice of bitterness against us, doubtless because they fear lest the hearts, which the weight of folly presses down beneath, should be drawn up on high by the voice of him that speaketh aright. Therefore, as we have said, because our enemies love us when mute, and hate us when we speak, it is rightly said in the case of Job keeping silence,

And none spake a word unto him.

xxvii. 53. Yet sometimes when they see the hearts of believers vacant through sloth, they do not cease to scatter the seeds of error by speech. But when they see the minds of the good busied on high, seeking the way back to their country, earnestly sorrowing over the toils of this place of exile, they rein in their tongues with anxious heed; in that they see that whilst they assail those sorrowing hearts with fruitless words, they are speedily made to hold their peace. And hence whereas it is well said, *none spake a word unto him*, the cause of their silence is immediately brought in by implication, when it is said,

For they saw that his grief was very great.

xxviii. 54. For when our hearts are pierced with violent grief from the love of God, the adversary fears to speak frowardly at random, for he sees that by provoking the fixed mind, he not only has no power to draw it to untoward ways, but that by its being stirred up, he may chance to lose even those whom he held bound.

55. Perhaps it may influence some that we have so made out these particulars, that what was well done by the friends should denote that which was to be ill done by heretics. Yet in this way it very often happens that a circumstance is virtue in the historical fact, evil in its meaning and import, just as an action is sometimes in the doing ground of condemnation, but in the writing, a prophecy of merit,

which we shall the sooner show, if we shall bring forward one testimony of Holy Writ to prove both points. For who, that hears of it, not only among believers but of unbelievers themselves also, does not utterly loathe this, that David walking upon his solar lusteth after Beershebah the wife of Uriah? Yet when he returns back from the battle, he bids him go home to wash his feet. Whereupon he answered at once, *The Ark of the Lord abideth in tents, shall I then take rest in my house?* [2 Sam. 11, 11] David received him to his own board, and delivers to him letters, through which he must die. But of whom does David walking upon his solar bear a figure, saving of Him, concerning Whom it is written, *He hath set his tabernacle in the sun?* [Ps. 19, 4. Vulg.] And what else is it to draw Beersheba to himself, but to join to Himself by a spiritual meaning the Law of the formal letter, which was united to a carnal people? For Beersheba is rendered 'the seventh well,' assuredly, in that through the knowledge of the Law, with spiritual grace infused, perfect wisdom is ministered unto us. And whom does Uriah denote, but the Jewish people, whose name is rendered by interpretation, 'My light from God?' Now forasmuch as the Jewish people is raised high by receiving the knowledge of the Law, it as it were glories 'in the light of God.' But David took from this Uriah his wife, and united her to himself, surely in that the strong-handed One, which is the rendering of 'David,' our Redeemer, showed Himself in the flesh, whilst He made known that the Law spake in a spiritual sense concerning Himself. Hereby, that it was held by them after the letter, He proved it to be alienated from the Jewish people, and joined it to Himself, in that He declared Himself to be proclaimed by it. Yet David bids Uriah 'go home to wash his feet,' in that when the Lord came Incarnate, He bade the Jewish people turn back to the home of the conscience, and wipe off with their tears the defilements of their doings, that it should understand the precepts of the Law in a spiritual sense, and finding the fount of Baptism after the grievous hardness of the commandments, have recourse to water after toil. But Uriah, who recalled to mind that the ark of the Lord was under tents, answered, that he could not enter into his house. As if the Jewish people said, 'I view the precepts of God in carnal sacrifices, and I need not to go back to the conscience in following a spiritual meaning.' For he, as it were, declares 'the ark of the Lord to be under tents,' who views the precepts of God as designed for no other end than to show forth a service of carnal sacrifice. Yet when he would not return home, David even bids him to his table, in that though the Jewish people disdain to return home into the conscience, yet the Redeemer at His coming avouches the commandments to be spiritual, saying, *For had ye believed Moses, ye would* [Vulg. *would perchance*] *have believed Me: for he wrote of Me*. [John 5, 46] And thus the Jewish people holds that Law, which tells of His Divinity, whereunto that people deigns not to give credence. And hence Uriah is sent to Joab with letters, according to which he is to be put to death, in that the Jewish people bears itself the Law, by whose convicting testimony it is to die. For whereas holding fast the commandments of the Law it strives hard to fulfil them, clearly it does itself deliver the judgment whereupon it is condemned. What, then, in respect of the fact, is more foul than David? What can be named purer than Uriah? What again in respect of the mystery can be discovered holier than David, what more faithless than Uriah? Since the one by guiltiness of life prophetically betokens innocency, and the other by innocency of life prophetically represents guilt. Wherefore it is with no inaptitude that by the things that are well done by the friends of Job we have represented to us those to be done amiss by heretics, in that it is the excellency of Holy Writ so to relate the past as to set forth the future; in such wise to vindicate the case in the fact, that it is against it in the mystery; so to condemn the things done, that they are commended to us as fit to be done in the way of mystery.

Moral

56. So then as we have completed the allegorical mysteries, unravelling them piece by piece, let us now proceed to follow out the sense of the moral truth, hastily touching thereupon, for the mind hastens forward to make out the parts of greater difficulty, and if it is for long wrapped up in the plain parts, it is hindered from knocking as it were fit at those which are closed. Oftentimes our old enemy, after he has brought down upon our mind the conflict of temptation, retires for a time from his own contest, not to put an end to his wickedness, but that upon those hearts, which he has rendered secure by a respite, returning of a sudden, he may make his inroad the more easily and unexpectedly. It is hence that he returns again to try the blessed man, and demands pains on the head of him,

whom nevertheless the Supreme Mercy while keeping fast yields up to him, saying,

Ver. 6. Behold, he is in thine hand: but save his life.

xxix.

57. For He so forsakes us that He guards us, and so guards us that by the permitted case of temptation, He shows us our state of weakness. And he immediately *went forth from before the face of the Lord*, and by smiting him whom He had thus gotten he wounded him *from the sole of his foot even to his crown*. Thus, viz. in that when he receives permission, beginning with the least, and reaching even to the greater points, he as it were rends and pierces all the body of the mind [*corpus mentis*] with the temptations which he brings upon it, yet he does not attain to the smiting of the soul [*animam*], in that deep at the bottom of all the thoughts of the heart, the interior purpose of our secret resolution holds out, in the midst of the very wounds of gratification which it receives, so that although the enjoyment may eat into the mind, yet it does not so bend the set intent of holy uprightness as to bring it to the very softness of consenting. Yet it is our duty to cleanse the mere wounds of enjoyment themselves by the sharp treatment of penance, and if aught that is dissolute springs up in the heart to refine it with the chastening hand of rigorous severity. And hence it is rightly added immediately,

Ver. 8. And he took him a potsherd to scrape the humour withal.

xxx.

58. For what do we understand by the 'potsherd,' saving forcibleness of severity, and what by the 'humour,' save laxity of unlawful imaginations? And thus we are smitten, and 'scrape off the humour with a potsherd,' when after the defilements of unlawful thoughts, we cleanse ourselves by a sharp judgment. By the potsherd too we may understand the frailness of mortality. And then to 'scrape the humour with a potsherd,' is to ponder on the course and frailty of our mortal state, and to wipe off the rottenness of a wretched self-gratification. For when a man bethinks himself how soon the flesh returns to dust, he readily gets the better of that which originating in the flesh foully assails him in the interior. So, when bad thoughts arising from temptation flow into the mind, it is as if humour kept running from a wound. But the humour is soon

cleansed away, if the frailty of our nature be taken up in the thought, like a potsherd in the hand.

59. For neither are these suggestions to be lightly esteemed, which though they may not draw us on so far as to the act, yet work in the mind in an unlawful way. It is hence that our Redeemer was come, as it were, 'to scrape the humour from our wounds,' when He said, *Ye have heard that it was said by them of old time, Thou shalt not commit adultery. But I say unto you, that whosoever looketh on a woman to lust after her, hath committed adultery with her already in his heart.* [Matt. 5, 27. 28.] 'The humour,' therefore, 'is wiped off,' when sin is not only severed from the deed, but also from the thought. It is hence that Jerubbaal saw the Angel when he was winnowing corn from the chaff, at whose bidding he forthwith dressed a kid and set it upon a rock, and poured over it the broth of the flesh, which the Angel touched with a rod, and thereupon fire coming out of the rock consumed it. [Judg. 6, 11. &c.] For what else is it to beat corn with a rod, but to separate the grains of virtues from the chaff of vices, with an upright judgment? But to those that are thus employed the Angel presents himself, in that the Lord is more ready to communicate interior truths in proportion as men are more earnest in ridding themselves of external things. And he orders a kid to be killed, i.e. every appetite of the flesh to be sacrificed, and the flesh to be set upon a rock, and the broth thereof to be poured upon it. Whom else does the 'rock' represent, saving Him, of Whom it is said by Paul, *And that rock was Christ?* [1 Cor. 10, 4] We 'set flesh then upon the rock,' when in imitation of Christ we crucify our body. He too pours the juice of the flesh over it, who, in following the conversation of Christ, empties himself even of the mere thoughts of the flesh themselves. For 'the broth' of the dissolved flesh is in a manner 'poured upon the rock,' when the mind is emptied of the flow of carnal thoughts too. Yet the Angel directly touches it with a rod, in that the might of God's succour never leaves our striving forsaken. And fire issues from the rock, and consumes the broth and the flesh, in that the Spirit, breathed upon us by the Redeemer, lights up the heart with so fierce a flame of compunction, that it consumes everything in it that is unlawful either in deed or in thought. And therefore it is the same thing here 'to scrape the humour with a potsherd,' that it is there to 'pour the broth upon the rock.' For the perfect mind is ever eagerly on the watch, not only that it may refuse to do

bad acts, but that it may even wipe off all that is become foul and soft in it, in the workings of imagination. But it often happens that war springs up from the very victory, so that when the impure thought is vanquished, the mind of the victor is struck by self-elation. Therefore it follows that the mind must be no otherwise elevated in purity, than that it should be heedfully brought under in humility. And hence, whereas it was said of the holy man, *And he took a potsherd, and scraped the humour withal*, it is forthwith fitly added,

And he sat down upon a dunghill.

xxxi.

60. For 'to sit down upon a dunghill' is for a man to entertain mean and abject notions of himself. For us to 'sit upon a dunghill,' is to carry back the eye of the mind, in a spirit of repentance, to those things which we have unlawfully committed, that when we see the dung of our sins before our eyes, we may bend low all that rises up in the mind of pride. He sits upon a dunghill, who regards his own weakness with earnest attention, and never lifts himself up for those good qualities, which he has received through grace. Did not Abraham sit by himself upon a dunghill, when he said, *Behold, now, I have taken upon me to speak unto the Lord, which am but dust and ashes?* [Gen. 18, 27] For it is plain to see in what place he had set himself, who, at the very moment that he was speaking with God, reckoned himself to be 'dust and ashes.' If he then thus despises himself who is raised to the honour of converse with the Deity even, we should consider with earnest thoughts of heart with what woes they are destined to be stricken, who, while they never advance a step towards the highest things, are yet lifted up on the score of the least and lowest attainments. For there are some, who, when they do but little things, think great things of themselves. They lift their minds on high, and account themselves to excel other men in the deserts of virtue. For surely, these inwardly quit the dunghill of humility within themselves, and scale the heights of pride; herein following the steps of him, the first that elevated himself in his own eyes, and in elevating brought himself to the ground, following the steps of him, who was not content with that dignity of a created being, which he had received, saying, *I will ascend into heaven; I will exalt my throne above the stars of God*. [Is. 14, 13] And it is hence that she, which is united to him by an evil alliance, even Babylon, i.e. 'the

confused multitude of sinners,' says, *I am, and none else beside me, I shall not sit as a widow*. [Is. 47, 8] Whosoever then swells within him, has set himself on high by himself. Yet doth he sink himself so much the deeper below, in proportion as he scorns to think the lowest things of himself according to the truth. There are some too that labour not to do aught that is virtuous, yet when they see others commit sin, they fancy themselves righteous by comparison with them. For all hearts are not wounded by the same or a similar offence. For this one is entrapped by pride, while that perchance is overthrown by anger, and avarice is the sting of one, while luxury fires another. And it very often chances that he, who is brought down by pride, sees how another is inflamed with anger; and because anger does not speedily influence himself, he now reckons that he is better than his passionate neighbour, and is as it were lifted up on the score of his righteousness in his own eyes, in that he forgets to take account of the fault, by which he is more grievously enchained. And it very often happens that he who is mangled by avarice, beholds another plunged in the whirlpool of luxury, and because he sees himself to be a stranger to carnal pollution, he never heeds by what defilements of the spiritual life he is himself inwardly polluted; and while he considers well the evil in another, which he is himself without, he forgets to take account in his own case of that which he has; and so it is brought to pass, that when the mind to be pronounced upon goes off to the cases of other men, it is deprived of the light of its own judgment, and so much the more cruelly vaunts itself against others' failings, in proportion as it is from negligence in ignorance of its own.

61. But, on the other hand, they that really desire to rise to the heights of virtue, whenever they hear of the faults of others, immediately recall the mind to their own; and the more they really bewail these last, so much the more rightly do they pronounce judgment on those others. Therefore, forasmuch as every elect person restrains himself in the consideration of his own frailty, it may be well said that the holy man in his sorrow sits down upon a dunghill. For he that really humbles himself as he goes on his way, marks with the eye of continued observation all the filth of sin wherewith he is beset. But we must know that it is in prosperity that the mind is oftenest touched with urgent temptations, yet that it sometimes happens that we at the same time undergo crosses without, and are wearied with

the urgency of temptation within, so that both the scourge tortures the flesh, and yet suggestion of the flesh pours in upon the mind. And hence it is well, that after the many wounds that blessed Job received, we have yet further the words of his illadvising wife subjoined also, who says,

Ver. 9. Dost thou still retain thine integrity? Curse God, and die.

xxxii.

62. For the illadvising wife is the carnal thought goading the mind, since it often happens, as has been said above, that we are both harrassed with strokes without, and wearied with carnal promptings within. For it is hence that Jeremiah bewails, saying, *Abroad the sword bereaveth; at home there is as death.* [Lam. 1, 20] Since 'the sword bereaveth,' when vengeance outwardly smites and pierces us, and 'at home there is as death,' in that indeed he both undergoes the lash, and yet the conscience is not clear of the stains of temptation within. Hence David says, *Let them be as chaff before the wind, and let the angel of the Lord persecute them.* [Ps. 35, 5] For he that is caught by the blast of temptation in the heart, is lifted up like dust before the face of the wind; and when in the midst of these strokes the rigour of God smites them, what else is it, but the Angel of the Lord that persecutes them?

63. But these trials are carried on in the case of the reprobate in one way, and of the Elect in another. The hearts of the first sort are so tempted that they yield consent, and those of the last undergo temptations indeed, but offer resistance. The mind of the one is taken captive with a feeling of delight, and if at the moment that which is prompted amiss is displeasing, yet afterwards by deliberation it gives pleasure. But these so receive the darts of temptation, that they weary themselves in unceasing resistance, and if at any time the mind under temptation is hurried away to entertain a feeling of delight, yet they quickly blush at the very circumstance of their delight stealing upon them, and blame with unsparing censure all that they detect springing up in themselves of a carnal nature. Hence it is rightly added immediately,

Ver. 10. Thou speakest as one of the foolish women speaketh. What? shall we receive good at the hand of God, and shall we not receive evil?

xxxiii.

64. For it is meet that the holy mind restrain by spiritual correction whatever of a carnal nature within it ut-

ters rebellious muttering, that the flesh whether by speaking severe things may not draw it into impatience, nor yet by speaking smooth ones melt it to the looseness of lust. Therefore let manly censure, reproving the dictates of unlawful imaginations, hold hard the dissolute softness of what is base in us, by saying, *Thou speakest as one of the foolish women speaketh*. And, on the other hand, let the consideration of the gifts repress the discontent of bitter thought, saying, *Shall we receive good at the hand of God, and shall we not receive evil?* And whoever desires to get the mastery of his vices, and goes forward to the eternal heights of inward recompense [*retributionis*] with the steps of a true purpose, the more he sees himself to be on every hand beset with the war of the vices, the more resolutely he arrays himself with the armour of the virtues, and fears the darts the less, in proportion as he defends his breast bravely against their assault.

65. Yet it very often happens, that whilst we are striving to stay ourselves in this fight of temptation by exalted virtues, certain vices cloak themselves to our eyes under the garb of virtues, and come to us as it were with a smooth face, but how adverse to us they are we perceive upon examination. And hence the friends of blessed Job as it were come together for the purpose of giving comfort, but they burst out into reviling, in that vices that plot our ruin assume the look of virtues, but strike us with hostile assault. For often immoderate anger desires to appear justice, and often dissolute remissness, mercy; often fear without precaution would seem humility, often unbridled pride, liberty. Thus the friends come to give consolation, but fall off into words of reproach, in that vices, cloaked under the guise of virtues, set out indeed with a smooth outside, but confound us by a bitter hostility. And it is rightly said,

Ver. 11. For they had made an appointment together to come to mourn with him and to comfort him.

xxxiv. 66. For vices make an appointment together under the cloak of virtues; in that there are certain ones, which are banded together against us by a kind of agreement, such as pride and anger, remissness and fear. For anger is neighbour to pride, and remissness to cowardice. Those then come together by agreement, which are allied to one another in opposition to us, by a kind of kinship in iniquity; but if we acknowledge the toilsomeness of our captivity, if we grieve in our inmost soul from love of our eternal home, the sins that steal upon the inopportunely joyful, will not be able to prevail against the opportunely sad. Hence it is well added,

Ver. 12. And when they lifted up their eyes afar off, and knew him not, they lifted up their voice, and wept.

xxxv.

67. For the vices do not know us in our afflictions, in that so soon as they have knocked at the dejected heart, being reproved they start back, and they, which as it were knew us in our joy, because they made their way in, cannot know us in our sadness, in that they break their edge on our very rigidity itself. But our old enemy, the more he sees that he is himself caught out in them, and that with a good courage, cloaks them with so much the deeper disguise under the image of virtues; and hence it is added, *They lifted up their voice, and wept; and they rent every one his mantle, and sprinkled dust upon their heads toward heaven.*

Ver. 18. So they sat down with him upon the ground seven days and seven nights.

xxxvi.

68. For by the weeping pity is betokened, discretion by the cutting of the garments, the affecting [al. 'effecting'] of good works by the dust upon the head, humility by the sitting. For sometimes the enemy in plotting against us feigns somewhat that is full of pity, that he may bring us down to an end of cruelty. As is the case, when he prevents a fault being corrected by chastisement, that that, which is not suppressed in this life, may be stricken with the fire of hell. Sometimes he presents the form of discretion to the eyes, and draws us on to snares of indiscretion, which happens, when at his instigation we as it were from prudence allow ourselves too much nourishment on account of our weakness, while we are imprudently raising against ourselves assaults of the flesh. Sometimes he counterfeits the affecting of good works, yet hereby entails upon us restlessness in labours, as it happens, when a man cannot remain quiet, and, as it were, fears to be judged for idleness. Sometimes he exhibits the form of humility, that he may steal away our affecting of the useful, as is the case when he declares to some that they are weaker and more useless than indeed they are, that whereas they look upon themselves as too unworthy, they may fear to administer the things wherein they might be able to benefit their neighbours.

69. But these vices which the old enemy hides under the semblance of virtues, are very minutely examined by the hand of compunction. For he that really grieves within, resolutely foredetermines what things are to be done outwardly, and what are not. For if the virtue of compunction moves us in our inward parts, all the clamouring of evil dictates is made mute; and hence it follows.

And none spake a word unto him; for they saw that his grief was very great.

xxxvii. 70. For if the heart feels true sorrow, the vices have no tongue against it. And when the life of uprightness is sought with an entire aim, the fruitless prompting of evil is closed up. But oftentimes if we brace ourselves with strong energy against the incitements of evil habits, we turn even those very evil habits to the account of virtue. For some are possessed by anger, but while they submit this to reason, they convert it into service rendered to holy zeal. Some are lifted up by pride. But whilst they bow down the mind to the fear of God, they change this into the free tone of unrestrained authority in defence of justice. Strength of the flesh is a snare to some; but whilst they bring under the body by practising works of mercy, from the same quarter, whence they were exposed to the goading of wickedness, they purchase the gains of pitifulness. And hence it is well that this blessed Job, after a multitude of conflicts, sacrifices a victim for his friends. For those whom he has for long borne as enemies by their strife, he one day makes fellow-countrymen by his sacrifice, in that whilst we turn all evil thoughts into virtues, bringing them into subjection, by the offering of the intention, we as it were change the hostile aims of temptation into friendly dispositions.

Let it suffice for us to have gone through these things in three volumes in a threefold method. For in the very beginning of this work we set firm the root of the tongue, as a provision against the bulk of the tree that should spring up, that we might afterwards produce the boughs of exposition according as the several places require.

BOOK IV.

Wherein Gregory, having in the Preface set forth in few words that the letter of Scripture is at times at variance with itself, and that the imprecations of Job, as of Jeremiah and David, cannot be understood without absurdity according to the sound which they convey, explains the words of Job in historical, mystical, and moral sense, from the commencement of the third chapter to the twentieth verse of the same.

Preface. HE who looks to the text and does not acquaint himself with the sense of the holy Word, is not so much furnishing himself with instruction as bewildering himself in uncertainty, in that the literal words sometimes contradict themselves; but whilst by their oppositeness they stand at variance with themselves, they direct the reader to a truth that is to be understood. Thus, how is it that Solomon says, *There is nothing better for a man than that he should eat and drink*; [Ecc. 2. 24] and adds not long after, *It is better to go to the house if mourning than to the house of feasting?* [Ecc. 7, 2] Wherefore did he prefer mourning to feasting, who had before commended eating and drinking? for if by preference it be good 'to eat and drink,' undoubtedly it should be a much better thing to hasten to the house of mirth than to the house of mourning. Hence it is that he says again, *Rejoice, O young man, in thy youth*; [Ecc. 11, 9] yet adds a little after, *for youth and pleasure are vanity*. [ver. 10. Vulg.] What does this mean, that he should either first enjoin practices that are reprehensible, or afterwards reprehend practices that he has enjoined, but that by the literal words themselves he implies that be, who finds difficulty in the outward form, should consider the truth to be understood, which same import of truth, while it is sought with humility of heart, is penetrated by continuance in reading. For as we see the face of strange persons, and know nothing of their hearts, but if we are joined to them in familiar communication, by frequency of conversation we even trace their very thoughts; so when in Holy Writ the historical narration alone is regarded, nothing more than the face is seen. But if we unite ourselves to it with frequent assiduity, then indeed we penetrate its meaning, as if by the effect of a familiar intercourse. For whilst we gather various truths from various parts, we easily see in the words thereof that what they import is one thing, what they sound like is another. But everyone proves a stranger to the knowledge of it, in proportion as he is tied down to its mere outside.

THE FIRST PART.

ii. See here, for instance, in that blessed Job is described as having cursed his day, and said, *Let the day perish wherein I was born, and the night in which it was said, There is a man child conceived*; [Job 3, 3] if we look no further than the surface, what can we find more reprehensible than these words? But who does not know that the day, in which he was born, could not at that time be in existence, for it is the condition of time to have no stay of continuance. For whereas by way of the future it is ever tending to be, so in going out by the past, it is ever hastening not to be. Wherefore then should one so great curse that, which he is not ignorant hath no existence? But perchance it may be said, that the magnitude of his virtue is seen from hence, that he, being disturbed by tribulation, imprecates a curse upon that, which it is evident has no existence at all. But this notion is set aside the moment the reasonableness of the thing is regarded, for if the object existed, which he cursed, it was a mischievous curse; but if it had no being, it was an idle one: but whoso is filled with His Spirit, *Who declareth, that every idle word that men shall speak, they shall give account thereof in the Day of Judgment*; [Matt. 12, 36] fears to be guilty of what is idle, even as of what is mischievous. To this sentence it is further added, *Let that day be turned into darkness; let not God regard it from above, neither let the light shine upon it. Let darkness and the shadow of death stain it; let a cloud dwell upon it; let it be enfolded in bitterness. As for that night, let darkness seize upon it. Lo, let that night be solitary, let no joyful voice come therein: let it look for light, and have none; neither let it see the dawning of the day*. How is it that that day, which he knows to have gone by with the flight of time, is said 'to be turned into darkness?' And whereas it is plain that it has no existence, wherefore is it wished for that 'the shadow of death might stain it?' or what cloud dwells upon it, what envelopement of bitterness enfolds it? or what darkness seizes upon that night, which no stay holds in being? Or how is it desired that that may be solitary, which in passing away had already become nought? Or how does that look for the light, which both lacks perception, and doth not continue in any stay of its own self? To these words he yet further adds,

Why died I not from the womb? why did I not give up the ghost when I came out of the belly? Why did the knees prevent me? or why the breasts

that I should suck? For now I should have lain still and have been quiet, I should have slept, and been at rest. [*Job 3, 11–13*]

If he had died at once from the womb, would he have got by this very destruction a title to a reward? Do abortive children enjoy eternal rest? For every man that is not absolved by the water of regeneration, is tied and bound by the guilt of the original bond. But that which the water of Baptism avails for with us, this either faith alone did of old in behalf of infants, or, for those of riper years, the virtue of sacrifice, or, for all that came of the stock of Abraham, the mystery of circumcision. For that every living being is conceived in the guilt of our first parent the Prophet witnesses, saying, *And in sin hath my mother conceived me.* [Ps.51, 5] And that he who is not washed in the water of salvation, does not lose the punishment of original sin, Truth plainly declares by Itself in these words, *Except a man be born of water and of the Spirit, he cannot enter into the kingdom of God.* [John 3, 5] How is it then, that he wishes that he had 'died in the womb,' and that he believes that he might have had rest by the boon of that death, whereas it is clear that the rest of life could in no wise be for him, if the Sacraments of Divine knowledge had in no wise set him free from the guilt of original sin? He yet further adds with whom he might have rested, saying, *With kings and counsellors of the earth which built desolate* [Vulg. *solitudines*] *places for themselves.* Who does not know that *the kings and counsellors of the earth* are herein far removed from 'solitude,' that they are close pressed with innumerable throngs of followers? and with what difficulty do they advance to rest, who are bound in with the tightened knots of such multifarious concerns! As Scripture witnesses, where it says, *But mighty men shall be mightily tormented.* [Wisd. 6, 6] Hence Truth utters these words in the Gospel; *unto whomsoever much is given, of him shall be much be required.* [Luke 12, 48] He implies besides, whom he would have had as fellows in that rest, in the words, *Or with princes that had gold, that filled their houses with silver.* [Matt. 19, 23] It is a rare thing for them that have gold to advance to rest, seeing that Truth says by Itself, *They that have riches shall hardly enter into the kingdom of heaven.* [Mark 10, 23] For what joys in the other life can they look for, who here pant after increase of riches? Yet that our Redeemer might further show this event to be most rare, and only possible by the supernatural agency of God, He says, *With men this is impossible; but with God all things are possible.* [Matt. 19, 26] Therefore because these words are, on the surface, at variance with reason, the letter itself thereby points out, that in those words the Saint delivers nothing after the letter.

iv. But if we shall first examine the nature of other curses in Holy Writ, we may the more perfectly trace out the import of this one, which was uttered by the mouth of blessed Job. For how is it that David, who to those that rewarded him evil, returned it not again, upon Saul and Jonathan falling in war, curses the mountains of Gilboa in the following words, *Ye mountains of Gilboa, let there be no dew, neither let there be rain upon you, nor fields of offerings; for there the shield of Saul is vilely cast away, as though he had not been anointed with oil?* [2 Sam. 1, 21] How is it that Jeremiah, seeing that his preaching was hindered by the hardness of his hearers, utters a curse, saying, *Cursed be the man, who brought tidings to my father, saying, A man child is born unto thee?* [Jer. 20. 15] What then did the mountains of Gilboa offend when Saul died, that neither dew nor rain should fall on them, and that the words of his sentence against them should make them barren of all produce of verdure? Why, forasmuch as Gilboa is by interpretation 'running down,' while by Saul's anointing and dying, the death of our Mediator is set forth, by the mountains of Gilboa we have no unfit representation of the uplifted hearts of the Jews, who, while they let themselves run down in the pursuit of the desires of this world, were mingled together in the death of Christ, i.e. of 'the Anointed.' And because in them the anointed King dies the death of the body, they too are left dry of all the dew of grace; of whom also it is well said, *that they cannot be fields of first fruits.* Because the high minds of the Hebrews bear no 'first fruits;' in that at the coming of our Redeemer, persisting for the most part in unfaithfulness, they would not follow the first beginnings of the faith; for Holy Church, which for her first fruits was enriched with the multitude of the Gentiles, scarcely at the end of the world will receive into her bosom the Jews, whom she may find, and gathering none but the last, will put them as the remnant of her fruits. Of which very remnant Isaiah hath these words, *For though thy people Israel shall be as the sand of the sea, yet a remnant of them shall return.* [Is. 10, 22] However, the mountains of Gilboa may for this reason be cursed by the Prophet's mouth, that whilst, the land being dried up, no fruit is produced, the possessors of the land might be stricken with the woe of that barrenness, so that they might themselves receive the sentence of the curse, who had obtained as the just reward of their iniquities to have the death of the King take place among them. But how is it that, from the lips of the Prophet, that man received the sentence of cursing, who brought to his father the tidings of his birth? Doubtless this is so much the more full of deeper mystery within, as it lacks human reason without. For perchance, if it had sounded at all reasonable without, we should never have been kindled to the pursuit of the interior meaning; and thus he the more fully implies something within, that he shows nothing that is reasonable without. For though the Prophet had come into this world from his mother's womb to be the subject of affliction, in what did the messenger of his birth do wrong? But what does the person of the Prophet represent 'carried hither and thither [*fluctuantis*]' except the mutability of man, which came by the dues of punishment, is thereby signified? and what is expressed by his 'father' but this world whereof we are born? And who is that man, who 'bring tidings of our birth to our father,' saving our old enemy, who, when he views us fluctuating in our thoughts, prompts the evil minded, who by virtue of this world's authority have the preeminence, to persuading us to our undoing, and who, when he has beheld us doing acts of weakness, commends these with applause [*favoribus*] as brave, and tells as it were of male children being born, when he gives joy that we have turned out corrupters of the truth by lying? He gives tidings to the father that a man child is born, when he shows the world him, whom he has prevailed with, turned into a corrupter of innocence. For when it is said to any one committing a sin or acting proudly, 'Thou hast acted like a man,' what else is this than that a man child is told of in the world? Justly then is the man cursed, who brings tidings of the birth of a man child; because his tidings betoken the damnable joy of our corrupter. Thus by these imprecations of Holy Scripture we learn what, in the case of blessed Job, we are to look for in his words of imprecation, lest he, whom God rewards after these wounds and these words, should be presumptuously condemned by the mistaken reader for his words. As then we have in some sort cleared the points, which were to be the objects of our enquiry in the preface, let us now proceed to discuss and to follow on the words of the historical form.

THE FIRST PART.

Historical

Ver. 1, 2, 3. After this Job opened his mouth, and cursed his day, And Job spake, and said, Let the day perish wherein I was born.

i. 1. That which is here said, *He opened his mouth*, must not be gone into negligently. For by the things which Holy Scripture premises but slightly, we are apprised that what comes after is to be expected with reverence. For as we know nothing what vessels that are closed contain inside, but when the mouth of the vessels is opened, we discover what is contained within; so the hearts of the Saints, which so long as their mouth is closed are hidden, when their mouth is opened, are disclosed to view. And when they disclose their thoughts, they are said to open their mouth, that with the full bent of our mind we may hasten to find out, as in vessels that are set open, what it is that they contain, and to refresh ourselves with their inmost fragrance. And hence when the Lord was about to utter His sublime precepts on the Mount, the words precede, *And He opened His mouth, and taught them*; [Matt. 5, 2] though in that place this too should be taken as the meaning, that He then opened His own mouth in delivering precepts, wherein He had long while opened the mouths of the Prophets. But it requires very great nicety in considering the expression, *After this*, namely, in order that the excellence of all that is done may be perceived in its true light by the time. For first we have described the wasting of his substance, the destruction of his children, the pain of his wounds, the persuasions of his wife, the coming of his friends, who are related to have rent their garments, to have shed tears with loud cries, to have sprinkled their heads with dust, and to have sat upon the ground for long in silence, and afterwards it is added, *After this Job opened his mouth, and cursed his day*; clearly that from the very order of the account, duly weighed, it might be concluded that he could never have uttered a curse in a spirit of impatience, who broke forth into a voice of cursing whilst his friends were as yet silent. For if he had cursed under the influence of passion, doubtless upon hearing of the loss of his substance, and upon hearing the death of his sons, his grief would have prompted him to curse. But what he then said, we have heard before. For he said, *The Lord gave, and the Lord hath taken away*. [Job 1, 21] Again, if he had cursed under the impulse of passion, he might well have uttered a curse when he was stricken in his body, or when he was mischievously advised by his wife. But what answer he then gave we have already learnt; for he says, *Thou speakest as one of the foolish women speaketh. What? shall we receive good at the hand of God, and shall we not receive evil?* [Job 2, 10] But after this it is set forth that his friends arrive, shed tears, seat themselves, keep silence, whereupon this is immediately subjoined, that he is said to have *cursed his day*. It is, then, too great an inconsistency to imagine that it was from impatience that he broke out into a voice of cursing, no man setting him on, no man driving him thereto, when we know that amidst the loss of all his goods, and the death of his children, amidst bodily afflictions, the evil counsels of his wife, he only gave great acknowledgments to his Creator with a humble mind. It is plain, then, with what feelings he spoke this when he was at rest, who even when stricken uttered such a strain of praise to God. For afterwards, when no longer stricken, he could not be guilty of pride, whom even his pain under the rod only showed to be full of humility. But as we know for certain that holy Scripture forbids cursing, how can we say that that is sometimes done aright, which yet we know to be forbidden by the same Holy Writ?

2. But be it known that Holy Writ makes mention of cursing in two ways, namely, of one sort of curse which it commands, another sort which it condemns. For a curse is uttered one way by the decision of justice, in another way by the malice of revenge. Thus a curse was pronounced by the decree of justice upon the first man himself, when he fell into sin, and heard the words, *Cursed is the ground for thy sake*. [Gen. 3, 17] A curse is pronounced by decree of justice, when it is said to Abraham, *I will curse them that curse thee*. Again, forasmuch as a curse may be uttered, not by award of justice, but by the malice of revenge, we have this admonition from the voice of Paul the Apostle in his preaching, where he says, *Bless, and curse not*; [Rom. 12, 14] and again, *nor revilers shall inherit the kingdom of God*. [1 Cor. 6, 10] So then God is said to curse, and yet man is forbidden to curse, because what man does from the malice of revenge, God only does in the exactness and perfection of justice. But when holy men deliver a sentence of cursing, they do not break forth therein from the wish of revenge, but in the strictness of justice, for they behold God's exact judgment within, and they perceive that they are bound to smite evils arising without with a curse; and are

guilty of no sin in cursing, in the same degree that they are not at variance with the interior judgment.

It is hence that Peter flung back the sentence of a curse upon Simon when he offered him money, in the words, *May thy money perish with thee*; [Acts 8, 20] for he who said, not *does*, but *may*, showed that he spoke this, not in the indicative, but in the optative mood. Hence Elias said to the two captains of fifty that came to him, *If I be a man of God, then let fire come down from heaven, and consume thee*. [2 Kings 1, 10] And upon what reasonable grounds of truth the sentences of either of the two were established, the issue of the case demonstrated. For both Simon perished in eternal ruin, and fire descending from above consumed the two captains of fifty. Thus the subsequent miracle [*virtus*] testifies with what mind the sentence of the curse is pronounced. For when both the innocence of him that curseth remains, and he that is cursed is by that curse swallowed up to the extent of utter destruction, from the end of either side we collect, that the sentence is taken up and launched against the offender from the sole Judge of what is within.

3. Therefore if we weigh with exactness the words of blessed Job, his cursing cometh not of the malice of one guilty of sin, but of the integrity of a judge, not of one agitated by passion, but of one sober in instruction; for he, who in cursing pronounced such righteous sentence, did not give way to the evil of perturbation of mind, but dispensed the dictates of wisdom. For, in fact, he saw his friends weeping and wailing, he saw them rending their garments, he saw how they had sprinkled their heads with dust, he saw them struck dumb at the thought of his affliction; and the Saint perceived that those whose hearts were set upon temporal prosperity, took him, by a comparison with their own feelings, for one brokenhearted with his temporal adversity. He considered that they would never be weeping for him in despair, who was stricken with a transient ill, except they had themselves withdrawn their soul in despair from the hope of inward soundness; and while he outwardly burst forth into the voice of grief, he showed to persons inwardly wounded the virtue of a healing medicine, saying,

Ver. 3. Let the day perish wherein was born.

4. For what is to be understood by 'the day of our birth,' save the whole period of our mortal state? So long as this keeps us fast in the

corruptions of this our mutable state of being, the unchangeableness of eternity does not appear to us. He, then, who already beholds the day of eternity, endures with difficulty the day of his mortal being. And observe, he says not, 'Let the day perish wherein I was created,' but, let the day perish wherein I was born. For man was created in a day of righteousness, but now he is born in a time of guilt; for Adam was created, but Cain was the first man that was born. What then is it to curse the day of his birth, but to say plainly, 'May the day of change perish, and the light of eternity burst forth?'

5. But inasmuch as we are used to bid perish in two ways, (for it is in one way that we bid perish, when we desire to anything that it should no longer be, and in another way that we bid it perish, when we desire that it should be ill therewith,) the words that are added concerning this day, *Let a cloud dwell upon it: let it be enveloped in bitterness* [Vulg.]; clearly show, that he wishes not this day to perish in such sort as not to be, but so that it may go ill with it; for that can never be 'enveloped in bitterness,' which is so wholly destroyed as not to be at all. Now this period of our mutable condition is not one day to perish, (i.e. to pass away,) in such a way, as to be in an evil plight, but so as to cease to be altogether, as the Angel bears witness in Holy Writ, saying, *By Him that liveth for ever and ever, that there should be time no longer.* [Rev. 10, 6] For though the Prophet hath it, *Their time shall endure for ever* [Ps. 81, 15], yet because time comes to an end with every moment, he designated their coming to an end by the name of 'time,' showing that without every way ending they come to an end, that are severed from the joys of the inward Vision. Therefore because this period of our mortal condition does not so perish as to be in evil plight, but so as not to be at all, we must enquire what it means that he desires it may perish, not so that it may not be, but that it may be in ill condition. Now a human soul, or an Angelic spirit, is in such sort immortal, that it is capable of dying, in such sort mortal, that it can never die. For of living happily, it is deprived whether by sin or by punishment; but its essential living it never loses, either by sin or punishment: it ceases from a mode of living, but it is not even by dying susceptible of an end to every mode of being. So that I might say in a word, that it is both immortally mortal, and mortally immortal. Whereas then he wishes that the day may perish, and soon after it is said that it is 'to be enveloped in bitterness,' whom should we think the holy man would express by

the name of 'day,' except the Apostate Spirit, who in dying subsists in the life of essential being? Whom destruction does not withdraw from life, in that in the midst of pains eternal an immortal death kills, while it preserves, him whose perishing, fallen as he is already from the glory of his state of bliss, is still longed for no otherwise than that being held back by the punishments, which he deserves, he may lose even the liberty of tempting.

6. Yea, he presents himself as the day, in that he allures by prosperity; and his end is in the blackness of night, for that he leads to adversity; thus he displayed day when he said, *In the day ye eat thereof, then your eyes shall be opened, and ye shall be as Gods*; [Gen. 3, 5] but he brought on night, when he led to the blackness of mortality; the day, therefore, is the proffered promise of better things, but the night is the very manifested experience of evils. The old enemy is the day, as by nature created good, but he is the night, as by his own deserts sunk down into darkness. He is day, when by promising good things he disguises himself as an Angel of light to the eyes of men, as Paul witnesses, saying, *For Satan himself is transformed as an angel of light*; [2 Cor. 11, 14] but he is night, when he obscures the minds of those that consent to him with the darkness of error. Well then may the holy man, who in his own sorrows bewailed the case of the whole human race, and who viewed nothing in any wise special to himself in his own special affliction, well may he recal to mind the original cause of sin, and soften the pain of the infliction by considering its justice. Let him look at man, and see whence and whither he has fallen, and exclaim, *Let the day perish wherein he was born, and the night in which it was said, There is a man child conceived*. As if he said in plain words, 'Let the hope perish, which the apostate Angel held forth, who, disguising himself as day, shone forth with the promise of a divine nature, but yet again showing himself as night, brought a cloud over the light of our immortal nature. Let our old enemy perish, who displayed the light of promises, and bestowed the darkness of sin; who as it were presented himself as day by his flattery, but led us to a night of utter darkness by sealing our hearts with blindness.' It proceeds;

Ver. 4. Let that day be turned into darkness.

ii. 7. This day shines as it were in the hearts of men, when the persuasions of his wickedness are thought to be for our good, and what they are within is never seen; but when his wickedness is seen as it is, the day of false promises is as it were dimmed by a kind of darkness spread before the eyes of our judgment, in this respect, that such as he is in intrinsic worth, such he is perceived to be in his beguilement, and so 'the day becomes darkness,' when we take as adverse even the very things, which he holds out as advantageous whilst persuading them. 'The day becomes darkness,' when our old enemy, even when lurking under the cloak of his blandishments, is perceived by us to be such as he is when ravening after us, that he may never mock us with feigned prosperity, as though by the light of day, dragging us by real misery to the darkness of sin. It proceeds;

Let not God regard it from above, neither let the light shine upon it.

8. As Almighty God was able to create good things out of **iii.**
nothing, so, when He would, He also restored the good things that were lost, by the mystery of His Incarnation. Now he had made two creations to contemplate Himself, viz. the Angelic and the human, but Pride smote both, and dashed them from the erect station of native uprightness. But one had the clothing of the flesh, the other bore no infirmity derived from the flesh. For an angelical being is spirit alone, but man is both spirit and flesh. Therefore when the Creator took compassion to work redemption, it was meet that He should bring back to Himself that creature, which, in the commission of sin, plainly had something of infirmity; and it was also meet that the apostate Angel should be driven down to a farther depth, in proportion as he, when he fell from resoluteness in standing fast, carried about him no infirmity of the flesh. And hence the Psalmist, when he was telling of the Redeemer's compassionating mankind, at the same time justly set forth the cause itself of His mercy, in these words, *And he remembered that they were but flesh* [Ps. 78, 39]. As if he said, 'Whereas He beheld their infirmities, so He would not punish their offences with severity.' There is yet another respect wherein it was both fitting that man when lost should be recovered, and impossible for the spirit that set himself up to be recovered, namely, in that the Angel fell by his own wickedness, but the wickedness of another brought man down. Forasmuch then as mankind is brought to the light of repentance by the coming of the Redeemer, but the apostate Angel is not recalled by any hope of pardon, or with any amendment of conversion, to the light of a restored estate, it may

well be said, *Let not God regard it from above, neither let the light shine upon it*. As though it were plainly expressed, 'For that he hath himself brought on the darkness, let him bear without end what himself has made, nor let him ever recover the light of his former condition, since he parted with it even without being persuaded thereto.' It goes on;

Let darkness and the shadow of death stain it.

iv. 9. By 'the shadow of death,' we must understand 'oblivion,' for as death ends life, so oblivion puts an end to memory. As therefore the apostate Angel is delivered over to eternal oblivion, he is overclouded with the shadow of death. Therefore let him say, *Let darkness and the shadow of death stain it*; i.e. 'So let him be overwhelmed with the blindness of error, that he never more rise up again to the light of repentance by recollection of God's regard. The words follow;

Let a cloud dwell upon it [Vulg.]*: and let it be enveloped in bitterness.*

v. 10. It is one thing that our old enemy suffers now, bound by the chains of his own wickedness, and another that he will have to suffer at the end. For in that he is fallen from the rank of the interior light, he now confounds himself within with the darkness of error; and hereafter he is involved in bitterness, in that by desert of a voluntary blindness, he is tortured with the eternal torments of hell. Let it be said then, 'What is it that he, who has lost the calm of the light interior, now endures as the foretaste of his final punishment? *Let a cloud dwell upon it*. Moreover let that subsequent doom be added also, which preys upon him without end.' *Let him be folded up in bitterness*; for everything folded up, shows, as it were, no end anywhere, for as it shows not where it begins, so neither does it discover where it leaves off. The old enemy then is said to be folded up in bitterness, in that not only every kind of punishment, but punishment too without end or limit awaits his Pride; which same doom then receives its beginning when the righteous Judge cometh at the last Judgment; and hence it is well added,

Ver. 6. As for that night, let a dark whirlwind seize upon it.

vi. 11. For it is written, *Our God shall come, and shall not keep silence; a fire shall devour before Him, and it shall be very tempestuous round about Him.* [Ps. 50, 3] Thus [Vulg. *tenebrosusturbo*] a dark whirlwind seizes upon that night, in that the apostate Angel is by that fearful tempest carried off from before the strict Judge to suffer eternal woe; thus this night is seized by a whirlwind, in that his blind Pride is smitten with a strict visitation. It goes on;

Let it not be joined unto the days of the year; let it not come into the number of the months.

12. By year we understand not inapplicably the preaching of supreme grace. For as in a year the period is completed by a connected series of days, so in heavenly grace is a complex life of virtue made complete. By a year too we may understand the multitude of the redeemed. For as the year is produced by a number of days, so by the assemblage of all the righteous there results that countless sum of the Elect. Now Isaiah foretells this year of a completed multitude, in these words; *The Spirit of the Lord is upon Me, because the Lord hath anointed Me to preach good tidings unto the meek: He hath sent Me to bind up the brokenhearted, to proclaim liberty to the captives, and the opening of the prison to them that are bound; To proclaim the acceptable year of the Lord* [Is. 61, 1]. For 'the acceptable year of the Lord is proclaimed,' in that the future multitude of the faithful is foretold as destined to be illumined with the light of truth. Now what is meant by 'the days,' but the several minds of the Elect? What by the months, but their several Churches, which constitute one Catholic Church? *So then let not that night be joined unto the days of the year, neither let it come into the number of the months.* For our old enemy, hemmed in with the darkness of his pride, sees indeed the coming of the Redeemer, but never returns to pardon with the Elect. And hence it is written, *For verily He took not on Him the nature of Angels, but He took on Him the seed of Abraham* [Heb. 2, 16]. For it was on this account that our Redeemer was made not Angel, but Man, because He must needs be made of the same nature as that which He redeemed, that He might at once let go the lost angel, by not taking his nature, and restore man, by taking his nature in Himself. These days, which abide in the interior light, may also be taken for the angelic spirits, and the months, for their orders and dignities. For every single spirit, in that he shines, is a 'day,' but as they are distinguished by certain set dignities, so that there are some that are Thrones, some Dominions, some Principalities, and some Powers, **vii.**

according to this distribution of ranks, they are entitled 'months.' But forasmuch as our old enemy is never brought back to merit light, and is never restored to the order of the ranks above, he is neither reckoned in the days of the year, nor in the months. For the blindness of the pride that he has been guilty of is so settled upon him, that he no more returns to those heavenly ranks of interior brightness. He no longer now mixes with the ranks of light that stand firm and erect, for that, in due of his own darkness, he is ever borne downwards to the depth. And for that he remains for ever an alien to the company of that heavenly land, it is yet further justly added,

Ver. 7. Lo, let that night be solitary, let it be worthy of no praise.

viii. 13. That night is made solitary, in that it is divided by an eternal separation from the company of the land above. Yet this may be also taken in another sense, viz. that he loses man, whom he had made his fellow in ruin, and that the enemy perishes alone together with his body [i.e. the wicked], while many that he had destroyed are restored by the Redeemer's grace. The night then is made solitary, when they that are Elect being raised up, our old enemy is made over alone to the eternal flames of hell. And it is well said, *Let it be worthy of no praise.* For when mankind, encompassed with the darkness of error, took stones for gods, in this, that they worshipped idols, what else did they but praise the deeds of their seducer? Hence Paul rightly remarks, *We know that an idol is nothing. But I say that the things which the Gentiles sacrifice, they sacrifice to devils.* [1 Cor. 8, 4; 10, 20] How else then is it with those that have bowed themselves to the worship of idols, but that they have 'praised the darkness of night?' But, lo! we see now that that night is known to be unworthy 'of any praise,' since now the worship of idols is condemned by the human race redeemed; and that 'night is left solitary',' in that there is none that goeth with the damned apostate spirit to suffer torments. It proceeds;

Ver. 8. Let them curse it that curse the day, that are ready to rouse up Leviathan.

ix. 14. In the old translation it is not so written, but, *Let him curse it that hath cursed the day, even him who shall take the great whale* [so LXX]. By which words it is clearly shown, that the destruction of Antichrist, to be at the end of the world, is foreseen by the holy man. For the evil spirit, who by rights is night, at the end of the world passes himself for the day, in that he shows himself to men as God, while he takes to himself deceitfully the brightness of the Deity, *and exalteth himself above all that is called God, or that is worshipped*. [2 Thess. 2, 4] The same therefore that curseth the day, curseth the night; in that He at this present time destroys his wickedness, Who will then by the light of His coming also extinguish the power of his strength. And hence it is well subjoined, *Who will take the great whale*. For the strength of this whale is taken as a prey in the water, in that the wiliness of our old enemy is overcome by the Sacrament of Baptism.

15. But that which in the Old Translation is spoken of the Author of all things, in this translation, which we get from the Hebrew and Arabian tongues, is related of His elect Angels. For it is of them that it is said, *Let them curse it that curse the day*. For that spirit in his pride desired to pass himself for day even with the Angelic Powers, at that time when as though in the power of the Deity he exalted himself above the rest, and drew after him such countless legions to destruction. But they, truly, who with humble spirits stood firm in the Author of their being, when they saw there was night in his perverse ways; trod under foot the day of his brightness by thinking humbly of themselves, who do now point out to us the darkness of his disguise, and show us how we should contemn his false glare. So let it be said of the night of darkness, which blinds the eyes of human frailty; *Let them curse it that curse the day*; i.e. 'Let those elect Spirits by condemning denounce the darkness of his erring ways, who see the grandeur of his shining already from the first a deceit.' And it is well added, *Who are ready to rouse up* [Vulg. thus] *Leviathan*. For 'Leviathan' is interpreted to be 'their addition.' Whose 'addition,' then, but the 'addition' of men? And it is properly styled 'their addition;' for since by his evil suggestion he brought into the world the first sin, he never ceases to add to it day by day by prompting to worse things.

Or indeed it is in reproach that he is called Leviathan, i.e. styled 'the addition of men.' For he found them immortal in Paradise, but by promising the Divine nature to immortal beings, he as it were pledged himself to add somewhat to them beyond what they were. But whilst with flattering lips he declared that he would give what they had not, he robbed them cunningly even of what they had. And hence the [al. The Lord by the P.] Prophet describes this same Leviathan in these words, *Leviathan, the bar-serpent* [Vulg. *serpentem vectem*]*: even Leviathan that crooked serpen*t. For this Leviathan in the thing, which he engaged to add to man, crept nigh to him with tortuous windings; for while he falsely promised things impossible, he really stole away even those which were possible. But we must enquire why he that had spoken of 'a serpent,' subjoining in that very place the epithet 'crooked,' inserted the word 'bar,' except perhaps that in the flexibility of the serpent we have a yielding softness, and in 'the bar,' the hardness of an obstinate nature. In order then to mark him to be both hard and soft, he both calls him 'a bar' and 'a serpent.' For by his malicious nature he is hard, and by his flatteries he is soft; so he is called 'a bar [E.V. *Piercing*],' in that he strikes even to death; and 'a serpent,' in that he insinuates himself softly by deceitful acts.

16. Now this Leviathan at this present time elect Spirits of the Angelic host imprison close in the bottomless pit. Whence it is written, *And I saw an Angel come down from heaven, having the key of the bottomless pit, and a great chain in his hand; and he laid hold on the dragon, that old serpent, which is the Devil and Satan, and bound him a thousand years*; [Rev. 20, 1–3] and cast him into the bottomless pit. Yet at the end of the world they call him back to more open conflicts, and let him loose against us in all his power. And hence it is written again in the same place; *Till the thousand years should be fulfilled, and after that he must be loosed*. For that apostate angel, whereas he was created so that he shone preeminent among all the other legions of the Angels, fell so low by setting himself up, that he is now prostrated beneath the rule of the orders of Angels that stand erect, whether that being put in chains by them, as they minister to our welfare, he should now lie buried from sight, or that they at that time setting him free for our probation, he should be let loose to put forth all his power against us. Therefore, because the proud apostate Spirit is restrained by those elect Spirits, who being humble would not follow him, and, they being the executioners, it is ordered, that he shall one day be recalled for the purpose of an open conflict, that he may be utterly destroyed, let it be well said, who are ready to rouse up Leviathan; but forasmuch as the artful adversary is not yet raised to wage open

war, let him show how that night now by hidden influences overshadows the minds of some men. It follows;

Ver. 9. Let the stars be darkened with the shadow thereof.

17. In Holy Scripture by the title of stars we have set forth x.
sometimes the righteousness of the Saints which shineth in the darkness of this life, and sometimes the false pretence of hypocrites, who display all the good that they do, that they may win the praise of men; for if well doers were not stars, Paul would never say to his disciples, *In the midst of a crooked and perverse 11.ation, among whom ye shine like lights in the world.* [Phil. 2, 15] Again, if among those that seem to act aright, there were not some that sought by their conduct to win the reward of man's esteem, John would never have seen stars falling from heaven, where he says, *The dragon put forth his tail, and drew the third part of the stars of heaven.* [Rev. 12, 4] Now a portion of the stars is drawn by the dragon's tail, in that, in the last efforts of Antichrist to win men, some that appear to shine will be carried off. For to draw the stars of heaven to the earth is by the love of earth to involve those in the froward ways of open error, who seem to be devoted to the pursuit of the heavenly life. For there are that as it were shine before the eyes of men by extraordinary deeds; but forasmuch as these very deeds are not the offspring of a pure heart, being struck blind in their secret thoughts, they are clouded with the darkness of this night, and these often lose the more outward deeds, which they do not practise with any purity of heart. And so because the night is permitted to prevail, whenever even amidst good works the purpose of the heart is not cleansed, let it be said with justice, *Let the stars be dark with the shadow thereof*; i.e. 'let the dark malice of our old enemy prevail against those who in the sight of men show as bright by good works, and that light of praise, which in the eye of man's judgment they had taken, let them lay aside;' for they are 'overshadowed with the darkness of night,' when their life is brought to shame by open error, so that verily they may also appear outwardly such in practice, as they do not shrink from appearing to the Divine eye in their secret hearts. It proceeds;

Ver. 9. Let it look for light, but have none; neither let it see the dawning of the day.

18. In the Gospel Truth declares, *I am the light of the world.* xi.

[John 8, 12] Now as this same Saviour of us men is one Person with the assembly of the good, for He is Himself the Head of the Body, and we all are the Body of this Head, so our old enemy is one person with the whole company of the damned; in that he as a head out-tops them all in iniquity, and they, whilst they minister in the things he prompts, hold fast to him like a body joined below to the head. And so it is meet that all that is said of this night, i.e. of our old enemy, should be applied to his body, i.e. to all wicked persons. Wherefore because our Redeemer is the light of mankind, how is it that it is said of this night, *Let it look for light, and have none*; but that there are some, who exhibit themselves as maintaining by words that faith, which they undo by works? Of whom Paul says, *They profess that they know God, but in works they deny Him*; [Tit. 1, 16] with these, indeed, either the things which they do are bad, or they follow after good deeds with no good heart. For they do not seek everlasting rewards as the fruit of their actions, but transitory partiality. And yet, because they hear themselves praised as Saints, they believe themselves to be really Saints, and in proportion as they account themselves unblameable according to the esteem they are in with numbers, they await in greater security the Day of strict account. Of whom the Prophet well says, *Woe unto you that desire the day of the Lord*. [Amos 5, 18] To these blessed Job utters the sentence due to them, saying in the temper of one foretelling the thing, and not as the wish of one that desired it, *Let it look for light, but have none*. For that night, I mean the adversary of darkness, in his members doth look for the light, but seeth none; in that whether it be they who retain the faith without works, these, trusting that they may be saved at the final Judgment by right of the same faith, will find their hope prove vain, because by their life they have undone the faith, which in the confession of the lips they have maintained; or they, who for the sake of human applause make a display of themselves in doing well, they vainly look for a reward of their good deeds at the hand of the Judge, when He cometh; for that whereas they do them out of regard to the notoriety of praise, they have already had their reward from the lips of men. As the Truth testifies, Which says, *Verily I say unto you, they have their reward* [Matt. 6, 2. 5.]; and here it is justly added, *Neither let it see the dawning of the day*.

19. For the dawn is the title of the Church, which is changed from the darkness of its sins into the light of righteousness. And hence the

Spouse, admiring her in the Song of Solomon, says, *Who is she that goeth forth as the morning arising?* [Cant. 6, 10] for like the dawn doth the Church of 'the Elect arise, in that she quits the darkness of her former iniquity, and converts herself into the radiance of new light. Therefore in that light, which is manifested at the coming of the strict Judge, the body of our enemy when condemned seeth no day-spring of the rising dawn, in that when the strict Judge shall come, every sinner, being overlaid with the blackness of his own deserts, knows not with what wondrous splendour Holy Church rises into the interior light of the heart. For then the mind of the Elect is transported on high, to be illuminated with the rays of the Divine Nature, and in the degree that it is penetrated with the light of that Countenance, it is lifted above itself in the refulgence of grace. Then doth Holy Church become a full dawn, when she parts wholly and for ever with the darkness of her state of mortality and ignorance. Thus at the Judgment she is still the dawn, but in the Kingdom she is become the day. For though together with the renewal of our bodies she already begins to behold the light at the Judgment, yet her vision thereof is more fully consummated in the Kingdom. Thus the *rising of the dawn* is the commencement of the Church in light, which the reprobate can never see, because they are closed in upon and forced down to darkness by the weight of their evil deeds from the sight of the Righteous Judge. And hence it is rightly said by the Prophet, *Let the wicked be taken out of the way, that he see not the glory of God.* [Is. 26, 10. LXX] It is hence that these words are uttered by the Psalmist concerning this dawn, *Thou shalt hide them in the secret of Thy Presence from the pride of men.* [Ps. 31, 20] For every Elect one at the Judgment is hid in the countenance of the Godhead in interior vision, whereas the blindness of the reprobate without is banished and confounded by the strict visitation of justice.

20. And this too we not irrelevantly interpret with reference to the present time likewise, if we minutely search the hearts of dissemblers. For the proud and hypocritical look on the deeds of the good on the outside, and they find that such are commended by men for their doings, and they admire their high repute, and they see that these receive praises for their good deeds, but they do not see how studiously they eschew such praises; they regard the overt acts, but are ignorant that these proceed from the principle of the interior hope alone. For all that shine with the true light of righteousness are

first changed from the darkness of the inward purpose of the heart, so that they wholly forsake the interior dimness of earthly coveting, and entirely turn their hearts to the desire of the light above, lest while they seem to be full of light to others, they be in darkness to themselves; thus persons that assume, because they regard the deeds of the righteous, but do not survey their hearts, imitate them in the things from whence they may obtain applause without, but not in the things whereby they may inwardly arise to the light of righteousness; and they as it were are blind to see the dayspring of the rising dawn, because they do not think it worth their while to regard the religious mind's intent.

Allegorical

21. The holy man, who was filled with the virtue of the prophetic Spirit, may also have his eye fixed upon the faithlessness of Judaea at the coming of the Redeemer, and in these words he may be speaking prophetically of the mischievous effects of her blindness, as though in the character of one expressing a wish, so as to say, *Let it look for light, but have none; neither let it see the dawning of the day*. For Judaea 'looked for the light but had none;' since by prophecy she waited indeed for the Redeemer of Man that should come, but never knew Him when He came; and the eyes of the mind, which she opened wide to the expectation, she closed to the presence of the Light; neither did she see the dayspring of the rising dawn, in that she scorned to pay homage to those first beginnings of Holy Church, and while she supposed her to be undone by the deaths of her members, was ignorant to what strength she was attaining. But as, when speaking of the faithless, he signified the members of the wicked head, he again turns his discourse to the head of the wicked itself, saying,

Ver. 10. Because it shut not up the doors of my mother's womb, nor hid sorrow from mine eyes.

xii.

22. What the womb of his mother is to each individual man, that the primary abode in Paradise became to the whole human race. For from it came forth the family of man as it were from the womb, and tending to the increase of the race, as if to the growth of the body, it issued forth without. There our conception was cemented, where the Man, the origin of mankind, had his abode, but the serpent opened the mouth of this womb, in that by

his cunning persuading he broke asunder the decree of heaven in man's heart. The serpent opened the mouth of this womb, in that he burst the barriers of the mind which were fortified with admonitions from above. Let the holy man then in the punishment which he suffers, cast the eyes of his mind far back to the sin. Let him mourn for this, which the neglect of darkness, that is, the dark suggestions of our old enemy lodged in man's mind; for this, that man's mind consented to his cunning suggestions to his own betrayal, and let him say, *Because it shut not up the doors of my mother's womb, nor hid sorrow from mine eyes.* Nor let this disturb us, that he complains that he only did not shut up, whom he abhors for having opened the gate of Paradise. For 'he opened,' he calls *shut not up*; and 'he entailed it,' *nor hid sorrow from me.* For he would as it were have 'hid sorrow,' if he had kept quiet, and have 'shut up,' if he had forborne from bursting in. For he is weighing well who it is he speaks of, and he reckons that it would have been as if the evil spirit had bestowed gains upon us if he had only not entailed losses upon our heads. Thus we say of robbers that they give their prisoners their lives, if they do not take them.

Moral 23. It is well to go over these points again from the beginning, and according to what we remark in practice in the present life, to review it in a moral sense. Blessed Job, observing how presumptuously mankind, after his soul fell from its original state, was lifted up in prosperity, and with what dismay it was dashed by adverse fortune, falls back in imagination to that unalterable state which he might have kept in Paradise, and in what a miserable light he beheld the fallen condition of our mortal state of being, so chequered with adversity and prosperity, he showed by cursing the same in these words;

Ver. 3. Let the day perish wherein I was born; and the night wherein it was said, There is a man child conceived.

24. It seems as it were like day, when the good fortune of this world smiles upon us, but it is a day that ends in night, for temporal prosperity often leads to the darkness of affliction. This day of good fortune the Prophet had condemned, when he said, *Neither have I desired man's day* ['*diem hominis*' Vulg.], *Thou knowest it.* [Jer. 17, 16] And this night our Lord declared He was to suffer at the final close

of His Incarnation, when he declared by the Psalmist as if in the past, *My reins also instructed me in the night season.* [Ps. 16, 7] But by 'the day' may be understood the pleasures of sin, and by 'the night' the inward blindness, whereby man suffers himself to be brought down to the ground in the commission of sin. And therefore he wishes the day may perish, that all the flattering arts which are seen in sin, by the strong hand of justice interposing, may be brought to nought. He wishes also that the 'night may perish,' that what the blinded mind executes even in yielding consent, she may put away by the castigation of penance.

25. But we must enquire why man is said to be born in 'the day' and conceived in 'the night?' Holy Scripture uses the title 'man' in three ways, viz, sometimes in respect of nature, sometimes of sin, sometimes of frailness. Now man is so called in respect of nature, as where it is written, *Let Us make man after Our image and likeness.* [Gen. 1, 26] He is called man in respect of sin, as where it is written, *I have said, Ye are all gods, and all of you are children of the Most High: but ye shall die like men.* [Ps. 82, 6. 7.] As though he had expressed it plainly, 'ye shall perish like transgressors.' And hence Paul says, *For whereas there is among you envying and strife and divisions, are ye not carnal, and walk as men?* [1 Cor. 3, 3] As though he had said, 'Ye that carry about minds at variance, do ye not still sin, in the spirit of faulty human nature?' He is called man, in relation to his weakness, as where it is written, *Cursed be the man that trusteth in man.* [Jer. 17, 5] As if he had said in plain words, 'in weakness.' Thus man is born in the day, but he is conceived in the night, in that he is never caught away by the delightfulness of sin, until he is first made weak by the voluntary darkness of his mind. For he first becomes blind in the understanding, and then he enslaves himself to damnable delight. Let it be said then, *Let the day perish wherein I was born, and the night wherein it was said, There is a man child conceived*: i.e. 'Let the delight perish, which has hurried man into sin, and the unguarded frailness of his mind, whereby he was blinded even to the very darkness of consenting to evil. For while man does not heedfully mark the allurements of pleasure, he is even carried headlong into the night of the foulest practices. We must watch then with minds alive, that when sin begins to caress, the mind may perceive to what ruin she is being dragged. And hence the words are fitly added,

Ver. 4. Let that day be darkness.

26. For 'the day becomes darkness,' when in the very commencement of the enjoyment, we see to what an end of ruin sin is hurrying us. We 'turn the day into darkness,' whenever by severely chastising ourselves, we turn to bitter the very sweets of evil enjoyment by the keen laments of penance, and, when we visit it with weeping, whereinsoever we sin in gratification in our secret hearts. For because no believer is ignorant that the thoughts of the heart will be minutely examined at the Judgment, as Paul testifieth, saying, *Their thoughts the meanwhile accusing or else excusing one another*; [Rom. 2, 15] searching himself within, he examines his own conscience without sparing before the Judgment, that the strict Judge may come now the more placably disposed, in that He sees his guilt, which He is minded to examine, already chastised according to the sin. And hence it is well added, **xiv.**

Let not God require it from above.

27. God requires the things, which He searches out in executing judgment upon them. He does not require those, which He so pardons as to let them be unpunished henceforth in His own Judgment. And so 'this day,' i.e. this enjoyment of sin, will not be required by the Lord, if it be visited with self-punishment of our own accord, as Paul testifies, when he says, *For if we would judge ourselves, we should not be judged of the Lord.* [1 Cor. 11, 31] 'God's requiring our day,' then, is His proceeding against our souls at the Judgment by a strict examination of every instance of taking pleasure in sin, in which same 'requiring' He then smites him the harder, whom He finds to have been most soft in sparing himself. And it follows well, *Neither let the light shine upon it*. For the Lord, appearing at the Judgment, illumines with His light all that He then convicts of sin. For what is not then brought to remembrance of the Judge, is as it were veiled under a kind of obscurity. So it is written, *But all things that are reproved are made manifest by the light*. [Eph. 5, 13] It is as though a certain darkness hid the sins of penitents, of whom the Prophet says, *Blessed is he whose transgression is forgiven, whose sin is covered.* [Ps. 32, 1] Therefore, as everything that is veiled is as it were hidden in darkness, that which is not searched out in vengeance, is not illumined with light at the Day of final account. **xv.**

For all those actions of ours, which He would not then visit with justice, the mercy of God in wotting of them still hideth in some sort from itself, but all is displayed in light, that is at that time manifest in the sight of all men. *Let*, then, *this day be darkness*, in this way, viz. that by penance we may smite the evil that we do. *Let not the Lord require this day, neither let the light shine upon it*, in this way, viz. that while we smite our own sin, He may not Himself fall thereupon with the visitations of the Final Judgment.

28. But the Judge will come Himself to pierce all things, and strike all things to the core. And because He is every where present, there is no place to flee to, where He is not found. But forasmuch as He is appeased by the tears of self-correction, he alone obtains a hiding-place from His face, who after the commission of a sin hides himself from Him now in penance. And hence it is with propriety yet further added of this day of enjoyment,

Ver. 7. Let darkness and the shadow of death stain it.

xvi. 29. Then indeed darkness stains the day, when the delight of our inclinations is smitten through with the inflictions of penance. By darkness moreover may be signified secret decisions. For what we see in the light we know, but in the dark we either discern nothing at all, or our eyes are bewildered with an uncertain sight. Secret decrees then are like a certain kind of darkness before our eyes, being utterly inscrutable to us. And hence it is written of God, *He made darkness His secret place;* [Ps. 18, 11] and we know well that we do not deserve pardon, but, by the grace of God preventing us, we are freed from our sins by His secret counsels. *Darkness*, therefore, *stains the day*, when the joy of gratification, which is a proper subject of tears, is in mercy hidden from that ray of just wrath by His secret determinations. And here the words aptly follow, *and the shadow of death*.

30. For in Holy Scripture, the *shadow of death* is sometimes understood of oblivion of mind, sometimes of imitation of the devil, sometimes of the dissolution of the flesh. For the *shadow of death* is understood of the oblivion of the mind, in that, as has been said above, as death causes that that which it kills should no longer remain in life, so oblivion causes that whatsoever it seizes should no longer abide in the memory. And hence too, because John was coming to proclaim to the Hebrew people That God, Whom they had

forgotten, he is justly said by Zacharias, *to give light to them that sit in darkness and in the shadow of death*; for 'to sit in the shadow of death,' is to turn lifeless to the knowledge of the love of God in a state of oblivion. *The shadow of death* is taken to mean the imitating our old enemy. For, since he brought in death, he is himself called death, as John is witness, saying, *and his name is death*. [Rev. 6, 8] And so by *the shadow of death* is signified the imitating of him. For as the shadow is shaped according to the character of the body, so the actions of the wicked are cast in a figure of conformity to him. Hence when Isaiah saw that the Gentiles had fallen away after the likeness of our old enemy, and that they rose up again at the rising of the true Sun, he justly records, as though in the past, what his eyes beheld as certain in the future, saying, *They that dwell in the land of the shadow of death, upon them a great light hath shined*. Moreover, *the shadow of death* is taken for the dissolution of the flesh, in that, as that is the true death whereby the soul is separated from God, so the shadow of death is that whereby the flesh is separated from the soul. And hence it is rightly said by the Prophet in the words of the Martyrs, *Though Thou hast sore broken us in the place of dragons, and covered us with the shadow of death*. [Ps. 44, 19] For those, who, we know, die not in the spirit, but only in the flesh, can in no wise say that they are 'covered with the true death,' but *with the shadow of death*.

31. How is it then that blessed Job demands *the shadow of death*, for putting out the day of evil enjoyment, but that for the obliterating of our sins in God's sight he calls for the Mediator between God and man, who should undertake for us the death of the flesh alone, and Who by the shadow of His own death, should do away the true death of transgressors? For He comes to us, who were held in the bands of death, both of the spirit and of the flesh, and His own single Death He reckoned to our account, and our two deaths, which He found, He dissolved. For if He had Himself undertaken both, He would never have set us free from either. But He took one sort in mercy, and condemned them both with justice. He joined His own single Death to our twofold death, and by dying He vanquished that double death of ours. And hence it was not without reason that He lay in the grave for one day and two nights, namely, in that He added the light of His own single Death to the darkness of our double death. He, then, that took for our sakes the death of the flesh alone, underwent *the shadow of death*, and buried from the eyes of God the

sin that we have done. Therefore let it be truly said, *Let darkness and the shadow of death stain it.* As though it were said in plain words; 'Let Him come, Who, that He may snatch from the death of the flesh and of the spirit, us, that are debtors thereto, may, though no debtor, discharge the death of the flesh.' But since the Lord lets no sin go unpunished, for either we visit it ourselves by lamenting it, or God by judging it, it remains that the mind should ever have a watchful eye to the amendment of itself. Therefore, in whatever particular each person sees that he is succoured by mercy, he must needs wipe out the stains thereof in the confession of it. And hence it is fitly added,

Let a shade dwell upon it.

xvii. 32. For because the eye is perplexed in the *shade*, therefore the perplexity of our mind in penitence is itself called *shade*, for as the shade obscures the light of day with a mass of clouds, so confusion overclouds the mind with troubled thoughts. Of which it is said by one, *There is a shame which is glory and grace.* [Ecclus. 4, 21] For when in repenting we recall our misdoings to remembrance, we are at once confounded with heaviness and sorrow, the throng of thoughts clamours vociferously in our breast, sorrow wears, anxiety wastes us, the soul is turned to woe, and, as it were, darkened with the shade of a kind of cloud. Now this *shade* of confusion had oppressed the minds of those to their good, to whom Paul said, *What fruit had ye then in those things whereof ye are now ashamed?* [Rom. 6, 21] *Let shade*, then, *seize* this day of sin, i.e. 'Let the chastening of penance with befitting sorrow discompose the flattery of sin.' And hence it is added with fitness,

Let it be enfolded in bitterness.

xviii. 33. For the day is enfolded in bitterness, when, upon the soul returning to knowledge, the inflictions of penance follow upon the caresses of sin. We 'enfold the day in bitterness,' when we regard the punishments that follow the joys of forbidden gratification, and pour tears of bitter lamenting around them. For whereas what is folded up is covered on every side, we wish 'the day to be folded in bitterness,' that each man may mark on every side the ills that threaten crooked courses, and may cleanse the wantonness of self-gratification by the tears of bitter sorrow.

34. But if we hear that day, which we have rendered the 'gratification of sin,' assailed with so many imprecations, that, surely, our tears poured around it may expiate whatsoever sin the soul is become guilty of by being touched with gratification through negligence, with what visitings of penitence is the night of that day to be stricken, i.e. the actual consent to sin? For as it is a less fault when the mind is carried away in delight by the influence of the flesh, yet by the resistance of the Spirit offers violence to its sense of delight; so it is a more heinous and complete wickedness not only to be attracted to the fascination of sin by the feeling of delight, but to pander to it by yielding consent. Therefore the mind must be cleansed from defilement by being wrung harder with the hand of penitence, in proportion as it sees itself to be more foully stained by the yielding of the consent. And hence it is fitly subjoined,

Ver. 6. As for that night, let a black tempest seize it.

35. For the awakened spirit of sorrow is like a kind of tempestuous whirlwind. For when a man understands what sin he has committed, when he minutely considers the wickedness of his evil doings, he clouds the mind with sorrow, and the air of quiet joy being agitated, as it were, he sweeps away all the inward tranquillity of his breast, by the whirlwind of penitence. For unless the heart, returning to the knowledge of itself, were broken by such a whirlwind, the Prophet would never have said, *Thou breakest the ships of Tarshish with a strong wind.* [Ps. 48, 7] For *Tarshish* is rendered, 'the exploring of joy.' But when the strong blast of penitence seizes the mind, it disturbs therein all the 'explorings' after a censurable joy, that it now takes pleasure in nought but to weep, minds nought but what may fill it with affright. For it sets before the eyes, on the one hand, the strictness of justice, on the other the deserts of sin, it sees what punishment it deserves, if the pitifulness of the sparing Hand be wanting, which is wont by present sorrowing to rescue from eternal woe. Therefore, 'a strong wind breaks the ships of Tarshish,' when a mighty force of compunction confounds, with wholesome terrors, our minds which have abandoned themselves to this world, like as to the sea. Let him say then, *As for that night, let a black tempest seize it*, i.e. let not the softness of secure ease cherish the commission of sin, but the bitterness of repentance burst on it in pious fury.

THE FIRST PART.

36. But we are to bear in mind, that when we leave sins unpunished, we are 'taken possession of by the night,' but when we correct those with the visitation of penitence, then we ourselves 'take possession of the night,' that we have made. And the sin of the heart is then brought into our right of possession, if it is repressed in its beginning. And hence it is said by the voice of God to Cain, harbouring evil thoughts, Thy *sin will lie at the door. But under thee shall be his desire, and thou shalt rule over him.* For 'sin lieth at the door,' when it is knocking in the thoughts, and 'the desire thereof is under,' and man 'ruleth over it,' if the wickedness of the heart, being looked to, be quickly put down, and before it grows to a state of hardness, be subdued by a strenuous opposition of the mind. Therefore that the mind may be quickly made sensible of its offence by repenting, and hold in under its authority the usurping power of sin, let it be rightly said, *As for that night let a black tempest seize it*; as though it were said in plain words, 'Lest the mind be the captive of sin, let it never leave a sin free from penance.' And because we have a sure hope that what we prosecute with weeping, will never be urged against us by the Judge to come, it is rightly added,

Let it not be joined unto the days of the year; let it not come into the number of the months.

XX. 37. The year of our illumination is then accomplished, when at the appearing of the Eternal Judge of Holy Church, the life of her pilgrimage is completed. She then receives the recompense of her labours, when, having finished this season of her warfare, she returns to her native country. Hence it is said by the Prophet, *Thou shalt bless the crown of the year with Thy goodness.* For the Crown of the year is as it were 'blessed,' when, the season of toil at an end, the reward of virtues is bestowed. But the days of this year are the several virtues, and its months the manifold deeds of those virtues. But observe, when the mind is erected in confidence, to have a good hope that, when the Judge comes, she will receive the reward of her virtues, all the evil things that she has done are also brought before the memory, and she greatly fears lest the strict Judge, Who comes to reward virtues, should also examine and weigh exactly those things, which have been unlawfully committed, and lest, when 'the year' is completed, the 'night' also be reckoned in. Let him then say of this night, *Let it not be joined unto the days of the year, let it not come into the number of the months.* As though he implored that strict Judge in such words as these; 'When, the time of Holy Church being completed, Thou shalt manifest Thyself for the final scrutiny, do Thou so recompense the gifts Thou hast vouchsafed, that Thou require not the evil we have committed. For if that 'night be joined unto the days of the year,' all that we have done is brought to nought, by the accounting of our iniquity. And the days of our virtues no longer shine, if they be overclouded in Thine eyes by the dark confusion of our night being added to the reckoning.'

38. But if we would not then have inquest made on our night, we must take especial care now to exercise a watchful eye in examining it, that no sin whatever may remain unpunished by us, that the froward mind be not bold to vindicate what it has done, and by that vindication add iniquity to iniquity. And hence it is rightly added,

Ver. 7. Lo, let that night be solitary, and worthy of no praise.

xxi.

39. There are some men that not only never bewail what they do, but who do not cease to uphold and applaud it, and verily a sin that is upheld, is doubled. And against this it is rightly said by one, *My son, hast thou sinned? add not again thereto.* [Ecclus. 21, 1] For he 'adds sin to sin,' who over and above maintains what he has done amiss; and he does not 'leave the night alone,' who adds the support of vindication also to the darkness of his fault. It is hence that the first man, when called in question concerning the 'night' of his error, would not have the same 'night' to be 'solitary,' in that while by that questioning he was called to repentance, he added the props of self-exculpation, saying, *The woman whom Thou gavest to be with me, she gave me of the tree, and I did eat*; i.e. covertly turning the fault of his transgression upon his Maker; as if he said, 'Thou gavest me occasion of transgressing, Who gavest me the woman.' It is hence that in the human race the branch of this sin is drawn out from that root so far as to this present time, that what is done amiss should be yet further maintained. Let him say then, *Let that light be solitary, and not worthy of any praise.* As though he besought in plain words, 'Let the fault that we have done remain alone, lest while it is praised and upheld, it bind us a hundredfold more in the sight of our Judge. We ought not indeed to have sinned, but would that, by not adding others, we would even leave those by themselves, which we have committed.'

THE FIRST PART.

40. But here it is to be impressed upon our minds, that he in a true sense bears hard upon his sin, whose heart is no longer set to the love of the present state of being by any longing for prosperity, who sees how deceitful are the caresses of this world, and reckons its smiles as a kind of persecution; and hence it is well added,

Ver. 8. Let them curse it that curse the day.

xxii. 41. As if he said in plain words; 'Let them strike the darkness of this night by truly repenting, who henceforth despise and tread upon the light of worldly prosperity.' For if we take 'the day,' for the gladness of delight, of this 'night' it is rightly said, *Let them curse it that curse the day.* In that, indeed, they do truly chastise the misdeeds committed with the visitations of penance, who are henceforth carried away by no sense of delight after deceitful goods. For of those whom other mischievous practices still delight, it is all false whereinsoever they are seen to bewail one set they have been guilty of. But if, as we have said above, we understand thereby the crafty suggestion of our old enemy, those are to be understood to curse the 'night,' that curse the 'day,' in that surely they all really punish their past sins, who in the mere flattering suggestion itself detect the snares of the malicious deceiver. But it is well added;

Who are ready to rouse up Leviathan.

xxiii. 42. For all they that with the spirit tread under foot the things which are of the world, and with a perfect bent of the mind desire the things that belong to God, *rouse up Leviathan* against themselves, in that they inflame his malice, by the incitements of their life and conduct. For those that are subject to his will, are as it were held in possession by him with an undisturbed light, and their tyrannizing king, as it were, enjoys a kind of security, while he rules their hearts with a power unshaken, but when the spirit of each man is quickened again to the longing after his Creator; when he gives over the sloth of negligence, and kindles the frost of former insensibility with the fire of holy love; when he calls to mind his innate freedom, and blushes that his enemy should keep him as his slave; because that enemy marks that he is himself contemned, and sees that the ways of God are laid hold of, he is stung that his captive struggles against him, and is at once fired with jealousy, at once pressed to the conflict, at once raises himself to urge countless temptations against the soul that withstands him, and stimulates himself in all the arts of mangling, that launching the darts of temptation he may pierce the heart, which he has long held with an undisputed title. For he slept, as it were, whilst he reposed at rest in the corrupt heart. But he is 'roused,' in challenging the fight, when he loses the right of wicked dominion. Let those then curse this light, that are ready to *rouse up Leviathan*, i.e. 'let all those gather themselves resolutely to encounter sin with the stroke of severe judgment, who are no wise afraid to rouse up Leviathan in his tempting of them.' For so it is written, *My son, if thou come to serve the Lord, stand in righteousness and in fear; and prepare thy soul for temptation*. For whosoever hastes to gird himself in the service of God, what else does he than prepare against the encounter of the old adversary, that the same man set at liberty may take blows in the strife, who, when slaving in captivity under tyrannizing power, was left at rest? But in this very circumstance that the mind is braced to meet the enemy, that some vices it has under its feet, and is striving against others, it sometimes happens that somewhat of sin is permitted to remain, nevertheless not so as to do any great injury.

43. And often the mind, which overcomes many and forcible oppositions, is unable to master one within itself, and that perchance a very little one, though it be most earnestly on the watch against it. Which doubtless is the effect of God's dispensation, lest being resplendent with virtue on all points, it be lifted up in self-elation, that while it sees in itself some trifling thing to be blamed, and yet has no power to subdue the same, it may never attribute the victory to itself, but to the Creator only, whereinsoever it has power to subdue with resolution; and hence it is well added,

Ver. 9. Let the stars thereof be overshadowed with darkness.

xxiv.

44. For the stars of this night are overshadowed with darkness, when even they that already shine with great virtues, still bear something of the dimness of sin, while they struggle against it, so that they even shine with great lustre of life, and yet still draw along with unwillingness some remains of the night. Which as we have said is done with this view, that the mind in advancing to the eminence of its righteousness, may through weakness be the better strengthened, and may in a more genuine manner shine

in goodness by the same cause, whereby, to the humbling of it, little defects overcloud it even against its will. And hence when the land of promise now won was to be divided to the people of Israel, the Gentile people of Canaan are not said to be slain, but to be made tributary to the tribe of Ephraim; as it is written, *The Canaanites dwelt in the midst of Ephraim under tribute.* [Jos. 16, 10. V.] For what does the *Canaanite*, a Gentile people, denote saving a fault? And oftentimes we enter the land of promise with great virtues, because we are strengthened by the inward hope that regards eternity. But while, amidst lofty deeds, we retain certain small faults, we as it were permit the Canaanite to dwell in our land. Yet he is made tributary, in that this same fault, which we cannot bring under, we force back by humility to answer the end of our wellbeing, that the mind may think meanly of itself even in its highest excellencies, in proportion as it fails to master by its own strength even the small things that it aims at. Hence it is well written again, *Now these are the nations which the Lord left, to prove Israel by them.* [Jud. 3, 1] For it is for this that some of our least faults are retained, that our fixed mind may ever be practising itself heedfully to the conflict, and not presume upon victory, forasmuch as it sees enemies yet alive within it, by whom it still dreads to be overcome. Thus Israel is trained by the Gentile people being reserved, in that the uplifting of our goodness meets with a check in some very little faults, and learns, in the little things that withstand it, that it does not subdue the greater ones by itself.

45. Yet this that is said, *Let the stars thereof be overshadowed with darkness*, may also be understood in another sense; for that *night*, viz. consent to the sin, which was derived to us by the transgression of our first parent, has smitten our mind's eye with such a dimness, that in this life's exile, beset by the darkness of its blinded state, with whatever force it strain after the light of eternity, it is unable to pierce through; for we are born condemned sinners after punishment has begun [*post poenam*], and we come into this life together with the desert of our death, and when we lift up the eye of the mind to that beam of light above, we grow dark with the mere dimness of our natural infirmity. And indeed many in this feeble condition of the flesh have been made strong by so great a force of virtue, that they could shine like stars in the world. Many in the darkness of this present life, while they show forth in themselves examples

above our reach, shine upon us from on high after the manner of stars; but with whatsoever brilliancy of practice they shine, with whatever fire of compunction they enkindle their hearts, it is plain that while they still bear the load of this corruptible flesh, they are unable to behold the light of eternity such as it is. So then let him say, *Let the stars thereof be overshadowed with darkness*; i.e. 'let even those in their contemplations still feel the darkness of the old night, of whom it appears that they already spread the rays of their virtues over the human race in the darkness of this life, seeing that, though they already spring to the topmost height in thought, they are yet pressed down below by the weight of the first offence. And hence it comes to pass that at the same time that without they give specimens of light, like the stars, yet within, being closely encompassed by the darkness of night, they fail to mount up to the assuredness of an immoveable vision. Now the mind is often so kindled and inflamed, that, though it be still set in the flesh, it is transported into God, and every carnal imagination brought under; and yet not so that it beholds God as He is, in that, as we have said, the weight of the original condemnation presses upon it in corruptible flesh. Oftentimes it longs to be swallowed up, just as it is, that if it might be so, it might attain the eternal life without the intervention of the bodily death. Hence Paul, when he ardently sought for the inward light, yet in some sort dreaded the evils [*damna*] of the outward death, said, *For we that are in this tabernacle do groan, being burthened, for that we would not be unclothed, but clothed upon, that mortality might be swallowed up of life*. [2 Cor. 5, 4. Vulg.] Therefore holy men long to see the true dawn, and, if it were vouchsafed, they would even along with the body attain that deep of inmost light. But with whatever ardour of purpose they may spring forth, the old night still weighs upon them, and those eyes of our corruptible flesh, which the crafty enemy has opened to concupiscence, the just Judge holds back from the view of His inward radiance. And hence it is well added,

Let it look for light and have none, neither let it see the dawning of the day.

46. For with whatever strength of purpose the mind, while yet in this pilgrimage, labours to see the Light as It is, the power is withheld, in that this is hidden from it by the blindness of its state under the curse. [Now the 'rising of the dawn' is the **XXV.**

brightness of inward truth, which ought to be ever new to us. And this the night assuredly seeth not, because our infirmity, blind by reason of sin, and still placed in the corruptible flesh, mounts not up to that light wherewith our fellow citizens above are already irradiated. For the rising of this dawn is in the interior, where the brightness of the Divine Nature is manifested ever new to the spirits of the Angels, and where that bliss of light is as it were ever dawning, which is never brought to an end.] [Note: this bracketed portion is found only in the Edition of Gussanville, and there without any notice to show where it comes from. (Ben.) It is not in the Oxford Mss.] But the *rising of the dawn*, is that new birth of the Resurrection, whereby Holy Church, with the flesh too raised up, rises to contemplate the sight of Eternity; for if the very Resurrection of our flesh were not as it were a kind of birth, Truth would never have said of it, *In the Regeneration, when the Son of Man shall sit upon the throne of His glory*. [Matt. 19, 28] This then, which He called a *regeneration*, He beheld as a *rising*. But with whatever virtue the Elect now shine forth, they cannot pierce to see what will be that glory of the new birth, wherewith they will then mount up together with the flesh to contemplate the sight of Eternity. Hence Paul says, *Eye hath not seen, nor ear heard, neither hath entered into the heart of man, the things which God hath prepared for them that love Him*. [1 Cor. 2, 9] Let him say then, *Let it look for light and have none, neither let it see the dawning of the day*. For our frail nature, darkened by its spontaneous fault, penetrates not the brightness of inward light, unless it first discharge its debt of punishment by death. It goes on;

Ver. 10. Because it shut not up the doors of my mother's womb, nor took away sorrow from mine eyes.

xxvi. 47. As has been likewise remarked above, the words, *it shut not up*, are 'it opened,' and *it took not away*, 'it brought upon me.' So that this *night*, i.e. sin, opened the door of the womb, in that to man, conceived unto sin, it unsealed the lust of concupiscence, whereof the Prophet says, *Enter thou into thy chambers, and shut thy doors*. [Isa. 26, 20] For we 'enter our chambers,' when we go into the recesses of our own hearts. And we 'shut the doors,' when we restrain forbidden lusts; and so whereas our consent set open these doors of carnal concupiscence, it forced us to the countless evils of our corrupt state. And so now we henceforth groan under the weight of mortality, though we came thereunto by our own free will, in that the justice of the sentence against us requires thus much, that what we have done willingly, we should bear with against our will. It proceeds;

Ver. 11, 12. Why died I not from the womb? Why did I not give up the ghost when I came out of the belly? Why did the knees prevent me? or why the breasts that I should suck?

xxvii.

48. Be the thought far from us, that blessed Job, who was endued with such high spiritual knowledge, and who had such a witness of praise from the Judge within, should wish that he had perished in abortive birth! But seeing, what we also learn by the reward which he received, that he has within the witness of his fortitude, the weight of his words is to be reckoned within.

49. Now sin is committed in the heart in four ways, and in four ways it is consummated in act. For in the heart it is committed by the suggestion, the pleasure, the consent, and the boldness to defend. For the suggestion comes of the enemy; the pleasure, of the flesh; the consent, of the spirit; and boldness to uphold, of pride. For the sin, which ought to fill the mind with apprehension, only exalts it, and in throwing down uplifts, while by uplifting it causes its more grievous overthrow; and hence that upright frame, wherein the first man was created, was by our old foe dashed down by these four strokes. For the serpent tempted, Eve was pleased, Adam yielded consent, and even when called in question he refused in effrontery to confess his sin. The serpent tempted, in that the secret enemy silently suggests evil to man's heart. Eve was pleased, because the sense of the flesh, at the voice of the serpent, presently gives itself up to pleasure. And Adam, who was set above the woman, yielded consent, in that whilst the flesh is carried away in enjoyment, the spirit also being deprived of its strength gives in from its uprightness. And Adam when called in question would not confess his sin, in that, in proportion as the spirit is by committing sin severed from the Truth, it becomes worse hardened in shamelessness at its downfall. Sin is likewise completed in act by the self-same four methods; for first the fault is done in secret, but afterwards it is done openly before men's eyes without the blush of guilt, and next it is formed into a habit, finally, whether by the cheats of false hope, or the stubbornness of reckless despair, it is brought to full growth.

50. These four modes of sin then, which either go on secretly in the heart, or which are executed in act, blessed Job views, and bewails the many stages of sin wherein the human race was fallen, saying, *Why died I not from the womb? Why did I not give up the ghost when I came out of the belly? Why did the knees prevent me? or why the breasts that I should suck?* For 'the womb of conception' at the first was the tongue of the evil suggestion. Now the sinner would 'perish in the womb,' if only man knew in the very suggestion itself that he would bring death upon himself. Yet 'he came forth from the belly,' in that, as soon as the tongue had conceived him in sin by its suggestions, the pleasure likewise, immediately hurried him forth; and after his coming forth, 'the knees prevented him,' in that having issued forth in the carnal gratification, he then completed the sin by the consent of the spirit, all the senses being made subservient like knees underneath. And 'the knees preventing him, the breasts did also give him suck.' For whereas, in the spirit's consenting to the sin, the senses were drawn into the service, the many reasonings of vain confidence followed, which nourished the soul thus born, in sin with poisoned milk, and lulled it with soothing excuses, that it should not fear the bitter punishment of death. And hence the first man waxed bolder after his sin, saying, *The women whom thou gavest to be with me, she gave me of the tree, and I did eat*. [Gen. 3, 12] And truly, he had fled to hide himself out of fear, yet when he was called in question, he made it appear how swoln he was with pride while he feared; for when punishment is feared as the present consequence of sin, and the face of God being lost is not loved, the fear is one that proceeds from a high stomach [*timor ex tumore*], and not from a lowly spirit. For he is full of pride who does not give over his sin, if be may go unpunished.

51. But, as we have said, sin is committed in these four ways, as in the heart, so also in the deed; for he says, *Why died I not in the womb?* For the womb to the sinner is the secret fault in man, which conceives the sinner under cover, and as yet hides its guilt in the dark. *Why did I not give up the ghost, when I came out of the belly?* For there is 'a coming out of the womb from the belly,' when the sinner does not blush to do openly as well the things, which he has been guilty of in secret. Thus they had as it were come out of the womb of their hiding place, of whom the Prophet spake it; *And they declare their sin as Sodom, they hide it not*, *Why did the knees prevent me?* [Is. 3, 9]

In that the sinner, when he is not confounded at his wickedness, is strengthened in the same by the further stays of most heinous custom. The sinner is as it were nursed on the knees, till he grow bigger, so long as the sin is confirmed by habitual acts, till it acquires strength. *Or why the breasts that I should suck?* For when the sin has once begun to issue into habit, then, alas! the sinner feeds himself either with the fallacious hope of God's mercy, or with the open recklessness of despair, that he never may return back to self-amendment, in so far as he either extravagantly colours to himself the pitifulness of his Maker, or is extravagantly terrified at the sin that he has done. Let the blessed man, then, take a view of man's fall, and mark down what precipice he has plunged himself into the pit of iniquity, saying, *Why died I not in the womb?* i.e. 'Why would I not, in the very secret act of sin in the heart, kill myself to the life of the flesh?' *Why did I not give up the ghost, when I came out of the belly?* i.e. 'Why, when I came forth in the overt act, died I not, was I not then at least instructed that I was undone?' For he would have 'given up the ghost' in his condemnation of himself, if he had known that he was lost. Why did the knees prevent me? i.e. 'Even after the open act of sin, why, yet further, did the custom too take me up in it, to make me stronger to commit sin, and to nurse and sustain me with habitual wicked acts?' *Why the breasts, that I should suck?* i.e. 'After I entered into the habit of sin, why did I rear myself to a more tremendous pitch of iniquity, either by reliance on false hope, or by the milk of a miserable despair?' For when the fault has been brought into a habit, the mind, even if it be inclined, by this time resists more feebly: for it becomes bound upon the mind by as many chains, as there are recurrences of the evil practice that clench it fast. Whence it happens that the mind, being sapped of strength, when it has no power to get free, turns to some resource or other of fallacious consolation, so as to flatter itself that the Judge, Who is to come, is of so great mercy, that even those, whom He shall find deserving of condemnation, He will never wholly destroy. Whereunto there is this worst addition, that the tongue of many like him abets him, since there are many who magnify with their praises these very misdeeds; whence it comes to pass that the fault is continually growing, nourished by applauses. Also then we neglect to heal the wound, which is counted worthy of the meed of praise. Hence Solomon says well, *My son, if sinners give thee suck, consent thou not.* [Prov.

1, 10. V.] For the wicked 'give suck,' whenever they either put wicked acts in our way to be done by their enticements, or applaud them with marks of favour when done. Does not he suck of whom the Psalmist says, *For the wicked man is commended in his heart's desire; and he that doeth iniquity receives a blessing,?* [Ps. 10, 3. Vulg. 9, 24]

52. We must also know, that those three modes of being sinners are more easily corrected as they come in their order downwards; but the fourth is not corrected but with difficulty. And hence our Saviour raises the damsel in the house, the young man without the gate, while Lazarus He raises in the grave; for he that sins in secret is as yet lying dead in the house, he is already being carried without the gate, whose iniquity is done openly, even to the shamelessness of commission in public; but he is pressed with the sepulchral mound, who, in the commission of sin, is over and above pressed and overlaid with the use of habit. But all these in mercy He restores to life; in that it is often the case that Divine grace enlighteneth with the light of its regard those that are dead not only in secret sins, but likewise in open evil practices, and that are overlaid with the weight of evil habit. But our Saviour knows indeed of a fourth being dead from the disciple's lips, yet never raises him to life; in that it is hard indeed for one, whom, after continuance in bad habit, the tongues of flatterers too get hold of, to be recovered from the death of the soul; and of such an one it is said with justice, *Let the dead bury their dead.* [Luke 9, 60] For 'the dead bury the dead,' as often as sinners load sinners with their approval. For what else is it to 'sin,' but to lie down in death? and to 'bury,' except it be to hide? But they that pursue the sinner with their applauses, bury the dead body under the mound of their words. Now Lazarus too was dead, yet he was never buried by the dead. For the believing women, who also gave tidings of his death to the Quickener, had laid him under the ground. And hence he forthwith returned back to the light; for when the soul is dead in sin, it is soon brought back, if anxious thoughts live over it. But sometimes, as we have likewise said above, it is not false hope that cuts off the mind, but a more deadly despair pierces it. And whereas this totally cuts off all hope of pardon, it supplies the soul with the milk of error in greater abundance.

53. Let the holy man then consider, what wickedness man has been guilty of, yet for the worse, after the first sin, and, after he had lost paradise, to what broken steeps he descended in this place of

exile, and let him say, *Why died I not in the womb?* i.e. 'When the suggestion of the serpent conceived me a sinner, O that I had then known the death that would come upon me; lest the suggestion should transport me to the length of delight, and should link me more closely to death.' *Why did I not give up the ghost when I came out of the belly?* As though he said, 'O that when I came out to the external gratification, I had known that I was parting with the internal light; so that I had at least died [i.e. died from sinning] at the point of this gratification only, that death might not inflict a sharper sting through the consent.' *Why did the knees prevent me?* As though he said, 'O that the consent had never caught me, my senses being made to bear up my frowardness, that my own consenting might not hurry me yet for the worse into shamelessness.' *Or why the breasts that I should suck?* As though he said, 'O that I had at least refused to flatter myself, after ill acts committed, that I might not attach myself thereby the more wickedly to my fault, the more softly I dealt with myself therein.' So then in these words of reproach, he charged himself with having sinned in our first parent. But had man never been brought down to the wretchedness of this place of banishment, by committing sin, let him say what peace he might have had. It proceeds;

Ver. 13. For now should I have lain still and been quiet; I should have slept, then had I been at rest.

xxviii.

54. For this was man set in Paradise, that, had he attached himself by the chains of love to an obedient following of his Creator, he might one day be transported to the heavenly country of the Angels, and that, without the death of the flesh. For he was made immortal in such sort, that, if he sinned, he would yet be capable of dying, and in such wise mortal, that, if he sinned not, he should even be capable of never dying, and that, by desert of a free choice, he might attain the blessedness of those realms, wherein there is neither possibility of sinning nor of death. There then, where, since the time of the Redemption, the Elect are conveyed, with the death of the flesh intervening, to the same place our first parents, if they had remained stedfast in the state of their creation, would undoubtedly have passed, and that, without the death of the body. Man then would have lain still and been quiet, he would have 'slept and been at rest,' in that being brought to the rest of his eter-

nal country, he would have found as it were a retreat from these clamours of human frailty. For since sin, he, as it were, is kept awake and crying aloud, who bears with struggling opposition the strife of his own flesh. This stillness of peace man, when he was created, enjoyed, when he received the freedom of his will, to encounter his enemy withal. And because he yielded himself up to him of his own accord, he forthwith found in himself what was to rise in clamours against him, forthwith met in the conflict with the riotings of his frail nature; and though he had been created by his Maker in peaceful stillness, yet, once of his own will laid low under the enemy, he had to endure the clamours of the fight. For the very suggestion of the flesh is a kind of outcry against the mind's repose, which man was not sensible of before the transgression, plainly because there was nought that he could be exposed to undergo from infirmity of his own. But since he has once voluntarily subjected himself to his enemy, now being bound with the chains of his sins, he serves him in some things even against his will, and suffers clamours in the mind, when the flesh strives against the Spirit. Did not clamours within meet his ears, who was pressed with the words of an evil law at variance with himself, saying, *But I see another law in my members, warring against the law of my mind, and bringing me into captivity to the law of sin which is in my members.* [Rom. 7, 23] Let then the holy man reflect in what a peace of mind he would have reposed, if man had refused to entertain the words of the serpent, and let him say, *For now should I have lain still and been quiet, I should have slept, then had I been at rest*; i.e. I should have withdrawn into the retirement of my breast to contemplate my Creator, had not the fault, the first sin of consent, betrayed me out of myself to the riotings of temptation; and let him add to the joys of this state of tranquillity, whom he would have had for his fellows in the enjoyment thereof saying,

Ver. 4. With the kings and counsellors of the earth.

xxix. 55. From things without sense we learn what to think of beings endowed with sense and understanding. Now the earth is rendered fruitful by the air, while the air is governed by the quality of the heaven. In like manner man is over the beasts, the Angels over man, and the Archangels are set over the Angels. Now that man has sovereignty over the beasts, we both perceive by the common use, and are instructed by the words of the Psalmist, who says, *Thou hast put all things under his feet; all sheep and oxen, yea, and the beasts of the field.* [Ps. 8, 6. 7.] And that the Angels are placed over man is testified by the Prophet, in these words, *But the prince of the kingdom of Persia withstood me.* [Dan. 10, 13] And that the Angels are under the governance of authority in superior Angels, the Prophet Zechariah declares; *And, behold, the Angel that talked with me went forth, and another angel went out to meet him, and he said unto him, Run, speak to this young man, saying, Jerusalem shall be inhabited as towns without walls.* [Zech. 2, 3. 4.] For in the actual ministration of the holy spirits, if the superior Powers did not direct the inferior, one Angel would never have learnt from the lips of another what he should say to a man. Therefore, forasmuch as the Creator of the Universe holdeth all things by Himself alone, and yet for the purpose of constituting the defined order characterizing a universe of beauty, He rules one part by the governance of another; we shall not improperly understand *the kings* to be the Angelic spirits, who the more devotedly they serve the Maker of all beings, have things subject to their rule the more. He would then have been 'at rest with kings;' in that, surely, man would have already had peace in company with the Angels, if he had refused to listen to the tongue of the Tempter. These too are rightly called 'counsellors,' for they 'consult' for the spiritual commonwealth, while they unite us to the kingdom as fellow-heirs with themselves. They are justly called 'counsellors;' for, whereas, from their lips we are made acquainted with the will of the Creator, it is in them assuredly that we find counsel to extricate ourselves from the misery that besets us here.

56. But since blessed Job is full of the Holy Spirit of Eternity, and since Eternity knows neither to have been nor to be about to be, whereto, as we know, neither things past depart, nor things future approach, as seeing all things in the present, he may, in the present inspiration of the Spirit, have his eyes fixed on the future preachers of the Church, who, when they leave the body, are separated by no intervals of delay from the inheritance of the heavenly country, as the fathers of old were. For as soon as they are parted asunder from the ties of the flesh, they enter into rest in their heavenly habitation, as Paul bears witness, who says, *For we know that if our earthly house of this tabernacle were dissolved, we have a building of God, an house not made with hands, eternal in the heavens.* [2 Cor. 5, 1] But before our Redeemer by His own death paid man's penalty, those even that fol-

lowed the ways of the heavenly country, [see Book xiii. §. 49.] the bars of hell held fast after their departure out of the flesh, not so that punishment should light on them, but that while resting in regions apart, they should find the guilt of the first sin a bar to their entrance into the kingdom, in that the Intercession of the Mediator was not yet come. Whence, according to the testimony of the same Mediator, the rich man, that is tormented in hell, beholds Lazarus at rest in the bosom of Abraham. Now if these had not been in the lower regions, he, in the place of his torment, would not have seen them; and hence this same Redeemer of us men, in dying to pay the debt of our sin, goes down into hell, that He may bring back to the realms of heaven all His followers, who had been held in that debt. But where man in a state of redemption now ascendeth, thither, if he had refused to sin, he might have reached even without the help of the Redemption. Let then the holy man consider that if he had not sinned, he would have ascended to that place, even without redemption, whereunto the holy Preachers, since the Redemption, must fain arrive at the cost of much labour, and let him show in company with whom he would now be at peace, saying, *With kings and counsellors of the earth*. For the kings are the holy Preachers of the Church, who know both how to order aright those that are committed to them, and to regulate their own bodies; who, while they check the motions of lust in themselves, rule over their thoughts, kept in due subjection according to the law of virtue. These too are rightly entitled, counsellors of the earth. For they are 'kings' in that they rule themselves, but counsellors of the earth, because they yield lifegiving counsel to the lifeless sinner. They are kings in that they know how to govern themselves, and counsellors of the earth, in that they lead earthly minds up to heavenly things by advice of their admonitions. Was not he 'a counsellor of the earth,' that said, *Now concerning virgins I have no commandment of the Lord, yet I give my judgment*; and again, *but she is happier if she so abide, after my judgment*. [1 Cor. 7, 25. 40.] It is justly added,

Which build desolate places for themselves.

XXX. 57. For all that either seek forbidden things, or that desire to appear somewhat in this world, are inwardly beset with a countless throng of thoughts, and while they stir up in their own bosom a host of desires, their mind, being laid prostrate, is miserably trodden by the foot of crowded resort. Thus one man has subjected himself to the law of lust, and he paints to his mind's eye representations of impure acts, and when the execution of the deed is not in his power, the thing is the more often done in the inward intent; the consummating of pleasure is sought, and the mind being struck powerless, borne hither and thither, disquieted at once and blinded, looks out eagerly for an opportunity of the foulest fulfilment in practice. That mind then, which is disordered by a rabble riot of thoughts, suffers as it were a kind of crowded population. Another man has submitted his neck to the dominion of Anger, and what does he employ himself about in imagination but quarrels which do not even exist? Such a man is often overlooking those that are before him, contradicting the absent, giving and receiving insults in imagination, making his reply severer than the insult received, and when there is none there to encounter him, he makes up a quarrel in his own breast with much uproar. He then that is pressed down by an intolerable weight of angry thoughts, has the misfortune of a rabble in his own bosom. Another has delivered himself over to the law of avarice, and, out of conceit with his own possessions, hankers after what belongs to another: it often happens that being unable to obtain what he longs for, he spends the day indeed in idleness, but the night in thought; he is a sluggard in useful work, because he is harassed with unlawful devices; he multiplies his schemes, and stretches his bosom the wider by all the contrivances and expedients of his invention; he is busy to reach the desired objects, and in order to obtain them he casts about for the most secret windings to serve for his occasions, and the moment that he reckons himself to have hit upon any crafty contrivance on an occasion, he is now in high glee as having obtained possession of his object, and now he is contriving what he may even add further to the thing when gotten, and is considering how it ought to be improved to a better condition; and whereas he is now in possession, and is bringing it to wear a better appearance, he is next considering the snares of those that are envious of him, and pondering what dispute they may fasten upon him, and making out what answer to give, and at the time he has nothing in his hands, the empty handed disputant is wearing himself out in defence of the thing which he desires. Thus although he has not got a particle of the object desired, yet he has already in his breast the fruit of his desire in the troublesomeness of the quarrel; and so he, that is overcome by the tumultuous instigations of avarice, has a vast population besetting him. Another one has subjected himself to the empire of pride, and while he lifts himself up against his fellow-creatures, he submits his heart to the vice, to his great misery. He covets the wreaths of elevated honours, he aims to exalt himself by his successes, and all that he desires to be, he represents to himself in the secret thoughts of his own breast. He is already as it seems seated on the judgment-seat, already sees the services of his subjects at his command, already shines above others, already brings evil upon one party, or recompenses another for having done this. Already in his own imagination he goes forth into public surrounded by throngs, already marks with what observance he is sustained in his high position; yet while fancying this, he is creeping by himself alone. Now he is treading one set under his feet, now he is elevating another, now he is gratifying his dislikes upon those he treads under foot, now he is receiving applause from the other whom he has elevated. What else is that man doing, who has such a multitude of fanciful imaginations pictured in his heart, save gazing at a dream with waking eyes? and thus, since he undergoes the misery of so many combinations of cases, which he pictures to himself, he plainly carries about within him crowds, that are engendered of his desires. Another has by this time learnt to eschew forbidden objects, yet he dreads lest he should lack the good things of this world, he is anxious to retain the goods vouchsafed him; he is ashamed to appear inferior among men, and he is full of concern lest he should become either a poor man at home, or an object of contempt in public. He anxiously inquires what may suffice for himself, what the needs of his dependants may require; and that he may sufficiently discharge the rights of a patron towards his dependants, he searches for patrons whom he may himself wait upon; but whilst he is joined to them in a relation of dependence, he is undoubtedly implicated in their concerns, wherein he often consents to forbidden acts, and the wickedness, which he has no mind for on his own account, he commits for the sake of other objects which he has not forsaken. For often, while dreading the diminution of his reputation in the world, he gives his approval to those things with his superiors, which in his own secret judgment he has now learnt to condemn. Whilst he anxiously bethinks himself what he owes to his patrons, what to his dependants, what gain he may make for himself, how he may promote his inclinations, he is in a manner overlaid with resort of crowds, as many in number as the demands of the cases whereby he is distracted.

58. But holy men, on the other hand, because their hearts are not set upon anything of this world, are assuredly never subject to the pressure of any tumults in their breast, for they banish all inordinate stirrings of desire from the heart's bed, with the hand of holy deliberation. And because they contemn all transitory things, they do not experience the licentious familiarities of the thoughts springing therefrom. For their desires are fixed upon their eternal country alone, and loving none of the things of this world, they enjoy a perfect tranquillity of mind; and hence it is said with justice, *Which built desolate places for themselves.* For to 'build desolate places' is to banish from the heart's interior the stirrings of earthly desires, and with a single aim at the eternal inheritance to pant in love of inward peace. Had he not banished from himself all the risings of the imaginations of the heart, who said, *One thing have I desired of the Lord, that will I seek after; that I may dwell in the house of the Lord?* [Ps. 27, 4] For he had betaken himself from the concourse of earthly desires to no less a solitude than his own self, where he would be the more secure in seeing nought without, in proportion as there was no insufficient object that he loved. For from the tumult of earthly things he had sought a singular and perfect retreat in a quiet mind, wherein he would see God the more clearly, in proportion as he saw Him alone with himself also alone.

59. Now they, who 'build for themselves solitary places,' are very properly also called 'consuls,' for they set up the mind's solitude in themselves in such wise, that whereinsoever they have the greater ability, they never cease to consult for the good of others through charity. Accordingly let us consider a little more particularly the case of him, whom we just now noticed as 'a consul,' and see in what manner he casts abroad the counters of the virtues, for the setting forth examples of a sublime life to the lines of people under him. Observe, in order to inculcate the returning good for evil, he makes confession on his own person, saying, *If I have returned on them that requited me evil, then should I deserve to fall empty before mine enemies.* [Ps. 7, 4] To excite the love of our Maker, he introduces himself saying, *But it is good for me to draw near to* [to cleave] *God.* To work an impression of holy humility, he shows the secrets of his heart, saying, *Lord, mine heart is not haughty, nor mine eyes lofty.* [Ps. 131, 1] He

excites us by his own example to imitate his unswerving zeal, saying, *Do not I hate them, O Lord, that hate thee, and am not I grieved with them that rise up against thee? I hate them with perfect hatred, I count them mine enemies*. [Ps. 139, 21. 22.] To light up in us the desire of our eternal home, he laments the length of this present life, and says, *Woe is me that my sojourn is prolonged*. [Ps. 120, 5. V.] Surely he shone forth in the magnificence of the consulship, who, by the example of his own conversation, casts before us so many of virtue's counters.

60. But let this *counsellor* tell whether he too builds a solitary place for himself. For he says, *Lo, I fled far off and remained in the wilderness*. He 'fleeth far off,' in that he raises himself from the throng of earthly desires in high contemplation of God; and he 'remains in the wilderness,' in that he persists in the retiring purpose of his mind. Of this solitude Jeremiah says well to the Lord, *I sat alone from the face of Thy hand, because Thou hast filled me with threatening*. [Jer. 15, 17] For the 'face of God's hand,' is the stroke of His righteous judgment, whereby He cast man out of Paradise, when he waxed proud, and shut him out into [*caecitatem* A.B.C.D.E.] the darkness of his present place of banishment. But 'His threatening' is the farther dread of a subsequent punishment. Accordingly after 'the face of His hand,' we are yet further terrified with 'His threats,' because both the penalty of our present banishment has already fallen upon us in the actual experience of His judgment, and, if we do not leave off from sinning, He further consigns us to everlasting punishments. Let the holy man then, here cast away, consider whence it was that man fell, and whither the justice of the Judge yet further hurries him, if he goes on to sin afterwards, and let him dismiss from his breast the countless hosts of temporal desires, and bury himself in the deep solitude of the mind, saying, *I sat alone from the face of Thy Hand; for Thou hast filled me with threatening*. As though he said in plain words, 'when I consider what I already suffer in experience of Thy judgment, I seek with trembling the withdrawal of my mind from the tumult of temporal desires; for I dread even still worse those eternal punishments, which Thou dost threaten.' Well then is it said of 'kings and counsellors,' *which built desolate places for themselves*. In that they, who know both how to govern themselves, and to advise for others, being unable as yet to obtain admission to that interior tranquillity, fashion a resemblance to it within themselves by pursuit of a quiet mind.

Ver. 15. Or with princes that have gold, who fill their houses with silver.

xxxi.

61. Whom does he call *princes*, but the rulers of holy Church, whom the Divine economy substitutes without intermission in the room of their predecessors? Concerning these the Psalmist, speaking to the same Church, says, *Instead of thy fathers thou hast children born to thee, whom thou mayest make princes in all lands.* [Ps. 45, 16] And what does he call gold, saving wisdom; of which Solomon says, *A treasure to be desired lieth at rest in the mouth of the wise?* [Prov. 21, 20] That is, he saw wisdom as gold, and therefore called it a treasure: and she is well designated by the name of 'gold,' for that, as temporal goods are purchased with gold, so are eternal blessings with wisdom. If wisdom had not been gold, it would never have been said by the Angel to the Church of Laodicea, *I counsel thee to buy of me gold tried in the fire.* [Rev. 3, 18] For we 'buy ourselves gold,' when we pay obedience first, to get wisdom in exchange, and it is to this very bargain that a certain wise man rightly stimulates us, in these words, *If thou desire wisdom, keep the commandments, and the Lord shall give her unto thee.* [Ecclus. 1, 26] And what is signified by the 'houses,' but our consciences? Hence it is said to one that was healed, *Go unto thine house.* [Matt. 9, 16] As though he had heard in plain words, 'After the outward miracles, turn back into thine own conscience, and weigh well what kind of person within thou shouldest show thyself before God.' And what too is represented by silver but the divine revelations, of which the Psalmist says, *The words of the Lord are pure words, as silver tried in the fire?* [Ps 12, 6] The word of the Lord is said to be like silver tried in the fire, because God's word, when it is fixed in the heart, is tried with afflictions.

62. Let the holy man then, full of the Spirit of Eternity, both sum up the things that shall be, and gather together in the open bosom of his mind all those, whom ages long after should give birth to, and consider with wonder and astonishment those Elect souls, with whom he would be enjoying rest in life eternal without the weariness of labour, had none ever been led into sin by the passion of pride, and let him say, *For now should I have lain still and been quiet; I should have slept; then had I been at rest with kings and counsellors of the earth, which built desolate places for themselves, or with princes that had gold, who filled their houses with silver.* For as, if no decay of sin had

ever ruined our first parent, he would not have begotten of himself children of hell, but they all, who must now be saved by the Redemption, would have been born of him Elect souls, and none else, let him look at these, and reflect how he might have been at rest in their company. Let him see the holy Apostles so ruling the Church they had undertaken, that they never ceased to give it counsel by the word of preaching, and so call them kings and counsellors. After these let him behold rulers arise in their room, who by living according to wisdom should have gold, and by preaching right ways to others should shine with the silver of sacred discourse, and let him call them real princes, the houses of whose conscience are full of gold and silver. But as it is not enough sometimes for the Spirit of Prophecy to foresee future events, unless at the same time it presents to the view of the prophet the past and by-gone, the holy man opens his eyes below and above, and not only fixes them on the future, but also recalls to mind the past. For he forthwith adds,

Ver. 16. Or as an hidden untimely birth I had not been; as infants which never saw light.

xxxii. 63. An abortive child, because it is born before the full period, being dead is forthwith put out of sight. Whom then does the holy man term 'abortives,' with whom he might 'have been at rest,' he reflects, saving all the Elect, who from the beginning of the world lived before the time of the Redemption, and yet studied to mortify themselves to this world. Those who had not the tables of the Law, 'died' as it were 'from the womb,' in that it was by the natural law that they fear their Creator, and believing the Mediator would come, they strove to the best of their power, by mortifying their pleasures, to keep even those very precepts, which they had not received in writing. And so that period, which at the beginning of the world produced our fathers dead to this life, was in a certain sense the 'womb of an abortive birth.' For there we have Abel, of whom we read not that he resisted his brother when he slew him. There Enoch, who approved himself such that he was carried up to walk with the Lord. There Noah, who hereby, that he was acceptable to the searching judgment of God, was, in the world, the world's survivor. There Abraham, who, while a pilgrim in the world, became the *friend of God*. There Isaac, who, by reason of his fleshly eyes waxing dim, by his age had no sight of things present, but by the efficacy of the prophetic Spirit lighted up future ages even with his extraordinary luminousness of sight. There Jacob, who in humility fled his brother's indignation, and by kindness overcame the same; who was fruitful indeed in his offspring, but yet being more fruitful in richness of the Spirit, bound that offspring with the chains of prophecy. And this *untimely birth* is well described as *hidden*, in that from the beginning of the world, while there are some few, whom we are informed of by Moses' mention of them, by far the largest portion of mankind is hidden from our sight. For we are not to imagine that during all the period up to the receiving of the Law, only just so many righteous men came forth, as Moses has run through in the most summary notice. And thus, forasmuch as the multitude of the righteous born from the beginning of the world is in great measure withdrawn from our knowledge, this *untimely birth* is called *hidden*. And it is also said, *not to have been*, because a few only being enumerated, the generality of them are not preserved among us by any written record for their memorial.

64. Now it is rightly added; *As infants which never saw light*. For they, who came into this world after the Law was received, were conceived to their Creator, by the instruction of the same Law; yet, though *conceived*, they never saw light, in that these never could attain to the coming of the Lord's Incarnation, which yet they stedfastly believed; for the Lord Incarnate says, *I am the Light of the world* [John 8, 12]; and that very Light declareth, *Many Prophets and righteous men have desired to see those things which ye see, and have not seen them*. [Matt. 13, 17] Therefore the fruit 'conceived never saw light,' in that, although quickened to entertain the hope of a future Mediator by the plain declarations of the Prophets, they were never able to behold His Incarnation. In all these then the inward conception brought forth a form of faith, but never carried this on so far as to the open vision of God's Presence; for that death intervening hurried them from the world before Truth made manifest had shed light thereon.

65. Thus the holy man then, full of the spirit of Eternity, fixes to his memory by the hand of the heart all that is transient; and because every creature is little in regard to the Creator, by the same Spirit, Which hath nought either in Itself or about Itself saving always to be, he views both what shall be, and what hath been, and directs the eye of his mind both below and above, and regarding things that are

coming as past, he burns in the core of his heart toward eternal Being, and says, *For now I should have lain still and been quiet*. For 'now' belongs to the present time, and what else is it for one to seek a rest always placed in the present, but to pant after that bliss of eternity, whereunto there is nought in coming or in going? Which always Being The Truth, by the lips of Moses, shows to be His own attribute, so as to communicate it to us in some degree in the words, *I AM THAT I AM, and He said, Thus shalt thou say unto the children of Israel, HE THAT IS hath sent me unto you*; and now, that he is contemplating things transient, and seeking an ever present bliss, and making mention of the light to come, and enumerating and considering the orders of the Elect children thereof, let him now show us in a little plainer terms the rest itself that appertains to this light, and let him show in plainer words, what is brought to pass therein every day relating to the life and conduct of the wicked. It proceeds;

Ver. 17. There the wicked cease from disturbance, and there the weary in strength be at rest.

xxxiii. 66. We have already said above, that herein, viz. that the hearts of sinners are possessed with a tumult of desires, they are grievously oppressed by a host of goading thoughts, but in this light, which the 'infants conceived' never saw, the wicked are said to 'cease from their disquietude' for this reason, that the coming of the Mediator, which the fathers under the Law had long waited for, the Gentiles found to the peace of their life, as Paul testifies, who says, *Israel hath not obtained that which he seeketh for, but the election hath obtained it*. [Rom. 11, 7] In this light then 'the wicked cease from disquietude,' inasmuch as the minds of the untoward, when they have come to the knowledge of the truth, eschew the wearisome desires of the world, and find rest in the quiet haven of interior love. Does not the Light Itself call us to this rest when It says, *Come unto Me, all ye that labour and are heavy laden, and I will give you rest; take My yoke upon You and learn of Me, for I am meek and lowly in heart: and ye shall find rest unto Your souls*; *For My yoke is easy, and My burthen is light*. [Matt. 11, 28–30] For what heavy yoke does He put upon our mind's neck, Who bids us shun every desire that causes disquietude? What heavy burthen does He lay upon His followers, Who warns us to decline the wearisome ways of the world? Now, by the testimony of the Apostle Paul, *Christ died for the ungodly*;

[Rom. 5, 6] and it was for this reason that the Light Itself condescended to die for the ungodly, that these might not continue in the disorderment of their state of darkness. So let the holy man consider with himself, that by the mystery of the Incarnation 'the Light' rescues the wicked from heavy toil, while It takes clean away all the aims of wickedness from their hearts; let him reflect how every converted person has already here below a taste, by inward tranquillity, of that rest which he desires to have throughout eternity, and let him say, *There the wicked cease from, disturbance, and the weary in strength are at rest.*

67. For all they that are strong in this world are by their might in one way strong, not *wearied out in strength*; but they that are endued with might in the love of their Maker, the more they be strengthened in the love of God, which is their object of desire, become in the same degree powerless in their own strength, and the stronger their longing for the things of eternity, the more they are wearied as to earthly objects by a wholesome failure of their strength. Hence the Psalmist, being wearied with the strength of his love, said, *My soul hath fainted in* [al. *toward* as V.] *Thy salvation*. [Ps. 119, 81] For his soul did faint while making way in God's salvation, in that he panted with desire of the light of eternity, broken of all confidence in the flesh. Hence he says again, *My soul longeth, yea, even fainteth for the courts of the Lord*. [Ps. 84, 2] Now when he said 'longeth,' he added rightly, and 'fainteth,' since that longing for the Divine Being is little indeed, which is not likewise immediately followed by a fainting in one's self. For it is but meet that he who is inflamed to seek the courts of eternity, should be enfeebled in the love of this temporal state. So that he should be cold to the pursuit of this world, in proportion as he rises with soul more inflamed to the love of God. Which love if he completely grasps, he then at the same time completely quits the world, and the more entirely dies to temporal things, the higher he is made to soar after the life to come by the inspirations of Eternity. Had not that soul found itself wearied in its own strength, which exclaimed, *My soul* [so V.] *was melted when he spake*; [Cant. 5, 6] clearly in that while the soul is touched by the inspirations of the secret communication, weakened in the seat of its own strength, it is 'melted' by the desire wherewith it is swallowed up, and finds itself wearied in itself by the same step whereby it is brought to see that there is a might without itself to which it soars.

THE FIRST PART.

Hence when the Prophet was telling that he had seen a vision of God, he adds, *And I, Daniel fainted and was sick certain days*; [Dan. 8, 27] for when the soul is held fast to the power of God, the flesh waxes faint in respect of its own strength. Thus Jacob, who held an Angel in his hold, immediately afterwards halted upon one foot; for he that regards things on high with a genuine love, already forswears to walk in this world with a doubleminded affection. For he rests upon one foot, who is strong in the love of God alone; and it must needs be that the other should wither, for when the virtue of the soul gains increase, it behoves assuredly that the strength of the flesh wax dull. Let blessed Job, then, review the deep recesses of the hearts of the faithful, and consider the haven of inward peace that they find, while in advancing unto God they are enfeebled in their own strength, and let him say, *There the weary in strength be at rest.* As if he taught in plain words, 'there the repose of light is the reward of those, whom the advancement of inward restoration wearies here.' Nor ought it to influence us, that after naming light he did not subjoin, *in this*, but *there*, for that which he beholds encompassing the Elect, he discovers to be our place as it were. Whence then the Psalmist, when contemplating the unchangeableness of Eternity, and saying, *But Thou art the same, and Thy years shall not fail*; [Ps. 102, 28] proclaims that this is the place of the Elect, by adding, *But the children of Thy servants shall dwell there.* For God, Who without position containeth all things, remains a place without locality to us who come to Him. And when we reach this place, our eyes are opened to see, what infinite vexation even our very repose of mind was in this life, for though the righteous by comparison with the bad already enjoy rest, yet in estimating the inmost Rest, they are altogether not at rest. Hence it is well added;

Ver. 18. There the former prisoners are alike without vexation.

xxxiv. 68. For though the just are possessed by no riot of carnal desires, yet the clog of corruption binds them down in this life with hard chains; for it is written, *For the corruptible body presseth down the soul, and the earthly tabernacle weigheth down the mind that museth upon many things.* [Wisd. 9, 15] So herein even, that they are still mortal beings, they are weighed down by the burthen of their state of corruption, and chained and bound by its clogs, in that they are not yet risen in that liberty of an incorruptible life. For they meet with one thing from the mind, and another from the body, and they are spent every day in the inward conflict with themselves. Are they not indeed bound with the hard chain of vexation, whose mind, without labour, is dissolved in ignorance, and is not trained without the strivings of labour? When forced it stands erect, of itself it lies prostrate, and yet as soon as raised up, it forthwith falls, by conquering itself with laborious effort, its eyes are opened to see heavenly things, but recoiling, it flees the light, which had illuminated it. Are they not bound fast with the hard chain of vexation, who when their fired soul draws them with a perfect desire to the bosom of inward peace, suffer perturbation from the flesh in the heat of the conflict? And though this now no longer encounters it face to face, as though drawn up with hostile front, yet it still goes muttering like a captive in the rear of the mind, and, though with fears, it yet defiles with vile clamouring the form of fair tranquillity in the breast. Therefore, though the Elect subdue all enemies with a strong hand, since they long for the security of inward peace, it is yet a grievous vexation to them to have something still to vanquish. And leaving these out of the question, they endure over and above those chains too, which a sore necessity outwardly fastens upon them; for to eat, to drink, and to be tired, are chains of corruption, and chains too, which can never be unloosed, save when our mortal nature is turned into the glory of an immortal nature; for we fill our body with food to sustain it, lest it fail from extenuation; and we thin it down by abstinence, lest it oppress by repletion. We quicken it by motion, lest it be killed by lying motionless, but by setting it down we soon stop its motions, that by that very activity it may not give under. We clothe it with garments as a succour to it, lest the cold destroy it, and cast off these succours so sought after, lest the heat should parch it. Exposed then to so many vicissitudes and chances, what else do we, but drudge to the corruptibility of our state of being, that howsoever the multiplicity of the services rendered to it may sustain that body, which the fretting care of a frail nature subject to change weighs to the ground. Hence Paul says well, *For the creature was made subject to vanity, not willingly, but by reason of him who hath subjected the same in hope. Because the creature itself also shall be delivered from the bondage of corruption into the glorious liberty of the sons of God.* [Rom. 8, 20. 21.] For 'the creature is made subject to vanity, not willingly,' in that man, who willingly left the footing of inborn firmness, being pressed down by the weight of a deserved mortality, is the unwilling slave of the corruption of his changeful condition. But this creature is then rescued from the slavery of corruption, when in rising again it is lifted uncorrupt to the glory of the sons of God. Here then the Elect are bound with vexation, in that they are still pressed down by the curse of their corrupt condition. But when we are stripped of our corruptible flesh, we are as it were loosened from those chains of vexation, whereby we are now held bound. For we already long to come into the presence of God, but we are still hindered by the clog of a mortal body. So that we are justly called 'prisoners,' in that we have not as yet the advance of our desire to God free before us. Hence Paul, whose heart was set upon the things of eternity, yet who still carried about him the load of his corruption, being in bonds exclaims, *Having a desire to be unloosed and to be with Christ*. [Phil. 1, 23] For he would not desire to be 'unloosed,' unless, assuredly, he saw himself to be in bonds. Now because he saw that these bonds were most surely to be burst at the Resurrection, the Prophet rejoiced as if they were already burst asunder, when he said, *Thou hast loosed my bonds. I will offer to thee the sacrifice of thanksgiving*. [Ps. 116, 16] Let the holy man then reflect that inward light is the haven that receives converted sinners, and let him say, *There the wicked cease from trouble*. Let him reflect, that holy men, being awearied with the exercising of desire, enjoy the deeper repose in that inmost bosom, and let him say, *And there the weary in strength are at rest*. Let him reflect, that being absolved from all the bonds of corruption at once and together, they attain those uncorrupt joys of liberty. *And the former prisoners are alike without vexation*. And it is well said, *the former prisoners*, for while that ever present bliss is in his view, all that shall be, and is going [B. 'and shall be gone'], seems as though past. For whilst the end of all things is awaited, all that passes away is accounted already to have been. But let him tell what all they, for whom the interior rest is there in store, shall meanwhile have done here. It goes on;

They have not heard the voice of the exactor. [*non exaudierunt*]

XXXV. 69. Who else is to be understood by the title of the 'exactor,' saving that insatiate prompter, who for once bestowed the coin of deceit upon mankind, and from that time ceases not daily to claim the debt of death? Who lent to man in Paradise the money of sin, but by the multiplying of wickedness is daily exacting it with usury? Concerning this exactor, Truth says in the Gospel, *And the Judge deliver thee to the officer* [V. *'exactori'*]. [Luke 12, 58] Therefore the voice of this exactor is the tempting of persuasion to our hurt. And we hear the voice of the exactor, when we are smitten with his temptation, but we do not bear it effectually [*exaudimus*] if we resist the hand that smites, for he 'hears' that feels the temptation, but he hears effectually who yields to the temptation. So let it be said of the righteous, *They have not heard the voice of the exactor*; for though they hear his prompting in that they are tempted, they do not hear it effectually, for that they take shame to yield thereto, but because whatsoever the mind loves with great affection, it is often repeating even in utterance of the lips; blessed Job, in that he views the crowds of inward peace with fulness of affection, again employs himself about the description [al. the distinguishing of them] of it, saying,

Ver. 19. The small and great are there; the servant is free from his master.

70. Forasmuch as there is to us in this life a difference in works, doubtless there will be in the future life a difference in degrees of dignity, that whereas here one surpasses another in desert, there one may excel another in reward. Hence Truth says in the Gospel, *In My Father's house are many mansions.* [John 14, 2] But in those 'many mansions,' the very diversity of rewards will be in some measure in harmony. For an influence so mighty joins us together in that peace, that what any has failed to receive in himself, he rejoices to have received in another. And thus they that did not equally labour in the vineyard, equally obtain all of them a penny. And indeed with the Father are 'many mansions,' and yet the unequal labourers receive the same penny, in that the blessedness of joy will be one and the same to all, yet not one and the same sublimity of life to all. He had seen the small and great in this light, who said in the voice of the Head; *Thine eyes did see My substance, yet being imperfect, and in Thy book were all My members written*. [Ps. 139, 16] He beheld 'the small and the great together,' when he declared, *He will bless them that fear the Lord, both small and great*. [Ps. 115, 13] And it is well added, *And the servant is free from his master*. For it is written, *Everyone that sinneth is the servant of sin* [John 8, 34]. For whosoever yields himself up to bad desire, submits the neck of his mind, till now free, to the dominion

of wickedness. Now we withstand this master, when we struggle against the evil whereby we had been taken captive, when we forcibly resist the bad habit, and treading under all froward desires, maintain against the same the right of inborn liberty, when we strike our sin by penitence, and cleanse the stains of pollution with our tears. But it oftentimes happens, that the mind indeed already bewails what it remembers itself to have done amiss, that already it not only forsakes its misdeeds, but even chastises them with the bitterest lamentations, yet while it recalls to memory the things that it has done, it is affrighted and sorely dismayed against the Judgment. It already turns itself with a perfect intention, but does not yet lift itself up in a perfect state of security, for while it weighs the rigid exactness of the final scrutiny, it trembles with anxiety between hope and fear, for it knows not, when the righteous Judge comes, what He will reckon, what He will remit of the deeds done. For it remembers what evil deeds it has committed, but it cannot tell whether it has worthily bewailed the commission of them, and it dreads lest the vastness of the sin exceed the measure of penance. And it is very often the case that 'Truth' already remits the sin, yet the troubled soul, whilst it is full of anxiety for itself, still trembles for the pardon thereof. So that in this present life the servant already escapes from his master, yet he is not free from him, in that by chastisement and penance man already forsakes his sin, yet he still fears the strict Judge for the recompensing of it. There then 'the servant will be free from his master,' when there will be no longer misgiving about the pardon of sin, when the recollection of its sin no longer condemns the soul, now secured, where the conscience does not tremble under a sense of guilt, but exults in the pardon of the same in a state of freedom.

72. But if man is reached there by no remembrance of his sin, how does he congratulate himself that he has been saved therefrom? Or how does he return thanks to his Benefactor for the pardon, which he has received, if by an intervening forgetfulness of his past wickedness, he knows not that he is a debtor to suffer punishment? For we must not pass over negligently that which the Psalmist says, *I will sing of the mercies of the Lord for ever*. [Ps. 89, 1] For how does he 'sing of the mercies of God for ever,' if he knows not that he has been miserable; and if he has no recollection of past misery, whence does he answer with praises the bestowal of mercy? And again, we

must enquire how the mind of the Elect can be in perfect bliss, if amidst its joys the memory of its guilt reaches it? Or how does the glory of indefectible light shine out, when it is overcast by the sin that is recalled to mind? But be it known, that just as oftentimes now in joy we call to mind sad things, so in the future life, we bring back the memory of past sin without any hurt to our bliss. For it very often happens, that in the season of health, we recall to mind past pains without feeling pain, and in proportion as we remember ourselves sick, the more we hug ourselves in health. And so in that blissful estate there will be a remembrance of sin, not such as to pollute the mind, but to attach us the more closely to our joy, that while the mind without pain remembers itself of its pain, it may the more clearly perceive itself to be a debtor to the physician, and so much the more cherish the health it has received, in proportion as it remembers what it has escaped of uneasiness. And so then, placed in that state of bliss, we so regard our evil deeds without loathing, as now being set in light, without any inward blindness of the heart, we see the darkness with our mind; for though that be dim which we perceive with the imagination, this comes from the sentence of light, not from the misfortune of blindness. And thus throughout eternity we render to our Benefactor the praise of His mercy, yet are in no degree oppressed with the consciousness of wretchedness; for whilst we review our evils without any evil betiding the mind, on the one hand there will never be ought to defile, the hearts that render praise on the score of past wickednesses, and again there will always be somewhat to inflame them to the praise of their Deliverer. Therefore, because the repose of inward light does in such sort transport the great ones into itself, that yet it does not leave the little ones, let it be rightly said, *the small and great are there*. Now forasmuch as the mind of the converted sinner is there touched by the recollection of his sin in such sort that he is not overwhelmed by any confusion at that recollection, it is fitly subjoined, *And the servant is free from his master.*

BOOK V.

He explains the remainder of chap. iii. from ver. 20. the whole of chap. iv. and the first two verses of chap. v.

i. 1. THOUGH the appointments of God are very much hidden from sight, why it is that in this life it is sometimes ill with the good and well with the wicked, yet they are then still more mysterious when it both goes well with the good here below, and ill with the wicked. For when it goes ill with the good, and well with the bad, this perhaps is found to be for that both the good, if they have done wrong in anything, receive punishment here that they may be more completely freed from eternal damnation, and the wicked meet here with the good things, which conduce to this life, that they may he dragged to unmitigated torments hereafter. And hence these words are spoken to the rich man, when burning in hell, *Son, remember that thou in thy lifetime receivedst thy good things, and likewise Lazarus evil things.* [Luke 16, 25] But when it is well with the good here and ill with the wicked, it is very doubtful, whether the good for this reason receive good things, that they may be set forward and advance to something better, or whether by a just and secret appointment they receive here the reward of their deeds, that they may prove void of the rewards of the life to come; and whether afflictions for this reason come upon the wicked, in order that by correcting, they may be the means of preserving them from everlasting punishments, or whether their punishment only begins here, that, one day to receive completion, it should lead to the final torments of hell. Therefore, because in the midst of the divine appointments the human mind is closed in by the great darkness of its uncertainty, holy men, when they see this world's prosperity to be their lot, are disquieted with fearful misgivings. For they fear lest they should receive here the fruits of their labours. They fear lest Divine Justice should see in them a secret wound, and in loading them with external blessings should withhold them from the interior. But when they exactly consider, that they never do good saving that they may please God only, nor triumph in the very exuberance of their prosperity, then indeed they less fear hidden judgments to their hurt in their good fortune, yet they ill endure that good fortune, in that it impedes the interior purpose of the heart, and they reluctantly submit to the caresses of this present life, forasmuch as they are not ignorant that they are in some degree retarded thereby in their interior longing. For honour in this world is more engrossing than the contempt thereof, and the rise of prosperity weighs upon them more than the pressure of a hard necessity. For sometimes when a man is outwardly straitened by the latter, he is the more entirely set at liberty to fix his desire upon the interior good; but by the other the mind, while forced to yield to the will of many, is kept back from the race of its own desire. And hence it is that holy men are in greater dread of prosperity in this world than of adversity. For they know that while the mind is under soft and beguiling impressions, it is sometimes apt to give itself up to be drawn away after external objects. They know that oftentimes the secret thought of the heart so beguiles it, that it does not see how it is changed. And they consider too, what the eternal blessings are which they desire, and they see what a mere nothing all is that courts and smiles upon us after the manner of things temporal, and their mind bears the worse all the prosperity of this world, in proportion as it is pierced with love of heavenly happiness; and it is planted so much the more erect in contempt of the delightfulness of the present life, the more it perceives that this is beguiling it by stealth in the disregard of eternal glory. Hence when blessed Job, having his eye fixed upon the rest above, had said, *The small and great are there; and the servant is free from his master.* He therefore adds,

Ver. 20. Wherefore is light given to one that is in misery?

2. In holy Scripture prosperity is sometimes represented by the title of light, and this world's adversity by the name of night. Hence it is well said by the Psalmist, *As is its darkness, so also is its light*. [Ps 139, 12. Vulg.] For as holy men thus trample upon the prosperity of this state by contemning it, as also they sustain its adverse fortune by trampling upon it, by an exceeding highmindedness laying under their feet alike the good and the ill of the world, they declare, *As its darkness, so also is its light*. As though they said in plain words, 'as its griefs do not force down the resoluteness of our fixed mind, so neither can its caresses corrupt the same.' But since these last, as we have said above, though they fail to lift up the mind of the righteous, do yet cause them disquietude; holy men, who know themselves to be in misery in this wearisome exile, shrink from shining in its prosperity. Hence it is well said at this time, *Wherefore is light given to one that is in misery?* for 'light is given to those in mis- ii.

ery,' when they, who, by contemplating things above, see themselves to be in misery in this our pilgrimage, have the brightness of transitory prosperity bestowed upon them; and when they are deploring grievously, that they are slow in returning to their country, they are over and above constrained to bear the burthen of honours. The love of eternal things is crushing them, and at the same time the glory of temporal things smiles upon them. When these reflect what the things are, which keep them down below, and what those are that they see not of the things above, what those are that set them up on earth, and what they have lost of heavenly blessings, they are stung with regret of their prosperity. For though they see that they are never wholly overwhelmed thereby, yet they anxiously consider that their thoughts are divided between the love of God, and the gifts of His hand; and hence when he says, *Wherefore is light given to him that is in misery?* he subjoins forthwith,

And life unto the bitter in soul?

iii. 3. For all the Elect are bitter in soul, in that either they never cease to punish themselves by weeping for the transgressions they have committed, or they afflict themselves with regrets, that banished here far from the face of their Creator, they are not yet admitted to the bliss of the eternal country; and of their hearts it is well said by Solomon, *The heart knoweth its own bitterness, and a stranger shall not intermeddle with his joy.* For the hearts of the reprobate are likewise in bitterness, for that they are afflicted even by their very bad passions themselves. Yet they know not of this very bitterness, because having voluntarily blinded their own eyes, they cannot estimate what they are undergoing; but on the contrary the heart of a good man knoweth its own bitterness, for it knows the hard condition of this place of exile, wherein it is cast forth to be torn in pieces; and it sees how tranquil is all that it has lost, how troubled the condition it has fallen into. Yet this embittered heart is one day brought back to its own joy, and *a stranger shall not intermeddle* therewith, in that he, who now casts himself forth without, away from this sorrow of the heart, in his aims, will then remain shut out from its interior festival.

4. They then that are *in bitterness of soul*, long to be wholly dead to the world, that, as they themselves aim at nothing in this present world, so they may not henceforth be fettered by the world with any

ties; and it very often happens that a person has already ceased to retain the world in his affections, but the world still ties down that person by its business, and he indeed is already dead to the world, but the world is not yet dead to him. For in a certain sense the world, still alive, regards [D. 'desires him' (as below)] him, so long as it strives to carry him away in its actions, when he is bent another way. Hence, since Paul both himself utterly contemned the world, and saw that he was become such an one as this world could not possibly desire, having burst the bonds of this life, and being henceforth at liberty, he rightly exclaims, *The world is crucified to me, and I unto the world.* For 'the world was crucified to him,' because being now dead to his affections it was no longer an object of love to him; and he had likewise 'crucified himself to the world,' in that he studied to show himself thereto in such a light, that, as though dead, he might never be coveted by it. For if there be a dead person, and one alive in the same place, though the dead sees not the living, yet the living person does see the dead, but if both are dead, neither can possibly see the other. Thus he, who no longer loves the world, but yet even against his will is loved by the world, though he himself being as it were dead sees nothing of the world, yet the world not being dead sees him; but if he neither himself retains the world in his affections, nor again is retained in the affections of the world, then both are mutually dead to one another; in that whereas neither seeks the other, it is as if the dead heeded not the dead. Therefore, because Paul neither sought the glory of the world, nor was himself sought out by the same, he glories both in being himself crucified to the world, and in the world being crucified to him. Now because there are many that desire this, who yet do not altogether rise up to the very extreme point of such a state of deadness, they may well lament and say; *Wherefore is light given to him that is in misery, and life unto the bitter in soul.* For 'life is given to those in bitterness,' when the glory of this world is bestowed upon the sad and sorrowful, in which same life they do not spare themselves the chastening of most urgent fear; for though they do not themselves hold to the world, yet they still dread being such as the world holds to; and except they were living to it in some slight degree, it would never surely love them for their serviceableness to its interests; just as the sea keeps living bodies in her own bosom, but dead ones she forthwith casts out from herself. It proceeds;

Ver. 21. Which long for death, but it cometh not.

iv. 5. For they desire to mortify themselves wholly, and to be entirely extinct of the life of temporal glory, but by the secret appointments of God they are often forced either to take the lead in command, or to busy themselves with dignities imposed on them, and in these circumstances they unceasingly look for a perfect mortification, but this expected death cometh not; in that the use of them is still alive to temporal glory even against their will, though they submit to that glory from the fear of God, and while they inwardly retain their aim after piety, they outwardly discharge the functions of their station, that they should neither quit their perfection in their inward purpose, nor set themselves against the dispensations of their Creator in a spirit of pride. For by a marvellous pitifulness of the Divine Nature it comes to pass, that, when he, who aims at contemplation with a perfect heart, is busied with human affairs, his perfect mind at once profits many that are weaker, and in whatever degree he sees himself to be imperfect, he rises therefrom more perfect to the crowning point of humility. For sometimes by the very same means, whereby holy men suffer loss in their own longings, they bear off the larger profits by the conversion of others, for, while it is not permitted them to give themselves thereto as they desire, it is their grateful office to carry off along with themselves others, whom they are associated with. And so it is effected by a wonderful dispensation of pity, that by the same means, whereby they seem to themselves to be the more undone [*destructiores*], they rise with richer resources to the building up [*constructionem*] of their heavenly Country.

6. Now sometimes they fail to attain the desires, that they have conceived, for this reason, that by the very interposing of the delay, they may be made to expand to the same objects with an enlarged embrace of the mind, and by a striking dispensation it is effected that that, which if fulfilled might perhaps become thin and poor, being kept back, gains growth. For they desire so to mortify themselves that, if it may be vouchsafed, they may already perfectly behold the face of their Creator, but their desire is delayed that it may gain increase, and it is fostered in the bosom of its slow advancement that it may grow larger. Hence the Bride, panting with desire of her Bridegroom, justly cries out, *By night on my bed I sought him, whom my*

soul loveth: I sought him, but I found him not. [Cant. 3, 1] The Spouse hides himself when He is sought, that not being found He may be sought for with the more ardent affection, and she in seeking is withheld, that she cannot find Him, in order that being rendered of larger capacity by the delay she undergoes, she may one day find a thousandfold what she sought. Hence when blessed Job said, *Which long for death, but it cometh not*; that he might the more minutely particularize this very desire of those seekers, he thereupon adds;

And dig for it as for hid treasures.

7. For all men that seek for a treasure by digging, the deeper they have begun to go, kindle to the work with the greater energy; for in the same proportion that they reckon themselves to be now, at this moment, approaching the buried treasure, they strive with increased efforts in digging for it. They, then, that perfectly desire the mortification of themselves, seek it as they that dig for hid treasures, for the nearer they are brought to their object, the more ardent they show themselves in the work. Therefore they never flag in their labour, but increase the more in the exercise thereof; for that in the degree, that they reckon on their reward as now nearer at hand, they spend themselves the more gladly in the work. Hence Paul says well to some, that were seeking the hid treasure of the eternal inheritance, *Not forsaking the assembling of ourselves together as the manner of some is; but consoling* [V. *consolantes*] *one another, and so much the more as ye see the day approaching.* [Heb. 10, 25] For to give consolation to the labourer, is to continue labouring in like manner to him, the sight of a fellow labourer being the alleviation of our own labour, as, when a companion joins us in a journey, the way itself is not shortened, yet the toilsomeness of the way is alleviated by the society of a companion. Therefore, whereas Paul looked for their consoling one another in their labours, he added these words, *and so much the more as ye see the day approaching.* As though he said, 'let your labour increase the more, that now the reward of your labour itself is nigh at hand.' As if he expressed himself in plain words, 'Do ye seek a treasure? Then ye should dig for it with the greater ardour, that ye have by digging reached by this time close to the gold ye were in quest of.' **v.**

8. Though this, that he says, *Which long for death and it cometh not; and dig for it as for hid treasures*, may be taken in another sense also.

For in that we cannot perfectly die to the world, unless we bury ourselves within the invisible depths of our own heart from all things visible, they that long for the mortifying of themselves, are well compared to those that dig for a treasure. For we die to the world by means of an unseen wisdom, of which it is said by Solomon, *If thou seekest her as silver, and diggest for her as for hid treasures*. [Prov. 2, 4] Since wisdom lieth not on the surface of things, for it is deep in the unseen. And we then lay hold on the mortification of ourselves, in attaining wisdom, if, relinquishing visible things, we bury ourselves in the invisible; if we so seek for her in the digging of the heart, that every imagination, which the mind conceives, of an earthly nature, she puts from her with the hand of holy discernment, and acquaints herself with the treasure of virtue which was hidden from her. For she soon finds a treasure in herself, if she thrust from her that heap of earthly thoughts, which lay as a wretched load upon her. Now because he describes death coveted as a treasure, he rightly subjoins;

Ver. 22. Which rejoice exceedingly and are glad, when they can find the grave.

vi. 9. For as the grave is that place wherein the body is buried, so heavenly contemplation is a kind of spiritual grave wherein the soul is buried. For in a certain sense we still live to this world, when in spirit we roam abroad therein. But we are buried in the grave as dead, when being mortified in things without, we secrete ourselves in the depths of interior contemplation. And therefore holy men never cease to mortify themselves with the sword of the sacred Word to the importunate calls of earthly desires, to the throng of unprofitable cares, and to the din of obstreperous tumults, and they bury themselves within before God's presence in the bosom of the mind. Hence it is well said by the Psalmist, *And Thou shalt hide them in the secret of Thy presence from the strife of tongues*. [Ps. 31, 20] Which though it be not until afterwards fully brought to pass, is yet even now in a great measure accomplished, when with the feeling of delight they are caught away into the inward parts from the strife of temporal desires, so that, whilst their mind wholly expands in every part to the love of God, it is not rent and torn by any useless anxiety. Hence it is that Paul had seen those disciples as dead, and as it were buried in the grave by contemplation, to whom he said, *Ye* *are dead, and your life is hid with Christ in God*. [Col. 3, 3] He, then, that seeks for death rejoices when he finds the grave; for whoso desires to mortify himself, is exceeding joyful on finding the rest of contemplation; that being dead to the world he may lie hid, and bury himself in the bosom of interior love from all the disquietudes of external things.

10. But since in addition to this, that he speaks of a treasure being dug up, the finding of a grave is further introduced, it is needful that our mind's eye should keep this in view, that the ancients buried their dead with their wealth. He, then, that seeks for a treasure, 'rejoices when he has found the grave,' in that when we, in quest of wisdom, turn the pages of Holy Writ, when we trace out the examples of those that have gone before us, we as it were derive joy from the grave, for we find the mind's wealth among the dead, who, because they [several Mss. 'for they who.'] are perfectly dead to this world, rest in secret with their riches beside them. And so he is made rich by the grave, who, following the example of the righteous, is raised up in the excellency of contemplation. But when he asks, saying, *Wherefore is light given to him that is in misery?* he intimates the reason for which he ventures to put such a question, by saying,

Ver. 23. Why is light given to a man whose way is hid, and whom God hath encompassed with darkness?

vii.

11. For 'man's way is hid to him,' in that though he already takes cognizance of the kind [*qualitate*] of life that he is leading, he does not yet know to what issue it tends. Though his affections are now fixed on things above, though he seeks them with all his longings, he is yet ignorant whether he shall persevere in the same longings. For forsaking our sins we strive after righteousness, and we know whence we are come, but we know nothing whereunto we may arrive. We know what we were yesterday, but we cannot tell what we may chance to be to-morrow. 'Man's way then is hid to him,' in that he so sets the foot of his labour, that, this notwithstanding, he can never foresee the issue of the accomplishment thereof.

12. Now there is also another 'hiding of our way.' For there are times when we are ignorant, whether the very things which we believe we do aright, are rightly done in the strict Judge's eye. For, as

we have also said a long way above, it often happens that an action of ours, which is cause for our condemnation, passes with us for the aggrandizement of virtue. Often by the same act, whereby we think to appease the Judge, He is urged to anger, when favourable. As Solomon bears witness, saying, *There is a way which seemeth right unto a man; but the end thereof are the ways of death.* [Prov. 14, 12] Hence, whilst holy men are getting the mastery over their evil habits, their very good practices even become an object of dread to them, lest, when they desire to do a good action, they be decoyed by a semblance of the thing, lest the baleful canker of corruption lurk under the fair appearance of a goodly colour. For they know that they are still charged with the burthen of corruption, and cannot exactly discern the things that be good. And when they bring before their eyes the standard of the final Judgment, there are times when they fear the very things which they approve in themselves; and indeed they are in mind wholly intent on the concerns of the interior, yet alarmed from uncertainty about their doings, they know not whither they are going. Hence after he had said, *Wherefore is light given to one that is in misery?* it is with propriety added, *to a man whose way is hid?* As though the words were, 'Why has that man this life's success for his portion, who knows not of his course of conduct, in what esteem it is held by his Judge. And it is rightly subjoined, *And whom God hath encompassed with darkness.* For man is 'encompassed with darkness,' since howsoever he may burn with heavenly longings, he is ignorant how it goes with him in the interior. And he is in great fear lest aught concerning himself should meet him in the Judgment, which is now hidden from himself in the aspirations of holy fervour. 'Man is encompassed with darkness,' in that he is closed in by the clouds of his own ignorance. Is not that man 'encompassed with darkness,' who most often neither remembers the past, nor finds out the future, and scarce knows the present? That wise man had seen himself to be encompassed with darkness, when he said, *And with labour do we find the things that are before us; but the things that are in heaven who shall search out?* [Wisd. 9, 16]

The Prophet beheld himself 'encompassed with' such 'darkness,' when he was unable to discover the interior springs of His inmost economy, saying, *He made darkness His secret place.* [Ps. 18, 11] For the Author of our being, in that, when we were cast out into this place of exile, He took from us the light of His vision, buried Himself from our eyes as it were 'in the secret place of darkness.'

13. Now as often as we attentively regard this same darkness of our blind estate, we stir up the mind to lamentation. For it weeps for the state of blindness, which it is under without, if it remember in humility that it is bereft of light in the interior, and when it looks to the darkness which surrounds it, it is wrung with ardent longing for the inward brightness, and rent with thought's whole effort, and that light above, which as soon as created it relinquished, now debarred, it makes the object of its search. Whence it very often happens that that radiance of inward joy bursts out amidst those very tears of piety; and that the mind, which had lain torpid in a state of blindness, being fed with sighs, receives strength to gaze at the interior brightness. Whence it rightly proceeds,

Ver. 24. For my sighing cometh before I eat.

14. For the soul's 'eating' is its being fed with the con- **viii.**
templations of the light above, and thus it sighs before it eats, in that it first travails with the groanings of sorrow, and afterwards is replenished with the cheer of contemplation. For except it sigh, it eats not, in that he that refuses to humble himself, in this exile we are in, by the groanings of heavenly desires, never tastes the delights of the eternal inheritance. For all they are starved of the food of truth, that take joy in the emptiness of this scene of our pilgrimage, but he 'sighs,' that 'eats,' because all who are touched with the love of truth, are at the same time fed with the refreshments of contemplation. The Prophet 'ate sighing,' when he said, *My tears have been my bread*. [Ps. 42, 3] For the soul is fed by its own grief, when it is lifted up to the joys above by the tears, which it sheds, and indeed it bears within its sorrowful sighings, but it receives food for its refreshing, the more the force of its love gushes out in weeping. And hence blessed Job still goes on with the violence of that weeping, adding,

And my roarings are poured out like overflowing waters.

15. Waters, that overflow, advance with a rush, and swell **ix.**
with billows evermore increasing. Now whilst the Elect set the judgments of God before the eyes of their mind, whilst they dread the secret sentence concerning them, whilst they trust to at-

tain to God, but yet are in fear lest they should not attain, while they call to mind their past doings, which they weep over, whilst they shrink from the events that still await them, in that they are unknown, there are gathered in them as it were a kind of billows, as of water, which spend themselves in the roarings of grief, as upon a shore beneath them. The holy man then saw how great are the billows of our thoughts in our penitential mourning, and he called the very waves of our grief overflowing waters, saying, *And my roarings are like overflowing waters*. Now there are times when the righteous, as we likewise said a little above, even in the midst of their very good works, are affrighted and give themselves to continual mourning, lest they should offend by some secret misdemeanour therein. And when God's scourges suddenly take hold of them, they imagine that they have done despite to the grace of their Maker, in that being either impeded by infirmities, or weighed down with sadness, they are not ready to perform works of mercy to their neighbours; and their heart turns to mourning, for that the body is become slack to its devout ministration. And whereas they see that they are not adding to their reward, they fear that their past deeds also have been displeasing. Hence when blessed Job described his roaring like overflowing waters, he thereupon added,

Ver. 25. For the thing that I greatly feared is come upon me, and that which I am afraid of is come unto me.

X. 16. The righteous therefore lament and fear, and torment themselves with bitter lamentations, because they dread to be given over, and though they rejoice in their own correction [*correptio*], the correction itself disturbs their fearful spirits, lest the evil, which they are undergoing should not be the merciful stroke of discipline, but the righteous visitation of vengeance. And the Psalmist reflecting thereupon says with justice, *Who knoweth the power of Thine anger?* [Ps. 90, 11] For the power of God's anger cannot be conceived by our faculties, in that His dispensation, by its undiscerned provisions concerning us, often takes us up in that very point where it is counted to abandon us, and in the very thing wherein it is supposed to take us up, it forsakes us. So that very often that is rendered grace to us, which we call wrath, and that is sometimes wrath, which we account to be grace. For strokes of affliction are the correction of some men, but others they lead to a frenzy of impatience, and there are some whom prosperity, in that it soothes them, calms from a state of madness, while there are others whom, seeing that it uplifts them, it wholly turns adrift from every hope of conversion. Now vice forces all men down beneath, but some the more easily return from thence, that they take the greater shame to themselves to have fallen thereunto. And attainments in virtue in every case raise men on high, yet sometimes some men, in that swelling thoughts are engendered from their virtues, fall down by the very pathway of their rise. And so forasmuch as the power of God's wrath is little known, under all circumstances it must needs be unceasingly feared. It proceeds;

Ver. 26. Did I not dissemble it? Did I not hold my peace? Did I not rest quiet? Yet wrath came upon me.

17. Though in every situation of life, we sin in thought, word, and deed, the mind is then hurried along in all these three ways with the greater freedom from control, when it is lifted up with this world's good fortune. For when it sees that it surpasses other men in power, feeling proudly, it thinks high things of itself, and when no opposition is offered by any to the authority of its word, the tongue has the more uncontrolled range along precipitous paths; and while it is permitted to do all that it likes, it reckons all that it likes to be lawfully permitted it. But good men, when supported by this world's power, bring themselves under severer discipline of the mind, in proportion as they know that, from the intolerance of power, they are persuaded to unlicensed acts, as if they were more licensed to do them [vid. b. xx.c.73.]. Thus they refrain their hearts from surveying their own glory, they check their tongues from unrestrained talk, they guard their actions from restless roaming. For it often happens that they that are in power lose the good things that they do, because they entertain high conceits, and while they reckon themselves to be of use for every purpose, they blast the merit even of the usefulness they have laid out. For in order that a man's deeds may be rendered of greater worth, they must needs always appear worthless in his own esteem, lest the same good action elevate the heart of the doer, and in elevating overthrow its author by selfelation, more effectually than it helps the very persons for whom it may chance to be rendered. For it is hence that the King of Babylon, while he was secretly revolving in his own mind, in **xi.**

the pride of his heart, saying, *Is not this great Babylon which I have builded?* was suddenly turned into an irrational beast. For he lost all that he had been made, because he would not humbly keep back what he had done; and because in the Pride of his heart he lifted himself up above men, he lost that very human faculty, which he had in common with man. And often they that are in power burst out at random into insulting language towards their dependants, and this merit, viz. that they serve their office of authority with vigilance, they lose by reason of their forwardness of speech, plainly considering with overlittle dread the words of the Judge, that he *who shall say to his brother without cause Thou fool*, [Matt. 5, 22] makes himself obnoxious to hell fire. Often they that are in power, whereas they know not how to refrain lawful actions, slide into such as are unlawful, and unquiet. For he alone is never brought down in things unlawful, who is careful to restrain himself at times even from things lawful. It is with the bands of this selfsame restraint that Paul showed himself to be bound for good, when he says, *All things are lawful to me, but all things are not expedient* [1 Cor. 6, 12]; and in order to show in what exceeding freedom of mind he was set at large by reason of this very restraint, he thereupon added, *All things are lawful for me, but I will not be brought under the power of any*. For when the mind pursues after the desires that it entertains, it is convicted of being enslaved to the things, by the love of which it is subdued. But Paul, 'to whom all things are lawful,' is 'brought under the power of none;' in that by restraining himself even from things lawful, those very objects, which, if enjoyed, would weigh him down, being contemned, he rises above.

18. Let blessed Job then declare for our better instruction what he was when in power, in these words, *Did I not dissemble?* For when we are in possession of power, it is both to be taken account of for purposes of utility, and to be kept out of sight because of Pride, in order that he that uses it, on the one hand, that he may render service therewith, may be aware that he has the power, and on the other, that he may not be elated, may not be aware that he has the power. Now what he was in word of mouth, let him add in these words, *Was I not silent?* What in respect of forbidden deeds, let him further subjoin, *Did I not rest quiet?* But the being *silent* and *quiet* admit of being yet more minutely examined into. Thus, to be *silent* is to

withhold the mind from the cry of earthly desires. For all tumult of the breast is a strong and mighty clamouring.

19. Moreover they rest, that bear themselves well in power, in that they prefer to lay aside, at intervals, the din of earthly business for the love of God, lest whilst the lowest objects incessantly occupy the mind, it should altogether fall away from the highest. For they know that it can never be lifted up to things above, if it be continually busied in those below with tumultuous care and concern; for what should that mind gain concerning God in the midst of business, which, even when at liberty, strives with difficulty to apprehend aught that concerns Him? And it is well said by the Psalmist, *Keep yourselves aloof, and know that I am God*. [Ps. 46, 10] For he that neglects to keep himself aloof to God, by his own judgment upon himself hides the light of God's vision from his eyes. Hence moreover it is declared by Moses, that those fish that have no fins should not be eaten. [Lev. 11, 10. 12.] For the fish, that have fins, are wont to make leaps above the water. Thus they only pass into the body of the Elect in the manner of food, who, whilst they yield themselves to the lowest charges, can sometimes by the mind's leaps mount up to things on high, that they may not always be buried in the deeps of care, and be reached by no breath of the highest love as of the free air. They, then, who are busied in temporal affairs, then only manage external things aright, when they betake them with solicitude to those of the interior, when they take no delight in the clamours of disquietudes without, but repose within themselves in the bosom of tranquil rest.

20. For men of depraved minds never cease to keep on the tumult of earthly business within their own breasts, even when they are unemployed. For they retain pictured in imagination the things, which their love is fixed on, and though they be employed in no outward work, yet within themselves they are toiling and labouring under the weight of an unquiet quiet. And if the management of these same things be accorded to them, they wholly go forth from themselves, and follow after these temporal and transient concerns by the path of their purpose of mind, with the unintermitted steps of the thoughts. But pious minds, on the one hand,. seek not such things when lacking, and on the other, they bear them with difficulty, when present, for they fear lest by the care of external things they be made to go out of themselves. Which same is well represented in the life of

those two brothers, concerning whom it is written, *And Esau was a cunning hunter, a man of the field; and Jacob was a plain man dwelling in tents.* [Gen. 25, 27. Vulg.] Or it is said in the other translation [so lxx.], *he dwelt at home.* For what is represented by Esau's hunting but the life of those, who, giving a loose to themselves in external pleasures, follow the flesh? and, moreover, he is described to be *a man of the field*, for the lovers of this world cultivate the external in the same proportion, that they leave uncultivated their internal parts. But Jacob is recorded to be *a plain man, dwelling in tents*, or *dwelling at home*, in that, truly, all, that seek to avoid being dissipated in external cares, abide plain men in the interior, and in the dwelling place of their conscience; for to 'dwell in tents,' or 'in the house,' is to restrain one's self within the secrets of the heart, nor ever to let themselves run loose without in their desires, lest, while men gape after a multitude of objects without, they be led away from themselves by the alienation of their thoughts. So let him, who was tried and trained in prosperity, say, *Did I not dissemble it? Did I not hold my peace? Did I not rest quiet?* For, as we have said above, when holy men receive the smiles of transitory prosperity, they 'dissemble' the favour of the world, as though they were ignorant of it, and with a resolute step they inwardly trample upon that, whereby they are outwardly lifted up. And they 'hold their peace,' in that they never clamour with the uproar of wicked doings. For all iniquity has its voice belonging to it in the secret judgments of God. Hence it is written, *The cry of Sodom and Gomorrah is great*. And they 'rest quiet,' when they are not only hurried away by no unruly appetite of temporal desires, but over and above eschew the busying themselves out of due measure with the necessary concerns of this present life.

21. But while they do this, they are still made to feel the strokes of a Father's hand, that they may come to their inheritance the more perfect, in proportion as the rod, striking in pity, is daily purifying them even from the very least sins. Thus they are unceasingly doing righteous acts, yet are perpetually undergoing severe troubles. For often our very righteousness itself, when brought to the test of God's righteous eye, proves unrighteousness, and that which is bright in the estimate of the doer, is foul in the Judge's searching sight. Hence when Paul said, *For I know nothing by myself*; he forthwith added, *Yet am I not hereby justified*; [1 Cor. 4, 4] and immediately implying the reason wherefore he was not justified, he says, *But he*

that judgeth me is the Lord. As though he said, 'For this reason I say that I am not justified herein, viz. that I know nothing by myself because I know that I am tested with greater exactness by Him, That judgeth me.' Therefore we must keep out of sight all that favours us outwardly, we must keep under control whatsoever is clamorous within, we must eschew the things that twine themselves about us as necessary, and yet in all of these we must still fear the chastisements of a strict inquisition; since even our very perfection itself does not lack sin, did not the severe Judge weigh the same with mercy in the exact balance of His examination.

22. And it is well added, *Yet indignation came upon me*. For with wonderful skilfulness of instruction, when about to tell of the chastisements, he premised the good deeds, that each man might hence be led to consider what punishments await sinners hereafter, if the righteous even are chastised here with strokes so strong. For it is hence that Peter says, *For the time is come that Judgment must begin at the house of God, And if the righteous scarcely be saved, where shall the ungodly and the sinner appear?* [1 Peter 4, 17. 18.] Hence Paul, after he said many things in commendation of the Thessalonians, straightway added, *So that we ourselves glory in you in the churches of God, for your patience and faith in all your persecutions and tribulations that ye endure; Which is a manifest token of the righteous judgment of God*. [2 Thess. 1, 4. 5.] As if he said, 'Whilst you, that act so uprightly, undergo so many hardships, what else is it than that ye are giving examples of the righteous judgment of God, since from your punishment it is to be inferred in what sort He smites those with whom He is wroth, if He suffers you to be thus afflicted, in whom He delights; or how He will strike those towards whom He shows righteous judgment, if He thus torments your own selves, whom with pitifulness He cherishes in reproving.

23. The first words, then, of blessed Job being ended, his friends that had come in pity to comfort him, set themselves by turns to the upbraiding of him; and while they launch out to words of strife, they drop the purpose of pity, which they had come for. And indeed they do this with no bad intent, but, though they manifest feeling for the stricken man, they supposed him to be no otherwise stricken than for his wickedness; and whereas guarded speech does not follow that good intention, the very purpose of mercy is turned into the sin of an offence. For it was their duty to consider to whom and on what

occasion they spake; in that he, to whom they had come, was a righteous man, and besieged with the strokes of God's hand; and so they should from his past life have estimated those words of his mouth, which they were unable to understand, and not have convicted him from present strokes, but have entertained fear for their own lives, and not as it were by reasoning have lifted themselves above, but by lamenting joined themselves to that stricken Saint, so that their knowledge might in no wise display itself in words, but that great teacher, grief, might instruct the tongue of the comforters to speak aright. And though they perchance might in anything be of a different mind, assuredly it was meet that they should express these feelings with humility, lest by words without restraint they should accumulate wounds upon the smitten soul.

24. For it often happens that, because they cannot be understood, either the doings or the sayings of the better men are displeasing to the worse; but they are not to be rashly censured by them, inasmuch as they cannot be apprehended in their true sense. Often that is done in pursuance of policy ['*dispensatorie,*' in economy] by greater men, which is accounted an error by their inferiors. Often many things are said by the strong, which the weak only decide upon, because they know nothing about them. And this is well represented by that Ark of the Testament being inclined on one side by the cows kicking, which the Levite desiring to set upright, because he thought it would fall, he immediately received sentence of death. [2 Sam. 6, 7] For what is the mind of the just man but the Ark of the Testament? which, as it is being carried, is inclined by the kicking of the cows; in that it sometimes happens that even he, who rules well, being shaken by the disorder of the people subject to him, is moved by nought else than love to a condescension in policy. But in this, which is done in policy, that very bending, that is, of strength is accounted a fall by the inexperienced; and hence there are some of those that are in subjection, who put out the hand of censure against it, yet by that very rashness of theirs they forthwith drop from life. Thus the Levite stretched forth his hand as it were in aid, but he lost his life in being guilty of offence, in that while the weak sort censure the deeds of the strong, they are themselves made outcasts from the lot of the living. Sometimes too holy men say some things condescending to the meanest subjects, while some things they deliver contemplating the highest; and foolish men, because they know

nothing of the meaning either of such condescension or elevation, presumptuously censure them. And what is it to desire to set a good man right for his condescension, but to lift up the ark that is inclined with the presuming hand of rebuke? what is it to censure a righteous man for unapprehended words, but to take the move he makes in his strength for the downfall of error? But he loses his life, who lifts up the ark of God with a high mind; in that no man would ever dare to correct the upright acts of the Saints, unless he first thought better things of himself. And hence this Levite is rightly called Oza, which same is by interpretation 'the strong one of the Lord,' in that the presumptuous severally, did they not audaciously conclude themselves 'strong in the Lord,' would never condemn as weak the saying and doings of their betters. Therefore while the friends of blessed Job leap forth against him, as if in God's defence, they transgress the rule of God's ordinance in behaving proudly.

25. But when any of the doings of better men are displeasing to the less good, they are by no means to hold their peace about the considerations which influence their minds, but to give utterance thereto with a great degree of humility, so that the purpose of him, whose feelings are pious, may, in a genuine manner, keep the form of uprightness, in proportion as he goes by the pathway of lowliness. Thus both all that we feel is to be freely expressed, and all that we express is to be uttered with the deepest humility, lest even what we intend aright we make other than right, by putting it forth in a spirit of pride. Paul had spoken many things to his hearers with humility, but it was with still more humility that he busied himself to appease them about that humble exhortation itself, saying, *And I beseech you, brethren, suffer the word of exhortation: for I have written a letter unto you in few words*. [Heb. 13, 22] And likewise bidding farewell to the Ephesians at Miletus, who were deeply grieved and loudly lamenting, he recalls his humility to their remembrance, in these words, *Therefore watch, and remember that by the space of three years I ceased not to warn everyone night and day with tears*. [Acts 20, 31] Again he says to the same persons by letter, *I therefore, the prisoner of the Lord, beseech you that ye walk worthy of the vocation, wherewith ye are called*. [Eph. 4, 1] Therefore let him infer from hence, if he ever thinks rightly at all, with what humility the disciple ought to address the Master, if the Master of the Gentiles himself, in the very things which he proclaims with authority, beseeches the disciples so sub-

missively. Let everyone collect from hence in what a spirit of humility he should communicate to those, from whom he has received examples of good living, all that he perceives aright, if Paul submitted himself in a humble strain to those, whom he himself raised up to life.

26. But Eliphaz, who is the first of the friends to speak, though he came with pity to console, yet in that he departs from meekness of speech, is ignorant of the rules of consoling; and while he neglects the guarding of his lips, he is guilty of excess, even to offering insult to the afflicted man, saying, *The tiger hath perished for lack of prey, the roaring of the lion, and the voice of the fierce lioness* [V. thus], *and the teeth of the young lions are broken* [Job 4, 10. 11.]: i.e. by the teeth of a *tiger* marking out blessed Job, as it were, with the fault of variedness; by *the roaring of the lion*, denoting that man's terribleness; by *the voice of the lioness*, the loquacity of his wife; and by the *broken teeth of the young lions*, signifying the gluttony of his sons brought to ruin. And hence the sentence of God rightly reproves the feeling of the friends, which had lifted itself up in swelling reproach, saying, *Ye have not spoken of Me the thing that is right, as My servant Job hath*. [Job 42, 7]

27. But I see that we must enquire, wherefore Paul makes use of their sentiments with so much weight of authority, if these sentiments of theirs be nullified by the Lord's rebuke? For they are the words of Eliphaz which he brought before the Corinthians, saying, *For it is written, He taketh the wise in their own craftiness*. [1 Cor. 3, 19. Job 5, 13] How then do we reject as evil what Paul establishes by authority? or how shall we account that to be right by the testimony of Paul, which the Lord by His own lips determined not to be right? But we speedily learn how little the two are at variance together, if we more exactly consider the words of that same Divine sentence, which assuredly having declared, *Ye have not spoken of Me the thing that is right*; thereupon added, *as My servant Job*. It is clear then that some things contained in their sayings were right, but they are overcome by comparison with one who was better; for among other things, which they say without reason, there are many forcible sentences they utter in addressing blessed Job; but when compared with his more forcible sayings they lose the power of their forcibleness. And many things that they say are admirable, were they not spoken against the afflicted condition of the holy man. So that in themselves they are great, but because they aim to pierce that righteous person,

that greatness loses its weight, for with whatever degree of strength, it is in vain that the javelin is sent to strike the hard stones, since it glances off the further with blunted point, the more it comes hurled with strength. Therefore, though the sayings of Job's friends be very forcible in some points, yet, since they strike the Saint's well-fenced life, they turn back all the point of their sharpness. And therefore because they are both great in themselves, and yet ought never to have been taken up against blessed Job, on the one hand let Paul, weighing them by their intrinsic excellence, deliver them as authoritative, and on the other let the Judge, forasmuch as they were delivered without caution, censure them in respect of the quality of the individual.

28. But, as we have said above that these same friends of blessed Job contain a figure of heretics, let us now search out how their words agree with heretics; for some of the opinions which they hold are very right, but in the midst of these they fall away to corrupt notions; for heretics have this especial peculiarity, that they mix good and evil, that so they may easily delude the sense of the hearer. For if they always said wrong, soon discovered in their wrongheadedness, they would be the less able to win a way for that, which they desire. Again, if they always thought right, then, surely, they would never have been heretics. But whilst with artfulness of deceiving they engage themselves with either, both by the evil they vitiate the good, and by the good they conceal the evil, to the end that it may be readily admitted; just as he that presents a cup of poison, touches the brim of the cup with honied sweets, and while this that has a sweet flavour is tasted at the first sip, that too which brings death is unhesitatingly swallowed. Thus heretics mix right with wrong, that by making a show of good things, they may draw hearers to themselves, and by setting forth evil they may corrupt them with a secret pestilence. Yet it sometimes happens that being collected by the preaching and admonitions of Holy Church, they are healed from such a contradiction in views, and hence the friends of blessed Job offer the sacrifice of their reconciliation by the hands of the same holy man, and even under attainder they are restored to the favour of the Supreme Judge. Of whom we have a fitting representation in that cleansing of the ten lepers. [Luke 14, 15] For in leprosy both a portion of the skin is brought to a bright hue, and a portion remains of a healthy colour. Lepers therefore are a figure of heretics, for in

that they blend evil with good, they cover the complexion of health with spots. And hence that they may be healed, they rightly cry out, *Jesus, Master* [*Preceptor,* Vulg.]. For whereas they notify that they have gone wrong in His words, they humbly call Him *Master* when they are to be healed, and so soon as they return to acknowledge the Master, they are at once brought back to the right state of health. But as on the sayings of his friends we have carried the preface to our interpretation somewhat far, let us now consider minutely the very words themselves which they spake. The account goes on ;

C. iv. 1, 2. Then Eliphaz the Temanite answered and said, If we assay to commune with thee, wilt thou be grieved?

xii. 29. It has been already declared above, what there is set forth in the interpretation of these names. Therefore, because we are in haste to reach the unexamined parts, we forbear to unfold again what has been already delivered. Accordingly this is to be heedfully observed, that they, that bear the semblance of heretics, begin to speak softly, saying, *If we assay to commune with thee, wilt thou, be grieved?* For heretics dread to incense their hearers at the outset of their communing with them, lest they be listened to with ears on the watch, and they carefully shun the paining of them, that they may catch their unguardedness, and what they put forward is almost always mild, while that is harsh which they cunningly introduce in going on. And hence at this time the friends of Job begin with the reverence of a gentle address, but they burst forth even to launching the darts of the bitterest invectives; for the roots of thorns themselves are soft, yet from that very softness of their own they put forth that whereby they pierce. It goes on;

But who can hold in [thus V.] *the discourse conceived?*

30. There be three kinds of men, which differ from one another by qualities carried forward in gradation. For there are some, who at the same time that they conceive evil sentiments to speak, restrain themselves in their speech by none of the graveness of silence; and there are others, who, whereas they conceive evil things, withhold themselves with a strong control of silence. And there are some, who being made strong by the exercise of virtue, are advanced even to so great a height, that, as to speaking, they do not even conceive any evil thoughts in the heart, which they should have to restrain by

keeping silence. It is shown then to which class Eliphaz belongs, who bears witness that he cannot 'withhold his conceived discourse.' Wherein too he made known this, that he knew that he would give offence by speaking. For he would never be anxious to withhold words that he cannot, unless he were assured beforehand that he would be inflicting wounds by the same; for good men check precipitancy of speech with the reins of counsel, and they take heedful thought, lest, by giving a loose to the wantonness of the tongue, they should by heedlessness of speech pierce their hearer's spirits [*conscientiam*]; hence it is well said by Solomon, *He that letteth out water is a head of strife.* [Prov. 17, 14] For 'the water is let out,' when the flowing of the tongue is let loose. And he that 'letteth out water,' is made the 'beginning of strife,' in that by the incontinency of the lips, the commencement of discord is afforded. Thus, as the wicked are light in mind, so they are precipitate in speech, and neglect to keep silence, thoroughly considering what they should say. And what a light spirit [*conscientia*] conceives, a lighter tongue delivers apace. Hence on this occasion Eliphaz infers from his own experience a thing, which in a feeling of hopelessness he believes concerning all men; saying, *But who can withhold his conceived discourse?* It proceeds;

Ver. 3, 4. Behold, thou hast instructed many, and thou hast strengthened the weak hands. Thy words have upholden him that was falling, and thou hast strengthened the feeble knees.

xiv.

31. If the text of the historical account be regarded in itself, it is of great service to the reader, that in blessed Job, instead of the ripping up of vices, proclaim is made of his virtues by his reviling friends; for the testimony to our manner of life is never so strong, as when commendable things are told by him, who aims to fasten guilt upon our head. But let us consider of what a lofty height that man was, who by instructing the ignorant, strengthening the weak, upholding the faltering, amid the cares of his household, amidst the charge of countless concerns, amidst anxious feelings for his children, amidst the pursuit of so many laborious occupations, devoted himself to putting others in the right way. And being busied indeed, he executed these offices, yet being free, he did service in the master's office of instruction. By exercising superintendence, he disposed of temporal things, by preaching, he announced eternal truths; uprightness of life, both by practice he showed to all behold-

ers, and by speech he conveyed to all that heard him. But all that are either heretics or bad men, in recording the excellencies of the good, turn them into grounds of accusation. Hence Eliphaz deduces occasion of reviling against blessed Job from the same quarter, whence he related commendable things of him; for it goes on,

Ver. 5. But now it is come upon thee, and thou faintest: it toucheth thee, and thou art troubled.

xv. 32. All men of froward mind assail the life of the righteous in two ways; for either they assert that what they say is wrong, or that what they say aright they never observe; and hence blessed Job is reproved by his friends further on for his mode of speech, whereas now he is torn in pieces for having spoken right things, but not having observed them. And so at one time the speech, and at another time the practice of the good meets with the disapproval of the wicked, in order that either the tongue being rebuked may hold its peace, or the life, being convicted by the testimony of that same tongue of theirs, may give way under the charge. And mark that first they bring forward commendations of the tongue, and afterwards complain of the weakness of the life. For the wicked, that they may not openly show themselves to be evil, sometimes say such good things of the just, as they know to be already received concerning them by others also. But as we have said above, these very points they forthwith strain to the increase of guilt, and from hence, that they spoke favourable things also, they point out that credit is to be given them in the reverse, and with more seeming truth they intimate evil things, in proportion as they commended the good with seeming zeal. Thus they wrest words of favourable import to the service of accusation, in that they afterwards more deeply wound the life of the righteous from the same source, whence a little before in semblance they vindicated it. But it often happens that their good qualities, which they first condemn when possessed, they afterwards admire, as if departed. And hence Eliphaz, as he declares them to be departed, subjoins the virtues of the holy man, enumerating them, and saying,

Ver. 6. Where is thy fear, thy strength, thy patience, and the perfectness of thy ways? [*thus V.*]

xvi. 33. All which same he makes to succeed that sentence which he set before, saying, *But now a stroke is come upon thee, and thou faintest; it toucheth thee, and thou art troubled.* Thus he declares that they were brought to nought all of them together, in this, that he blames blessed Job's being troubled by the scourge. Yet it is to be well taken notice of, that though he chides unbefittingly, yet the ranks of virtues he fitly describes; for in enumerating the virtues of blessed Job, he marked out his life in four stages, in that he both added strength to fear, and patience to strength, and to patience, perfection. Since one sets out in the way of the Lord with fear, that he may go on to strength; for as in the world boldness begets strength, so in the way of God boldness engenders weakness; and as in the way of the world fear gives rise to weakness, so in the way of God fear produces strength; as Solomon witnesses, who says, *In the fear of the Lord is strong confidence.* [Prov. 14, 26] For 'strong confidence' is said 'to be in the fear of the Lord,' in that, in truth, our mind so much the more valorously sets at nought all the tenors of temporal vicissitudes, the more thoroughly that it submits itself in fear to the Author of those same temporal things. And being stablished in the fear of the Lord, it encounters nothing without to fill it with alarm, in that whereas it is united to the Creator of all things by a righteous fear, it is by a certain powerful influence raised high above them all. For strength is never shown saving in adversity, and hence *patience* is immediately made to succeed to *strength*. For every man proves himself in a much truer sense to have advanced in 'strength,' in proportion as he bears with the bolder heart the wrongs of other men. For he was little strong in himself, who is brought to the ground by the wickedness of another. He, in that he cannot bear to face opposition, lies pierced with the sword of his cowardice. But forasmuch as perfection springs out of patience, immediately after patience we have the perfectness of his ways introduced. For he is really perfect, who feels no impatience towards the imperfection of his neighbour; since he that goes off, not being able to bear the imperfection of another, is his own witness against himself, that he is not yet perfectly advanced. Hence Truth says in the Gospel, *In your patience possess ye your souls.* [Luke 21, 19] For what is it to possess our souls, but to live by the rule of perfection in all things, to command all the motions of the mind from the citadel of virtue? He then that maintains patience possesses his soul, in that from hence he is endued with strength to encounter all adversities, whence even by overcoming himself he is made master of himself; and as he quells himself in a manner worthy of all praise, he comes forth unquelled with dauntless front, because by conquering himself in his pleasures, he makes himself invincible to reverses. But as Eliphaz rebuked him with reviling, so now he adds a few words, as if in exhortation, saying,

Ver. 7. Remember, I pray thee, who ever perished being innocent? or where were the righteous cut off?

xvii. 34. Whether it be heretics, of whom we have said that the friends of blessed Job bore an image, or whether any of the froward ones, they are as blameable in their admonitions, as they are immoderate in their condemnation. For he says, *Who ever perished being innocent? or where were the righteous cut off?* Since it often happens that in this life both 'the innocent perish,' and 'the righteous are 'utterly cut off,' yet in perishing they are reserved to glory eternal. For if none that is innocent perished, the Prophet would not say, *The righteous perisheth, and no man layeth it to heart*. [Is. 51, 1] If God in His providential dealings did not carry off the righteous, Wisdom would never have said of the righteous man, *Yea, speedily was he taken away, lest that wickedness should alter his understanding*. [Wisd. 4, 11] If no visitation ever smote the righteous, Peter would never foretell it, saying, *For the time is come that judgment must begin at the house of God*. [1 Pet. 4, 17] They then are really righteous, who are furnished forth by the love of the Country above to meet all the ills of the present life. For all that fear to endure ills here, for the sake of eternal blessings, clearly are not righteous men. But Eliphaz does not take account either that the righteous are cut off, or that the innocent perish here, in that oftentimes they that serve God, not in the hope of heavenly glory, but for an earthly recompense, make a fiction in their own head of that which they are seeking after, and, taking upon themselves to be instructors, in preaching earthly immunity, they show by all their pains what is the thing they love. It goes on ;

Ver. 8, 9. Even, as I have seen, they that plough iniquity, and [V. *so*] *sow sorrows, and reap the same, by the blast of God do they perish, and by the breath of His nostrils are they consumed.*

xviii. 35. To 'sow griefs' is to utter deceits, but to 'reap griefs' is to prevail by so speaking. Or, surely, they 'sow griefs,' who do froward actions, they 'reap griefs,' when they ate punished for this forwardness. For the harvest of grief is the recompense of condemnation, and whereas it is immediately introduced that they that 'sow and reap griefs,' 'perish by the blast of God,' and are 'consumed by the breath of His nostrils,' in this passage the 'reaping of grief' is shown to be not punishment as yet, but the still further perfecting of wickedness, for in 'the breath of His nostrils' the punishment of that 'reaping' is made to follow. Here then they 'sow and reap griefs,' in that all that they do is wicked, and they thrive in that very wickedness, as is said of the wicked man by the Psalmist, *His ways are always grievous; Thy judgments are far above out of his sight: as for all his enemies, he puffeth at them.* [Ps. 10, 5] And it is soon after added concerning him, under his tongue is labour and grief. So then he 'sows griefs,' when he does wicked things, he 'reaps griefs,' when from the same wickednesses he grows to temporal greatness. How then is it that they 'perish by the blast of God,' who are for the most part permitted to abide long here below, and in greater prosperity than the righteous? For hence it is said of them again by the Psalmist, *They are not in trouble as other men, neither are they plagued like other folk.* [Ps. 73, 5] Hence Jeremiah says, *Wherefore doth the way of the wicked prosper?* [Jer. 12, 1] For because, as it is written, *For the Lord is* [Vulg.] *a long-suffering rewarder* [Ecclus. 5, 4], He oftentimes for long bears with those, whom He condemns for all eternity. Yet sometimes He strikes quickly, in that He hastens to the succour of the pusillanimity of the innocent. Therefore Almighty God sometimes permits the wicked to have their own way for long, that the ways of the righteous may be more purely cleansed. Yet sometimes He slays the unrighteous with speedy destruction, and by their ruin He strengthens the hearts of the innocent. For if He were now to smite all that do evil, on whom would He yet have to show forth the final Judgment? And if He never at any time smote any man, who would ever have believed that God regarded human affairs? Sometimes then He strikes the bad, that He may show that He does not leave wickedness unpunished. But sometimes He bears with the wicked for long, that He may teach the heedful what judgment they are reserved for.

36. Thus this sentence of the cutting off of the wicked, if it be not spoken of all men in general at the end of this present state of being,

is undoubtedly to a great degree made void of the force of truth; but it will then be true, when iniquity shall no longer have reprieve. And perchance it may be more lightly taken in this sense, since neither 'the innocent perishes' nor 'the upright is cut off,' in that though here he is worn out in the flesh, yet in the sight of the eternal Judge he is renewed with true health. And they that 'sow and reap griefs,' 'perish by the blast of God,' in that in proportion as they go on here deeper in doing wickedly, they are the more severely stricken with the damnation to follow. But whereas he premises this sentence with the word, *Remember*, it is clearly evident that something past is recalled to mind, and not anything future proclaimed. Then therefore Eliphaz would have spoken more truly, if he had believed that these things were wrought on the head of the wicked in general by final vengeance.

37. But this point, that God is said to 'breathe,' claims to be more particularly made out. For we, when we 'breathe,' draw the air from the outside within us, and, thus drawn within, we give it forth without. God then is said to 'breathe' in recompensing vengeance, in that from occasions without He conceives the purpose of judgment within Him, and from the internal purpose sends forth the sentence without. When God 'breathes' as it were, somewhat is drawn in from things without, when He sees our evil ways without, and ordains judgment within. And again as if by God 'breathing,' the breath is sent forth from within, when from the internal conception of the purpose, the outward decree of condemnation is delivered. And so it is rightly said that they, that 'sow griefs,' perish 'by the breath of God,' for wherein they execute wicked deeds outwardly, they are deservedly stricken from within. Or, surely, when God is said to 'breathe,' in that the breath of His wrath is immediately introduced, by the designation of His 'breathing' may be denoted that very visitation of His. For when we are wroth, we kindle with the breath of rage. To show the Lord then meditating vengeance, He is said to 'breathe' in His indignation, not that in His own Nature He is capable of turning or change, but that after long endurance, when He executes vengeance upon the sinner, He, Who continueth tranquil in Himself, seems in commotion to them that perish. For whereas the condemned soul sees the Judge arrayed against its doings, He is exhibited to it as troubled, in that it is itself troubled by its own guiltiness before His eyes. But after he had in appearance

exhorted him with clemency, he openly subjoins language of reproach, saying,

Ver. 10. The roaring of the lion, and the voice of the lioness, and the teeth of the young lions are broken.

xix.

38. For what does he call *the roaring of the lion* but, as we have said a little above, the severe character of that man? what *the voice of the lioness*, but his wife's loquacity? what the *teeth of the young lions*, but the greediness of his children? For because his sons had perished when feasting, they are denoted by the term of 'teeth;' and while unsparing Eliphaz rejoices that they are all 'broken,' he denounces them as deservedly condemned. And he yet further doubles the cruelty of his reproaches, when he adds;

Ver. 11. The tiger perisheth for lack of prey, and the stout lions' whelps are scattered abroad. [Vulg. *thus*]

xx.

39. For whom does he denote by the name of 'tiger' but blessed Job, marked with the stamp of changeableness or covered with the spots of dissimulation? For every dissembler, in that he desires to appear righteous, can never show himself pure in all things; for while he assumes some virtues in hypocrisy, and secretly gives way to vicious habits, some concealed vices speedily break out upon the surface, and exhibit the hide of overlaid hypocrisy, like a coat for sight, varied with their admixture, so that it is very often a marvel how one, who is seen to be master of such great virtues, should be at the same time stained with such damnable deeds. But truly every hypocrite is a tiger, in that while he derives a pure colour from pretence, it is striped with the intermediate blackness of vicious habits. For it often happens that while he is extolled for pureness of chastity, he renders himself foul by the stain of avarice. Often while he makes a fair show by the good quality of bountifulness, he is stained with spots of lust. Often while he is clad in the bright array of bountifulness and chastity, he is blackened by ferociousness in cruelty, as if from a zealous sense of justice. Often he is arrayed in bounty, chastity, pitifulness, in a fair outside, but is marked with the interspersed darkness of pride. And thus it comes to pass, that whereas by the intermixture of vicious habits, the hypocrite does not present an unstained appearance in himself, the tiger, as it were, cannot be of one colour. And this same 'tiger' seizes the prey, in

that he usurps to himself the glory of human applause. For he, that is lifted up by usurped praise, is as it were glutted with the prey. And it is well that the applause that hypocrites have is called 'prey.' For it is nought else than a prey, when the things of another are taken away by violence. Now every hypocrite, in that by counterfeiting the life of righteousness he seizes for himself the praise that belongs to the righteous, does in truth carry off what is another's. Thus Eliphaz, who knew that blessed Job had walked in ways worthy to be praised in the period of his wellbeing, concluded from the stroke that came after that he had maintained these in hypocrisy, saying, *The tiger perisheth for lack of prey*. As if he had said plainly, 'The shifting of thine hypocrisy is at end, because the homage of applause is also taken from thee, and thine hypocrisy is in 'lack of prey,' in that being stricken by the hand of God, it lacks the favourable regards of man.'

40. But in the translation of the Septuagint, it is not said 'the tiger,' but 'the *Myrmicoleon perisheth for lack of prey*.' For the Myrmicoleon is a very little creature, a foe to ants, which hides itself under the dust, and kills the ants laden with grains, and devours them thus destroyed. Now 'Myrmicoleon' is rendered in the Latin tongue either 'the ants' lion,' or indeed more exactly 'an ant and lion at once.' Now it is lightly called 'an ant and lion;' in that with reference to winged creatures, or to any other small-sized animals, it is an ant, but with reference to the ants themselves it is a lion. For it devours these like a lion, yet by the other sort it is devoured like an ant. When then Eliphaz says, the Ant-lion perisheth, what does he censure in blessed Job under the title of 'Ant-lion' but his fearfulness and audacity? As if he said to him in plain words, 'Thou art not unjustly stricken, in that thou hast shown thyself a coward towards the lofty, a bully towards those beneath thee.' As though he had said in plain terms, 'Fear made thee crouch towards the crafty sort, hardihood swelled thee full towards the simple folk, but 'the Ant-lion' no longer hath prey,' in that thy cowardly self elation, being beaten down with blows, is stayed from doing injury to others.' But forasmuch as we have said that the friends of blessed Job contain a figure of Heretics, there is a pressing necessity to show how these same words of Eliphaz are to be understood in a typical sense likewise.

Allegorical

Ver. 10. The roaring of the lion, and the voice of the lioness, and the teeth of the young lions, are broken.

xxi.

41. Forasmuch as the nature of everything is compounded of different elements, in Holy Writ different things are allowably represented by anyone thing. For the lion has magnanimity, it has also ferocity: by its magnanimity then it represents the Lord, by its ferocity the devil. Hence it is declared of the Lord, *Behold, the Lion of the tribe of Judah, the Root of David hath prevailed.* [Rev. 5, 5] Hence it is written of the devil, *Your adversary, the devil, like a roaring lion, walketh about seeking whom he may devour.* [1 Pet. 5, 8] But by the title of a 'lioness' sometimes Holy Church, sometimes Babylon is represented to us. For on this account, that she is bold to encounter all that withstand, the Church is called a 'lioness,' as is proved by the words of blessed Job, who in pointing out Judaea forsaken by the Church, says, *The sons of the traders have not trodden, nor the lioness passed by it.* [Job 28, 8. Vulg.] And sometimes under the title of a lioness is set forth the city of this world, which is Babylon, which ravins against the life of the innocent with terribleness of ferocity, which being wedded to our old enemy like the fiercest lion, conceives the seeds of his froward counsel, and produces from her own body reprobate sons, as cruel whelps, after his likeness. But the 'lion's whelps' are reprobate persons, engendered to a life of sin by the misleading of evil spirits, who both all of them together constitute that great city of the world which we have declared before, even Babylon; and yet these same sons of Babylon severally are called not 'a lioness' but 'a lioness's whelps.' For as the whole Church together is denominated Sion, but the several individual Saints the sons of Sion, so both the several individuals among the reprobate are called the children of Babylon, and all the reprobate together are designated the same Babylon.

42. But so long as good men remain in this life, they keep watch over themselves with anxious heed, lest the lion that goeth about surprise them by guile, i.e. lest our old enemy slay them under some show of virtue; lest the voice of the lioness stun their ears, i.e. lest the glory of Babylon catch away their minds from the love of the heavenly country; lest 'the teeth of the young lions' bite them, i.e. lest the promptings of the reprobate gain power in their heart. But, on the other hand, heretics are already as if secured touching holiness, because they fancy that they have surmounted all obstacles by the preeminent merit of their life. And hence it is said here, *The roaring of the lion, and the voice of the lioness, and the teeth if the young*

lions are broken. As though it were expressed in plain words; 'We for this reason are never beaten and bruised with any strokes, for that we tread under at once the might of the old enemy, and the lust of earthly glory, and the promptings of all the reprobate, overcoming them by the preeminence of our life.' Hence it is further added;

Ver. 11. The tiger perisheth for lack of prey, and the lions' whelps are scattered abroad.

xxii. 43. By the title of a 'tiger' he again represents him, whom he formerly designated by the name of a 'lion.' For Satan both for his cruelty is called 'a lion,' and for the variousness of his manifold cunning he is not unsuitably designated 'a tiger.' For one while he presents himself to man's senses lost as he is, one while he exhibits himself as an Angel of light. Now by caressing he works upon the minds of the foolish sort, now by striking terror he forces them to commit sin. At one time he labours to win men to evil ways without disguise, at another time he cloaks himself in his promptings under the garb of virtue. This beast, then, which is so variously spotted, is rightly called 'a tiger,' being with the LXX called an 'Ant-lion,' as we have said above. Which same creature, as we have before shown, hiding itself in the dust kills the ants carrying their corn, in that the Apostate Angel, being cast out of heaven upon the earth, in the very pathway of their practice besets the minds of the righteous, providing for themselves the provender of good works, and whilst he overcomes them by his snares, he as it were kills by surprise the ants carrying their grains. And he is rightly called 'Ant-lion,' i.e. 'a lion and ant.' For as we have said, to the ants he is 'a lion,' but to the birds of the air, 'an ant,' in that our old enemy, as he is strong to encounter those that yield to him, is weak against such as resist him. For if consent be yielded to his persuasions, like a lion he can never be sustained, but if resistance be offered, like an ant he is ground in the dust. Therefore to some he is 'a lion,' to others 'an ant,' in that carnal minds sustain his cruel assaults with difficulty, but spiritual minds trample upon his weakness with virtue's foot. Heretics then, because they are full of pride by pretension to sanctity, say as it were in exultation, *The Ant-lion*, or probably, *the tiger perisheth for lack of prey.* As though the words were plainly expressed, 'The old foe has no prey in us, in that, as far as regards our purposes, he already lies defeated.' Now it is for this reason that he is again mentioned under the title of 'an Ant lion,' or of 'a tiger,' who had been already set forth by the 'roaring of the lion broken,' because whatever is said in joy, is repeated over and over. For when the mind is full of exultation, it redoubles the expressions. And hence the Psalmist, from true joy, frequently repeats this, that he was assured that he had been heard, saying, *the Lord hath heard the voice of my weeping. The Lord hath heard my supplications. The Lord hath received my prayer.* [Ps. 6, 8. 9.]

44. But when holy men are glad of heart that they have been rescued from some evil habits, they possess [Lit. 'shake'] themselves with great fear even in that very gladness. For though they be now rescued from the commotion of any single storm, yet they call to mind that they are still tossing in the treacherous waves of an uncertain sea, and they so exult in hope that they tremble in fear, and so tremble in fear that they exult in confidence of hope. Whence it is said by the same Psalmist, *Serve the Lord with fear, and rejoice with trembling.* [Ps. 2, 11] But on the other hand, they, whom a specious show of sanctity fills with big thoughts, when they get the better of any one evil habit, immediately erect their heart in pride, and as it were glory in the perfection of their lives, and for this, that perchance they have been once snatched from the perils of the storm, they already forget that they are still at sea, they look upon themselves as great in all things, and imagine that they have wholly overcome their old adversary; they regard all men below them, in that they believe that their wisdom places them above all. Whence it is added;

Now a secret word was spoken to me.

xxiii.

45. 'A secret word,' heretics pretend to hear, that they may bring a certain reverence for their preaching over their hearers' minds. And hence they preach with a secret meaning, that their preaching may seem to be holy, in proportion as it is at the same time hidden. Now they are loath to have a common sort of knowledge, lest they should be placed on a par with the rest of their fellow-creatures, and they are ever making out new things, which whilst others know nothing of, they plume their own selves on the preeminence of their knowledge before inexperienced minds. And this knowledge, as we have said, they teach is occult; for, that they may be able to show it to be wonderful, they affirm that they ob-

tained it by secret means. Hence with Solomon the woman, bearing the semblance of heretics, says, *Stolen waters are* [Vulg.] *sweeter, and bread eaten in secret is more pleasant*. [Prov. 9, 17] Whence in this place too it is added;

And mine ear as it were by stealth received the veins [Vulg.] *of the whispering thereof.*

They 'receive the veins of whispers by stealth,' in that abandoning the grace of knowledge in fellowship, they do not enter thereinto by the door, as the Lord witnesses, *Who says, He that entereth not by the door into the sheepfold, but climbeth up some other way, the same is a thief and a robber; But he that entereth in by the door is the shepherd of the sheep.* [John 10, 1. 2.] Therefore he 'receives the veins of divine whispers by stealth,' who, whilst the door of public preaching for receiving the knowledge of His excellency is forsaken, searches out the gaps and chinks of a froward understanding. But because the thief and robber, who enters by another way, both loves the darkness, and abhors the clearness of the light, it is properly added;

Ver. 13. In the horror of a vision of the night, when deep sleep falleth on men.

xxiv. 46. It often happens, that while heretics are bent to discourse of things above them, they become their own witnesses against themselves, that what they deliver is not true. For in a vision of the night the sight is uncertain. Therefore they declare that they received 'the inklings [*rimas*] of whispers' in 'the tenor of a vision of the night,' for, that the things, which they teach, may be made to appear sublime to others, they declare that they themselves can scarcely comprehend them. But it may be inferred from hence how far that can be rendered certain to their hearers, which they themselves beheld but dubiously. And so is it marvellously ordered, that while they run on speaking of sublime things, in the exposure of folly, they are entangled in the very words of their sublimity. Now to what height they rear themselves for singularity of wisdom, is shown, when he adds in the same breath, *when deep sleep falleth upon men*. As if it were openly said by heretics, 'When men are asleep beneath, we wake to receive heavenly truths, in that to us all that is known, to the knowledge whereof the dull hearts of men cannot arise.' As if they said in plain words, 'In things, wherein our understanding rises erect, the faculties of the rest of the world lie asleep.' But sometimes, when they see that this is disregarded by the hearer, they feign that they are themselves in fear of what they say. Whence it is added;

Ver. 14. Fear came upon me and trembling, which made all my bones to shake.

xxvi.

47. For because they desire to appear objects of wonder for the loftiness of their instructions, they affect to be awed at the accounts which they make up. And whilst it is a less difficulty to hear than to speak, they are bold enough to put forth that, which, forsooth, they feign that they the very same persons were scarcely able to hear. Whence it is added yet further;

Ver. 15, 16. And when a spirit passed before my face, the hair of my flesh stood up. There stood one, but I knew not the face of him.

48. That they may show that they have been made acquainted with incomprehensible mysteries, they relate, not that 'a spirit' stood still, but that it 'passed by before their face.' And they pretend that they beheld a countenance they knew not, that they may prove themselves to be known to Him, Whom the human mind is not equal to know. And here it is further added;

An image was before mine eyes, and I heard the voice as it were of a light breath of air.

xxvii.

49. Heretics often picture God to themselves by a sensible form [*imaginaliter*], seeing that they are unable to behold Him spiritually. And they tell that they hear His 'voice as of a light breath of air,' in that for the obtaining the knowledge of His secret things, they delight to have as if a particular freedom of intercourse with Him. For they never teach the things, which God reveals openly, but such as are breathed into their ears in a secret manner. All this, then, we have said, to indicate what we are to look for in the words of Eliphaz, as he bears the semblance of heretics. But forasmuch as the friends of blessed Job would never have been the friends of one so great, unless they had evidently learned something of truth, which same, while they go wrong in uttering sentences of rebuke, yet do not altogether totter in the knowledge of the truth, let us return upon these same words a little way back, that

we may make out more exactly how the things which are said concerning the perception of truth, may be delivered in a true sense by persons viewing things aright. Now sometimes heretics utter things both true and lofty, not that they themselves receive them from above, but because they have learnt them in the controversy of Holy Church, nor do they apply them to the furtherance of conscientious living, but to the display of scientific skill. Whence it very commonly happens, that by knowing they tell high truths, yet in living they know nothing what they tell. Therefore, whether as they represent heretics, who hold, not the life, but the words of knowledge, or whether in the person of the friends of blessed Job, who, doubtless, with regard to their knowledge of the truth, might in seeing realize what they aimed in teaching to give utterance to, let us more minutely examine these sayings which we have gone through, that, while the words of Eliphaz are carefully gone into, it may be shown what knowledge he possessed, though in that knowledge he failed to retain humility, who appropriated to himself peculiarly a benefit common to all. For he says,

Ver. 12. Now a hidden word was spoken to me.

xxviii. 50. For the invisible Son is called 'the hidden Word,' concerning Whom John says, *In the beginning was the Word.* [John 1, 1] Which he the same person teaches to be 'hidden' in that he adds, *and the Word was with God, and the Word was God.* But this 'hidden Word' is delivered to the minds of the Elect, when the power of the Only-Begotten Son is made manifest to believers. By 'the hidden word' we may also understand the communication of inward Inspiration, concerning which it is said by John, *His anointing teacheth you of all things.* [1 John 2, 27] Which same inspiration on being communicated to the mind of man lifts it up, and putting down all temporal interests inflames it with eternal desires, that nothing may any longer yield it satisfaction but the things that are above, and that it may look down upon all, that, from human corruption, is in a state of uproar below. And so to hear 'the hidden word' is to receive in the heart the utterance of the Holy Spirit. Which same indeed can never be known save by him, by whom it may be possessed. And hence it is said by the voice of Truth concerning this hidden utterance, *And I will pray the Father, and He shall give you another Comforter, that He may abide with, you for ever; even The*

Spirit of Truth, whom the world cannot receive. [John 14, 16. 17.] For as that 'Comforter,' after the Ascension of the Mediator, being another Consoler of mankind, is in Himself invisible, so He inflames each one that He has filled to long after the invisible things. And because worldly hearts are set upon the things that are seen alone, the world receiveth Him not, because it doth not rise up to the love of the things that are unseen. For worldly minds, in proportion as they spread themselves out in interests without, contract the bosom of the heart against the admission of Him. And because out of mankind there are few indeed, who, being purified from the pollution of earthly desires, are opened by that purification to the receiving of the Holy Spirit, this word is called 'a hidden word,' since, surely, there are particular persons that receive that in the heart, which the generality of men know nothing of. Or truly this same inspiration of the Holy Spirit is 'a hidden word,' in that it may be felt, but cannot be expressed by the noise of speech. When, then, the inspiration of God lifts up the soul without noise, 'a hidden word' is heard, in that the utterance of the Spirit sounds silently in the ear of the heart. And hence it is added;

And mine ear as it were stealthily received the veins of the whispering thereof.

xxix.

51. The ear of the heart 'receives stealthily the veins of heavenly whispering,' in that both in a moment and in secret the inspired soul is made to know the subtle quality of the inward utterance. For except it bury itself from external objects of desire, it fails to enter into the internal things. It is both hidden that it may hear, and it hears that it may be hidden; in that at one and the same time being withdrawn from the visible world its eyes are upon the invisible, and being replenished with the unseen, it entertains a perfect contempt for what is visible. But it is to be observed that he does not say, *Mine ear received as it were by stealth the whispering thereof*; but *the veins of the whispering thereof*; for 'the whispering of the hidden word' is the very utterance of inward Inspiration itself; but 'the veins of the whispering' is the name for the sources of the occasions whereby that inspiration itself is conveyed to the mind. For it is as if It opened 'the veins of its whispering,' when God secretly communicates to us in what ways He enters into the ear of our understandings. Thus at one time He pierces us with love, at another time

with terror. Sometimes He shows us how little the present scene of things is, and lifts up our hearts to desire the eternal world, sometimes He first points to the things of eternity, that these of time may after that grow worthless in our eyes. Sometimes He discloses to us our own evil deeds, and thence draws us on even to the point of feeling sorrow for the evil deeds of others also. Sometimes He presents to our eyes the evil deeds of others, and reforms us from our own wickedness, pierced with a wonderful feeling of compunction. And so to 'hear the veins of Divine whispering by stealth,' is to be made to know the secret methods of divine Inspiration, at once gently and secretly.

52. Though we may interpret whether 'the whispering' or 'the veins of whispering' in another way yet. For he that 'whispers' is speaking in secret, and he does not give out, but imitates a voice. We, therefore, so long as we are beset by the corruptions of the flesh, in no wise behold the brightness [*claritatem*] of the Divine Power, as it abides unchangeable in itself, in that the eye [*acies*] of our weakness cannot endure that which shines above us with intolerable lustre from the ray of His Eternal Being. And so when the Almighty shows Himself to us by the chinks [*rimas*] of contemplation, He does not speak to us, but whispers, in that though He does not fully develope Himself, yet something of Himself He does reveal to the mind of man. But then He no longer whispers at all, but speaks, when His appearance is manifested to us in certainty. It is hence that Truth says in the Gospel, *I shall show you plainly of the Father*. [John 16, 25] Hence John says, *For we shall see Him as He is*. [1 John 3, 2] Hence Paul says, *Then shall I know even as also I am known*. [1 Cor. 13, 12.] Now in this present time, the Divine whispering has as many veins for our ears as the works of creation, which the Divine Being Himself is Lord of; for while we view all things that are created, we are lifted up in admiration of the Creator. For as water that flows in a slender stream is sought by being bored for through veins, with a view to increase it, and as it pours forth the more copiously, in proportion as it finds the veins more open, so we, whilst we heedfully gather the knowledge of the Divine Being from the contemplation of His creation, as it were open to ourselves the 'veins of His whispering,' in that by the things that we see have been made, we are led to marvel at the excellency of the Maker, and by the objects that are in public view, that issues forth to us, which is hidden in concealment.

For He bursts out to us in a kind of sound as it were, whilst He displays His works to be considered by us, wherein He betokens Himself in a measure, in that He shows how Incomprehensible He is. Therefore, because we cannot take thought of Him as He deserves, we hear not His voice, yea, scarcely His whispering. For because we are not equal to form a full and perfect estimate of the very things that are created, it is rightly said, *Mine ear as it were by stealth received the veins of whispering*; in that being cast forth from the delights of paradise, and visited with the punishment of blindness, we scarcely take in 'the veins of whispering;' since His very marvellous works themselves we consider but hastily and slightly. But we must bear in mind, that in proportion as the soul being lifted up contemplates His excellency, so being held back it shrinks from His righteous perfectness [*rectitudinem*]. And hence it is rightly added;

Ver.13. In the horror of a vision of the night.

XXX.

53. *The horror of a vision of the night* is the shuddering of secret contemplation. For the higher the elevation, whereat the mind of man contemplates the things that are eternal, so much the more, terror-struck at her temporal deeds, she shrinks with dread, in that she thoroughly discovers herself guilty, in proportion as she sees herself to have been out of harmony with that light, which shines in the midst of darkness [*intermicat*] above her, and then it happens that the mind being enlightened entertains the greater fear, as it more clearly sees by how much it is at variance with the rule of truth. And she, that before seemed as it were more secure in seeing nothing, trembles with sore affright from her very own proficiency itself. Though, whatever her progress in virtue, she does not as yet compass any clear insight into eternity, but still sees with the indistinctness of a certain shadowy imagining. And hence this same is called *a vision of the night*. For as we have also said above, in the night we see doubtfully, but in the day we see steadily. Therefore because, as regards the contemplating the ray of the interior Sun, the cloud of our corruption interposes itself, nor does the unchangeable Light burst forth such as It is to the weak eyes of our mind, we as it were still behold God 'in a vision of the night,' since most surely we go darkling under a doubtful sight. Yet though the mind may have conceived but a distant idea concerning Him, yet in contemplation of His Greatness, she recoils with dread, and is filled with a greater

awe, in that she feels herself unequal even to the very skirts of the view of Him. And falling back upon herself, she is drawn to Him with closer bonds of love, Whose marvellous sweetness, being unable to bear, she has but just tasted of under an indistinct vision. But, because she never attains to such an height of elevation, unless the importunate and clamorous throng of carnal desires be first brought under governance, it is rightly added,

When deep sleep falleth upon men.

xxxi. 54. Whoever is bent to do the things which are of the world, is, as it were, awake, but he, that seeking inward rest eschews the riot of this world, sleeps as it were. But first we must know that, in holy Scripture, sleep, when put figuratively, is understood in three senses. For sometimes we have expressed by sleep the death of the flesh, sometimes the stupefaction of neglect, and sometimes tranquillity of life, upon the earthly desires being trodden underfoot. Thus, by the designation of sleep or slumbering the death of the flesh is implied; as when Paul says, *And I would not have you to be ignorant, brethren, concerning them which are asleep.* [1 Thess. 4, 13] And soon after, *Even so them also which sleep in Jesus will God bring with Him.* [ver. 14] Again, by sleep is designated the stupefaction of neglect; as where it is said by that same Paul, *Now it is high time to awake out of sleep.* [Rom. 13, 11] And again, *Awake, ye righteous* [Vulg.], *and sin not.* [1 Cor. 15, 34] By sleep too is represented tranquillity of life, when the carnal desires are trodden down; as where these words are uttered by the voice of the spouse in the Song of Songs, *I sleep, but my heart waketh.* [Cant. 5, 2] For, in truth, in proportion as the holy mind withholds itself from the turmoil of temporal desire, the more thoroughly it attains to know the things of the interior, and is the more quick and awake to inward concerns, the more it withdraws itself out of sight from external disquietude. And this is well represented by Jacob sleeping on his journey. He put a stone to his head and slept. He beheld a ladder from the earth fixed in heaven, the Lord resting upon the ladder, Angels also ascending and descending. For to 'sleep on a journey' is, in the passage of this present life, to rest from the love of things temporal. To sleep on a journey is, in the course of our passing days, to close those eyes of the mind to the desire of visible objects, which the seducer opened to the first of mankind, saying, *For God doth know that in the day ye eat* *thereof, then your eyes shall be opened.* [Gen. 3, 5] And hence it is soon afterwards added, *She took of the fruit thereof, and did eat, and gave also unto her husband with her, and he did eat. And the eyes of them both were opened.* [ver. 6, 7.] For sin opened the eyes of concupiscence, which innocence kept shut. But to 'see Angels ascending and descending,' is to mark the citizens of the land above, either with what love they cleave to their Creator above them, or with what fellow-feeling in charity they condescend to aid our infirmities.

55. And it is very deserving of observation, that he that 'lays his head upon a stone,' is he who sees the Angels in his sleep, surely because that same person by resting from external works penetrates internal truths, who with mind intent, which is the governing Principle of man, looks to the imitating of his Redeemer. For to 'lay the head upon a stone' is to cleave to Christ in mind. Since they that are withdrawn from this life's sphere of action, yet whom no love transports above, may have sleep, but can never see the Angels, because they despise to keep their head upon a stone. For there are some, who fly indeed the business of the world, but exercise themselves in no virtues. These, indeed, sleep from stupefaction, not from serious design, and therefore they never behold the things of the interior, because they have laid their head, not upon a stone, but upon the earth. Whose lot it most frequently is, that in proportion as they rest more secure from outward actions, the more amply they are gathering in themselves from idleness an uproar of unclean thoughts. And thus under the likeness of Judaea the Prophet bewails the soul stupefied by indolence, where he says, *The adversaries saw her, and did mock at her sabbaths.* [Lam. 1, 7] For by the precept of the Law there is a cessation from outward work upon the Sabbath Day. Thus her 'enemies looking on mock at her sabbaths,' when evil spirits pervert the very waste hours of vacancy to unlawful thoughts. So that every soul, in proportion as it is supposed to be devoted to the service of God, by being removed from external action, the more it drudges to their tyranny, by entertaining unlawful thoughts. But good men, who sleep to the works of the world, not from inertness, but from virtue, are more laborious in their sleep than they would be awake. For herein, that by abandoning they are made superior to this world's doings, they daily fight against themselves, maintaining a brave conflict, that the mind be not rendered dull by neglect, nor, subdued by indolence, cool down to the harbouring of impure de-

sires, nor in good desires themselves be more full of fervour than is right, nor by sparing itself under the pretext of discretion, may slacken its endeavour after perfection. These are the things she is employed withal: she both wholly withdraws herself from the restless appetite of this world, and gives over the turmoil of earthly actions, and in pursuit of tranquillity, bent on virtuous attainments, she sleeps waking. For she is never led on to contemplate internal things, unless she be heedfully withdrawn from those, which entwine themselves about her without. And it is hence that Truth declares by His own mouth, *No man can serve two Masters.* [Matt. 6, 20] Hence Paul says, *No man that warreth entangleth himself with the affairs of this life, that he may please him that hath chosen him to be a soldier.* [2 Tim. 2, 4] Hence the Lord charges us by the Prophet, saying, *Be still* [*Vacate*, be at leisure], *and know that I am the Lord.* [Ps. 46, 10] Therefore, because inward knowledge is not cognisable by us, except there be a rest from outward embarrasments, the season of the hidden word, and of the whisperings of God, is in this place rightly set forth, when it is said, *In the horror of a vision of the night, when deep sleep falleth upon men*, in that truly our mind is never caught away after the force and power of inward contemplation, unless it be first carefully lulled to rest from all agitation of earthly desires. But the human mind, lifted on high by the engine as it were of its contemplation, in proportion as it sees things higher above itself, the more terribly it trembles in itself. And hence it is fitly added,

Ver. 14. Fear came upon me and trembling, which made all my bones to shake.

xxxii. 56. What is denoted by 'bones' but strong deeds? Of which also it is said by the Prophet, *He keepeth all their bones.* [Ps. 34, 20] And it often happens that the things which men do, they reckon to be of some account, because they know not, how keen is the discernment of His inward sifting; but when, transported on the wings of contemplation, they behold things above, in some sort they melt away from the security they felt in their presumption, and quake in sight of God the more, in proportion as they do not even reckon their excellences fit for the searching eye of Him, Whom they behold. For it is hence that he, who had gained ground in doing strong deeds, being lifted up by the Spirit, exclaimed, *All my hones shall say, Lord, who is like unto Thee?* [Ps. 35, 10] As though he said, 'My flesh is without words, in that my infirmities are wholly silent before Thee, but my bones sing the praises of Thy greatness. In that the very things, which I thought to be strong in me, tremble at the view of Thee.' It is hence that Manoah shrinking at the vision of the Angel, says, *We shall surely die, for we have seen The Lord*. [Judg. 13, 22. 23.] Whom his wife immediately comforts, with these words, *If the Lord were pleased to kill us, He would not have received a burnt-offering, and a meat-offering at our hand*. But how is it that the man becomes fearful at the vision of the Angel, and the woman bold; but that as often as heavenly things are shown us, the spirit indeed is shaken with affright, yet hope has confidence? For hope lifts itself to dare greater feats from the same cause, whereby the spirit is troubled, in that it sees the first the things that are above. Therefore because, when the mind, being lifted on high, beholds the higher depths of the secrets of heaven, all that is most solid of human strength trembles, it is well said here, *Fear came upon me and trembling, which made all my bones to shake*. As though it were expressed in plain words; 'When I perceived the secrets of inmost subtlety, in that quarter where I thought myself in my own eyes strong, I faltered in the sight of the Judge.' For contemplating the strictness of Divine Justice, we justly fear even for the very works themselves, which we flattered ourselves we had so done that they were strong. For our uprightness, when drawn parallel to the inward rule, if it meets with strict judgment, comes cross, with many sinuosities of its windings, to the inward uprightness. And hence, when Paul both perceived that he had the bones of the several virtues, and yet that these same bones trembled under the searching scrutiny, he says, *But with me it is a very small thing that I should be judged of you, or of man's judgment; yea, I judge not mine own self; for I know nothing against myself*: [1 Cor. 4, 3. 4.] Yet because, when the 'veins' of the divine 'whispering' were heard, these same bones quaked, he thereupon added, *For I am not hereby justified; but he that judgeth me is the Lord*. As though be were to say, 'I remember that I have done light things, yet I presume not on my merits; for our life is brought to the scrutiny of Him, under Whom even the bones of our strength are dismayed.

57. But when the mind is suspended in contemplation, when, exceeding the narrow limits of the flesh, with all the power of her ken, she strains to find something of the freedom of interior security, she cannot for long rest standing above herself, because though the spirit

carries her on high, yet the flesh sinks her down below by the yet remaining weight of her corruption. And hence it is added,

Ver. 15. And as a spirit passed before my face, the hair of my flesh stood up.

xxxiii. 58. 'A spirit passes before our face,' when we are brought to the knowledge of invisible things, and yet see these same not stedfastly, but with a hasty glance. For not even in the sweetness of inward contemplation does the mind remain fixed for long, in that being made to recoil by the very immensity of the light it is called back to itself. And when it tastes that inward sweetness, it is on fire with love, it longs to mount above itself, yet it falls back in broken state to the darkness of its frailty. And advancing in high perfection, it sees that it cannot yet see that which it ardently loves, which yet it would not love ardently did it not in some sort see the same. Thus the spirit is not stationary, but 'passes by;' because our contemplation both discloses to us, that pant thereafter, the heavenly light, and forthwith conceals the same from us failing from weakness. And because in this life, whatever degree of virtue a man may have advanced to, he still feels the sting of corruption, *For the corruptible body presseth down the soul, and the earthy tabernacle weigheth down the mind that museth upon many things* [Wisd. 9, 15]; therefore it is rightly added,

The hair of my flesh stood up.

59. For 'the hairs of the flesh' are all the superfluities of human corruption. 'The hairs of the flesh' are the imaginations of the former life, which we so cut away from the mind, that we let no grief for the loss of them disturb our peace. And it is well said by Moses, *Let the Levites shave* [Vulg. thus] *all the hairs of their flesh*. [Numb. 8, 7] For a 'Levite' is rendered 'taken.' And thus it behoves the 'Levites' to shave all 'the hairs of the flesh,' in that he who is 'taken' into the divine ministrations, ought to show himself clear of all imaginations of the flesh before the eyes of God, that the mind never put forth unlawful thoughts, and so deform the fair appearance of the soul as it were by sprouting hairs. But whatever perfection of holy living may have raised the condition of any man, yet there still springs up to him from his old state of life somewhat to bear. And hence the same hairs of the Levites are commanded to be shaven, not to be plucked

out, for the roots still remain in the flesh to the shaven hairs, and grow again to be again cut off, in that while we are to use great diligence in cutting off all rank thoughts, yet they never can be wholly and entirely cut off. For the flesh is ever engendering a rank produce, which the spirit should ever be cutting away with the knife of heedfulness. Yet it is then that we see these things with more exactness, when we penetrate into the heights of contemplation; and hence it is rightly said, *Whilst a Spirit passed before my face, the hair of my flesh stood up.*

60. For when the human mind is lifted up on the tower of contemplation, it the more cruelly torments itself for its superfluities, in proportion as it perceives that which it loves to be infinitely refined; and when it beholds that beautiful Being, which it longs for, above its own height, it severely judges everything infirm in itself, which it bore with tranquillity before. Therefore when 'the Spirit passeth by,' 'the hairs quake,' in that before the power of compunction, all rank thoughts flee away, that nought that is loose, nought that is dissipated, any longer gives pleasure, for severity of inward visitings kindles the inspired soul even against its own self; and when that which riseth up in the heart of an unlawful kind, is cut away with unintermitted strictness, it very often happens that the invigorated soul enters into its ray of contemplation with a somewhat larger range, and almost arrests the spirit which was 'passing by.' Yet does not this same lingering of contemplation fully discover the force of the Divine nature, for its vastness transcends all human powers thus enlarged and elevated. And hence it is well added;

Ver. 16. There stood a certain one, but I could not discern the form thereof. [V. *thus*]

xxxiv.

61. For we do not speak of a certain one, saving surely in the case of him, whom we are either unwilling or unable to express. Now with what feeling it is here said a certain one, is clearly set forth, in that it immediately comes in, *but I could not discern the form thereof.* For the human soul, being by the sin of the first of mankind banished from the joys of paradise, lost the light of the invisible, and poured itself out entire in the love of the visible, and was darkened in the interior sight, in proportion as it was dissipated without, to the deformment of itself. Whence it comes to pass that it knows nothing, saving the things that it acquaints itself with by the

palpable touch, so to say, of the bodily eyes. For man, who, had he been willing to have kept the commandment, would even in his flesh have been a spiritual being, by sinning was rendered even in soul carnal, so as to imagine such things only as he derives to the soul through the images of bodily substances. For body is the property of heaven, earth, water, animals, and all the visible things; which he unceasingly beholds; and while the delighted mind wholly precipitates itself into these, it waxes gross, loses the fineness of the inward sense; and whereas it is now no longer able to erect itself to things on high, it willingly lies prostrate in its weakness in things below. But when with marvellous efforts it strives to rise up from the same, it is great indeed, if the soul, thrusting aside the bodily form, be brought to the knowledge of itself, so as to think of itself without a bodily figure, and by thus thinking of itself to prepare itself a pathway to contemplate the substance of Eternity.

62. Now in this way it shows itself to its own eyes as a kind of ladder, whereby in ascending from outward things to pass into itself, and from itself to tend unto its Maker. For when the mind quits bodily images, entering into itself, it mounts up to no mean height; for though the soul be incorporeal, yet because she is incorporate with the body, she is known by that property of hers, which is confined within the local bounds of the flesh. And whereas she forgets things known, acquaints herself with such as are unknown, remembers what has been consigned to oblivion, entertains mirth after sadness, is adjudged to punishment [*addicitur*] after joy; she herself shows by her own diversity in herself, how widely she is removed from the Substance of eternal Unchangeableness. Which is always the same, even as It Is; Which every where present, every where invisible, every where whole and entire, every where incomprehensible, is by the longing mind discerned without seeing, heard without uncertainty, taken in without motion, touched without bodily substance, held without locality. Now when the mind that is used to corporeal objects represents to itself this same Substance, it is loaded with the phantasms of divers images. And whilst it banishes these from the eyes of its attention with the hand of discernment, making everything give place thereto, it at last beholds It in some degree. And if it does not as yet apprehend what It is, it has surely learnt what It is not. And so because the mind is carried away into unaccustomed ground, when it pries into the Essence of the Deity, it is

rightly said here, *A certain one stood, but I could not discern the form thereof.*

63. And it is well said, it stood still; for every created thing, in that it is made out of nothing, and of itself tends to nothing, has not the property to stand, but to run to an end. But a creature endowed with reason, by this very circumstance, that it is created after the image of its Maker, is fixed that it should not pass into nothing. Now no irrational creature is ever fixed, but only, so long as, by the service of its appearing, it is completing the form and fashion of the universe, it is delayed in passing away. For though heaven and earth abide henceforth and for ever, still they are at this present time of themselves hastening on to nought; yet for the use of those, whom they serve, they remain to be changed for the better. To 'stand' then is the attribute of the Creator alone, through Whom all things pass away, Himself never passing away, and in Whom some things are held fast, that they should not pass away. Hence our Redeemer, because the fixed state of His Divine Nature could not be comprehended by the human mind, showed this to us as it were in passing, by coming to us, by being created, born, dead, buried, by rising again, and returning to the heavenly realms. Which He well shadowed out in the Gospel by the enlightening the blind man, to whom when passing on He vouchsafed a hearing, but it was standing still that He healed his eyes. For by the economy of His Human Nature He had His passing on, but the standing by the power of His Divine Nature, in that He is every where present. Thus the Lord is said to hear the complaints of our blind condition in passing, in that being made Man He has compassion on human misery; but He restores light to the eyes standing still, in that He enlightens the darkness of our frail state by the efficacy of His Divine Nature. It is well then that, after it has been said, *Then a spirit passed before my face*, it should be added, *but I could not discern the form thereof*. As if it were in plain words, 'Him, Whom I perceived in passing, I discovered never to pass.' He then that 'passes' is the same as He that 'stands still.' He 'passes,' in that when known He cannot be detained, He 'stands still,' in that, so far as He is known, He is seen to be unchangeable. Therefore, because He, That is ever the Same, is seen by a hasty glance, God at the same time appears both passing and standing still. Or surely His 'standing' is His never varying with any change; as it is said to Moses, *I AM THAT I AM*. And as James represents Him, say-

ing, *With Whom is no variableness, neither shadow of turning*. [Jam. 1, 17] Now whereas every man, that apprehends something of the Eternal Being by contemplation, beholds the Same through His coeternal Image, it is rightly subjoined;

An image was before mine eyes.

xxxv. 64. For the Image of the Father is the Son, as Moses teaches in the case of man at his creation; *So God created man in His own Image; in the Image of God created He him*. [Gen. 1, 27] And as the Wise Man, in the setting forth of Wisdom, says concerning the same Son, *For She is the brightness* [*candor*] *of the everlasting light*. [Wisd. 7, 26] And as Paul hath it, *Who being the brightness* [*splendor*] *of His glory, and the express Image of His Person*. [Heb. 1, 3] When then His Eternity is perceived as far as the capability of our frail nature admits, His Image is set before the eyes of the mind, in that when we really strain towards the Father, as far as we receive Him we see Him by His Image, i.e. by His Son. And by That Image, Which was born of Himself without beginning, we strive in some sort to obtain a glimpse of Him, Who hath neither beginning nor ending. And hence this same Truth says in the Gospel, *No man cometh to the Father but by Me*. [John 14, 6] And it is well added,

And I heard the voice as it were of a light breath.

xxxvi. 65. For what is signified by 'the voice of a light breath,' but the knowledge of the Holy Spirit, Which proceeding from the Father, and receiving of that which belongeth to the Son, is gently imparted to the knowledge of our frail nature? Yet when It came upon the Apostles, It is demonstrated by an outward sound, like a vehement blast, where it is said, *And suddenly there came a sound from heaven as of a rushing mighty wind*. [Acts 2, 2] For when the Holy Spirit imparts Itself to the knowledge of frail humanity, It is both represented by 'the sound of a rushing mighty wind,' and also by the 'voice of a gentle breath,' clearly, in that when It comes, It is both 'vehement' and 'gentle;' 'gentle,' in that It tempers the knowledge of Itself to our perceptions, so as to be in some sort brought under our cognizance; 'vehement,' in that however It may temper that same, yet by Its coming, It confounds while It illumines the darkness of our frail condition. For It touches us but lightly by Its enlightening influence, yet it shakes our emptiness with fearful might.

66. So God's voice is heard as if of 'a light breath,' in that the Divine Being never imparts Himself as He is to those that contemplate Him while still in this life, but to the purblind eyes of our mind He discovers His brightness [*claritatem*] but scantily. Which is well represented by the very receiving of the Law itself, when it is said that Moses ascended, and God descended upon the Mount. For 'the Mount' is our very contemplation itself, whereinto we ascend, that we may be elevated to see those things which are beyond our frail nature; but the Lord descends thereupon, in that, when we advance much, He discloses some little concerning Himself to our perceptions, if either 'little' or 'somewhat' can be said to be in Him, Who, being always One and abiding the Same, cannot be understood by parts, and yet is said to be *participated* by His faithful servants, whereas 'part' is nowise admissible in His Substance. But because we are unable to express Him with perfect speech, being hindered by the scanty measure of our human nature, as by the impotency of the infant state, we give back an echo of Him in some sort with stammering utterance. But that when we are lifted up in high contemplation, it is somewhat refined that we attain unto in the knowledge of the Eternal One, is shown by the words of Sacred Story, when the illustrious Prophet Elijah is instructed in the knowledge of God. For when the Lord promised him that He would pass by before him, saying, *And, behold, the Lord passeth by, a great and strong wind rending the mountains, and breaking in pieces the rocks before the Lord*; He thereupon added, *But the Lord is not in the wind: and after the wind a quaking, but the Lord is not in the quaking: and after the quaking a fire, but the Lord is not in the fire: and after the fire, a still small voice*. [1 Kings 19, 11. 12.] [V. *the whisper of a gentle air*] For the wind before the Lord overturns the mountains, and shatters the rocks, in that the affright, which rushes in upon us from His coming, both casts down the exaltation of our hearts, and melts their hardness. But the Lord is said not to be in the 'wind of quaking' and in the fire, but it is not denied that He is 'in the still small voice,' in that verily when the mind is hung aloft in the height of contemplation, whatever it has power to see perfectly and completely is not God, but when it sees something of great fineness, this is the same as that he hears belonging to the incomprehensible substance of the Deity. For we as it were perceive a still small voice, when by a moment's contemplation we taste with finest sense the savour of incomprehensible truth.

Accordingly then only is there truth in what we know concerning God, when we are made sensible that we cannot know anything fully concerning Him. Hence it is well added in that place, *And it was so when Elijah heard it, that he wrapped his face in his mantle, and went out and stood at the entering in of the cave.* After the still small voice, the Prophet covers his face with his mantle, because in that very refined contemplation he learns in what a cloak of ignorance man is shrouded; for to draw the mantle over the face is to veil the mind by the consideration of its own infirmity, that it may never presume to seek things above it, that it never rashly open the eyes of the understanding beyond itself, but close them with a feeling of awe to that which it cannot apprehend. And he, in doing such things, is described to have *stood at the entering in of the cave.* For what is our cave but this dwelling-place of our corrupt nature, wherein we are still held fast from remaining oldness? But when we begin to take in something of the knowledge of the Divine Being, we as it were already stand 'in the entering in of our cave;' for whereas we cannot make perfect progress, yet panting after the knowledge of the truth, we already catch something of the breath of liberty. So to 'stand at the entering in of the cave,' is, forcing aside the obstruction of our corrupt nature, to begin to issue forth to the knowledge of the truth. And hence upon the cloud descending on the Tabernacle, the Israelites seeing it afar off are related to have stood at the entering in of their tents, [Ex. 33, 9] in that they, who in some sort behold the coming of the Deity, as it were already issue forth from the habitation of the flesh. Therefore because with whatever amplitude of virtue the human mind may have enlarged its compass, yet it scarcely knows the very outermost extremes that belong to the interior things, it is rightly said here, *And I heard the voice as of a light breath*; but as at the time that the knowledge of the Deity shows us after all but little concerning Itself, It is perfectly instructing the ignorance of our infirmness; let him that 'heard the voice of a light breath,' declare all that he learnt by that same hearing. It goes on;

Ver. 17. Shall mortal man be more just than God? Shall a man be more pure than his Maker?

xxxvii. 67. Human righteousness compared with the righteousness of God is unrighteousness, for even a candle is seen to shine bright in the dark, but being set in the ray of the sun its light is darkened. What then did Eliphaz learn when he was transported in contemplation, saving that man cannot be justified in comparison with God? For we believe that what we do outwardly is righteous, but when we never at all acquaint ourselves with the things of the interior, we are as it were blind whilst set in the ray of the sun. But when we, little as we can, discern the one, it is not a little [*non utcunque*] that we judge the others, in that a man judges the darkness more exactly, in proportion as the brightness [*claritas*] [A.B.C.D. 'reality'] of light is more truly manifested to him. For he, that seeth light, knoweth what to account of the darkness, as he, that is ignorant of the whiteness of light, lets pass even dark objects for light ones. And it is rightly added, *Shall a man be more pure than his Maker?* For whoso murmurs at the stroke, what does he, but charge the justice of the striker? Thus a man accounts himself more pure than his Maker, if he stirs complaint against the scourge, and without doubt he makes Him give place to himself, Whose judgment he blames in the case of his own affliction. Thus, that man may never dare charge his Judge with offence, let him humbly bethink himself that He is the Author of Nature; for He, That with marvellous skill made man out of nothing, does not pitilessly afflict him that He has made; which Eliphaz then learnt when he 'heard the voice as it were of a light breath.' For by the contemplation of the greatness of God we learn, how humbly we should abase ourselves with fear under His visitation. And he, that hath a taste of things above, bears with resignation all events below, in that he perfectly sees within, whereat he should reckon that which he does without. For he miscounts himself righteous, who knows not the rule of the Supreme Righteousness. And it often happens that a piece of wood is counted straight, if it be not applied to the rule; but so soon as it is put thereto, we discover the degree of distortion wherewith it swells out, in that, truly, the straight line cuts off and condemns that, which the cheated eye approved as good. Thus Eliphaz, in that he beheld things above, delivered a strict judgment on all below, and though it was not rightly he reproved blessed Job, yet by comparison with the Creator of all things he rightly describes the measure of the creature, saying,

Ver. 18, 19. Behold, His servants are not stedfast, and in His Angels He found folly: How much more in them that dwell in houses of clay, whose foundation is in the dust, which shall be consumed as by the moth?

xxxviii. 68. Though the Angelical nature, by being fixed in contemplation of the Creator, remains unchangeable in its own state, yet hereby, that it is a created being, it admits in itself the variableness of change. Now to be changed is to go from one thing into another, and to be without stability in one's self. For every single being tends to some other thing by steps, as many in number as it is subject to motions of change. And it is only the Incomprehensible Nature, which knows not to be moved from its fixed state, in that It knows not to be changed from this, that It is always the Same. For if the essence of the Angels had been strange to the motion of change, being created well by its Maker, it would never have fallen in the case of reprobate spirits from the tower of its blessed estate. But Almighty God in a marvellous manner framed the nature of the highest spiritual existences good, yet at the same time capable of change; that both they, that refused to remain, might meet with ruin, and they, that continued in their own state of creation, might henceforth be stablished therein more worthily in proportion as it was owing to their own choice, and become so much the more meritorious in God's sight, as they had staid the motion of their mutability by the stablishing of the will. Whereas then this very Angelical nature too is in itself mutable, which same mutability it has hereby overcome, in that it is bound by the chains of love to Him, Who is ever the Same, it is now rightly said, *Behold, His servants are not stedfast*. And there is forthwith added a proof of this same mutability, in that it is brought in from the case of the apostate spirits, *And in His Angels He found folly*. And from the fall of these He rightly draws the consideration of human frailty, when he appends thereto; *How much more in them that dwell in houses of clay, whose foundation, is earthly, which shall be consumed as by the moth*. For we inhabit houses of clay, in that we subsist in earthly bodies. Which Paul considering says well; *But we have this treasure in earthen vessels*. [2 Cor. 4, 7] And again, *For we know that if our earthly house of this tabernacle were dissolved, we have a building of God, an house not made with hands*. [5, 1] 'The earthly foundation' too is the substance of the flesh; which the Psalmist had earnestly contemplated in himself, when he said, *My* *bones are not hid from Thee, which Thou madest in secret, and my substance in the lower parts of the earth.* [Ps. 139, 15] Now the moth springs from the garment, and in its production destroys that very garment, whereupon it is produced. And the flesh is as a kind of garment to the soul, but this same garment has withal its moth, in that from itself there arises carnal temptation, whereby it is rent and torn. For our garment is as it were consumed by a kind of moth of its own, in that the corruptible flesh engendereth temptation, and by this is brought to destruction. Man is consumed as if by a moth, in that he has arising from himself that, whereby he is to be broken in pieces. As though it were in plain words, 'If those spirits cannot be of themselves unchangeable, which are kept down by no infirmity of the flesh, by what inconceivable temerity do men account themselves to hold on stedfastly in good, who, wherein they have their understanding elevating them on high, have the clog of carnal frailty acting as an impediment to them, so that through the evil, of a corrupting tendency they contain a cause in themselves, whence they turn old from the interior newness?

69. The holy Doctors may likewise be understood by 'the Angels,' according as it is said by the Prophet, *For the Priest's lips should keep knowledge, and they should seek the law at his mouth, for he is the Angel* [*Angelus*] *of the Lord of hosts.* [Mal. 2, 7] With whatever degree of virtue these may shine, they can never be altogether without sin, so long as they are engaged in the journey of this life, in that their step is doubtless brought into contact either with the mire of unlawful practice, or with the dust of the thought of the heart. Now they 'dwell in houses of clay,' who rejoice in this ensnaring life of the flesh. Paul had been brought to contemn the inhabiting this house of clay, when he said, *But our conversation is in heaven.* [Phil. 3, 20] Let him say then, *Behold, His servants are not stedfast, and in His Angels He hath found folly: how much more in them that dwell in houses of clay, whose foundation is in the dust, which are consumed as by the moth?* As if he had said in plain words, 'If the pathway of the present life cannot be passed through without defilement by those, who proclaiming the things of eternity, gird themselves up to encounter those of time, what evils do they undergo, who rejoice to be plunged in the delights of the fleshly habitation?' 'For His servants are not stedfast,' for when the mind strains toward things on high, it is dissipated by the conceits of its own flesh, so that oftentimes whilst the mind

pants after the things of the interior, while it looks at heavenly objects alone, smitten by a momentary carnal delight, it lies low severed from itself, and he that felt joy that he had surmounted the hindrances of his frailty, prostrated by an unexpected wound, is only filled with woe. Perverseness then is found even in His Angels, so long as those very men, who proclaim His truth, the surprisals of a deceitful life do at times lie heavy on. So then if even those are smitten by the wickedness of this world, whom a holy purpose presents erect against the same, with what strokes are not they pierced, whom nothing less than [*ipsa*] delight in their frailty brings to the ground before its darts? And these are well described to be 'consumed,' as it were, 'with a moth.' For a moth does mischief, and makes no sound. So the minds of the wicked, in that they neglect to take account of their own losses, lose their soundness, as it were, without knowing it. For they are losing innocency from the heart, truth from the lips, continency from the flesh, and in the course of time, life from the sum of their age. But they see not one whit that they are unceasingly letting go these same, in that they are busied with all their heart in temporal concerns. Thus they are 'consumed as it were with a moth,' in that they suffer the canker of sin without sound, whilst they remain ignorant what losses in life and innocency of heart they are undergoing. Hence it is well added,

Ver. 20. They shall be cut off from morning to evening.

xxxix. 70. For the sinner is 'cut off from morning to evening,' in that from the beginning of his life to the end thereof he is ever getting wounded by the commission of sin. For the reprobate by increase in wickedness are at all times redoubling blows upon themselves, cut off by which, they may fall headlong into the pit. And it is well said of them by the Psalmist, *Bloody and deceitful men shall not halve their days*. [Ps. 55, 23] For to 'halve our days' is to part off the time of our life misspent in pleasure, for the purpose of penitential mourning, and in parting off to recover the same to a good use. But the wicked never 'halve their days,' in that not even in the end of their time do they change their frowardness of heart. Contrary whereunto Paul rightly exhorts, saying, *Redeeming the time, because the days are evil*. [Eph. 5, 16] For we 'redeem the time,' when by tears we recover our past life, which by rioting we had lost. It goes on,

And because none understandeth, they perish for ever.

71. That is to say, 'none' of those, who 'shall be cut off from morning unto evening.' 'None understandeth,' whether of those that perish, or of those who follow the lost ways of the perishing. Whence it is elsewhere written, *The righteous perisheth, and no man layeth it to heart: and merciful men are taken away, none considering.* [Is. 57, 1] Thus, whereas the wicked are set upon temporal things alone, and are unconcerned to learn what blessings are in store for the Elect for everlasting, while they look to the affliction of the just, but never learn what is the recompense of that affliction, they put forth the foot of their conversation into the pit, for they willingly shut their eyes to the light of understanding. For being decoyed by foolish pleasures, whilst for objects, which they see, they entertain an affection, which belongs to time, being meanwhile strangers to themselves, they never see whereunto they are hurrying for all eternity. It is possible too that by the morning may be denoted the prosperous fortune of this world, and by the evening the adverse fortune thereof. So then 'the wicked are cut off from morning to evening,' in that by running riot through prosperity they are brought to ruin, and being made impatient by adversity they are lifted up to madness. These would never be cut off from morning to evening, by sin, if they either took prosperity for the salve or adversity for the knife to their sore. **xl.**

72. But forasmuch as the assemblage of the human race is never so forsaken, that the whole is let to go to destruction, there be some, that look down upon the enjoyments of the present life, even when they are present, consider that they are transient, and in the love of the eternal world tread them underfoot. And while they set the step of judgment on this first stage, they mount with invigorated soul to a loftier height, so that they not only contemn all temporal things, for that they must be quickly parted with, but have no desire to attach themselves thereto, even if they might last for ever. And they withdraw their love from the things created in beauty, because they stretch forth by the steps of the heart toward the Father of all Beauty Himself. And there are some that love the good things of the present life, yet never in any wise attain unto them, who pant after temporal blessings with all their hearts' desire, who covet the glory of the world, yet never can make themselves master thereof. For

these, so to speak, the heart draws them on to seek the world, the world drives them back to search out the heart. For it often chances that, being bruised by those very adversities which they suffer, they are brought back to reason, and returning back into themselves, they consider how little there is in that, which they were seeking after, and forthwith betake themselves to weeping for the foolishness of their desire, and conceive the stronger yearnings for eternal things, in proportion to the folly in which they grieve that they once spent themselves for those of time. Hence, the wicked having been described, it is well added,

Ver. 21. But they that have been left shall be taken away from among them.

xli. 73. Whom else do we understand by 'the left,' but all the despised of this world? whom whilst the present life chooses not for any use of honour, it 'leaves' as being the least and most worthless. But the Lord is said to 'take away those that are left' of the world, in that He condescends to make choice of the despised of this life, as Paul bears witness, saying, *Not many wise men after the flesh, not many mighty, not many noble are called: but God hath chosen the foolish things of the world to confound the wise; and God hath, chosen the weak things of the world to confound the things that are mighty*. [1 Cor. 1, 26. 27.] Which is well represented in the Book of Kings by the Egyptian servant fainting in the way, whom the Amalekite abandons taken sick upon the journey, but David finds, refreshes with food, and makes the guide of his route; he pursues the Amalekite, finds him feasting, and utterly destroys him [1 Sam. 30, 13]. For what does it mean that the Egyptian servant of the Amalekite turns faint upon the journey, but that the lover of this present world, covered with the blackness of his sins, is often abandoned in weakness and contempt by the same world, so that he is no longer able to run therewith, but being broken down by adversity, grows helpless. But David finds him, in that our Redeemer, Who is in a true sense 'strong of hand,' sometimes turns to the love of Himself those, whom He finds despised as to the glory of the world, in that He refreshes them with the knowledge of the Word. He chose him the guide of his way, in that He makes him even the preacher of Himself. And he, that had no power to follow the Amalekite, becomes the guide of David, in that he, whom the world forsook as worthless, not only when converted entertains the Lord in his affections [*suas mentes*, al. *su mente*], but by preaching Him brings Him home even to the hearts of others also. And with this same guide David discovers and annihilates the Amalekite as he feasted, in that Christ breaks up the joy of the world by those very men as preachers, whom that world scorned to have for its companions. Therefore because it very often happens that those, whom the world abandons, are chosen of the Lord, it is rightly said in this place, *Those, that may have been left, shall be taken from amongst them*. It proceeds;

They shall die, even without wisdom.

xlii.

74. How is it that he set forth above the death of the wicked, saying, *Because none understandeth they shall perish for ever*; and concerning the Elect of God thereupon subjoined, *And they that have been left shall be taken away from among them*; yet forthwith adds that which cannot accord with those Elect ones, saying, *They shall die even without wisdom?* For if they be taken away from among the wicked by the hand of God, how are they said 'to die without wisdom?' Why, doubtless it is the fashion of Holy Writ, in relating anything, after inserting a sentence that concerns another case, to return straightway to its former subject. Thus after he had said, *And because there is none that understandeth, they shall perish for ever*; he immediately brought in the lot of the Elect, saying, *But they that have been left shall be taken away from among them*. And again directing the eye of his meaning to that destruction of the wicked, which he had foretold, he suddenly subjoined, *they shall die, even without wisdom*. As if he said, 'Those of whom I said that 'not understanding, they should perish for ever,' will assuredly 'die without wisdom.'' But we shall the better show that this is at times the way with Holy Writ, if we produce therefrom a similar instance to this. For when Paul the Apostle was counselling his beloved disciple for the settling the offices of the Church, that he might not by chance without due order promote any to Holy Orders, he said, *Lay hands suddenly on no man, neither be partaker of other men's sins. Keep thyself pure*. [1 Tim. 5, 22] And forthwith directing his words to his bodily infirmities, he says, *Drink no longer water, but use a little wine for thy stomach's sake, and thine often infirmities*. [ver. 23] And he immediately subjoins; *Some men's sins are open beforehand, going before to judgment, and some men they follow after*. [ver. 24] What connection then has that, which he add-

ed concerning the sins of different men being hidden and manifest, with this, that he forbad him in his weak health to drink water? but that after the insertion of a clause concerning his weakness of health he came back again at the end to that, which he had said above, *Lay hands suddenly on no man, neither be partaker of other men's sins.* For in order to show with what anxious heed these same sins are to be inquired into, after introducing a charge to prudence directed against the annoyance of bad health, he straightway put in, that in some men they lay exposed to view, in some hidden from sight, saying, *Some men's sins are open beforehand going before to judgment, and some men they follow after.* As then in this sentence Paul does not chime in with these same words, to which, speaking of the weakness of Timothy's health, he subjoined it, but he has returned to that which he made mention of before after an interruption; so when in this place Eliphaz said concerning the Elect, *They that have been left shall be taken from among them*, by subjoining thereupon, *they die even without wisdom*; he forthwith recurs to that, which he delivered concerning the wicked, saying, *And because none understandeth, they shall perish for ever.*

75. Now it is for this reason that the wicked look down upon the Elect, because they are going toward a life that is invisible through a death that is visible; of whom it is well said in this place, *They die even without wisdom.* As though it were said in plain words, "They equally indeed eschew death and wisdom; and wisdom they wholly get quit of, but they do not escape the snares of death. And whereas doomed, as they are, to die one day, they might in dying have received life, while they dread the death, which will most surely come, they part both with life and wisdom together." But, on the other hand, the righteous die in wisdom, for that death, which they cannot wholly avoid, when it threatens them for the sake of the truth, they refuse to put off to a later day, and whilst they undergo the same with resignation, they turn the punishment of their race into an instrument of virtue; that life may be received back from the same quarter, whence, for the deserts of the first sin, it is forced to its end. But because Eliphaz delivered these things with a true meaning against the wicked; in accounting blessed Job to be worthy of blame, he puffed himself up in pride of wisdom. And hence, after declarations so good and righteous, he subjoins words of mocking, and says,

Chap. V. 1. Call now, if there be any that will answer thee.

76. For Almighty God often passes by the prayer of that man in his trouble, who slights His precepts in the season of rest. Hence it is written, *He that turneth away his ear from hearing the law, even his prayer shall be abomination.* [Prov. 28, 9] Now for us 'to call,' is to beseech God with humble prayer; but for God to 'answer,' is to vouchsafe an accomplishment to our prayers; and so he says, *Call now, if any will answer thee.* As though he said in plain words, 'However thou mayest cry out in thy distress, thou hast not God answering thee, in that the voice in tribulation findeth not Him, Whom the mind in tranquillity disregarded. Where he adds in yet further derision, **xliii.**

And turn thee to some one of the Saints?

77. As though he said in scorn, 'The Saints too thou canst never obtain for abettors in thy distress, whom thou wouldest not have for companions in thy mirth. And after this mocking he forthwith adds the sentence, saying, **xliv.**

Ver. 2. For wrath killeth the foolish man, and envy slayeth the silly man.

Moral 78. Which same sentence would have been true, had it not been delivered against the patience of so great a man. But let us weigh well the thing that is said, though it be made to recoil by the virtue of his hearer, that we may show how right the matter is, which is put forth, if it were not unjustly put forth against blessed Job; since it is written, *But Thou, Lord, Judgest with tranquillity.* [Wisd. 12, 18] We must above all things know, that as often as we restrain the turbulent motions of the mind under the virtue of mildness, we are essaying to return to the likeness of our Creator. For when the peace of the mind is lashed with Anger, torn and rent, as it were, it is thrown into confusion, so that it is not in harmony with itself, and loses the force of the inward likeness. Let us consider then how great the sin of Anger is, by which, while we part with mildness, the likeness of the image of the Most High is spoilt. By Anger wisdom is parted with, so that we are left wholly in ignorance what to do, and in what order to do it; as it is written, *Anger resteth in the bosom of a fool* [Ecc. 7, 9]; in this way, that it withdraws the light of understanding, while by agitating it troubles the **xlv.**

mind. By Anger life is lost, even though wisdom seem to be retained; as it is written, *Anger destroyeth even the wise*. [Prov. 15, 1. LXX] For in truth the mind being in a state of confusion never puts it in execution, even if it has power to discern anything with good judgment. By Anger righteousness is abandoned, as it is written, *The wrath of man worketh not the righeousness of God*. [Jam. 1, 20] For whereas the agitated mind works up to harshness the decision of its reasoning faculty, all that rage suggests, it accounts to be right. By Anger all the kindliness of social life is lost, as it is written, *Be not the companion of an angry man; lest thou learn his ways, and get a snare to thy soul*. [Prov. 22, 24. 25. not V.] And the same writer, *Who can dwell with* [not V.] *a man whose spirit is ready to wrath* [thus V.]? [Prov. 18, 14] For he that does not regulate his feelings by the reason that is proper to man, must needs live alone like a beast. By Anger, harmony is interrupted; as it is written, *A wrathful man stirreth up strife, and an angry man diggeth up sins*. [Prov. 15, 18. not as V. or LXX] For 'an angry man diggeth up sins,' since even bad men, whom he rashly provokes to strife, he makes worse than they were. By Anger the light of truth is lost; as it is written, *Let not the sun go down upon your wrath*. [Eph. 4, 26] For when wrath brings into the mind the darkness of perturbation, God hides therefrom the ray of the knowledge of Himself. By Anger the brightness [*splendor*] of the Holy Spirit is shut out. Contrary whereunto, it is written according to the old translation, *Upon whom shall My Spirit rest, saving upon him that is humble and peaceful, and that trembleth at My words?* [Is. 66, 2] For when He mentioned the humble man, He forthwith subjoined the word 'peaceful;' if then Anger steals away peace of mind, it shuts its dwelling place against the Holy Spirit, and the soul being left void by Its departure, is immediately carried into open frenzy, and is scattered away to the very surface from the inmost foundation of the thoughts.

79. For the heart that is inflamed with the stings of its own Anger beats quick, the body trembles, the tongue stammers, the countenance takes fire, the eyes grow fierce, and they that are well known are not recognised. With the mouth, indeed, he shapes a sound, but the understanding knows nothing what it says. Wherein, then, is he far removed from brain-struck [*arreptitiis*] persons, who is not conscious of his own doings? Whence it very often comes to pass that anger springs forth even to the hands, and as reason is gone the fur-

ther, it lifts itself the bolder. And the mind has no strength to keep itself in, for that it is made over into the power of another. And frenzy employs the limbs without in dealing blows, in proportion as it holds captive within the very mind, that is the mistress of the limbs. But sometimes it does not put out the hands, but it turns the tongue into a dart of cursing. For it implores with entreaty for a brother's destruction, and demands of God to do that, which the wicked man himself is either afraid or ashamed to do. And it comes to pass that both by wish and words he commits a murder, even when he forbears the hurting of his neighbour with the hands. Sometimes when the mind is disturbed, anger as if in judgment commands silence, and in proportion as it does not vent itself outwardly by the lips, inwardly it burns the worse, so the angry man withholds from converse with his neighbour, and in saying nothing, says how he abhors him. And sometimes this rigorousness of silence is used in the economy of discipline, yet only if the rule of discretion be diligently retained in the interior. But sometimes whilst the incensed mind foregoes the wonted converse, in the progress of time it is wholly severed from the love of our neighbour, and sharper stings arise to the mind, and occasions too spring up which aggravate her irritation, and the mote in the eye of the angry man is turned into a beam, whilst anger is changed into hatred. It often happens that the anger, which is pent up within the heart from silence, burns the more fiercely, and silently frames clamorous speeches, presents to itself words, by which to have its wrath exasperated, and as if set in judgment on the case, answers in exasperation exceeding cruelly: as Solomon implies in few words, saying, *But the expectation of the wicked is wrath*. [Prov. 11, 23] And thus it is brought to pass that the troubled Spirit finds louder riot in its silence, and the flame of pent-up anger preys upon it the more grievously. Hence a certain wise man said well before us, *The thoughts of the angry man are a generation of vipers, they devour the mind which is their mother*.

80. But we are to know that there be some, whom anger is somewhat prompt in inflaming, but quickly leaves them; while there are others whom it is slow in exciting, but the longer in retaining possession of. For some, like kindled reeds, while they clamour with their voices, give out something like a crackle at their kindling: those indeed speedily rise into a flame, but then they forth with cool down into their ashes; while others, like the heavier and harder kinds of

wood, are slow in taking fire, but being once kindled, are with difficulty put out; and as they slowly stir themselves into heat of passion, retain the longer the fire of their rage. Others again, and their conduct is the worst, are both quick in catching the flames of anger, and slow in letting them go; and others both catch them slowly, and part with them quickly. In which same four sorts, the reader sees clearly that the last rather than the first approaches to the excellence of peace of mind, and in evil the third is worse than the second. But what good does it do to declare how anger usurps possession of the mind, if we neglect to set forth at the same time, how it should be checked?

81. For there are two ways whereby anger being broken comes to relax its hold upon the mind. The first method is that the heedful mind, before it begins to do anything, set before itself all the insults which it is liable to undergo, so that by thinking on the opprobrious treatment of its Redeemer, it may brace itself to meet with contradiction. Which same, on coming, it receives with the greater courage, in proportion as by foresight it armed itself the more heedfully. For he, that is caught by adversity unprovided for it, is as if he were found by his enemy sleeping, and his foe dispatches him the sooner, that he stabs one who offers no resistance. For he, that forecasts impending ills in a spirit of earnest heedfulness, as it were watching in ambush awaits the assault of his enemy. And he arrays himself in strength for the victory in the very point wherein he was expected to be caught in entire ignorance. Therefore, before the outset of any action, the mind ought to forecast all contrarieties, and that with anxious heed, that by taking account of these at all times, and being at all times armed against them with the breastplate of patience, it may both in foresight obtain the mastery, whatever may take place, and whatever may not take place, it may account gain. But the second method of preserving mildness is that, when we regard the transgression of others, we have an eye to our own offences, by which we have done wrong in the case of others. For our own frailty, being considered makes excuse for the ills done us by others. Since that man bears with patience an injury that is offered him, who with right feeling remembers that perchance there may still be somewhat, in which he himself has need to be borne with. And it is as if fire were extinguished by water, when upon rage rising up in the mind each person recalls his own misdoings to his recollection;

for he is ashamed not to spare offences, who recollects that he has himself often committed offences, whether against God or against his neighbour, which need to be spared.

82. But herein we must bear in mind with nice discernment that the anger, which hastiness of temper stirs is one thing, and that which zeal gives its character to is another. The first is engendered of evil, the second of good. For if there was no anger originating in virtue, Phinees would never have allayed the fierceness of God's visitation by his sword. Because Eli lacked such anger, he quickened against himself the stirrings of the vengeance of the Most High to an implacable force. For in proportion as he was lukewarm towards the evil practices of those under his charge, the severity of the Eternal Ruler waxed hot against himself. Of this it is said by the Psalmist, *Be ye angry, and sin not*. [Ps. 4, 5 Vulg.] Which doubtless they fail to interpret aright, who would only have us angry with ourselves, and not with others likewise, when they sin. For if we are bidden to love our neighbours as ourselves, it follows that we should be as angry with their erring ways as with our own evil practices. Of this it is said by Solomon, *Anger* [so Vulg.] *is better than laughter; for by the sadness of the countenance the heart is made better*. [Ecc. 7, 3] Of this the Psalmist says again, *Mine eye is* [V. thus] *disturbed because of anger* [*prae ira*. Vulg. *a furore*]. [Ps. 6, 8] For anger that comes of evil blinds the eye of the mind, but anger that comes of zeal disturbs it. Since necessarily in whatever degree he is moved by a jealousy for virtue, the world of contemplation, which cannot be known saving by a heart in tranquillity, is broken up. For zeal for the cause of virtue in itself, in that it fills the mind with disquietude and agitation, presently bedims the eye thereof, so that in its troubled state it can no longer see those objects far up above, which it aforetime clearly beheld in a state of tranquillity. But it is brought back on high with a more penetrating ken by the same means, whereby it is thrown back for a while so as to be incapable of seeing. For the same jealousy in behalf of what is right after a short space opens wider the scenes of eternity in a state of tranquillity, which in the mean season it closes from the effects of perturbation. And from the same quarter whence the mind is confounded so as to prevent its seeing, it gains ground, so as to be made clear for seeing in a more genuine way; just as when ointment is applied to the diseased eye, light is wholly withheld, but after a little space it recovers this in truth and reality by the same means, by

which it lost the same for its healing. But to perturbation contemplation is never joined, nor is the mind when disturbed enabled to behold that, which even when in a tranquil state it scarcely has power to gaze on; for neither is the sun's ray discerned, when driving clouds cover the face of the heavens; nor does a troubled fountain give back the image of the beholder, which when calm it shows with a proper likeness; for in proportion as the water thereof quivers, it bedims the appearance of a likeness within it.

83. But when the spirit is stirred by zeal, it is needful to take good heed, that that same anger, which we adopt as an instrument of virtue, never gain dominion over the mind, nor take the lead as mistress, but like a handmaid, prompt to render service, never depart from following in the rear of reason. For it is then lifted up more vigorously against evil, when it does service in subjection to reason; since how much soever our anger may originate in zeal for the right, if from being in excess it has mastered our minds, it thereupon scorns to pay obedience to reason, and spreads itself the more shamelessly, in proportion as it takes the evil of a hot temper for a good quality; whence it is necessary that he who is influenced by zeal for right should above all things look to this, that his anger should never overleap the mind's control, but, in avenging sin, looking to the time and the manner, should check the rising agitation of his mind by regulating it with nicety of skill, should restrain heat of temper, and control his passionate emotions in subjection to the rule of equity, that the punisher of another man may be made more just, in proportion as he has first proved the conqueror of himself; so that he should correct the faults of transgressors in such away, that he that corrects should himself first make advancement by self-restraint, and pass judgment on his own vehemency, in getting above it, lest by being immoderately stirred by his very zeal for right, he go far astray from the right. But as we have said, forasmuch as even a commendable jealousy for virtue troubles the eye of the mind, it is rightly said in this place, *For wrath killeth the foolish man*; as if it were in plain terms, 'Anger from zeal disturbs the wise, but anger from sin destroys the fool;' for the first is kept in under the control of reason, but the other lords it over the prostrate mind in opposition to reason. And it is well added,

And envy slayeth the little I one.

xlvi.

84. For it is impossible for us to envy any but those, whom we think to be better than ourselves in some respect. And so he is 'a little one,' who is slain by jealousy. For he bears witness against his very own self, that he is less than him, by envy of whom he is tormented. It is hence that our crafty foe, in envying of the first man, despoiled him, in that having lost his estate of bliss, he knew himself to be inferior to his immortality. It is hence that Cain was brought down to commit the murder of his brother; in that when his sacrifice was disregarded, he was maddened that he, whose offering God accepted, was preferred to himself; and him, whose being better than himself was his aversion, he cut off, that he might not be at all. Hence, Esau was fired to the persecution of his brother; for, the blessing of the firstborn being lost, which, for that matter, he had himself parted with for a mess of pottage, he bewailed his inferiority to him, whom he surpassed by his birth. Hence his own brethren sold Joseph to Ishmaelites, that were passing by, in that upon the mystery of the revelation being disclosed, they set themselves to resist his advancement, that he might never become superior to themselves. Hence Saul persecutes his servant David by throwing a lance at him, for he dreaded that man growing beyond his own measure, whom he perceived to be daily waxing bigger by his great achievements in the virtues. Thus he is a 'little one,' who is slain by envy; in that except he himself proved less, he would not grieve for the goodness of another.

85. But herein we must bear in mind, that though in every evil thing that is done, the venom of our old enemy is infused into the heart of man, yet in this wickedness, the serpent stirs his whole bowels, and discharges the bane of spite fitted to enter deep into the mind. Of whom also it is written, *Nevertheless, through envy of the devil came death into the world.* For when the foul sore of envy corrupts the vanquished heart, the very exterior itself shows, how forcibly the mind is urged by madness. For paleness seizes the complexion, the eyes are weighed down, the spirit is inflamed, while the limbs are chilled, there is frenzy in the heart, there is gnashing with the teeth, and while the growing hate is buried in the depths of the heart, the pent wound works into the conscience with a blind grief. Nought of its own that is prosperous gives satisfaction, in that a self-inflicted pain wounds the pining spirit, which is racked by the prosperity of another: and in proportion as the structure of another's

works is reared on high, the foundations of the jealous mind are deeper undermined, that in proportion as others hasten onward to better things, his own ruin should be the worse; by which same downfall even that is brought to the ground, which was believed to have been raised in other doings with perfect workmanship. For when envy has made the mind corrupt, it consumes all that it may have found done aright. Whence it is well said by Solomon, *A sound heart is the life of the flesh: but envy the rottenness of the bones*. [Prov. 14, 30] For what is denoted by 'the flesh,' saving weak and tender things? and what by the 'bones,' saving strong deeds? And it is most common that some with real innocency of heart should appear to be weak in some points of their practice, whilst some now perform deeds of strength before the eyes of men, but yet towards the excellences of others they are inwardly consumed with the plague of envy; and so it is well said, *A sound heart is the life of the flesh*. In that where inward innocency is preserved, even if there be some points weak without, yet they are sometime made strong and fast. And it is rightly added, *But envy the rottenness of the bones*. For by the bad quality of envy even strong deeds of virtue go for nought before the eyes of God. Since the rotting of the bones from envy is the spoiling of the strong things even.

86. But why do we say such things concerning envy, unless we likewise point out in what manner it may be rooted out? For it is a hard thing for one man not to envy another that, which he earnestly desires to obtain; since whatever we receive that is of time becomes less to each in proportion as there are many to divide it amongst. And for this reason envy wrings the longing mind, because that, which it desires, another man getting either takes away altogether, or curtails in quantity. Let him, then, who longs to be wholly and entirely void of the bane of envy, set his affections on that inheritance, which no number of fellowheirs serves to stint or shorten, which is both one to all and whole to each, which is shown so much the larger, as the number of those that are vouchsafed it is enlarged for its reception. And so the lessening of envy is the feeling of inward sweetness arising, and the utter death of it is the perfect love of Eternity. For when the mind is withdrawn from the desire of that object, which is divided among a multitude of participators, the love of our neighbour is increased, in proportion as the fear of injury to self from his advancement is lessened. And if the soul be wholly rav-

ished in love of the heavenly land, it is also thoroughly rooted in the love of our neighbour, and that without any mixture of envy. For whereas it desires no earthly objects, there is nothing to withstand the love it has for its fellow. And what else is this same charity but the eye of the mind, which if it be reached by the dust of earthly love, is forthwith beaten back with injury from its gaze at the inward light? But whereas he is 'a little one,' who loves earthly things, and a great one that longs after the things of eternity, it may be suitably enough rendered in this sense likewise, *And envy slayeth the foolish one*; in that no man perishes by the sickness of this plague, except him that is still unhealthy in his desires.

THE SECOND PART.

BOOK VI.

The whole of the fifth chapter, beginning at the third verse, is explained first in a spiritual sense, a few parts in an allegorical, and a great many in a moral sense.

Mystical SAVING the historical verity, I proposed to myself to make out the sayings of blessed Job and of his friends by the mystical mode of interpretation: for it is plain to all that are acquainted with the truth, that Holy Writ takes care to hold out in promise the Redeemer of the world in all its statements, and that it has aimed to represent Him by all the Elect as by His members. And hence blessed Job is in the Latin tongue rendered 'grieving,' that both by his name and by his wounds the Passion of our Redeemer might be signified, of Whom the Prophet says, *Surely He hath borne our griefs, and carried our sorrows.* [Is. 53, 4] And the Tempter, having robbed him of everything, slew both his servants and his children; in that at the time of His Passion he smote with the weapon of faithlessness not only the Jewish people, that served Him out of fear, but the very Apostles also themselves, that were regenerated in His love. The body of blessed Job is mangled with wounding, for our Redeemer does not disdain to be pierced with nails upon the stock of the Cross. And he received wounds, from the sole of the foot to the very crown of his head, in that not only in her last and lowest members, but even up to the very highest, Holy Church, which is His Body, is harassed with persecution by the raging Tempter. Hence also Paul said, *And fill up that which is behind of the afflictions of Christ.* [Col. 1, 24] And his wife strives to persuade him to curse, in that all the carnal minds within the pale of Holy Church prove abettors of the cunning Tempter. For she, who prompts him to cursing, represents the life of the carnal sort; since, as we have already said above, all persons of unchastened habits within the pale of Holy Church, in proportion as they are brought nigh to the good by their faith, pinch them harder by their life. For because they cannot be avoided, as being of the number of the faithful, they are borne by the faithful as the greater harm, in proportion [see Preface, § 14] as it is nearer home. But his friends, who come as if to administer consolation, but run out into words of bitter upbraiding, bear the likeness of heretics, who, in striving to defend God against the righteous, only offend Him.

2. These things then, which have been more fully delivered above, I have endeavoured to gather into a small compass after their mystical representation, that by this very repetition it might be recalled to the recollection of my reader, that I minister to the spiritual understanding. And yet, when occasion of usefulness demands, I also busy myself to make out with minute exactness the letter of the history, but when it is needed I embrace both at the same time, that the allegory may put forth spiritual fruit, which same nevertheless is produced by the historical verity as from the root. Now the friends of blessed Job, who, we have said, bear the likeness of heretics, we by no means condemn for their words throughout; for whereas it is delivered against them by the sentence from above, *For ye have not spoken before Me the thing that is right;* [Job 42, 7] and it is thereupon added, *Like My servant Job*; it is plainly manifest that that is not altogether set at nought, which is only disapproved by comparison with what is better. For they incautiously slip into censure of him, but yet, as they are the friends of so great a man, from familiar intercourse with him they learnt many mystical truths. Whence, as we have also said above, Paul uses their very words, and by taking these in aid of his statement, he testifies that they were delivered from a source of truth. Which same nevertheless Truth does rightly censure, in that no sentence, however full of force, should be delivered against a holy man. Accordingly the words of Eliphaz may be considered in a mystical sense, whereby he addresses blessed Job, saying,

Ver. 3. I have seen the foolish taking root; but suddenly I cursed his beauty. [*so V.*]

ii. 3. For the Jewish people showed itself to be 'foolish,' in that it slightly regarded the very Presence of Eternal Wisdom in the flesh. And it waxed strong, as it were, by taking root, in that it had power over the life of the Elect to the extinction thereof in time. And Eliphaz despises such an one, cursing him, in that all heretics, whom we have said the friends of blessed Job bear a figure of, while they boast themselves in the name of Christ, censure in a way of authority the unbelief of the Jews. Concerning which same foolish one it is forthwith added,

Ver. 4. His children are far from safety, and they are crushed in the gate, neither shall there be any to deliver them.

4. They all are 'the children' of this foolish man, who are generated by the preaching of that unbelief, and these 'are far from safety,' for though they enjoy the temporal life without trouble, they are stricken the worse with eternal vengeance, as the Lord says concerning these same sons of such an one, *Woe unto you, Scribes and Pharisees, hypocrites, for ye compass sea and land to make one proselyte, and when he is made ye make him twofold more the child of hell than, yourselves.* [Matt. 23, 15] It follows, *And they are crushed in the gate, neither shall there be any to deliver them.* Who else is to be understood by the name of *gate*, but the Mediator between God and Man, *Who says, I am the door; by Me if any man enter in, he shall be saved.* [John 10, 9] The sons, then, of this foolish man advance without the gate, and they are 'crushed in the gate,' for the evil offspring of the Jews, before the Mediator's coming, prospered in the observance of the Law, but in the presence of our Redeemer itself they fell away from the service of the Divine Being, proving outcasts by the deserts of their faithlessness. And verily there is none 'to rescue them,' for while they strive by their persecution to kill the Redeemer Himself, they cut themselves off from the proffered means of their rescue. And it is well added concerning him,

Ver. 5. Whose harvest the hungry eateth up, and the armed one shall seize him.

5. Now 'the harvest' of this foolish man was the crop of Sacred Writ. For the words of the Prophets are like so many grains of the ears, which the foolish man had, but did not eat. For the Jewish people indeed held the Law as far as the letter, but, from an infatuated pride, as to the sense thereof, they went hungering. But 'the hungry eateth the harvest' of this foolish one, in that the Gentile folk eats by taking in the words of the Law, in which the Jewish people toiled and laboured without taking them in. These hungry ones of faith the Lord foresaw, when He had said by the Evangelist, *Blessed are they that hunger and thirst after righteousness, for they shall be filled.* [Matt. 5, 6] Of these hungry ones Hannah says **iv.**

prophesying, *They that were full, have hired out themselves for bread, and they that were hungry were satisfied*. [1 Sam. 2, 5] And as he lost the harvest, it is rightly added how the foolish man himself too perishes, where it is said, *And himself shall the armed one seize*. The old enemy, being 'armed,' seized the Jewish people, for he extinguished in them the life of faith by the darts of deceitful counsel, that in the very point, wherein they imagined themselves to be rooted in God, they might resist His dispensation. And Truth forewarns the Disciples of this, saying, *Yea, the time cometh that whosoever killeth you will think that he doeth God service*. [John 16, 2] It follows.

And the thirsty shall drink his riches.

v. 6. The riches of this 'foolish' one 'the thirsty drink,' in that by the streams of Sacred Writ, which the Jewish people possessed in the display of pride, the converted minds of the Gentiles are watered. And hence it is said to those same persons by the Prophet, *Ho, every one that thirsteth, come ye to the waters; and he that hath no silver, come ye*. [Is. 55, 1] For that the divine oracles are denoted by the word 'silver,' is testified by the Psalmist in these words, *The words of the Lord are pure words, as silver tried in the fire*. [Ps. 12, 6] They then that 'have no silver,' are bidden to the 'waters,' in that the Gentile world which had never received the precepts of Holy Writ, is satisfied with the outpouring of Divine Revelation, which they now drink of the more eagerly, in proportion as they thirsted for it long time in a state of drought. Thus the very same Divine oracles are called at once 'harvests' and 'riches;' 'harvests,' because they refresh the hungering soul; 'riches,' because they array us in a rare richness of moral excellences. The same things are said both to be 'eaten,' and to be 'drunk,' for this reason, that whereas there are certain things therein that are obscure, which we understand not without they be interpreted, these same we in a manner swallow eating; and whereas certain other things indeed, that are easy to be understood, we so take as we find them, these we drink as if unchewed, in that we swallow them unbroken. These things we have run through in brief mode under their mystical signification, lest perchance we might seem to have passed over anything; but because they could not be the friends of blessed Job, except in some points they also shone conspicuous for high moral worth, it remains that in their words we examine the force of their import in a moral sense, that, whilst the weight and substance of their speech is made out, it may be shown what sort of teaching they were masters of.

Ver.3. I have seen the foolish taking root, but suddenly I cursed his beauty.

Moral 7. 'The foolish' is as it were made fast in the earth by 'taking root,' in that he is fixed in the love of earth with all his heart's desire. And hence Cain is recorded to have been the first that builded a city in the earth, that it might be plainly shown, that that same man laid a foundation in the earth, who was turned adrift from the firm hold of our heavenly country. The foolish man as it were lifts himself up by 'taking root,' when he is buoyed up in this world with temporal good fortune, so that he obtains whatsoever he desires, is subject to no crosses, prevails against the weak without meeting with resistance, gainsays those that do well with authority, is ever attaining to better circumstances by means of worse practices, so that from the very cause that he is forsaking the path of life, he lives for the time the happier. But when the weak see that the wicked flourish, they are alarmed, and being troubled in their own breasts by the prosperity of sinners, they inwardly falter in the mind's footsteps. It was the likeness of these same that the Psalmist took when he declared, *But as for me, my feet were almost gone, my step, had well nigh slipped; for I was envious at the sinner, when I saw the prosperity of the wicked*. [Ps. 73, 2. 3.] **vi.**

8. But when the strong see their glory, they forthwith fix their minds upon the punishment which is to follow after that glory, and with deep thought of heart within they contemn that, which swells the proud without with the bigness of empty inflation. It is then well said, *I have seen the foolish taking root, but suddenly I cursed his beauty*. For to 'curse the beauty' of the fool is to condemn his glory by an advised sentence, for he is the more frightfully drowned in torments, the higher he is lifted up in sins; for the being lifted up is transient, but the being punished is perpetual; for he, that meets with honour on his road, will meet with condemnation on his arrival; and he is as it were coming to a prison through pleasant meadows, who is going on to ruin through this world's prosperity. But it is to be observed, that, when he says that he 'cursed the beauty of the fool,' he directly adds, *suddenly*; for it is the way with man's weak mind to vary according to the modification of the objects

which it beholds. Thus it often happens that his judgment is led by the mere appearance of the object presented, and his bias and feeling are framed according to the thing which is before his eyes. For often persons, while they see the glory of certain individuals, are charmed with the appearances thereof, and account it something great, and heartily wish they might themselves obtain the like; but when they see the children of glory severally either overthrown of a sudden, or perchance even brought to death, they acknowledge with a sigh that human glory is altogether nought, so as to exclaim at once, 'See what a nothing is man!' Which indeed they would say with more propriety, if when they saw man in possession of glory, then thinking of his destruction, they had felt that transitory power is nought. For it is then that we are to reflect what a nothing human exaltation is, when by its successes it mounts above others; then we ought to reflect with what speed happiness will flee away, when it flourishes, as if for ever, before the eyes of men. For that the glory of a perishable being is nothing in the actual hour of death, any of the weak sort can presently consider. For then even they hold it cheap, who even until death follow after it with affection. So that it is well said*, I have seen the foolish taking root, but suddenly I cursed his beauty*. As if he said plainly; 'Against the beauty of the foolish I admitted no delay in my cursing, for as soon as I discerned it, I saw along with it the punishment that comes after; for I should not have cursed suddenly, if any delight in that glory had kept hold of me, but I cursed without tardiness, for beholding his punishments which are destined to endure, I condemned his power without hesitating.' But because in every case the more the wicked make way in this world, the greater numbers they drag to destruction, it is rightly subjoined, *Let his children be* [al. *his children shall be*] *far from safety*. For the children of the foolish one are they, that after his copy are brought forth in this world's ambition; who truly are so much the further from safety, in proportion as in the practice of iniquity they are stricken by no infirmity. Of these it is well added,

Ver. 4. And they shall be crushed in the gate; neither shall there be any to deliver them.

vii. 9. For as the entrance of a city is called the 'gate,' so is the day of Judgment the gate of the Kingdom, since all the Elect go in thereby to the glory of their heavenly country. And hence when Solomon saw this day approaching for the recompensing of Holy Church, he said, *Her husband is known in the gates, when he sitteth among the elders of the land*. [Prov. 31, 23] For the Redeemer of mankind is the 'husband' of Holy Church, Who shows Himself 'renowned' in the gates. Who [A.B.C.D. 'because he'] first came to sight in degradation and in mockings, but shall appear on high at the entering in of His kingdom: and 'He sitteth among the elders of the land,' for that He shall decree sentence of condemnation together with the holy preachers of that same Church, as Himself declares in the Gospel, *Verily I say unto you, Ye which leave followed Me, in the Regeneration, when the Son of Man shall sit on the throne of His glory, ye also shall sit upon twelve thrones, judging the twelve tribes of Israel*. [Matt. 19, 28] Which same Isaiah also foretelling long before uses these words, *The Lord will enter into judgment with the ancients of His people*. [Is. 3, 14] Of these gates Solomon says again, *Give her of the fruit if her hands, and her own works shall praise her in the gates*. [Prov. 31, 31] For Holy Church then receives of 'the fruit of her hands,' when the recompensing of her labours lifts her up to the entertainment of heavenly blessings, for her 'works then praise her in the gates,' when the words are spoken to her members in the very entrance to His kingdom; *For I was an hungred, and ye gave Me meat; I was thirsty, and ye gave Me drink; I was a stranger, and ye took Me in; naked, and ye clothed Me*. [Matt. 25, 35] The children then of this foolish man are lifted up *before* 'the gate,' but '*in* the gate they shall be crushed;' in that the followers of this world carry themselves proudly in the present life, but in the very entrance of the kingdom they are struck with an everlasting visitation. And it is well added, *Neither is there any to deliver them*. For 'Truth' delivers from eternal woe those whom in temporal weal She straitens by discipline. He, then, that now refuses to be straightened, is left then without the means to be 'delivered,' For Him, Whom they care not to have as a Father in training, the wicked in the season of their calamity never find a deliverer in succouring. It proceeds;

Whose harvest the hungry one shall eat up.

viii.

10. Even the foolish man has a 'harvest,' when any wicked man is vouchsafed the gift of a right understanding, is instructed in the sentences of Holy Writ, speaks good words, yet never in any wise does the thing that he says; gives forth the words of

God, yet does not love them; by his praise magnifies them, by his practice tramples on them. Thus because this foolish man both understands and speaks that, which is right, yet does not love this in his doings, while he has a harvest, he goes starving. Which same 'the hungry eateth up,' in that he, who pants after God with holy desires, learns what he hears, and practises what he has learnt. And, whilst he is invigorated by the right preaching of a wrong teacher, what else is this than that he is filled with the produce of the foolish? Did not 'Truth' charge His 'hungry ones' to eat up the 'harvest' of the foolish, when, they being inflamed by holy desires, He charged them concerning the Pharisees, saying, *All therefore whatsoever they bid you observe, observe and do; but do not ye after their works.* [Matt. 23, 3] As though He said plainly; 'By speaking they rear the harvest of the word, but by evil living they touch it not. Let this harvest then be the refreshment for your hunger, for it is for you that they reserve it in their own infatuated loathing.' And it is well added,

Ver. 5. And the armed man shall seize him.

ix. 11. For our old enemy is conquered as an unarmed man, when, by openly prompting evil things to the mind of man, he aims to destroy all the good together. But he comes 'armed,' when, leaving some good things untouched, he covertly works the ruin of others. For often he does not tempt some people in the understanding, nor oppose them in their meditation on Holy Writ, yet he undoes the life of those in practice, who, while they are praised for the excellence of knowledge, neglect to have regard to the shortcomings of their works, and while the mind is decoyed in the delightfulness of good esteem, no remedy is applied to the wounds of the life; and thus the 'armed' enemy has swallowed up this man, whom under the cloak of deceit, whilst leaving on one side, he has got the better of on another. It goes on,

And the thirsty shall drink [so. V.] *his riches.*

x. 12. Often the foolish man has a fountain of inward liquid, but he does not drink thereof; in that he is vouchsafed parts to understand, yet he disdains to acquaint himself with the sentences of Holy Writ by the reading of them; he knows that he has ability to understand by studying, yet he gives over in disdain all study of the lessons of truth. 'The riches' of the mind too are the words of Divine utterance, yet the foolish man regards these riches with his eyes, while he never applies them to the purpose of his own adornment. For on hearing the words of the law he sees indeed that they are great, yet he does not put himself to pains to understand them with any earnestness of love. But, reversely, another man has a thirst, but has not ability; love draws him to meditation, but the dulness of his sense withstands him, and often in the science of the Divine law, he from time to time finds out that by application, which the man of parts remains ignorant of from carelessness. Thus 'the thirsty drink up the riches of this foolish man,' as often as those precepts of God, which the quickwitted know nothing of from disdaining them, the duller sort follow after with warm affection. In these verily the eye of love lights up the shades of dulness; for thirst uncloses that to the slower sort, which disdain shuts up to the quicker. And they for this reason get to the depths of understanding, because they do not scorn to practise even the very least things that they have learnt, and while they aid the understanding with the hands, they lift themselves above the level of the clever. Hence it is well said by Solomon, *The lizard climbeth with his hands, and is in kings' palaces.* [Prov. 30, 28] For commonly 'birds,' which have a wing that lifts them up to fly, dwell in the bushes, and the 'lizard,' which has no wings for flying, 'climbing with hands,' occupies the abode of royalty, in that often any that are quickwitted, while they grow slack from carelessness, continue in bad practices, and the simple folk, which have no wing of ability to stand them in stead, the excellency of their practice bears up to attain to the walls of the eternal kingdom. Whereas then 'the lizard climbeth with his hands,' he 'is in kings' palaces;' in that the plain man, by earnestness of right practice, reaches that point, whereunto the man of ability never mounts. But having heard this, a question occurs to our mind, wherefore either the gift of understanding is bestowed on a heedless man, or any earnest mind is hindered by its slowness? To which an answer is speedily given, in that it is forthwith added,

Ver. 6. There is nothing in the earth without cause. [so Vulg.]

13. For on this account it often happens that even a slothful man receives ability, that he may be the more deservedly punished for his carelessness, because he scorns to acquaint himself with that which he might attain to without labour. And on this account **xi.**

the earnest person is straitened with slowness of understanding, that he may obtain so much the larger rewards of compensation, the more he toils in anxiety to find out. Therefore 'there is nothing in the earth without cause,' since slowness stands the earnest mind in stead for a reward, and to the slothful quickness only thrives for punishment. But for the understanding of those things that be right, we are at one time instructed therein by earnestness of labour, at another time by pains of affliction. Hence after it has been said, *There is nothing in the earth without cause*, it is fitly added thereupon,

Neither doth trouble spring out of the ground.

xii. 14. For 'trouble springeth out of the ground,' as it were, when man, being created after the image of God, is scourged by things without sense. But because it is by reason of the hidden deserts of men's souls that the open scourges of chastisements are sent forth, it happens at the same time that 'trouble springeth not out of the ground,' since it is the perversity of our sense, which requires that it should be stricken by things that have no sense. For thus we see that for our correction the looked for rain is withheld from the parched earth, and the vaporous air is scorched by the fiery heat of the sun; the sea rages with bursting tempests, and some embarked to cross its bosom it cuts off, and others are debarred the longed-for passage by the rampant water; the earth not only yields sparingly the produce of her fertility, but also destroys the seeds she has received. In all which circumstances we clearly discern that which a wise man testifies concerning God, *And the world shall fight with Him against the unwise*. [Wisd. 5, 20] For 'the world fights with the Lord against the unwise,' when even the very contrariety of the elements does service in the chastisement of offenders. Yet neither doth 'trouble Spring out of the ground,' for each insensate thing is put in motion to our annoyance, only by the impulse of our own doings. 'Trouble does not spring out of the ground,' for chastisement never a whit springs from that creature that strikes the blow, but from that one, without doubt, which, by committing sin, drew forth the severity of the stroke. But we must take great and diligent heed, that, when in outward circumstances we are afflicted with a weight of grief, we reach forward in hope to things above; that the mind may attain the heights above, in proportion as we are chastened by the external punishment. And hence it is justly subjoined,

Ver. 7. Man is born to labour, and the bird to flying.

15. For 'man is born to labour,' in that he, who is furnished with the gift of reason, bethinks himself that it is wholly impossible for him to pass through this season of his pilgrimage without sorrowing. Hence when Paul was recounting his woes to his disciples, he justly added, *For yourselves know that we are appointed thereto.* [1Thess. 3, 3] But even in that the flesh is afflicted with scourges, the mind is lifted up to seek higher things, as Paul again bears witness, saying, *But though our outward man perish, yet the inward man is renewed day by day.* [2 Cor. 4, 16] So then, 'man is born to labour, and a bird to flying,' for the mind flies free on high for the very same reason that the flesh toils the sorer below. **xiii.**

16. By the designation of 'man' too, may be represented the life of the carnal sort. And hence Paul says, *For whereas there is among you envying and strife and divisions, are ye not carnal?* [1 Cor. 3, 3] Soon after which he subjoins and says, *Are ye not men?* [ver. 4, Vulg.] In this life, then, 'man is born to labour,' for every carnal person, in seeking to obtain transitory things, is overcharging himself with the burthen of his desires. For it is sore labour to be seeking this same glory of the present life, at times to win it so sought, and to guard it with diligence when won. It is sore labour, with infinite pains to lay hold of that, which he, that shall lay hold, knows can never remain for long. But holy men, forasmuch as they have no fondness for transitory objects, are not only laid under no burthen of temporal desires, but even, if crosses on any occasion arise, in these very straits and faintings are free from trouble. For what is there more severe than scourges? and yet it is written concerning the Apostles when scourged, *And they departed from the presence of the council, rejoicing that they were counted worthy to suffer shame for His Name.* [Acts 5, 41] What then can be labour to the minds of those, to whom even the chastisement of stripes is not labour? Man then is 'born to labour,' for he really feels the ills of the present state, who is agape after the good things thereof. For that mind which hangs on the attraction of things above, has beneath it whatsoever is set in motion against it from without. Therefore it is well added, *and a bird to flying.* For the soul withdraws itself from the painfulness of labour, in proportion as it raises itself through hope toward things on high. Was not Paul like a 'bird born to flying,' who in undergoing such

countless crosses, said, *Our conversation is in heaven?* [Phil. 3, 20] And again, *We know that if our earthly house of this tabernacle were dissolved, we have a building of God, an house not made with hands, eternal in the heavens.* [2 Cor. 5, 1] Like a bird, then, he had mounted above the scenes below, whom, while yet lingering on earth in the body, the wing of hope was already bearing up in the heights. But forasmuch as none by his own strength can transport himself on high, so as to be raised to the invisible world, while he is borne down by visible things, it is immediately added with propriety,

Ver. 8. Wherefore I will entreat the Lord, and unto God would I make my address.

xiv. 17. As though he said in plain words, 'Him I petition, by Whom I know that these things are bestowed.' For if he imagined that he had them by himself, he would not need to make his prayer to God. It goes on;

Which doeth great things and unsearchable, marvellous things without number.

xv. 18. Who may see to the bottom of the marvellous works of Almighty God, how He made all things of nothing, how the very framework of the world is arranged with a marvellous mightiness of power, and the heaven hung above the atmosphere, and the earth balanced above the abyss, how this whole universe consists of things visible and invisible, how He created man, so to say, gathering together in a small compass another world, yet a world of reason; how constituting this world of soul and flesh, He mixed the breath and the clay by an unsearchable disposal of His Might? A part, then, of these things we know, and a part we even are. Yet we omit to admire them, because those things which are full of marvels for an investigation deeper than we can reach, have become cheap from custom in the eyes of men. Hence it comes to pass that, if a dead man is raised to life, all men spring up in astonishment. Yet every day one that had no being is born, and no man wonders, though it is plain to all, without doubt, that it is a greater thing for that to be created, which was without being, than for that, which had being, to be restored. Because the dry rod of Aaron budded, all men were in astonishment; every day a tree is produced from the dry earth, and the virtue residing in dust is turned into wood, and no man wonders. Because five thousand men were filled with five loaves, all men were in astonishment that the food should have multiplied in their teeth; every day the grains of seed that are sown are multiplied in a fulness of ears, and no man wonders. All men wondered to see water once turned into wine. Every day the earth's moisture being drawn into the root of the vine, is turned by the grape into wine, and no man wonders. Full of wonder then are all the things, which men never think to wonder at, because, as we have before said, they are by habit become dull to the consideration of them; but when he said, *which doeth great things*, he did well in immediately adding, *and unsearchable*. For it was but little to do great things, if the things that were done could have been searched to the bottom. And it is lightly added, marvellous things without number. As it would have been but an inferior greatness, if the things, which He created 'unsearchable,' He had made but few in number.

19. But herein it ought to be impressed upon us, that the Divine miracles should both ever be under our consideration in earnestness of mind, and never sifted in intellectual curiosity. For it often happens that the thought of man, when, seeking the reason of certain things, it fails to find it out, plunges into a whirlpool of doubt. Hence it comes to pass that some men reflect that the bodies of the dead are reduced to dust, and while they are unable to infer the power of the Resurrection from reasoning, they despair of their being able to be brought back to their former condition. Things that are marvellous then are to be believed on a principle of faith, but not to be pried into by reason. For, if reason set them open before our eyes, they would no longer be marvellous. But when the mind may chance to falter in these, it is needful that such things as it knows by custom, yet does not infer by reason, should be recalled to mind, that by the weight of a similar circumstance one may supply strength to the faith, which one finds to be undermined by one's own shrewdness. For, when the dust of the human flesh is thought on, the mind of some is shaken, and despairs of the time, when dust shall return to flesh, and through the lineaments of the limbs form a body restored to life, when that dryness of earth shall flush into freshness through the living limbs, and fashion itself in distinct parts by the forms and shapes of them. This indeed can never be comprehended by reason, yet it may be easily believed from example. For who would imagine that from a single grain of seed a huge tree would rise

up, unless he had it as a certain fact by experience? In that extreme minuteness of a single grain, and with next to no dissimilarity within itself, where is the hardness of the wood buried, and a pith either tender or hard compared with the wood, the roughness of the bark, the greenness of the root, the savour of the fruits, the sweetness of the scents, the variety of the colours, the softness of the leaves? Yet because we know this by experience, we do not doubt that all these spring from a single grain of seed. Where then is the difficulty that dust shall return into limbs, when we have every day before our eyes the power of the Creator, Who in a marvellous manner, even from a grain creates wood, and in a still more marvellous manner from the wood creates fruit? *Which doeth great things and unsearchable; marvellous things without number.* For the greatness of the Divine works can neither be made out in respect of kind and quality, nor reckoned in respect of quantity. Hence it is still further added,

Ver. 10, 11. Who giveth rain upon the face of the earth, and sendeth waters upon all things. Who setteth up on high those that be low; and those which mourn He exalteth with safety.

xvi. 20. Forasmuch as we believe that the friends of blessed Job were enlightened by their intercourse with him, we must needs handle these words of Eliphaz in a mystical manner. Thus Almighty God 'gives rain upon the earth,' when He waters the withered hearts of the Gentiles with the grace of heavenly preaching, and He 'sendeth waters upon all things,' in that by the fulness of the Spirit He fashions the barrenness of lost man to fruitfulness; as 'Truth' says by His own lips, *Whosoever drinketh of the water that I shall give him, shall never thirst.* But by the title of the universe man is denoted, in that in him there is set forth a true likeness and a large participation in common with the universe. For everything that is either is, yet does not live; or is and lives, yet does not feel; or is and lives and feels, yet neither understands nor discriminates; or is and lives and feels and understands and discriminates. For stones are, yet do not live. Trees both are and live, yet do not feel. For their verdure is called the life of herbs and of trees, as is declared by Paul concerning seeds, *Thou fool! that which thou sowest is not quickened except it die.* [1 Cor. 15, 36] Brute creatures both are and live and feel, yet do not understand. Angels both are and live and feel, and by understanding they exercise discernment. Man, then, in that

Mystical

he has it in common with stones to be, with trees to live, with animals to feel, with angels to discern, is rightly represented by the title of the 'universe,' in whom after some sort the 'universe' itself is contained. And hence 'the Truth' says to His disciples, *Go ye into all the world, and preach the Gospel to every creature.* That is, He would have every creature to be taken for man only, in whom He created something common with all things.

21. Though in this place, 'all things' may be understood in another sense also. For the grace of the Holy Spirit in bringing the rich under its influence, does not keep back the poor; while it abases the strong, it does not forbid the weak to come to it; while it gathers together the noble, at the same time it lays hold of the base-born; while it takes up the wise, it disdains not the foolishness of the unskilful. God, then, 'sendeth waters upon all things,' Who by the gift of the Holy Spirit calleth to the knowledge of Himself from every class of men.

22. Again it may be that by the designation of 'all things,' the mere diversities of characters are set before us. For one is lifted up by pride, another is bent down by the weight of fear, one burns with lust, another pants with avarice, one lets himself sink from listlessness, another is fired with rage. But while, by the teaching of Holy Writ, humility is given to the proud man, confidence bestowed upon the fearful, the lustful cleansed from impurity by devotedness to chastity, the avaricious by moderation cooled from the heat of his covetous desires, the careless liver made erect by the uprightness of an earnest mind, the passionate man restrained from the hastiness of his headlong disposition, God 'sendeth water upon all things,' for He adapts the power of His Word in each severally according to the diversity of their characters, that each may find in His revelation that, whereby he may yield the produce of the virtue that he needs. Hence it is said by a wise man of the sweetness of manna, *Thou didst send them from heaven bread prepared without their labour, having in itself all delight, and the sweetness of every taste.* [Wisd. 16, 20] For the manna contained in itself all manner of delight and the sweetness of every taste, for this reason, that in the mouth of the spiritual sort it yielded a taste, according to the eater's will, in that the Divine Word, being at the same time suited to all minds, yet never at variance with itself, condescends to the kind and character of its hearers; and whereas every elect person understands it with profit according

to his own fashion, he as it were turns the manna he received into a taste at will. And forasmuch as after the toils of good practice comes the glory of compensation, it is rightly subjoined after the sending of water, *Who setteth up on high those that be low, and those which mourn He exalteth with safety*.

23. 'Those that be low are set on high,' in that they, who are now despised for the love of God, shall then come as judges along with God, as 'Truth' pledges this which we have just named to the same humble ones, saying, *Ye which have followed Me, in the Regeneration, when the Son of Man shall sit on the throne of His glory, ye also shall sit upon twelve thrones, judging the twelve tribes of Israel*. [Matt. 19, 28] Then 'those that mourn the Lord exalts with safety,' in that they who, being inflamed with desire of Him, flee prosperity, endure crosses, undergo tortures at the hands of persecutors, chasten their own selves with grieving, are then vouchsafed a safety so much the more exalted, as they now from devout affection kill themselves to all the joys of the world. Hence it is that it is said by Solomon, *The heart knoweth his own soul's bitterness, and a stranger doth not intermeddle with his joy*. [Prov. 14, 10] For the human mind 'knoweth its own soul's bitterness,' when inflamed with aspirations after the eternal land, it learns by weeping the sorrowfulness of its pilgrimage. But the 'stranger doth not intermeddle with his joy,' in that he, that is now a stranger to the grief of compunction, is not then a partaker in the joy of consolation. Hence it is that 'Truth' says in the Gospel, *Verily, verily I say unto you, that ye shall weep and lament, but the world shall rejoice; and ye shall be sorrowful, but your sorrow shall be turned into joy*. [John 16, 20] And again, *And ye therefore now have sorrow, but I will see you again, and your heart shall rejoice, and your joy no man taketh from you*. [ver. 21. 22] The Lord, then, is said 'to exalt with safety those which mourn,' in that to all, who for His sake are stricken with grief in time, He vouchsafes true salvation for their comfort. But at the same time nothing hinders but that this may be understood of God's Elect even in this life.

24. For those that be 'low are set on high,' in that when they abase themselves in humility, they mount above all sublunary things in the discernment of a lofty mind. And, while they reckon themselves to be worthless in all things, by the discriminating view of a right mind, they surmount and trample upon the glory of this world. Let us look at lowly Paul. Mark how he says to his disciples, *For we*

preach not ourselves, but Christ Jesus the Lord, and ourselves your servants for Christ's sake. [2 Cor. 4, 5] Let us see this 'humble man set up on high.' He says, *Know ye not that we shall judge Angels?* [1 Cor. 6, 3] and again, *And hath raised us together, and made us sit together in heavenly places.* [Eph. 2, 6] Perchance at that moment the chain was holding him outwardly fast bound. Yet he had been 'set on high' within, who, by the certainty of his hope, was already sitting in heavenly places. Holy men then are objects of scorn without, and as unworthy persons have every indignity put upon them, yet in sure confidence that they are meet for the heavenly realms, they look with certainty for the glory of the Eternal world. And when they are hard pressed without in the assaults of persecution, they fall back within into the fortified stronghold of their mind; and thence they look down upon all things passing far below them, and amongst them they see passing even themselves as in the body. They dread no threats, for even tortures they so endure as to set them at nought. For it is hence that it is said by Solomon, *But the righteous shall be bold as a lion.* [Prov. 28, 1] Hence it is written again by the same, *The righteous man shall not be grieved by anything that shall happen to him.* Prov. 12, 21] For because all the righteous are seated on the lofty height of their purposed mind, whereas in dying they are not sensible of death, it is so in a marvellous manner, that the missiles of the reprobate at the same time both strike them, and do not reach them. Those then that are 'low are set up on high,' in that from the very circumstance that they despise themselves in all things, they are rendered the more secure against them all.

25. Contrary to which it is rightly delivered by the Prophet to the lost soul under the likeness of Babylon, *Come down and sit in the dust, O virgin daughter of Babylon, sit on the ground; there is no throne for the daughter of the Chaldeans.* [Is. 47, 1] For here I think the human mind is called a virgin, not as undefiled, but as unproductive. And forasmuch as Babylon is rendered 'confusion,' the barren soul is rightly named the daughter of Babylon, who, in that she never puts forth good works, whilst she is framed on no method of a right life, is as it were engendered of the parentage of confusion. But if she is called a virgin not as being barren but undefiled, after that she is fallen from the state of saving health, it is only to the increase of her 'confusion' that she is called that which she once was. And it is fitly that the Divine voice, in rebuking her, says to her, *Come down*; for the human

mind is stationed on high, when it covets the rewards above; but it 'comes down' from this station, when being overcome it yields itself cowardly to decaying worldly desires. And it is immediately subjoined to her with justice, *And sit in the dust*. For 'coming down she sits in the dust,' in that quitting heavenly scenes, she grovels in the very lowest, being stained with earthly imaginations. And here it is yet further added by way of repetition, *Sit on the ground*. As if in uttering reproaches he said in plain words, 'Because thou refusedst to lift thyself by a heavenly conversation, laid prostrate beneath thyself, be degraded in earthly courses.' And hence it is forthwith added by a necessary consequence, *There is no throne for the daughter of the Chaldeans*. For the Chaldeans are translated 'fierce.' And they are very fierce, who, pursuing their own wills, refuse to spare even their own lives. Earthly desires are 'fierce,' which render the mind hard and insensible not only to the precepts of the Creator, but also to the blows of stripes. But the 'daughter of the fierce ones has no throne,' in that the mind that is born to the love of the world by bad desires, and is by those same desires rendered obdurate, herein that she yields herself to earthly concupiscence, parts with the seat of judgment, and she sits as mistress upon no throne within her, in that she lacks the balance of discernment, and is withheld from the sitting of her judgment, because she ranges abroad among external lusts. For it is clear that that mind, which has lost the seat of counsel within, in a thousand ways dissipates itself without in desires. And because it shut the eyes to doing what it understands, it is deservedly blinded, so as not even to know what it does; and oftentimes by a deserved visitation it is left in its own will, and is set loose under those very toilsome services of the world, which it pants after with solicitude. Hence it is fitly added in that place, *For thou shall no more be called tender and delicate. Take the millstones, and grind meal.* [Is. 27, 2] It is well known that parents spare their tender daughter, nor charge her with hard and servile employments. So Almighty God as it were calls a daughter tender when He recalls the well-beloved soul of each person from the wearisome services of this world, that, whilst it is charged with external works, it be not hardened to internal desires. But the 'daughter of the Chaldeans' is not called 'soft and tender,' in that the mind, which is abandoned to evil inclinations, is left in this world's travail, the thing which it most anxiously desires. So that like a handmaid she drudges in the service of the world without, who refuses as a daughter to love God within. Hence she is bidden to 'take the millstone, and grind meal.' A millstone is whirled round in a circle, and the meal is thrown out. Now each separate course of this world's action is a mill, which, while it heaps up a multitude of cares, as it were whirls the minds of men in a circle, and she as it were throws forth the meal from herself, in that, when the heart is turned wrong, she is ever producing infinitely little thoughts. But it sometimes happens that he, who while at rest is accounted of some worth, on being placed in any scene of action is stripped bare. Hence we have it forthwith subjoined in that place, *Uncover thy baseness, make bare the shoulder, uncover the thighs, pass over the rivers.* For in the execution of a work 'baseness is uncovered,' in that the base and abject soul is made known in the manifestation of working, whereas before while at rest, it was accounted great. The mind 'makes bare the shoulder,' when it brings to light its practice, which was kept from view. It 'uncovers the thighs,' in that it plainly discovers, by what strides of desire it reaches after the advantages of the world. Furthermore 'it passes over the rivers,' in that it unceasingly pursues the courses of this present life, which are daily running out to their end. And, whilst it gives over one set, and follows after another, it is as it were ever going on from river to river. These things we have delivered by way of discussion in few words, in order to show where that mind lies grovelling, which has been unseated from the throne of a holy purpose. For if it ever cease to pant after the things which are above it, it plunges even unceasingly below itself. But it is fixed on high, if, abandoning the love of temporal things, it is bound fast to the hope of a changeless eternity.

Literal 26. It is well said then, *Who setteth up on high those that be low.* And it is fitly added, *And those which mourn He exalteth with safety.* Oftentimes in this world even any that be glad of heart are 'exalted,' whilst they are swoln by the mere gloriousness of their fortune, but 'those that mourn, the Lord exalts to safety,' in that he raises His sorrowing children to glory by the solid substance of true joy; for they are exalted by safety, and not by madness, who, set fast in good works, rejoice with a sure hope in God. For there are some, as we have said, who both do misdeeds, and yet do not cease to rejoice. Of whom Solomon says, *Who rejoice to do evil, and delight in the things that be froward.* [Prov. 2, 14] And again, *There be wicked men, who are as secure, as though they had the deeds of the righteous.* [Ecc. 8, 14. Vulg.] These, truly, are not 'exalted by safety,' but by foolishness, which same are full of pride when they ought to be loaded with sorrow, and for the very reason that these wretched persons let themselves out in exultation, they are wept over by all good men. Verily not unlike to the senses of madmen, they account that insanity, in which they surpass others, to be strength. They know not that it comes from disease, that they are able to do more than the sane, and they as it were esteem themselves to have increased in powers, whilst they are drawing near to the end of life by accessions of sickness. These because they have no perception of reason, are wept for, and they laugh, and they expand in an extraordinary exultation of heart, in the very same proportion that from insensibility they are ignorant of the evil they are undergoing. Those then that 'mourn' the Lord 'exalts with safety,' in that the mind of the Elect is full of joy, derived, not from the madness of the present life, but from the certain prospect of eternal salvation. Hence it is fitly added immediately afterwards, with respect to this very destruction of the wicked,

Ver. 12. He disappointeth the devices of the crafty, so that their hands cannot perform their enterprise.

xvii. 27. The minds of the lost are ever awake to evil imaginations, but very often the Providence above counteracts them, and though not even when they are crushed with adversities do they amend the wickedness of their counsel, yet that they may never prevail against the good, He puts a check upon their power. And against these it is brought to pass by marvellous retribution, that whilst the effect of their evil doing is lacking to them, still conscience gives them over convicted to the just sentence of the Judge. Whereas then they devise evil things, they show what they themselves are about; but, whereas they cannot 'perform their enterprize,' they, against whom it was imagined, are protected; and hence is yet further added aright,

Ver. 13. He taketh the wise in their own craftiness, and the counsel of the froward is carried headlong.

xviii. 28. For oftentimes, some that are puffed up with human wisdom, when they see that the decrees of God are contrary to their inclinations, set themselves to oppose them with crafty manoeuvres, and that they may bend the power of the dispensation of the Most High to meet their own wishes, they busy themselves in cunning contrivances, they devise schemes of excessive refinement. But they are only executing the will of God by the very way they are labouring to alter it, and whilst they strive to withstand the purpose of the Almighty, they are obeying His behests; for it often happens that that renders good service to His provident ordering, which on the part of human efforts makes a silly opposition to Him. Therefore the Lord taketh the wise in their own craftiness, when the acts of man even then conveniently serve His purposes, when they are opposed to them. Which we shall the better show, if we bring forward a few instances of actual facts.

Joseph's Brethren.

29. Joseph had been visited by a dream, how that his brother's sheaves fell down before his sheaf; he had been visited by a dream, how that the sun and moon together with the other stars worshipped him. And because he related these things guilelessly to his brethren, envy and fear of his future dominion over them forthwith smote their breasts; and when they saw him coming to them, they said with malice burning against him, *Behold this dreamer cometh. Come now therefore, and let us slay him, and we shall see what good his dreams will do him.* [Gen. 37, 19. 20.] And fearing to become subject to his dominion, they let down the dreamer into a well, and sell him to Ishmaelites that were passing by. He, then, having been brought into Egypt, subjected to slavery, condemned on the charge of lust, being vouchsafed aid for the merits of his chastity, and set up for his judgment in prophecy, was advanced over the whole of Egypt; and by the wisdom from on high with prudent foresight he collected stores of corn, and thus met the impending peril of a scarcity. And when the famine poured itself over the earth, Jacob, being distressed for the providing of food, sent his sons into Egypt. They find Joseph, whom they did not know, master of the distribution of corn, and that they might win the favour to have food given them, they were forced to worship the distributor thereof with their necks bent down to the earth. Now then let us consider the course of the transaction; let us consider how the power of God 'took the wise in their own very craftiness.' Joseph had for this reason been sold, that he might not be worshipped, yet he was for this reason worshipped, because he was sold; for they dared to try a thing in

craft, that the counsel of God might be changed; but by resisting they helped on the decree of God, which they strove to get quit of. For they were constrained to execute the will of God by the very act by which they laboured craftily to alter the same. Thus whilst the Divine purpose is shunned, it is fulfilling; thus while human wisdom resists, it is 'caught.' Those brethren feared lest Joseph should grow to an height above themselves. But that which was arranged by the Divine disposal, their precautions were the cause and occasion of bringing about. Human wisdom then was 'caught' in itself, when in the very way that its purpose was to oppose the will of God, it did service toward the completion thereof.

30. Thus, whereas Saul saw David, his subject, grow up in a daily advance in valorous achievements, he betrothed his daughter to him in marriage, and demanded that an hundred foreskins of the Philistines should be given by him for her dowry, that when the soldier thus challenged sought to exceed his own measure, being delivered over to the swords of his enemies, he might bring his life to an end; according as it is written, *The king requireth not any dowry, but an hundred foreskins of the Philistines, to be avenged of the king's enemies. But Saul thought to make David fall by the hands of the Philistines.* [1 Sam. 18, 25] But David, strengthened by the favourable aid of the interior Disposal, engaged himself to give the hundred, and he brought back two hundred foreskins. By the convincing force of which deed Saul being overcome, was 'caught' in the purpose of his wisdom by Providence above; for by the very means that he looked to destroy the life of the rising soldier, he raised to the highest pitch the fame of his merits. *Saul.*

31. But because the very Elect sometimes strive to be sharp-witted in a degree, it is well to bring forward another wise man, and to show how the craft of mortal men is comprehended in the Inner Counsels. For Jonah desired to be sharp-witted in prudence, when being sent to preach the repentance required of the Ninevites, because he feared that, if the Gentiles were chosen, Judaea would be forsaken, he refused to discharge the office of that preaching. He sought a ship and settled to fly to Tharsis, but straightway a storm arises, the lot is cast, that it may be found out to whose fault it is owing that the sea is in commotion. Jonah is found in the offence, he is plunged into the deep, devoured by the whale *Jonah.*

swallowing him, and there he is brought by the beast carrying him, where he despised to go of his own accord. See, the tempest of God finds out the runagate, the lot binds him, the sea receives him, the beast encloses him, and because he sets himself against paying obedience to his Maker, he is carried a culprit by his own prison to that place, whither he was sent. When God commanded, man would not administer the prophecy; when God breathed on it, the beast vomits the Prophet. God then 'taketh the wise in their own craftiness,' when He brings back even that to serve the purpose of His will, by which the will of man sets itself in contradiction to Him.

The Jews. 32. Let us, yet further, look well into the wisdom of the Hebrews, that we may see what in its foresight it resisted, what by so resisting it brought about. Surely, when a multitude of believers was gathering together at the miracles of our Redeemer, when the priests of the people, kindled by the torches of envy, declared that all the world were going after Him, saying, *Perceive ye how ye prevail nothing? Behold, the world is gone after Him* [John 12, 19]; that they might cut away from Him the strength of so great a concourse, they endeavoured to put an end to His power by death, saying, *It is expedient that one man die, and not that the whole nation perish.* [John 11, 50] Yet the death of our Redeemer availed to the uniting of His Body, i.e. of the Church, and not to the severing away of it. And hence it is commanded by the Law, that in representation of our Sacrifice, the throat of the turtledove or the pigeon should be cut, and not entirely severed, so that even after death the head should cleave to the body, in that verily *the Mediator between God and man* [1 Tim. 2, 5], i.e. the Head of all of us, and the Sacrifice of the true cleansing, from the very cause that He underwent death; was more truly joined to us. After the cutting, then, the head of the turtledove adheres to its body, for neither does the death that intervenes sever Christ from His Church. His persecutors then did that which they laboured after with pernicious intent, they brought death upon Him; that so they might cut off from Him the devotedness of the faithful; but faith only gained growth from thence, whence the cruelty of the faithless looked to extinguish it. And while they reckon that they are cutting off His miracles by persecuting Him, in truth they were forced to extend them without knowing it. Therefore the Lord took the wise in their own craftiness, when He reduced even that to the service of His pitifulness, in which the fierceness of man raged against Him.

33. For the Just and Merciful One, as He disposes the deeds of mortals, vouchsafes some things in mercy, and permits other things in anger; and the things which He permits He so bears with, that He turns them to the account of His purpose. And hence it is brought to pass in a marvellous way, that even that, which is done without the Will of God, is not contrary to the Will of God. For while evil deeds are converted to a good use, the very things that oppose His design, render service to His design. For hence it is said by the Psalmist, *The works of the Lord are great, sought out unto all His wills.* [Ps. 111, 2. Vulg.] For His works are so great, that by everything that is done by man, His Will is sought out; for it often happens that it is done by the very act, whereby it was thought to be thrown aside. Hence again it is said, *Whatsoever the Lord pleased, that did He in Heaven and in earth.* [Ps. 135, 6] Hence Solomon says, *There is no wisdom, nor understanding, nor counsel against the Lord.* [Prov. 21, 30] It remains that, in all that we do, we search out the potency of the Supreme Will, to which same, when we know it, all our conduct ought devoutly to render service, and to follow it as the guide of its course, lest it serve the same even against its will, if it declines it from pride. For the potency of the Divine purpose cannot be evaded, but he that bridles himself in under His nod, tempers it to himself with great efficacy; and he lightens the weight thereof to himself, who willingly bears it on the bowed shoulder of the heart. But as we have above made mention of His persecutors, let us proceed to show how the words that are subjoined likewise fit their blindness. It goes on;

Ver. 14. They shall meet with darkness in the day-time, and grope in the noonday as in the night.

xix. 34. They 'meet with darkness in the day-time,' for in the very presence of Truth, they were blinded by the deceitfulness of unbelief. For we see clearly in the day-time, but in the night the pupil of our eye is dimmed. Therefore whilst the persecutors beheld the miracles of Divine Power, and yet doubted of His Divine Nature, they were subjected to 'darkness in the day-time,' for they lost their eyesight in the light. Hence it is that 'Light' Itself admonishes them, saying, *Walk while ye have the light, lest darkness come upon you.* [John 12, 35] It is hence that it is said of Judaea, *Her sun is gone* *down, while it was yet day.* [Jer. 15, 9] It is hence that the Prophet again took up in himself the strain of persons in a state of penitence, in these words, *We stumble at noonday as in the night, we are in dismal places as dead men.* [Is. 59, 10] Hence again He says, *Watchman, what of the night? Watchman, what of the night? The watchman said, The morning cometh, and also the night.* [Is. 21, 11. 12] For 'the watchman came by night,' in that the Guardian of the human race even showed Himself manifest in the flesh, and yet Judaea, being close pressed by the darkness of her faithlessness, never knew Him. Where it is well added in the voice of the watchman, *The morning cometh, and also the night.* For by His presence hath a new light shone out upon the world, and yet the former darkness remained in the hearts of unbelievers. And it is well said, *They shall grope in the noonday as in the night*; for we search out by groping that which we do not see with our eyes. Now the Jews had seen His undisguised miracles, and yet they still went on seeking Him, as it were groping for Him, when they said, *How long dost Thou make us to doubt? If Thou be the Christ, tell us plainly.* [John 10, 24] See, the light of miracles was before their eyes, yet stumbling in the darkness of their own hearts, they continued to grope in seeking for Him. And this same blindness of theirs burst out into cruelty, and their cruelty even to the extent of overt acts of persecution. But the Redeemer of mankind could not for long be held by the hands of His persecutors. Hence it is forthwith added;

Ver. 15. But He shall save the poor from the sword of their mouth, and from the hand of the mighty.

35. For it is this very Poor Man of whom it is said by Paul, *Though He was rich, yet for our sakes He became poor.* [2 Cor. 8, 9] And because the Jews in accusing betrayed the Lord, Whom, when so betrayed, the Gentiles put to death, by 'the sword of the mouth' may be signified the tongue of the Hebrews, that were His accusers, of whom the Psalmist says, *Whose teeth are spears and arrows, and their tongue a sharp sword.* [Ps. 57, 4] For, as the Gospel also witnesses, they cried out, *Crucify Him, Crucify Him.* Luke 23, 21; John 19, 6] But by 'the hand of the violent' may be set forth the very Gentile world itself, which crucified Him, which in our Redeemer's death fulfilled in act the words of the Hebrews; God then 'saved this Poor One both from the hand of the violent,' and from 'the sword of the **XX.**

mouth,' in that our Redeemer, in His human Nature, was subjected both to the powers of the Gentiles, and to the tongues of the Jews by dying, but in the power of His Divine Nature He overcame them by rising again. By which same resurrection what else is brought to pass than that our weakness is strengthened to conceive the hope of the life hereafter? And hence it is well added immediately afterwards,

Ver. 16. And so the needy shall have hope.

xxi. 36. For when the poor man is rescued, 'the needy' is restored to hope, for the lowly people of the faithful is shaken with dismay at our Redeemer dying, but is established firm by His rising again, for the very first poor ones of His people, viz. the chosen Preachers, were smitten by the sight of His death, but restored by the manifesting of His resurrection. When, then, the poor man is saved, 'the needy' recovers hope, for by the Lord rising again in the flesh, every faithful soul is strengthened to have a confident expectation of eternal life. But, now, the Truth has already come in an open manifestation, He has already undergone the death of the flesh, and destroyed the same by rising again, already the glory of the Ascension has ennobled His Resurrection, and yet the tongue of the Hebrews does not yet cease to urge Him with insults; and He indeed suffers them with patience, that by such sufferance He may turn some, and others that refuse to be turned He may one day visit with severer punishment. For the tongue of unbelievers will then be struck dumb from their habit of unbridled speech, when it shall see Him coming as a just Judge, Whom now it has judged unjustly. And hence it is well added,

And iniquity shall stop her mouth.

xxii. 37. For now iniquity still opens wide her mouth, in that the tongue of unbelievers never ceases to urge with insults the Redeemer of the human race. But she shall then 'stop her mouth,' when this same, which she will not shut in good will, she shall shut in punishment. Yet this may also be well understood of the conversion of the persecutors. For when 'the poor is saved,' whilst 'the needy' returns to hope, iniquity is struck dumb, her mouth being stopped, in that by the miracle of His Resurrection shining out, whilst a full number of unbelievers is brought to the faith, it has ceased from the mocking and abuse of its Redeemer.

For its mouth, which it opened in mocking God, it has now shut in the dread of Him.

Moral 38. It is good to run through these points in a moral sense, putting aside the signification of the Jewish people, and to trace out in what manner they are transacted by wicked men in general. For the minds of the wicked, when they see some things done well by their neighbours, are strained upon the stretched rack of their jealousy, and they undergo the grievous chastisement of their own malice, when with a consuming heart they see good in others. Therefore it is well said, *They meet with darkness in the day time*. For when their mind is grieved for the superiority of another, there is an overshadowing from the ray of the light; for oftentimes while they view the unconcealed good qualities in their neighbours, they look closely if there be any evil points lying concealed from sight, and they busy themselves in eager scrutinies, if they may chance to find somewhat with which they may be able to charge them. Sound limbs indeed are all they see, but, with the eyes of the heart closed, they seek by feeling to find a sore. And hence it is rightly subjoined, *And grope in the noonday as in the night*. The day of good deeds shines outwardly in a neighbour, but they 'grope as it were in the night,' because inwardly they are under the darkness of their jealous feeling. They busy themselves to get to some points which they may censure, they seek out an opening for detraction, but forasmuch as they are unable to find this, they search about in blindness without. Which is well set forth in that occasion, when from the Angels protecting Lot, the inhabitants of Sodom could not find the doorway in his house, as it is written, *And they pressed sore upon the man, even Lot, and came near to break the door. But the men put forth their hand, and pulled Lot into the house to them, and shut to the door. And they smote the men that were at the door of the house with blindness, both small and great, so that they wearied themselves to find the door*. [Gen. 19, 9–11] What does it mean that, when the wicked are up in arms against him, Lot is brought back into the house, and defended, but that every righteous man, while he encounters the assaults of evil ones, is brought back into his interior, and abides undismayed. But the men of Sodom cannot find the door in Lot's house, because the corrupters of souls detect no opening of accusation against the life of the righteous man. For, stricken with blindness, they as it were go round and round the house, who, under the influence of envy scrutinize words and deeds; but because in the life of the just, strong and praiseworthy conduct fronts them every way, groping at random they feel nothing else than the wall. Therefore it is well said, *And grope in the noonday as in the night*. For while the good, which they see, it is out of their power to impeach, being blinded by wickedness, they search out for impeachment evil which they see nothing of.

39. And here it is properly subjoined, *But he shall save the poor from the sword of their mouth, and from the hand of the mighty*. For the 'poor' is everyone that is not set up in his own eyes. And hence 'Truth' says in the Gospel, *Blessed are the poor in spirit, for theirs is the kingdom of heaven*. [Matt. 5, 3] Now a person is drawn into sin in two ways. For either he is led on by pleasure, or overcome by fear. For 'the sword of the mouth' is the mischievousness of persuasion, but 'the hand of the mighty' is the opposition of power. But because he that is truly humble, who is here called 'the poor,' as he covets none of the good things of this world, so also undauntedly sets at nought even its adverse fortune, it is well said, *But He saveth the poor from the sword of their mouth, and from the hand of the mighty*. As if it were put plainly; 'God doth so firmly establish the souls of the humble in Himself, that neither the alluring arts of persuasion can draw them, nor the pains of punishment break them in to the practice of sin. For hope rears the spirit into the eternal world, and therefore it is not sensible of any of the ills without, that it falls under. And hence it is subjoined, *So the needy shall have hope*. Unto the fruits of which same hope, verily, when the poor man attaineth, everyone that is exalted is struck dumb; and hence it is yet further added, *And iniquity shall stop her mouth*. For the wicked man detracts from the good, and the righteous ways, which he cares not to practise, he never ceases to pull in pieces by slander, but iniquity at that time stoppeth her mouth, when her eyes are opened to see how great is the glory of the recompense provided for righteous souls. For then he is not at liberty to speak against the good, in that torments hold his tongue tied by the deserved retribution of his misdeeds. Hence it is well delivered by Hannah, speaking in prophecy, *He will keep the feet of his Saints, and the wicked shall be silent in darkness*. [1 Sam. 2, 9] But that every elect soul may escape eternal woe, and the poor mount up to everlasting glory, he must be bruised here below with continual stripes, that he may be found purified in the Judgment. For we are

every day borne downwards by the mere weight of our infirmity, but that by the wonderful interposition of our Maker we are relieved by succouring stripes. Hence it is added,

Ver. 17. Behold, happy is the man whom God correcteth.

xxiii.

40. The highest virtue is to avoid sins, that they should never be done, and second to that, at least to amend them when they have been committed. But for the most part we not only never at all avoid sins that threaten, but we do not even open our eyes to them, when committed. And the mind of sinners is enveloped in the deeper darkness, in proportion as it does not see the deficiency of its own blindness. Hence it is very often brought to pass, by the bountifulness of God's gift, that punishment follows upon transgression, and stripes unclose the eyes of the transgressor, which self-security was blinding in the midst of evil ways. For the inactive soul is touched with the rod, so as to be stimulated, in order that he, that has lost, by being self-secure, the firm seat of uprightness, may mark, upon being afflicted; where he is laid prostrate; and thus to him [A.B.C.D. 'huic'] the very sharpness of the correction becomes the source of light; and hence it is said by Paul, *But all things that are proved, are made manifest by the light* [Eph. 5, 13]; for proof of saving health lies in the force of the pain. Hence it is that Solomon says, *For healing will cause great offences to cease*. [Ecc. 10, 4. Vulg.] Hence again he says, *For whom the Lord loveth He correcteth, even as a father the son in whom he delighteth*. [Prov. 3, 12] Hence the Lord addresses John by the voice of the Angel, saying, *As many as I love, I rebuke and chasten*. [Rev. 3, 19] Hence Paul says, *Now no chastening for the present seemeth to be joyous, but grievous, nevertheless afterward it yieldeth the peaceable fruit of righteousness, unto them that are exercised thereby*. [Heb. 12, 11] Although therefore grief and happiness can never meet together, yet it is rightly said here, *Happy is the man whom the Lord correcteth*. For by this means, that the sinner is straitly visited with the pain of correction, he is sometimes trained to happiness, which knows no intervention of pain. It proceeds,

Therefore despise not thou the chastening of the Lord.

xxiv.

41. Whosoever is smitten for a fault and lifted up in murmuring against the stroke, 'reproves the chastening of the Lord.' For he lays to His charge, that he has this put upon him

unjustly. But they that are stricken, not for the cleansing of guilt, but for the testing of their fortitude, when they inquire into the causes of the stroke, must by no means be said to 'reprove the correction of the Lord;' for their aim is to discover in themselves what they are ignorant of. And hence blessed Job, breaking out into a voice of liberty, amidst the visitings of the scourge, the more rightly questions the judgments of the smiter concerning him, the more he is really ignorant of causes for his suffering in himself. Eliphaz, then, forasmuch as he reckoned that he was visited, not with the trial of probation, but of purification, when he spoke with freedom amidst the stripes, supposed that he 'reproved the correction of the Lord.' And we have said that he at the same time bears the likeness of heretics with great fitness, in that whatsoever is done aright by Holy Church, is ever, in their judgment, turned and twisted awry, to some fault of crookedness. But forasmuch as it is with a good intention that he is led to speak, yet he takes no heed to discriminate who he is speaking to, he yet further subjoins, and proclaims the dispensations of the supreme governance, saying,

Ver. 18. For He maketh sore, and bindeth up; He woundeth, and His hands shall make whole.

XXV. 42. In two ways Almighty God wounds those, whom He is minded to bring back to saving health; for sometimes He smites the flesh, and consumes the hardness of the heart by the fear of Him. Thus He recalls to saving health, by dealing wounds, when He afflicts His own Elect outwardly, that they be quickened with inward life. Whence He also says by Moses, *I will kill and I will make alive, I will wound and I will heal* [Deut. 32, 39]; for He 'kills,' that He may 'make alive,' He 'wounds,' that He may 'heal;' in that He for this reason applies stripes without, in order that He may heal the wounds of sin within. But sometimes, even if strokes without should seem to have ceased, He inflicts wounds within, in that He strikes the hardness of the heart with the desire of Himself; yet in wounding He heals, in that when we are pierced with the dart of His dread, He recalls us to a right sense. For our hearts are not well sound, when they are wounded by no love of God, when they feel not the wofulness of their pilgrimage, when they do not go sorrowing with the least degree of feeling for the infirmity of their neighbour. But they are 'wounded,' that they may be 'healed,' in that

God strikes unfeeling souls with the darts of His love, and straightway makes them full of feeling, through the burning heat of charity, and hence the spouse says in the Song of Songs, *For I am wounded with love.* [Cant. 2, 5. LXX] For the diseased soul, laid prone upon the litter of this place of banishment in blind self-security, neither beheld the Lord, nor sought to see Him. But on being struck with the darts of His love, it is wounded in its innermost parts with a feeling of pious affection, burns with the desire of contemplation; and in a marvellous manner she is made alive by wounding, who aforetime lay dead in a state of health: she glows, she pants, and yearns to see Him already, from Whom she turned. By being smitten, then, she is brought back to a state of soundness, who is recalled to a secure state of inward repose by the disturbing of her self-love. But when the wounded soul begins to pant after God, when, setting at nought all the alluring arts of the world, it stretches forth in desire to the land above, all is forthwith turned to its trial, whatsoever aforetime was accounted pleasing and alluring in this world. For they that had a fond affection for him living in sin, cruelly assault him when he lives aright. The soul that is raised up toward God, is subject to rude assaults from the flesh, wherein it formerly lay grovelling in enjoyment, the slave of evil habits; former pleasures recur to the mind, and push hard the resisting soul with a grievous conflict. But because that, while we are afflicted with transitory labour, we are rescued from everlasting pain, it is fitly subjoined;

Ver. 19. He shall deliver thee in six troubles, yea, in seven there shall no evil touch thee.

xxvi.

43. For what is denoted by the number 'six,' which is followed by 'the seventh,' saving the labour and course of the present life? For God, finishing all things on the sixth day, created man, and God rested on the seventh day; and this same seventh day is without an evening, for there is no longer any end to close the rest that followeth. When all things, then, are completed, the rest followeth, in that after the good works of the present life, the recompense of eternal rest follows. Therefore 'in six troubles the Lord delivers us,' that 'no evil may touch us in the seventh,' in that by the training of His fatherly pity, He exercises us with the labours of the present life, but at the coming of the Judge, He hides us from the scourge, that He may then bring us out the more sure for His salva-

tion, in proportion as we are now scored the more cruelly with scourges. And immediately reckoning up with fitness both the ills of the present life, and the aids of Protection from above, adds,

Ver. 20. In famine He shall redeem thee from death, and in war from the power of the sword.

xxvii. 44. As the 'famine' of the flesh is the withdrawal of the support of the body, so the hunger of the soul is the silence of divine revelation. Hence it is rightly delivered by the Prophet, *I will send a famine in the land, not a famine of bread, nor a thirst of water, but a famine of hearing the word of the Lord.* [Amos 8, 11] And forasmuch as when the divine communication leaves the human soul, the temptation of the flesh gains force against it, it is fitly brought in, *And in war from the power of the sword.* For we suffer a war, when we are assailed by the temptations of our flesh. Concerning which same war the Psalmist says, *Cover my head in the day of battle.* [Ps. 140, 7] Therefore, whereas the reprobate, whilst their strength fails from a 'famine' of the word of God, are furthermore pierced with 'the sword of war,' the Lord both 'in famine redeems' His Elect 'from death,' and 'in war' He hides them 'from the sword.' For while He refreshes their souls with the food of His word, He makes them strong to resist the temptations of the body. Yet there be some, who, though they recruit themselves, out of the store of the word of God, from the famine of the interior, though they be already stayed up against the temptations of the body by the virtue of continency, yet still fear to be stricken with the slanders of their fellow-creatures, and oftentimes, whilst they dread the arrows of the tongue, they strangle themselves with the noose of sin. And hence it is fitly added,

Ver. 21, Thou shalt be hid from the scourge of the tongue.

xxviii. 45. 'The scourge of the tongue' is the taunting of insults offered. They strike the righteous 'with the scourge of the tongue,' who pursue their deeds with mockery. For oftentimes the tongue, while it utters jibes, recalls from a good deed, and puts itself out like a scourge, in that it cuts the back of the cowardly soul. Which 'scourge of the tongue,' the Prophet had seen plotting against the elect soul, when He said, promising the aid that is above, *Surely He shall deliver thee from the snare of the hunter, and from the rough* *word*. [Ps. 91, 3. Vulg.] For 'hunters' seek nothing else than flesh, but we are 'delivered from the snare of the hunters and from the rough word,' when we overcome both the snare of carnal persons, and the reproaches of sneers, by setting them at nought. For their words are 'rough,' which are arrayed against our righteous ways. And to 'escape the roughness of words,' is to trample down the mockings of calumniators by shutting our eyes to them, the holy soul then is hidden from 'the scourge of tongues,' in that whilst in this world it never seeks the honour of applause, neither does it feel the insults of calumny. But there be some that already set at nought the words of the scornful, already care nothing for their jeers, yet they still stand in dread of the pains and tortures of the body. For our old adversary, in order to withdraw us from a right bent of mind, assaults us in diverse modes, and prosecutes the tempting of us one while by a famine of the word, another while by the conflict of the flesh, now by the scourge of talk, now by the distress of persecution. But because every perfect person, when once he has overcome the evil habits in himself, straightway goes on to brace his mind to meet the inflictions of suffering, it is properly subjoined,

Neither shalt thou be afraid of calamity when it cometh.

46. For holy men, for that they see that they are engaged with an adversary of manifold form, equip themselves variously in their conflict. For against a famine, they have the sustenance of God's word; against the sword of war, they have the shield of continency; against the scourge of the tongue, the defence of patience; against the hurt of outward misfortune, they have the aid of inward love. Hence in a marvellous method it is brought to pass, that the more manifold the temptations which the craft of the enemy brings upon them, so much the richer in virtues are the wary soldiers of God rendered. And forasmuch as all the Elect severally, whilst they bear with courageous hearts the conflicts of the present life, are providing for themselves security under the terrors of the future Judgment, it is rightly subjoined; **xix.**

Ver. 22. In destruction and famine thou shalt laugh.

47. For the lost shall then suffer 'destruction and famine,' when, being condemned in the last Judgment, they are parted asunder from the sight of 'the Bread' eternal. For it is written, **xxx.**

Let the wicked be taken away, that he see not the glory of God. [Is. 26, 10. lxx.] And the Lord declares by His own lips, *I am the living Bread, Which came down from heaven.* [John 6, 51] Thus at one and the same time both 'destruction and famine' combine to torture those, who not only feel torments without, but farther suffer death within by the plague of starvation. Hell 'destroys,' in that it burns, famine kills, in that the Redeemer hides His face from them. For well and justly they have their recompense both within and without, in that the wretched people both by thought and by deed did commit offence. Whence it is well said by the Psalmist, *Thou shalt make them as a fiery oven in the time of Thine anger: the Lord shall confound them in His wrath, and the fire shall devour them.* [Ps. 21, 9] For that, which is 'devoured' by fire, is kindled from the outside. But an oven is set on fire within. And so in the time of God's anger all the unrighteous are both 'made as a fiery oven,' and also 'devoured by the fire,' in that at the appearing of the Judge, when all the multitude of them is banished from the sight of Him, both within the conscience is set on fire from the misery of want [*'Desiderium'*], and without hell torments the flesh.

48. 'The scourge of the tongue' too may be understood to mean the sentence of the final doom, whereby the Just Judge says to the lost, *Depart from Me, ye cursed, into everlasting fire, prepared for the devil and his angels.* [Matt. 25, 41] The righteous man then is 'hidden from the scourge of the tongue,' and from the coming woe, because in that exceeding strictness of doom, he is then comforted with the, mild voice of the Judge, when it is said, *For I was an hungred, and ye gave Me meat: I was thirsty, and ye gave Me drink: I was a stranger, and ye took Me in: naked, and ye clothed Me: I was sick, and ye visited Me: I was in prison, and ye came unto Me.* [ver. 35, 36.] Before which it is premised; *Come, ye blessed of My Father, inherit the kingdom prepared for you from the foundation of the world.* [ver. 34.] Therefore 'in destruction and famine' the righteous man 'shall laugh;' for, when the final vengeance smites all the wicked, he himself joys in the glory of a meet reward. Nor does he at that time any longer compassionate the damned by virtue of his human nature. For, incorporated into the Divine Justice by resemblance [*per speciem*], he is, by the unshaken force of interior strictness, made thoroughly firm. For the souls of the Elect, being reared up in the clear light of the Righteousness above, are touched by no sense of compassion, in that the height of

their bliss makes them strangers to misery. Hence also it is well said by the Psalmist; *The righteous also shall see this, and shall fear, and shall laugh at him, and shall say, Lo, this is the man that made not God his helper.* [Ps. 52, 6. 7.] For now the righteous see the wicked and fear, then they shall see and laugh. For because they may now fall in imitation of them, here they are holden of fear, but because they cannot then advantage the damned, there they entertain no sympathy. Therefore, that they should not commiserate those that are doomed to eternal woe, they read in that very justice of the Judge wherein they exist in bliss. For, a thing which it is not right to imagine of them, they lower the character of the happiness vouchsafed them, if, when placed in the kingdom, they wish for something which they never can accomplish. But whosoever orders himself after the precepts of life, already tastes here below the first-fruits of that secure estate which shall last for ever, so that he has no fear of our old enemy; nor at the coming on of the crisis of death in any degree dreads his violent assault. For to the righteous the beginning of their recompense is most commonly nothing else than the very security of their minds in dying. Hence it is rightly added,

Neither shalt thou be afraid of the beast of the earth.

xxxi.

49. For our crafty foe is called 'a beast of the earth,' in that he ravins with the violence of his savage nature, to seize upon the souls of sinners at the hour of their death. For those whom he deludes by flattery during their lifetime, he seizes with cruelty when they are dying. Contrary whereunto the Lord gives a promise concerning the Church of the Elect through the Prophet, *The evil beast shall not go up thereon.* [Is. 35, 9] They then in dying fear the 'beast of the earth,' who when living fear not the power of their Maker. For good men, because they submit themselves from the core of their heart to the dread of God, put away every weight of fear arising from the adversary's coming. For it is hence that the Psalmist beseeches the Lord, in these words, *Lest he tear my soul as a lion.* [Ps. 7, 2] Hence again he says, *Hear my voice, O God, in my prayer, preserve my soul from fear of the enemy.* [Ps. 64, 1. 2.] For while they live they perfectly fear the Judge, that when they die they may not dread the accuser. Well then is it said, *Neither shalt thou be afraid of the beast of the earth.* As if it were in plain words, 'Forasmuch as thou art not now overcome by the enemy in his alluring address, thou

shalt not hereafter fear him in his rage. But when we live well, it is very needful to be on our guard, that the mind, looking down upon others, be not lifted up by the pride of standing alone. Hence it is that the blessing of fellowship is fitly called to mind, where the words are immediately introduced thereupon,

But with the stones of the countries shall be thy covenant.

xxxii. 50. The Churches of the nations are like separate countries in the world, which, while they be planted in one faith, are separated by a diversity of customs and of tongues. What then do we take the stones of the countries to mean but the Elect ones of the Church, to whom it is declared by the voice of him who was the first among the teachers, *Ye also as lively stones are built up a spiritual house?* [1 Pet. 2, 5] Concerning whom the Lord by His Prophet promises Holy Church, saying, *Behold, I will lay thy stones in order*. [Is. 54, 11] Whoso then lives aright, joins himself in covenant 'with the stones of the countries.' For herein, that he conquers the desires of the world, without doubt he ties his life to an imitation of the Saints that have gone before. But when he is departing from the practice of the world, the assaults of malicious spirits increase, which nevertheless, the more they afflict a man in sorrow of heart, bow him the more humbly to his Creator. And hence it is added,

And the beasts of the earth shall be peacemakers to thee.

xxxiii. 51. First it is to be observed, that he does not say, 'made peaceful,' but, 'peacemakers,' that is to say, not that they are at peace, but that they make peace; for the crafty foes in making plots distress, but the distressed soul delights the more in her return to the heavenly home, the more she lives toiling in this woful place of exile, and most truly abases herself to the gracious regard of her Helper, when she considers the most violent plots of the enemy against her. The beasts of the earth then are rendered 'peacemakers' to the Elect, in that the malignant spirits, when they bear down the hearts of the good by their hostility, drive them to the love of God against their will. Thus there arises a firmer peace with God, from the same source, whence a tougher fight is occasioned us by our adversaries.

52. By the 'beasts of the earth' too may be understood the motions of the flesh, which, while they gall the mind by prompting

conduct which is contrary to reason, rise up against us like beasts. But when the heart is bowed down under the Divine Law, even the incitements of the flesh are reduced, so that, though in tempting us they give a low muttering, yet they never mount so high as to the execution of the deeds, as to the madness of open biting. For who that still subsists in this corruptible flesh, completely tames these beasts of the earth, when that preeminent Preacher that was caught up to the third heaven, says, *But I see another law in my members, warring against the law of my mind, and bringing me into captivity to the law of sin, which is my members.* [Rom. 7, 21] But it is one thing to see these beasts raging in the field of practice, and another to hold them ravening within the door of the heart. For when they be forced back within the bars of continence, though they still roar by tempting, yet, as we have said, they go not such lengths as the bite of unlawful practice. The beasts of the field then are peacemakers, in that though the motions of the flesh beat high in the desire, yet they never assail us with the open resistance of deeds, (though by this same circumstance, that they are called 'peacemakers,' even this same that we have said of malicious spirits is not unsuitably understood.) For the motions of the flesh 'make peace' for us with God, when they offer opposition by tempting us. For the mind of the righteous man, in that his way is directed to the realms above, is sore bestead by a grievous war arising from the corruptible body. And if at any time it be hindered in heavenly aspirations by any enjoyment of this world however slight, by that very war of temptation, which it undergoes, it is urged on to set all its affections in that, which is disturbed by no opposition. Whence it comes to pass that it recalls to mind the interior repose, and fleeing from the enticements of the flesh, sighs after it with a full affection. For temptation constrains every man to mark from whence and whereunto he is fallen, who after he has forsaken the peace of God, feels a strife rise up against him from out of himself, and then he more truly sees what he has lost of the assured love of God, who having fallen down to himself, finds his own self insulted within himself. The beasts of the earth then make peace for us, in that the motions of the flesh, whilst by offering temptation they irritate us, urge us forwards to the love of the interior repose. Now it is rightly added,

Ver. 24. And thou shalt know that thy tabernacle shall be in peace.

THE SECOND PART.

xxxiv. 53. In holy Scripture full peace is described in one way, and peace in its beginning in another. For 'Truth' gave to His Disciples peace in its beginning, when He said, *Peace I leave with you; My peace I give unto you.* [John 14, 27] And Simeon desired to have perfect peace, when he besought saying, *Now lettest Thou Thy servant depart in peace, according to Thy word.* [Luke 2, 29] For our peace begins in longing for the Creator, but it is perfected by a clear vision. For it will then be perfect, when our mind is neither blinded by ignorance, nor moved by the assaults of its fleshly part. But forasmuch as we touch upon its first beginnings, when we either subject the soul to God or the flesh to the soul, the 'tabernacle' of the righteous man is said to 'have peace,' in that his body, which he inhabits by his mind, is held in from the froward motions of its desires under the controlling hand of righteousness. But what advantage is it to restrain the flesh by continence, if the mind is uninstructed to expand itself by compassion in the love of our neighbour? For that chasteness of the flesh is as nothing, which is not recommended by sweetness of spirit. Whence after the 'peace of the tabernacle' it is fitly subjoined,

And thou shalt visit thy likeness, and shalt not sin.

xxxv. 54. For the *likeness* of man is another man. For a fellow-creature is rightly called our 'likeness,' in that in him we discern what we ourselves are. Now in the visiting of the body we go to our neighbour by the accession of steps, but in the spiritual visiting, we are led not by the footstep but by affection. He then 'visits his likeness,' whoever direct his way to one, whom he sees to be like to himself in nature, by the footsteps of love, so that by seeing his own case in another, he may collect from himself how to condescend to another's weakness. He 'visits his likeness,' who, that he may remodel another in himself, takes account of himself in another. For hence 'Truth,' in telling by the mouth of Moses what had been done, denoted what was to be done, saying, *And the earth brought forth grass and herb yielding seed after his kind, and the tree yielding fruit, each one bearing seed after his kind.* [Gen. 1, 12] For 'the tree produces seed after its kind' when our mind gathers from itself thought for another, and produces the fructification of well doing. Hence the wise man says, *Do not that to any, which thou wouldest not have done to thyself.* [Tob. 4, 15] Hence the Lord says in the Gospel,

Therefore all things whatsoever ye would that men should do to you, do ye even to them. [Matt. 7, 12] As if He said in plain words, 'Visit your likeness in another man, and from your own selves learn what conduct it behoves you to exhibit to others.' Hence Paul says, *And unto the Jews I became as a Jew, that I might gain the Jews; to them that are under the law, as under the law, that I might gain them that are under the law; to them that are without law, as without law, (being not without law to God, but under the law to Christ.)* [1 Cor. 9, 20. 21.] And soon after, *I am made all things to all men, that I might save all.* [ib. 22] Not indeed that the great Preacher, to become like a Jew, broke away into faithlessness; nor, that he might become 'as one under the law,' did he turn back to the fleshly sacrifice; nor, that he might become 'all things to all men,' did he change his singleness of mind into variety of deceit; but by lowering himself, not by falling, he drew near to the unbelievers, to this end, that by taking each one into himself and transforming himself into each one, by sympathizing with them, he might gather what it was, that, if he himself were like them, he would justly have desired should be bestowed upon him by others; and might go along with every erring person so much the more to the purpose, in proportion as he had learnt the method of his salvation by the consideration of his own case. Well then is it said, *And thou shalt visit thy likeness, and shalt not sin.* For sin is then perfectly conquered, when everyone sees from the likeness of himself, how to expand in the love of his neighbour. But when the flesh is kept in check from evil practices, when the mind is exercised in virtuous habits, it remains that every one should by word of mouth reach the life, which in his own ways he observes. For he gathers abundant fruits of his preaching, who sows before the seeds of welldoing. Whence after the 'peace of the tabernacle' and the 'visiting of our likeness,' it is rightly subjoined,

Ver. 25. Thou shalt know also that thy seed shall be manifold, and thine offspring as the grass of the earth.

xxxvi.

55. For after the 'peace of his tabernacle,' after 'the visiting of our likeness,' the manifold seed of the righteous man ariseth, in that after the macerating of the members and the fulness of the moral virtues, the word of preaching is bestowed upon him so much the more productive, in proportion as it is anticipated in his breast by the tillage of perfect practice. For he receives

eloquence to speak well, who expands the bosom of his heart by the exercises of right living. Nor does the conscience hinder the speaker, when the life goes before the tongue. It is hence that the Egyptians, who, by Joseph's management, were subjected to a state of public servitude, when they humble themselves by submitting their persons to the king's power, carry away corn even for seed. For we receive, even when free, fruit to eat, when we are at the same time fed by the sacred word, and yet in the gratification of our pleasures roam after different objects, which we seek after in this world. But when we become slaves, we receive corn for seed too, in that while we are made wholly subject to God, we are replenished further with the word of preaching. And since a vast progeny of faithful souls succeeds, when holy preaching is first bestowed, after the multiplying of the seed, it is rightly subjoined, *And thine offspring as the grass of the earth*. The progeny of the righteous is compared to the grass of the earth, in that he who is born in a copy of him, while he quits the decaying glory of the present life, comes out green with hope in the things of eternity. Or truly, the progeny of the righteous springeth up like 'the grass,' in that while he shows forth by his living what he declares by his preaching, an innumerable multitude of followers arises. But whosoever already looks down upon all earthly objects of desire, whoever spreads himself out in the labours of an active life, finds it by no means suffice him to do great things without, unless by contemplation he also have power to penetrate into interior mysteries. Hence too the words are thereupon fitly introduced,

Ver.26. Thou shalt come to thy grave in fulness, like as a shock of corn cometh in in his season.

xxxvii. 56. For what is denoted by the name of the grave, saving a life of contemplation? which as it were buries us, dead to this world, in that it hides us in the interior world away from all earthly desires. For they being dead to the exterior life, were also buried by contemplation, to whom Paul said, *For ye are dead, and your life is hid with Christ in God*. An active life also is a grave, in that it covers us, as dead, from evil works; but the contemplative life more perfectly buries us, in that it wholly severs us from all worldly courses. Whoever then has already subdued the insolencies of the flesh in himself, has this task left him, to discipline his mind by the exercises of holy practice. And whosoever opens his mind in holy works, has over and above to extend it to the secret pursuits of inward contemplation. For he is no perfect preacher, who either, from devotion to contemplation, neglects works that ought to be done, or, from urgency in business, puts aside the duties of contemplation. For it is hence that Abraham buries his wife after death in a double [*in spelunca agri duplici* Vulg.] sepulchre, in that every perfect preacher buries his soul, dead to the desires of the present life, under the covering of good practice and of contemplation, that the soul which aforetime, sensible of the desires of the world, was living in death, may as it were, without being obnoxious to sense, lie buried from carnal concupiscence under an active and contemplative life. It is hence that the Redeemer of mankind in the day time exhibits His miracles in cities, and spends the night in devotion to prayer upon the mountain, namely, that He may teach all perfect preachers, that they should neither entirely leave the active life, from love of the speculative, nor wholly slight the joys of contemplation from excess in working, but in quiet imbibe by contemplation, what in employment they may pour back to their neighbours by word of mouth. For by contemplation they rise into the love of God, but by preaching they return back to the service of their neighbour. Hence with Moses, whilst a heifer is slaughtered in sacrifice, scarlet wool twice dyed is enjoined to be offered together with hyssop and cedar wood. For we slay a heifer, when we kill our flesh to its lust of gratification; and this we offer with hyssop and cedar and scarlet wool, in that together with the mortifying of the flesh, we burn the incense of faith, hope, and charity. The hyssop is of use to purify our inward parts; and Peter says, *purifying their hearts by faith*. [1 Pet. 1, 3] Cedar wood never decays by rotting, in that no end finishes the hope of heavenly things. Whence too Peter says, *He hath begotten us again by a lively hope by the resurrection of Jesus Christ from the dead; to an inheritance incorruptible, undefiled, and that fadeth not away*. Scarlet wool flames with the redness of its hue, in that charity sets on fire the heart she fills. Whence also 'Truth' says in the Gospel, *I am come to send fire on the earth*. But scarlet wool twice dyed is ordered to be offered, that in the sight of the internal Judge our charity may be coloured with the love both of God and of our neighbour, that the converted soul may neither so delight in repose for the sake of the love of God, as to put aside the care and service of our neighbour, nor busying itself for the love of our neighbour, be so wedded, thereto, that entirely forsaking quiet, it extinguish in itself the fire of love of the Most High. Whosoever then has already offered himself as a sacrifice to God, if he desires perfection, must needs take care that he not only stretch himself out to breadth of practice, but likewise up to the heights of contemplation.

57. But herein it is above all things necessary to know, that the compositions [*'conspersio,'* dough, paste.] of souls are infinitely varied one with another, for there are some of such inactivity of mind, that, if the labours of business fall upon them, they give way at the very beginning of their work, and there be some so restless, that if they have cessation from labour, they have only the worse labour, in that they are subject to worse tumults of mind, in proportion as they have more time and liberty for their thoughts. Whence it behoves that neither the tranquil mind should open itself wide in the immoderate exercising of works, nor the restless mind stint itself in devotion to contemplation. For often they, who might have contemplated God in quiet, have fallen, being overcharged with business; and often they, who might live advantageously occupied with the service of their fellow-creatures, are killed by the sword of their quiescence. It is hence that some restless spirits, whilst by contemplation they hunt out more than their wits compass, launch out even to the length of wrong doctrines, and, whilst they have no mind to be the disciples of Truth in a spirit of humility, they become the masters of falsities. It is hence that 'Truth' says by His own lips, *And if thy right eye offend thee, pluck it out, and cast it from thee; for it is profitable for thee to enter into life with one eye, rather than having two eyes be cast into hell fire.* For the two lives, the active and the contemplative, when they be preserved in the soul, are accounted as two eyes in the face. Thus the right eye is the contemplative life, and the left the active life. But, as we have said, there be some, who are quite unable to behold the world above, and spiritual things, with the eye of discernment, yet enter upon the, heights of contemplation, and therefore, by the mistake of a perverted understanding, they fall away into the pit of misbelieve. These then the contemplative life, adopted to an extent beyond their powers, obliges to fall from the truth, which same persons the active life by itself might have kept safe in lowliness of mind in the firm seat of their uprightness. To these 'Truth' rightly addresses the warning which we said before, *And if thy right eye offend thee, pluck it out, and cast it from thee; for it is good for thee to enter into*

life with one eye, rather than having two eyes to be cast into hell fire. As if He said in plain words; 'When thou art not qualified for the contemplative life by a fitting degree of discretion, keep more safely the active life alone, and when thou failest in that which thou choosest as great, be content with that which thou heedest as very little, that if by the contemplative life thou art forced to fall from the knowledge of the truth, thou mayest by the active life alone be able to enter into the kingdom of heaven at least with one eye.' Hence He says again, *But whoso shall offend one of these little ones which believe in Me, it were better for him that a millstone were hanged about his neck, and that he were drowned in the depth of the sea.* [Matt. 18, 6] What is denoted by 'the sea,' but this present state of being? what by 'the millstone,' but earthly practice, which while it binds down the neck of the soul by foolish desires, sends it out into the round of labour. Thus there are some, who, while they quit earthly courses and rise beyond the powers of their understanding in pursuance of the exercises of contemplation, having laid aside humility, not only cast themselves into error, but separate any that be weak from the bosom of unity; and thus 'it would be better for him, that offends one of the least, with a millstone fastened to his neck, to be cast into the sea,' in that indeed it would have been more expedient for the froward mind, if, busied with the world, it were employed in earthly matters, than, in the exercises of contemplation, to be free to work the destruction of numbers. On the other hand, if it were not that the contemplative life suited some minds more than the active life, the Lord would never say by the voice of the Psalmist, *Be still, and know that I am God.* [Ps. 46, 10]

58. But herein it is necessary to know, that often at one and the same time love stimulates inactive souls to work, and fear keeps back restless souls in the exercise of contemplation. For a weight of fear is an anchor of the heart, and very often it is tossed by the stormy sea of thoughts, but is held fast by the moorings of its self-control; nor does the tempest of its disquietude make shipwreck of it, in that perfect charity holds it fast on the shore of the love of God. Whence it is necessary that whoever eagerly prosecutes the exercises of contemplation, first question himself with particularity, how much he loves. For the force of love is an engine of the soul, which, while it draws it out of the world, lifts it on high. Let him then first examine whether in searching after the highest things he loves, whether in

loving he fears, whether he knows either how to apprehend unknown truths, while he loves them, or not being apprehended to reverence them in cherishing fear. For in contemplation, if love does not stimulate the mind, the dulness of its tepidity stupefies it. If fear does not weigh on it, sense lifts it by vain objects to the mist of error, and when the door of secret things, being closed against it, is slow in being opened, merely by its own presumption alone it is forced the farther off there-from, for it strives to force a way to that which it seeks after without finding, and when the proud mind takes falsehood for truth, in proportion as it is advancing the step as if inwards, it is directing it without. Thus it is for this reason that the Lord, when about to give the Law, came down in fire and in smoke; in that He both enlightens the lowly by the clearness of His manifestation of Himself, and darkens the eyes of the highminded by the dimness of error. First then the soul must be cleansed from all affection for earthly glory, and from the gratification of carnal concupiscence, and next it is to be lifted up in the ken of contemplation. Hence too, when the Law is given to them, the people are forbidden the Mount, namely, that they who, by the frailty of their minds, still have their affections set upon earthly objects, may not venture to take cognizance of things above. And hence it is rightly said, *And if a beast touch the mountain, it shall be stoned*. [Ex. 19, 13] For 'a beast touches the mountain,' when the mind, which is bowed down to irrational desires, lifts itself to the heights of contemplation. But it is 'smitten with stones,' in that being unable to bear the highest things, it is killed by the mere blows of the weight on high.

59. Let all then that strive to lay hold of the summit of perfection, when they desire to occupy the citadel of contemplation, first try themselves, by exercising, in the field of practice, that they may heedfully acquaint themselves, if they now no longer bring mischiefs upon their neighbours, if when brought upon them by their neighbours, they bear them with composure of mind, if when temporal advantages are put in their way, the mind is never dissipated by joy, if, when they are withdrawn, it is not stung by overmuch regret, and then let them reflect, if, when they return inwardly to themselves, in this work of theirs of exploring spiritual things, they never draw along with them the shadows of corporeal objects, or when drawn along, as they may be, if they drive them off with the hand of discretion [al. *districtionis,* severity]; if, when they long to behold the unen-

compassed light, they put down all images of their own compass, or in that which they seek to reach unto above themselves, conquer that which they are. Hence it is rightly said here, *Thou shalt come to thy grave in abundance*. For the perfect man does 'come to the grave in abundance,' in that he first gathers together the works of an active life, and then by contemplation wholly hides from this world his fleshly sense, which is now dead. Hence too it is fitly subjoined,

Like as a shock of corn cometh in in his season.

60. For the season for action comes first, for contemplation last. Whence it is needful that every perfect man first discipline his mind in virtuous habits, and afterwards lay it up in the granary of rest. For it is hence that he, who was left of the legion of devils at the bidding of our Lord, seats himself at His Saviour's feet, receives the words of instruction, and eagerly desires to leave his country in company with the Author of his recovery, but That very 'Truth' Himself, Who vouchsafed to him recovery, tells him, *Return first unto thine own house, and show what great things God hath done unto thee*. [Luke 8, 39. &c.] For when we have the least particle imparted to us of the knowledge of God, we are no longer inclined to return to our human affairs, and we shrink from burthening ourselves with the wants of our neighbours. We seek the rest of contemplation, and love only that which refreshes without toil. But after we are cured, the Lord sends us home. He bids us relate the things that have been done with us, so as that in fact the soul should first spend itself in labour, and that afterwards it may be refreshed by contemplation.

61. It is hence that Jacob serves for Rachel, and gets Leah, and that it is said to him, *It is not the custom in our country to give the youngest before the first-born*. For Rachel is rendered 'the beginning seen,' but 'Leah,' 'laborious.' And what is denoted by Rachel but the contemplative life? What by Leah, but the active life? For in contemplation 'the Beginning,' which is God, is the object we seek, but in action we labour under a weighty bundle of wants. Whence on the one hand Rachel is beautiful but barren, Leah weak eyed, but fruitful, truly in that when the mind seeks the ease of contemplation, it sees more, but it is less productive in children to God. But when it betakes itself to the laborious work of preaching, it sees less, but it bears more largely. Accordingly after the embrace of Leah, Jacob attains to Rachel, in that every one that is perfect is first joined to an

active life in productiveness, and afterwards united to a contemplative life in rest. For that the life of contemplation is less indeed in time [i.e. age], but greater in value [*merito*] than the active, we are shown by the words of the Holy Gospel, wherein two women are described to have acted in different ways. For Mary sat at our Redeemer's feet, hearing His words, but Martha eagerly prosecuted bodily services; and when Martha made complaint against Mary's inactivity, she heard the words, *Martha, Martha, thou art careful and troubled about many things; but one thing is needful: and Mary hath chosen that good part, which shall not be taken away from her*. [Luke 10, 41. 42.] For what is set forth by Mary, who sitting down gave ear to the words of our Lord, saving the life of contemplation? and what by Martha, so busied with outward services, saving the life of action? Now Martha's concern is not reproved, but that of Mary is even commended. For the merits of the active life are great, but of the contemplative, far better. Whence Mary's part is said to be 'never taken away from her,' in that the works of the active life pass away together with the body, while the joys of the contemplative life are made more lively at the end. Which is well and briefly set forth by the Prophet Ezekiel, when, beholding the flying creatures, he says, *And the likeness of the hands of a man were under their wings*. [Ezek. 10, 21] For what can we suppose meant by the wings of the creatures, saving the contemplations of the Saints, by which they soar aloft, and quitting earthly scenes, poise themselves in the regions of heaven? What do we understand by the 'hands,' saving deeds? For whereas they open themselves in the love of their neighbour, the good things, which abound to them, they administer even by bodily ministration; but 'the hands are under the wings,' in that they surpass the deeds of their action, by the excellence of contemplation.

62. Moreover by 'the grave' it may be that not only our contemplation in this life is understood, but the rest of our eternal and interior reward, wherein we more thoroughly rest, the more perfectly is killed in us the life of corrupt existence. He then 'goes down to the grave in abundance,' who, after he has stored up the works of the present life, being perfectly dead to his mutable condition of existence, is buried in the depth of the true light. Whence also it is said by the Psalmist, *Thou shalt hide them in the secret of Thy presence, from the provoking of men*. [Ps. 31, 20] And the comparison that is added brings this home to us with effect, where it is subjoined, *Like as a*

shock of corn cometh in in his season. For corn in the field is touched by the sun, in that in this life the soul of man is illumined by the regard of the light above. It receives the showers, in that it is enriched by the word of Truth; it is shaken by the winds, in that it is tried with temptations; and it bears the chaff 'growing' along with it, in that it bears the life of daily increasing wickedness in sinners, directed against itself; and after it has been carried away to the barn, it is squeezed by the threshing weight, that it may be parted from the bold of the chaff, in that our mind, being subjected to heavenly discipline, whilst it receives the stripes of correction, is parted from the society of the carnal sort in a cleaner state; and it is carried to the granary with the chaff left behind, in that while the lost remain without, the Elect soul is transported to the eternal joys of the mansion above. Well then is it said, *Thou shalt come to thy grave in abundance, like as a shock of corn cometh in in his season*; in that, whereas the righteous after sufferings meet with the rewards of the heavenly land, it is like as if the grains after pressing and squeezing were carried away to the granary. And it is in another's season indeed that they feel the strokes, but in their own that they rest from being struck. For to the Elect the present life is another's season, whence to some that were yet unbelievers 'Truth' says, *My time is not yet come, but your time is alway ready*. [John 7, 6.] And again, *But this is your hour, and the power of darkness*. [Luke 22, 53.] Thus 'he cometh to his grave in abundance, like as a shock of corn cometh in in his season,' in that he receives the rest eternal, who, that he may be set free of the chaff, which is destined to be burnt, first feels here below the pressure of discipline. But whereas Eliphaz in the course of his address mentioned 'the tabernacle,' 'the stones,' 'the beasts,' 'the seed,' 'the herbs,' and 'the grave,' he himself intimates that he did not speak of these according to the letter, in that after all of them he thereupon subjoins;

Ver.21. Lo this, as we have searched it, so it is.

xxxviii.

63. Assuredly it is clear, that in these words he says nothing upon a view of the surface, in that a thing, that is 'searched,' is not set before the face. He then, who shows that he had 'searched' these things, proves that in outward words inward things were what he had in view. And after the whole he is brought to the foolishness of boasting, in that he thereupon adds;

THE SECOND PART.

And now thou hast heard it, turn it in thy mind.

XXXIX. 64. With whatever lessons of instruction the mind may be furnished, it argues great want of skill to wish to instruct one that is superior, whence the very things which are rightly delivered by the friends, are not pronounced right by the interior Judge. For they lose the efficacy of their rightness herein, that they are not suited to the hearer. For even medicines lose their efficacious properties when they be administered to sound limbs. In all, then, that is said, it is necessary that the occasion, the time, and the individual, be taken into account, whether the truth of the sentiment confirms the words delivered, whether the fitting time calls for it, whether the character of the person does not impugn both the truth of the sentiment, and the suitableness of the time. For he launches his darts in a manner to deserve praise, who first looks at the enemy that he is to strike. For he masters the horns of the strong bow amiss, who in sending the arrow with force, strikes a fellowcountryman.

BOOK VII.

He explains the whole of the sixth chapter, except the three last verses, part allegorically and in part morally.

Literal

i.

1. Some men's minds are more tormented by scourges than reproaches, but some are more wounded by reproaches than by scourges. For oftentimes the tortures of speech assail us worse than any pains, and while they make us rise up in our vindication, they lay us low in impatience. Whence, that no temptation whatever might be lacking to blessed Job, not only scourges strike him from above, but the sayings of his friends in talk gall him, being sorer than scourges, that the soul of the holy man, being driven hither and thither, might, burst forth in the emotion of wrath and haughtiness, and that all the purity he had lived in might be defiled by head-strong pride of speech. But when touched by the scourges, he gave thanks, when galled with words, he answered aright, and being smitten he makes it appear how little he esteemed the well-being of the body. In speaking too he shows how, wisely he held his peace. But there were a few things mixed with his words, which, in the judgment of men, might seem to transgress the limits of patience; of which we shall take a true view, if in the examination of them we weigh well the sentence of the Most High Judge. For it was He, Who both in the first instance gave blessed Job the first place in opposition to the adversary, saying, *Hast thou considered My servant Job, that there is none like him in the earth, a perfect and an upright man, one that feareth God and escheweth evil?* [Job 1, 8] It was He, Who after the trial rebuked his friends, saying, *For ye have not spoken before Me the thing that is right, as My servant Job hath*. It remains then, that when the mind wavers with uncertainty in the discoursings of blessed Job, it estimate their weight from the beginning, and ending of that same account. For one who was to fall could never have been commended by the Eternal Judge, nor could one who had fallen be awarded the first place. If then, when we be caught in the tempest of embarrasment, we have regard to the first and last points in this history, the vessel of the soul is as it were held fast at prow and stern by the rope of its reflections, that it be not forced on the rocks of error, and so we are not overwhelmed by any storms arising from our ignorance, if we hold to the tranquil shore of the sentence of the Most High. For, mark, he says a thing which might urge the read-

er's mind with no slight questioning. Yet who could dare to pronounce that not right, which sounds right in God's ears?

Chap. vi. 2, 3. Oh that my sins [so Vulg.] *were throughly weighed, whereby I have deserted wrath, and the calamity that I suffer laid in the balances. It should be found heavier even as the sand of the sea.*

ii. 2. Who else is set forth by the title of 'the balances,' but the Mediator between God and man, Who came to weigh the merit of our life, and brought down with Him both justice and loving-kindness together? But putting the greater weight in the scale of mercy, He lightened our transgressions in pardoning them. For in the hand of the Father having been made like scales of a marvellous balancing, in the one scale He hung our woe in His own Person, and in the other our sins. Now by dying He proved the woe to be of heavy weight, and by releasing it showed the sin to be light in mercy's scale, Who vouchsafed this instance of grace first, that He made our punishment to be known to us. For man, being created for the contemplation of his Maker, but banished from the interior joys in justice to his deserts, gone headlong into the wofulness of a corrupt condition, undergoing the darkness of his exile, was at once subject to the punishment of his sin, and knew it not; so that he imagined his place of exile to be his home, and so rejoiced under the weight of his corrupt condition as in the liberty of a state of salvation. But He Whom man had forsaken within, having assumed a fleshly nature, came forth God without; and when He presented Himself outwardly, He restored man, who was cast forth without, to the interior life, that He might henceforth perceive his losses, that he might henceforth lament the sorrows of his blind state. Man's woe then was found to be heavy in the balance, in that the ill, which he was laid under, he only knew in his Redeemer's appearing presence. For not knowing the right, he bore with delight the darkness of his state of condemnation. But after he saw a thing for him to delight in, he likewise perceived a thing to grieve over, and what he underwent he felt was grievous, in that what he had lost was made known as sweet. Let then the holy man, thrown out of the barriers of silence by the sayings of his friend in discourse, and filled with the overflowing of the prophetic spirit, exclaim with his own voice, yea, with the voice of mankind, *Oh that my sins were thoroughly weighed, whereby I have deserved wrath, and the calamity that I suffer laid in the bal-*

Mystical

ances together! It should be found heavier even as the sand of the sea. As if it were in plain words, 'The evil of our condition under the curse is thought light, in that it is weighed without the Redeemer's equity [*aequitate*] being as yet known, but oh that He would come, and hang in the scale of His Mercy the wofulness of this dismal exile, and instruct us what to seek back for after that exile. For if He makes known what we have lost, He shows that to be grievous which we endure.' But this same misery of our pilgrimage is fitly compared to the sand of the sea, (for the sand of the sea is forced without by the chafing of the waters,) in that man too in transgressing, because he bore the billows of temptation unsteadily, was carried out of himself from within. Now of great weight is the sand of the sea, but the calamity of man is said to be 'heavier than the sand of the sea,' for his punishment is shown to have been hard, at the time when the sin is lightened by the merciful Judge. And because every man that owns the grace of the Redeemer, everyone that longs for a return to his Country, now that he is instructed, groans beneath the burthen of his pilgrimage; after the longing for the balances, the words are rightly subjoined;

Therefore my words are full of grief.

3. He that loves sojourn abroad instead of his own country, **iii.**
knows not how to grieve even in the midst of griefs. But the words of the righteous man are full of grief, for so long as he is subject to present ills, he sighs after something else in his speech; all that he brought upon himself by sinning is set before his eyes, and that he may return to the state of blessedness, he weighs carefully the judgments whereby he is afflicted. Whence it is added,

Ver.4. For the arrows of the Almighty are in me.

4. For by the epithet of 'arrows' sometimes the utterances **iv.**
of preaching, sometimes the arrows of visitation are denoted. Now the utterances of preaching are represented by 'arrows;' for in this, that they smite men's vices, they pierce the hearts of evil doers. Concerning which arrows it is said to the Redeemer at His coming, *Thine arrows are sharp, O Thou Most Mighty; the people shall fall under Thee in the heart.* [Ps. 45, 5. lxx.] Of Him Isaiah says, *I will send those that escape of them to the nations, into the sea, into Africa, and into Lydia, holding the arrow, into Italy, and into Greece.* [Is. 66, 19] Again by 'ar-

rows' is represented the stroke of visitation, as where Elisha bids king Joash, 'shoot an arrow,' and when he shoots, says, *For thou shalt smite the Syrians, till thou hast consumed them*. [2 Kings 13, 17] Whereas then the holy man surveys the sorrows of his pilgrimage, because he groans under the strokes of the visitation of the Lord, let him say, *Therefore my words are filled with grief. For the arrows of the Almighty are within me*. As though he said in plain words, 'I being under curse of exile have no joy, but as laid under the Judgment, I am full of pain, for I see and know the force of the stroke.' But there are a great number that are chastised with tortures, but not amended. Contrary to which it is fitly subjoined,

The indignation whereof drinketh up my spirit.

v. 5. For what else is the 'spirit of man,' but the spirit of pride? Now 'the arrows of the Lord drink up the spirit of man,' when the awards of heavenly visitation keep back the chastened soul from self-elation. 'The arrows of the Lord drink up the spirit of man,' in that, when he is intent upon outward things, they draw him within. For the spirit of David was drunk up when he said, *When my spirit failed within me, Thou knewest my ways*. [Ps. 142, 3] And again, *My soul refused to be comforted, I remembered God and was troubled, I complained and my spirit failed*. Therefore 'the indignation of the arrows drinketh up the spirit' of the righteous, for the decrees from above, in wounding, work a change in the Elect, whom they find in any sins; so that the soul being pierced, quits its hardness or heart, and the blood of confession runs down from the wound that brings health. For they consider whence and whereunto they have been cast down, they consider from how high bliss they have fallen, and to what miseries of their corrupt condition, and they not only groan in the midst of the things which they are suffering, but furthermore dread that which the strict Judge threatens sinners with concerning the fires of hell. Whence the words are rightly subjoined;

And the terrors of God do set themselves in array against me.

vi. 6. The mind of the righteous not only considers well what it is now undergoing, but also dreads what is in store. It sees all that it suffers in this life, and fears lest hereafter it suffer still worse things. It mourns that it has fallen into the exile of this blind state away from the joys of Paradise; it fears, lest, when this exile is quitted, eternal death succeed. And thus it already undergoes sentence in suffering chastisement, yet still dreads the threats of the Judge to come as the consequence of sin. Hence the Psalmist says, *Thy fierce wrath goeth over me; Thy terrors cut me off.* [Ps. 88, 16] For after that 'the fierce wrath of the Internal Judge goeth over, His terrors still do cut us off,' in that we already suffer one evil by condemnation, and still dread another from everlasting vengeance. Let the holy man then, weighing well the ills that he is subject to, exclaim, *The arrows of the Lord are within me, the indignation whereof drinketh up my spirit.* But being in dread of worse things to last for ever, let him add, *The terrors of God do set themselves in array against me.* As if he said in plain words, 'Being stricken indeed I feel grief for my present circumstances, but this is the worst feature in my grief, that even in the midst of punishment I still fear eternal woes.' But forasmuch as he already longs for the bringing in of the balances, he already weighs the evils into which the human race has fallen, though he was placed among a Gentile people, yet because he was full of the gift of prophetic inspiration, in the following words he shows with what ardent desire the coming of the Redeemer is thirsted for, whether by the Gentile world or by Judaea, saying,

Ver. 5. Doth the wild ass bray when he hath grass? or loweth the ox at his full manger?

Allegorical 7. For what is denoted by 'the onager,' that is, the wild ass, saving the Gentile people, which, as nature has produced it without the stalls of training, so has continued roaming abroad in the field of its pleasures? What is represented by 'the ox,' saving the Jewish people, which being bowed down to the yoke of the dominion above, in gathering together proselytes unto hope, drew the ploughshare of the Law through all the hearts that it was able? But we learn from the witness of blessed Job's life to believe, that many even of the Gentiles looked for the coming of the Redeemer. And at the birth of the Lord, we have learnt by Simeon's coming in the spirit into the Temple, with what longing desire holy men of the Israelitish people coveted to behold the mystery of His Incarnation. Whence too the same Redeemer says to His Disciples, *For I tell you that many prophets and kings have desired to see those things which ye see, and have not seen them.* [Luke 10, 24] The 'grass' of the wild ass then, and the ox's 'fodder,' is this very Incarnation of the **vii.**

Mediator, by which both the Gentile world and Judaea are together filled to the full. For because it is said by the Prophet, *All flesh is grass* [Is. 40, 6]; the Creator of the universe taking flesh of our substance, willed to be made 'grass,' that our flesh might not remain grass for ever; and so 'the wild ass' then found 'grass,' when the Gentile people received the grace of the Divine Incarnation. Then 'the ox' had not an empty manger, when to the Jewish people, looking for His Flesh, the Law showed Him forth, Whom it prophesied to them whilst long kept in expectation of Him. Whence too the Lord, when He was born, is placed in a manger, that it might be signified, that the holy animals, which under the Law had long been found an hungred, are filled with 'the fodder' of His Incarnation. For at His birth He filled a manger, Who gave Himself for food to the souls of mortal beings, saying, *He that eateth My Flesh, and drinketh My Blood, dwelleth in Me, and I in him*. [John 5, 56] But because both the longings of the Elect from among the Gentiles were for long deferred, and the holy men severally of the Hebrew people groaned long while in expectation of their redemption, blessed Job, in giving forth the mysteries of prophecy, rightly implies the causes of distress in the case of either people, by saying, *Will the wild ass bray while he hath grass? Or will the ox low over his full manger?* As though it were in plain speech, 'The Gentile world for this reason groans, because the grace of the Redeemer does not yet yield it refreshment, and Judaea on this account draws out her lowings, for that in holding the Law, but not seeing the author of the Law, standing before the manger she goes hungering. And because this same Law, before the coming of our Mediator, was held not in a spiritual but in a carnal manner, it is rightly added,

Ver. 6. Can that which is unsavoury be eaten without salt?

viii. 8. In the Law, the virtue of the hidden meaning is the salt of the letter. Whosoever, then, being intent upon carnal observances, refused to understand it in a spiritual sense, what else did he but eat 'unsavoury food?' But this 'salt,' 'Truth,' on being known, put into the food, when He taught that the savour of a hidden sense lay at the bottom of the Law, saying, *For had ye believed Moses, ye might* [Vulg. *forsitan*] *have believed Me, for he wrote of Me*. [John 5, 46] And again, *Have salt in yourselves, and have peace one with another*. [Mark 9, 50] But because before our Redeemer's coming,

Judaea held the Law in a carnal way, the Gentile world refused to bend themselves to its precepts, which enjoined hard things. Thus it would not eat unsavoury meat. For before that it got the relish of the Spirit, it shrunk from keeping the force of the letter. For which of the Gentiles would bear this, which is therein enjoined, to cut their children's flesh for a religious service? to cut off the sins of speech by death? And hence it is well added yet further;

Or can anyone taste, what by being tasted brings death? [Vulg.]

ix.

9. For the Law, if tasted in a carnal way, 'brought death,' in that it seized the misdeeds of transgressors with a severe visitation; it 'brought death,' in that both by the injunction it made known the sin, and did not by grace put it away, as Paul testifies, saying, *The Law made nothing perfect*. And again, *Wherefore the Law is holy, and the commandment holy and just and good*. And soon after, *But sin, that it might appear sin, working death in me by that which is good*. But the Gentile world, when turned to Christ, in that it understands Him to be sounding in the words of the Law, being straitened by its desires looks for Him, Whom it ardently loves, in a spiritual way amongst carnal precepts. And hence in the voice of the Church it is immediately added by the Prophetic Spirit,

Ver. 7. The things which my soul refused to touch are for straitness become my meat.

x.

10. For he goes very far wrong, who imagines that the words of blessed Job were delivered with an eye to the historical fact alone. For what would the holy man, and one too borne up by the proclaim of His Maker, have said, that was great, or rather what that was true, if he had said that 'unsavoury meat could not be eaten?' or who had offered deadly food for him to eat, that he should subjoin, *Or who can taste, what by being tasted brings death*? And if we imagine that was said of his friends' discourse, we are withheld from this view by the sentence that is subjoined, in which he says, *The things that my soul refused to touch are for straitness become my meat*. For never let it be thought that the holy man, when established in soundness of state, at any time looked down upon the words of his friends; who, as we learn afterwards by himself attesting it, was humble even to his servants, His words then are not void of mystical senses, which, as we gather from the end of the history, the internal Arbiter Himself

THE SECOND PART.

commends. And these would never have gone on commanding such deep veneration even to the very ends of the world, if they had not been pregnant with mystical meaning.

11. Let blessed Job then, in that he is a member of holy Church, speak in her voice also, saying, *The things which my soul refused to touch are for my straitness become my meat*. For the Gentile world, after conversion, made eager by the fever of her love, hungers for the food of Holy Scripture, which being filled with pride it disdained for long. And yet these words agree with the voice of Judaea also, if they be a little more attentively made out. For from the training of the Law, and from the knowledge of the One God, she herself had salt, and looked down upon all the Gentiles as brute creatures. But because, when instructed by the precepts of the Law, she disdained to admit to herself the communion of the Gentiles, what did she but loath to take 'unsavoury food?' For the Divine decree had forbidden, on the menace of death, that the Israelitish people should join in a league with strangers, and pollute the way of life in holy religion. Whence too it is added, *Or can anyone taste, what, by being tasted, brings death?* But because this same Judaea, in the portion of the Elect, was converted to the faith of the Redeemer, the light which she had become acquainted with she laboured by the Holy Apostles to deliver to the faithless of her offspring. But the pride of the Hebrew people rejected the ministry of her preaching, whence she immediately turned aside her words of exhortation for the gathering together of the Gentiles, as it is said also by the same Apostles, *It was necessary that the word of God should first have been spoken to you; but seeing that ye have put it from you, and have judged yourselves unworthy of everlasting life, lo, we turn to the Gentiles*. [Acts 13, 46] Whence too in this place it is fitly subjoined, *The things which my soul refused to touch are now for my straitness become my meat*. For Judaea, having disdained the life of the Gentiles, refused as it were for long to touch her, whose society she scorned to admit; but on coming to the grace of the Redeemer, being rejected by the unbelieving Israelites, while by the Holy Apostles she stretches out herself for the gathering together of the Gentiles, she as it were takes that for food with a hungry appetite, which before with loathing she disdained as unworthy. For she underwent 'straitness' in her preaching, who saw that what she spoke was despised among the Hebrew people. But for her 'straitness' she ate the food which she had for long despised, in that being rejected by the

obduracy of the Jews, she yearns to take to her the Gentile folk, whom she had contemned. Seeing then that we have delivered these points in a figurative sense, it remains that we go into them in their moral import.

Moral 12. The holy Man, longing for the coming of the Redeemer under the name of a 'balance,' whilst he opens his mind in discourse, instructs us to earnestness of life; whilst he tells his own tale, marks some things that belong to us; whilst he brings forward what we are to acknowledge concerning himself, strengthens unto life us that be trembling and weak. For now indeed we live by the faith of our Mediator, and yet still, for the cleansing out of our faults, endure heavy scourges of inward visitation; whence also, after longing for the balance, he adds,

Ver. 4. For the arrows of the Lord are within me, the indignation whereof drinketh up my spirit.

13. Now see, as has been remarked above, we are at the same time pierced by the stroke of Divine correction, and yet that is still worse, which we apprehend of the terribleness of the Judge to come, and of His everlasting visitation. Whence the words are thereupon introduced, *And the terrors of God do set themselves in array against me.* But the mind ought to be dispossessed of fear and sadness, and be drawn out in aspirations after the eternal land alone. For we then show forth the noble birth of our Regeneration, if we love Him as a Father, Whom with slavish soul we now dread as a Master. And hence it is spoken by Paul, *For ye have not received the spirit of bondage again to fear, but ye have received the spirit of the adoption of sons, whereby we cry, Abba, Father.* [Rom. 8, 15] Therefore let the soul of the Elect lay aside the weight of fear, exercise itself in the virtue of love, long for the worthiness of its renewal, pant after the likeness or its Maker; whom so long as it is unable to behold, it must needs await hungering after His eternal Being, i.e. after its own internal meat. Whence it is also justly added, **xi.**

Ver. 5. Doth the wild ass bray when he hath grass? Or loweth the ox over his full manger?

14. Who else are denoted by the term of 'the wild ass,' saving they who being set in the field of faith, are not bound by the reins of any ministration? Or whom does the designation of **xii.**

'the ox' set forth, saving those, whom within the bounds of Holy Church, the yoke of Orders taken upon them constrains to the ministry of preaching? Now the 'grass' of the wild ass, and the ox's 'fodder,' is the inward refreshing of the faithful folk. For some within the pale of Holy Church are held after the manner of an ox by the bands of the employment taken upon them, others after the manner of a 'wild ass' know nothing of the stalls of Holy Orders, and pass their time in the field of their own will. But when any one in the secular life glows with aspirations after the interior vision, when he yearns for the food of the inward refreshing, when seeing himself starved in the darkness of this pilgrim state, he refreshes himself with what tears he may, it is as if 'the wild ass brayed,' not finding 'grass.' Another one too is subject to the obligation of the Order he has taken upon him, he spends himself in the labour of preaching, and longs to be henceforth refreshed by eternal contemplation; but forasmuch as he does not see the likeness of His Redeemer, it is as if the chained ox lowed at the empty manger. For because being set at the widest distance from the interior wisdom, we see nothing of the verdure of the eternal inheritance, like brute animals we go hungering after the longed for grass. Of which same grass it is said by the voice of our Redeemer, *By Me if any man enter in, he shall be sated, and shall go in and out, and find pasture*. [John 10, 9] But most often, which is wont to be a grievous woe to those that love, the life of the wicked is arrayed against the holy aims of the good, and when the soul is transported in heavenly aspirations, the purpose of mind, which we have began with well, is dashed to the ground, being crossed by the words and practices of the foolish; so that the soul, which had already soared up to things above in the efforts of contemplation, for the defeating of the foolishness of the froward, girds itself for the encounter down below. Whence also it is added,

Ver. 6. Or can that which is unsavoury be eaten, not seasoned with salt? Or can anyone taste, what by being tasted brings death?

xiii. 15. For the words and the practices of the carnal introduce themselves like food into our minds, so as to be swallowed up in the belly of complacence. But any of the Elect eateth not that which is 'unsavory,' for setting apart in judgment the words and the deeds of the froward, he puts them away from the mouth of his heart. Paul forbade unsavoury meat to be offered for the food of souls, when he said to his disciples, *Let your speech be alway with grace, seasoned with salt*. [Col. 4, 6] And to the Psalmist also the words of the children of perdition tasted unsavoury in the mouth of the heart, when he said, *The wicked have related tales to* [so V.] *me which are not after Thy Law*. [Ps. 119, 85] But often, when the words of the wicked press themselves with importunity into our ears, they beget in the heart a war of temptation. And though both reason reject and the tongue censure them, yet that is with difficulty mastered within, which without is sentenced with authority. Whence it is necessary that that should never even reach the ears, which the mind must keep off from the avenue of the imagination by exercising watchfulness. Holy men, then, whereas their hearts pant with aspirations after Eternity, lift themselves to such an exalted elevation of life, that to hear any longer the things that are of the world they account to be a grievous burthen bearing them down. For they reckon that to be impertinent and insufferable, which does not tell of what their hearts are full of.

16. Now it often happens that the mind is already transported to the realms on high in desire, is already entirely parted asunder from the foolish converse of earthly men, but is not yet braced to prefer the crosses of the present life for the love of God; already it seeks the things on high, already it contemns the grovelling follies below, but it does not yet turn itself to the endurance of the adversity which it has to bear. And hence it is added,

Or can anyone taste that, which by being tasted brings death?

17. For it is hard to seek after that which torments, to follow that which makes life depart. But very often the life of the righteous stretches itself up to such a height of virtue, that both within it rules in the citadel of interior reason, and without, by bearing with it, brings the folly of some to conversion; for we must needs bear with the weaknesses of those, whom we are striving to draw on to strong things. For neither does any man lift up one that is fallen, save he, who in compassion bends the uprightness of his position. But when we compassionate the weakness of another, we are the more strongly nerved as to our own; so that, from love of the things of futurity, the soul prepares itself to meet the ills of the present time, and looks out for the hurts of the body, which it used to fear. For its heavenly

aspirations being enlarged, it is more and more straitened, and when it sees how great is the sweetness of the eternal land, it fervently loves for the sake of that the bitter tastes of the present life. Whence after the disdain of 'unsavoury meat,' after the impossibility of the tasting of death, it is with propriety subjoined,

Ver. 7. The things which my soul refused to touch are for my straitness become my meat.

xv. 18. For the soul of the righteous, going on in its progress, whereas before, when it cared for its own interests alone, it loathed to bear the burthens of another, and, too little sympathizing with others, could not stand against adversities, now that it constrains itself to bear with the weakness of its neighbour, acquires strength to overcome adversity, so that for the love of truth it seeks the hurts of the present life with so much the more courage afterwards, that before it fled from them in its weakness. For by its bending it is made erect, by its drawing towards another it is stretched out, by its fellow-feeling it is strengthened, and when it opens itself out in the love of our neighbour, it as it were gathers from reflection, with what resoluteness to lift itself up to its Maker. For charity, which lowers us according to the force of our sympathy, lifts us the higher upon the height of contemplation, and enlarged manifold it already burns with bigger desires, already beats high to attain to the life of the Spirit, even though through the torments of the body. What then aforetime he refused to touch, this same for straitness he afterwards eateth, who scarce containing his desires, now for love of his heavenly Country loves even the very pains, which for long he had feared. For if the mind is bent towards God with a strong purpose, whatever bitter betides it in this present life it accounts sweet, all that annoys it reckons rest, and it longs to pass even through death, that it may more completely possess itself of life. It desires to be utterly annihilated below, that it may more truly mount on high. But all this I may be falsely representing to be the case with the mind of a righteous man in general, and with the mind of blessed Job, if he do not himself subjoin the words,

Ver. 8–10. Oh that I might have my request, and that God would grant me the thing that I long for! Even that He That hath begun would

destroy me. Let him let loose His hand, and cut me off! Let this be my comfort; that He should afflict me with sorrow, and not spare.

19. But perchance he entreats such things through stubbornness, perchance, in that he wishes to be entirely annihilated, he charges the injustice of the smiter. Far be the thought! For with what feeling he begs it, he shows in the following words, saying, *Nor will I gainsay the speech of the Holy One.* So then he never murmurs against the injustice of Him that dealeth the blow, who even amidst the strokes calls his smiter 'the Holy One.' But we ought to know that it is sometimes the adversary, and sometimes God that bruises us with affliction. Now by the bruising of the adversary, we are made defaulters in virtue; but when we are broken by the bruising of the Lord, from vicious habits we are made strong in virtue. This bruising the Prophet had foreseen when he said, *Thou shalt rule them with a rod of iron, Thou shalt dash them in pieces like a potter's vessel.* [Ps. 2, 9] The Lord 'rules and breaks us with a rod of iron,' in that by the strong rule of righteousness in His dispensation, while He reanimates us within, He distresses us without. For as He abases the power of the flesh, He exalts the purpose of the spirit; and hence this bruising is compared to a potter's vessel, as is also delivered by Paul, *But we have this treasure in earthen vessels.* [2 Cor. 4, 7] And describing at the same time the dashing in pieces and the ruling [Vulg. has, *Thou shalt rule them,* for, *Thou shalt break them*], he says, *Though our outward man perish, yet the inward man is renewed day by day.* Let the holy man who is eager to draw near to God even through strokes, exclaim in the spirit of humility, **xvi.**

Ver. 9. That He That hath begun would bruise me!

20. For very often the Lord begins to work in us the bruising of our vicious habits, but when the mind is lifted up at the very first step of its progress, and when it already exalts itself as on the ground of its virtuous attainments, it opens an entrance to the adversary, that rages against it, who penetrating into the depths of the heart, dashes in pieces all that he may find therein springing from the earnestness of a good beginning, and shows himself the more violent in the breaking of it in proportion as he is the sorer grieved that it had made progress, though but a little way. Whence too, as the Gospel is witness, by the voice of 'Truth,' the unclean **xvii.**

spirit, which went out alone, returns with seven other spirits to the neglected dwelling-place of the conscience. Lest then, after the beginnings of divine correction, the old adversary snatch him unawares, and drag him along for the breaking in pieces of his virtues, the holy man fitly beseeches, saying, *That He That hath begun would bruise me*. As if he said in plain words, 'That which He has begun in me may He not cease to perfect by smiting me, lest He deliver me over forsaken to the adversary to bruise me.' Hence it is fitly subjoined,

That He would let loose His hand, and cut me off.

xviii. 21. For oftentimes being swoln with the confidence of lengthened prosperity, we are lifted up in a certain kind of frame of self-elation, and when our Creator sees that we are lifted up, but does not exercise His love towards us by stripes, He as it were keeps His hand hid, as to the smiting of our evil ways. Did He not tie the hand of His affection, when He said to the people, when guilty of transgression, *I will not any more be wroth with thee*; and, *My jealousy is departed from thee*. [Ezek. 16, 42] Therefore, 'That He would let loose His hand,' means, 'that He would exercise His affection.' And it is rightly added, 'and cut me off.' For whenever either the sudden pain of the scourge, or the trial of our weakness, falls upon us in a state of security, and elated with the abundance of our virtuous attainments, the pride of our hearts, being cut down, is precipitated from the height of its seat, so that it dares do nothing of itself, but levelled by the blow of its frailty, seeks the hand of one to lift it. Hence it is that, when holy men are looked upon with admiration on the grounds of the secret dispensation of God's providence towards them, they the more dread their very prosperity itself: they long to be subjected to trial, they covet to be stricken, that fear and pain may discipline the unwary mind, lest when an enemy breaketh out of ambush on this road of our pilgrimage, its self-security cause its greater downfal. Hence the Psalmist says, *Examine me, O Lord, and prove me*. [Ps. 26, 2] Hence he says again, *For I am ready for the scourges*. [Ps. 38, 17] For because holy men see that the wound of their inward corruption cannot be without putridity, they gladly set them under the hand of the physician for lancing, that the wound being opened, the venom of sin may run out, which, with a whole skin, was inwardly working their destruction. Hence it is yet further added;

Ver. 10. And let this be my consolation, that afflicting me with pain He spare not.

22. The Elect, when they know that they have done unlawful things, but find upon careful examination that they have met with no afflictions in return for those unlawful deeds, with the immense force of their fear, are in a ferment with alarm, and labour and travail with dark misgivings, lest grace should have forsaken them for ever, seeing that no recompensing of their ill-doing keeps them safe in the present life; they fear lest the vengeance which is suspended be stored to be dealt in heavier measure at the end; they are eager to be stricken with the correction of a Father's hand, and they reckon the pain of the wound to be the medicine of saving health. Therefore it is rightly said in this place, *Let this be my consolation, that afflicting me with grief He spare not.* As if it were in plain words, 'May He, Who spares people here for this cause, that He may strike them for ever and ever, therefore strike me here, that, by not sparing me, He may spare me for ever. For I console myself in being afflicted, in that conscious of the rottenness of human corruption, by being wounded I gain assurance for the hope of saving health.' And that he uttered it not with a swoln but with a humble mind, he makes plain, as we have before said, by the addition, in the words,

Neither will I gainsay the words of the Holy One.

23. Most often the words of God to us are not the sounds **xx.**
of speech, but the enforcement of deed. For He speaks to us
in that which He works upon us in silence. Blessed Job then would be gainsaying the words of God, if he murmured at His blows; but what feelings he entertains for his smiter is shown by him, who, as we have already said, calls Him 'Holy One' from whom he is submitting to blows. It goes on;

Ver. 11. What is my strength, that I should hold up? And what is mine end that I should deal patiently?

24. It is necessary to bear in mind, that the 'strength' of **xxi.**
the righteous is of one sort, and the strength of the reprobate
of another. For the strength of the righteous is to subdue the flesh,

THE SECOND PART.

to thwart our own wills, to annihilate the gratification of the present life, to be in love with the roughnesses of this world for the sake of eternal rewards, to set at nought the allurements of prosperity, to overcome the dread of adversity in our hearts. But the strength of the reprobate is to have the affection unceasingly set on transitory things, to hold out with insensibility against the strokes of our Creator, not even by adversity to be brought to cease from the love of temporal things, to go on to the attainment of vain glory even with waste of life, to search out larger measures of wickedness, to attack the life of the good, not only with words and by behaviour, but even with weapons, to put their trust in themselves, to perpetrate iniquity daily without any diminution of desire. Hence it is that it is said by the Psalmist to the Elect, *Be of good courage, and let your heart be strengthened, all ye that hope in the Lord*. [Ps 31, 24] Hence it is declared by the Prophet to the reprobate, *Woe unto you that are mighty to drink urine, and men of strength to mingle strong drink*. [Is. 5, 22] Hence it is declared by Solomon, that all the holy without any weakening of desire contemplate the interior rest. *Behold his bed, which is Solomon's, threescore valiant men are about it, of the most valiant of Israel*. [Cant. 3, 7] Hence the Psalmist directing his meaning against the children of perdition in the voice of the Redeemer in His Passion, says, *Lo, they have surprised my soul: the mighty have rushed forth against me*. [Ps. 59, 3] How well did Isaiah comprehend both sorts of strength in the words, *But they that wait upon the Lord shall change* [*mutabunt* E.V. marg.] *their strength*. [Is. 40, 31] For in that he said not they will 'take,' but they will 'change,' he clearly made known that that which is laid aside is of one sort, and that which is entered upon of another sort.

25. Are not the reprobate also 'strong,' who take such pains in running after the concupiscence of this world, boldly expose themselves to perils, welcome insults for the sake of gain, never give back from the lust of their appetites conquered by any opposition, grow obdurate with scourges, and for the sake of the world undergo the ills of the world, and so to say in seeking the pleasures thereof are parting with them, nor yet in parting with them ever weary. Whence it is well said by Jeremiah in the voice of mankind, *He hath made me drunken with wormwood*. [Lam. 3, 15] For one that is drunk knows nothing what he is undergoing. He then is 'drunken with wormwood,' who alienated from the faculty of reason through the

love of the present life, whilst whatsoever he undergoes for the sake of the world he accounts but light, is blind to the bitterness of the toil which he is enduring, in that in enjoyment he is led on to the several things in which in chastisement he is wearied out. But on the other hand the righteous man makes it his aim to be weak for undergoing the perils of the world for the world's sake, looks to his own end, marks how transitory the present life is, and refuses to undergo toils without for the sake of that, the enjoyment of which he has overcome within. Let blessed Job then, pressed by the adversities of the present life, say in his own voice, yea, in the voice of all the righteous, *What is my strength that I should hold up? And what is mine end that I should deal patiently?* As if he made it known in plain words, saying, 'I cannot submit to the ills of the world for the sake of the world, for now I am no longer strong in the desire thereof. For while I look to the end of the present life, why do I bear the burthen of that, the longing for which I tread under my feet?' And because the unrighteous severally, as we have said, bear the toils thereof with stronger resolution in proportion as they feed with greater avidity on its enjoyment, therefore he rightly subjoins without delay that same strength of the reprobate, in the words,

Ver. 12. Neither is my strength the strength of stones, nor is my flesh of brass?

xxii.

26. For what have we here denoted by 'brass' and 'stones' save the hearts of the insensate, who oftentimes even receive the strokes of the Most High, and yet they are not softened by any strokes of discipline? Contrary whereunto, it is said to the Elect through the Prophet, by promise from the Lord, *I will take the stony heart out of you, and will give you a heart of flesh.* [Ezek. 11, 19] Paul also says, *Though I speak with the tongues of men and of Angels, and have not charity, I am become as sounding brass, or a tinkling cymbal.* [1 Cor. 13, 1] For we know that stones when struck cannot give a clear sound, but when brass is struck a very sonorous sound is made by the striking of it; which, because like stones it is without life, has no sense contained in the sound. And there be some, who, like to stones, have become so hardened as to the precepts of religion, that, when the stroke of the visitation of the Most High is proving them, they never return the sound of humble confession. But some differing in no respect from the metallic nature of brass, when they re-

ceive the strokes of the smiting of the Most High, give forth the sound of devout confession; but because they do not send out the tones of humility from the heart, when they have been brought back to a state of sound health, they know nothing what they have vowed. The one then, being struck like stones, have no tones at all, while the other in nothing omit the resemblance of brass, who when under the stroke utter good things which they do not feel. The one sort refuse even words to the worship of the smiter. The other sort, in promising what they never fulfil, cry out without any life. Let the holy man then, who amidst the scourges eschewed the hardness of the reprobate, exclaim, *Neither is my strength the strength of stones, nor is my flesh of brass.* As though he made open confession in plain words, saying, 'Under the lash of discipline I keep clear of similarity to the reprobate. For neither have I become like stones so hardened that under the impulse of the stroke I turned dumb in the duty of confession; nor again, like brass do I give back the voice of confession, while I know not the meaning of the voice.' But because under the scourge the reprobate are strong unto weakness, and the Elect weak unto strength, blessed Job, while he declares that he is not strong of a diseased sense, makes it plain that he is strong of a state of saving health. So let him instruct us whence he received this same strength, lest if he ascribes to himself the powers that he has, he be running vigorously to death. For very often virtue possessed kills worse than if it were wanting, for while it lifts up the mind to self-confidence, it pierces it with the sword of self-elation, and while as it were it quickens by imparting strength, slays by filling with exaltation, i.e. it forces on to destruction the soul, which, through self trust, it uproots from trust in the interior strength. But forasmuch as blessed Job is both rich in virtue, and yet has no confidence in himself, and, that I may say so, in powerlessness is possessed of powers, he fitly subjoins these words, saying,

Ver. 13. Lo, there is no help to me in myself.

xxiii. 27. It is now made clear to whom the mind of the stricken man had recourse for hope, seeing that he declares that there was no hope to him in himself; but because he intimates that in himself he was weak, for the earning [or 'to (show) the merit of.'] of yet greater strength, let him add how he was even forsaken by his neighbours, *My friends also departed from me* [V. thus]. But mark, he that was despised without, is seated within upon the throne of judgment. For at the moment that he declares himself forsaken, he forthwith breaks out into pronouncing sentence, in the words,

Ver.14. Whoso taketh away pity from his friend, forsaketh the fear of the Lord.

xxiv.

28. Who else is here denoted by the name of a friend, saving every neighbour, who is united to us in a faithful attachment in proportion as, having received from us good service in this present time, he effectually aids us toward attaining hereafter the eternal country? For because there are two precepts of charity viz. the love of God and the love of our neighbour, by the love of God the love of our neighbour is brought into being, and by the love of our neighbour the love of God is fostered. For he that cares not to love God, verily knows nothing how to love his neighbour, and we then advance more perfectly in the love of God, if in the bosom of this love we first be suckled with the milk of charity towards our neighbour. For because the love of God begets the love of our neighbour, the Lord, when going on to say in the voice of the Law the words, *Thou shalt love thy neighbour*, prefaced it by saying, *Thou shalt love the Lord thy God*; [Matt. 22, 37. 39. Deut. 6, 5; 10, 12] for this reason, that in the soil of our breast He might first fix the root of His love, so that afterwards in the branches the love of our brethren should shoot forth. Again, that the love of God grows to strength by the love of our neighbour, is testified by John, where he says, *For he that loveth not his brother, whom he hath seen, how can he love God, Whom he hath not seen?* [1 John 4, 20] Which love of God, though it has its birth in fear, yet it is changed by growing into affection.

29. But oftentimes Almighty God, to make known how far anyone is from the love of Him and of his neighbour, or what proficiency he has made therein, regulating all things in a marvellous order, puts down some by strokes, and sets up others by successes; and as often as He forsakes certain persons in their temporal estate and condition, He shows the evil that lurks in the hearts of certain others. For very often the persons that courted us in the season of prosperity without an equal, are the very ones to persecute us in distress. For when a man in a prosperous condition is beloved, it is very doubtful whether his good fortune or the individual be the object of love. But the loss of prosperity puts to the test the force of

the affection. Whence a certain wise man says rightly, *A friend cannot be known in prosperity; and an enemy cannot be hidden in adversity.* [Ecclus. 12, 8] For neither does prosperity show a friend, nor adversity hide an enemy, in that both the first is often hidden by awe for our high fortune, and the latter is disclosed to view from presuming on our adverse condition. Let the holy man then, set in the midst of scourges, exclaim, *He that taketh away pity from his friend, forsaketh the fear of the Lord*; in that doubtless he that contemns his neighbour in consequence of his adversity, is clearly convicted never to have loved him in his prosperity. And since Almighty God smites some for this reason, that He may both discipline the individuals stricken, and afford to those that are not stricken opportunity for doing good; whosoever disregards one that is smitten, puts away from him an occasion of virtue, and lifts himself up the more wickedly against his Maker, in proportion as he views Him as neither merciful in the saving of himself, nor just in the wounding of another. But we must observe that blessed Job in such sort describes his own case, that the life of all the Elect People is at the same time set forth by him. For seeing that he is a member of that People, when he describes what he himself undergoes, he is also relating what that People is subject to, saying,

Ver. 15. My brethren have passed by me like a brook which passeth by rapidly in the hollows.

XXV. 30. Because the mind of the reprobate is set on present things alone, for the most part it proves a stranger to the scourge now, in proportion as hereafter it remains an exile from the inheritance. But oftentimes the lost hold the same faith by which we live, receive the same Sacraments of faith, are bound in the unity of the same religion, yet they are unacquainted with the bowels of compassion; of the force of that love, with which we are inflamed, both towards God and our neighbour, they know nothing. Therefore they are rightly called both 'brethren,' and those that 'pass by,' in that by faith they come forth from the same mother's womb with ourselves, but are not rooted in one and the same earnestness of charity towards God and our neighbour. Whence they are also fitly likened to a 'brook which passes by rapidly in the valleys.' For a brook flows from the highlands down below, and while it gathers its waters from the winter rains, is dried up by the summer heats; for they that from love of earthly objects quit the hope of the land above, seek the valley as it were from the uplands, and these are replenished with the winter season of the present life; but the summer of the Judgment to come dries them up, in that so soon as the sun of the rigour of the Most High waxes hot, it turns the joy of the reprobate into drought. Therefore it is rightly said, *Rapidly passeth by in the valleys*. Since for a torrent to pass by rapidly to the valleys, is for the mind of the froward, without any pains or hindrance to descend to the lowest aims. For all ascending is in painstaking, but all descending is in pleasure, in that in effect the step is strained to reach a higher level, but in relaxation, it is let down to a lower one. For it is a matter of much toil to get a stone up to the top of a mountain, but it is no labour to let the same down from the top to the bottom. Surely, that same is propelled down without let, which did not reach the top without mighty pains. The crop is sown by long application, it is nourished by a long course of shower and sunshine, yet it is consumed by a single instantaneous spark. By little and little buildings mount to a height, but by instantaneous falls they come to the ground. A vigorous tree lifts itself in the air by slow accessions of growth, but all that it has in a long course reared on high, is brought down at once and together. Therefore forasmuch as ascending is with pains and descending with pleasure, it is rightly expressed in this place, *My brethren have passed by me like a brook which passeth by rapidly in the valleys;* which too may be taken in another sense likewise.

31. For if we understand the valleys to be the regions of punishment below, then all the unrighteous 'pass away rapidly like a brook to the valleys,' in that in this life, which; they go after with all the desire of their heart, they can never stay for long, since for all the days that they add to their age, they are as it were daily tending by so many steps to their end. They wish for the periods to be lengthened to them, but forasmuch as when granted they cannot hold; for as many additions as they are allowed to their life, they are losing just so many from their period of living; therefore the moments of time, in so far as they pursue, they are fleeing from; in so far as they get them, they are parting with them. Thus they 'pass away rapidly to the valleys,' who indeed draw out to a great length their desires for the pleasures, but on a sudden are brought down to the dungeons of hell. For because even that period which is protracted by any length

of life whatever, if it be closed by an ending; is not long, those wretched persons learn from the end that: that was but short, which they held only in letting go. Whence also it is well said by Solomon, *But if a man live many years and rejoice in them all; yet let him remember the days of darkness; for they shall be many: and when they have come, the past shall be convicted of vanity*. [Eccles. 11, 8] For when the foolish mind meets on a sudden with evil which never passes away, it is made to understand by undergoing the eternal durations thereof, that the thing which could pass away was vain. But we should know that the greater number desire to do right, but there are some things calculated to cross and thwart their weak minds arising from the present life; and whereas they fear to undergo crosses in the lowest things, they offend against the rule of right set by the decree above. Whence it is rightly subjoined,

Ver. 16. Over those that fear the frost, the snow rushes down.

xxvi. 32. For the frost congeals below, but the snow falls down from above. And often there are persons, who, while they fear temporal adversities, expose themselves to the severity of everlasting visitation. Concerning whom it is rightly declared by the Psalmist, *There were they in great fear where no fear was*. [Ps. 14, 5] For this man already longs to defend the truth with freedom, yet being affrighted in that very longing that he feels, he shrinks from the indignation of a human power, and while on earth he fears man in opposition to the truth, he undergoes from heaven the wrath of Truth. That man, conscious of his sins, is already desirous to bestow upon the needy the things which he is possessed of, yet dreads lest he himself come to need them so bestowed. When, being alarmed, he provides with reservation for his own use succours of the flesh for the future, he starves the soul from the sustenance of mercy, and when he fears want on earth, he cuts off from himself the eternal plenitude of the heavenly cheer. Therefore it is well said, *Over those that fear the frost, the snow rushes down*. In that all who apprehend from below what ought to be trodden under the feet, undergo from above what is deserving of apprehension, and when they will not pass by what they might have trodden beneath them, they meet with a judgment from heaven which they can in no sort sustain. Now by acting thus they attain the glory of the world in time, but what will they do in the hour of their call, when terror-stricken they quit at once all the things which they kept here with grievous apprehensions? And hence it is rightly subjoined,

Ver. 17. What time they be dissipated they shall perish.

33. For all persons that are ruled by concern for the present life, are brought to nought by the loss of it, and then they are undone without, who have for long been undone within by disregarding the things of eternity. Concerning whom it is rightly added, *When they have become hot, they shall be dissolved from their place.* For every wicked man when he 'has become hot is dissolved from his place,' in that, in drawing near to the Judgment of the Interior Severity, when he has now begun to be heated in the knowledge of his punishment, he is severed from that gratification of his flesh whereunto he had long time clung. Hence it is that it is delivered by the Prophet against the reprobate, *And vexation alone shall only give understanding to the hearing* [Is. 28, 19]; in that verily they never understand the things of eternity, saving when they are already made to undergo punishment for those of time without remedy. Thus the mind is heated, and inflames itself with the fires of a fruitless repentance, it shrinks from being led to punishment, and holds fast to the present life in desire, but it is dissolved from its place, in that panting from the gratification of the flesh, its hardness is melted by suffering chastisement. But seeing that we have heard what all the wicked will undergo in the hour of their removal, let us hear further some of the ways in which their course is perplexed in the career of their freedom. It goes on, **xxvii.**

Ver. 18. The paths of their steps are involved. [V. *involutae*]

34. All that is involved is folded back into itself. And there are some who as it were resolve, with all the purpose of their heart, to resist the vicious habits that mislead them, but when the crisis of the temptation comes full upon them, they do not hold out in their purposed resolution. For one swoln with the bad daring of pride, when he sees that the rewards promised to humility are great, lifts himself up against himself, and as it were puts away the swelling and turgid bigness of pride, and vows to prove himself humble under whatever insults; but when he has been suddenly assailed with the injuriousness of a single word, he straight-way returns to his accustomed haughtiness, and is brought into such a **xxviii.**

swelling temper of mind, that he does not at all remember that he had made it his object to win the blessed attainment of humility. Another, fired with avarice, is out of breath with eagerness in adding to his means. When he sees that all things speedily pass away, he arrests his mind, which is roaming abroad through covetous desires, he determines henceforth not to set his heart on anything, and to hold what he has already gotten only under the reins of great control; but when objects that delight him are suddenly presented to his eyes, thereupon the heart beats high in the ambition to obtain them, the mind cannot contain itself, it looks about for an opportunity of getting them, and unmindful of the moderation which it had covenanted with itself, in longings for the attainment of them, disquiets itself with goading thoughts. Another is polluted by the corruption of lust, and is now bound and chained with long usage, but he sees how excellent is the pureness of chastity, and finds it a foul disgrace to be mastered by the flesh. Therefore he resolves to restrain the dissoluteness of his pleasures, and seems to set himself with all his powers to make a stand against habit; but upon the image being either presented to his eyes, or recalled to his recollection, when he is moved by a sudden temptation, at once he becomes all adrift from his former state of preparation; and the same man, that had set up against it the shield of resolution, lies pierced with the javelin of self-indulgence, and he being unstrung is overcome by lust, like as if he had never made ready any weapons of resolve against it. Another is set on fire with the flames of anger, and is uncontrolled even to the extent of offering insults to his neighbours, but when no occasion of rage comes across his spirit, he considers how excellent the virtue of mildness is, how high the loftiness of patience, and sets himself in order to be patient even against insult: but when any slight matter arises to ruffle him, he is in a moment kindled from his heart's core to words and insults. So that not only the patience he had promised never returns to his remembrance, but that the mind neither knows its own self, nor those revilings which it utters. And when he has fully satisfied his rage, it is as if he returned after exercise to a state of tranquillity, and then he calls himself in again into the chambers of silence, when not patience, but the gratification of its hastiness has given a check to the tongue. Therefore even late, and after the insults have been offered, he scarcely restrains himself, seeing that fiery horses too are often checked from their career, not by the hands of the controller, but by the limits of the ground. Therefore it is well said of the reprobate, *The paths of their way are involved.* For in resolve they aim at right courses indeed, but are ever doubling back into their accustomed evil ones, and being, as it were, drawn out without themselves, they return back to themselves in a round, who indeed desire good ways, but never depart from evil ways. For they wish to be humble, yet without being despised; to be content with their own, yet without suffering need; to be chaste, yet without mortification of the body; to be patient, yet without undergoing insults; and when they seek to make virtuous attainments, yet eschew the toils thereof, what else is this than that at one and the same time they know nothing of the conflicts of war in the field, and desire to have the triumphs for war in the city.

35. Not but that this, that their ways are described as 'involved,' may be further understood in another sense also; for it often happens with some people that they stoutly gird themselves up to encounter some vices, but neglect to overcome others, and while they never lift themselves up against these, they are reestablishing against themselves even those which they had subdued. For one has now subdued the flesh from the dominion of lust, but he has not yet reined in the mind from avarice; and while he keeps himself in the world for the practising of avarice, and does not quit earthly courses, when the juncture of the occasion breaks out, he falls into lust also, which sin he seemed to have already subdued. Another has overcome the violence of avarice, but he has never subdued the power of lust, and when he is providing the costs of fulfilling his lustful passion, he submits the neck of the heart to the yoke of avarice too, which he had for long got the mastery of. Another has now laid low rebellious impatience, but has not yet subdued vainglory; and when for this he winds himself into the honours of the world, being pierced with the irritation of cases that chance, he is brought back a captive to his impatience, and whilst vainglory lifts up the soul to the vindication of itself, being overcome it submits to that which it had got the upper hand over. Another has subdued vainglory, but has not yet brought down impatience. And when in impatience he utters a thousand threats to those that offer opposition, being ashamed not to execute what he says, he is brought back under the dominion of vainglory, and being subdued, by means of something else, he becomes liable to that, which he was rejoicing that he had fully conquered. Thus then

the vices retain a hold over their runaway by mutual aid in turn, and they as it were receive him back, when already gone, under the rule of their dominion, and hand him over to each other by turns for vengeance. Thus 'the paths of the ways of the wicked are involved,' in that although by mastering one evil habit, they free the foot, yet, while another sways them, they entangle it in the very one, which they had conquered.

36. But sometimes while the paths of their ways are involved, at once not a single sin is overcome, and one sin is done by occasion of another. For oftentimes to theft there is joined the deceit of denial, and often the sin of deceit is increased by the guilt of perjury. Often a misdeed is committed with shameless assurance, and often (which becomes worse than any fault) there is even a glorying in the commission of the misdeed. For though self-exaltation is apt to arise on the score of virtue, yet sometimes the foolish mind exalts itself on the grounds of the wickedness it has done. And when transgression is joined to transgression, what else is this than that the steps of the froward are bound in involved ways and entangled chains? Hence it is rightly delivered by Isaiah against the froward soul, under the likeness of Judaea, *And it shall be an habitation of dragons, and a pasture for ostriches, and the demons shall meet with the onocentaurs, and the satyr shall cry to his fellow*. For what is denoted by the 'dragons,' saving malice, and what by the name of 'ostriches,' saving hypocrisy; as an ostrich has the appearance of flight, but has not the use of flying, for that hypocrisy too impresses upon all beholders an image of sanctity in connection with itself, but knows not to maintain the life of sanctity. Therefore in the perverse mind the dragon lies down and the ostrich feeds, in that both lurking malice is cunningly covered, and the guise of goodness is set before the beholder's eyes. But what is represented by the title of 'onocentaurs,' saving those that be both lecherous and high-minded? for in the Greek tongue, 'onos' signifies 'an ass,' and by the designation of an 'ass' lust is denoted, according to the testimony of the Prophet, who says, *Whose flesh is as the flesh of asses* [Ezek. 23, 20]; but by the name of a 'bull' the neck of pride is set forth, as it is spoken by the Psalmist in the voice of the Lord concerning the Jews in their pride, *Many bulls have compassed me; strong bulls of Bashan have beset me round*. [Ps. 22, 19] Thus they are 'onocentaurs,' who, being subject to vicious habits of lust, lift up their neck on account of the very same cause for which they ought to have

been abased, who, in serving their fleshly gratifications, all sense of shame being put far from them, not only do not grieve that they have lost the way of uprightness, but further even exult in the working of confusion. Now 'the demons' meet with the 'onocentaurs,' in that the evil spirits readily serve to their wish all those whom they see rejoicing in the things which they ought to have bewailed; and it is fitly subjoined there, *And the hairy satyr* [Lat. *pilosus*] *shall cry to his fellow*. Now what others are represented by the title of 'the hairy one,' saving they which the Greeks call 'Pans,' and the Latins 'Incubi,' whose figure begins in the human form, but terminates in the extremity of a beast? Therefore by the designation of 'the hairy one' is denoted the ruggedness of every sin, which even if in any case it begins as if in a pretext of reason, yet always goes on to irrational motions; and it is like a man ending in a beast, whilst the sin, beginning in a copy of reason, draws him out even to a result devoid of reason. Thus often the pleasure of eating is subservient to gluttony, and it pretends to be subservient to the requirement of nature, and while it draws out the belly into gluttony, sets up the limbs in lasciviousness. Now 'the satyr crieth to his fellow,' when one wickedness perpetrated leads to the perpetration of another, and as if by a kind of voice of thought, a sin already committed invites another sin which yet remains to be committed. For oftentimes, as we have said, gluttony says, 'If you do not sustain the body with plentiful support, you can hold on in no useful labours;' and when it has kindled the mind by the desires of the flesh, immediately lust too in her turn forms words of her own prompting, saying, 'if God would not have human creatures united together in a bodily sort, He would never have made members in themselves suited to the purposes of so uniting;' and when it suggests these things as if in reason, it draws on the mind to unrestrained indulgence of the passions, and often when found out, immediately it looks out for the support of deceit and denial, and does not reckon itself guilty, if, by telling lies, its life may be protected. Thus 'the satyr crieth to his fellow,' when, under some semblance of reasoning, a sin following out of the occasion of a preceding sin ensnares the froward soul; and when harsh and rugged sins sink it low, it is as if 'the satyrs' ruled it, gathered together in it in concord; and thus it comes to pass that the ways of their paths are always involving themselves worse and worse, when sin taking occasion of sin enchains the lost soul.

THE SECOND PART.

37. But here it is necessary to know that sometimes the eye of the understanding is first dulled, and then afterwards the mind being taken captive roams at random amidst outward objects of desire, so that the blinded soul knows nothing where it is being led, and willingly surrenders itself to the allurements of the fleshly part; while at other times the desires of the flesh first burst forth, and after long custom in forbidden courses, they close the eye of the heart. For often the mind discerns light ways, but does not lift itself up fearlessly against bad practices, and it is overcome while offering resistance, when the very thing that it does in exercising discernment is outdone by the pleasurable emotion of its partner [*carnis suae*] the flesh. For that it very often happens that first the eye of contemplation is parted with, and afterwards the mind is subjected to the toils of the world through the desires of this our flesh, Samson is witness on being taken captive by the Philistines [Allophylis, as usual in V. and LXX.], who after he had lost his eyes was put to the mill, because the evil spirits, after that by the piercings of temptation they force out the eye of contemplation within, send it without into a round of labour. Again, that it often happens that both right practice is parted with externally, and yet the light of reason still retained in the heart, the Prophet Jeremiah instructs us, who, while he relates the captivity of Zedekiah, tells us the course of the captivity of the interior, in these words, *Then the king of Babylon slew the sons of Zedekiah in Reblatha before his eyes; also the king of Babylon slew all the nobles of Judah. Moreover he put out Zedekiah's eyes.* [Jer. 39, 6. 7.] The king of Babylon is our old enemy, the master of the confusion of the interior, who first slaughters the sons before the eyes of the parent beholding it, in that he oftentimes so destroys good works, that the very man who is taken captive perceives with terror that he is parting with them. For the soul very often groans, but yet being subdued by the enjoyments of its fellow the flesh, the good things which it begot it loses while it loves them; it sees the ills, which it undergoes, and yet never lifts the arm of virtue against that king of Babylon. But whilst having its eyes open it is struck with the doing of iniquity, by being used to sin it is one day brought to this, that it is bereft of the very light of reason itself also. Whence the king of Babylon, after his sons had been first put to death, plucked out Zedekiah's eyes, in that the evil spirit, after that good deeds have been first put away, afterwards takes away the light of understanding likewise. Which rightly befals

Zedekjah in Reblatha, for 'Reblatha' is rendered 'these many.' For he at last has even the light of reason too closed, who is weighed down by bad habit in the multitude of his iniquities. But in whatever way sin may come forth, or from whatever occasion it may spring, yet the ways of the reprobate are always 'involved,' so that, being abandoned to depraved lusts, they either do not pursue good things at all, or pursuing them with a weak aim, they never stretch out the unimpeded steps of the mind in pursuit of them. For either they do not set out with right aims, or, breaking down in the very way, they never attain to them. Whence it generally happens that tiring of them they return to their own ways, prostrate themselves from their settled purpose of mind in the enjoyments of the flesh, mind only the things that are transitory, and take no heed of those which are calculated to abide with them. Whence it is fitly subjoined,

They shall walk unto emptiness, and perish.

38. For they all 'walk unto emptiness,' who bring with them nothing of the fruit of their labour. Thus one man spends himself in the attainment of honours, another is in a fever with multiplying his means, another pants after the obtaining of applause; but because everyone at his death leaves all such things here, he has lost his labour on emptiness, who has brought nothing with him before the presence of the Judge. Contrary whereto it is well delivered in the Law, *Thou shalt not appear before the face of the Lord empty.* [Ex. 23, 15] For he that has not provided for himself the wages of life earned by well doing, 'appears before the Lord empty.' [Deut. 16, 16] Hence it is said of the just by the Psalmist, *But they shall doubtless come again with rejoicing, bringing their sheaves with them.* [Ps. 126, 6] For they come to the inquisition of Judgment, 'bringing their sheaves with them,' who exhibit in themselves those good works, whereby they may obtain life. Hence the Psalmist says again concerning every Elect person, *Who hath not taken his soul in vain.* [Ps. 24, 4] For everyone 'takes his soul in vain,' who, taking account of present things only, pays no heed to those that shall follow him to last for ever. He 'takes his soul in vain,' who, being unconcerned for the life thereof, prefers to it the care of the flesh; but the righteous do not 'take their soul in vain,' in that whatsoever they do through the instrumentality of the body, with stedfast purpose they make all tell to its weal, that even though the deed pass away, still the cause of the deed may nev-

er pass, in that after life it procures the rewards of life. But the reprobate are indifferent to take account of these; for verily 'going walking into emptiness,' in pursuing life they flee from it, and in finding it they lose it. But we are more effectually withheld from imitating the wicked, if we calculate their losses by the end. Whence it is well added even with a charge,

Ver. 19. Consider the paths of Tema, the ways of Sheba, and wait a little while. [V. *thus*]

39. For Tema is rendered 'the south wind,' and Sheba 'a net.' What is here set forth by 'the south wind,' which dissolves the limbs it blows on with its warm breath, saving dissolute laxity of life? and what by 'the net,' save the fettering of practice? For they that aim at the things that are eternal with a dissolute mind, of their own free will fetter themselves by the irregularity of their efforts, that they should never advance towards God with a free step, and while they entangle themselves with the loose practices of their behaviour, they as it were set their feet to be held in the meshes [*maculis*] of a net. For as we said a little way above, that there are persons who are drawn back into bad habits, already got the better of, by means of other open evil habits not yet overcome, so there are some that fall back into those which they had abandoned by means of others, which are cloked with the title of respectability, or the honourableness of praise. Thus there are very many, who now no longer aim at the things of another, and who with the love of tranquillity begun are parted from the jarrings of this world, thirst to be instructed in Holy Writ, long to give themselves to heavenly contemplations, yet they do not abandon with a perfect freedom of soul all concern about their domestic affairs, and often while they are employed in the service of the same in a lawful way, they are involved in the unlawful jarrings of this world at the same time; and while they are eager to protect their earthly interests with anxious care, they quit that repose of the heart, which they sought for; and whilst their substance, that is escaping from them, is guarded with continual caution, the word of divine knowledge which has been conceived in the heart is let loose; in that, according to the declaration of 'Truth,' the thorns choke the seed that has sprung up, when the importunate cares of earthly things put out the word of God from the recollection [Matt. 13, 22]. Therefore they are walking in a net with their steps all

abroad, who, while they do not perfectly forsake the world, fetter themselves in their steppings, that they cannot step.

40. And there are very many, who not only do not covet what belongs to another, but even abandon all that they possessed in the world, who despise themselves, do not aim at any glory of the present life, sever themselves from this world's courses of action, and whatever prosperity may smile upon them, they well nigh tread it under their feet; yet being tied with the chain of earthly relationship, while they imprudently obey the dictates of the love of kindred, it often happens that by the instrumentality of relations they turn back to those habits which they had even together with self-contempt already subdued; and whereas they love their fleshly kin beyond what needs, being drawn back without, they are separated from the Parent of the heart. For we often see men, who, as far as concerns their own interest, henceforth no longer entertain any desires of the present life, who have quitted the world both in practice and in profession, yet for their inordinate affection for relations, burst into the courts of justice, busy themselves with the discord of earthly things, part with the freedom of interior repose, and restore in their hearts the interests of the world that were long undone. Whither then are those walking but into a net, whom perfection of life commenced had already set free from the present world, but whom the excessive love of earthly kin still binds?

41. For they that follow after the reward of the eternal espousals with close pursuits, and not with loose steps, as they disregard themselves for the love of God, so they lay aside everything whereby they see they are hindered; and since it is necessary for God's sake that they should render service to all that they are able, for God's sake they refuse their private services even to their relations. Hence it is that when one said, *Suffer me first to go and bury my father*, he thereupon heard from the lips of 'Truth,' *Follow Me, and let the dead bury their dead, but go thou and preach the kingdom of God*. [Luke 9, 59. 60.] Wherein it is to be observed, that whereas the chosen disciple is withheld from the burial of his father, for the sake of God it is not permitted a devout person to do for a dead father, from carnal affection, that which, for God's sake, he ought to do for strangers likewise. Hence again 'Truth' says, *If any man come to Me, and hate not his father, and mother, and wife, and children, and brethren, and sisters, yea, and his own life also, he cannot be My disciple*. [Luke 14, 26] In which

same place, forasmuch, as after the hatred of our kindred we have the hatred of our own life brought in, it is plainly shown that we are bidden to hold our relations in hatred in such sort as ourselves, that urging them [A.B.E. ourselves] away to the interests of eternity, and putting aside carnal favour towards them, when it is a hindrance in the way, we might learn by a proportioned skill of discrimination, at once to love them suitably, and to hate them savingly, so that in love hatred might be so taught to arise, that we might be able to love more really in hatred. Hence again it is said by Moses, *Who said unto his father and to his mother, I know you not, and to his brethren, I recognize you not, nor knew they their own children; these have observed Thy word and Thy covenant, and kept Thy judgments.* [Deut. 33, 9] For he longs to know God more familiarly who, from love of religion, desires to know no longer those whom he has known after the flesh. For the knowledge of God is lessened by a grievous curtailment, if it be shared with acquaintance with the flesh. Everyone then must be put without the pale of kindred and acquaintance, if he would be more genuinely united to the Parent of all, that those same ones, whom for the sake of God he makes light of for a good end, he may the more substantially love, in proportion as he renounces in them the destructible affection of carnal attachment.

42. We ought indeed, even in a temporal way, to benefit more than the rest those to whom we are more nearly united; for a flame too extends its burning to things put by it, but that particular thing, wherein it originates, it first sets burning. We ought to acknowledge the tie of earthly relationship, and yet to disown it, when it obstructs the progress of the mind, that the faithful soul, being inflamed in devotion to divine things, may at once not look with contempt on the things which are joined to it below, and that by regulating these aright in itself, it may mount above them in the love of things on high. Therefore with wise caution we must be on our guard, that no favouring of the flesh steal upon us, and divert the step of the heart from the right path, lest it hinder the efficacy of heavenly love, and sink the soaring mind; downwards under a superincumbent weight. For everyone ought so to sympathize in the wants of his kindred, that yet by such sympathy he never let the force of his purpose be impeded, so that affection indeed should fill the bowels of the heart, yet not divert it from its spiritual resolve. For it is not that holy men do not love their fleshly kin, to give them

all things necessary, but they subdue this very fondness within themselves from love of spiritual things, in order so to temper it by the control of discretion, that they may be never led by it, yea in a small measure, and in the very least degree, to deviate from the straight path. And these are well conveyed to us by the representation of the cows, which going along towards the hilly lands under the Ark of the Lord, proceed at one and the same time with fondness and with hardened feeling; as it is written, *And the men did so: and took two milk cows, and tied them to the cart, and shut up their calves at home: and they laid the Ark of the Lord upon the cart.* [1 Sam. 6, 10] And soon after; *And the cows took the straight way to the way of Beth-shemesh, and they went along by one way, lowing as they went, and turned not aside to the right hand or to the left.* [ver. 12] For observe, when the calves were shut up at home, the cows which are fastened to the waggon bearing the Ark of the Lord, moan and go their way, they give forth lowings from deep within, and yet never alter their steps from following the path. They feel love indeed shown by compassion, but never bend their necks behind. Thus, thus must they needs go on their way, who being placed under the yoke of the sacred Law, henceforth carry the Lord's Ark in inward knowledge, so as never for this, that they take compassion on the necessities of relations, to deviate from the course of righteousness which they have entered upon. For 'Beth-shemesh' is rendered 'the house of the sun.' Thus to go to Beth-shemesh with the Ark of the Lord placed on them, is in company with heavenly knowledge to draw near to the seat of light eternal. But we are then really going on towards Beth-shemesh, when in going the path of righteousness, we never turn aside into the adjoining side-paths of error, not even for the sake of the affection we bear to our offspring; kindness to whom ought indeed to have a place in our mind, but never to turn it back, lest that mind, if it be not touched by a feeling of affection, be hard, or being too much touched, if it is turned aside, be slack.

43. It is well to look at blessed Job, in whom the yoke of God's fear had worn the neck of the heart, and see under what controlling influence of discretion he bears the Ark of the Lord's sentence. For when the calves are gone he lows, in that, when tidings of his children's death were brought 'him, 'he fell upon the ground with his head shaven,' yet he goes by the right way whilst lowing, in that his lips in groaning are opened to utter the praises of God, whereas, he

exclaims without delay, *The Lord gave, and the Lord hath taken away; blessed be the name of the Lord*. [Job 1, 21] But minds that are not gifted with discretion know nothing of this rule of life, and in the degree that they seek the ways of the Lord negligently, they are turned back foolishly to the paths of the world.

44. Rightly then does the holy man after 'the paths of Theman' make mention of 'the ways of Saba.' For they whom the south wind of a mischievous warmth has relaxed, are verily held bound in the net of entanglement. But in describing the deeds of the wicked, he rightly admonishes them to 'consider' these things; for we delight in froward practices in doing them, but when seen in others we pass sentence upon them, and the actions, which in our own case we think to be little deserving of sentence, we learn to be as base as they really are by the conduct of others; and so it comes to pass that the mind is brought back to itself, and takes shame to do the thing that it censures. For it is as though an ugly face in a mirror caused disgust, as often as the mind sees in a similar life, what to feel abhorrence for in itself. Therefore he says, *Consider the paths of Teman, the ways of Sheba, and wait a little*. As if it were in plain words; 'Look to the harms of another's luke-warmness, and then you will the more surely take hope in relation to eternal things, if with the eye of the heart rightly directed you look at that which may disgust you in others.'

45. And it is well said, wait a little; for it often happens, that whereas the short period of the present life is loved as if it were to last for long, the soul is dashed from its eternal hope, and being beguiled with present objects, is thrown back by the blackness of self-despair. And when it imagines that the period is long which remains for it to live, at once upon quitting life it meets that eternity, which it may not avoid. Hence it is that it was spoken by one that was wise, *Woe unto you that have lost patience*. For truly they 'lose patience,' who, whilst they reckon to tarry long amongst visible things, part with the hope of the invisible. And while the mind is rivetted to present objects, life is ended, and they are suddenly brought to unlooked-for punishments, which, being deceived by their presumptuous expectations, they flattered themselves they would either never meet with, or not till late. Hence 'Truth' says, *Watch therefore, for ye know neither the day nor the hour*. [Matt. 25, 13] Hence again it is written, *The Day of the Lord so cometh as a thief in the night* [1 Thess. 5, 2]; for because it is never seen drawing near to

seize upon the soul, it is likened to a thief in the night. Therefore it ought to be the more apprehended as always coming, in proportion as it cannot be foreknown by us when it is about to come. Whence holy men too, in that they have their eyes incessantly fixed on the shortness of life, do as it were pass through life daily undergoing death; and prepare themselves on a more solid basis for the things that shall last, in proportion as they are ever reflecting by the end that transitory things are nought. For hence the Psalmist, seeing that the life of the sinner fleeth at a quick pace, exclaims, *For yet a little while and the sinner shall not be*. [Ps. 37, 10] Hence again he says, *As for man, his days are as grass*. [Ps. 103, 15] Hence Isaiah says, *All flesh is grass, and all the goodliness thereof is as the flower of the field*. [Is. 40, 6] Hence James rebukes the spirit of the presumptuous, saying, *For what is your life? it is even a vapour that appeareth for a little time*. [James 4, 14] Therefore it is rightly said, *wait a little*, in that both that is unmeasurable which follows after without limit, and all but little that is closed by an end. For that ought not to seem long to us, which by the course of its allotted period is tending not to be; which while it is carried on by moments, its very own moments, whilst they delay, are themselves urging forwards; and from the very same cause, from which it is seen to be in our possession, it results that it ceases to be in our possession. But blessed Job, after he had brought in the shortness of the present life in terms of contempt, therefore in the voice of all the Elect rises up justly against the wicked, subjoining,

Ver. 20. They are confounded, because I have hoped.

46. When the wicked inflict evils upon the good, if they see them to be shaken from the interior hope, they are overjoyed at their deceiving taking effect, for they account the spread of their error to be the greatest gain, in that they rejoice have fellows in perdition, but whilst the good man's hope is rooted within, and never bent to the ground by outward evils, confusion seizes the soul of the wicked, in that whilst they are unable to get at the innermost parts of the distressed, they are ashamed to prove themselves cruel for no end. Therefore let the holy man say in his own voice, let him say in the endurance of the Church universal in affliction and groaning, Who, amidst the contrarieties of the wicked, without any default of mind, longs for the joy of the heavenly recompense, and by dying holds on

to life; *They are confounded, because I have hoped*. As though it were in plain words, 'because the wicked by hard persecutions fail to soften the force of my rigid mind, surely being covered with shame they lose the labours of their cruel ways.' And hence at once he looks on the blessings of the Retribution to come as henceforth here, and marks what an arraignment awaits the wicked at the Judgment, adding,

They came even unto me, and were ashamed.

xxxii. 47. For lost sinners 'come even to Holy Church' on the Day of Judgment, in that they are then brought even to the beholding of her glory, that for the greater punishment of their guilt they may see in their rejection what they have lost. Then shame covers the wicked, when conscience bearing witness convicts them in the sight of the Judge. Then the Judge is beheld without, and the accuser is felt within. Then every sin is called up before the eyes, and the soul, over and above the burnings of hell, is worse tortured by its own fire. Concerning these it is rightly said by the Prophet, *Lord, let Thy hand be exalted, that they see not, let them see and be confounded*. [Is. 26, 11] For now their merits darken the understanding of lost sinners, but then the knowledge of their guilt enlightens it, so that both now they in no wise see what is to be followed, and then they perceive it, after they have lost it. For now they do not care to understand the things of eternity, or they refuse to make them their object, when understood; but then assuredly, both understanding and longing after them, they have them disclosed to their sight, when they can no longer obtain them thus longed for. *Allegorical*

48. Which same words of blessed Job, moreover, are in an especial manner suited to his friends, who set themselves to shake the mind of the holy man by bitter upbraidings. For he says, *They were confounded because I have hoped*. As if it were in plain words, 'Whilst they fail by foolish revilings to turn me to despair, they are themselves confounded by the madness of their fool-hardiness.' *They came even up unto me, and were ashamed*. As though he expressed it, 'Seeing the sores of my body, but ignorant of the constancy of my mind, whilst they took upon them to reproach me for unrighteousness, they did not yet 'come up unto me,' but striking with cruel *Literal*

reproaches, whereas they find that my soul stands firm amidst adversity, 'coming to me,' as it were, 'they are ashamed.' For herein they 'come to me,' in that they know me in the interior of my heart, and there they are 'covered with shame,' where outward loss moves me not, standing with firm mien.' Now there are some, who do not know how to fear God, saving when they are either affrighted by adversity experienced in their own person, or known in others; whom prosperity uplifts from presumptuousness, and crosses dismay from weakness. Of the number of which same, blessed Job charged his friends with being, in that he immediately adds; saying,

Ver. 21. For now ye are come, to see my stroke, and are afraid.

xxxiii.

49. As though he said in plain words, 'I feared God then, when, buoyed up with prosperity, I felt no hurts of the scourge. But ye, who fear not God from love, dread Him from the stroke of the rod alone. It goes on;

Ver. 22, 23. Did I say, Bring unto me? or, Give me of your substance? or, Deliver me from the enemy's hand? or, Redeem me from the hand of the mighty?

Allegorical

xxxiv.

50. If these words are referred to the person of Holy Church, as we have said that blessed Job's friends bear the likeness of heretics, he rightly declares that he does not 'want their substance.' For the 'substance' of heretics is not unsuitably taken for carnal wisdom, by which whilst they are wickedly sustained, they as it were show themselves rich in words, which Holy Church does not go after, in proportion as she goes beyond it by spiritual understanding. But oftentimes, while heretics maintain wrong things concerning the Faith, they utter various refined sayings against our old Enemy concerning the temptations of the flesh. For sometimes they as it were show in themselves healthy limbs of practice, in the same degree that as wounded in faith they are held in the head by the fangs of the envenomed serpent. But Holy Church is not minded to hear refined sayings concerning temptation from those, who, whilst they deliver some truths that relate to practice, are leading men onward into the falsities of misbelief. Whence it is rightly said in this place, *Did I say, Bring unto me? or, Give me aught of your substance? or, Deliver me from the enemy's hand? or, Redeem me from the hand of the mighty?* For he calls the strength of Sa-

tan, 'the enemy's hand,' and the powers of evil spirits, 'the hand of the mighty.' Whom he in this respect calls mighty, in that whereas they were created void of fleshly infirmity, no impotency being mixed therewith obstructs their wicked efforts. But with regard to this which is subjoined,

Ver. 24. Teach me, and I will hold my tongue, and cause me to understand wherein I have erred.

XXXV. 51. It seems doubtful under the scale of what pointing this should hang, whether it be joined to what he had brought in, *Did I say*, or whether the sentence is spoken disjoined from the preceding, so that it is said thereby in reproach, *Teach me, and I will hold my tongue, and cause me to understand wherein I have erred.* Which same however agrees with either pointing, for by neither does he depart from the path of sound meaning. But since we have delivered these things in course allegorically, it remains for us to examine the words of the history in a moral sense.

52. Blessed Job had undergone the loss of his property; being given over to the strokes of evil spirits, he was suffering the smarts of their wounds; yet in loving the wise foolishness of God, he had trodden under foot the foolish wisdom of the world with inward scorn. Therefore in opposition to the rich of this world he is called poor, in opposition to the powerful he is called oppressed, in opposition to the wise he is called a fool. He answers the three, that as poor he seeks not their substance, nor as oppressed their aid against the strong, nor as a fool does he seek the lore of earthly wisdom. For in that the holy man is carried off above himself in spirit, both being poor he is not straitened by want, and being oppressed he suffers nothing, and being of free will foolish, he does not gaze with admiration at carnal wisdom. Hence it is that another poor and oppressed man says, *We are perplexed, yet not in despair, persecuted, but not forsaken we are cast down, yet perish not.* [2 Cor. 4, 8. 9.] Hence it is that teaching the wisdom of a holy foolishness, he says, *But God hath chosen the foolish things of the world to confound the wise.* [1 Cor. 1, 27] And, *if any man among you seemeth to be wise in this world, let him become a fool, that he may be wise.* [3, 18] Hence making manifest both the gloriousness of oppression, and the riches of chosen poverty, he says, *As dying, and behold we live; as chastened, and not*

Moral

killed; as sorrowful, yet alway rejoicing; as poor, yet making many rich; as having nothing, and yet possessing all things. [2 Cor. 6, 9]

53. It is well on this point to lift up the eyes of the mind, and to see in the Elect of God, who are suffering oppression without, what a fortress of strength they are masters of within. For all that is high and exalted without, in their secret view is grovelling, from the contempt they feel. For transported above themselves in the interior, they fix their mind on high, and all that they meet with in this life, they look upon as passing away far below unconnected with themselves, and so to speak, while they strive by the Spirit to become quit of the flesh, almost the very things they are undergoing, they are blind to. For in their eyes whatsoever is exalted in time, is not high. For as though set upon the summit of a high mountain, they look down upon the flats and levels of the present life, and rising above themselves in spiritual loftiness, they see made subject to themselves, within, all that swells highest without in carnal glorying; and hence they spare no Powers that are contrary to truth, but those whom they see to be uplifted by pride, they abase by the authority of the Spirit. For it is hence that Moses, coming from the wilderness, encounters the king of Egypt with authority, saying, *Thus says the Lord God of the Hebrews, How long wilt thou refuse to humble thyself before Me? let My people go, that they may serve Me*: [Ex. 10, 3] and when Pharaoh, being driven hard by the plagues, said, *Go ye, sacrifice to your God in this land* [Ex. 8, 25]; he thereupon answered with increased authority, *It is not meet so to do; for we shall sacrifice the abominations of the Egyptians to the Lord our God*. It is hence that Nathan encounters the king when guilty; to whom first offering a similar instance of the transgression committed, and holding him convicted by the voice of his own sentence, he thereupon added, saying, *Thou art the man, who hast done this thing*. [2 Sam. 12, 7] It is hence that the Man of God, being sent to Samaria to destroy idolatry, when king Jeroboam threw frankincense upon the altar, not fearing the king, not held back by the dread of death, with undaunted spirit, put forth the authority of a free voice against the Altar, saying, *O Altar, Altar, thus says the Lord; Behold, a child shall be born to the house of David, Josiah by name, and upon thee shall he offer the priests of the high places*. [1 Kings 13, 2] It is hence that when proud Ahab, being bowed down to the service of idols, ventured to upbraid Elijah, saying, *Art thou the man that troubleth Israel?* [1 Kings 18, 17] Elijah forthwith struck the fool-

ishness of the king in his pride with the authoritativeness of a free rebuke, saying, *I have not troubled Israel, but thou and thy fathers house, in that ye have forsaken the commandments of the Lord, and have followed Baalim*. [ver. 18] It is hence that Elisha, following his master's true loftiness, confounded for the guilt of unbelief Joram the son of Ahab, when he came to him with the king Jehoshaphat, saying, *What have I to do with thee? Get thee to the prophets of thy father and to the prophets of thy mother*. [2 Kings 3, 13] And, *As the Lord of hosts liveth, before Whom I stand, surely were it not that I regard the presence of Jehoshaphat the king of Judah, I would not look toward thee, nor see thee*. [ver. 14] Hence it is that the same man held Naaman fixed before the door of his house, when he came to him with horses and chariots, and did not meet him, set up as he was with abundance of talents and raiment; that he did not open the door of his house to him, but charged him by a messenger that he should wash seven times in the Jordan. Hence too this same Naaman was going away enraged, saying, *Behold, I thought he will surely come out to me*. It is hence that Peter, when the priests and elders, raging furiously even in scourging, forbade him to speak in the Name of Jesus, straightway made answer with great authority, saying, *Whether it be right in the sight of God to hearken unto you more than unto God, judge ye. For we cannot but speak the things which we have seen and heard*. [Acts 4, 19. 20.] It is hence that when Paul saw the chief Priest sitting in judgment [al. making resistance] against the Truth, and when his officer had struck him a blow on the cheek, he uttered not a curse, as being moved to wrath, but filled with the Spirit, prophesied with a free voice, saying, *God shall smite thee, thou whited wall: for sittest thou to judge me after the law, and commandest me to be smitten contrary to the law?* [Acts 23, 3] It is hence that Stephen not even when doomed to die dreaded to put forth authoritativeness of voice in utterance against the power of his persecutors, saying, *Ye stiff necked and uncircumcised in heart and ears, ye do alway resist the Holy Ghost: as your fathers did, so do ye*. [Acts 7, 51]

54. But that holy men burst into such high words from passionate affection for Truth, and not from the sin of pride, they themselves plainly point out, in that by other doings and other sayings they make it appear with what great humility they are adorned, and with what great charity they are inflamed toward those whom they rebuke. For pride begets hatred, humility only love. Thus the words which love makes bitter, flow, surely, from the fountain head of

humility. Accordingly, how could Stephen utter reproach in pride, who with bended knee prayed for those whom he reproached, when they went on to worse and stoned him, saying, *Lord, lay not this sin to their charge.* [ver. 60] How did Paul in pride utter words of bitterness against the Priest and Chief of his nation, who in humility lowers himself to the service of his disciples, saying, *For we preach not ourselves, but Christ Jesus our Lord, and ourselves your servants for Christ's sake?* [2 Cor. 4, 5] How did Peter resist the rulers from Pride? when in compassion to their erring course, he as it were makes excuse for their guilt, saying, *I wot that through ignorance ye did it, as did also your rulers. But those things which God before had showed by the mouth of all His prophets, that Christ should suffer, He hath so fulfilled.* [Acts 3, 17. 18.] And he draws them in pity to life, saying, *Repent ye therefore, and be converted, that your sins may be blotted out.* [ver. 19] How was it from pride that Elisha refused to come to the sight of Naaman, who not only let himself be seen, but even be taken hold of by a woman? concerning whom it is written, *And when she came to the Man of God to the hill, she caught him by the feet, but Gehazi came near to thrust her away. And the Man if God said, Let her alone, for her soul is in bitterness.* [2 Kings 4, 27] How was it in pride that Elijah uttered words of reproach against the proud king, seeing that he ran humbly before his chariot, as it is written, *And he girded up his loins, and ran before Ahab?* How was it of Pride that the man of God disregarded the presence of Jeroboam, who out of pity straightway restored his withered right hand to its former soundness? As it is written, *And it came to pass, when king Jeroboam heard the saying of the man of God, which had cried against the altar in Bethel, that he put forth his hand from the altar, saying, Lay hold on him. And his hand dried up.* [1 Kings 13, 4] And shortly after, *And the man of God besought the face of the Lord, and the king's hand was restored him again, and became as it was before.* [ver. 6] For as pride cannot give birth to miraculous powers, we are shown, in what a Spirit of humility the voice of upbraiding issues, in that signs go along with it. How did Nathan swell high in words of rebuke against king David, who when there was sin lacking that deserved rebuke, fell on his face upon the ground in his sight? as it is written, *And they told the king, saying, Behold, Nathan the Prophet. And when he was come in before the king, he bowed himself before the king with his face to the ground.* [1 Kings 1, 23] How could Moses, when he freely withstood the Egyptian king, indulge contempt for him, who while he held familiar communing with God worshipped with self-abasement Jethro his relation who was following him? to whose advice he paid such ready obedience, that after the secret communications of God, he accounted that great gain, which came to him without from the lips of man.

55. From one set of deeds of the Saints, then, we learn what account we are to take of another. For holy men are neither free spoken out of pride, nor submissive out of fear. But whenever uprightness uplifts them to freedom of speech, thought of their own weakness preserves them in self-abasement. For though, in chiding them, they smite as from above the misdoings of offenders, yet judging themselves the more exactly in their own eyes, they in a manner take their place amongst the refuse, and as they pursue after wickedness in others, so much the fiercer do they return to keep themselves in check; and, on the other hand, as they never spare themselves in doing better, they are the more watchful in rebuking the deeds of other men. For what, that is derived from the powers of man without, shall strike them with wonder, who alike look down upon themselves, even at the moment that now they have well nigh gotten hold of the summit of interior height. And so for this reason it is right for them to sit in judgment on the loftiness of earthly exaltation without, for that no load of swelling humour weighs down the eye within. Hence when blessed Job disregards earthly wisdom, and powers, and substance, in those friends that were full of harsh words, saying, *Did I say, Bring unto me? or, Give me of your substance? or, Deliver me from the enemy's hand ? or, Redeem me from the hand of the mighty? Teach me, and I will hold my tongue, and cause me to understand wherein I have erred*; what opinion he entertains about himself, he makes appear a little below, saying, *Yea, ye overwhelm the fatherless.* Thus it is clearer than the light what a weak nature he sees himself to be possessed of, in that he calls himself *fatherless*. It goes on;

Ver. 25. Wherefore have ye detracted from the words of truth; when there is none of you that is able to convict them?

56. He must himself be pure from evil, who makes it his concern to correct the evil practices of other men, so as not to be taken up with earthly imaginations, not to give way to grovelling desires, in order that he may the more clearly see what things others ought to avoid, in proportion as he himself the more thoroughly eschews

them by knowledge and by practice. For the eye which dust weighs upon, never clearly sees the spot upon the limb, and the hands that hold mud can never cleanse away the overcast dirt. And this according to the older of the old Translation, the voice of God rightly conveyed in sense to David, busied about external wars, when It says, *Thou shalt not build a temple, for thou art a man of blood.* [1 Chron. 22, 8; 28, 3.] Now he builds God's Temple, who is devoted to correcting and forming the minds of his neighbours. For we are God's Temple, who are framed to life by His indwelling, as Paul bears witness, saying, *For the temple of God is holy, which temple ye are.* [1 Cor. 3, 17] But a man of blood is forbidden to build a temple to God, in that he who is still devoted to carnal practices, must needs blush to instruct the minds of his neighbours spiritually. Therefore it is well said, *Wherefore have ye detracted from the words of truth, when there is none of you that is able to convict them?* As if it were in plain words; 'With what rashness do ye blame all ye hear, who knowing nothing of the causes of my stroke, still utter words that deserve blame.' It goes on,

Ver. 26. Ye only set in order speeches to upbraid, and ye speak words against the wind.

57. There are two sorts of speech, which are very troublesome and mischievous to mankind, the one which aims to commend even froward things, the other which studies to be always carping even at right ones. The one is carried downward with the stream, the other sets itself to close the very channels and streams of truth. Fear keeps down the one, pride sets up the other. The one aims to catch favour by applause; anger, in order that it may be manifested in contention, drives forward the other. The one lies grovelling at command; the other is always swelling high in opposition. Accordingly, blessed Job convicts his friends of being of this kind, when he says, *Ye do but set in order speeches to upbraid.* But he proceeded to make known whence it is that men come even to the effrontery of unjust upbraiding, when he added, *And ye speak words to the wind.* For to 'speak, words to the wind' is to talk idly. For often when the tongue is not withheld from idle words, a loose is even given to the rashness of foolish reviling. For it is by certain steps of its descent, that the slothful soul is driven into the pitfall. Thus while we neglect to guard against idle words, we are brought to mischievous ones, so that it first gives sat-

isfaction to speak of the concerns of others, and afterwards the tongue by detraction carps at the life of those of whom it speaks, and sometimes even breaks out into open revilings. Hence the incitements are sown of angry passions, jars arise, the fire-brands of animosity are kindled, peace is altogether extinguished in men's hearts. Hence it is well said by Solomon, *He that letteth out water is a beginning of brawls*. [Prov. 17, 14] For to let out water is to let the tongue loose in a flood of words, contrary to which he at the same time declares in a favourable sense, saying, *The words of a man's mouth are as deep waters*. [Prov. 18, 4] He then that letteth out water is a beginning of brawls, for he who neglects to refrain his tongue, dissipates concord. Hence it is written contrariwise, *He that silenceth a fool, softeneth wrath*. [Prov. 26, 10. Vulg.]

58. But that everyone that is given to much talking cannot maintain the straight path of righteousness, the Prophet testifies, in that he says, *For an evil speaker shall not be led right upon the earth*. [Ps. 140, 11] Hence again Solomon says, *In the multitude of words there wanteth not sin*. [Prov. 10, 19] Hence Isaiah says, *And the cultivation of righteousness, silence*; so pointing out that the righteousness of the interior is desolated, when we do not withhold from immoderate talking. Hence James says, *If any man among you think himself to be religious, and bridleth not his tongue, but deceiveth his own heart, this man's religion is vain*. [James 1, 26] Hence he says again, *Let every man be swift to hear, slow to speak*. [1, 19] Hence he adds again, *The tongue is an unruly evil, full of deadly poison*. [3, 8] Hence 'Truth' warns us by his own lips, saying, *Every idle word that men shall speak, they shall give account thereof in the day of judgment*. [Matt. 12, 36] For an idle word is such as lacks either cause of just occasion, or purpose of kind serviceableness. If then an account is demanded for idle speech, it is very deeply to be considered what punishment followeth after that much talking, wherein we sin even by words of pride.

59. Furthermore, be it known that they are lost to the whole estate of righteousness altogether, who let themselves go in mischievous words. For the mind of man, like water, both when closed round is collected on high, in that it seeks anew the source whence it descended, and when let loose it comes to nought, in that it dissipates itself to no purpose down below. For the mind is as it were drawn out of itself in so many streams, as it lets itself out in superfluous words from the strict control of silence. And hence it has no

power to turn back within to the knowledge of itself, in that being dissipated without in much talking, it loses the strength of interior reflection. Therefore it lays itself bare in every part to the inflictions of the plotting enemy, in that it does not hedge itself about with any defence for its safe-keeping. Whence it is written, *He that hath no rule over his own spirit in his talk is like a city that is broken down and without walls.* For because it is without the wall of silence, the city of the mind lies open to the darts of the enemy, and when it casts itself forth of itself in words, it exhibits itself exposed to the adversary, and he gets the mastery of it without trouble, in proportion as the soul that he has to overcome combats against its own self by much talking.

60. But herein be it known, that when we are withheld from speaking by excess of fear, we are sometimes confined within the strait bounds of silence beyond what need be. And whilst we avoid the mischiefs of the tongue without caution, we are secretly involved in worse. For oftentimes while we are overmuch restrained in speech, we are subject to a mischievous degree of much talking in the heart, that the thoughts should be hot within, the more that the violent keeping of indiscreet silence confines them, and most often they let themselves take a wider range in proportion as they reckon themselves to be more secure, in that they are not seen by censors without. Whence the mind is sometimes lifted up in pride, and, as it were, regards as weak those persons whom it hears engaged in talk. And when it keeps the mouth of the body shut, it never knows to what degree it is laying itself open to evil by entertaining pride. For it keeps the tongue down, but it sets the heart up. And whereas it never takes heed to itself from inattention, it censures all the world more freely to itself, in proportion as it does it at the same time the more secretly. And most frequently oversilent people, when they meet with any wrongs, are driven into bitterer grief, the more they do not give utterance to all that they are undergoing. For if the tongue declared with calmness the annoyance inflicted, grief would flow away from our consciousness. For closed wounds give more acute pain, in that when the corruption that ferments within is discharged, the pain is laid open favourably for our recovery. And generally whilst over-silent men fix their eyes on the faults of any, and yet hold in the tongue in silence, they are, as it were, withdrawing the use of the salve, after the wounds have been seen. For they

the more effectually become the cause of death, that they refused by speaking to cast out the poison which they might. And hence if immoderate silence were not a thing to blame, the Prophet would newer say,

Woe is me, for I have held my peace.

61. What then have we here to do, saving that the tongue must be heedfully kept in under the poise of a mighty control, but not that it must be indissolubly chained, lest either being let loose it run out into mischief, or being bound up, it be also slack to render service. For hence it is said by one, *A wise man will hold his tongue till he sees opportunity,* that when he accounts it convenient, strictness of silence being laid aside, by speaking such things as are meet, he may devote himself to answer the end of usefulness. Hence Solomon says, *A time to keep silence, and a time to speak.* For the seasons for changes are to be weighed with discretion, lest either when the tongue ought to be restrained, it let itself out to no purpose in words, or when it might speak to good purpose, it keep itself in from sloth. Which the Psalmist considering comprehended in a brief petition, saying, *Set a watch, O Lord, before my mouth; and a door of guard on my lips.* [Ps. 141, 3] For a door is opened and shut. He then who prayed not that a bar should be set to his lips, but a door, openly showed that the tongue ought both to be held in by self-control, and let loose on grounds of necessity, that both the voice should open the discreet mouth at the fitting time, and on the other hand silence close it at the fitting time. And because neither the friends of Job, nor all heretics, whose likeness they bear, know how to observe this, they are said to 'utter words to the wind.' In that the sayings which the weightiness of discretion does not establish firmly, the breath of levity carries along.

BOOK VIII.

He explains part of the sixth Chapter, from verse 27, and the whole of the seventh and eighth Chapters. In the course of this exposition, from verse 11, to the end of the eighth Chapter, he speaks at length on the sin of hypocrisy.

Literal and Allegorical

1. WE have already in the preceding book considered the point, that blessed Job is making known to us the force of his humility, when he says,

Ver. 27. Yea ye overwhelm the fatherless, and ye strive to overthrow your friend.

For he shows what great weakness he considers himself to be of, who calls himself 'fatherless.' But because charity even when wounded cannot quit love, he at once complains that they would have him overthrown, and yet witnesses that he is their friend. Whose words, as we have often said already, in such wise specially apply to himself, that yet by them, in the Spirit of Prophecy, we have at the same time set forth the sentiment ['sententia.' see l. xxiii. § 31] of the faithful People, in the voice of the Church Universal. Which same People, while encountering the opposition of heretics, both regards itself as weak in humility, and yet never abandons the greatness of keeping love entire. For the People of Holy Church, as it is the child of a dead Father, is not unfitly called 'fatherless,' in that henceforth indeed through faith it follows His life of Resurrection, but does not as yet see Him by His appearing. Now heretics 'overwhelm the fatherless,' when they bear hard upon the lowliness of the faithful People, by clamorous and false charges, and yet he is a 'friend,' whom they set themselves to 'overthrow,' in that God's faithful People never cease with loving affection to call to the Truth, the very persons whom they suffer as persecutors. But herein it is necessary to be known, that holy men neither dread from weakness to be exposed to falsehoods, nor in being harmed ever hold their peace as to the Truth. Whence it is added;

Ver. 28. But fulfil what ye have begun; give ear, and see if I lie.

2. For because he does not fear to endure adversities, let him say, *But fulfil what ye have begun*; and because he does not withhold the announcements of the Truth from his very persecutors themselves, let him add, *Give ear, and see if I lie*. As if he said in plain words, 'Neither do I tremble at the mischiefs done me before, nor **ii.**

do I withhold the succours of correction from ungrateful hearers, in that I both have exercise through being driven to straits by misfortune, and gain increase by being kindly devoted to my very persecutors themselves.' For the mind of the Saints, in this war of temptations, being at once defended by the shield of patience, and begirt with the swords of love, obtains resolution for the enduring of bad treatment, and puts forth kindness in the recompensing good, so as both to receive stoutly the weapons of enmities, and return forcibly the darts of love. For he does not in any way go armed to the wars, who either taking a shield, uses no swords, or using swords, is not protected by a shield. And hence the soldier of God, encountered by a war of adversity, ought both to hold before him the shield of patience, lest he perish, and being prompt to preach he should launch the darts of love, that he may win the victory. The sum of which armour Paul briefly informs us of, saying, *Charity suffereth long, and is kind*. [1 Cor. 13, 4] But when one of either is wanting, charity is not, i.e. if bearing with the wicked without kindness, he has no love; or again if showing himself without patience, he neglect to bear with the wicked whom he loves. Therefore that true charity may be retained by us, it must needs be that both patience support kindness, and again kindness support patience, that building up a large edifice as it were in our breast, both patience may give strength to the tower of kindness, and kindness give grace to the firmly founded edifices of patience. Therefore let blessed Job, as being prompt to patience, say, *But fulfil what ye have begun*; and as endued with kindness let him add, *Give ear, and see I lie,*

iii. 3. But because Holy Church, being well trained in the school of humility, does not enjoin as by authority the right instructions which she delivers to those that be gone astray, but wins acceptance for them by reason, it is well said in this place, *See if I lie*. As though it were in plain words, 'In all that I declare, give no credence to me upon grounds of authority, but consider on grounds of reason whether they be true. And if at any time she says what cannot be comprehended by reason, she reasonably advises that human reasoning should not be looked for in hidden truths.' But it often happens that heretics, when they meet with opportunity for reasoning, give themselves a loose in the brawlings of strife. Hence it is immediately subjoined with propriety,

Ver. 29. Answer, I pray you, without strife.

4. For neither do heretics try to attain truth by their investigations, but to appear to be the winners; and whereas they desire to show for wise without, they are bound within in their foolishness with the chains of their own pride; hence it comes to pass that they look out for contests of rivalry, and concerning God, Who is our Peace, they know not how to speak with peaceableness, and by the article of peace they become contrivers of strife. To whom it is well spoken by Paul, *But if any man seem to be contentious, we have no such custom, neither the Churches of God.* [1 Cor. 11, 16] Now it is rightly added,

And speaking that which is just, judge ye.

5. For everyone that speaks, whilst he waits for his hearer's sentence upon his words, is as it were subjected to the judgment of him, by whom he is heard. Accordingly he that fears to be condemned in respect of his words, ought first to put to the test that which he delivers; that there may be a kind of impartial and sober umpire sitting between the heart and the tongue, weighing with exactness whether the heart presents right words, which the tongue taking up with advantage may bring forward for the hearer's judgment. Therefore let blessed Job, while managing his own case against his friends, yet telling our proceedings against heretics, blame precipitancy in speakers, and gather words to suit their mind, saying, *And speaking that which is just, judge ye.* As if it were in plain words, 'If in this, that ye come out to us in the issuing forth of the tongue, ye would not be found fault with, retain within the balances of justice, that what is delivered without, may find acceptance by the weightiness of truth, the more in proportion as the scales of discretion weigh it well within, and because those put forth a right judgment about the sayings of others, who are used first to sit in judgment on their own; after that he had said, speaking that which is just, judge ye, he immediately adds with propriety, **iv.**

Ver. 30. And ye shall not find iniquity in my tongue, nor shall foolishness sound through my jaws.

6. As if it were expressed in plain words, 'The more exactly ye weigh your own words, the more truly ye estimate those of others, and when what ye say begins to be right, ye will recognise **v.**

what ye hear to be just. For my tongue never sounds of folly to you, unless it be what comes from your own inward thoughts.' Thus Holy Church makes it her aim first to prove the allegations of her enemies to be false, and then to make known the announcements of the truth, for so long as they reckon themselves to hold right notions, they obstinately assail the right things that they hear. Therefore it is necessary beforehand that heretics should feel their error, lest they gainsay the truth when it is heard. For neither if the tiller of the soil neglect to root up the briars of the field by the cutting of the share, will the earth bring to a crop the seed received into her bosom; and 'when the physician does not get rid of the corruption, by opening the wound, healthy flesh never forms in the corrupt spot. First then in destroying what is bad, let him say, *And speaking that which is just, judge ye*; but afterwards in teaching what is right, let him add, *And ye shalt not find iniquity in my tongue, nor shall foolishness sound through my jaws*. Now it is the way with heretics to deliver some things openly, to hold others in secret, for by the 'tongue,' plain speaking is denoted, but by the 'jaws [*fauces*],' the secret harbouring.

7. Neither in the tongue then of Holy Church does 'iniquity resound,' nor 'foolishness in her jaws,' for the things that she proclaims in open utterance, at the same time she preserves in inward faith; nor does she teach one thing in public and keep another to herself in secret; but she both delivers what she thinks by giving utterance to it, and keeps what she delivers by living accordingly; and whatever is let out belonging to the feast of heavenly wisdom by the tongue of preaching, she tastes this same by the jaws of silent expectation. And let blessed Job, both as an individual member of the whole Church, in telling his own case, and as showing what is the heart of all of the Elect, make known all that he feels, that the testimony of his speech may manifest the uprightness of his mind. It proceeds,

Chap. vii. 1. The life of man upon earth is a warfare.

vi. 8. In this passage in the old Translation the life of man is not called 'a warfare' at all, but 'a trial,' yet if the meaning of either word be regarded, the sound that meets the ear outwardly is different, yet they make one and the same concordant meaning. For what is represented by the title of 'a trial,' saving our contest with evil spirits? and what by the designation of 'a warfare,' *Moral* but an exercising against our enemies? So that trial is itself 'a warfare,' in that whilst a man is watching against the plots of evil spirits, surely he is spending himself under arms for the fight. But we are to observe that this life of man is not said to *have* 'trial,' but it is described as itself *being* 'trial.' For having of free will declined from the upright form wherein it was created, and being made subject to the rottenness of its state of corruption, whilst out of self it begets mischiefs against self, it henceforth becomes the very thing it undergoes. For whereas by letting itself down, it relinquished the erect seat of the interior, what did it find in itself save the shifting of change? And though it now erect itself thence to seek things on high, it directly drops down to its own level from the impulse of a slippery changeableness. It desires to stand up in contemplation, but has not the strength. It strives to fix firmly the step of thought, but is enfeebled by the slippings of its frailty. Which same burthens of a changeful lot, forasmuch as it sought them out of free will, so it bears them against the will. Man might have possessed his fleshly part in quiet, if created aright as he was by his Maker, he had been willing to be possessed by Him; but, whereas he aimed to lift himself up against his Maker, he straightway experienced in himself insolency from the flesh. Now forasmuch as together with guilt punishment is also inherited along with it by birth, we are born with the engrafted evil of a frail nature; and we as it were carry an enemy along with us, whom we get the better of with toilsome endeavours. And so the life of man is itself 'a trial,' in that it has that springing up to it from itself, whereby it is liable to be destroyed. And though it is ever cutting down by the principle of virtue all that it begets in the principle of frailty, yet it is ever begetting in frailty somewhat to cut down by virtue.

9. And so the life of man is in such a way 'a trial,' that though we are henceforth restrained from the commission of sin, yet in our very good works themselves we are clouded now by the recollection of evil deeds, now by the mists of self-deception [*seductionis*], now by the suspension of our own purpose of mind. Thus one man henceforth restrains the flesh from excess, and yet he is still subject to images thereof, in that the things, which he has done willingly, come to mind against his will, and what he accounted pleasure he bears as punishment. But because he fears to be drawn again into the conquered evil habit, he restrains his greedy appetite by the forcible

means of a singular abstinence, and by his abstinence his face is rendered pale; then when paleness is observed in his countenance, his life is commended as deserving of the reverential regard of his fellow-creatures, and presently with the words of commendation vainglory enters into the mind of this man of abstinence, which while the mind having received a shock cannot get the better of, it seeks to blot from the face the paleness whereby that entered in, and so it comes to pass that being tied fast with the knots of infirmity, either in avoiding the paleness of abstinence, it again dreads to be brought under the dominion of excess, by food, or subduing by abstinence the impulse to excess, it apprehends its paleness serving to vainglory. Another man getting the better of the downfall of pride, henceforth lays hold of the state of humility with all the desire of his heart, and when he sees people that are full of pride breaking out so far as to the oppressing of the innocent, being inflamed by the incitement of zeal, he is forced to lay aside in some degree the thing he determined on, he displays the force of the side of right, and withstands the evil-minded not with mildness, but with authority. Whence it is very commonly the case, that either by pursuit of humility he is led to abandon zeal for the right, or again by zeal for right he interrupts the pursuit of humility, which he maintained. And when the authoritativeness of zeal and lowliness of purpose scarcely admit of being preserved together, the man is made a stranger to himself in his embarrassment. So that he is in a great dilemma lest in a deluded mind either pride pass itself off for the high tone of zeal, or timid inactivity feign itself humility. Another man, considering how great is the sin of deceit, determines to fortify himself in the citadel of truth, so that henceforth no false word should proceed out of his lips, and that he should wholly cut himself off from the sin of lying. But it very frequently happens that, when the truth is spoken, the life of a neighbour is borne hard upon; and whilst the person fears to bring injury upon another, he is brought back, as in an aim of pity, to that evil habit of deceit which he had for long kept under; and so it comes to pass, that though wickedness has no place in his mind, yet the shadow of falsehood dims therein the rays of truth. And hence oftentimes, because when a man is urged with questions he cannot keep silence, either by telling a falsehood he slays his own soul, or by speaking the truth bears hard upon the life of a neighbour. Another man, incited by the love of his Maker, aims by unintermitted prayer to withhold his mind from all earthly thoughts, and to place it in safety in the secret deeps of inward repose; but in the very mounting of his prayer, whilst he is striving to ascend from things below, he is struck back by the vision of them, and the eye of the mind is stretched to gaze on the light, but from bodily habit it is dimmed by the images of earthly things arising. Whence it very often comes to pass, that the mind of the person so striving, being exhausted by its own weakness, either giving over prayer, is lulled asleep in sloth, or if it continue long in prayer, the mist of rising images gathers thick before its eyes.

10. And so it is well said, *The life of man is a trial upon earth*, since there also he met with the guiltiness of a downward course, where he thought to lay hold on the advancement of an upward one, and the mind is only thrown into disorder by the same act whereby it strove to arise out of its disorder, so that it is thrown back upon it-self shivered by the very means, by which it was already getting above itself collected and compacted. This man being a stranger to instruction in the Divine Law, is kept down by his ignorance, that he should do nothing for the attaining of salvation. That man being en-dued with the knowledge of the Divine Law, while he is delighted that understanding is vouchsafed to him beyond other men, in that he exults with a selfish delight, wastes in himself the gift of under-standing which he has received. And in the Judgment he is shown to light worse than others by the same thing, whereby he is exhibited brighter than others for a season. The first, because he is lifted high by no gifts of extraordinary powers, eschews the more plain path of uprightness too, and as if accounting himself an alien to the heavenly benefit, does evil things as though with more security, in proportion as he has never been vouchsafed the high endowments of the heaven-ly gift. The other the spirit of Prophecy replenishes, uplifts to the foreknowledge of events, and shows him things to come as now pre-sent. But whilst oftentimes and in many cases he is lifted above him-self, so that he does really contemplate future events, his mind being drawn off into self-confidence, fancies that that spirit of Prophecy, which cannot always be had, is always with him, and when he takes every notion that he may have for prophecy, because that he ascribes this to himself even when he has nothing of it, he even loses it in the degree that he might possess it. And so it comes to pass, that he is brought back in sorrow behind the standard of other men's merits by

the very means, whereby he was advanced before it in gladness of heart in the esteem of all. And so, *The life of man is a trial upon earth*, in that either being a stranger to extraordinary powers, it is unable to mount to the heavenly prize, or enriched with spiritual gifts, it is one day ruined the worse by occasion of its extraordinary powers.

11. But whereas we have said a little above that 'a trial' is the same as 'a warfare,' it is above everything to be borne in mind, that something more is signified to us by the title of 'warfare,' than by the name of 'trial.' For to our apprehension there is this addition made by the expression of 'a warfare,' namely, that by warfare there is made daily progress towards an end. And whilst the space of warfare goes on increasing in a regular course, the whole warfare of men [B. & C. 'of a man'] is at the same time diminishing. And so, *the life of man is a warfare upon earth*, in that, as we have said above, each one of us, while by the accessions of time he is daily advancing to the end of life, in adding to his life, is making an end to live. For he looks for the days to come round, but as soon as they are come for the lengthening of life, they are already taken away from the amount of life; for while the step of the traveller too is advancing over the ground in front, what remains of the way is lessening. Thus our life is 'a warfare,' in that in the same degree that it is drawn out to its enlargement, it is brought to an end, so as not to be. Therefore it is well said, *The life of man is a warfare upon earth*; for whilst by the several periods of time it seeks to gain ground, by that very period which it adds but in losing, it is made to pass away as it grows. And hence the very course of a warfare itself is described in the words that are immediately added,

Are not his days also like the days of an hireling?

vii. 12. The hireling longs for his days to pass the quicker, that he may attain without delay to the reward of his toil; and so the days of man imbued with a knowledge of the Truth and of the things of eternity, are justly compared to 'the days of an hireling,' because he reckons the present life to be his road, not his country, a warfare, not the palm of victory, and he sees that he is the further from his reward, the more slowly he is drawing near to his end. Moreover we must bear in mind, that the hireling spends his strength in labours that belong to others, yet procures for himself a reward that is his own. Now it is uttered by the Redeemer's voice,

My Kingdom is not of this world. [John 18, 36] All we, then, who being endued with the hope of heaven, wear ourselves out with the toiling of the present life, are busied in the concern of another. For it often happens that we are even compelled to serve the sons of perdition, that we are constrained to give back to the world what belongs to the world, and we are spent indeed with another man's work, yet we receive a reward of our own, and by this, that we manage uncorruptly the interests of others, we are made to arrive at our own. In reverse of which, 'Truth' says to certain persons, *And if ye have not been faithful to that which is another man's, who shall give you that which is your own.* [Luke 16, 12] Moreover it is to be remembered, that an hireling anxiously and heedfully looks to it, that never a day pass clear of work, and that the expected end of the time should not come empty for his rewarding. For in his earnestness of labour he sees what he may get in the season of recompense. Thus when his work advances, his assurance in the reward is increased, but when the work is at a stand-still, his hope sickens in respect of the recompense. And hence each of the Elect reckoning his life as the days of an 'hireling,' stretches forward to the reward the more confident in hope, in proportion as he holds on the more stoutly for the advancement of labour. He considers what the transitory course of the present life is, he reckons up the days with their works. He dreads lest the moments of life should pass void of labour. He rejoices in adversity, he is recruited with suffering, he is comforted by mourning, in that he sees himself to be more abundantly recompensed with the rewards of the life to come, the more thoroughly he devotes himself for the love thereof by daily deaths. For it is hence that the citizens of the Land above say to the Creator of it in the words of the Psalmist, *Yea, for Thy sake are we killed all the day long.* [Ps 44, 22] Hence Paul says, *I die daily, brethren, for your glory.* [1 Cor. 15, 31] Hence he says again, *For the which cause I also suffer these things; but I am not confounded, for I know Whom I have believed, and am persuaded that He is able to keep that which I have committed unto Him against that day.* [2 Tim. 1, 12] Therefore holy men for all the labours which they now exercise, while committing them to 'Truth,' already hold so many pledges of their recompense shut up in the chamber of hope. Yet oppressive heat is now felt under toil, that one day refreshment may be had in rest. Whence it is rightly added immediately afterwards,

THE SECOND PART.

Ver. 2, 3. As a servant earnestly desireth the shadow, and as an hireling looketh for the end of his work, so am I made to possess months of vanity, and I have numbered me wearisome nights.

viii. 13. Since for 'a servant to desire the shadow,' is after the heat of trial and the sweat of labour to seek the cool of eternal repose. Which shadow that servant desired, who said, *My soul thirsteth for God, the living God; when shall I come and appear before God?* [Ps. 42, 2] And again, *Woe is me that I sojourn in Mesech*. [Ps. 120, 5] Who as if after hard toil retreating from the heat, and seeking a covering that he might attain the rest of coolness, says again, *For I will enter into the place of the wonderful Tabernacle, even to the house of God*. [Ps. 42, 4] Paul panted to lay hold of this 'shadow,' having *a desire to depart and to be with Christ*. [Phil. 1, 23] This shadow they had already attained unto in the fulness of the desire of their hearts, who said, *We which have borne the burthen and heat of the day*. [Mat. 20, 12] Now he that is said to 'desire' the shadow, is rightly styled 'a servant,' in that each one of the Elect, so long as he is bound fast by the condition of frailty, is held in under the yoke of corruption, in its exercising dominion over him, as though under the harrassing effect of heat; which same person, when he is stripped of corruption, is then made known to himself as free and at rest. And hence it is well said by Paul also, *Because the creature itself also shall be delivered from the bondage of corruption, into the glorious liberty of the children of God*. [Rom. 8, 21] For the Elect are now, pressed down by the penalty of a corrupt state, but then they are exalted high by the glory of an incorrupt. And in the same degree that, relatively to the burthens of our present constraint, there is nought of liberty now manifested in the sons of God, relatively to the glory of the liberty to ensue, nought of servitude will then appear in the servants of God. And so the servile garb of corruption being cast off, and the nobility of liberty bestowed, the creature is turned into the gloriousness of the sons of God, in that in being united to God by the Spirit, it is proved as it were to have surmounted and overcome this very thing, that it is a created being. Now he that still 'desires the shadow' is 'a servant,' in that so long as he is subject to the heat of temptation, he is bearing on his shoulders the yoke of a wretched condition, and it is rightly added there, *and as an hireling looks for the reward of his work*.

14. For an hireling, when he looks at the work to be done, at once resigns his spirit in consequence of the length and burthensomeness of the labour; but when he recalls his sinking spirit to take thought of the reward of his work, he immediately sets afresh his vigour of mind for the exercising of his labour, and what he reckoned a grievous burthen in respect of the work, he esteems light and easy on the grounds of the recompense. Thus, thus, do each of the Elect, when they meet with the crosses of this life, when insults upon their good name, losses in their substance, pains of the body are brought upon them, reckon the things grievous, which they are tried with; but when they stretch the eyes of the mind to the view of the heavenly country, by comparison with their reward they see how light is all they undergo. For that which is shown to be altogether insupportable for the pain, is by forecasting reflection rendered light for the recompense. It is hence that Paul is always being lifted up bolder than himself against adversities, in that 'as an hireling he looketh for the end of his work.' For he accounts what he undergoes to be a heavy burthen, but he reckons it light in consideration of the reward. For he does himself declare how great the burthen is of what he suffers, in that he bears record that he was 'in prisons more abundantly, in stripes above measure, in deaths oft,' &c. who 'of the Jews five times received folly stripes save one.' [2 Cor. 11. 23. &c.] Who was 'thrice beaten with rods, once stoned, thrice suffered shipwreck, a night and a day was in the deep of the sea; who endured perils of waters, of robbers, of his own countrymen, of the heathen, in the city, in the wilderness, in the sea, among false brethren; 'who in weariness and painfulness, in fastings often, in cold and nakedness,' had labour and toil, who sustained 'fights without, within fears,' who declares himself pressed down above strength, saying, that we were pressed out of measure, above strength, insomuch that we were weary even of life. But in what sort he wiped off him the streams of this hard toil with the towel of his reward, he himself tells, when he says, *For I reckon that the sufferings of this present time are not worthy to be compared, with the glory to come, which shall be revealed in us.* Thus, 'as an hireling, he looketh for the end of his work,' who while he considers the increase of the reward, reckons it of no account that he labours well nigh spent. But it is well added, *So am I made to possess months of vanity, and wearisome nights have I numbered me.*

THE SECOND PART.

15. For the Elect serve the Creator of things, and yet are often driven to straits by the want of things; they hold fast in God by love, and yet they lack the supports of the present life. So they who do not aim at present objects by their actions, as to the profits of the world, spend 'months of vanity.' Moreover they are subject to 'wearisome nights,' in that they bear the darkness of adversity not only to the extent of want, but oftentimes to the anguish of the body. For to undergo contempt and want is not hard to virtuous minds; but when adversity is turned to the paining of the flesh, then surely wearisomeness is felt from pain. It may also be not unsuitably interpreted, that each one of the Saints as a hireling spends 'months of vanity,' in that he now already bears the toil, but does not yet hold the reward; the one he undergoes, the other he looks for; but 'he numbers him wearisome nights,' in that by exercising himself in virtuous habits, he is accumulating upon his own head the ills of the present life: for if he does not aim to advance in spirit, he finds the things of the world perchance less galling to him.

Allegorical

16. Yet, if this sentence be referred to the voice of Holy Church, the meaning thereof is traced out with a little more particularity. For she herself has 'months of vanity,' who in her weak members has to bear earthly actions running on to nought without the meed of life. She 'numbers to herself wearisome nights,' in that in her strong members she bears manifold afflictions. For in this life there be some things that are hard, and some that are empty, and some that are both hard and empty at one and the same time. For from love of the Creator to be tried with the afflictions of the present life, is hard indeed, but not empty. For love of the present world to be dissolved in pleasures, is empty indeed, but not hard. But for the love of that world, to be exposed to any adversities, is at one and the same time both empty and laborious, in that the soul is at once 'afflicted by adversity, and not replenished with the compensation of the reward. And so in those who being now placed within the pale of Holy Church, still let themselves out in the pursuit of their pleasures, and are thenceforth not enriched with the fruit of good works, she passes 'months of vanity,' in that she spends the periods of life without the gift of the reward. But in those who, being devoted to everlasting aims, meet with the crosses of this world, 'she numbers herself wearisome nights,' in that she as it were

in the obscurity of the present life undergoes the darkness of woe. But in those who at one and the same time love this transitory world, and yet are wearied with its contradiction, she sustains at once 'days of vanity,' and 'wearisome nights,' in that neither does any recompense coming after reward their lives, and, yet present affliction straitens them. But it is rightly that she never says that she has 'days,' but 'months of vanity' in these. For by the name of 'months,' the sum and total amount of days is represented, and so by the 'day,' we have each individual action set forth: but by 'months,' the conclusion of those actions is implied. But it often happens that when we do anything in this world, being buoyed up by the eager intentness of our hope, this particular thing that we are about, we never think empty; but when we are come to the end of our doings, failing to obtain the object of our aims, we are grieved that we have been labouring for emptiness, and so we spend not only days, but likewise 'months of vanity,' in that not in the beginning of our actions, but only at the end, we bethink ourselves that we have been toiling in earthly practices without fruit. For when trouble follows upon our actions, it is as if the months of vanity of our life were brought home to us: in that it is only in the consummation of our actions that we learn, how vain was all our toil therein.

17. But because in the sacred word sometimes 'night' is put for ignorance, according to the testimony of Paul, who says to his disciples instructed in the life to come; *Ye are all the children of the light, and the children of the day; we are not of the night, nor of darkness.* [1 Thess. 5, 5] To which words he prefixed, *But ye, brethren, are not in darkness, that that day should overtake you as a thief.* [ib. 4] In this place the voice of Holy Church may be understood in the person of those of her members, who after the darkness of their state of ignorance are brought back to the love of righteousness, and being enlightened by the rays of truth, wash out with their tears all that they have done amiss. For every one that has been enlightened looks back to see how polluted all that was that he laboured at, in love with the present life. And therefore Holy Church in the case of these, in whom there is a return to life, compares her toils to 'a servant' in a state of heat, and to 'an hireling longing for the end of his work,' in the words, *As a servant earnestly desireth the shadow, and as an hireling looketh for the end of his work; so am I made to possess months of vanity, and wearisome nights have I numbered me.* For in drawing the comparison

there are two things which he premised, as also in the describing of weariness there are two which he thereupon added. For to the one oppressed with heat he gave 'months of vanity,' in that in proportion as the refreshing of eternity is more the object of our desire, it is more clearly seen how vainly we spend our labour for this life. But to the one in expectance he brought in 'wearisome nights,' in that the more that at the end of our works we look at the reward we are to have given us, the more we lament that we so long knew nothing of the thing that we now aim at. And hence the very solicitude of the penitent is carefully set forth, so that it is said, 'that he numbered to himself wearisome nights,' in that the more truly we return to God, the more exactly we consider, while we grieve over them, those toils which we underwent in this world from ignorance. For as everyone finds that to become more and more sweet which he desires of the things of eternity, so that which he was undergoing for the love of the present world, is made appear to him proportionably burthensome. Now if the following words be considered with reference to the historical import alone, doubtless we have the mind of one in sorrow described by them, viz. how in the different impulses of desire he is variously urged by the force of grief. For it goes on,

Ver. 4. When I lie down, I say, When shall I arise? and again I look for the evening.

ix. 18. For in the night, day is desired, in the day, evening is longed for; in that grief will not let the things that are before us give satisfaction, and while it saddens the heart in the experience of the present, it is ever stretching it to something beyond in expectation, as it were by a consolatory longing. But because at one and the same time the afflicted mind is drawn out in desire, and yet its grief, even though beguiled by longings, is not ended; it is rightly added, *And I shall be filled with pains even until the darkness.* But the cause of this grief is set forth, when the words are immediately introduced,

Ver. 5. My flesh is clothed with worms and clods of dust: my skin is dried up and shrunken.

x. 19. But we shall make out these words more exactly and more applicably, if we go back to the order of the foregoing interpretation. For by sleep the torpor of inaction, and by rising the exercising of action, is represented. By the name of the evening moreover, because it accords with sleep, we have set forth again the desire of inaction. But Holy Church, as long as she is leading a life of corruption, never ceases to bewail the inconveniences of her condition of mutability. For man was created for this end, that, with mind erect, he might mount to the citadel of contemplation, and that no touch of corruption should cause him to swerve from the love of his Maker; but herein, that he moved the foot of his will to transgression, turning it away from the innate stedfastness of his standing, he immediately fell away from the love of his Creator into himself. Yet in forsaking the love of God, that true stronghold of his standing, he could not stand fast in himself either; in that by the impulse of a slippery condition of mutability, being precipitated beneath himself through corruption, he also came to be at strife with himself. And now, in that he is not secured by the stedfastness of his creation, he is ever being made to vary by the fit of alternating desire, so that both at rest he longs for action, and when busied pants for rest. For because the stedfast mind, when it might have stood, would not, it is now no longer able to stand even when it will, in that in leaving the contemplation of its Creator, it lost the strength of its health, and wherever placed is ever seeking some other place through uneasiness. And so in setting forth the fickleness of the human mind, let him say, *When I go to sleep, I say, When shall I arise? and again I shall look for the evening.* As if it were expressed in plain words; 'Nothing it receives sufficeth the mind, in that it has lost Him, Who might have truly sufficed to it. Thus in sleep I long for rising, and at rising I look for evening, for both when at rest I aim at the employment of action, and when employed I look for the inaction of repose.'

20. Which nevertheless may be understood in another sense also. For to sleep is to lie prostrate in sin. For if the designation of 'sleep' did not denote sin, Paul would never say to his disciples, *Awake, ye righteous, and sin not.* [1 Cor. 15, 34] And hence too he charges his hearer, saying, *Awake, thou that sleepest, and arise from the dead, and Christ shall give thee light.* [Eph. 5, 14] And again; *That now it is high time for us to arise out of sleep.* [Rom. 13, 11] Hence too Solomon upbraids the sinner, saying, *How long wilt thou sleep, O sluggard?* [Prov. 6, 9] Therefore each one of the Elect, when he is oppressed with the sleep of sin, strives to rise to keep the watch of righteousness. But

often when he has risen he feels himself lifted up by the greatness of his virtuous attainments. And hence after attainments in virtue he desires to be tried with the adversities of the present life, lest he fall the worse from presumption in his virtuous achievements. For if he had not known that he was preserved more effectually by trial, the Psalmist would never have said, *Examine me, O Lord, and prove me*. [Ps. 26, 2] And so it is well said here, *When I go to sleep, I say, When shall I arise? and again I shall look for the evening*; in that both in the sleep of sin, we look for the light of righteousness, and when successes in virtuous attainments elevate the mind, adversity is wanted for our aid, so that when the soul is exalted above what it ought to be in rejoicing at its own excellencies, it may be established by sorrow coming forth, through the encounters of the present life. Hence it is not said, *I shall dread the evening*, but, *I shall look for*. For we 'look for' favourable things, we dread those that are adverse to us. And so the good man 'looks for evening,' in that when he needs to be tried with affliction, adversity itself is made success to him.

21. By the designation of 'evening' there may also be understood the tempting of sin, which oftentimes assaults the mind the sharper, in proportion as the spirit transports it higher to the regions above. For never in this life is sin so entirely abandoned in the practising of righteousness, that we continue without flinching in the self-same righteousness; in that although right principle does already drive out sin from the dwelling of the heart, yet the very sin, that is so banished, taking her seat at the doors of our thought, knocks for it to be opened to her. And this Moses too conveyed in spiritual signification, when he described the parts of time being made in a bodily way, saying, *And there was light*, and adding soon after, *And the evening was made* [Vulg. *factum est*]. [Gen. 1, 3. 5.] For the Maker of all things foreseeing man's guilt, then exhibited in Time what now passes in the human mind. For the light draws on to eventide, in that the shades of temptation follow the light of righteousness. But because the light of the Elect is not put out by temptation, not night; but evening, is recorded as made. Since it often happens, that in the heart of the righteous temptation shades the light of righteousness, but it does not put an end thereto; it forces it to the paleness of a flickering state, but does not utterly quench it. And so the Elect both after sleep long for the rising, and after rising look for evening, in that they use both to awake from sin to the light of righteousness,

and when placed in that same light of righteousness, they are ever making themselves ready to encounter the snares of temptation; which same they do not dread, but look for, as they are not ignorant that even trials promote the interest of their righteousness.

22. But with whatever degree of virtue they may have striven against their corruption, they cannot have entire health, until the time that the day of their present life is ended. And hence it is added, *And I shall be full of pains even until the darkness*. For one while adversities burst upon them, at another time successes themselves beguile them by insidious joviality; at one time evil propensities making head stir up a war of the flesh, at another time being brought under, they invite the mind to pride. Therefore the life of good man is *full of pains even until the darkness*, in that so long as the period of their state of corruption is going on, it is shaken by tribulation both internal and external; nor does it experience assurance of health, saving when it leaves behind it for good the day of temptation. And hence this same cause of these pains is brought in immediately afterwards, when it is said, *My flesh is clothed with corruption and foulness of dust*. For, as we have said a little above, man wilfully forsook his innate stability, and plunged himself into the abyss of corruption: and hence now he either goes slipping in impure works, or defiled by forbidden thoughts. For, so to speak, being judicially bowed down beneath its own sin, our nature its very self is put out of the pale of nature, and, when let loose, it is carried even to the length of bad works, while, being held in, it is dimmed by the pressing imagination of bad works. Thus in the fulfilment of a forbidden deed, 'corruption' [*putredo*] taints the flesh, while in the lightness of evil thought, dust as it were rises up before the eyes. By consenting to evil practices we are wasted with corruption, but by suffering in the heart the images of evil deeds, we are defiled with the stains of dust; and so he says, *My flesh is clothed with foulness of dust*. As if it were in plain words; 'The carnal life that I am subjected to, either the corruption of wanton practice defiles, or the cloud of wretched thought compasses about in the recollection of evil ways.

23. And yet if we take this in the voice of the Holy Church Universal, doubtless we find her at one time sunk to the earth by the 'corruption' of the flesh, at another time by 'the defilement of dust.' For she has many in her, who whilst they are devoted to the love of the flesh, turn corrupt with the putrefaction of excess. And there

are some that keep indeed from the gratification of the flesh, yet grovel with all their heart in earthly practices. So let Holy Church say in the words of one of her members, let her say what she undergoes from either sort of men, *My flesh is clothed with corruption, and the defilements of dust*. As if she told in plain words, saying, 'There are very many that are members of me in faith, yet these are not sound or pure members in practice: in that either being mastered by foul desires, they run out in the rottenness of corruption; or, being devoted to earthly practices, they are besmeared with dust. For in those, whom I have to endure, that are full of wantonness, I do plainly lament for the flesh turned corrupt; and in those, whom I suffer from, that are seeking the earth, what else is this but that I carry it defiled with dust?'

24. And hence it is properly added at the same time concerning both sorts; *My skin is dried up and shrivelled*. For in the body of the Church, those that are devoted to outward concerns alone are suitably called 'the skin,' which same by becoming dry is contracted, in that the soul of carnal men, while their hearts are set on present objects, and covet what is close at hand, have no mind, as it were, to be made to stretch out after the things of the future world in long-suffering. These, while they disregard the richness of the interior hope, are dried up that they become shrivelled; in that if hopelessness did not parch their hearts, the fever of a little mind would never contract them. Thus it was this contraction that the Psalmist dreaded, when in fear of the drought of the same he said, *May my soul be satisfied as with marrow and fatness*. [Ps. 63, 5] For the soul is 'satisfied with marrow and fatness,' when it is refreshed by the infusion of heavenly hope against the heat of present longings. And so the 'skin' being dried up shrivels, when the heart being given to outward objects, and dried up in hopelessness, is not stretched out in love of its Creator, but is folded up into itself, so to say, by wrinkled thought.

25. But it is to be considered that carnal minds only delight in present things, because they never weigh well how transitory the life of the flesh is. For if they regarded the speed of its flight, they would never love it even when it smiled upon them. But Holy Church, in her elect members, daily minds how quick a flight belongs to outward things, and therefore she sets firm the foot of serious purpose in the interior. And hence it is well added;

Ver. 6. My days are past more swiftly than a web is cut off by the weaver.

Moral 26. By a very suitable image the time of the flesh is compared to a web. For as the web advances by threads, so this mortal life by the several days; but in proportion as it grows to its bigness, it is advancing to its cutting off. For as we have also said above, whilst the time in our hands passes, the time before us is shortened. And of the whole space of our lives those portions are rendered fewer that are to come, in proportion as those are many in number that have gone by. For a web, being fastened above and below, is bound to two pieces of wood that it may be woven; but in proportion as below the part woven is rolled up, so above the part that remains to be woven is being unwound, and by the same act, by which it augments itself in growth, that is rendered less which remains. Just so with the periods of our life, we as it were roll up below those that are past, and unwind at top those that are to come, in that in the same proportion that the past become more, the future have begun to diminish. But because not even does a web suffice for the setting forth of our span of time, for the rapid course of our life surpasses the speed and quickness even of that too, it is well said in this place, *My days are past away more swiftly than a web is cut off by the weaver.* For to the web there is a delay of growth, but to the present life there is no delay of coming to an end. For in the one when the hand of the workman is stopped, the end of the arrival is deferred, but in this latter, because we consume without end time ending every instant, even while resting we are brought to the end of our way, and along the course of our passage, we go on even in sleeping. Therefore the Elect, seeing that the moments of the present life run past at speed, never in this journey of most rapid motion fix the purpose of their hearts. And hence it is well added upon that, **xi.**

And are spent without any hope.

27. The minds of lost sinners are bound fast with such love for the days of their present life, that they long to live for ever here in the same way. So that, if it were possible, they desire never to have the course of their life brought to an end. For they are too indifferent to take account of the future, they place all their hope in transitory things, they aim to have nothing but such objects as pass **xii.**

away. And while they think too much of transitory things, and never look forward to those that shall remain, the eye of their heart is so closed in insensible blindness, that it is never fixed on the interior light. Whence it often happens, that distress already shakes the frame, and approaching death cuts off the power of the breath of life, yet they never cease to mind the things that are of the world. And already the avenger is dragging them to judgment, and yet they themselves, occupied with the concerns of time, in the busy management of them, are only thinking how they may still live on in this world. In the act of leaving everything, they dispose of all as if they were entering upon the possession of them, in that the hope of living is not broken, at the very moment when life is at an end. They are already being forced to judgment in feeling [*per sententiam*], yet they still cleave to the hold of their goods in solicitude. For by the hardened soul death is still believed to be far off, even when his touch is felt. And the soul is so separated from the flesh, that by keeping itself in excessive love for things present, when it is led to everlasting punishment, it does not know this mere thing, whither it is being led; and in leaving all that it would not love with bounds, it suddenly finds without bounds things that it never anticipated. But, on the other hand, the mind of the righteous is stretched in intentness after the eternal world, even when the present life goes smoothly along with it. It enjoys the high health of the flesh, yet the spirit is never hindered by dependence on it. No atom [*articulum*] of death as yet breaks forth, still he daily regards it as present to him. For because life is unceasingly slipping by, the expectation of living is wholly cut short for him. Therefore it is well said of the passing days, *And are spent without hope*. As if it were declared in plain terms; 'I have not placed confidence of heart in the present life, in that all that is passing I have dismissed from my hopes, treading it under foot.' And hence it is rightly added immediately after,

Ver. 7. O remember that my life is wind.

xiii. 28. For those men love the life of the flesh as enduring, who do not consider how infinite is the eternity of the life to come; and whereas they take no thought of the sure stedfastness of the everlasting state, they take their exile for their home, darkness for light, going for standing. Since they that know nothing of greater things can never judge rightly of the least. For the order of judging requires that we should be above that which we are striving to try. Since if the mind is not able to rise above all things, it has no certain sight at all in relation to those, by which it is surpassed. And so it is for this reason that the lost soul is inadequate to estimate the course of the present life, because from love of the same it is bowed down to the admiration thereof. But holy men, in proportion as they lift their hearts towards the eternal world, bethink themselves how short-lived that is which is closed by an ending. And all that is passing is rendered worthless to their senses, forasmuch as that pours in its light through the rays of intelligence, which once received never departs. And as soon as they contemplate the infinite extent of eternity, they cease any longer to desire as great whatsoever has an end to limit it. But the mind when lifted up is carried beyond the limits of time, even when by the flesh it is held fast in time, and it looks down from a greater height on all that is to have an end, the more truly it knows the things without end. Now this very consideration of the short span of man's estate is itself an offering of singular efficacy [*virtutis*] to our Maker. Whence a sacrifice of this merit is here rightly offered together with prayer, when it is said, *O remember that my life is wind*. As if it were said in plain words, 'Regard with loving-kindness one that is quickly gone, in that I claim to be looked upon by Thee with greater pity, even in proportion as I myself do not turn away mine eyes from the contemplation of my short span.' But seeing that when the season of our present life is cut short, there is no more return to the work of earning our forgiveness, it is rightly added,

Mine eye shall no more return to see good.

xiv.

29. The eye of the dead 'no more returneth to see good,' in that for the setting forth of good works, the soul once snipped of the flesh knows no return. It is hence that the rich man, whom the fire of hell was devouring, knew that he could never restore himself by doing works; for he never turned himself to do good to himself, but to his brethren that were left; *I pray thee, father Abraham, that thou wouldest send him to my father's house; for I have five brethren, that he may testify unto them, lest they also come into this place of torment*. [Luke 16, 27. 28.] For hope even though unfounded is used to cheer the stricken soul; but the lost, that they may feel their woe the keener, lose even hope as to pardon. And hence when he was

given over to avenging flames, he was not anxious to help himself, as we said, but his brethren, in that he knew that he would never be without the torments of those fires, the punishment of despair being superadded. Hence Solomon says, *Whatsoever thy hand findeth to do, do it with thy might; for there is no work, nor device, nor knowledge, nor wisdom, in the grave, whither thou goest.* [Eccles. 9, 10] So 'the eye shall no more return to see good,' in that the soul, on meeting with its recompense, is never again recalled to tell to the account of practice. Therefore forasmuch as all that is seen is fleeting, and the things that follow are to endure, blessed Job rightly combined the two in one verse, saying, *O remember that my life is wind: mine eye shall no more see good.* For looking at the transitoriness of things present, he says, *O remember that my life is wind.* But contemplating the eternity of those that come after, he added, *Mine eye shall no more return to see good.* And here, furthermore, he justly proceeds to take upon him the voice of the whole race of man destitute of the benefit of redemption, saying,

Ver. 8. The eye of man shall not see me.

XV. 30. For 'the eye of Man' is the pity of the Redeemer, which softens the hardness of our insensibility, when it looks upon us. Hence, as the Gospel witnesses, it is said, *And the Lord turned, and looked upon Peter. And Peter remembered the word of the Lord. And he went out, and wept bitterly.* [Luke 22, 61. 62.] But the soul when divested of the flesh 'the eye of Man' doth not henceforth at all regard, in that it never delivers him after death, whom grace doth not restore to pardon before death. For hence Paul says, *Behold, now is the accepted time, behold, now is the day of salvation.* [2 Cor. 6, 2] Hence the Psalmist says, *For His mercy is for the present state of being*; [Ps. 118, 1] for this reason, that the man whom mercy doth not rescue now, after the present state of being, justice alone consigns to punishment. Hence Solomon says, *And if the tree fall toward the south or toward the north, in the place where the tree falleth there it shall be.* [Eccles. 11, 3] For when, at the moment of the falling of the human being, either the Holy Spirit or the Evil Spirit receives the soul departed from the chambers of the flesh, he will keep it with him for ever without change, so that neither once exalted, shall it be precipitated into woe, nor once plunged into eternal woes, any further arise to take the means of escape. Therefore let the holy man, contemplating the ills of mankind, viz. how he is removed from the present world without the knowledge of his Redeemer, and buried in everlasting flames without remedy, and taking up their voice in his own person, give utterance to the words, *And the eye of man shall not see me*. Forasmuch as the man whom the grace of the Redeemer doth not now look upon to correct, it doth not then visit to keep from destruction. For the Lord, when He cometh to judgment, looketh on the sinner to smite, but He doth not look on him to acknowledge him in bestowing the grace of salvation. He taketh account of sins, and knoweth not the life of those that perish. Hence after that the holy man had averred that he could no more be 'seen by the eye of Man' after the present life, he rightly added at once;

Thine eyes are upon me, and I shall not stand.

xvi.

31. As though he said in plain words; 'Thou, when thou comest in severity to Judgment, both seest not, to save, and yet seest, to smite, in that him, whom Thou lookest not on in the present life with the pitifulness of Thy saving care, hereafter looking on Thou dost extinguish by Thy law of justice. For now the sinner casts away the fear of God, and yet lives, blasphemes and yet prospers, because the pitiful Creator would not in seeing punish him, whom He would rather by waiting for bring to amendment; as it is written, *And winkest at the sins of men for their repentance*. [Wisd. 11, 23] But when the sinner is then looked upon, he 'does not stand,' in that when the strict Judge minutely examines his deserts, the convicted sinner cannot bear up against his torments.

32. Not but that this likewise accords with the voice of the righteous, whose mind is ever anxiously fixed on the coming Judgment. For they have fears for everything that they do, whilst they heedfully consider who are the persons, and before what a Judge they will have to stand. They behold the power of His Mightiness, and they consider what an amount of guilt they are tied and bound with from their own imperfection. They reckon up the evil deeds of their own doing, and multiply over against them the benefits of their Creator. They reflect how rigidly He judges wicked deeds, how minutely He examines good ones; and they foresee without a shadow of doubt that they will be lost, if they be judged apart from pity: for even this very life that we seem to live righteously is sin, if, when He takes account of our lives, the mercy of God does not make allowance for

it in His own eyes. For it is hence written in this very book, *Yea, the stars are not pure in His sight.* [Job 25, 5] For strictly judged in His sight those very persons do also bear spots of defilement, that shine bright in the purity of holiness. Therefore it is well said, *Thine eyes are upon me, and I shall not stand.* As if it were said in plain terms by the voice of the righteous man, 'If I be sifted with an exact scrutiny, I cannot stand up in undergoing judgment, for life cannot bear up against punishment, if the mercilessness of just retribution bears hard upon it.' Now both the sin and the punishment of that same human race is well added in few words, where it is said immediately afterwards,

Ver. 9. As the cloud is consumed and vanisheth away; so he that goeth down to hell shall come up no more.

xvii. 33. For a cloud is suspended in the higher regions, but it is condensed and driven by the wind that it flies, and it is scattered by the heat of the .sun that it vanishes. Thus, thus verily is it with the hearts of men, which by the faculty of reason bestowed upon them dart on high, but driven by the blasts of the evil spirit, they are forced hither and thither by the bad impulses of their desires, but by the searching eye of the Judge above they are melted as if by the heat of the sun, and being once consigned to the regions of woe, never return for the benefit of working. Let the holy man then, in setting forth the elevation, the career, and the eclipse of the human race, exclaim, *As the cloud is consumed and vanisheth away, so he that goeth down to the grave shall come up no more.* As if he spake in plain words, saying, 'In flying on high he is brought to nought, who by exalting himself is advancing to destruction, whom, if sin once force to punishment, mercy never more restores to pardon.' Hence it is yet further added,

He shall return no more to his own house.

xviii. 34. As the house of the body is a bodily habitation, so that becomes to each separate mind 'its own house,' whatsoever thing it is used to inhabit in desire. And so 'there is no more returning to his own house,' because, when once a man is given over to eternal punishments, he is henceforth no more recalled thither, where he had attached himself in love. Moreover by the designation of hell the despair of the sinner may also be set forth, of which it is said by the Psalmist, *In hell, who shall confess to Thee?* [Ps. 6, 5] Whence again it is written, *When the ungodly man cometh into the pit of sinners, he contemneth*. [Prov. 18, 3] Now whosoever yields himself to ungodliness, doth assuredly quit the life of righteousness by a proper death. But when a man after sin is furthermore overwhelmed by a mountain of despair, what else is this but that after death he is buried in the torments of hell? Therefore it is rightly said, *As the cloud is consumed, and vanisheth alway, so he that goeth down to hell shall come up no more*; in that it very often happens, that with the commission of wickedness despair also is united, and the way of returning is henceforth cut off. But the hearts of the despairing are rightly compared to clouds, in that they are at once darkened with the mists of error, and thick with the number of sins; but being consumed, they vanish away, in that being lighted up by the blaze of the final Judgment, they are scattered to the winds. 'The house' too is often understood for the dwelling-place of the heart. Hence it is said to one that was healed, *Go to thine house* [Mark 5, 19]; in that it is most meet that the sinner after pardon should turn back into his own mind, so as not to do aught a second time which may justly subject him to the scourge. But he that has 'gone down to hell,' shall no more 'ascend into his own house,' in that him, that despair overwhelms, it puts forth without from the habitation of the heart. And he cannot return back within, because when he has been ejected without, day by day he falls urged on into worse extremes. For man was made to contemplate his Creator, that he might ever be seeking after His likeness, and dwell in the festival [*solemnitate*] of His love. But being cast without himself by disobedience, he lost the seat of his mind, in that being left all abroad in dark ways, he wandered far from the habitation of the true light. Whence it is further added with propriety,

Neither shall his place know him any more.

xix.

35. For 'the place' of man, but not a local place, the Creator Himself became, Who created him to have his being in Himself, which same place man did then forsake, when on hearing the words of the deceiver, he forsook the love of the Creator. But when Almighty God in the work of redemption showed Himself even by a bodily appearing, He Himself, so to say, following the footsteps of His runagate, came as a place where to keep man whom He had lost. For if the Creator could not in any sense be styled 'a

place,' the Psalmist, in praising God, would never have said, *The children of thy servants shall dwell there* ['there' is not in V. or LXX.]. [Ps. 102, 29] For we never say *there*, except when we mark out a place in a particular manner. But there are very many, who even after they have received the succour of the Redeemer, are precipitated into the darkness of despair, and they perish the more desperately, in proportion as they despise the very offered remedies of mercy. And so it is rightly said concerning him that is damned, *Neither shall his place know him any more.* For he is not known by his Creator in His sorer severity at the Judgment, in the same degree that he is not recalled even by His gifts to the grace of restoration. And hence it is particularly to be observed, that he does not say, 'Nor shall he know his own place any more;' but, *Neither shall his place know him any more.* For whereas that 'knowing' is ascribed not to the person, but to the place, the Creator Himself is manifestly set forth, by the name of 'a place,' Who, when He cometh in strictness for the final account, shall say to all that abide in iniquity, *I know you not whence ye are.* [Luke 13, 25] But the Elect severally, in proportion as they consider that lost sinners are unsparingly cut off, day by day purify themselves with greater diligence from the stains of the iniquity they have done; and when they see others on the brink of ruin grow cold in the love of life, they earnestly inflame themselves to tears of penitence. Hence it is well added,

Ver. 11. Therefore also I will not refrain my mouth.

XX. 36. For that man 'refrains his mouth,' that is ashamed to confess the evil he has done. For to put the mouth to labour is to employ it in the confession of sin done, but the righteous man doth 'not refrain his mouth,' in that forestalling the wrath of the searching Judge, he falls wroth upon himself in words of self-confession. Hence the Psalmist says, *Let us come before His Presence with confession.* [Ps. 95, 2] Hence it is delivered by Solomon, *He that coveteth his sins shall not prosper, but whoso confesseth, and forsaketh them shall have mercy.* [Prov. 28, 13] Hence it is written again, *The just man is first the accuser of himself.* [Ib. 18, 17] But the mouth is never opened in confession, unless at the thought of the searching Judgment the spirit is in straits from fear; and hence it is fitly said afterwards,

I will speak in the anguish of my spirit.

xxi.

37. For 'anguish of the spirit' sets the tongue in motion, so that the voice of confession is levelled against the guilt of evil practice. Moreover it is to be borne in mind, that oftentimes even the reprobate make confession of sins, but are too proud to weep for them. But the Elect prosecute with tears of severe self-condemnation those sins of theirs which they disclose in words of confession. Hence it was well that after blessed Job had pledged himself not to spare his lips, he added directly the anguish of the spirit. As if he avowed plainly, saying, 'The tongue doth in such sort tell of guilt, that the spirit is not ever let go loose amidst other things, free of the sting of sorrow; but in telling my sins, I disclose my wound, and in thinking over my sins for their amendment, I seek the cure of the wound in the medicine of sorrow.' For he that tells indeed the evil deeds he has done, but holds back from lamenting what he has told, he as it were by taking off the covering discovers the wound, but in deadness of mind he applies no remedy to the wound. Therefore it is needful that sorrow alone should wring out the voice of confession, lest the wound, being exposed, but neglected, in proportion as it is henceforth more freely touched through the knowledge of our fellowcreatures, fester so much the worse. Contrariwise the Psalmist had not only disclosed the sore of his heart, but was furthermore applying to it thus laid bare the remedy of sorrow, when he said, *I acknowledge my sin unto Thee, and my iniquity will I think on.* [Ps. 32, 5] For by so 'acknowledging' he discovered the hidden sore, and by thus 'thinking on' it, what else did he, than apply a remedy to the wound? But to the mind that is distressed, and anxiously thinking on its own ills, there arises a strife in behalf of self against self. For when it urges itself to the sorrows of penitence, it rends itself with secret upbraiding. And hence it is justly added afterwards,

I will converse with the bitterness of my spirit.

xxii.

38. For when we are in trouble from dread of God's judgment, whilst we bewail some things done wrong, seeing that by the mere force of our bitterness alone we are stirred up to enter into ourselves more observantly, we find in ourselves other things also to bewail more largely. For it often happens that what

escaped us in our insensibility, is made known to us more exactly in tears. And the troubled mind finds out more surely the ill that it has done and knew not of, and its conflict discovers to it in a true point of view how far it had deviated from the peace which is of truth, in that its guilt, which while secure it thought not of, it finds out in itself when disturbed. For the bitterness of penance gaining ground urgently brings home to the confounded heart the unlawful things it has committed, exhibits the Judge arrayed against them in severity, strikes deep the threats of punishment, smites the soul with consternation, overwhelms it with shame, chides the unlawful motions of the heart, and disturbs the repose of its mischievous self-security, all the good gifts that the Creator has vouchsafed to bestow upon him, all the evil that he himself has done in return for the good things of His hand, are reckoned up, how that he was created by Him in a wonderful way, that he was sustained freely and for nought, that he was endowed with the substance of reason at his creation, that he was called by the grace of his Creator, that he himself even when called refused to follow, that the pitifulness of Him that calleth did not disregard him, not even when deaf and resisting, that he was enlightened with gifts, that of his own free will, even after these gifts received, he blinded himself by wicked deeds, that he was cleared from the wrong doings of his state of blindness by the strokes of fatherly solicitude, that by means of the pains of these strokes he was restored to the joys of saving health by the remedy that mercy applied, that being subject to certain bad practices, though not of the worst sort, he does not cease to sin even in the midst of these strokes; that the grace of God even when slighted did not abandon its sinner. And thus whereas it upbraids with so much keenness the agitated mind at one time by a display of the gifts of God, another time by the reproaches of its own behaviour, the bitterness of spirit has a tongue of its own in the heart of the righteous, which speaks to it the more searchingly, in proportion as it is heard within. And hence it is not at all said, 'I will talk *in* the bitterness of my spirit,' but *I will converse with the bitterness*; in that the force of grief, which taking each sin separately, stimulates the deadened mind to lamentations, as it were shapes words of converse to it, wherein it being chidden might find itself out, and henceforth rise up with better heed to the safe keeping of itself. And so let the righteous man say in his own voice; as bearing a figure of Holy Church, let him say in ours too; *I will converse with the bitterness of my spirit*. As if he spake it in plainer words, saying, 'Within I hold converse with the anguish of my heart against mine own self, and without I hide myself from the lash of the Judge.' Now the mind that is borne hard upon by the pangs of penitence is gathered up close into itself, and severed by strong resolution from all the gratifications of the flesh, it longs to advance to things above, yet it still feels opposition from the corruption of the flesh. And hence it is rightly added immediately,

Ver. 12. Am I a sea or a whale, that thou hast compassed me about with a prison?

xxiii.

39. Man is 'compassed about with a prison,' in that he very often both strives to mount on high by the strides of virtuous attainments, and yet is impeded by the corruption of his fleshly part. Of which same the Psalmist rightly prays that he might be divested, saying, *Bring my soul out of prison, that I may praise Thy Name*. [Ps. 142, 7] But what have we set forth by the designation of 'the sea,' saving the hearts of carnal men tossed with swelling thoughts? and what by the name of 'a whale,' except our old enemy? who when in taking possession of the hearts of the children of this world he makes his way into them, does in a certain sort swim about in their slippery thoughts. But the whale is made fast in prison, in that the evil Spirit, being cast down below, is kept under by the weight of his own punishment, that he should have no power to fly up to the heavenly realms, as Peter testifies, who says, *God spared not the Angels that sinned, but cast them down to hell, and delivered them into chains of darkness to be reserved unto judgment*. [2 Pet. 2, 4] 'The whale' is fast bound in prison, in that he is prevented from tempting the good as much as he desires. The sea too is 'compassed about with a prison,' in that the swelling and raging desires of carnal minds, for the doing of the evil that they long for, are clogged by the straitness of their inability. For they often long to have power over their betters, yet by the Divine ordering, that regulates all things marvellously, they are made to bow beneath them. They desire, being exalted high, to injure the good, yet being brought under their power, they look for consolation from them. For the sake of fulfilling the gratification of the flesh, they covet length of years in the present life, yet they are carried off from it with haste. Concerning such it is well said by the Psalmist, *And He put the waters as it were in a*

skin. [Ps. 78, 13. V. thus] For 'the waters are in a skin' when their loose desires, in that they find not the execution in deed, are kept down under a carnal heart. Therefore the whale and the sea are hemmed in by the close pressure of a prison, in that whether as regards the evil spirit or his followers, in whose minds he gathers himself and sets rolling therein the waves of tumultuous thoughts, the rigour of the Most High confines them, that they should have no power to accomplish the evil things that they are set upon.

40. But holy men, in proportion as they contemplate the Mysteries of heavenly truths with more perfect purity of heart, pant after them with daily increased ardour of affection. They long to be henceforth filled to the full at that fountain head, whence they as yet taste but a little drop with the mouth of contemplation. They long entirely to subdue the promptings of the flesh, no longer to be subject to anything unlawful in the imaginations of the heart springing from the corruption thereof. But because it is written, *For the corruptible body presseth down the soul, and the earthy tabernacle weigheth down the mind that museth upon many things*, [Wisd. 9, 15] therefore they henceforth rise above themselves in purpose of mind, but being still subject to the capricious motions of their imperfect nature, they lament that they are confined in the prison-house of corruption. *Am I a sea or a whale, that Thou dost compass me about with a prison?* As if it were in plain words; 'The sea or the whale, i.e. the wicked and their prime mover, the Evil Spirit, because they desire to have a loose given them for the mere liberty of committing iniquity alone, are justly held bound in the prison of the punishment inflicted on them. But I, that already long for the liberty of Thine eternal state, why am I still enclosed in the prison of mine own corruption?' Not that this is either demanded in pride by the righteous, in that being inflamed with the love of the Truth they desire completely to surmount the narrow compass of their imperfect condition; nor yet that it is unjustly ordered by the Author of the just, in that in delaying the wishes of His Elect, He puts them to pain, and in paining purifies, that they may one day be the better enabled by that delay, for the receiving that they desire. But the Elect, so long as they are kept away from the interior rest, turn back into their own hearts, and being there buried from the tumults of the flesh, as it were seek a retreat of infinite delight. But therein they often feel the stings of temptation, and are subject to the goadings of the flesh, and there they meet with the

hardest toils, where they had looked for perfect rest from toil. Hence the holy man after the prison of his state of corruption that he told of, hastening to return to the tranquil regions of the heart, seeing that he experienced in the interior also all that same strife, to escape which he fled from things without, adds immediately, saying,

Ver. 13, 14. When I say my bed shall comfort me, I shall be eased in speaking with myself on my couch, then Thou scarest me with dreams, and terrifiest me through visions.

xxiv.

41. For in Holy Writ a 'bed,' a 'couch,' or 'litter,' is usually taken for the secret depth of the heart. For it is hence that under the likeness of each separate soul, the Spouse, urged by the piercing darts of holy love, says in the Song of Songs, *By night on my bed I sought him, whom my soul loveth*. [Cant. 3, 1] For 'by night and on the bed is the beloved sought,' in that the appearance of the Invisible Creator, apart from every image of a bodily appearing, is found in the chamber of the heart. And hence 'Truth' says to those same lovers of Him, *The kingdom of God is within you*. [Luke 17, 21] And again, *If I go not away, the Comforter will not come*. [John 16, 7] As if it were in plain words; 'If I do not withdraw My Body from the eyes of your fixed regard, I lead you not by the Comforter, the Spirit, to the perception of the unseen.' Hence it is said by the Psalmist of the just, *The Saints shall be joyful in glory, they shall rejoice upon their beds* [Ps. 149, 5]; in that when they flee the mischiefs from things without, they exult in safety within the recesses of their hearts. But the joy of the heart will then be complete, when the fight of the flesh shall have ceased without. For so long as the flesh allures, because as it were the wall of our house is shaken, even the very bed is disturbed. And hence it is rightly said by that Psalmist, *Thou hast made all his bed in his sickness*. [Ps. 41, 3] For when temptation of the flesh moves us, our infirmity being made to tremble disturbs even the bed of the soul. But what do we understand in this place by 'dreams' and 'visions' saving the representations of the last searching Judgment? What we already have some slight glimpse of through fear, but do not see it as it really is. Thus holy men, as we have said, ever turn back to the secret recesses of the heart, when from the world without, they either meet with successes beyond their wishes, or with adversities beyond their strength, and, wearied with their toils without, they seek as a bed, or litter, the resting-

places of the heart. But whilst by certain pictures of their imagination they see how searching the judgments of God are, they are as it were disturbed in their very repose on their beds by the vision of a dream. For they behold after what sort the strict Judge cometh, Who while with the power of infinite Majesty He lights up the secret recesses of the heart, will bring back every sin before our eyes. They bethink themselves what the shame of that is, to be confounded in the sight of the whole human race, of all the Angels and the Archangels. They reflect what agony is in store after that confounding, when at one and the same time guilt shall prey upon the soul imperishably perishing, and hell fire upon the flesh unfailingly failing. When, then, the mind is shaken by so terrific a conception, what else is this but that a sad dream is presented upon the bed? Therefore let him say, *When I say, My bed shall comfort me, and I shall be eased talking with myself on my couch*; *then Thou scarest me with dreams, and terrifiest me through visions.* As if he confessed openly, saying, 'If fleeing from external things, I turn back into the interior, and am anxious in some sort to rest upon the bed of my heart, there, whilst Thou dost set me to [A.B.D. 'teach me'] the contemplation of Thy severity, Thou makest me to fear horribly by the mere images my foresight raises up.' Now it is well said, *And I shall be eased, talking with myself in my bed*, in that when we return wearied to the silence of our hearts, as it were holding converse on our beds, we handle the secret words of thought within ourselves. But this very converse of ours is turned into dread, in that thereby there is more forcibly presented to us in imagination the view, which holds out the terrors of the Judge.

42. But lest anyone should be at pains to make out these words after the literal sense, it is of great importance to find out in how many ways the mind is affected by images from dreams. For sometimes dreams are engendered of fulness or emptiness of the belly, sometimes of illusion, sometimes of illusion and thought combined, sometimes of revelation, while sometimes they are engendered of imagination, thought, and revelation together. Now the two which we have named first, we all know by experience, while the four subjoined we find in the pages of Holy Writ. For except dreams were very frequently caused to come in illusion by our secret enemy, the Wise Man would never have pointed this out by *Literal*

saying, *For dreams and vain illusions have deceived many,* [Ecclus. 34, 7] or indeed, *Nor shall ye use enchantments, nor observe dreams.* [Lev. 19, 26. Vulg.] By which words it is shown us how great an abomination they are, in that they are joined with 'auguries.' Again, excepting they sometimes came of thought and illusion together, Solomon would never have said, *For a dream cometh through the multitude of business.* [Eccl. 5, 3] And unless dreams sometimes had their origin in a mystery of a revelation, Joseph would never have seen himself in a dream appointed to be advanced above his brethren, nor would the espoused of Mary have been warned by the Angel in a dream to take the Child and to fly into Egypt. Again, unless dreams sometimes proceeded from thought and revelation together, the Prophet Daniel, in making out the vision of Nebuchadnezzar, would never have set out with thought as the root; *As for thee, O king, thy thoughts came into thy mind upon thy bed, what should come to pass hereafter, and He That revealeth secrets maketh known to thee what shall come to pass.* [Dan. 2, 29] And soon afterwards, *Thou, O king, sawest and beheld a great image. This great image, that was great, and its stature lofty, stood before thee, &c.* [ver. 31] Thus while Daniel declares in awful terms the dream about to be fulfilled, and shows in what thoughts it had its rise, it is made plain and manifest that the thing very frequently proceeds from thought and revelation combined.

43. Now it is clear, that since dreams shift about in such a variety of cases they ought to be the less easily believed, in proportion as it less easily appears from what influencing cause they spring. For it often happens that to those, whom the Evil Spirit cuts off when awake through the love of the present life, he promises the successes of fortune even whilst they sleep, and those, whom he sees to be in dread of misfortunes, he threatens with them the more cruelly by the representations of dreams, that he may work upon the incautious soul by a different kind of influence, and either by elevating it with hope or sinking it with dread, may disturb its balance. Often too he sets himself to work upon the souls of the Saints themselves by dreams, that at least for a passing moment they may be thrown off the line of steady thought, though by their own act they straightway shake the mind clear of the delusive phantasy. And our designing foe, in proportion as he is utterly unable to get the better of them when awake, makes the deadlier assault upon them asleep. Whom yet the dispensation of the Highest in loving-kindness alone allows to

do so in his malevolence, lest in the souls of the Elect their mere sleep, though nothing else, should go without the meed of suffering. Therefore it is well spoken to Him that ruleth over all, *When I say, my bed shall comfort me, I shall be eased talking with myself on my couch; then Thou scarest me with dreams, and terrifiest me through visions.* Surely in that God ordereth all things wonderfully, even He Himself doth that thing, which the Evil Spirit seeks to do unjustly, whilst He letteth it not be done saving justly. Now forasmuch as the life of the righteous is at once assaulted on watch by temptation, and harassed in dreaming by illusion; undergoes without the mischiefs of its corruption, and within painfully carries in itself unlawful thoughts; what may it do in order to pluck the foot of the heart out of the mazes of such numberless entanglements? Yea, thou blessed man, with what dismay and trouble thou art every way compassed about we have learnt; now let us be informed, what plan thou dost devise to encounter the same. It goes on,

Ver. 15. So that my soul chooseth hanging and my bones death.

XXV. 44. What is then represented by the soul but the bent of the soul, and by the bones, the strength of the flesh? Now everything that is hung is assuredly lifted up from things beneath; therefore 'the soul chooseth hanging that the bones may die,' in that whilst the mind's intent lifts itself on high, it extinguishes all the strength of the exterior life in itself. For the Saints know it for a most certain truth, that they can never enjoy rest in the present life, and so they 'choose hanging,' in that quitting earthly objects of desire, they raise the mind on high. But whilst hung on high they inflict death on their bones, in that for love of the land above, having their loins girt in press and pursuit after virtuous attainments, all wherein they were afore time strong in the world, they load with the chain of self-abasement. It is well to mark how Paul had his soul suspended aloft, who said, *Nevertheless I live: yet not I, but Christ liveth in me.* [Gal. 2, 20] And again; *Having a desire to depart and to be with Christ.* [Phil. 1, 23] And, *For to me to live is Christ, and to die is gain.* [ver. 21] Who recalling to mind the achievements of earthly strength, reckoned up as it were so many bones in himself, saying, *An Hebrew, of the Hebrews, as touching the Law a Pharisee; concerning zeal, persecuting the Church of God.* [Phil. 3, 5. 6.] But by that 'hanging' of his soul, how that he does to death these bones in him- *Moral* self, he immediately declares, in that he adds, *But what things were gain to me, these I counted loss for Christ*. [ver. 7] Which same bones he implies were still more mercilessly dealt with to destruction in himself, when he adds, *For whom I have made all things loss, and do count them but dung*. [ver. 8] But in what manner he hung without life and his bones all dead, he shows, in that he adds in that place, saying, *That I may win Christ, and be found in Him, not having mine own righteousness, which is of the law, but that which is through the faith of Jesus Christ*. [ver. 9] But whereas by bringing together his declarations we have avouched Paul to have been suspended aloft dead to the world, let us now show whether blessed Job, being filled with the same Spirit, eschews the concupiscence of the exterior life. It goes on,

Ver. 16. I have given over hope, I will not live any longer.

xxvi.

45. There be some of the righteous, who so entertain the desire of heavenly things, that, notwithstanding this, they are not broken off from the hope of things earthly. The inheritance bestowed on them by God they keep for the supply of necessities, the honours awarded them on a temporal footing they retain; they do not covet the things of others, they make a lawful use of their own. Yet these are strangers to those same things that they have, in that they are not bound in affection to those very goods which they keep in their possession. And there are some of the righteous, who bracing themselves up to lay hold of the very height of perfection, whilst they aim at higher objects within, abandon all things without, who bare themselves of the goods possessed by them, strip themselves of the pride of honours, who by continuance in a grateful sorrow affect their hearts with longing for the things of the interior, refuse to receive consolation from those that are exterior, who whilst in spirit they drink of the inward joys, wholly extinguish in themselves the life of corporeal enjoyment. For it is said by Paul to such as these, *For ye are dead, and your life it hid with Christ in God*. [Col. 3, 3] The Psalmist spoke in their voice, when he said, *My soul longeth, yea, even fainteth for the courts of the Lord*. [Ps. 84, 2] For they 'long' but do not 'faint,' who are already imbued indeed with heavenly desires, but notwithstanding are still not tired of the enjoyments of earthly objects. But he 'longeth, yea, even fainteth, for the courts of the Lord,' who whilst he desires the eternal world, doth not hold on in the love of the temporal. Hence the Psalmist says

again, *My soul fainteth for Thy salvation.* [Ps. 119, 81] Hence 'Truth' bids us by His own lips, saying, *If any man will come after Me, let him deny himself.* [Luke 9, 23] And again; *Whosoever he be of you that forsaketh not all that he hath, he cannot he My disciple.* [Luke 14, 33] Thus the holy man, his soul parted from earthly objects of desire, sets himself in the number of such as those, when he says, *I have given over hope, I will not live any longer.* Since for a righteous man 'to give over hope' is to quit the good things of the present life, in making choice of eternity, and to put no trust in temporal possessions. And whilst doing this, he declares that he 'will not live any longer,' in that by a quickening death he is daily killing himself to the life of passion. For be it far from us to think that the holy man should despair of the bountifulness of God's mercy, that he should withdraw the step of the heart from advancing in the interior way, that forsaking the love of the Creator he should as it were stop on the road lacking a guide, and pierced with the sword of rifling despair, be brought to ruin. But lest we seem violently to wrest his sayings according to the caprice of our own view, we ought to form our estimate of what is promised by that which follows after. For in what sense he said this, he does himself immediately point out, in that he adds,

Spare me, O Lord, for my days are nothing.

xxvii. 46. For neither do the two words agree together, *I have given over hope*, and, *spare me.* For he that 'gives over hope,' no longer begs to be spared; and he who is still anxious to be spared, is surely far from 'giving over hope.' It is on one sort of grounds then that he 'gives over hope,' and on another that the holy man prays to be spared; in that whilst he abandons the good things of this transitory life in 'giving over the hope' thereof, he rises more vigorous in hope for the securing of those that shall endure. So that in 'giving over hope,' he is the more effectually brought to the hope of pardon, who seeks the things to come so much the more determinately, in proportion as he more thoroughly forsakes those of the present time in giving up hope. And we are to take notice, that when teaching us the strength of his heart, he delivered indeed but one sentiment about himself, but in teaching it to us he has repeated it a third time. For what he had said above, *My soul chooseth hanging*, it was in repeating this, that he added the words, *I have given over hope*, and in aiming at the blessings of eternity, and putting behind those of time, he last of all brought in this, *Spare me*. And what he said above, *And my bones death*, this same it was that he added, *I will not live longer*, and this he delivered to end with, *for my days are nothing*. But he lightly considers that his 'days are nothing,' because as we have often remarked already a little above, holy men, the more thoroughly they are acquainted with things above, in the same proportion they look down upon the things of earth from a loftier height. And therefore they see that the days of the present life are 'nothing,' because they have the eyes of their illumined soul fixed in the contemplation of eternity. And when they return thence to themselves, what do they find themselves to be but dust? And being conscious of their frailty, they are in dread of being judged with severity; and when they regard the force of that vast Energy, they tremble to have it put to the test what they are. And hence it is further added with propriety,

Ver. 17. What is man, that Thou shouldest magnify him? and that Thou shouldest set Thine heart upon him?

Literal **xxviii.**

47. God magnifieth man, in that He enriches him with the bountiful gift of reason, visits him with the inspiration of grace, exalts him with the greatness of imparted virtue; and whereas he is nothing in himself, yet through the bounty of His lovingkindness He vouchsafes to him to be a partaker of the knowledge of Himself. And the Lord 'setteth His heart upon man' so magnified, in that after His gifts He brings forth judgment, weighs merits with exactness, rigidly tries the weights of life, and exacts punishment from him afterwards the more strictly, in proportion as He prevents him here more bounteously by the benefit bestowed. So then let the holy man view the immensity of the Supreme Majesty, and recall the eye of reflection to his own frailty. Let him see that flesh cannot comprehend that which Truth through the Spirit teaches concerning Himself. Let him see that man's spirit, even when it is lifted up, is not able to bear the Judgment, which God holds over it, on a trial of strict recompensing, and let him say, *What is man, that Thou shouldest magnify him? and that Thou shouldest set Thine heart upon him?* As though he cried out in plain words, saying, 'Man is magnified with a spiritual gift, but yet he is flesh, and after Thy gifts, Thou takest strict account of his ways; yet if he be judged with pity set aside, the weight that rests over him from Thine

exactness, not even the spirit that is raised to righteousness has strength to sustain, seeing that though Thy gifts draw him out beyond his own compass, yet at the inquest of Thy strict scrutiny his own frailty contracts him.' And hence it is fitly added still further;

Ver. 18. And that Thou shouldest visit him in the dawn, and try him suddenly?

xxix. 48. Which is there of us that does not know that it is called the 'dawn,' when the night season is now changing into the brightness [*claritatem*] of light? so we too are closed in by the darkness of night, when we are dimmed by the practice of wickedness; but the night is turned into light, when the darkness of our erring state is illuminated by knowledge of the Truth. The night is turned into light, when the splendour of righteousness lights up our hearts, which the blindness of sin lay heavy upon. This dawn Paul saw rise in the minds of the disciples, when he said, *The night is far spent, the day is at hand.* [Rom. 13, 12] And so the Lord 'visits us at the dawn,' in that He illumines the darkness of our state of error with the light of the knowledge of Himself, uplifts us with the gift of contemplation, exalts us to the stronghold of virtue. But it is to be observed, that after God 'visits him at the dawn,' He 'tries man suddenly,' in that both in drawing near He advances our souls to virtuous heights, and in withdrawing Himself He suffers them to be assaulted with temptation. For if after the bestowal of the gifts of virtue, she is never moved by any assault of temptation, the soul boasts that she has these of herself. Therefore that she may at one and the same time enjoy the gifts of a firm state, and humbly acknowledge her own state of infirmity, by the visitation of grace she is lifted up on high, and by the withdrawal of the same, it is proved what she is in herself. Which is well intimated to us in the history of the book of sacred reading, wherein Solomon is recorded both to have received wisdom from on high, and yet directly after that very wisdom was received, to have been assailed by the disputing of the harlots. [1 Kings 3, 16, &c.] For immediately after he had received the grace of that great enlightenment, he was exposed to the strife of base women; for that oftentimes when the visiting of the interior bounty illuminates our mind with virtues vouchsafed it, even filthy imaginations forthwith disorder it, that the soul, which being lifted up exults in the immensity of the gift, being at the same time struck by temptation, may discover what she is. So Elijah both being visited at the dawn, opened the doors of heaven by a word, and yet being 'tried suddenly,' fleeing helpless through the desert, was in dread of a single woman. [1 Kings 19, 3] Thus Paul is carried to the third heaven, and penetrating into the secrets of Paradise, he is held in contemplation; and yet when he returns to himself, travails against the assaults of the flesh, and is subject to another law in his members, by whose rebellion within him he grieves to see the law of the Spirit hard bestead. [2 Cor. 12, 2] Therefore God 'visits at the dawn,' but, after this visiting, He 'tries suddenly,' in that He both lifts up by the gift vouchsafed, and by the same being for a while withdrawn, shows unaided [*ipsum*] man to himself. Which doubtless we are so long subject to, until the time, when the pollution of sin being clean taken away, we be renewed to the substance of promised incorruption. Hence it is fitly added yet further,

Ver. 19. How long wilt Thou not depart from me, nor let me alone until I swallow down my spittle.

XXX.

49. The spittle runs into the mouth from the head, but from the mouth it is carried into the belly by being swallowed. And what is our head saving the Deity, through Whom we derive the original of our being, so as to be 'creature,' as Paul bears witness, who declares, *The head of every man is Christ, and the head of Christ is God*; and what is our belly, saving the mind, which, whilst it takes its food, i.e. heavenly perception, being invigorated, doth surely rule the members of the several actions. For except Holy Writ did sometimes describe the mind by the name of 'the belly,' Solomon surely would never have said, *The spirit of man is the candle of the Lord, searching all the inward parts of the belly*; [Prov. 20, 27] forasmuch as whilst the grace of heavenly visitation illumines us, it discloses even all the depths of the mind that are hidden from our sight. What then is meant by the term 'spittle,' but the savour of interior contemplation, which runs down from the head to the mouth, in that issuing from the brightness of the Creator [*de claritate conditoris*], whilst we are still set in this life, it but just touches us with a taste of revelation. And hence the Redeemer at His coming mixed the spittle with clay, and restored the eyes of him that was born blind, [John 9, 6] in that heavenly grace enlightens the carnal bent of our hearts, by a mixture of the contemplation of Itself, and from his original

blindness restores man anew to perception. For whereas nature henceforth brought him forth in this place of exile, since he was banished from all the joys of Paradise, man was produced from his birth, as it were, without eyes. But, as the holy man teaches, this spittle runs into the mouth indeed, but that it should not reach into the belly, it is not swallowed down, in that the contemplation of the Divine Being grazes the sense, but does not perfectly refresh the mind, because the soul is unable perfectly to behold what as yet, the mist of corruption impeding the view, it sees by a hasty glimpse.

50. For see how the soul of the Elect already bears down all earthly desires beneath itself, already mounts above all the objects that it sees are of a nature to pass away, is already lifted up from the enjoyment of external delights, and closely searches what are the invisible good things, and in doing the same is carried away into the sweetness of heavenly contemplation; already very often it sees something of the interior world as it were through the mist, and with burning desire strives to the utmost to be admitted to the spiritual ministries of the Angels, feeds on the taste of the Light Incomprehensible, and being carried out of self disdains to sink back again into self; for forasmuch as the body, which is in the way to corruption, still weighs down the soul, it has not power to attach itself to the Light for long, which it sees in a momentary glimpse. For the mere infirmity of the flesh by itself drags down the soul, as it mounts above itself, and brings it down, as it aspires, to provide for low cares and wants. And so spittle flowing from the head touches the mouth, but never reaches to the belly; in that our understanding indeed is henceforth watered with the dews of heavenly contemplation, but the soul is not at all fully satisfied. For in the mouth is the taste, but fulness in the belly; and so we cannot 'swallow down our spittle,' in that we are not suffered to fill ourselves with the excellency of heavenly brightness [*claritatis*], which we taste as yet but in a sip. But whereas this very same that we are already in some slight degree made acquainted with above us, comes from the pitifulness of One that spareth, while that we cannot as yet obtain a perfect perception of it is of the punishment of the old curse still, it is rightly said now, *How long dost Thou not spare me, nor let me alone, till I swallow down my spittle?* As if it were in plain words; 'Then Thou dost perfectly spare man, when Thou admittest Him to the perfect measure of the contemplation of Thee; that being transported he may behold

Thy brightness [*claritatem*] in the interior, and no corruption of his flesh without should hold him back. Then 'thou lettest me alone till I swallow down my spittle, when Thou replenishest me with the savour of Thy brightness [*claritatis*] even to the very overflow of fulness, that I should never henceforth go a hungered, with but a taste of the mouth, through lack of food, but be stedfastly stayed in Thee, the belly of my interior being watered.' But whoso would obtain the good that he desires must acknowledge the evil that he has done. The account goes on.

Ver.20. I have sinned; what shall I do unto Thee, O Thou Preserver of men?

xxxi.

51. Observe how he confesses the ill that he has done, but the good that he should present to God in compensation, he no where can find, in that all virtue whatever of human practice is without power to wash out the guilt of sin, except His mercifulness in sparing foster it, and not His justice in judging press hard upon it. Whence it is well said by the Psalmist, *Because Thy mercy is better than the life*; [Ps. 63, 3] in that howsoever innocent it may seem to be, yet with the strict Judge our life doth not set us free, if the lovingkindness of His mercy loose not to it the debt of its guilt. Or indeed when it is said, *What shall I do unto Thee?* it is plainly, shown us that those very good things, which we are commanded to practise, are not a gain to Him that imposes the command, but to ourselves. Whence it is said again by the Psalmist, *My goodness extendeth not unto Thee*. [Ps. 16, 2] Now the abjectness of our destitution is set forth, when God is called the 'Preserver of men,' in that if His preserving hand defend us not in the face of the snares of the secret adversary, the eye of our heedfulness sleeps on watch, as the Psalmist again bears record, who says, *Except the Lord keep the city, the watchman waketh but in vain*. [Ps. 127, 1] For it is through ourselves, that we have been brought to the ground, but to rise again by our own strength is beyond our ability. The fault of our own will laid us low once, but the punishment of our fault sinks us worse day by day. We strive by the efforts of our earnest endeavours, to lift ourselves to the uprightness we have lost, but we are kept down by the weight of our just dues. And hence it is fitly added, *Why hast Thou set me opposite to Thee, so that I am a burthen to myself?*

THE SECOND PART.

xxxii. 52. Then did God 'set man opposite to Him,' when man forsook God by sinning. For being taken captive by the persuasions of the Serpent, he became the enemy of Him, Whose precepts he despised. But the righteous Creator 'set man opposite to Himself,' in that He accounted him an enemy by pride. And this very oppositeness of sin is itself made a weight of punishment to man, that he being wrongly free, might serve his own corruption, who while serving rightly exulted in the freedom of incorruption. For quitting the healthful stronghold of humility, he was brought by growing proud to the yoke of infirmity, and in erecting only bowed down the neck of the heart, in that he who refused to submit to the behests of God, prostrated himself beneath his own necessities; which we shall show the better, if we set forth those burthens, first of the flesh and afterwards of the spirit, which he is made subject to after being cast down to the ground.

53. For to say nothing of this, that he is liable to pains, that he gasps with fever; the very state of our body, which is called health, is straitened by its own sickness. For it wastes with idleness, it faints with work; failing with not eating, it is refreshed by food so as to hold up; going heavily with sustenance, it is relieved by abstinence, so as to be vigorous; it is bathed in water, not to be dry; it is wiped with towels, not by that very bathing to be too wet; it is enlivened by labour, that it may not be dulled by repose; it is refreshed by repose, that it faint not under the exertion of labour; worn with watching, it is recruited by sleep; oppressed with sleep, it is roused to activity by watching, lest it be worse wearied by its own rest; it is covered with clothing, lest it be pierced by the hardship of cold; fainting under the heat it sought, it is invigorated by the blowing of the air. And whereas it meets with annoyances from the very quarter whence it sought to shelter itself from annoyances, being badly wounded, so to say, it sickens by its own cure. Therefore fevers set aside and pains not in action, our very breath itself is sickness, whereunto there is never wanting the necessity of administering a cure. Since whatever the comforts we seek out for occasion of life, we as it were meet with so many medicines of our sickness; but the very medicine itself too is turned into a sore, in that attaching ourselves a little too long to the remedy we sought, we are more brought down in that which we prudently provide for our refreshment. Thus was presumption to be amended, thus was pride to be

laid low. For whereas we once took to us a high spirit, so every day we carry the mud that runneth down.

54. Our very mind too itself being banished from the secure delight of interior secresy, is now beguiled by hope, now tormented by fear; one while cast down by grief, at another time made light by a false mirth; it obstinately attaches itself to transitory objects, and is continually afflicted by the loss of them, in that it is also continually undergoing change by a course that carries it away; and being made subject to things changeable, it is also made to be at odds with its own self. For seeking what it has not got, it anxiously obtains it, and so soon as it has begun to possess the same, is sick of having obtained what it sought after. Oftentimes it loves what it once despised, and despises what, it used to love. It learns by dint of pains what are the things of eternity, but it forgets them in a moment, if it cease to take pains. It takes a long time to seek, that it may find, but a little concerning the things above, but speedily falling, back into its wonted ways, not even for a little space does it hold on in the things it has found. Desiring to be instructed, with difficulty it gets the better of its ignorance, and being so instructed it has a harder contest against the pride of knowledge; with difficulty it subjects to itself the usurping power of its fleshly part, yet it is still subject to the images of sin within, the works whereof it has already in vanquishing bound down without. It raises itself in quest of its Creator, but being thrown back, it is bewildered by the beguiling mist of corporeal attachments. It desires to survey itself, and to see how being incorporeal it bears rule over the body, and it cannot. It asks in a wonderful way what it is unable to answer itself, and remaining ignorant is at a loss under that, which it inquires with a wise purpose. Viewing itself as large and scanty at once, it knows nothing how to form a true estimate of itself, in that if it were not large it would not be seeking matters of so deep enquiry, and again if it were not little, it would at least find that which it asks of itself.

55. Well therefore is it said, *Thou hast set me opposite to Thee, so that I am a burthen to myself*, in that whilst man being banished is both subject to annoyances in the flesh, and to perplexities in the mind, surely he carries about his own self as a grievous burthen. On every side he is beset with sicknesses, on every side he is hard bestead with infirmities, that he who, having abandoned God, thought to suffice to himself for his repose, might find nought in himself but a turmoil

of disquietude, and might try to fly from himself so found, but having set his Creator at nought, might not have where to fly. The burthens of which state of infirmity that wise man rightly regarding, exclaims, *An heavy yoke is upon the Sons of Adam, from the day that they go out of their mother's womb, till the day that they return to the mother of all things*. [Ecclus. 40, 1] But blessed Job regarding these things, and seeking with groans wherefore they were so ordered, does not reproach justice, but interrogates mercy; that in asking he may himself in self-abasement deal a blow to that, which the Divine pity might in sparing alter. As if he said in plain words; 'Wherefore dost Thou despise man set as in opposition to Thee, Who, I am assured, wouldest not that even he should perish whom Thou art thought to despise?' Whence he proceeds in a right way both to express humility in confession, and to subjoin the voice of free inquiry in the words,

Ver. 21. And why dost Thou not take away my transgression, and remove mine iniquity?

xxxiii. 56. By which same words, what else is intimated but the desire of the expected Mediator, concerning Whom John says, *Behold the Lamb of God, Which taketh away the sin of the world*. [John 1, 29] Or rather sin is then completely taken away from mankind, when our corruption is changed in the glory of incorruption. For we can never be free from sin so long as we are held fast in a body of mortality, and therefore he longs for the grace of the Redeemer, i.e. for the wholeness [*soliditatem*] of the Resurrection, who is looking to have his iniquity entirely 'taken away.' Hence immediately after adding both the punishment which was his due by birth, and the Judgment which he dreads in consequence of his own doings, he proceeds,

For now shall I sleep in the dust, and if Thou shalt seek me in the morning, I shall not abide.

xxxiv. 57. It was said to the first man on his sinning, *Dust thou art, and unto dust shalt thou return*. [Gen. 3, 19] Now by the 'morning,' is meant that manifestation of souls, which, when the thoughts are laid bare at the coming of the Judge, is as it were brought to light after the darkness of night. Of which same morning, it is said by the Psalmist, *In the morning I shall stand before Thee* *and shall see.* [Ps. 5, 3. Vulg.] Now God's 'seeking' is His searching man with a minute inquest, and, in searching, judging him with rigorous strictness. Therefore let blessed Job, surveying the miseries of man's fallen condition, see how that he is both already closely pressed by a present punishment, and in yet worse plight as concerns the future, and let him say, *For now shall I sleep in the dust, and if Thou shalt seek me in the morning, I shall not abide.* As if he openly lamented, saying, 'In the present life indeed I already undergo the death of the flesh, and yet still further from the Judgment to come I dread a worse death, even the doom of Thy severity. I suffer destruction for sin, yet further on coming to Judgment I dread my sins being brought up again even after my dissolution. Therefore looking at the external death, let him say, *For now shall I sleep in the dust*, and dreading the interior let him add, *And if Thou shalt seek me in the morning, I shall not abide.* For however strong in righteousness, even the very Elect by no means suffice to themselves for innocency, if they be strictly examined in Judgment. But they find it now for an alleviation of their withdrawal hence, that they know in their humility that they never can suffice. Therefore they shelter themselves under the covering of humility from the sword of such a grievous visitation, and in proportion as awaiting the terribleness of the Judge to come, they tremble with continual alarm, so there is an unceasing progress in their becoming better prepared. It goes on,

C. viii. 1, 2. Then answered Bildad, the Shuhite, and said, How long wilt thou speak these things? and how long shall the breath [V. so.] *of the words of thy mouth be multiplied?*

XXXV.

58. To the unrighteous the words of the righteous are ever grievous, and such as they hear spoken for edification, they bear as a burthen put upon them. As Bildad, the Shuhite, plainly indicates in his own case, when he says, *How long wilt thou speak these things?* For he that says *how long*, shows that he cannot any longer bear words of edification. But whereas unfair men are too proud to be set right, they find fault with the things that are spoken well; and hence he immediately adds, *And how long shall the breath of the words of thy mouth be multiplied?* When multiplicity is blamed in the speech, surely it is thereby denied that there is weight of meaning in the sense. For the power of speakers on the highest matters is distinguished by a fourfold quality. For there be some whom fulness

in speaking and thinking combined give width and compass, and there be some whom meagreness both of thought and utterance reduces to small dimensions; and there are some who are furnished with ability in speaking, but not with penetration in thinking; and there are some, who have penetration of thought to support them, but from barrenness of expression are made silent. For we discover the same in man that we often see in things without sense. Thus it very often happens that both an abundant supply of water is obtained from the deep of the earth, and that it is conveyed by ample channels upon the surface; and very often a scanty quantity lies concealed in the heart of the earth, and hardly finding a crevice to issue by, strains itself out in scanty dimensions without. Very often too the smallest quantity springs up out of reach of the eye, and when it finds an outlet gaping wide whereby it may issue forth from an ample opening, it swells out in a thin stream, and the big channels open themselves wide, but there is not aught for them to pour forth; and very often an ample store springs up out of sight, but being confined by narrow channels, it dribbles out in the smallest quantities. Just so in one sort the ample mouth delivers what the copious fountain of the wit supplies; in another, neither does thought furnish sense, nor the tongue pour it forth. In others, the mouth indeed is wide to speak, but for the giving out that which thought has provided for it, the tongue gets nothing at all; whilst in others, a full fountain of thought abounds in the heart, but a disproportionate tongue, like a scanty channel, confines it. In which same four sorts of speaking, the third only is obnoxious to blame, which appropriates to itself by words that, to the level whereof it doth not rise in wit. For the first is worthy of praise, in that it is powerful and strong in both particulars. The second deserves commiseration, which in its littleness lacks both. The fourth calls for aid, in that it has not power to embody what it thinks. But the third is worthy to be despised and ought to be restrained, in that while it lifts itself high in speech it is grovelling in sense; and like limbs swoln with inflation, it goes forth to the ears of the hearers big but void. And it is this which Bildad hurls as an accusation against blessed Job, saying, *And how long shall the words of the breath of thy mouth be multiplied?* For he that attributes multiplicity of words to the mouth, doubtless finds fault with the barrenness of the heart. As if he said in plain words, 'Thou art raised by abundance of breath in word of mouth, but thou art stinted by scantiness of sense.' But when bad men blame right things, lest they should themselves appear not to know what is righteous, the good things that are known of all men, and which they have learnt by hearsay, they deliver as unknown. And hence Bildad adds directly,

Ver. 3. Doth God pervert judgment? Or doth the Almighty pervert justice?

xxxvi.

59. These things blessed Job had neither in speaking denied, nor yet was ignorant of them in holding his tongue. But all bold persons, as we have said, speak with big words even well known truths, that in telling of them they may appear to be learned. They scorn to hold their peace in a spirit of modesty, lest they should be thought to be silent from ignorance. But it is to be known that they then extol the rectitude of God's justice, when security from ill uplifts themselves in joy, while blows are dealt to other men; when they see themselves enjoying prosperity in their affairs, and others harassed with adversity. For whilst they do wickedly, and yet believe themselves righteous, the benefit of prosperity attending them, they imagine to be due to their own merits; and they infer that God does not visit unjustly, in proportion as upon themselves, as being righteous, no cloud of misfortune falls. But if the power of correction from above touch their life but in the least degree, being struck they directly break loose against the policy of the Divine inquest, which a little while before, unharmed, they made much of in expressing admiration of it, and they deny that judgment to be just, which is at odds with their own ways; they canvass the equity of God's dealings, they fly out in words of contradiction, and being chastened because they have done wrong, they do worse. Hence it is well spoken by the Psalmist against the confession of the sinner, *He will confess to Thee, when Thou doest well to him.* [Ps. 49, 18] For the voice of confession is disregarded, when it is shaped by the joyfulness of prosperity. But that confession alone possesses merit of much weight, which the force of pain has no power to part from the truth of the rule of right, and which adversity, the test of the heart, sharpens out even to the sentence of the lips. Therefore it is no wonder that Bildad commends the justice of God, in that he experiences no hurt therefrom.

Allegorical

60. Now whereas we have said that the friends of

blessed Job bear the likeness of heretics, it is well for us to point out briefly, how the words of Bildad accord with the wheedling ways of heretics. For whilst in their own idea they see Holy Church corrected with temporal visitations, they swell the bolder in the bigness of their perverted preaching, and putting forward the righteousness of the Divine probation, they maintain that they prosper by virtue of their merits; but they avouch that she is rewarded with deserved chastisements, and thereupon without delay they seek by beguiling words a way to steal upon her, in the midst of her sorrows, and they strike a blow at the lives of some, by making the deaths of others a reproach, as if those were now visited with deserved death, who refused to hold worthy opinions concerning God. Hence Bildad the Shuhite, after he pleaded the justice of God, thereupon adds,

Ver. 4–6. Even if thy children have sinned against Him, and He have left them in the hand of their transgression; yet if thou wilt seek to God at dawn, and make thy supplication to the Almighty; if thou wilt walk pure and upright; surely now He will awake for thee, and make the habitation of thy righteousness at peace.

xxxvii. 61. As if the preachers of falsities were to say to afflicted Catholics, 'Provide for your lives, and learn what wrong things ye maintain from the condemnation of those that are dead from among you. For except your misbelief were displeasing to the Creator of all things, He would never take from you such numbers by destruction let loose to rage against them.' For he says, *If thy children have sinned against Him, and He have left them in the hand of their transgression.* As though he said in plain speech, 'They are left in the hand of their own wickedness, that refused to follow the life of our right rule.' Yet if thou wilt arise to God at dawn, and make thy supplication to the Almighty. For inasmuch as heretics think that the light of truth rests with themselves, they bid and summon Holy Church, as being in the night of error, to come to the dawning of the truth, that in the knowledge of God it may be led to rise, as in the dawning light, and by the prayer of penitence wash off past misdeeds. *If thou wilt walk pure and upright*; that is to say, pure in thought, upright in practice. Surely now He will awake for thee. As if it were in plain words, 'that He, Who now forbears to put forth the power of His protecting hand to thy tribulations, is as if asleep to the succouring of one going wrong.' And make the habitation of thy righteousness at peace, i.e. 'does away with the crosses of the present life, and vouchsafes without delay security in repose.' For because men that are bad reckon temporal enjoyment as a special blessing of Divine recompensing, what they themselves go after with solicitous concern, they promise to others as something great. Hence it very often happens that they either pledge themselves to regain them when lost, or draw on the minds of their hearers after still greater rewards of this world. Which Bildad openly expresses, when he adds upon that,

Ver. 7. Insomuch that though thy beginning was small, yet thy latter end shall greatly increase.

xxxviii.

62. But if it is counsel within the soul that he calls 'the habitation of righteousness,' the leaders of false opinions promise afflicted Catholics 'the habitation of their righteousness at peace,' in that if they draw them to their own views, then indeed they hold their peace from opposition. For those who have let themselves be drawn into that which is wrong, are the more lulled to rest in temporal peace, in proportion as they are parted the wider from eternal peace. Moreover they promise that the riches of understanding shall be increased to all that follow them. And hence it is added, *Insomuch that though thy beginning was small, yet thy latter end shalt greatly increase*. Then because they do not easily obtain credit to their words, in that their life is often shown to be worthy of contempt, they put forward the opinions of the Fathers of old, and turn the right line they take into a proof of their own erring way. Hence it is added, .

Ver. 8. For inquire, I pray thee, of the former age, and diligently search into the memory of the fathers.

xxxix.

63. They give us notice that 'the former generation' and 'the memory of the fathers' are not seen but 'searched,' because they will not have that to be seen therein, which lies open before the eyes of all men. But sometimes, like good men, they give some instruction of a moral kind, and show how the present may be gathered from the past; and from the things which are even now withdrawn from our eyes by passing away, they show how little there is in the things that are seen before our eyes. Whence it is yet further added,

Ver. 9. For we are but of yesterday, and know nothing, because our days upon earth are but a shadow.

xl. 64. And so the generation of old is set before us to be inquired of, that the period of the present life may be shown to pass away like a shadow; in this way, that if we recall to mind the things that have been and are now over, we clearly see how swiftly that also will be gone which we have in our hands. But it often happens that heretics go along with us in extolling the same fathers whom we venerate; but their sense being perverted, they strike at us by those very commendations of them. Hence it is yet further added,

Ver. 10. Shall not they teach thee, and tell thee, and utter words out of their heart?

xli. 65. We must mark what he had said before, *And the inspiration* ['spiritus,' as before] *of the words of thy mouth is multiplied.* But now when the fathers are brought to mind, he says, *They shall utter words out of their heart.* As though heretics abhorring the life of Holy Church said, 'Thou hast abundance of inspiration in thy mouth, in thy heart thou hast none of it. But they are to be heard in opposition, who, in uttering words from the heart, have taught the right thing by living like it.' But oftentimes the wicked, whereas the evil of their own crookedness is unknown to them, boldly pull in pieces the uprightness of others, and while they usurp to themselves authority of pronouncing rebukes against good men, they either deliver those good sentiments, which they have imbibed not by seeing but by hearing them, or else with lying lips lay that evil to the charge of others, which they are themselves guilty of committing. But when they give utterance to good thoughts, which they scorn to observe, it is to be remarked that very frequently Truth so speaks by the lips of her adversaries, that in putting their tongue in motion it smites their life. So that in telling of the highest perfection of righteousness while they know nothing of it, they themselves are rendered at once both judges by their words and accusers by their deeds.

Historical

Hence Bildad subjoins words of wondrous truth against hypocrites, but he is running himself through with the point of his discourse. For unless he were himself in some slight degree a pretender of righteousness, he would never venture to teach a good man with so much temerity. And indeed they are words of singular force that he speaks, but they ought to have been addressed to fools, not to a wise man; to the wicked, not to a good person; in that he proclaims himself no less than insane, who, when the gardens are parched, pours water into the river. But in the mean time, laying aside the question to whom the thing is said, let us weigh well and minutely what it is that is said, that the sentiments delivered may edify ourselves, even though they assail the character of their Author. It goes on,

Ver. 11. Can the rush grow up without moisture? can the flag grow without water?

Moral To whom Bildad compares 'the rush' and 'the flag,' he himself immediately discloses, when he adds;

Ver. 12, 13. Whilst it is yet in his greenness, and not cut down, it withereth before any other herb. So are the paths of all that forget God, and the hypocrite's hope shall perish.

66. So that by the name of 'a rush' or 'a flag,' he denotes the life of the hypocrite, which has an appearance of greenness, but has no fruit of usefulness for the services of man, which continuing dry in barrenness of practice, is green with only the colour of sanctity alone. But neither does a rush grow without moisture, nor a flag without water, in that the life of hypocrites receives indeed the infused grace of the heavenly gift for the doing of good works, but in whatsoever it does seeking praises without, it proves void of fruit of the infused grace vouchsafed it. For they often perform wonderful deeds of miraculous power, they expel demons from bodies possessed, and by the gift of prophecy, by knowing anticipate things to come, yet they are separated from the Giver of so many blessings in the bent of the thought of their heart. For through His gifts they seek not His glory, but their own applause. And whereas by the benefits vouchsafed them they raise themselves in their own praise, they are assailing their Benefactor with the very gifts of His bounty. For they behave themselves proudly against Him that gave them, from the very circumstance whereby they should have been rendered the more thoroughly humble towards Him. But a judgment the more unsparing smites them hereafter, in proportion as heavenly Goodness now pours upon them even in their ingratitude the dew of

His blessing in larger measure. And the fulness of the gift turns to the increase of condemnation to them, because when they are watered they bear no fruit, but under a hue of green rear themselves on high in barrenness. These 'Truth' well describes in the Gospel, saying, *Many shall say to Me in that day, Lord, Lord, have we not prophesied in Thy Name? and in Thy Name have cast out devils? and in Thy Name done many wonderful works? And then will I profess unto them, I never knew you; Depart from Me, ye that work iniquity*. [Matt. 7, 22. 23.] Thus neither the rush nor the flag lives without water, because hypocrites do not take the greenness of good works, save by gift from above; but because they appropriate it to the use of their own applause, they grow green indeed in the water, but barren.

67. Now it is well added, *Whilst it is yet in his flower, nor plucked with the hand, it withereth before any other herb*. 'The rush in his flower' is the hypocrite in esteem. Now the rush springing up with sharp edges is not plucked with the hand, in that the hypocrite, having his feelings sharpened by presumption, disdains to be rebuked for his wickedness. In his flower he gashes the hand that plucketh him, in that the hypocrite in the midst of applause, that no one may dare to rebuke him, by his cutting tongue wounds the life of the rebuker without delay. For he desires not to be holy, but to be called holy; and when he may chance to be rebuked, it is as if he were lopped off in the full bloom of his reputation. He is enraged to be found out in his wickedness, he forbids the man that brings his guilt home to him to address him, in that he is as it were pained by being touched in a secret wound. Such as he was known to the ignorant, he would wish to be accounted of all men, and readier to lay down his life than to be reprimanded, he is made worse by censure, because he accounts the word of disinterested goodness as the dart of deadly smiting. Hence in exasperated passion he directly rises in abuse, and looks about for all the evil he can rake together against the life of his rebuker. He longs to prove him beyond all comparison guilty, that he may make himself out innocent, not by his own doings, but by the guilt of others; so that often the person repents that he has uttered a word of censure, and that just as from the hand of one plucking anything, so from the mind of the person chiding, there runs out as it were the blood of sorrow, if I may say so. Hence it is well said by Solomon, *Reprove not a scorner, lest he hate thee*. For it is not proper for the good man to fear, lest the scorner should utter abuse at him

when he is chidden; but lest being drawn into hatred, he should be made worse.

68. And here it is necessary to be known, that the excellencies of good men, as they begin from the heart, go on increasing to the very end of the present life; but the practices of hypocrites, seeing that they are not rooted in secret, often come to nought before the present life is ended. For very frequently they devote themselves to the study of sacred scholarship, and because they prosecute it not for providing a store of merits, but for procuring commendations, the moment that they get hold of the sentence of human applause, and thereby secure the boon of transitory success, they give themselves with all their heart to worldly concerns, and are completely emptied of sacred scholarship, and by their way of acting afterwards, they show how much they love the things of time, who before only had those of eternity alone on their lips. But it is very often the case that they exhibit an appearance of maturity put on, they show fair by the composure of silence, by the forbearance of long suffering, by the virtue of continence; but when by means of these they have reached the height of the honour that they aimed at, and when respect is henceforth bestowed on them by all men, they immediately begin to let themselves out in wantonness of self-gratification, and they are their own witnesses against themselves that they held none of their good derived from the heart, in that they parted with it so soon.

But sometimes there are persons found who give all they possess, and lavish all their goods upon the needy, yet before the end of their life, inflamed with the itch of avarice, they covet the goods of others, who seemed to be giving their own with a lavish hand; and afterwards with determined cruelty they go after that, which they had given up before with pretended piety. And hence it is rightly said in this place, *Whilst it is yet in his flower, and not yet plucked with the hand, it withereth before any other herb*. For as to their fleshly part even the righteous are herbs, as the Prophet bears witness, who says, *All flesh is grass*. But 'the rush' is said to 'wither before all other herbs;' in that while the righteous continue in their goodness, the life of hypocrites is dried up from the greenness of assumed uprightness. Even the rest of the herbs wither, because the deeds of the righteous come to an end together with the life of the flesh. But the 'rush' precedes the withering of the herbs, for before the hypocrite passes out of the flesh, he gives over the deeds of virtuous habits which he had manifested in himself. Concerning which same it is also well said by the Psalmist, *Let them be as the grass upon the housetop, which withereth afore it be plucked up*. [Ps. 129, 6] For 'the grass upon the housetop' springeth up aloft, but it is never set firm with a rich soil, forasmuch as the hypocrite is seen practising the highest acts, but he is not stablished therein in purity of intention. Which same grass even when not plucked up soon withereth, for this reason, that the hypocrite at one and the same time still exists in the present life, and yet already parts with the practices of holiness as with the appearance of greenness. For because he went about to do good works without the purpose of a right heart, by losing these he shows that he flourished without a root.

69. But as we have before said, who he is to whom Bildad likens 'a rush' or 'a flag,' he makes plain at the moment, where he adds, *So are the paths of all that forget God, and the hypocrite's hope shall perish*. For what does the hypocrite hope for from all his deeds, saving the observance of honour, the reputation of applause, to be feared by his betters, to be called a Saint by all men? But the hope of the hypocrite can never endure, for, from not making eternity his aim, he hastes away from all that he holds in his hand. For the bent of his mind is not fixed in that glory which is possessed without end; but while he gapes after transient applause, he loses in the getting the thing that he toils for, as 'Truth' testifieth, Who says, *Verily I say unto you, they have had their reward*. [Matt. 6, 2] Now this hope of being vouchsafed a reward cannot be maintained for long, seeing that honour is bestowed for the works exhibited, but life is pressing on to its close; praises are reechoed, but then along with them the periods of time are speeding to an end. And because the soul is in no wise rooted in the love of the eternal world, it slips away together with the very objects that it is centered in. For no one can attach himself to the moveable, and remain himself unmoved. For he that embraces transitory things is drawn into transition by the mere circumstance, that he is entangled with things running out their course. Therefore let him say, *And the hypocrite's hope shall perish*. For the applause of man, which he seeks with mighty pains, being driven on by the items of time, does run to nought. And it is well added,

Ver. 14. His own folly shall not satisfy him.

70. For it is infinite folly to labour painfully, and pant after the breath of applause, to apply one's self to the heavenly precepts with hard toil, but to aim at the reward of an earthly kind of recompense. For that I may so express myself, he that in return for the good that he practises looks for the applause of his fellowcreatures, is carrying an article of great worth to be sold at a mean price. From that whereby he might have earned the kingdom of heaven, he seeks the coin of passing talk. His practice goes for little, in that he spends a great deal, and gets back but very little. Whereunto then are hypocrites like but to luxuriant and untended vines, which put forth fruit from their fertility, but are never lifted from the earth by tending? All that the rich branches bud forth, stray beasts tread under foot, and the more fruitful they see it is, the more greedily they devour it, thus cast away and laid low, in that the works of hypocrites while they show fair, come forth as if rich, but whilst they aim at human praises, it is as if they were left forsaken upon the ground. And the beasts of this world, i.e. the evil spirits, devour them, because they turn them to account to the end of perdition, and they seize upon them with greater avidity, in proportion as great things are more clearly known. Hence it is well said by the Prophet, *The standing stalk, there is no bud in them, and they shall yield no meal; if so be it yield, the strangers shall swallow it up.* [Hos. 8, 7. Vulg.] For the stalk is without a bud, when the life lacks the merit of virtuous habits. The stalk yieldeth no meal, when he that thrives in this world understands nothing refined, and yields no fruit of good practice.

xliii.

71. But very often even when it has yielded meal, strangers eat it up, in that even when hypocrites do show forth good works, the wishes of evil spirits are satisfied therewith. For those who do not aim to please God by them, do not feed the Owner of the land, but strangers. Thus the hypocrite, like a fruitful and neglected vine, cannot keep his fruit, because the cluster of good works lies prone upon the ground. Yet he is fed by his very own insanity itself, in that on the score of good practice he is esteemed of all men, he is set before others, he holds the minds of men in subjection, he is raised to the higher posts; he is fed high with applause. Now this folly of his satisfies him in the mean season, but it shall not satisfy him, in that when the season of retribution comes, it displeases him under punishment that he was foolish. Then he will perceive that he did fool-

ishly, when, for the gratification of applause, he receives the sentence of God's rebuke. Then he sees that he has been senseless, when for the transitory glory that he obtained, everlasting torments are his bitter portion. Then punishments disclose the true knowledge to light, in that by them it must at once be concluded that all was nought that could pass away; and hence it is rightly added,

And whose trust shall be a spider's web.

xliv. 72. The assurance of the hypocrite is rightly called like the webs of spiders, in that all the pains and labour they spend to acquire glory, the wind of the life of mortality blows to shreds. For as they never seek the things of eternity, they lose together with time all temporal good things. Moreover it is to be considered that spiders draw their threads in a regular order, for that hypocrites as it were regulate their works by the rule of discernment. The spider's web is woven with pains, but it is scattered by a sudden blast, in that whatsoever the hypocrite does with laborious effort, the breath of man's regard carries off; and whilst in the ambition of applause his work comes to nought, it is as if his labour went to the wind. For it often happens that the works of hypocrites last even to the very end of the present life, but, forasmuch as they do not thereby seek the praise of their Creator, they were never good works in the sight of God. Thus it is very often the case, as we have said above, that they are upheld by scholarship in the sacred Law, that they deliver lessons of instruction, that they fortify by testimonies every notion that they entertain; but they do not hereby seek the life of their hearers, but applause for themselves. For neither do they know how to put forth anything else but what may stir the hearts of their hearers to the quick, to pay the recompense of praise, not what may kindle them to shed tears. For the heart being preoccupied with external desires, is not hot with the fire of divine love, and so words that issue from a cold heart, can never warm their hearers to heavenly affection. For neither can anyone thing that is not itself alight in itself kindle any other thing. Hence it is very often brought to pass, that at one and the same time the sayings of hypocrites fail to instruct the hearers, and make the very persons themselves that utter them worse by being exalted with praises. For as Paul bears witness, *Knowledge puffeth up, but charity edifieth*. [1 Cor. 8,

1] Thus, whereas charity setteth not up in 'edifying,' knowledge in puffing up overthrows. Very often hypocrites chasten themselves with extraordinary mortification, wear down all the strength of their body, and as it were while living in the flesh utterly kill the life of the flesh, and so by abstinence verge upon death, that they live well nigh dying every day; but they seek the eyes of men for all this, they look for the renown of admiration, as 'Truth' testifieth, Which says, *For they disfigure their faces, that they may appear unto men to fast*. [Matt. 6, 16] For their faces become pallid, the body is made to shake with weakness, the breast labours with hard and broken breathings. But amidst all this, talk of admiration is looked for from the lips of neighbours, and nothing else is aimed at by such great pains, saving human esteem. Which same are well represented by that Simon, who in the season of our Lord's Passion bore the Cross in compulsion, of whom it is written, *And as they came out they found a man of Cyrene, Simon by name, him they compelled to bear His cross*. [Matt. 27, 32] For what we do by compulsion, we do not practise from a heartfelt devotedness of love. And so for him to bear the Cross of Jesus in compulsion, is to submit to the mortification of abstinence for some other aim than needs to be. Does he not bear the Cross of Jesus under compulsion, who as after the commandment of the Lord subdues the flesh, yet does not love the spiritual Country? And hence the same Simon bears the Cross, but doth not die; in that every hypocrite chastens his body in abstinence, but yet, in the love of glory, lives on to the world.

73. Contrariwise it is well said by Paul of the Elect; *For they that are Christ's have crucified the flesh with the vices and lusts*. For we 'crucify the flesh with the vices and lusts,' if we so restrain our appetite, that henceforth we look for nothing of the glory of the world. Since he that macerates the flesh, but pants after honours, has inflicted the Cross on his flesh, but from concupiscence lives the worse to the world, in that it often happens that in the semblance of holiness, he unworthily obtains the post of rule, which except he displayed something of merit in himself, he would never attain to receive by any pains whatever. But that which he gains for enjoyment is passing, and what ensues in punishment is enduring. Now his assurance of sanctity is placed in the lips of man, but when the inward Judge tries the secrets of the interior, no witnesses of the life are sought from without. Therefore it is well said, *Whose trust shall be a spider's web*;

since on the witness of the heart appearing, all passes by wherein his confidence consists, founded without in human applause. And hence it is yet further added with justice,

Ver. 15. He leaneth upon his house, but it shall not stand; he shall prop it, but it shall not rise up.

xlv. 74. As the house of our exterior life is the building which the body lives in, so the house of our thought is anything whatever that the mind is centered in by affection. For everything that we love, we as it were make our dwelling-place by reposing in it. Whence Paul, because he had fixed his heart in things above, being still upon earth indeed, yet a stranger to earth, said, *Our conversation is in heaven*. [Phil. 3, 20] So the mind of the hypocrite in whatever it does minds nothing else but the fame of its own reputation, nor cares where it is carried [*'ducitur'*] after by its deserts, but what it is called [*'dicatur'*] in the mean season. Therefore his house is delight of popularity, which he as it were dwells in at rest, in that in all his works he throws himself back thereupon within his mind. But this house can never stand, because praise fleeth away with life, and the applause of man does not hold in the Judgment. Hence the foolish virgins too, who took no oil in their vessels, because their glory was in the voices of others and not in their own consciences, confounded by the presence of the Bridegroom, say, *Give us of your oil, for our lamps are going out*. [Matt. 25, 8] For to seek oil from our neighbours is to beseech the fame of good works from the testimony of another man's mouth. For the empty soul, when it finds that it has retained nothing within by all its labours, looks about for testimony from without. As if the foolish Virgins said plainly, 'When ye behold us cast away without reward, say ye what ye have seen in our practice.'

75. But the hypocrite leans in vain then upon this house of applause, since no human testimony stands him in stead in the Judgment; for the same praise, which he afterwards claims in testimony, he before received in reward. Or surely the hypocrite leans upon his house, when beguiled by vain caresses, he is as it were lifted up in assurance of his holiness; for hypocrites do many things evil in secret, but a few things good in public. And when they receive praises from the good that appears, they turn away the eyes of observation from the concealed ill, and they esteem themselves such as they hear without, not such as they know themselves within. Whence it very

often happens that they also come to the Judgment of the Most High with confidence, because they imagine themselves such in the sight of the Interior Judge, as they were held to be by men without. Yet 'the house of the hypocrite cannot stand,' for in the terror of a sifting search, all the foregoing assurance of holiness falls to the ground. And when he knows that the testimony of another man's lips is wanting to him, he betakes himself to reckoning up his own works. Hence it is still further added, *He shall prop it, but it shall not rise up*. For that which cannot stand by itself, is propped to make it stand; for when the hypocrite sees his life tottering in the Judgment, he sets himself to make it stand in propping it, by the enumeration of his deeds. Do not they prop the dwelling-place of their own praise on every hand, who in reckoning up their own deeds in the Judgment, as we said before, say, *Lord, Lord, have we not prophesied in Thy Name? and in Thy Name have cast out devils? and in Thy Name done many marvellous works?* [Matt. 7, 22. 23.] But the house of praise, stayed up by all these statements, cannot rise, because the Judge says directly, *I never knew you; depart from Me, ye that work iniquity*. And it is to be had in mind that anything, that rises, lifts itself from below to a higher elevation, and so 'the house of the hypocrite cannot rise,' in that in all that he may have done after the heavenly precepts, he never lifted his soul from off the earth, so that with justice he is not then lifted up to the meed of recompense, who in that which he sets forth now, lies prostrate in the desire of temporal glory. But whereas we have heard how the life of the hypocrite, represented by the name of 'a rush,' is rejected in the Judgment, let us hear what sort of person he is held by men before the strict Judge appeareth. It proceeds,

Ver. 16. It is seen moist before the sun cometh.

xliv.

76. Oftentimes in Holy Writ the Lord is represented by the title of the Sun, as it is said by the Prophet, *But unto you that fear My Name shall the Sun of righteousness arise*. [Mal. 4, 2] And as the ungodly that are cast away in the Judgment, are described in the book of Wisdom, as saying, *We have erred from the way of truth, and the light of righteousness hath not shined unto us, and the Sun rose not upon us*; [Wisd. 5, 6] therefore, 'before the sun the rush is seen moist,' in that before God's severity burns hot in the Judgment, every hypocrite shows himself bedewed with the grace of holiness. He is seen as it were flourishing, because he is accounted righteous, he wins the

post of honour, he is strong in his high repute for sanctity, reverence is awarded to him by all men, his credit for praise is magnified. Thus this rush is full of moisture in the night, but on the coming of the sun it is dried up, in that the hypocrite is accounted holy by all men in the darkness of the present life, but when the searching Judge cometh, he will appear as wicked as he is. So then let him say, *He appears moist before the sun*, because now he shows himself flourishing to the eyes of men, but then he shall wither up in the scorching heat of the Divine Judgment. The account goes on;

And his produce [germen] issueth forth in his springing up.

xlvii. 77. For every herb in general is first raised out of the ground by springing up, it is subject to the influences of the air and heat, it is fed by the sun and showers, and then at length it is made to open itself to put forth the produce of its seed. But the rush is produced along with its flower, and so soon as it springs out of the earth, it puts forth its produce of seed with itself. Therefore by the rest of the herbs the Saints in general are well denoted, but the hypocrite by 'the rush,' because the righteous, before they spring up in the practice of holy conversation, undergo the winter season of this life, and the heats of bitter persecutions press them hard; and then, when they do what is right, they never look here for the reward of their, righteousness, but when they depart forth from the labours of the present world, on coming to their eternal Country, they enter upon the enjoyment of their looked-for reward. But contrariwise the hypocrite, in that he springs up in good practice at once, goes about to win the glory of the present world. As it were like a rush he springs up with his produce, who in return for this, that he is beginning to live well, aims at the outset to be held in honour by all men. So that the 'produce in the springing up,' is a reward at the outset. For often there are those that abandon the paths of overt wickedness, and put on the garb of holiness, and the moment they have touched the bare threshold of good living, forgetting what they were, they will not be henceforth chastened by penance for the iniquities they have committed, but they long to be commended for goodness begun; they are eager to get above the rest, even though better men than themselves. And for the most part whilst present prosperity follows them to their wish, they become infinitely worse than they were by the wearing of sanctity; but being busied with countless concerns, and distracted by that same busying, they not only never bewail the things that they have done, but still fill up more that should be bewailed.

78. For they that quit the world, ought not to be promoted to external [i.e. public] offices, unless in humility they be for some long time established in the contempt of that world. For the good soon comes to an end, which is made known to the world before the time. Thus with shrubs too that have been planted, if, before they are fastened with a firm root, the hand touch and shake them, it causes them to wither away, but, if the root be fixed deep, and, being sprinkled with the dews of the earth, be set fast, such as these the hand may even push, and not hurt: these even blasts of wind may buffet and wave, yet not overthrow. Thus, that the life of practice we have entered upon may not be uprooted, the root of the heart must be fixed long and vigorously in the deep of humility, that when from the mouths of men the breath of calumny or of applause blows strong, though it bend it a little either way, it may not root up the mind from its seat, but that after such bending it may return to its own upright standing, if it but hold strong in the root in its own self. What among things in course of growth is stronger than a rising wall? yet if, while it is in the act of erecting, it is pushed, it is at once destroyed without an effort; but if for a space of time it be allowed to dry from its wetness, often it is never a jot moved even by the strokes of the battering rams. In this way, in this self-same way, our goodness on the one hand being unseasonably displayed comes to nought, and on the other hand being longer kept hidden, is fairly secured; in that when the hand of human employment touches the recent life of our conversation, as it were it pushes the fresh brick wall, and easily destroys it, because it has not as yet got rid of the moisture of its own weakness. But when in its long lying at rest, the soul holds itself in, as it were like a dry wall, it grows hard against blows, and everything that strikes it, now it is solid, bounds off it at once shattered. It is hence that Moses forbade the life of aught that made the beginning to be employed in services for men, saying, *Thou shalt do no work with the firstling of thy bullock, nor shear the firstling of thy sheep*. [Deut. 15, 19] For to 'do work with the firstling of the bullock' is to display the beginning of a good conversation in the employment of public business. Moreover 'to shear the firstlings of sheep,' is to lay bare of the covering of its concealment the good we

have begun before the eyes of men. And so we are forbidden to 'work with the firstling of the bullock,' and we are hindered from 'shearing the firstlings of our sheep,' in that even if we begin anything strong, we ought not to be too ready to execute it in public. And when our life commences something simple and harmless, it is meet that it quit not the coverings of its secresy, that it may not bare that thing naked to the eyes of the world, the fleece being as it were withdrawn.

79. So let the firstlings of the bullocks and the sheep avail for the Divine sacrifices alone, that whatsoever we begin strong and harmless, we may sacrifice in honour of the Judge of the interior upon the altar of our hearts. Which same we may be sure is accepted the more gladly by Him, in proportion as being kept concealed from men it is stained by no desire of applause. But it often happens that the beginnings of a new method of life have still a mixture of the carnal life, and therefore they ought not to be too ready to make themselves known, lest while the good that pleases is applauded, the soul being beguiled by the praises of itself have no power to discover in itself the evil that lies concealed. Hence it is rightly said by Moses again, *And when ye shall have come into the land that I shall give you, and shall have planted all manner of trees bearing fruit, then ye shall take off their foreskins. The fruits that are put forth shall be unclean, unto you, ye shall not eat of them*. [Lev. 19, 23] For 'the trees bearing fruit' are works fruitful in virtue, and so we 'take off the foreskins of the trees,' when suspecting ourselves of the mere weakness of a beginning in itself, we do not give our approval to the beginnings of our good practices, but the fruits that are put forth, we count unclean, and do not make them answer for good for us, in that when the beginnings of good practice are applauded, it is meet that the mind of the doer should not be fed thereby; lest whilst the praise bestowed is plucked with delight, the fruit of good works be eaten prematurely. He, then, that receives the praise of virtue in its beginning from the mouths of men, as it were eats the fruit of the tree that he has planted before the time,

80. Hence 'Truth' says by the Psalmist, *It is vain for you to rise up before the light: rise up after ye have sat*. [Ps. 127, 2. Vulg.] For 'to: rise up before the light' is to take one's pleasure in the night-time of the present life, before the shining of Eternal Retribution is revealed. So we are to sit first, that we may rise afterwards in a right

way. For whoever doth not now humble himself by his own act and deed, the glory to ensue does not exalt such an one. Therefore what it is there to rise before the light, it is here for the hypocrite to put forth the produce in his springing up, for in setting his heart on human applauses, in the self-same place, where he springs up to good works, there he desires directly to obtain the glorying of his recompense. Had not they 'put forth their produce in their springing up,' of whom 'Truth' said, *They love the uppermost rooms at feasts, and the chief seats in the synagogues, and greetings in the markets, and to be called of men Rabbi?* [Matt. 23, 6, 7] Therefore seeing that for this reason, viz. because they are beginning to do well, they endeavour to obtain honour of men, as it were, like a rush, 'in their springing up they rise with their produce.' These same, whilst they aim to practise right things, first anxiously look about for witnesses of those same works, and canvass with secret calculation, if there be persons to see the things they are about to do, or if those who see them can report them in a proper way. But if it chance to happen that no one witnesses their doings, then, surely, they reckon them to be lost to them, and they account the eyes of the interior Umpire as off them, because they have no mind to receive at His hands the reward of their works hereafter. And whereas when the hypocrite does anything, he aims to be seen by many eyes, it is yet further added with truth concerning this same 'rush,'

Ver. 17. His roots will be wrapped about the heap of rocks, and he will dwell among the stones.

xlviii.

81. For what do we understand by the name of 'roots' save the hidden thoughts, which issue forth out of sight, but rise up in the display of works in open day? as it is also said by the Prophet concerning the seed of the Word, *And the remnant that is escaped of the house of Judah shall again take root downward and bear fruit upward.* [Is. 37, 31] For to 'take root downward,' is to multiply good thoughts in the secret depths, but 'to bear fruit upward,' is to show forth by the doing of practice what one has thought that is right. Now by the title of 'stones' in Holy Writ men are denoted, as it is said to Holy Church by Isaiah, *And I will make thy battlements jasper, and thy gates of carved stones.* [Is. 54, 12] And he made it plain what it was that he called those stones, where he added, *All thy children taught of the Lord.* As it is also expressed by Peter in giving ad-

monition, *Ye also, as lively stones, are built up a spiritual house.* [1 Pet. 2, 5] Here therefore, whereas they are called 'stones,' but are not in any wise called 'living stones,' by the bare appellation of stones may be set forth the lost and the Elect mixed together. Therefore this rush, 'which abideth in the place of stones, wrappeth his roots about the heap of rocks,' in that every hypocrite multiplies the thoughts of his heart, in seeking out the admiration of men; for in all that hypocrites do, seeing that in their secret thoughts they look out for the applauses of their fellow-creatures, like rushes as it were they 'send out roots into the heap of the rocks.' For on the point of acting they imagine their praises, and when applauded, they dwell upon them secretly with themselves in the thoughts of their heart. They rejoice that they have distinguished themselves first and foremost in the esteem of men; and while they are puffed up and swoln in themselves by their applause, they often themselves secretly wonder at what they are. They long to appear day by day higher than themselves, and grow to a height by extraordinary arts in practice. For as habits of virtue enfeeble everything bad, so presumption strengthens the same. For it forces the mind to grow quick, and to be in high condition at the expense of strength, in that what the prime quality of health withholds, the love of applause enjoins. Whence too, as we said, they look out for witnesses of their deeds; but if, it chance that witnesses of the thing are wanting, they themselves relate what they have done, and when they begin to be elated with applause, they add a little, by lying, to these works of theirs, which they describe themselves to have done. But even when they do give true accounts, by the act of telling them they are making them alien to them, in that when they are rewarded with the desired acknowledgments of esteem, they are dispossessed of their inward recompensing of them.

82. For in this, that they publish their good, they point out to the evil spirits, like enemies plotting against them, what to make spoil of. Whose life, truly, is represented by that sin of Hezekiah, which is well known to everyone, who after that by a single prayer, and in the space of a single night, he had laid low an hundred fourscore and five thousand of his enemies, by an Angel smiting them, after that he had brought back the sun close to its setting into the higher regions of the heavens, after that he had spun out the web of life to longer dimensions, now already narrowed by the end approaching, showed to the welcomed messengers of the king of Babylon all the good

treasures that he possessed, but directly heard from the voice of the Prophet, *Behold, the days come, that all that is in thine house shall be carried away into Babylon: nothing shall be left, says the Lord.* [2 Kings 20, 17] In this way, in this self-same way, do hypocrites, after they are grown to a height by great attainments in virtue, because they are indifferent to guard against the plots of evil spirits, and will not remain hidden in those attainments, by displaying their good things, make them over to the enemy; and by betraying it to view, they lose in a moment whatsoever they perform by taking pains in a long course of time. Hence it is said by the Psalmist, *And He delivered their strength into captivity, and their glory into the enemy's hand.* [Ps. 78, 61] For the 'strength' and 'glory' of presumptuous men is 'given over into the enemy's hand,' in that every good thing, that is exhibited in the desire of praise, is made over to our secret adversary's right of possession; for he calls his enemies to the spoil, who reveals his treasures to their knowledge; since so long as we are severed from the safety of the Eternal Land, we are walking along a way until robbers lying in wait. He then that dreads to be robbed on the road, must of necessity bide the treasures that he carries. O wretched beings, who by going after the praises of men, waste to themselves all the fruits of their labours, and whilst they aim to show themselves to the eyes of others, blast all that they do. Which same when the evil spirits prompt to boastfulness, taking them for a prey they strip bare their works, as we have said. Whence 'Truth' in setting forth by the Prophet the rancour of our old enemies, under the form of a particular people, says, *He hath laid my vineyard waste, and barked my fig-tree: he hath made it clean bare, and despoiled* [V. so.] *it; the branches thereof are made white.* [Joel 1, 7] For by spirits lying in wait the vineyard of God is made a desert, when the soul that is replenished with fruits is wasted with the longing after the praise of men. That people barks the fig-tree of God, in that carrying away the misguided soul in the appetite for applause, in the degree that it draws her on to ostentation, it strips her of the covering of humility, and 'making it clean bare despoils it,' in that so long as it is withdrawn from sight in its goodness, it is as it were clothed with the bark of its own covering. But when the mind longs for that it has done to be seen by others, it is as though 'the fig-tree despoiled' had lost the bark that covered it. And it is properly added there, *The branches thereof are made white*; in that his works being displayed to the eyes of men, turn ,white; a name for sanctity is gotten, when right practice is made appear, but whereas upon the bark being removed, the branches of this fig-tree wither, it is to be observed with due discrimination that the deeds of presumptuous men, when they are paraded before human eyes, by the same act whereby they aim to win favour, are rendered dry and sapless. Therefore the mind that is shown to view in boasting is rightly called a fig-tree barked, in that it is at once white, in so far as it is seen, and within a little of withering, in so far as it is denuded of the covering of the bark. The things we do, therefore, are to be kept within, if we expect to receive from the Umpire within the recompense of our work. It is hence that 'Truth' says in the Gospel, *But when thou doest alms, let not thy left hand know what thy right hand doeth, that thine alms may be in secret; and thy Father, which seeth in secret, shall reward thee openly*. [Matt. 6, 3. 4.] It is hence that it is said of the Church of the Elect by the Psalmist, *The king's daughter is all glorious within*. [Ps. 45, 13] Hence Paul says, *For our glory* [V. so.] *is this, the testimony of our conscience*. [2 Cor. 1, 12] For the king's daughter is the Church, which is begotten in good practice by the preaching of spiritual Princes. But 'her glory is within,' in that what she does she holds not for the boasting of outward display. Paul describes his 'glory' as 'the testimony of his conscience,' in that not aiming at the applause of another's man's lips, he knows no such thing as placing the satisfactions of his life out of himself.

83. Therefore the things that we do must be kept concealed, lest by carrying them negligently on the journey of the present life, we lose them, through the invasion of the spirits that hunt for spoil. And yet 'Truth' says, *Let them see your good works, that they may glorify your Father which is in heaven*. [Matt. 5, 16] But assuredly it is one thing when in the display of our works the glory of the Giver is our aim, and quite another when our own praise is the thing sought for in the gift of His bounty. And hence again in the Gospel the same 'Truth' says, *Take heed that ye do not your works before men, to be seen of them*. Therefore when our works are displayed to men, we must first weigh well, in entering into the heart, what is aimed at by the prosecution of such display. For if we make the glory of the Giver our end, even our works that are made public we keep hidden in His sight. But if we desire to win our own applause by them, they are thenceforth cast out of His sight without, even though they be known nothing of by numbers.

84. Now it belongs to those that are exceeding perfect, so to seek the glory of their Maker by the works shown, as not to know what it is to exult in self-congratulation upon the praise bestowed upon them. For then only is a praiseworthy work displayed to men without harm, when the praise awarded is genuinely trodden under in the mind's contempt. Which same as the weak sort do not perfectly get above in contemning it, it remains of necessity that they keep out of sight the good that they do. For often from the very first beginning of the display, they seek their own praise. And often in the displaying of their works, they desire to publish the gloriousness of the Creator, but being received with applause, they are carried off into desire of their own praise. And whilst they neglect to call themselves to account within, being dissipated without, they do not know what they do, and their work ministers to their pride, and they fancy that they are rendering it in the service of the Giver. Thus 'a rush abideth among the stones,' in that the hypocrite stands there, where he sets fast the purpose of his mind. For whilst he goes about to get the testimony of numbers, he takes his stand, as it were, in the heap of stones. But the same hypocrite that is represented by the designation of 'a rush,' whilst he brings his body under by abstinence, whilst by bestowing in alms all that he possesses, he spends himself in efforts of pity, whilst he gets instruction in the knowledge of the sacred Law, whilst he employs the word of preaching; who that beheld him so filled with bounty, would account him a stranger to the grace of the Giver? And yet the Hand of heavenly Dispensation vouchsafes to him the gifts of works, and withholds the lot of the inheritance. It lavishes endowments for working, yet disowns the life of the worker. For when the gift vouchsafed is applied toward his own praise, in the eye of the interior Light, he is darkened by the shadow of pride. Hence it is well added,

Ver. 18. If He destroy him from his place, then He shall deny him, saying, I have not known thee.

xlix.

85. The hypocrite is 'destroyed from his place,' when he is parted from the applause of the present life, by death intervening. But the interior Witness 'denieth' him, thus destroyed, and asserts that He knows him not, in that in justly condemning the life of the pretender, 'Truth' knows him not, nor recognises the good works he has done, in that he never put them forth in a right

purpose of mind. And hence when He cometh to Judgment, He will say to the foolish virgins, *Verily I say unto you, I know you not*. [Matt. 25, 12] In which same whilst He sees corruptness of mind, He condemns even incorruptness in the flesh. But would that their own ruin alone were enough for hypocrites, and that their wicked pains did not vehemently urge others to a life [al. 'a way'] of duplicity. For it is the way with everyone, to wish that, such as he is himself, others of a like sort should be joined with him, and to avoid difference in life, and to inculcate as a pattern for imitation the thing that he loves. Whence also according to the view of hypocrites every degree of simplicity of character is criminal. For they sit in judgment on open characters, and purity of heart they term stupidity; and all whom they desire to be attached to themselves, they turn out of the path of simplicity, and then, as though their folly were cast out, they reckon that they have enlightened those persons, in whom they force to a surrender that fortress of wisdom, purity of heart. But forasmuch as the hypocrite is condemned not for his own frowardness alone, but for the added ruin of his followers also, after that he is said not to be known by the Judge, the words are rightly brought in upon that;

Ver. 19. Behold, this is the joy of his way [al. 'of his life'], that out of the earth others also should grow.

l. 86. As though it were in plain words, 'When the Judge cometh, he is not acknowledged, but receives punishment a thousand fold, because he rejoiced in his wickedness more amply in proportion as he spread evil among others also.' For he that is not satisfied with being wicked himself here, must be tormented There with the due of the guilt of others also. Now then let the hypocrites rejoice, and triumph to have gotten the suffrages of their fellow-creatures. Let the simplicity of good men be looked down upon, and be called foolishness by the craft of the double-dealing. Speedily doth the contempt of the single-minded pass, speedily the glorying of the double-dealing run to an end. And hence it is fitly added,

Ver. 20. Behold, God will not cast out a perfect man, neither will He stretch out His hand to the evil.

li. 87. In that assuredly when the Strict One appeareth in the Judgment, He will at once lift up the despisedness of the simple by glorifying them, and break in pieces the greatness of the evil-minded [*malignorum*] by condemning them. For hypocrites are called evil-minded, who do good acts but not well, and practise everything right only in eagerness after praise. Now anyone, to whom we stretch out our hand, we plainly lift up from below. Thus God does not stretch out His hand to the evil-minded, in that all that seek earthly glory He leaves below, and how right soever the things that they do may seem to be, He doth not advance them to the joys above. Or, as may well be, hypocrites are for this reason called evil-minded, because they make a show of being wellminded toward their neighbours, and cover over the arts of their wicked designs. For in all that they either do or say, they show simplicity externally, but they are inwardly conceiving in the subtleties of double-mindedness; they counterfeit purity on the outside, but they conceal an evil heart at all times under the semblance of purity. In respect of whom it is well spoken by Moses, *Thou shalt not wear a garment woven of woollen and linen together*. [Deut. 22, 11] For by 'woollen' is denoted simplicity, by 'linen' subtlety. And it is the fact that a garment made of 'wool and linen' hides the linen within and shows the wool on the outside. And so he 'puts on a garment of woollen and linen together,' who in the mode of speech or behaviour that he adopts conceals within the artfulness of an evil purpose, and exhibits without the simplicity of an innocent mind. For whereas it is impossible to detect craftiness under the semblance of purity, it is as if linen were hidden under the thickness of wool. But after the condemnation of the double-minded, the recompensing of the righteous is duly exhibited, when it is added thereupon,

Ver. 21. Till He fill thy mouth with laughing, and thy lips with shouting.

lii.

88. For the 'mouth' of the righteous will then be 'filled with laughing' when the tears of their pilgrimage being done, their hearts shall be filled to the full with exulting in eternal joy. Concerning this laughing 'Truth' says to His disciples, *Verily, verily, I say unto you, that ye shall weep and lament, but the world shall rejoice; and ye shall be sorrowful, but your sorrow shall be turned into joy*. [John 16, 20] And again, *But I will see you again, and your heart shall rejoice, and your joy no man taketh from you*. [ver. 23] Concerning this laughing of Holy Church, Solomon says, *And she shall laugh in the last day*. [Prov.

31, 25] Of this it is said again, *Whoso feareth the Lord, it shall go well with him at the last*. [Ecclus. 1, 3] Not that there shall be laughter of the body, but laughter of the heart. For now from rioting in dissipation there springs a laughter of the body, but then from joy in security there will arise a laughter of the heart. Therefore when all the Elect are replenished with the delight of open vision, they spring forth into the joyousness of laughter in the mouth of the interior. But we call it shouting [*jubilum*], when we conceive such joy in the heart, as we cannot give vent to by the force of words, and yet the triumph of the heart vents with the voice what it cannot give forth by speech. Now the mouth is rightly said to be filled with laughter, the lips with shouting, since in that eternal land, when the mind of the righteous is borne away in transport, the tongue is lifted up in the song of praise. And they, because they see so much as they are unable to express, shout in laughter, because without compassing it they resound all the love that they feel.

89. Now it is said 'till,' not that Almighty God so long forbears to raise up the evil until he take to Him His Elect to the joys of their jubilee, as if afterwards He saved from the punishment those whom first leaving in sin He sentences to damnation, but that He never does it even before the Judgment, when it may seem doubtful to men, whether it is to be done. For that after the jubilee of His Eject people He does not stretch out His hand to the evil-minded, is already plain from the mere severity of the final reckoning by itself. As the Psalmist also spake in this manner, *The Lord said unto my Lord, Sit Thou on My right hand, until I make Thine enemies Thy footstool*. [Ps. 110, 1] Not that the Lord never sat on the Lord's right hand, after that by smiting His enemies He made them subject to His power, but that He is set over all things in eternal blessedness, even before He treads under His feet the hearts of those that rebel against Him. Wherein it is made plain that His enemies being brought under, He still rules without end even afterwards. Thus it is said in the Gospel of the espoused of Mary, *And knew her not, till she had brought forth her first-born Son*. [Matt. 1, 25] Not that he did know her after the birth of the Lord, but that he never touched her even when he did not know her to be the Mother of his Creator. For because it was impossible that he could have touched her after he knew that the Mystery of our Redemption was transacted from her womb, plainly it was necessary that the Evangelist should bear witness of that time, of

which there might be misgivings entertained by reason of Joseph's ignorance. And so it is expressed here in like manner, *Behold, God will not cast away a perfect man, neither will He stretch out His hand to the evil-minded; till He fill thy mouth with laughter, and thy lips with shouting*. As if it were expressed in plain speech; 'Not even before the Judgment does He abandon the life of the faithful, nor even before He appears does He forbear from smiting the minds of the evil-disposed by abandoning them.' For that the sons of perdition He torments without end, and that after that He shall have appeared His Elect reign for evermore, assuredly there is no doubt. It goes on;

Ver. 22. They that hate thee shall be clothed with confusion.

90. 'Confusion clothes' the enemies of the good in the final Judgment; for when they see before the eyes of their mind their past misdeeds running over in excess to them, their own guilt clothes them on every side, weighing them down. For they then bear the memory of their doings in punishment, who now, as though strangers to the faculty of reason, sin with hearts full of joy. There they see how greatly they should have eschewed all that they loved. There they see how woful that was, which they now hug themselves for in their sin. Then guilt spreads a cloud over the mind, and conscience pierces itself with the darts of its remembrances. Who then can adequately estimate how exceeding great will be the confusion of the wicked Then, when both the Judge Eternal is discerned without, and sin is set in review before the eyes within? who are on this account brought to such a pass, because they loved transient things alone. And hence it is rightly added upon that; **liii.**

And the tents of the wicked shall not abide.

91. For a tent is put together that the body may be preserved from heat and cold. What then is here set forth by the name of a dwelling-place, save the building of earthly prosperity, whereby the wicked are multiplying above their heads things to fall, that they may shelter themselves from the exigencies of the present life as from heat and rain. Thus they go about to rise in honours, lest they should appear contemptible. They pile up the good things of earth, and heap them high, lest they ever come to pine with the cold of want. They scorn to take thought of what is to come, and busy themselves with all their heart, that nought may be lacking in the **liv.**

present scene of things. They aim to spread their name, that they may not live unknown, and if everything is forthcoming to their hearts' content, they regard themselves as proof in all things, and blessed in their condition. Thus in the place where they rear a dwelling-place of the interior, there surely they have their tents fixed. They bear crosses with impatience, they rejoice in prosperity without restraint. They mind alone the things that are before them, nor do they draw their breath by the yearning after their heavenly home in the remembrance thereof. They are glad that the good things are theirs, which their heart is bent on having; and there, where they rest in the body, they bury the soul too, making it a thing extinct, in that being slain with the instrument of worldly solicitude, that pile of earthly things, which they heap together hunting for them without, they are always carrying on them within in thought.

92. But contrariwise the good neither take the blessings offered them here below as anything great, nor very much dread the ills brought upon them. But both whilst they use present advantages, they forecast inconveniences to come, and when they lament for present evils, they are comforted in the love of the good things to follow. And they are cheered by temporal support, just as a wayfarer enjoys a bed in a stable; he stops and hurries to be off; he rests still in the body, but is going forward to something else in imagination. But sometimes they even long to meet with afflictions, they shrink from finding all go well in transient things, lest by the delightfulness of the journey, they be hindered in arriving at their home; lest they arrest the step of the heart on the pathway of their pilgrimage, and one day come in view of the heavenly land without a recompense. They delight to be little accounted of, nor do they grieve to be in affliction and necessity. Thus they that never fortify themselves against the adversities of the present time, as it were will not have a tent against the heat and rain. And hence Peter is justly rebuked, because when he was not yet confirmed in perfectness of heart, upon the brightness of 'Truth' being made known, he goes about to set up a tent upon earth. [Matt. 17, 4] And thus the righteous are indifferent to build themselves up here below, where they know themselves to be but pilgrims and strangers. For because they desire to have joy in their own, they refuse to be happy in what belongs to another. But the unrighteous, the further they are removed from the inheritance of the eternal Country, fix the foundations of

the heart so much the deeper in the earth. It is hence that in the very beginning of man's creation Enoch is born seventh in the elect family. It is hence that Cain calls his firstborn son Enoch, and names the city that he built after him. [Gen. 4, 17] For 'Enoch' is rendered 'Dedication.' And so the wicked dedicate themselves in the beginning. For in this life, which is first, they plant the root of the heart, that they may flourish here to their content, and wither root and branch to the Country that follows after. But to the righteous, Enoch is born the seventh, in that the festal dedication of their lives is kept for the end. It is hence, as Paul testifies, Abraham dwells *in tents* [so Vulg.], *for he looked for a city which hath foundations, whose builder and maker is God*. [Heb. 11, 9] It is hence that Jacob goes humbly [Vulg. like E.V. *paullatim*] following the flocks of sheep, and Esau coming to meet him lords it with a throng of numerous attendants, in that here both the Elect are without pride, and the lost swell with satisfaction in the good things of the flesh. Hence the Lord says to Israel, *If thou shalt choose one from the people of the land and set him for a king over thee, he shall not multiply horses and horsemen to himself*. [Deut. 17, 15. 16.] And yet the first king 'chosen from among his brethren,' so soon as he had attained the height of power, chose for himself three thousand horsemen; he immediately launched into pride, burst forth in the building up of the height he had attained, in that without he could not keep under on a level of equality all that made his spirit within rise high above the level of others. That rich man had as it were erected for himself a fenced dwelling place, who said, *Soul, thou hast much goods laid up for many years: take thine ease, eat, drink, and be merry*. [Luke 12, 19] But because that dwelling is not bottomed upon the foundation of Truth, he heard at the same moment, *Thou fool, this night thy soul shall be required of thee: then whose shall these things be, which thou hast prepared?* [ver. 20] Therefore it is well said, *And the dwelling-place of the wicked shall come to nought*. In that the lovers of this fleeting life, whilst they diligently build themselves up in present things, are suddenly hurried into eternity.

THE SECOND PART.

BOOK IX.

He explains the ninth Chapter, together with the whole of the tenth.

i. 1. BAD minds, if they have once broken out into the eagerness of opposition, whether what they hear from those that withstand them be right or wrong, assail it with contradictory replies; for whereas the speaker is unwelcome from being in opposition, not even what is right is welcome when he utters it. But, on the other hand, the hearts of the good, whose dislike rises not at the speaker but at the offence, in such sort pass sentence on what is amiss, as to adopt still any right things that are said. For they sit the most even umpires in deciding the sense of their opponents' words, and they so reject what is put forth amiss, that notwithstanding they set the seal upon what they recognise to be delivered in truth. For among a wilderness of thorns the ear [*spica*] is generally to be found growing up from seed good for fruit. Therefore it must be managed with care by the hand of the tiller, that, whilst the thorn [*spina*] is removed, the ear be cherished, so that he, who is eager to root up what pricks, may have sense to preserve what gives nourishment. Hence in that Bildad the Shuhite had said well in enquiry, *Doth God pervert judgment, or doth the Almighty pervert justice?* in that he had delivered true and forcible sentiments against hypocrites, blessed Job, seeing that they were delivered against the wicked in general, admirably treads under foot the prosecution of his own defence, and at once sanctions the truths he had heard, saying,

Historical

Ver. 2. I know it is so of a truth, and that man put with God is not justified.

ii. 2. For man being put under God receives righteousness; being put with God he loses it: for everyone that compares himself with the Author of all good things, bereaves himself of the good which he had received. For he that ascribes to himself blessings vouchsafed to him, is fighting against God with His own gifts. Therefore by whatsoever means he being in contempt is lifted up, it is meet that being so set up he be brought to the ground by the same. Now because he sees that all the worth of our goodness is evil if it be strictly accounted of by the Judge of the interior, the holy man lightly subjoins;

Ver. 3. If thou wilt contend with Him, thou shalt not be able to answer Him one of a thousand.

3. In Holy Scripture, the number a thousand is wont to be taken for totality. Hence the Psalmist says, *The word which He commanded to a thousand generations*; when it is sufficiently plain that from the very beginning of the world up to the coming of our Lord no more than seventy-seven generations are reckoned up by the Evangelist. What then is represented in the number a thousand, save, until the bringing forth of the new offspring, the complete whole of the race foreseen. Hence it is said by John, *And shall reign with Him a thousand years* [Rev. 20, 6]; for that the reign of Holy Church is made complete by being perfected in entireness. Now forasmuch as a unit being multiplied is brought to ten, and ten being taken into itself is expanded to one hundred, which again being multiplied by ten is extended to a thousand, since we set out with one to get to one thousand, what is here denoted by the designation of 'one' but the commencement of good living? what by the fulness of the number 'a thousand,' but the perfection of that good life? Now to contend with God is not to ascribe to Him but to take to one's self the glory of one's goodness. But let the holy man consider that the man who has already received even the chiefest gifts, if he is lifted up for what has been vouchsafed him, parts with all that he had received, and let him say, *If he will contend with Him, he cannot answer Him one of a thousand*. For he, that 'contends' with his Maker, is unable to 'answer Him one of a thousand,' in that the man that sets himself up on the score of perfection, proves that be lacks the very beginning of good living. For we cannot 'answer Him one of a thousand,' since when we are lifted up for perfection of good life, we show that we have not so much as begun this. Now we are then more really moved by our weakness, when by reflection, we are led to form an estimate how infinite is the power of the Judge. **iii.**

Ver. 4. He is wise in heart, and mighty in strength.

4. What wonder is it, if we call the Maker of the wise, 'wise,' Whom we know to be Wisdom itself? and what wonder is it that he describes Him to be 'mighty,' Whom there is none that doth not know to be this very Mightiness itself? But the holy man, by the two words set forth in praise of the Creator, conveys a **iv.**

meaning to us, whereby to recall us in trembling to the knowledge of ourselves. For God is called 'wise,' in that He exactly knows our secret hearts, and it is added that He is 'mighty,' in that He smites them forcibly, so known. And so He can neither be deceived by us, because He is wise, nor be escaped, because He is strong. Now, as wise, He beholds all things, Himself unseen, then, as strong, without let or hindrance, He punishes those whom He condemns. Who ordains this likewise here with mightiness of wisdom, that when the human mind exalts itself against the Creator, it should confound itself by that very self-exaltation. And hence it is added,

Who hath resisted Him, and had peace?

v. 5. For He that creates all things marvellously, Himself regulates them, that after having been created, they should agree with themselves; and thus whereinsoever there is resistance made to the Creator, that agreement in peace is broken up, in that those things can never be well regulated, which lose the management of regulation above. For whatsoever things if subjected to God might have continued at peace, being left to themselves by their own act work their own confusion, in that they do not find in themselves that peace, which coming from above they contend against in the Creator. Thus that highest Angelical Spirit, who being in subjection to God might have stood at the height, being banished, has to bear the burthen of himself, in that he roams abroad in disquietude in his own nature. Thus the first parent of the human race, in that he went against the precept of his Creator, was thereupon exposed to the insolence of the flesh, and because he would not be subject to His Maker in obedience, being laid low beneath himself, even the peace of the body was forthwith lost to him. Thus it is well said, *Who hath resisted Him, and had peace?* In that by the same act, whereby the froward mind lifts itself against its Maker, it works its own confusion in itself. Now we are said to resist God, when we try to oppose His dispensations. Not that our frailty does resist His unchangeable decree, but what it has not the power to accomplish, it yet attempts. For often human weakness knows in secret the power of His dispensation, and yet aims, if it might be able, to reverse it. It sets to work to resist, but shivers itself to pieces by the very sword of its opposition. It struggles against the interior disposition of things, but, being overcome by its own efforts, is bound fast. Therefore to have peace whilst resisting can never be; for whereas confusion follows after pride, that which is foolishly done in sin is marvellously disposed to the punishment of the doer; but the holy Man, being filled with the influence of the Spirit of prophecy, while he regards in general the confounding of human pride, thereupon directs the eye of the mind to the special fate of the Jewish people, and shows by the ruin of a single people the punishment that awaits all that are lifted up. For he immediately adds in these words,

Ver. 5. Which removed the mountains, and they knew not whom He overturned in His anger.

Allegorical

vi.

6. Oftentimes in Holy Writ by the title of 'mountains,' the loftiness of Preachers is set forth. Of whom it is said by the Psalmist, *The mountains shall receive peace for Thy people*. [Ps. 72, 3] For the Elect Preachers of the eternal Land are not unjustly called 'mountains,' in that by the loftiness of their lives they leave the low bottoms of earthly regions, and are brought near to heaven. Now 'Truth' 'removed the mountains' when He withdrew the holy Preachers from the stubbornness of Judaea. Whence too it is rightly said by the Psalmist, *The mountains shall be carried into the heart of the sea*. [Ps. 46, 2] For 'the mountains were removed into the heart of the sea,' when the Apostles in their preaching, thrust off by the faithlessness of Judaea, came to the understanding of the Gentiles. Hence they themselves say in their Acts, *It was necessary that the word should first have been spoken to you but seeing ye put it from you and Judge yourselves unworthy of everlasting life, lo, we turn to the Gentiles*. [Acts 13, 46] Now this same 'removing of the mountains' they themselves 'knew nothing of, who were overthrown in the wrath of the Lord;' for when the Hebrew people drove the Apostles from their coasts, they supposed that they had made gain, in that they had parted with the light of preaching, since as their deserts demanded, being struck with a just visitation, they were blinded by so great a delusion of the understanding, that their losing the light they accounted to be joy; but upon the rejection of the Apostles, Judaea is at once brought to destruction by the hands of the Roman Emperor Titus, and she is dispersed and scattered abroad among all nations. And hence it is rightly added to the removing of the mountains,

Ver. 6. Which shaketh the earth out of her place and the pillars thereof shall tremble.

vii. 7. For 'the earth was shaken out of her place,' when the Israelitish people, rooted out of the borders of Judaea, submitted the neck to the Gentiles, because she would not be subjected to the Creator. Which same earth had pillars, in that the erection of her stubbornness, which was to be destroyed, rose upon the Priests and Rulers, the Teachers of the Law and the Pharisees. For in these she held in her the edifice of the letter, and in her season of peace, carried the burthen of carnal sacrifices like a fabric overlaid. But when 'the mountains were removed,' the 'pillars were shaken,' in that when the Apostles were withdrawn from Judaea, they were no more themselves allowed to live therein, who drove out from thence the proclaimers of life. For it was meet that they being brought into subjection should lose that earthly country, for the love of which they had not been afraid to assail the soldiers of the heavenly country. But upon the holy Teachers being drawn out, Judaea waxed altogether gross, and by the righteous inquest of Him That judgeth, she shut the eyes of the mind in the darkness of her delusion. Hence it is yet further continued;

Ver. 7. Which commandeth the sun, and it riseth not, and shutteth up the stars as under a seal.

viii. 8. Now sometimes in Holy Writ by the title of 'sun,' we have the brightness of the Preachers represented, as it is said by John, *And the sun became black as sackcloth of hair*. [Rev. 6, 12] For at the end of time the sun is exhibited 'like sackcloth of hair,' in that the shining life of them that preach is set forth before the eyes of the lost as hard and contemptible. And they are represented by the brightness of stars also, in that whilst they preach right doctrines to sinners, they enlighten the darkness of our night. And hence upon the removal of the Preachers it is said by the Prophet, *The stars of the rain are withholden*. Now whereas the sun shines in the day time, the stars illumine the shades of night. And very often in Holy Writ by the designation of *day* is denoted the eternal Country, and by the name of *night*, the present life. Holy preachers become like the sun to our eyes, inasmuch as they open to us the view of the true light; and they shine like stars in the dark, when for the purpose of helping our necessities they manage earthly things in an active life. They, as it were, shine as the sun in the day, whilst they raise the eye of our mind to contemplate the land of interior brightness, and they glitter like stars in the night, in that even whilst they are engaged in earthly action, they guide the foot of our practice, every moment on the point of stumbling, by the example of their own uprightness. But because when the Preachers were driven out, there was none who might either show the brightness of contemplation, or disclose the light of an active life to the Jewish people continuing in the night of their unbelief, (for the Truth, which being cast off abandoned them, when the light of preaching was removed, blinded them in reward of their wickedness,) it is rightly said, *Which commandeth the sun, and it riseth not, and shutteth up the stars as under a seal.* For He would not let the sun rise to that people, from whom He turned away the heart of the Preachers, and He 'shut up the stars as under a seal,' in that while He kept His Preachers to themselves in silence, He hid the heavenly light from the darkened perceptions of the wicked.

9. But it is to be considered, that we shut up anything under seal with this view, that when the time suits, we may bring it out to the light. And we have learnt by the testimony of Holy Writ, that Judaea, which is now left desolate, shall be gathered into the bosom of the Faith at the end. Hence it is declared by Isaiah, *For though thy people Israel be as the sand of the sea, yet a remnant of them shall be saved.* [Is. 10, 22] Hence Paul says, *Until the fulness of the Gentiles should come in, and so all Israel should be saved.* [Rom. 11, 25. 26.] Therefore He That removes His Preachers now from the eyes of Judaea, and afterwards exhibits them, has as it were 'shut up the stars under a seal,' that the rays of the spiritual stars being first hidden and afterwards beaming forth, she both being now cast off may not see the night of her misbelief, and then by being enlightened may find it out. It is hence that those two illustrious Preachers were removed, but their death delayed, that they might be brought back in the end for the purpose of preaching; of whom it is said by John, *These are the two olive trees and the two candlesticks standing before the Lord of the earth.* [Rev. 11, 4] One of whom 'Truth' by His own lips gives promise of in the Gospel, saying, *Elias truly shall first come, and restore all things.* [Matt. 17, 11] They then are as if the 'stars' were 'shut up under a seal,' who both at this present are concealed that they appear not, and hereafter shall appear that they may stand Him in good stead.

THE SECOND PART.

Yet the Israelitish people, which shall be gathered in full measure in the end, in the immediate infancy of Holy Church is pitilessly hardened. For it rejected the Preachers of the Truth, it spurned the message of succour. Yet this is effected by the marvellous contrivance of the Creator with this view, that the glory of the persons preaching, which if received might have lain hid in one people, being rejected might be spread abroad among all the nations. Hence too it is fitly added immediately afterwards ;

Ver. 8. Which alone spreadeth out the heavens.

ix. 10. For what is denoted by the name of 'the heavens,' but this very heavenly life of the persons preaching, of whom it is said by the Psalmist, *The heavens declare the glory of God*. [Ps. 19, 1] Thus the same persons are recorded to be the heavens, and the same to be the sun; the heavens indeed, in that by interposing [*intercedendo*] they shield; the sun, in that by preaching they display the power of light. And so, upon the 'earth being shaken' 'the heavens were spread out,' in that when Judaea ravened in the violence of persecution, the Lord spread wide the life of the Apostles, for all the Gentiles to acquaint themselves withal. And whilst she in judgment being made captive is scattered over the world, they by grace are every where amplified in honour. For 'the heavens' were of small compass, so long as one people contained so many mighty preachers. For to which of the Gentiles would Peter have been known, if he had continued in the preaching to the Jewish people alone? Who would have known of Paul's virtues, unless Judaea by persecuting him had transmitted him to our knowledge? See how already they, that were thrust off with scourges and with insults by the Israelitish people, are held in honour throughout the length and breadth of the world. The Lord alone then 'has spread out the heavens,' Who, by the wondrous ordering of His secret counsel, from the very cause, that He let His Preachers be persecuted in one people, caused them to spread out even to the comers of the world. But yet neither did this Gentile folk itself, which was devoted to the present world, when the tongues of the Apostles rebuked its iniquities, gladly welcome the words of life. For it forthwith swelled up in the pride of opposition, and roused itself to the cruelty of persecution. But she that sets herself to gainsay the words of preaching, is speedily subdued in wonderment at miraculous signs. Hence too the words are fitly added in praise of the Creator,

And treadeth upon the wave of the sea.

11. For what is denoted by the title of 'the sea,' but this world's bitterness raging in the destruction of the righteous? Concerning which it is said by the Psalmist too, *He gathereth the waters of the sea together as in a skin.* [Ps. 33, 7. Vulg.] For the Lord 'gathereth the waters of the sea together as in a skin,' when, disposing all things with a wonderful governance, He restrains the threats of the carnal pent up in their hearts. Thus 'the Lord treadeth upon the waves of the sea.' For when the storms of persecution lift up themselves, they are dashed in pieces in astonishment at His miracles. Since He that brings down the swellings of man's madness, as it were treads the waters standing up in a heap. Thus when the Gentile world saw that her form and fashion was undone through the preaching of the Apostles, when the rich sons of this world beheld poor men's deeds arrayed against their arrogance, when the wise men of this generation marked that the words of unlettered men were set in opposition to them, they swelled thereupon in a storm of persecution. Yet they who, being moved by the opposition of words, burst out in storms of persecution, are calmed, as we have said, by wonder at the miraculous signs. So the Lord set as many steps upon these waves, as He exhibited miracles to the persecutors in their pride. Whence it is well said again by the Psalmist, *Marvellously the floods lift up their waves; marvellous is the Lord on high.* [Ps. 93, 3. 4.] For against the life of the Elect the world has lifted itself wonderfully in waves of persecution, but the Creator of things above has still more marvellously put these down in the exaltation of the Preachers' power; for He showed that His ministers prevailed more in miracles above all that the powers of the earth had swelled unto in anger. Which the Lord moreover well delivered by the lips of Jeremiah, while relating outward things, telling of inward ones; *I have placed the sand for the bound of the sea, by a perpetual decree that it cannot pass it; and though the waves thereof toss themselves, yet can they not prevail: though they roar, yet can they not pass over it.* [Jer. 5, 22] For 'the Lord has placed the sand for the bound of the sea;' in that He has made choice of the despised and poor to dash in pieces the glory of the world. 'The waves of which same sea toss themselves,' when

the powers of the world leap forth in the uproar of persecution. Yet they cannot pass over the sand, in that they are broken in pieces by the miracles and the humility of the despised and scorned. But whilst the sea rages, while it is lifted up in the waves of its madness, yet whereas it is trodden upon by the manifestation of interior Power, Holy Church makes way, and by the accessions of time she rises to the station of her own rank [or 'the establishing of her own order'] Hence it is rightly added immediately afterwards,

Ver. 9. Which maketh Arcturus, Orion, and Hyades, and the chambers of the south.

xi. 12. The word of Truth never follows the vain fables of Hesiod, Aratus, or Callimachus, that in naming Arcturus it should take the last of the seven stars for the tail of the bear, or as if Orion were holding a sword as a mad lover; for these names of the stars were invented by the votaries of carnal wisdom, but Holy Scripture for this reason makes use of these words, that the things which it aims to convey instruction about, may be represented by the customariness of their usual designation. For if he had spoken of any stars he might wish by names unknown to us, man, for whom this very Scripture was made, would assuredly have known nothing what he heard. Thus in Holy Writ the wise ones of God derive their speech from the wise ones of the world, in like sort as therein God the very Creator of man, for man's benefit, takes in Himself the tones of human passion, i.e. so as to say, *It repenteth Me that I have made man upon the earth* [Gen. 6, 6. 7.]; whereas it is plain and undoubted that He, Who beholds all things before they come, after He has done anything, never repents by feeling regret. What wonder is it, then, if spiritual men use the words of carnal men, when the Ineffable Spirit Himself, Which is the Creator of all things, in order to draw the flesh to the understanding of Him, in His own case frames His speech of the flesh? Thus in Holy Writ, when we hear the familiar names of the stars, we learn what stars the discourse runs on. And after we have well weighed what stars are described, it remains that from their motions we be led to raise ourselves to the mysteries of the spiritual meaning. For not even after the letter is there anything strange, in that it is said that God created Arcturus, and the Orions, and the Hyades, concerning Whom it is an acknowledged truth, that there is nothing of any sort in the world but He Himself made it. But the holy man declares that the Lord made these, by which he means properly to denote things that are done in a spiritual way.

13. For what is represented by the name of Arcturus, which being set in the polar region of the heavens shines bright with the rays of seven stars, except the Church universal, which is represented in the Apocalypse of John by the seven Churches and the seven candlesticks? Which same, while She contains in Herself the gifts of sevenfold grace, beaming with the brightness of highest virtue, as it were gives light from the polar region of Truth. And it is furthermore to be considered, that Arcturus is ever turned about, and never sunk from sight, in that Holy Church ever undergoes the persecutions of the wicked without ceasing, and yet endures without failing 'even unto the end of the world.' For oftentimes because the sons of perdition have persecuted her even to the death, they have been persuaded that they had as it were utterly extinguished her, but she returned with manifold increase to the rearing of her full growth, in proportion as she travailed in dying amidst the hands of Her persecutors. Thus while Arcturus is turned about, he is set on high, for Holy Church is then more strongly reinvigorated in the Truth, when she spends herself more fervently for the Truth.

14. Hence too after Arcturus he immediately subjoins the 'Oriones' with propriety. For they arise in the very heaviest of the winter season, and they stir up storms by their rising, and put sea and land in commotion. What then is denoted by 'the Oriones,' after 'Arcturus,' saving the Martyrs? who, while Holy Church is set on high to take her stand of preaching, destined to undergo the weight of the persecutors and harassing treatment, came into the face of heaven, as it were, in the winter season. For when they were born, the sea and the land were troubled, in that when the Gentile world grieved that its method of life was undone, on their courage appearing, it set up for their destruction not only the fiery and turbulent, but the mild among men also. And thus the winter lowered in 'the Oriones,' in that when the constancy of the Saints shone out, the frozen soul of the unbelievers lashed itself into a tempest of persecution. And so 'the heavens' gave forth the Oriones, when Holy Church sent out her Martyrs, who whilst they had boldness to speak what is right to the uninstructed, brought upon themselves everything most heavy from the adverse bitterness of cold.

THE SECOND PART.

15. Now he justly subjoins the Hyades directly, which, when the springtide is waxing, go forth into the face of heaven, and, when the sun is now putting out the power of his heat, are given to sight. For they are attached to the beginnings of that sign, which the wise of this world call 'the Bull,' at which the sun begins to increase, and arises with more fervent heat, to lengthen out the periods of the day. Who, then, after 'the Oriones,' are denoted by the title of 'the Hyades,' saving the Doctors of Holy Church, who; when the Martyrs were taken away, came at that period to the world's knowledge, when faith now shines forth the brighter, and the winter of infidelity being forced back, the sun of truth flows deeper through the hearts of the faithful. These, when the storm of persecution was overpast, and the nights of long infidelity consummated, then arose to Holy Church, when the year now opens brighter in the vernal season of belief. Nor are the holy Doctors improperly denoted by the designation of 'Hyades,' for in the Greek tongue rain is called 'Hyetus;' and the 'Hyades' have received their name from the rains, surely because at their rising they bring showers. Thus they are well represented by the title of 'the Hyades,' who, brought out in the settled frame of Holy Church, as it were into the face of heaven, upon the parched earth of the human heart poured down the showers of holy preaching. For if the word of preaching were not rain, Moses would never have said, *Let my doctrine be waited for as the rain*. [Deut. 32, 2] 'Truth' would never have said by the lips of Isaiah, *I will also command the clouds that they rain no rain upon it;* [Is. 5, 6] and that which we brought forward a little above, *Therefore the stars of the showers are withholden*. [Jer. 3, 3] Thus while the Hyades come bringing showers, the sun is led on to the higher regions of heaven; in that, when the knowledge of the Doctors appears, while our minds drink in the showers of preaching, the heat of faith increases. And the earth being irrigated is rendered productive in fruit, when the light of the sky is fired; in that we yield the fruit of good works the more plentifully, the brighter we burn within our breasts through the flame of sacred instruction. And while heavenly lore is displayed to view by them more and more day by day, it is as if the springtide of interior light were opened upon us, that the new Sun may glow brightly in our souls, and being by their words made known to us, may daily surpass itself in brilliancy. For the end of the world being close at hand, the knowledge from above advances, and waxes bigger with

the progress of time. For hence it is said by Daniel, *Many shall run to and fro, and knowledge shall be increased*. [Dan. 12, 4] Hence the Angel says to John in the former part of the Revelation, *Seal up those things, which the seven thunders uttered*; [Rev. 10, 4] and yet at the end of that Revelation he bids him, saying, *Seal not the sayings of the prophecy of this book*. [Ib. 22, 10] For the first part of the Revelation is commanded to be sealed, but the end not to be sealed; for whatever was hidden in the beginnings of Holy Church, the end clears up day by day. But some imagine that 'the Hyades' are named from the Greek letter which is rendered by 'Y;' which, if it be so, is not opposed to the sense which we have given: the Doctors are not unsuitably represented by those stars which have their name from letters; but, though 'the Hyades' are not unlike the look of that letter, yet it is a fact that a shower is called 'Hyetus,' and that those at their rising bring with them rain.

16. Therefore let the holy man, viewing the order of our redemption, feel wonder, and wondering let him cry out, in the words, *Which alone spreadeth out the heavens, and treadeth upon the waves of the sea. Which maketh Arcturus, the Oriones, and Hyades*. For, when the heavens were spread out, the Lord made 'Arcturus,' in that, when the Apostles were brought to honour, He stablished the Church in heavenly conversation, and when Arcturus was made, He framed 'the Oriones,' in that the faith of the Church Universal being established, He launched forth the Martyrs against the storms of the world. And when 'the Oriones' were launched in heaven, He set forth 'the Hyades,' in that when the Martyrs proved strong against adversities, He vouchsafed the teaching of Masters, to water the drought of human hearts. These then are the ranks of the spiritual stars, which while they stand out conspicuous by the highest virtues, are ever shining from above.

17. But what remains after these things, saving that Holy Church, receiving the fruit of her toils, should attain to behold the inner depths of the Country above? And hence, whereas he had said, *Which maketh Arcturus, the Oriones, and the Hyades*; he rightly added directly, *and the chambers of the South*. For what is here denoted by the name of 'the South,' saving the fervour of the Holy Spirit? with which he that is replenished, kindles to the love of the spiritual Country. And hence it is said by the voice of the Spouse in the Song of Solomon, *Arise, O north wind, and come thou south, blow upon my gar-*

den, that the spices thereof may flow out. For upon the 'south wind' coming, the 'north wind' arising departs, when our old enemy, who had bound up our soul in inactivity, being expelled by the coming of the Holy Spirit, takes himself away. And 'the south wind blows upon the garden' of the Spouse, that 'the spices thereof may flow down;' in that, whensoever the Spirit of Truth has filled Holy Church with the excellences of His gifts, He scatters far and wide from her the odours of good works. And thus 'the chambers of the South' are those unseen orders of the Angels, and those unfathomed depths of the heavenly Country, which are filled with the heat of the Holy Spirit. For thither are brought the souls of the Saints, both at this present time divested of the body, and hereafter restored to the same anew, and like stars they are concealed in hidden depths. There all the day, as at midday, the fire of the sun burns with a brighter lustre, in that the brightness of our Creator, which is now overlaid with the mists of our mortal state, is rendered more clearly visible; and the beam of the orb seems to raise itself to higher regions, in that 'Truth' from Its own Self enlightens us more completely through and through. There the light of interior contemplation is seen without the intervening shadow of mutability; there is the heat of supreme Light without any dimness from the body; there the unseen bands of Angels glitter like stars in hidden realms, which cannot now be seen by men, in proportion as they are deeper bathed in the flame of the true Light. Thus it is altogether marvellous that, in the sending of the Apostles, the Lord stretched out the Heavens; that, in moderating the swellings of persecution He trode the waves of the sea, and kept them down; that in the stablishing of the Church, He set 'Arcturus' in his place; that in making the Martyrs proof against afflictions, He sent forth 'the Oriones;' that in the Doctors being replenished in peace, He gave forth 'the Hyades;' but after these it is beyond all comparison marvellous, that He should have provided for us the haven of the heavenly Land, as 'the chambers of the South.'

18. All this is beautiful, that is seen as it were in the face of heaven of God's ordering; but infinitely and incomparably more beautiful is that, to which we are brought without its being able to be seen. Hence the Spouse justly repeats a second time in the commendation of His Bride; *Behold thou art fair, my love; behold thou art fair: thou hast doves' eyes, besides that which lieth hidden within.* [Cant. 4, 1] He de-

scribes her 'fair,' and says again 'fair,' in that there is one sort of beauty of life and conduct, wherein she is now seen, and another beauty of rewards, wherein she will then be lifted up in the likeness of her Creator; and because her members, which are all the Elect, go about all things with simplicity, her eyes are called 'doves' eyes;' which shine with extraordinary light, for that they glitter even with the signs of miraculous power. But how great is all this marvel, which is able to be seen! That marvel relating to things of the interior is more wonderful, which is not now able to be seen, concerning which it is fitly added in that place, *Besides that which lieth hidden within*. For the glory of the visible world is great, but the glory of the secret recompensing far beyond comparison. That, then, which is denoted by the name of 'stars' by blessed Job, is in the words of Solomon represented by the title of 'eyes;' and what is described by Solomon, *Besides that which lieth within*, blessed Job conveys to us, when he extols 'the chambers of the South.' But see; the holy man in admiring things without, and contemplating those of the interior, telling of things manifest, and diving into things secret, aims to describe all that is done both within and without; but when shall the tongue of flesh unfold the works of the Supreme Greatness? And hence with just propriety directly afterwards, by giving up the attempt, he measures the compass of these same works the more effectually, saying,

Ver. 10. Which doeth great things past finding out; yea, and wonders without number.

xii.

19. For then we more thoroughly compass the deeds of Divine Might, when we acknowledge that we can never compass them; we then speak with greater eloquence, when we are silent on these, being struck dumb with astonishment. Since for the describing of God's works our insufficiency finds in itself how it may put forth its tongue sufficiently, that what it cannot suitably understand, it may suitably extol by being dumb. Whence it is well said by the Psalmist, *Praise Him in His mighty acts; praise Him according to His excellent greatness*. [Ps. 150, 2] For He 'praises God according to His excellent greatness,' who sees that he breaks down in the fulfilling of His praise. Therefore let him say, *Which doeth great things past finding out; yea, and wonders without number*: viz. 'great,' in power, 'past finding out,' in reason, 'without number,' in multitude.

THE SECOND PART.

Therefore the works of God which he could not compass by speaking, he more eloquently defined by proving deficient. But in the review of things, why are we carried so far without ourselves, considering that we know nothing of the very thing that is done to our own selves? Hence it is fitly added,

Ver. 11. Lo, if He come to me, I see Him not: if He passeth on, I perceive him not.

xiii. 20. For the human race being shut out from the interior joys, in due of sin, lost the eyes of the mind; and whither it is going with the steps of its deserts, it cannot tell. Thus, often that is the gift of grace which it takes to be wrath, and often that is the wrath of God's severity, which it supposes to be grace. For very commonly it reckons gifts of virtue as grace, and yet being uplifted by those gifts is brought to the ground; and very often it dreads the opposition of temptations as wrath, and yet being bowed down by those temptations, arises the more solicitous to the safe keeping of its virtuous attainments. For who would not reckon himself to be nigh to God, when he sees that he is magnified with gifts from on high, when either the gift of prophecy or the mastership of teaching is vouchsafed him, or when he is empowered to exercise the grace of healing? Yet it often happens that whilst the mind is made to sit loose by self-security in its virtues, from the adversary plotting against it, it is pierced 'with the weapon of unexpected sin, and is for ever put far away from God by the very means whereby for a time it was brought near to Him without the caution of heedfulness. And who would not look upon himself as now abandoned by Divine grace, when after experiencing purity, he sees that he is sorely pressed by the temptations of the flesh, that things unbefitting crowd on the mind, and before the eyes of fancy there pass things disgraceful and impure? Yet, when such things as these harass but not subdue, they do not slaughter by the effect of corrupting, but preserve by their effect of humbling, that the mind, finding itself weak under temptation, may wholly betake itself to the assistance of the Divine Being, and completely give over all confidence in itself; and thus it is brought to pass, that it attaches itself to God the deeper by the same thing, by which it was made to lament its having fallen away the lower from God. Therefore the coming and going of God are not at all discoverable by our faculties, so long as the issue of alternating states is hidden from our eyes; in that there is no certainty concerning the trial, whether it be a test of virtue or an instrument of our destruction; and concerning gifts we never find out whether they are the reward here of such as are given up, or whether they are a support on the road to bring men to their native Country. Thus let man, once banished from the interior joys, view the doors of the secret place of the Spirit shut against him, and cast forth to himself without, let him groan in the flesh, and seeing the losses which his blindness entails upon him, exclaim, *Lo, if He come to me, I see Him not; if He passeth on, I perceive Him not*. As if he lamented openly, saying, 'Since I have once lost my eyes by my own act and deed, as I am bearing the darkness of a self-sought night, now I neither know the rising nor the setting of the sun.' Yet man, who is pressed down by the infliction of infirmity, and heavy laden with the darkness of his blind estate, is going forward to the Judgment of the Light above, that he may render an account of his actions. And hence it is added immediately afterwards,

Ver. 12. If He question on a sudden, who will answer Him?

21. God 'questions suddenly' when He calls us unexpectedly to the strict searching of His scrutiny. But man cannot answer to His questioning, for that, if he be then sifted, all pity laid aside, even the life of the righteous sinks under the scrutiny. Or, surely, He questions, when He deals us hard blows, that, when the mind entertains great thoughts of itself in peace and quiet, it may find itself out in trouble, what sort it really is of. And very commonly because it is smitten, it utters groans; but it is unable to make answer, because the very distastefulness of his stroke is displeasing to him, yet looking to himself man holds his peace, and dreads to scrutinize the Divine decrees, because he knows himself to be but dust. Hence it is said by Paul, *Nay, but, O man, who art thou that repliest against God?* [Rom. 9, 20] He that is called by the name of 'man' (homo) is proved to be unable to 'reply against God.' For by this circumstance, that he was taken from the dust of the earth, he is not worthy to scrutinize the judgments of the Most High. Hence too it is fitly subjoined here, **xiv.**

Or, who will say unto Him, What doest Thou?

22. The acts of our Maker ought always to be reverenced **xv.**

without examining, for they can never be unjust. For to seek a reason for His secret counsel is nothing else than to erect one's self in pride against His counsel. So when the motive of His acts cannot be discovered, it remains that we be silent under those acts in humility, for the fleshly sense is not equal that it should penetrate the secrets of His Majesty. He then who sees no reason in the acts of God, on considering his own weakness does see reason wherefore he sees none. Hence also it is added by Paul afterwards, *Shall the thing formed say to Him that formed it, Why hast Thou made me so?* For in proportion as it sees itself to be 'a thing formed' by God's workmanship, it rebukes itself so as not to kick back against the hand of Him that wrought it; for He, Who in loving-kindness exalted what was not, never in injustice abandons that which is. So let the mind be brought to itself under the stroke, and what it cannot comprehend, let it cease to require, lest if the cause of God's wrath be searched out, It be called forth in larger measure for being searched out, and lest wrath, which humility might have pacified, pride kindle to an unextinguishable height. Hence it is moreover fitly added concerning this same Wrath,

Ver. 13. God, Whose wrath none can resist, and under Whom they that bear the world are bowed down.

xvi. 23. It is very strange that it is declared that none can resist God's wrath, seeing that the divine Oracles witness that many have withstood the wrathfulness of the visitation of Heaven. Did not Moses resist God's wrath, when standing up for the fallen people, He restrained the very impulse of the stroke from above, by the oblation of his own death, saying, *Yet now if Thou wilt forgive their sin:—and if not, blot me, I pray Thee, out of the book, which Thou hast written?* [Exod. 32, 32] Did not Aaron resist God's wrath, when between the living and the dead he took a censer, and assuaged the fire of visitation with the fumes of incense? [Numb. 16, 47. &c.] Did not Phinees resist God's wrath, when slaughtering them that went a whoring with strange women in the very act, he offered his zeal to the Divine wrath, and pacified fury with the sword? [Ib. 25, 11] Did not David resist God's wrath, who by presenting himself to the Angel, as he dealt destruction, won the grace of propitiation, even before the appointed time? [2 Sam. 24, 25] Did not Elijah resist God's wrath, who when the earth was now for long dried up, brought back by a word the showers withdrawn from the heavens? [1 Kings 18, 44] In what sense then was it said that none can resist the wrath of God, when it is proved by existing examples that numbers have resisted it? However, if we minutely consider both these words of blessed Job, and the deeds of those persons, we both find it to be true that there is no resisting the Divine Wrath, and also true that many have often resisted it. For all Saints that encounter the wrath of God, obtain it from Himself, that they should be thus set in the way to meet the force of His stroke; and so to say having Him with them, they lift up themselves against Him, and the Divine Power arms them in alliance with Itself against Itself. Since in that which they achieve against the wrath of Him dealing cruelly without, the grace of Him so angered encourages them within, and He bears up those serving Him inwardly, whom He submits to resisting Him outwardly. Thus He bears the supplicant's contradiction which He inspires, and that is forced upon Him as though He were unwilling, which is by Himself commanded to be done. For He says to Moses, *Now therefore let Me alone, that My wrath may wax hot against them, and that I may consume them, and I will make of thee a great nation*. [Ex. 32, 10] What is it to say to His servant, *Let Me alone*; but to give him boldness to supplicate? As if He said in plain words, 'Consider how thou prevailest with Me, and know that thou mayest obtain whatsoever thou beseechest for the People.' And that the thing is done with this mind, is witnessed by the pardon which is immediately subjoined. But when the Wrath above moveth Itself, so to say, from the heart's core, human opposition cannot stay It; and no man's entreaty presents itself to any purpose, when once God ordains anything whilst angered from His inward Deep. For it is hence that Moses, who blotted out by his entreaties the guilt of the whole People in God's sight, and whilst he offered himself in the way, appeased the force of the Divine indignation, when he came to the rock Horeb, and for the bringing forth the water gave way to distrust, could never enter the Land of Promise from the Lord being wroth. And oftentimes he is distressed on this score, often he is troubled by his regret making itself felt, and yet he could never remove from himself the anger of an ordained retribution, who by God's good pleasure removed it even from the very people. Hence David, who afterwards by prayer held back the sword of the Angel from the fallen People, first fled from his son with bare feet howling and lamenting, and until he received to the full the cup of vengeance for the transgression he had done, he could never abate the wrath of the Lord for himself. [2 Sam. 24, 10] Hence Elijah, that as a mortal man he might as it were feel some little of God's visitation, he, who opened the heavens with a word, fled in terror through the wilderness from a woman's indignation; and he proves weak for himself in his dismay, who appeases God's fury for others through his intercession. Thus there is both a possibility of resisting the wrath of God, when He, That is wroth Himself, vouchsafes aid; and there is no possibility at all of resisting it, when He both rouses Himself to deal vengeance, and doth not Himself inspire the prayer that is poured forth to Him. Hence it is said to Jeremiah, *Therefore pray not thou for this people, neither take to thee praise and prayer for them; for I will not hear in the time of their crying to Me*; [Jer. 7, 16] and again, *Though Moses and Samuel stood before Me, yet My mind could not be toward this people.* [Jer. 15, 1]

Literal

24. Wherein it may be usefully enquired wherefore, so many more ancient fathers being set aside, Moses and Samuel alone are preferably and preeminently singled out for the utterance of prayer? Which however we easily learn, if we weigh well the claims of that charity which is bidden to love even enemies. For that prayer comes with a special recommendation to the ears of our Creator, which exerts itself to make intercession for our enemies too; and hence 'Truth' says by His own lips, *Pray for them that despitefully use you and persecute you*. [Matt. 5, 44] And again, *When ye stand praying, forgive, if ye have ought against any*. [Mark 11, 25] Now when we revolve the deeds of the fathers of old time as Holy Writ describes them, we find that it was Moses and Samuel, who prayed for their adversaries. For one of them had to fly from the persecution of that infuriated People, and yet he interceded for the persecutor's life: the other being deposed from the rule of the People, says to his own adversaries themselves, *God forbid that I should sin against the Lord in ceasing to pray for you*. [1 Sam. 12, 23] Therefore in the difficult work of deprecating wrath, what is it to bring forward Moses and Samuel, but to show the more plainly that not even they if they stood forward would stay His wrath, who might for this reason have interceded the sooner for their friends, that they were used to intercede with Him even for their enemies. Hence it is said to that same Judaea, *I have wounded thee with the wound of an enemy, with the chas-*

tisement of a cruel one. And again, *Why criest thou for thine affliction? Thy sorrow is incurable.* [Jer. 30, 14. 15.] Let the holy man then regard how the wrath of God is restrained by no man's intercession, when once it is inexorably called forth, and let him say, *God, Whose wrath none can resist.* And this we rightly reduce to a particular sense, if we reflect on the woes of that same Israelitish People, which the Saviour, Who was made manifest in the mystery of His economy; abandoned in their pride, and called the Gentiles to the grace of the knowledge of Him. And hence it is rightly subjoined directly, *Under Whom they that bear the world are bowed down.*

25. For they do bear the world, who sustain the cares and concerns of the present world. Since every one is necessitated to bear the burthens of as great things as he is a leader of in this world; and hence a ruler of the earth is not unsuitably designated in the Greek tongue 'basileus.' For 'laus' means 'people.' Basileus therefore is the title 'basis laou' which in the Latin tongue is rendered 'basis populi,' or, 'the base of the people;' since it is he that bears up the people upon himself, in that he controls its motions, himself steadied by the weight of power. For in proportion as he bears the burthens of his subjects, like a base he supports a column raised upon it. Let blessed Job, then, full of the power of the prophetic Spirit, see how Judaea is forsaken, and the rulers of the Gentiles are bowed to the worship of the Divine Being, and let him say, *God, Whose wrath none can resist, under Whom they that bear the world are bowed down.* As though he plainly owned, saying, 'Both the People, that was once subject to Thee, Thou forsakest in Thy severity, and the powers of the Gentiles, that set up their heads, Thou bendest low in Thy mercy.'

26. Though hereby, that it is said, *Under Whom they that bear the world are bowed down*; we may also understand the Angelical powers; for these bear the world, in that they execute the charges of the governing of the universe, as Paul bears witness, when he says, *Are they not all ministering spirits, sent forth to minister for them that shall be heirs of salvation.* [Heb. 1, 14] Thus he says, *God, Whose wrath none can resist, under Whom they that bear the world are bowed down.* As if he beheld the humiliation of every created being, and said in fear and trembling, 'Which of frail mortals resists Thy nod, before Whose might the Angelic Powers themselves bow down themselves?' Or, surely, since, when we are bowed down, we see nothing of things

above us, those subtlest spirits must needs have been erect, if they completely reached the power of His Majesty; but 'they that bear the world, are bowed down under God,' for though when they are lifted up they behold the loftiness of the Divine Nature, yet not even the Angelic Powers attain to comprehend It. Which Same the righteous man failing from infirmity to fathom, and yet in some degree estimating It from the ministrations of the most exalted spirits being subject to Him, falls back to the consideration of himself with heedful humility, and makes himself little in his own eyes compared with the omnipotence of the Supreme Majesty; saying,

Ver. 14. How great am I that I should answer Him, and talk with Him in my words?

xvii. 27. As though he said in plain words, 'If that created being is unable to take thought of Him, which is not burthened by the flesh, in what spirit do I dispute about His judgments, who am straitened by the burthen of corruption?' But as God's words to us are oftentimes His judgments, declaring the sentence of our actions, so our words to God are the deeds which we set forth; but man 'cannot reason with God in his words,' in that, in the eye of His exact judgment, he maintains no assurance in his actions. Hence it is fitly added,

Ver. 15. Who, though I possessed anything righteous, yet would I not answer, but I would make supplication to my Judge.

xviii. 28. For, as we have often said, all human righteousness is proved unrighteousness, if it be judged by strict rules. And so there is need of prayer following after righteousness, that this, which if sifted to the bottom might be brought down, may be firmly established in the mere pitifulness of the Judge. And when this is possessed fully by the more perfect sort, it is said that they possess a something of it. In that the human mind both with difficulty puts in practice the truths apprehended by it, and the things which it apprehends are the merest outskirts. Therefore let him say, *Who, though I possessed anything righteous, yet would I not answer, but I would make supplication to my Judge.* As if he owned in plainer words; 'And if I should grow to the practising of virtue, I am made vigorous to life, not by merit, but of pardoning grace.' Therefore we must be strenuous in prayer, when we do right, so that all the righteous ways we live in we may season by humility; but very often it happens that our very supplication is tost to and fro by such a multitude of temptations, that it seems almost cast off from the presence of the Judge. And often our pitiful Creator receives it, but because it cannot put forth itself undefiled, as it is minded, it dreads the sentence of condemnation upon its head. Hence it goes on,

Ver. 16. And when I have called and He hath answered me, yet do I not believe that He hath hearkened unto my voice.

xix.

29. For very often the mind is set on fire with the flame of Divine love, and is uplifted to behold heavenly things and secret mysteries. It is now transported on high, and pierced with full affection, is made strange to things below; but being struck with sudden temptation, the soul which with set purpose had been established erect in God, pierced with arising temptations is bowed low; so that it cannot discern itself, and being held fast between good and evil practices, cannot tell on which side it is strongest. For very often it is brought to this pass, to wonder how it so lays hold of the highest truths, when unlawful thoughts defile it; and again how it admits unlawful thoughts, when the fervour of the Holy Spirit with power transports it above itself. Which alternate motions of thought in the mind being viewed aright by the Psalmist, he exclaims, *They mount up to the heaven, they go down again to the depths.* [Ps. 107, 26] For we mount up to the heaven, when we enter into the things above, but we go down to the depths, when we are suddenly cast down from the height of contemplation by grovelling temptations. Thus whilst the motions of the mind alternate between vows and vices, too truly they cloud for themselves the certainty of their being heard. Therefore it is rightly said, *When I have called and He hath answered me, yet do I not believe that He hath hearkened unto my voice.* In that the mind is rendered fearful from its mere changeableness, and by that which it is unwillingly subject to, imagines itself cast off and rejected.

30. It is interesting to observe with what exactness the holy man passes judgment on himself, that the judgments of God may find nought in him to take hold of. For having an eye to his own frailty, he says, *How much less shall I answer, and talk in my words with Him?* Not relying upon the claims of his own righteousness, but betaking himself to the hope alone of entreating, he adds, *Who, though I had*

anything righteous, yet would I not answer, but I would make supplication to my Judge. But apprehensive for the very entreaty itself, he adds, *And when I have called, and He hath answered me, yet do I not believe that He hath hearkened unto my voice.* Why does he shrink with so great apprehension, why does he tremble with such sore misgiving? but that his eye is fixed on the dreadfulness of the Judge, in the last strict reckoning, and not supporting the power of His searching eye, all that he does seems little worth in his account? Whence he adds thereupon,

Ver. 17. For He shall break me with a tempest.

xx. 31. In every case that sinner is 'broken with a tempest,' who seemed to be stablished in tranquillity, in that the man whom the long-suffering Above bears with for long, the last strict Judgment destroys. And this is rightly called 'a tempest,' because it is manifested in a commotion of the elements, as the Psalmist witnesses, when he says, *God shall come manifest, and He shall not keep silence; a fire shall devour before Him, and a mighty tempest round about Him.* [Ps. 50, 3] And hence another Prophet also says, *The Lord, His way is in the whirlwind and in the storm.* [Nahum 1, 3] In which same whirlwind the righteous man is never broken, for this reason, because here he is ever in fear and anxiety, lest he should be broken. For whilst still set in the journey of the present life, he bethinks himself how severe towards the actions of men the Requirer of works will appear, Who then condemns even without works some that are only bound with the guilt of original sin. Whence the holy man rightly adds thereupon in the voice of mankind,

And multiplieth my wounds even without cause.

xxi. 32. For there be some that are withdrawn from the present light, before they attain to show forth the good or evil deserts of an active life. And whereas the Sacraments of salvation do not free them from the sin of their birth, at the same time that here they never did aright by their own act; there they are brought to torment. And these have one wound, viz. to be born in corruption, and another, to die in the flesh. But forasmuch as after death there also follows, death eternal, by a secret and righteous judgment 'wounds are multiplied to them without cause.' For they even receive everlasting torments, who never sinned by their own will.

And hence it is written, *Even the infant of a single day is not pure in His sight upon earth.* Hence 'Truth' says by His own lips, *Except a man be born of water and of the Spirit, he cannot enter into the kingdom of God.* [John 3, 5] Hence Paul says, *We were by nature the children of wrath even as others.* [Eph. 2, 3] He then that adding nothing of his own is mined by the guilt of birth alone, how stands it with such an one at the last account, as far as the calculation of human sense goes, but that he is 'wounded without cause?' And yet in the strict account of God it is but just that the stock of mortality, like an unfruitful tree, should preserve in the branches that bitterness which it drew from the root. Therefore he says, *For He shall break me with a tempest, and multiply my wounds without cause.* As if reviewing the woes of mankind he said in plain words; 'With what sort of visitation does the strict Judge mercilessly slay those, whom the guilt of their own deeds condemns, if He smites for all eternity even those, whom the guilt of deliberate choice does not impeach?'

33. Now that these same sayings are not inconsistent with the case of blessed Job in a special sense, we shall acquaint ourselves, if we pursue the enquiry, how truly they were delivered. For considering himself with exactness, and judging himself in every action, he tells us with what great dread and apprehension he views the force of the severity of the Most High, adding, *For He will break me with a tempest.* As if it were in plain words, 'For this reason I ever fear Him even in time of quiet, because I cannot but know how He may come in the whirlwind, by His scourges:' which same scourges he both in fearing forecast, and in forecasting underwent. Whence he adds, *And will multiply my wounds even without cause.* For as we have often said already, blessed Job was never stricken that the stroke might blot out sin in him, but that it might add to his merit. Therefore in asserting himself wounded without cause, he declares that concerning himself openly, which 'Truth' witnesses of him in secret, saying, *Although thou movedst Me against him, to destroy him without cause.* The holy man then does not say from pride that which he says only in truth. Nor is he out of proportion with the rule of righteousness by those words, by which he is not at variance with the Judge. Who goes on to set forth the continuance of those wounds, when he adds,

He will not suffer me to take my breath, but filleth me with bitterness.

THE SECOND PART.

xxii. 34. It is often an exercise of virtue to the just, to be subject to ills from without by themselves; but that the conflict of a complete trial may discipline their powers, sometimes at one and the same time they are rent with torments without, and chastened with temptations within. Hence the holy man declares himself to be full of bitterness, in that whilst he is bearing scourges outwardly, there is a heavier weight, which from the adversary's tempting he carries in his interior; but withal the force of his sorrow is abated by considering the equity and the power of the Smiter. Whence he adds,

Ver. 19. If I speak of strength, lo, He is strong; if of equity in judgment, none dareth bear witness for me.

xxiii. 35. For He tries the counts of our lives, Who does not make them out by the testimony of another; in that He, Who is one day revealed as a strict inflicter of punishment, Himself was for long the silent witness of the sin. For it is on this account that the Prophet says, *I am judge and witness.* [Jer. 29, 23. Vulg.] Hence he says again, *I have long time holden My peace; I have been still, and refrained Myself; now will I cry like a travailing woman.* [Is. 42, 12] For a woman in travail casts forth with pain, what she has long borne in her womb with burthensomeness. And so after a long silence, like a travailing woman, the Lord utters His voice, in that what He now bears silently in Himself, He one day as it were reveals with pain in the avenging of the Judgment. But it deserves our enquiry; this righteous man, if any had ventured to give testimony in his behalf, would he have cleared him of guilt? And if no other gave testimony to him, then, at least, is he himself at all events of strength to offer testimony in his own behalf? It follows,

Ver. 20. If I desire to justify myself; mine own, mouth shall condemn me; if I say I am perfect, it shall also prove me perverse.

xxiv. 36. As if it were in plain words; 'Why should I speak about others, when I cannot bear testimony concerning myself?' But whereas thou art not competent to witness to thine own innocency, dost thou know the fact that thou art innocent? He proceeds,

Ver. 21. Though I were perfect, even this my soul shall not know.

xxv.

37. Most commonly if we know the good things that we do, we are led to entertain pride; if we are ignorant of them, we cannot keep them. For who would not, in however slight degree, be rendered proud by the consciousness of his virtue? or who, again, would keep safe within him that good, which he does not know of? what then remains as a provision against either of these evils, saving that all the good things that we do, in knowing we should not know; so that we both look upon them as right things, and as a mere nothing, that thus the knowledge of their rightness may quicken the soul to a good guard, and the estimation of their littleness may never exalt it in pride? But there are some things which are not easy to be ascertained by us, even when they are doing. For often we are inflamed with a right earnestness against the sins of transgressors, and when we are transported by passion beyond the bounds of justice, we account this the warmth of just severity. We often take upon ourselves the office of preaching, that we may in this way minister to the service of our brethren; but unless we be acceptable to the person, whom we address, nothing that we preach is received with welcome; and while the mind aims to please on useful grounds, it lets itself out after the love of its own praise in a shameful way, and the soul which was busied in rescuing others from captivity to bad habits, being itself made captive, begins to drudge to its own popularity. For the appetite for the applause of our fellow-creatures is like a kind of footpad, who as people are going along the straight road joins them from the side, that the wayfarer's life may be barbarously taken by the dagger drawn out of sight. And when the intention of purposed usefulness is drawn off to our own interests, in a way to make one shudder, sin accomplishes that identical work, which goodness began. Oftentimes even from the very beginning the thought of the heart seeks one thing, the deed exhibits another.

38. Often not even the thought itself proves faithful to itself, in that it sets one object before the mind's eye, and is hurrying far from it after another in real purpose. For very often we find persons who covet earthly rewards, and stand up in defence of justice, and these account themselves innocent, and exult in being the vindicators of right; who if the prospect of money be withdrawn, instantly cease from their defence of justice; and yet they look upon themselves as defenders of justice, and maintain themselves right to themselves,

who the while aim not at rightness but money. In opposition to whom it is well said by Moses, *That which is just, thou shalt follow justly*. [Deut. 16, 20] For he followeth unjustly that which is just, who is moved to the defence of just dealing not by his feeling for virtue, but by his love of temporal rewards. He 'followeth unjustly that which is just,' who is not afraid to drive a trade with that justice, which he makes his plea. And so 'justly to follow what is just' is in the vindication of justness to make that same justness our end and aim. We often do right things, and are far from looking for rewards, far from seeking applause from our fellowcreatures, yet the mind being set up in self-confidence, scorns to please those from whom it seeks nothing, sets at nought their opinions, and drives itself miserably free along the precipices of pride, and is the worse overwhelmed beneath sin from the same source, whence it boasts, its sins as if subdued, that it is subject to no covetous desires.

39. Often while we sift ourselves more than is meet, by our very aim at discernment we are the more undiscerningly led wrong, and the eye of our mind is dimmed, in proportion as it strives to perceive more; for he too, who determinately looks at the sun's rays, turns darksighted, and is necessitated to see nothing from the very thing in which he strives to see too much. Therefore whereas, if we are backward in our examination, we know nothing at all of ourselves, or, if we search ourselves with an exact scrutiny, we are very often dimsighted to distinguish between virtue and vice, it is rightly said here; *Though I were perfect, my soul shall not know it*. As if it were expressed plainly, 'With what foolhardiness do I find fault with God's judgments upon me, who do not know mine own self by reason of the darkness of my weak condition?' Whence it is well said by the Prophet, *The deep uttered his voice from the height of his imagining*. [Hab. 3, 10. LXX.] For the deep sustains a height of imagining, when the human mind, dim with the immensity of thought, even in its very searching does not penetrate itself, but to 'utter his voice from the height' is that whilst it is unable to fathom itself, it is constrained to rise up in admiration, so that it never should venture to dive into that which is above it, in proportion as, in taking thought itself of its own incomprehensible being, it cannot make out what it is. But the hearts of the righteous, because they cannot examine themselves to perfection, with difficulty bear this exile of dimsightedness; and hence it is added, *and I shall be weary of my life*. The

righteous man is weary to live, in that both by doing works he does not cease to seek after life, and yet cannot discover the merits of that same life; since he draws the balances of trial out from the bosom of interior Justice, and in himself is disabled for the effecting of discovery from the very cause that, being transported above himself, he is enlarged in the power of inquiring. But the alleviation of our darkness lies in the just and incomprehensible power of the Creator being recalled to mind, which both never leaves the wicked without taking vengeance, and surpasses the righteousness of the just by the boundlessness of its incomprehensibility; and hence it is fitly subjoined,

Ver. 22. This is one thing, that I have spoken, He destroyeth both the perfect and the wicked.

40. The 'perfect man is destroyed' by the Creator, in **xxvi.**
that whatever his pureness may have been, it is swallowed up by the pureness of the divine immensity. For though we take heed to preserve pureness, yet by consideration of the interior Perfection it is shown, that this which we practise is not purity; 'the wicked' likewise is 'destroyed' by the Creator, in that whilst God ordereth all things marvellously, his wickedness is caught in the noose of his own artifices. For he is even unwittingly involving himself in punishment on the same grounds whereon he wittingly exults in doing anything. Whereas therefore Almighty God at once surpasses the perfection of the righteous by pureness, and penetrating the craft of the wicked condemns it, it is rightly said, *This is one thing, therefore I said it; He destroyeth the perfect and the wicked.* As if it were expressed in plain words; 'I have spoken this word of reflection to myself, that neither being perfect, shall I appear perfect, if I be strictly examined; nor being wicked, if I would lie hid in myself, am I withdrawn from the piercings of heavenly probing, in that the strict Judge in comprehending all things, penetrates the subterfuges of wickedness in a marvellous way; and in ordering for the best, condemns the same by its 'own devices.' Or, indeed, He is Himself said to destroy both the perfect and the wicked, in that though they be separated in the life of the soul, yet in due of the first sin, they are alike dragged to the death of the flesh. And hence it is said by Solomon; *The learned dieth equally as the unlearned.* [Eccl. 2, 16] And

again, *All things are subject to vanity, and all go to one place; all are of the dust, and all turn to dust again.* [Eccl. 3, 20] It proceeds:

Ver. 23. If He scourge, let Him slay once for all, and not laugh at the trial of the innocent.

xxvii. *Mystical*

41. Who would not suppose that this was uttered in pride, unless he heard the sentence of the Judge, Who pronounces, *For ye have not spoken of Me the thing that is right, as My servant Job hath.* [Job 42, 7] Therefore it follows, that no one dare to find fault with the author's words, which it appears the Judge commends. But they must be sifted in their inner sense with the greater wariness and nicety, in proportion as they sound the harder on the outside. Thus the holy man surveying the woes of mankind, and considering whence they came, how that man, in consequence of the promise of his enemy, desiring to obtain the knowledge of good and evil, lost his very self too, so that he may say with truth, *Though I were perfect, yet my soul shall not know it;* how that after the punishment of exile he is further subject to the scourges of corruption, and even after being tormented is still tending to the death of the body, or indeed to the death of the soul, so that he may well say, *He destroyeth the perfect and the wicked*; in opposition to this he begs the grace of the Mediator, saying, *If he scourge, let him slay once for all.* For in that we have both in spirit departed from God; and that in flesh we return to dust, we are obnoxious to the punishment of a double death. But there came unto us One, Who in our stead should die the death of the flesh only, and join His single Death to our twofold death, and set us free from either kind. Concerning which it is said by Paul, *For in that He died, He died unto sin once.* [Rom. 6, 10] Thus let the holy man survey the ills of our state of corruption, and let him seek the one Death of the Mediator, which should cancel our two deaths, and in longing for this, let him say, *If He scourge, let Him slay once for all.*

42. But mark how that seems as though it were at war with humility, which is immediately introduced, *And not laugh at the trial of the innocent.* And yet we shall easily perceive this to be a very great piece of humility, if we consider it in a humble spirit. For it is plain to all persons that desire, when deferred, is in every case a pain; as Solomon bears witness, who says, *Hope deferred maketh the heart sick.* [Prov. 13, 12] Now for God to 'laugh,' is His refusing to take pity

upon the suffering of man. Hence the Lord says again, by Solomon, to the children of perdition continuing in sin, *I also will laugh at your calamity* [Prov. 1, 26]; i.e. 'I will not compassionate you in your distress with any pity.' Thus before the coming or our Redeemer, the Elect had all of them their pain, in that with ardent longing, they desired to behold the mystery of His Incarnation, as He Himself bears record, when He says, *For I tell you that many Prophets and Kings have desired to see these things which ye see, and have not seen them*; [Luke 10, 24] and so the 'pains of the innocent' are the desires of the righteous. For so long then as the Lord, taking no pity, deferred the wishes of His Elect, what did He else, but 'laugh at the pains of the innocent?' Therefore let the holy man, considering the gifts of the Redeemer that should come, and enduring with pain the delay of his wishes, express himself in the words, *If He scourge, let Him slay once for all, and not laugh at the pains of the innocent*. As if he besought in plain words, saying, 'Whereas our life is every day bruised with the scourge of vengeance on account of sin, let Him now appear, Who for our sake may undergo death once for all, without sin, that God may no more 'laugh at the pains of the innocent,' if He Himself come subject to suffering in the flesh, in desire of Whom our soul chastens itself.'

43. Or indeed if He uses the expression of God's 'laughing' for His joy, the Lord is said 'to laugh at the pains of the innocent,' in that the more ardently He is sought of us, the more graciously He rejoices over us. For we as it were cause a kind of joy to Him by our pain, when by holy desires, we chasten ourselves for the love of Him. Hence the Psalmist says, *Appoint a solemn day in frequency, even unto the horns of the altar*. [Ps. 118, 27. Vulg.] For he 'appointeth a solemn day to the Lord in frequency,' whosoever is continually chastening himself in the desire of Him; and it is enjoined that this same day of solemnity be carried even to the horns of the altar, in that it is necessary that every man chasten himself for so long time, until he attains to the height of the heavenly sacrifice, i.e. unto eternal bliss. Thus the holy man, for that he longs to have his desire fulfilled and no longer deferred, says with humility, *Nor laugh at the pains of the innocent*. As if he said, 'Let Him, gladly welcoming our petitions, no longer defer, but by manifesting bring to light Him, who chastens us in the expecting of Himself.' Now that blessed Job prayed that He in particular might be slain once for all, Who at 'the end' of the

world underwent for our sake the death of the flesh alone, he immediately makes appear, in that he at the same time subjoins the very course of His Passion; saying,

Ver. 24. The earth is given into the hand of the wicked. He covereth the faces of the judges thereof.

xxviii. 44. For what is denoted by the designation of 'the earth,' saving the flesh? who by the title of 'the wicked,' save the devil? The 'hands' of this wicked one were they, who were the aggressors in the death of our Redeemer. Thus 'the earth is given into the hands of the wicked,' in that our Redeemer's Soul our old enemy could never corrupt, by himself tempting Him. But His Flesh he being permitted did by means of his ministers deprive of life for three days; and unknown to himself, by that very permission, he ministered to the dispensation of God's pitifulness. For assailing our Redeemer with three temptations, he had no power to defile the heart of God. But when he set on the mind of Judas to bring about the death of His fleshly part, and when he gave him a band of soldiers and officers from the Chief Priests and Pharisees, then that wicked one stretched forth his hands upon 'the earth.' The judges of this earth were the Priests and Rulers, Pilate and the scoffing soldiers; and so this wicked one 'covered the faces of the judges thereof,' in that he veiled the mind of the persecutors, that they should not know their Maker, with a cloud of wickedness. Whence it is said by Paul, *But even unto this day, when Moses is read, the vail is upon their heart* [2 Cor. 3, 15]; and he says again, *For had they known it, they would not have crucified the Lord of glory*. [1 Cor. 2, 8] And so the face of the judges proved to be covered, in that the mind of the persecutors not even by His miracles ever knew Him to be God, Whom it had power to hold fast in the flesh. But forasmuch as our old enemy is one person with all the wicked, Holy Scripture very often so speaks of the head of the wicked, i.e. the devil, that it suddenly goes off to his body, i.e. to his followers. Therefore it may be that by the name of 'the wicked one,' the faithless and persecuting People is denoted, with which this also which is added accords;

If it is not he, who then is it?

xxix. 45. Who then shall anywhere be accounted wicked, if that People, which persecuted Pity Itself, be not wicked?

But the holy man, after regarding the faithlessness of the Jewish People, calls back the eye of his mind to himself, grieves that he cannot behold Him Whom he loves, is sad and sorrowful that he is withdrawn from the present world, before the Saving Health of the world is manifested; and hence he adds,

Ver.25. Now my days are swifter than a post: they are fled away, they have seen no good.

xxx.

46. For the business of a post is to tell what is coming after; and so all of the Elect that were born before the coming of the Redeemer, in that either by mode of life only, or by word of mouth likewise, they bore tidings of Him, were like a kind of post in the world. But whereas they foresee themselves withdrawn before the wished for season of Redemption, they mourn that they pass away 'swifter than a post,' and they lament that their days are short, because they are never extended so far as to see the light of the Redeemer; whence it is justly said, *They flee away, they see no good.* All things that have been created are good, as Moses bears record, who says, *And God saw everything that He had made, and, behold, it was very good.* [Gen. 1, 31] But that good alone is primarily good, whereby all those are good, which are not primarily good, and of this good, 'Truth' says in the Gospel, *None is good save one, that is, God.* [Luke 18, 19] Therefore because the days of the former fathers were ended before ever God was manifested to the world in the flesh, it is rightly said of those days, that they fled away, and saw no good. As if it were in plain words, 'They have passed away before the looked-for season, because they might not attain to the present appearing of the Redeemer.' Whence it is yet further added;

Ver. 26. They are passed away as the ships carrying fruits.

xxxi.

47. They that traverse seas transporting fruits, do themselves indeed enjoy the smell of the same, but the food thereof they convey to others. What else then did the ancient Fathers show themselves, saving ships carrying fruits? They indeed in foretelling the mystery of God's Incarnation, themselves enjoyed the sweet odour of hope, but to ourselves they brought down the fruit by the completion of that hope. For what they but smelled at in expecting, we are replenished with in seeing and receiving. And hence That same Redeemer says to His disciples, *Other men laboured, and ye*

are entered into their labours. [John 4, 38] And their days are likened to ships, because they pass by on their way, and very properly to those bearing fruits, for all the Elect severally, whom they carried before the Redeemer's coming, through the Spirit of prophecy, they were enabled to refresh with the expectation, but not to feed with the manifest appearing. Or, surely, whereas when ships carry fruits, they mix chaff with them, in order that they may transport them to land without injury, the days of the Fathers of yore are rightly described as like to ships bearing fruits, for in that the sayings of the Ancients tell of the mysteries of the spiritual life, they preserve these by means of the intermingled chaff of the history, and they bring down to us the fruit of the Spirit under a covering, when they speak to us carnal things. For often whilst they relate circumstances proper to themselves, they are exalted to the secrets of the Divine Nature. And often while they gaze at the loftiness of the Divine Nature, 'they are suddenly plunged into the mystery of the Incarnation. Hence it is still further added with fitness,

As the eagle that hasteth to the prey.

xxxii. 48. For it is of the habits of the eagle to gaze at the sun's rays with unrecoiling eye; but when it is pressed by need of sustenance, it turns the same pupil of the eye, which it had fixed on the rays of the sun, to the ken of the carcass, and though it flies high in air, it seeks the earth for the purpose of getting flesh. Thus, surely, thus was it with the old fathers, who as far as the frailty of human nature permitted it, contemplated the sight of the Creator with uplifted soul, but foreseeing Him destined to become incarnate at the end of the world, they as it were turned away their eyes to the ground from gazing at the rays of the sun; and they as it were descend from highest to lowest, whilst they see Him to be God above all things, and Man among all things; and whilst they behold Him, Who was to suffer and to die for mankind, by which same Death they know that they are themselves restored and fashioned anew to life, as it were like the eagle, after gazing at the rays of the sun, they seek their food upon the dead Body. It is good to view the Eagle gazing at the rays of the Sun, which says, *The mighty God, The Everlasting Father, the Prince of Peace.* [Is. 9, 6] But let him come down from the high flight of his lofty range to earth, and seek below the food of the carcass. For he adds a little while after, saying, *The chastisement of* *our peace was upon Him, and with His stripes we are healed.* [Is. 53, 5] And again, *And He is man, and who shall know Him?* [Jer. 17, 9. LXX] Thus the mind of the righteous man being lifted up to the Divine Nature, when it sees the grace of the Economy in His Flesh, as it were 'hasteth' suddenly from on high like an 'eagle to the prey.' 'But mark; that Israelitish People, which was for long watered with the Spirit of prophecy above measure, lost those same gifts of prophecy, and never continued in that faith, which in foreseeing it had proclaimed, and, by disowning, put away from itself that Presence of the Redeemer, which, by foretelling, it clearly delivered to all its followers. Hence, immediately, his speech is suitably made to turn, in sympathy, to their obduracy, and it is shown how the Spirit of prophecy is taken away from them. For it is subjoined,

Ver. 27. If I say, I will never speak thus; I change my countenance, and am tormented with grief.

xxxiii.

49. For the Jewish People would not speak as before, in that it denied Him, Whom it had foretold; but with changed countenance it is tormented with grief, in that while it defiled with the foulness of unbelief the aspect of its inward man, by which it might have been known by the Creator, setting out with present evils, it brought itself under the sentence of everlasting vengeance. For its face being as it were changed, it is not known by the Creator, in that upon faith in a good conscience being gone, it is condemned. But doubtless it remains for her, that the pain of punishment torment her, whom her Creator knowing not disowns. Seeing, then, that we have gone through these points under the signification of our Redeemer, now let us go over them again, to make them out in a moral sense.

Ver.25. Now my days have been swifter than a post, they are fled away, they have seen no good.

Moral

50. For as we have already said, the first man was so created that by the accessions of time his life could only be extended, but not spun to an end; but because by his own act and deed he fell into sin, in that he touched that which was forbidden, he was made subject to a transitory career, which man now, oppressed by fondness for the present life, both undergoes and longs for without ceasing. For, that he may not come to an end, he longs to live on,

yet by the accessions to life, he is daily advancing to his end, nor does he well discover the added portions of time, what nothings they are, when those things are done and over in a moment which seemed to be long in coming. Let the holy man then view the grounds of his position, and in the voice of mankind bewail the woes of a transitory career, saying, *Now my days have been swifter than a post; they are fled away, they have seen no good*. As if it were in plain words, 'Man was created for this end, that he might see good,' which is God; but because he would not stand in the light, in flying therefrom he lost his eyes; for in the same degree that by sin he began to let himself run out to things below, he subjected himself to blindness, that he should not see the interior light.' And of those days it is further added with fitness, *They are passed away as the ships carrying fruits*. For ships, when they 'carry fruits,' convey the produce of the land through the waves. Now the land of man was Paradise, which might have kept him unshaken, if by force of innocency he could have stood fast, but, because by sin he fell into the waves of a changeful state, after the land he came into the seas of the present life. Furthermore the fruits of the land were the word of commandment, the power of good works vouchsafed him, the perception of his Creator implanted in his nature. But these fruits, which we refused to eat on the land, we carry through the seas, in that we would not keep unmoved in Paradise the blessings of so many benefits vouchsafed to us, and now we endeavour to preserve them in the midst of temptations. Hasting to our bourn, we are driven forward by the breath of the present life, we are worn out with the tossing of our mutable condition. But whereas by the mystery of the Cross we are made fast to the good gifts implanted in our nature, it is as if we carried fruits by means of wood. And yet this may also be understood in another sense. For ships that carry fruits have sweetness of smell, but have no gravity of weight; and man, when he became an outcast from the joys of Paradise, lost the power of contemplation, and parted with the vigour of his native strength; and when he lifts up himself to seek anew the things above, he is sweetened indeed by the perfume of the memory, but yields no weight of life in meet proportion. Thus he is filled with the odours of fruits, and yet the vessel of our soul is lightly driven hither and thither without steadiness, in that we both call to mind the high state of Paradise with a remembrance of a sweet smell, and are subject to the troublesome waves of temptation arising from the flesh. Hence it is fitly subjoined, *As the eagle that hasteth to the prey*. For the eagle is suspended in an exceeding lofty flight, and poised in swift speeding skywards, but from the hunger of the belly, he seeks the ground, and suddenly plunges himself downward from on high. Thus, thus the race of man in our first parent fell from on high deep down below, whereas the dignity of its state by creation had hung it aloft in the high region of reason as in the freedom of the skies: but because, contrary to the commandment, he touched the forbidden fruit, he descended to the earth, through the lust of the belly; and it is as if he fed upon flesh after flying, for that he lost those free inhalings of contemplation, and now solaces himself with corporeal delights below. Thus 'as the eagle that hasteth to the prey,' our days pass swiftly by; for in proportion as we seek things below, we are hindered from maintaining ourselves in life.

51. But when we revolve such things in our mind by continual reflection, we are silently pressed with the hard questions, why did Almighty God create one, who He foresaw would perish? Why was He, Who is chief in power and chief in goodness, not so minded as to make man such that he could not perish? But when the mind silently asks these questions, it fears lest, by its very audacity in questioning thus, it should break out into pride, and holds itself in with humility, and restrains the thoughts of the heart. But it is the more distressed, that amid the ills that it suffers it is over and above tormented concerning the secret meaning of its condition. Hence here too it is fitly added; *If I shall say, I will never speak thus; I change my countenance, and am tormented with grief*. For we say, that 'we never ought to speak thus,' when transgressing the limit of our frail nature in pushing our enquiries, we reproach ourselves in dread, and are withheld by bethinking ourselves of heavenly awe, in which same withholding, the face of our mind is altered, in that the mind, which in the first instance, failing to comprehend them, boldly investigated things above, afterwards, finding out its own infirmity, begins to entertain awe for what it is ignorant of. But in this very change there is pain, for the mind is very greatly afflicted that, in recompense of the first sin, she is blinded to the understanding of things touching her own self. All that she undergoes she sees to be just. She dreads lest in her pain she be guilty of excess from liberty of speech, she imposes silence on the lips, but the awakened grief is

increased by the very act by which it is restrained. Let him say then; *If I shall say, I will never speak thus; I change my countenance, and am tormented with grief.* For we are then for the most part most grievously afflicted, when, as it were by a studied endeavour after consolation, we try to lighten to ourselves the ills of our afflicted condition; but whoever once considers with minute attention the ills of man propagated by the condemnation of our first parent, it follows that he must be afraid to add his own deeds thereto. Hence after the holy man had brought in matters of common concern, he at once subjoins those of special interest, saying,

Ver. 28. I was afraid of all my works, knowing that Thou wouldest not spare me, when guilty of transgression.

xxxiv. 52. What were the works that blessed Job practised, the text of this sacred history makes plain. For he studied to propitiate his Maker by numberless burnt offerings; in that according to the number of his sons, as it is written, rising up early in the morning, he offered burnt offerings for each, and purified them not only from impure actions, but likewise from bad thoughts. Of whom it is recorded, by the witness of Scripture, *For Job said, It may be that my sons have sinned, and cursed* [Lat. *blessed*] *God in their hearts.* [Job 1, 5] He exercised the feeling of sympathy, in that he declares of himself, when he was importuned by the interrogations of his friends, *Did not I weep for him that was in trouble?* [Job 30, 25] He discharged the office of pity, as he says, *I was an eye to the blind, and a foot was I to the lame.* [Job 29, 15] He kept pureness of chastity in heart, in that he discovers himself openly with adjuration, saying, *If mine heart have been deceived by a woman.* [Job 31, 9] He held the very topmost point of humility, from the grounds of his heart, who says, *If I did despise to be judged with my manservant or my maidservant, when they contended with me.* [ver. 13] He bestowed the bounties of liberality, who says, *Or have eaten my morsel myself alone, and the fatherless hath not eaten thereof?* [ver. 17] And again; *If his loins have not blessed me, and if he were not warmed with the fleece of my sheep.* [ver. 20] He displayed the kindness of hospitality, who says, *The stranger did not lodge in the street; but I opened my doors to the traveller.* [ver. 32] And in the midst of these things, for the consummation of his virtues, by that more excellent way of charity, he even loved his very enemies, in that he says, *If I rejoiced at the destruction of him that hated me.* [ver.

29] And again, *Neither have I suffered my mouth to sin, by wishing a curse to his soul.* [ver. 30] Why then was the holy man 'afraid for his works,' in that he ever practised these, by which God is wont to be softened towards transgressions? How then is it, that while doing works to be admired, he even fears for these same, being in alarm, when he says, *I was afraid of all my works*, save that we gather from the deeds and the words of the holy man, that if we really desire to please God, after we overcome our bad habits, we must fear the very things themselves that are done well in us?

58. For there are two particulars which must of necessity be seriously apprehended in our good works, viz. sloth and deceit. And hence it is said by the Prophet, as the old translation has it, *Cursed be he that doeth the work of the Lord deceitfully and negligently*. [Jer. 48, 10] Now it is to be carefully noted, that sloth comes of insensibility, deceit of self-love, for over little love of God gives magnitude to the first, while self-love, miserably possessing the mind, engenders the other. For he is guilty of deceit in the work of God, whosoever loving himself to excess, by that which he may have done well, is only making the best of his way to transitory good things in compensation. We must bear in mind too that there are three ways in which deceit itself is practised, in that, surely, the object aimed at in it is either the secret interest of our fellow creatures' feelings, or the breath of applause, or some outward advantage; contrary to which it is rightly said of the righteous man by the prophet, *Blessed is he that shaketh his hands clear of every favour*. [Is. 33, 15] For as deceit does not consist only in the receiving of money; so, no doubt, a favour is not confined to one thing, but there are three ways of receiving favours after which deceit goeth in haste. For a favour from the heart, is interest solicited in the opinion, a favour from the mouth is glory from applause, a favour from the head a reward by gift. Now every righteous man 'shaketh his hands clear of every favour,' in that in whatever he does aright, he neither aims to win vainglory from the affections of his fellow creatures, nor applause from their lips, nor a gift from their hands. And so he alone is not guilty of deceit in doing God's work, who while he is energetic in studying right conduct, neither pants after the rewards of earthly substance [*corporalis rei*], nor after words of applause, nor after favour in man's judgment. Therefore because our very good actions themselves cannot escape the sword of ambushed sin, unless they be guarded every day by anx-

ious fear, it is rightly said in this place by the holy man, *I was afraid of all my works*. As if he said with humble confession, 'What I have done publicly, I know, but what I may have been secretly subject to therein, I cannot tell.' For often our good points are spoilt by deceit robbing us, in that earthly desires unite themselves to our right actions; oftentimes they come to nought from sloth intervening, in that, love waxing cold, they are starved of the fervour in which they began. And so because the stealth of sin is scarcely got the better of even in the very act of virtue, what safeguard remains for our security, but that even in our virtue, we ever tread with fear and caution?

54. But what he adds after this presents itself as a very great difficulty to the mind; *I know that Thou wouldest not spare one that offendeth*. For if there be no 'sparing of one that offendeth,' who can be rescued from death eternal, seeing that there is no one to be found clear of sin? Or does He spare a penitent, but not one that offendeth, in that whilst we bewail our offences we are no longer offending? Yet how is it that Peter is looked at, while he is denying, and that by the look of his denied Redeemer he is brought to tears? How is it that Paul, when he was bent to do out the name of our Redeemer upon earth, was vouchsafed to hear His words from heaven? Yet was sin punished both in the one and in the other. In that of Peter on the one hand it is written, as the Gospel is witness, *And Peter remembered the word of Jesus, and went out, and wept bitterly*. [Luke 22, 61. 62.] And of Paul, that very same 'Truth' Which called him, says, *For I will show him how great things he must suffer for My Name's sake*. [Acts 9, 16] Therefore God never doth 'spare him that offendeth,' in that He never leaves his sin without taking vengeance on it. For either man himself in doing penance punishes it in himself, or God in dealing with man in vengeance for it, visits it with His rod, and thus there is never any sparing of sin, in that it is never loosed without vengeance. Thus David after his confession obtained to hear, *The Lord also hath put away thy sin*. [2 Sam. 12, 13] And yet being afterwards scourged 'with numberless afflictions, and a fugitive, he discharged the obligation of the sin which he had been guilty of. So we by the water of salvation are absolved from the sin of our first parent; and yet in clearing off the obligations of that same sin, although absolved, we still undergo the death of the flesh. Therefore it is well said, *I know that thou wouldest not spare one that offendeth*. In that either by ourselves or by His own self He cuts off even when He lets off our

sins. For from His Elect He is studious to wipe off by temporal affliction those spots of wickedness, which He would not behold in them for ever. But it oftentimes happens that when the mind is fearful more than behoves, when it is shaken with alarm, when it is pressed with ill-omened misgivings, it feels weary that it should live, in that it questions the attaining to life even through pains and labour. And hence it is thereupon added,

Ver.29. But if even so I be wicked, why, then, have I laboured in vain?

5. For if we be examined pity set aside, our work which **xxxv.**
we look to have recompensed with a reward is deserving of punishment. 'Therefore the holy man shrinking under secret judgment, says, *But if even so I be wicked, why, then, have I laboured in vain?* Not that he repents of having laboured, but that it grieves him even amidst labours to be in uncertainty about the reward. But we must bear in mind that the Saints so doubt that they trust, and so trust that notwithstanding they do not slumber in security. Therefore because it is very often the case that the mind, even when bent upon right courses, is full of fears, it follows that after the good deed is done, deprecating tears be had recourse to, in order that the humility of entreaty may bear up the deserts of right practice to eternal rewards. But yet we must bear in mind that neither our life nor our tears have power to make us perfectly clean, so long as the mortal condition of our state of corruption holds us fast bound. And hence it is rightly added,

Ver. 30, 31. If I wash myself with snow water, and if my hands shine as if never so clean; yet shalt Thou stain me with filthiness, and mine own clothes shall abhor me.

56. For 'snow water' is the weeping of humility; which **xxxvi.**
same, in that it excels all other virtues in the eyes of the strict Judge, is as it were white by the colour of preeminent merit. For there are some to whom there is lamenting but not humility, in that when they are afflicted they weep, yet in those very tears, they either set themselves in disdain against the life of their neighbours, or they are lifted up against the dispensation of their Maker. Such have water, but not 'snow water,' and they can never be clean, because they are not washed in the tears of humility. But he had washed himself clean from sin with snow water, who said with con-

fidence, *A broken and a humbled heart, O God, Thou shalt not despise*. [Ps. 51, 17] For they that afflict themselves with tears but turn rebels by murmuring, 'break' their heart indeed, but disdain to be 'humbled.' Though 'snow water' may also be understood in another sense. For water of the spring and stream issues out of the earth, but snow water is let fall from the sky. And there are very many, who torment themselves in the wailings of supplication, yet with all their pains in bewailing they spend themselves upon earthly objects of desire alone. They are pierced with anguish in their prayers, but it is the joys of transitory happiness that they are in search of. And so these are not washed with 'snow water,' because their tears come from below. For it is as if they were bathed in water of earth, who are pierced with grief in their prayers, on account of earthly good things. But they who lament for this reason, because they long for the rewards on high [or 'from on high'], are washed clean in snow water, in that heavenly compunction overflows them. For when they seek after the everlasting land by tears, and inflamed with longing for it lament, they receive from on high that whereby they may be made clean. Now by 'the hands' what else is denoted saving 'works?' Whence it is said to certain persons by the Prophet; *Your hands are full of blood*, [Is. 1, 15] i.e. 'your works are full of cruelty.'

57. But it is to be observed, that the holy man does not say, 'And make my hands shine ever so clean,' but *as if never so clean*. For so long as we are tied and bound by the penalty of a corrupt state, we never by whatsoever right works appropriate real cleanness to ourselves, but only imitate it. And hence it is fitly added, *Yet Thou shalt stain me with filth*. For God 'to stain us with filth' means His showing us to be stained with filth; in that in proportion as we more truly rise up to Him by good works, the more exactly we are made to know the filthiness of our life, by which we are rendered at variance with His pureness. Thus he says, *If I wash myself with snow water, and make my hands shine as if never so clean; yet shalt Thou stain me with filthinesses*. As if it were expressed in plain words, 'Though I be steeped in tears of heavenly compunction, though I be exercised in the courses of good works, yet in Thy pureness I perceive that I am not pure.' For the flesh itself, which is still subject to corruption, beats off the spirit when it is intent on God, and stains the beauty of the love of Him by foul and unhallowed movements of thought.

58. Hence too it is added, *And mine own clothes shall abhor me.* For what is denoted by the name of 'clothes' saving this earthly body, with which the soul is endued and covered, that it may not be seen naked in the subtleness of its substance? For hence Solomon says, *Let thy garments be always white*, [Eccl. 9, 8] i.e. the members of the body clean from filthy acts. Hence Isaiah says, *A garment mixed in blood shall be for burning*. [Is. 9, 5. Vulg.] For to 'mix garments in blood' is to defile the body with fleshly desires; which same the Psalmist dreaded to be defiled with, when he said, *Deliver me from bloodguiltiness, O God, Thou That art the God of my health*. [Ps. 51, 16] Hence it is delivered to John by the voice of the Angel, *Thou hast a few names in Sardis, which have not defiled their garments*. [Rev. 3, 4] But according to the way of Holy Writ, our clothes are said 'to abhor us,' in that they make us to be abhorred; in like manner as it is also said of Judas by Peter, *Now this man purchased a field with the reward of iniquity*. [Acts 1, 18] For Judas never could have purchased the potter's field, which was bought with the price of blood, in that restoring the thirty pieces of silver, he straightway punished the guilt of the betrayal by a death with greater guilt inflicted on himself, but 'he purchased' is rendered, he 'was the cause of purchasing.' So in this place, *Mine own garments shall abhor me*, means, 'shall make me to be abhorred.' For whilst the members set themselves up against the spirit, whilst they break in upon the engagements of holy desire, 'by the tumult of temptations that are caused by them, the soul being set in its own conflict learns how meanly it is still regarded by the Divine Being, in that while it fully desires to go through with the chastising of self and is not able, it is defiled by the dust of filthy thoughts. He felt this 'abhorrence of the clothes,' who said, *But I see another law in my members warring against the law of my mind, and bringing me into captivity to the law of sin, which is in my members*. [Rom. 7, 23] These very garments, in which he could not be entirely pleasing, he anxiously desired to lay aside, one day to be resumed much better, saying, *O wretched man that I am, who shall deliver me from the body of this death?* [Rom. 7, 24] Therefore let the righteous man say, *If I wash myself as with snow water, and make my hands shine as if never so clean, yet shalt Thou still stain me with filthiness, and mine own clothes shall abhor me*. In that howsoever he might have been transported on high in the compunctious visitings of contemplation, however he might have braced himself in practice by the exercise of pains, yet he

is still sensible of somewhat unmeet derived from a body of death, and sees himself to be abominable in many things, which he bears about him from his load of corruption. And this too becomes a worse affliction to him, that he often cannot make out by what means he is an offender. He undergoes scourges, but knows nothing what in him is greater, or what less, that displeases the severe Judge. And hence it is added,

32. For He is not a man, such as I am, that I should answer Him, or that He can be heard with me in Judgment on an equal footing.

xxxvii. 59. When we 'contend with another in judgment on an equal footing,' we both learn what is urged against us, and in all we allege we are heard, and in proportion as we apprehend the points openly objected, we reply with boldness to the points propounded. In this way forasmuch as the invisible Judge sees all that we do, it is as if He hears things that we say. But because we never know fully the thing that displeases Him, it is as if what He Himself says, we know not. Thus the holy man, considering the 'abhorrence of his own clothes,' is the more filled with fears, that he cannot 'be heard with Him in judgment on an equal footing.' In that so long as he is burthened with the load of his corruption, he meets with this worst evil in his punishment, that he does not even know the view that his Reprover takes. As though he said in plain words; 'Herein I am not heard on an equal footing, in that while all that I do is open to view, yet I myself cannot tell under what liabilities I am arrested.' It goes on,

Ver.32. Neither is there any that is able to convict both of us, and to lay his hand upon us both.

xxxviii. 60. It sounds hard that any should be sought who might convict God, but it will not be hard, if we recall to mind what He Himself says by another Prophet; for He charges us by Isaiah, *Cease to do evil, learn to do well. Seek judgment, relieve the oppressed, judge the fatherless, plead for the widow. Come, and convict* [*argu-ite*] *Me, says the Lord*. [Is. 1, 16—18.] For one whom we convict, we encounter with the authority of reason. And what is this, that when the Lord bids us do holy actions, He adds, *Come, and convict Me*, but that He plainly intimates the great assurance He vouchsafes to good works? As if it were said in plain words, 'Do right, and then no longer meet the motions of My displeasure by the groan of entreaty, but by the confident voice of authority.' For it is hence that John says, *If our heart condemn us not, then have we confidence toward God*. [I John 3, 21] It is hence that Moses, in that he is acceptable in rendering service, is heard while keeping silence, where it is said to him when he was silent, *Wherefore criest thou unto Me?* [Ex. 14, 15] It is hence that he withholds Him waxing wrath, when he hears the words, *Now therefore let Me alone, that My wrath may wax hot against this people*. [Ex. 32, 10] It is hence that the Lord complains that He had no one to convict Him, where it is said by the Prophet, *And I sought for a man among them that should make up the hedge, and stand in the way against Me for the land, that I should not destroy it, but I found none*. [Ez. 22, 30] It is hence that Isaiah laments bitterly, saying, *And we all do fade as a leaf; and our iniquities like the wind have taken us away. And there is none that calleth upon Thy Name, that stirreth up himself to take hold of Thee*. [Is. 64, 6. 7.]

61. Now any of the righteous may sometimes be able to resist the visitations of a present judgment, by the merits of a derived innocency, but they have no power by their own goodness to rid mankind of the woes of the death to come. Therefore let the holy man bethink himself whereunto the human race has run out, let him cast his eye on the woes of eternal death, which it is plain that human righteousness can never withstand, let him see how frowardly man has offended, let him see how severely the wrath of the Creator is directed against man, and let him call for the Mediator between God and man, God and Man in one, forasmuch as he beholds Him destined to come long after; let him lament and say, *Neither is there any that is able to convict both of us, and to lay his hand upon us both*. For the Redeemer of Mankind, who was made the Mediator between God and Man through the flesh, because that He alone appeared righteous among men, and yet, even though without sin, was notwithstanding brought to the punishment of sin, did both convict man, that he might not sin, and withstand God, that He might not smite; He gave examples of innocency that He took upon Him the punishment due to wickedness. Thus by suffering He convinced both the One and the other, in that He both rebuked the sin of man by infusing righteousness, and moderated the wrath of the Judge by undergoing death; and He 'laid His hand upon both,' in that He at once gave examples to men which they might imitate, and exhibited in Himself

those works to God, by which He might be reconciled to men. For before Him there never was forthcoming One, Who interceded for the guiltinesses of others in such wise, as not to have any of His own. Therefore none could encounter eternal death in the case of others, in the degree that he was bound by the guilt of his own. Therefore there came to men a new Man, as to sin a rebuker, as to punishment a befriender. He manifested miracles, He underwent cruel treatment. Thus He laid His hand upon both, for by the same steps by which He taught the guilty good things, He appeased the indignant Judge. And He did this too the more marvellously by His very miracles themselves, in that He reformed the hearts of offenders by mildness rather than by terror. Hence it is added,

Ver.34. Let Him take away His rod from Me, and let not His fear terrify me.

xxxix. 62. For in the Law God held the rod, in that He said, 'If any man do this or that, let him die the death.' But in His Incarnation He removed the rod, in that He showed the paths of life by mild means. Whence it is said to Him by the Psalmist, *Set forward, go forth prosperously and rejoice, because of truth, and meekness, and righteousness.* [Ps. 45, 3] For He had no mind to be feared as God, but put it into our hearts that as a Father He should be loved; as Paul clearly delivers; *For ye have not received the Spirit of bondage again to fear, but ye have received the Spirit of adoption of sons, whereby we cry, Abba, Father.* [Rom. 8, 15] Hence too it is fitly added here, *Mystical*

Ver.35. Then would I speak, and not fear Him.

xl. 63. For the holy man, because he beholds the Redeemer of the world coming in meekness, does not assume fear towards a Master, but affection towards a Father. And he looks down on fear, in that through the grace of adoption he rises up to love. Hence John says; *There is no fear in love, but perfect love casteth out fear.* [1 John 4, 18] Hence Zachariah says, *That we being delivered out of the hand of our enemies might serve Him without fear.* [Luke 1, 74] Therefore fear had no power to raise us from the death of sin, but the infused grace of meekness erected us to the seat of life. Which is well denoted by Elisha when he raised the child of the Shunamite. [2 Kings 4] He, when he sent his servant with a staff, never a whit restored life to the dead child; but upon coming in his own person, and spreading himself upon the dead body, and contracting himself to its limbs, and walking to and fro, and breathing several times into the mouth of the dead body, he forthwith quickened it to the light of new life through the ministering of compassion. For God, the Creator of mankind, as it were grieved for His dead son, when He beheld us with compassion killed by the sting of iniquity. And whereas He put forth the terror of the Law by Moses, He as it were sent the rod by the servant. But the servant could not raise the dead body with the staff; because, as Paul bears witness, *The Law made nothing perfect*. [Heb. 7, 19] But when He came in His own Person, and spread Himself in humility upon the dead body, He contracted Himself to match the limbs of the dead body to Himself. *Who, being in the form of God, thought it not robbery to be equal with God; but made Himself of no reputation, and took upon Him the form of a servant, and was made in the likeness of men; and found in fashion as a man*. [Phil. 2, 6—8.] He 'walks to and fro' also, in that He calls Judaea nigh at hand, and the Gentiles afar off. He breathes upon the dead body several times, in that by the publishing of the Divine gift, He bestows the Spirit of sevenfold grace upon those that lie prostrate in the death of sin. And afterwards it is raised up alive, in that the child, whom the rod of terror could not raise up, has been brought back to life by the Spirit of love. Therefore let him say in himself, and in the voice of mankind, *Let Him take His rod away from me, and let not His fear terrify me*. Then would I speak, and not fear Him. Where it is fitly added,

For I cannot respond whilst I fear.

Literal 64. We are said to respond to any one, when we pay back deeds worthy of his doings. Therefore to 'respond' to God, is to render back our services in return for His previous gifts. And hence it is that certain of the Psalms, in which holy practice is set forth for imitation are prenoted as written 'to respond.' Thus God created man upright, and bore with him in long-suffering, when he let himself out to do froward deeds. Every day He beholds sin, and yet does not quickly cut off the periods of life. He lavishes His gifts in loving-kindness, and exercises patience towards evildoers. Man ought to respond to so many benefits, yet 'he is not able to respond whilst he fears,' in that everyone that continues to dread with a slavish fear the Creator of mankind, assuredly **xli.**

does not love Him. For we then only render real services to God, when we have no fear of Him through the confidence of our love, when affection, not fear, directs us to good works, when sin is now no longer pleasing to our mind, even if it were allowed us. For everyone that is restrained by fear alone from the practice of evil, would gladly do evil things if liberty were given him. He then is in no whit really righteous, who is still not free from the hankering after evil; and so it is well said, *For I cannot respond while I fear.* In that we do not render real service to God, so long as we obey His commandments from fear, and not much rather from love. But when the love of His sweetness is kindled in our mind, all desire of the present life goes for little, fondness is turned into weariness, and the mind endures with sorrow this same, which she formerly served, under the dominion of an accursed love. Hence it is added with propriety,

Chap. x. 1. My soul is weary of my life.

xlii. 65. Now whensoever the present life has once begun to grow tasteless, and the love of the Creator to become sweet, the soul inflames itself against self, that it may accuse self for the sins, wherein it formerly vindicated itself, being ignorant of the things above. Whence he yet further adds with propriety,

I will let my speech go against myself.

xliii. 66. He as it were employs his speech in behalf of himself, who tries to defend by excuses the evil things he has done. But he 'lets his speech go against himself,' who begins to accuse himself of that which he has done amiss. Now very frequently even when we commit sin, we go on to try the things we have done. The mind of itself brings what it does to trial; but forasmuch as it does not at all forsake this in the desire, it is ashamed to acknowledge what it has done; but when it now comes down upon the indulgence of the flesh with the whole weight of its judgment, it lifts itself with a bold voice in the acknowledgment of that self-accusing. Whence it is rightly said here, *I will let my speech go against myself*; in that the resolute mind begins to let loose against itself words of abhorrence, which aforetime from a feeling of shame it kept to itself through weakness. But there be some that confess their sins in explicit words, but yet know nothing how to bewail in confessing them.

And they utter things with pleasure, that they ought to bewail. Hence it is further added with propriety;

I will speak in the bitterness of my soul.

xliv.

67. He that tells his sins abhorring them, must needs likewise 'speak of them in the bitterness of his soul,' that that very bitterness may punish whatsoever the tongue accuses of in the warrant of conscience. But we must bear in mind, that from the pains of penitence, which the mind inflicts upon itself, it derives a certain degree of security; and rises with the greater confidence to meet the inquest of the heavenly Judge, that it may make itself out more thoroughly, and ascertain how each particular is appointed towards, it. Hence it is forthwith added;

Ver. 12. I will say unto God, Do not condemn me; show me wherefore Thou so judgest me.

xlv.

68. Whereas he declares himself a sinner 'in the bitterness of his soul,' what else does he say to God, but that he may not be condemned, in that the bitterness of his present penance does away with the pains of ensuing wrath? Now God judgeth man in this life in two ways, seeing that either by present ills He is already beginning to bring upon him the torments to come, or else by present scourges He does away with the torments to come. For except there were some whom the just Judge, as the due of their sins, did both now and hereafter visit, Jude would never have said, *The Lord afterwards destroyed them that believed not*. [Jude 5] And the Psalmist would not say of the wicked, *Let them cover themselves with their own confusion as with a lined cloak* [*diploide*]. [Ps. 109, 29] For we mean by 'a lined cloak' a double garment. And so they are 'clothed with confusion as with a double garment,' who according to the due reward of their sin are at once visited with both a temporal and an everlasting judgment. For chastisement delivers those alone from woe, whom it alters. For those whom present evils do not amend, they conduct to those which are to ensue. But if there were not some whom present punishment preserves from eternal woe, Paul would never have said, *But when we are Judged we are chastened of the Lord, that we should not be condemned with the world*. [1 Cor. 11, 32] Hence it is spoken to John by the voice of the Angel, *As many as I love I rebuke and*

chasten. [Rev. 3, 19] Hence also it is written, *For whom the Lord loveth He chasteneth, and scourgeth every son whom He receiveth*. [Heb. 12, 6]

69. Therefore it often happens that the mind of the righteous man, in order to be made more secure, is the more penetrated with fear, and when he is beset with scourges, he is troubled with misgivings about the Judgment of the Most High. He fears lest all that he suffers should be the forerunner of the doom to ensue, and in his heart he questions the Judge, in that under His visitation he is full of doubts about the merit of his life. But when the goodness of his life is brought before the eyes of the mind, it is as if comfort were given in answer by the Judge, in that He never strikes to destroy him, whom by so striking He keeps in innocency of life and conduct. Therefore it is justly said here, *Show me wherefore Thou so judgest me*. As if it were expressed in plain words, 'Whereas Thou exercisest judgment upon me by scourging me, show me that by these scourges Thou art making me secure against the Judgment.' Which same however may also be understood in another sense. For very often the righteous man receives scourges for trial, and examining his life with the keenest eye of enquiry, though he both feel and own himself to be a sinner, yet for what particular sin he is smitten he cannot at all make out, and he trembles the more under the rod, in proportion as he knows nothing the reasons of his being smitten. He prays that the Judge would show him to himself, that what He in striking aims at, he may himself also chastise in himself by weeping. For he is well assured that That most just Avenger never afflicts anyone of us unjustly, and he is moved with excessive alarm, in that he is both put to pain under the lash, and cannot entirely discover in himself what there is for him to lament. Hence it is further added; *Historical*

Ver. 3. Is it good unto Thee that Thou shouldest calumniate and oppress the poor [Vulg. *me*]*, and the work of Thine hands, and help the counsel of the wicked?*

xlvi. 70. This same is so said by way of interrogation, that it is denied. As though it were in plain terms; 'Thou That art supremely good, I know dost not hold it good to oppress the poor man by calumny. And therefore I know that that is not unjust that I am suffering, and I am the more grieved, that cannot tell the causes of its justness.' But observe that he does not say, *That Thou shouldest* *oppress the innocent*, but, *the poor man*. For he who doth not represent his innocency, but his poorness to the severity of the Judge, does not now put on a bold front on the ground of his own life, but shows of how little strength he sees himself to be. Where also he fitly subjoins, *The work of Thine hands*. As if he said plainly, 'Thou canst not ever unfeelingly oppress him, whom Thou rememberest Thyself to have made of Thy mere grace.'

71. Now the words are excellently put in, *And help the counsel of the wicked*. For whom does he here call wicked, save the malignant spirits, who as they cannot themselves return back to life, mercilessly look out for fellows in destruction. Whose counsel it was that God's stroke should visit blessed Job, that he who showed himself righteous while at peace, might at all events commit sin under the scourge. Now the Lord did not 'help the counsel of the wicked,' in that whilst He gave up the flesh of the righteous man to their arts of temptation, He withheld his soul. It is this counsel that the evil spirits incessantly persevere in against the good, that those, whom they see serving God in innocency while at rest, on being stricken by misfortune may go headlong into a whirlpool of sin. But the sharpness of their counsel is brought to nought, in that our pitiful Creator qualifies the strokes in accordance with our powers, that the infliction may not exceed our virtue, and by the craftiness of the strong ones man's weakness be thrown out of course. Hence it is well said by Paul, *But God is faithful, Who will not suffer you to be tempted above that ye are able, but will with the temptation also make a way to escape, that ye may be able to bear it*. For except the merciful God tempered His trials to correspond with our powers, there is surely no man who could sustain the cunning plots of evil spirits without being brought to the ground, in that excepting the Judge assign a measure to our temptations, by this alone He at once throws down one standing, in that He puts upon him a burthen too much for his strength. Now blessed Job, in the way of denying, so put in a question the things which he uttered, even as in asking he denies the things which he thereupon subjoins, saying,

Ver.4—7. Hast Thou eyes of flesh? or shalt Thou see as man seeth? Are Thy days as the days of man? Are Thy years as the time of man, that Thou inquirest after mine iniquity, and searchest after my sin? To know that I have done nothing ungodly.

THE SECOND PART.

xlvii. 72. Eyes of flesh see not the deeds of the periods of time, save in time, in that both they themselves came out with time to see, and are closed with time, and man's sight follows any deed and does not prevent it, seeing that it but just glimpses at things existing, and sees nothing at all of things to come. Moreover the days and years of men differ from the days and years of Eternity, in that our life, which is begun in time and ended in time, Eternity, whilst it frames it within the boundlessness of its bosom, doth swallow up. And whereas the immensity of the same extends beyond us on this side and on that side, His 'TO BE eternally' spreads without beginning and without end: whereunto neither things gone by are past, nor things still to come, as though they did not appear, are absent; in that He, Who hath it always TO BE, seeth all things present to His eyes, and whereas He doth not stretch Himself by looking behind and before, He changes with no varieties of sight. And so let him say; *Hast thou eyes of flesh? or shalt Thou see as man seeth? Are Thy days as the days of man? Are Thy days as the days of man, that Thou inquirest after mine iniquity, and searchest after my sin? To know that I have done nothing ungodly.* As if, humbly inquiring, he said, 'Wherefore dost Thou search me by scourges in time, when even before time was Thou didst know me perfectly in Thine own self? Wherefore dost Thou make inquest concerning my sins by smiting, whom by the mightiness of Thine eternity Thou didst never but know before Thou fashionedst me?' The weight of Whose power he immediately goes on to describe, where he adds; *And there is none that can deliver out of Thine hand.*

xlviii. 73. As if he expressed it in plain words; 'What is left to Thee, saving to spare, Whose power no man can resist? For in proportion as there is none who might stay Thy visitation by the merits of his own excellence, let Thy pitifulness the more easily obtain from Thee [lit. 'from Itself.'] to spare.' But because being conceived in sin, and born in wickedness, we either do evil things of malice, or even in doing good things go wrong out of heedlessness, we have not wherewith the strict Judge may be rendered propitious towards us; but while we are unable to present our work as worthy of His regard, it remains that for the propitiation of His favour we offer to Him His own work. Hence it is added;

Ver. 8. Thine hands have made me and fashioned me, altogether round about: and dost Thou thus suddenly cast me down?

xlix.

74. As if He said to Him in humility; 'Whereas that which I have done being submitted to a just examination is not meet for the propitiating of Thee, consider in Thy mercy lest that should perish which is Thy doing [*quod fecisti*].' By which same words too the wicked doctrine of Manichaeus [some Mss. 'of Manes.'] is destroyed, who feigning that there are two Principles, strives to maintain that the spirit was made by God, but the flesh by Satan. For the holy man, being full of the grace of the prophetic Spirit, views events to come long afterwards, and foreseeing the shoots of divers errors, treads them underfoot, saying, *Thine hands have made me and fashioned me altogether round about*. For he, who declares himself both 'made and fashioned altogether round about' by God, leaves to the race of darkness no part either in his spirit or in his flesh. For he described himself as 'moulded' [*plasmatum*] in virtue of the interior image, but he spoke of being 'fashioned together round about' in so far as he consists of a covering of flesh.

75. But it is to be observed, that herein that he declares himself made by the hands of God, he is setting before the Divine Mercy the dignity of his creation; for though all things were created by the Word, Which is coeternal with the Father, yet in the very account of the Creation, it is shown how greatly man is preferred above all animals, how much even above things celestial, yet without sense. For, *He commanded, and they all were created*. [Ps. 148, 5] But when He determines to make Man, this which is to be thought of with awe is premised; *Let Us make man in Our Image, after Our Likeness*. [Gen. 1, 26] Nor yet is it written concerning him as it is of the rest of things created; *Let there be, and it was so*. [ver. 6. 7.] Nor as the waters the fowl, so did the earth produce Man; but before he was made it was said, *Let Us make*; [ver. 20] that whereas it was a creature endowed with reason that was being made, it might seem as if it were made with counsel. As if by design he is formed out of earth, and by the inspiration of his Creator set erect in the power of a vital spirit in this way, that he who was made after the image of his Creator, might have his being not by word of command, but by the greater eminence of action. That, then, which Man in the work of his creating received preeminently upon earth above all other creatures, this,

being laid under the scourge, he represents to the pitifulness of his Artificer, saying, *Thine hands have made me and fashioned me altogether round about: and dost Thou thus suddenly cast me down?* As if it were in plain words; 'Why dost Thou despise me with such light esteem, when Thou createdst me with such circumstances of dignity? and him whom by reason Thou settest above all other things, why dost Thou by sorrow set below them?' Yet this preeminence, that we possess, shines bright by reason of the 'Likeness,' but is very far removed from the perfection of blessedness by reason of the flesh, in that whilst the spirit mixes with dust, it is in a certain measure united with weakness. Which weakness blessed Job presents to the pitifulness of the Judge, when he subjoins;

Ver. 9. Remember, I pray Thee, that Thou hast made me as the clay.

l. 76. The spirits of the Angels did for this reason sin without forgiveness, because they might have stood the stronger in proportion as no mixture with flesh held them in bonds. But man for this reason obtained pardon after sin, that in a body of flesh he got that wherein he should be beneath himself. And hence in the eye of the Judge this frailty of the flesh alone is a ground for showing pity; as where it is said by the Psalmist, *But He is full of compassion, and will forgive their iniquity, and not destroy them; yea, many a time turned He His anger away from them, and did not stir up all His wrath, and remembered that they were but flesh*. [Ps. 78, 38. 39.] And so man was 'made as the clay' in that he was taken out of clay, for the making of him. For clay is made, when water is sprinkled [*se conspergit*] in with earth. Therefore man is made as clay, in that it is as if water moistened dust, while the soul waters the flesh. Which name the holy man excellently represents to the pitifulness of the Judge, when he beseeches saying, *Remember, I pray Thee, that Thou hast made me as the clay*. As if he said in plain words; 'Consider the frailty of the flesh, and remit the guilt of my sin.' Where moreover the death of that flesh is openly added, in that the words are immediately brought in;

And wilt Thou bring me unto dust again?

li. 77. As if he begged openly, saving, 'Remember, I pray Thee, that by the flesh I came from earth, and by the death thereof, I tend to earth. Thus regard the substance of my origin, and the penalty of my end, and be the readier to spare the sin of a transient being;' but as he has given out the sort and kind of man as created, he now subjoins the order of man as propagated, saying,

Ver. 10, 11. Hast Thou not poured me out like milk, and curdled me like cheese? Thou hast clothed me with skin, and flesh, and hast fenced me with bones and sinews.

78. For man when fashioned was moulded like clay, but being propagated he is 'poured out like milk' in the seed, and is 'curdled like cheese' in the flesh, and he is 'clothed with skin and flesh,' and is rendered firm by bones and sinews. Therefore by clay we have set forth to us the character of the first creating, but by milk the order of the subsequent conception, in that by the stages of curdling, it goes on little by little to be wrought strong into bones. But the account of the body as it was created is but slender praise of God, unless at the same time there be afterwards set forth the marvellous inspiration of its quickening. Hence it is added, **lii.**

Thou hast granted me life and mercy.

79. But the Creator vouchsafes to us blessings in vain, except He Himself keep safe all whatsoever He giveth. It follows, *And Thy visitation hath preserved my spirit.* Now all this that we have spoken of the exterior man, in what sense it may accord with the interior man, it is well to unfold and exhibit in few words, **liii.**

Remember, I beseech Thee, that Thou hast made me as the clay.

Moral 80. For our interior man proves like clay, in that the grace of the Holy Spirit is, infused into the earthly mind, that it may be lifted up to the understanding of its Creator. For the thinking faculty in man, which is dried up by the barrenness of its sin, through the power of the Holy Spirit grows green, like land when it is watered. Now it very often happens that whilst we use without let or hindrance the endowments of virtue by gift from above, by being used to such uninterrupted prosperity we are lifted up to self-confidence. Whence it very often happens that the same Holy Spirit, Which had exalted us, leaves us for a time, in order to show mere man to himself. And this is what the holy man immediately sets forth, when he adds, *And wilt Thou, bring me into dust again?* For as by the withdrawal of the Spirit the soul is left for a space under temptation, it is as if the ground were dried of its former moisture; that by being so forsaken it may be made sensible of its weakness, and learn how man was dried up without the infusion of heavenly grace. And he is fitly described as being 'brought into dust again,' in that when he is left to himself he is caught up by the breath of every temptation. But whereas on being left we are exposed to shocks, those gifts which we knew when we were inspired, we now think of more nicely. Whence he adds, *Hast Thou not poured me out like milk, and curdled me like cheese?* For when by the grace of the Holy Spirit our mind is withdrawn from the way of its former conversation, it is as if 'milk poured out,' in that it is formed in the sort of tenderness and delicacy of a new beginning. And it is 'curdled like cheese,' in that it is bound up in the consistency of consolidating thought, never from henceforth to let itself go loose in desires, but concentrating itself in a single affection, to rise up into a substantial remoulding. But it very often happens that the flesh, from old habit, murmurs against this spiritual embryo, and the soul meets with war from the man which it bears about without it. And hence he adds, *Thou hast clothed me with skin and flesh.* For the interior man is 'clothed with skin and flesh,' since wherein it is raised up to things above, it is straitly blockaded with the besieging of fleshly motions. Now one that is going on to righteousness our Creator never forsakes under temptation, Who by the inspiration of His Grace preventeth even him that is sinning; but the soul that is lifted up He both lets loose to wars without, and endues with strength within. And hence it is yet further fitly subjoined, *And hast fenced me with bones and sinews.* With 'flesh and skin we are clothed,' but we are 'fenced with bones and sinews,' in that though we receive a shock by temptation assaulting us from without, yet the hand of the Creator strengthens us within, that we should not be shattered. And so by the promptings of the flesh, He abases us in respect of His gifts, but by the bones of virtue He strengthens us against temptations. Therefore he says, *Thou, hast clothed me with skin and flesh, and hast fenced me with bones and sinews.* As if it were in plain words, 'Without Thou dost abandon me to undergo trial, yet within, that I may not perish, Thou keepest me by bracing me with virtue.' And for this reason He gives us righteousness to live as we ought, because in His loving-kindness He spares the past misdeeds whereby we have done amiss. And hence it is further added with propriety,

Thou hast granted me life and mercy.

81. For 'life' is granted, when goodness is inspired into evil minds, but 'life' cannot be had without 'mercy,' in that the Lord does not aid us to obtain the endowments of righteousness, unless He first in mercy remit our past iniquities. Or surely, He 'grants us life and mercy,' in that by the same mercy, with which He prevents us that we may lead a good life, continuing on afterwards He keep us safe. For except He add mercy, the life which He vouchsafes cannot be preserved; since we are daily growing old by the mere customariness of our human life, and by the impulse of the outward man we are carried out of interior life by loose thought; so that unless heavenly visiting either by piercing our hearts quicken us in love, or by scourging us renew us in fear, the soul is wholly and entirely ruined by a sudden downfall, when it seemed to be made new by a long course of devotion to virtue. Hence he subjoins, *And Thy visitation hath preserved my spirit*. For the visitation of the Most High preserves man's spirit, when, it being richly endowed with graces, He does not cease either to scourge it with the rod, or to pierce it with love. For if He bestows gifts, but does not raise it up by continually restoring it, the blessing is speedily lost, which is not preserved by the Giver. But mark how the holy man, whilst he views himself in a humble light, discovers the secrets of Divine mercy destined to be universally bestowed, and whilst he truly confesses his own weakness, he is suddenly transported on high to learn the calling of the Gentiles. For he forthwith adds,

Ver. 13. Though Thou hide these things in Thine heart; yet I know that Thou rememberest all.

Historical 82. As if it were in plain words; 'Why do I tremble for myself, who know that Thou dost gather in one even all nations? Which nevertheless Thou 'hidest in Thine heart,' in that Thou dost not yet make it known by open revelation, but Thou That 'rememberest all,' givest me, doubtless, assurance of pardon.' But it is to be borne in mind, that in certain deeds we are both made certain of pardon, and after the commission of the sins are strengthened to have confidence of our absolution by subsequent chastisement and penance, yet we are still touched with the remembrance of the wickedness we have committed, and, unwilling and **liv.**

abhorring it, are preyed upon by unlawful thoughts. And hence it is fitly subjoined,

Ver. 14. If I have sinned, and Thou sparedst me at the hour, wherefore dost Thou not let me be clean from mine iniquity?

lv. 83. The Lord 'spareth sin at the hour,' when the moment that we yield tears, He does away with the guilt of sin. But He doth not 'let us be clean from our iniquity,' in that of free will indeed we committed the sin, but sometimes against our will we undergo the remembrance of it with a sense of pleasure; for often that, which has been put away from the sight of the just Judge by tears intervening, recurs to mind, and the conquered habit strives to insinuate itself again for the entertaining of delight, and is renewed again in the former contest with revived assault, that what it once did in the body, it may afterwards go through in the mind by intruding thought; which same that spiritual wrestler knew how to regard with heedful eye, who said, *My scars* [V. *cicatrices*] *stink, and are corrupt through my foolishness*. For what are 'scars' but the healings of wounds? And so he who lamented his scars, beheld his pardoned wickednesses return to his remembrance for the entertaining of delight. Since for scars to grow corrupt is for wounds of sins, already healed, again to insinuate themselves in the tempting of us, and at their suggestions, after the skin of penitence has grown over; to be sensible of the stench and pain of sin again. Wherein there is at once both nothing done outwardly in deed, and sin is committed within in the thought alone, and the soul is laid under a close bond of guilt except it do away with it by heedful lamentation.

84. Whence it is well said by Moses, *If there be among you any man that is not clean by reason of a dream that chanceth him by night, then shall he go abroad without the camp, he shall not come within the camp: but it shall be when evening cometh on he shall wash himself with water: and when the sun is down he shall come into the camp again.* [Deut. 23, 10. 11.] For 'the dream that chanceth by night' is the secret tempting, whereby there is something foul conceived in the heart in dark thought, which nevertheless is not fulfilled in the deed of the body. Now, if there be any that is 'not clean by reason of a dream that chanceth him by night,' he is bidden to go abroad without the camp, in that it is meet that he that is defiled with impure thought, *Moral*

should look upon himself as unworthy the society of the faithful, that he should set before his eyes the deserts of his sin, and look down upon himself in the scale of good men. And so for 'one unclean to go abroad out of the camp' is for one hard bestead by the assaults of impurity, to look down upon himself by comparison with men of continency. And 'when evening cometh on he washes himself with water,' in that seeing his offence he has recourse to tears of penitence, that by weeping he may wash out everything that hidden defilement brings home to the soul's charge. 'And when the sun is down he shall come into the camp again,' in that when the heat of temptation has subsided, it follows that he should again take confidence to join the company of the good. For after washing with water, when the sun is set, he returns to the camp, who after tears of penance, when the flame of unlawful thought is quenched, is restored to assume the claims of the faithful, that he should not any longer account himself far removed from others, who rejoices that he is clean by the departure of the inward burning.

But herein be it known that it is for this reason that we are sometimes driven to straits by the impulse of unlawful thought, because we are ready to employ ourselves in certain courses of earthly conduct, though not unlawful. And when even in the very least things we come in contact with earthly conduct in desire, the might of our old enemy gaining strength against us, our mind is defiled by no little urgency of temptation. And hence the Priest of the Law is enjoined to consume with fire the limbs of the victim cut into pieces, the head, and the parts about the liver; but the inwards and the legs he is to wash with water first. [Lev. 1, 5. 12.] For we offer our own selves a sacrifice to God, when we dedicate our lives to the service of God, and we set the members of the sacrifice cut into pieces upon the fire, when we offer up the deeds of our lives dividing them in the virtues. The head and the parts contained about the liver we burn, when in our faculty of sense, whereby all the body is governed, and in our hidden desire we are kindled with the flame of divine love. And yet it is bidden, that the feet and the inwards of the victim be washed with water. For with the feet the earth is touched, and in the inwards dung is carried, in that it very often happens that already in the desire of our hearts we burn for eternity, already with an entire feeling of devotion we pant in longing desire for the mortification of ourselves; but whereas by reason of our frailty there is still a mixture of earth in what we do, even some of the things forbidden which we have already subdued, we are subject to in thought, and while unclean temptation defiles our thoughts, what else is this than that 'the inwards' of the victim carry dung? But that they may be fit to be burnt, let them be washed, in that it is necessary that tears of fear wash out the impure thoughts of the heart, for love from on high to consume them in acceptance of the sacrifice, and whatever the mind is subject to, proceeding either from untried conflict, or from the remembrance of former practice, let it be washed, that it may burn with so much the sweeter odour in the sight of its Beholder, in proportion as when it begins to draw near to Him, it sets upon the altar of its prayer along with itself nought earthly, nought impure. Therefore let the holy man regard the wretchedness of the human mind, how often it defiles itself with unhallowed thoughts, and after the Judge's remission of the guilt of our doings, even whilst he bewails his own case, let him show to us ours, for ourselves to bewail, saying, *If I have sinned, and thou sparedst me at the hour, wherefore dost thou not let me be clean from mine iniquity?* As if he said in plain words; 'If Thy forgiveness has taken away my sin, why does it not sweep it from my memory also?' Oftentimes the mind is so shaken from its centre at the recollection of sin, that it is prompted to the commission thereof far worse than it had been before subjected to it, and when entangled it is filled with fears, and being driven with different impulses, throws itself into disorder. It dreads lest it should be overcome by temptations, and in resisting, it shudders at this very fact, that it is harassed with the long toils of conflict. Hence it is fitly subjoined,

Ver. 15. If I be wicked, woe unto me; and if I be righteous, yet will I not lift up my head: I am full of affliction and misery.

lvi. 85. Yea, the wicked man has 'woe,' and the righteous man 'affliction,' in that both everlasting damnation follows the lost sinner, and each one of the Elect is purified by the pains of temporary affliction. The wicked man lifts up his head, yet when so lifted up he cannot escape the woe that pursues him. The righteous man, faring ill with the toils of his conflict, is not suffered to lift up his head, but while hard pressed, he is freed from everlasting affliction. The one sets himself up in pleasure, but is plunging himself into the punishment that succeeds. The others sinks himself to the earth in sorrow, yet hides himself from the weight of eternal visitation. Thus let the holy man consider how man either in striving against evil, is afflicted with present trouble, or giving up the contest, he is delivered over to eternal anguish, and let him say, *If I be wicked, woe unto me; and if I be righteous, yet will I not lift up my head: I am full of affliction and misery*; as if he lamented openly, saying, 'Either bowed down under the desires of the flesh, I am exposed to eternal punishment, or if I fight against unlawful impulses, I am tormented with present woe, seeing that I am not quit of the toils of the fight.' But the Providence of the Most High does for this reason suffer us who serve Him with all the bent of the mind, to be buffeted by the assaults of our flesh, lest our mind, by presuming on its own security, dare to lift itself up in pride, that whereas, when a shock comes it is filled with fears, it may set the foot of hope the stronger, in the aid of its Maker alone. Hence it is further added fitly,

Ver. 16. And by reason of pride, Thou wilt take me like a lioness.

lvii.

86. When a lioness hunts for food for her whelps, she rushes with ravening jaws into the pitfall. For as the account goes from certain countries, they make a pit in her path, and deposit a sheep in it, that the lioness in her ravening appetite may be provoked to precipitate herself into it, and they make it both narrow and deep at the same time, that she may have room to tumble into it in circling round it, but never get out by taking a leap. There is another pit too dug, which is to be close to the former, but which is joined to the one in which the sheep is, by the opening of the part at the bottom. And in this is put a cage, that the lioness tumbling in, forasmuch as she is pressed by terrors from above, when she goes about as it were to hide herself in the more secret part of the pit, may of her own will go into the cage; her savage temper being now no longer an object of fear, seeing that she is lifted up enclosed in the cage. For the beast that threw itself of its own accord into the pit is brought back to the regions above hedged round with bars. Thus, thus is it that the mind of man is taken, which being created in the liberty of free will, whilst it craved to feed the desires of the flesh, was like a lioness seeking food for her cubs, and fell into the pit of self-deception, in that at the suggestion of the enemy it stretched forth the hand to take the forbidden food, but it quickly found a cage in the pit, in that coming by its own act to death, it exposed itself at

once to the prison house of its own corruption, and is brought back to the free air by grace intervening. But whereas it tries to do many things, and has no power, it is bound by the hindrances of that same corruption, as though by the bars of a cage. It is now free of that pit of damnation into which it had fallen, in that receiving help from the hand of Redemption, in being brought back to pardon, it has got above the punishment of the death to follow. But yet, being shut in close, it feels the cage, in that it is encircled by the bands of heavenly discipline, that it may not roam through the desires of the flesh. And she that of her own will went down into the pit; returns to the free air in confinement, in that she both fell into sin by the liberty of the will, and yet the grace of the Creator holds her in by constraint, and against her will, from following her own motions. And so after the pit she has the cage to bear, in that being rescued from eternal punishment, she is withheld from the motions of a froward liberty, under the controlling hand of the heavenly Artificer. Therefore he says aright, *And by reason of pride, Thou wilt take me like a lioness*; in that both when free, man brought death upon himself through food, and on being brought back to pardon, he lives shut up under discipline for his greater good. Therefore like a lioness he was taken by reason of pride, in that the discipline, that belongs to his corrupt condition, now keeps him down from the very same cause, that not fearing the transgression of the commandment he boldly leapt into the pit.

87. But if for a short space we turn aside the eye of our mind from the sin of our first parent, we find that we ourselves are every day taken like the lioness, by the evil habit of pride. For it often happens that by the virtues that have been vouchsafed him, man is lifted up into the boldness of self-presumption, but by a wonderful ordering of Providence, some object is set before his eyes for him to fall therein. And whilst he seeks something in sin, what else is this but that he longs for the prey in the pit? With open mouth he falls by his own act, but has no power to rise by his own strength. And whereas he sees that of himself he is nothing, assuredly he learns Whose aid he must seek. Yet the heavenly Compassion draws him, thus taken out of the pit, as it were, in that as soon as his weakness is known, It restores him to pardon. And so like a lioness, by reason of pride that man hastes back to the upper regions within the cage, who when he is lifted up in the score of virtuous attainments, after he has fallen into evil desires, is bound fast in humility. For whereas

he had in the first case brought himself to destruction by his presuming on self, it is brought to pass by wonderful pitifulness, that he now lives walled in by the knowledge of his own weakness. And because the holy man sees that this often happens to his fellow creatures, he adopts in his own person the cry of peril that belongs to us, that when we read of his lamentations, we may be instructed what the things are in ourselves that we ought to lament. Now when pride uplifts the mind, the piercing sense of love for the Highest departs from us, but when grace from above descends upon us, immediately it prompts us to longings for itself in tears. And hence it is fitly subjoined,

And returning, Thou dost torture me marvellously.

lviii.

88. When we are forsaken by our Creator, we do not at all feel even the very ills of our abandonment. For in proportion as our Creator goes far off from us, our mind becomes more hardened in insensibility, loves nothing that is of God, entertains no longing for things above, and because it has no warmth of interior love, it lies frozen towards the earth, and in a pitiable way it becomes every day the more self-secure, in proportion as it becomes worse; and whereas it no longer remembers whence it has fallen, and no longer dreads the punishments to come, it knows nothing how deeply it is to be bewailed. But if it be touched by the inspiration of the Holy Spirit, at once it wakes up to the thought of its ruin, rouses itself in the pursuit after heavenly things, glows with the hot emotions of love towards the Highest, takes thought of the ills which every way beset it round about, and she weeps while making progress, who before was going to ruin in high glee. Therefore it is well said to the Creator, *And returning Thou dost torture me marvelously.* For by the same act whereby Almighty God in visiting our soul lifts it to the love of Himself, He makes it the more to sorrow in tears. As if it were in plain words, 'In going from me Thou dost not influence me, because Thou renderest me insensible, but when Thou returnest, Thou dost torture me, because whilst Thou dost cause Thyself to enter into me, Thou showest to me mine own self, and how deeply I am to be pitied.' And hence he never says that he is tortured judicially, but 'marvellously,' since while the mind is transported on high in weeping, with a feeling of joy it marvels at the pains of its piercing sorrow, and it is its joy to be so touched, be-

cause it sees that by its anguish it is lifted up on high. But often when heavenly Pity sees us slacken in the exercising ourselves in holy desires, It presents to our view the example of those that cleave to Itself, that the mind which is unbraced by indolence, in proportion as it observes in the case of others the advancement of minds well awake, may take shame for the dulness of sloth in itself. Hence it is rightly added,

Ver. 17. Thou renewest Thy witnesses against me, and multipliest Thy wrath: and pains war in me.

lix. 89. For 'God's witnesses' are they, who bear witness by the practice of holy works, what are the rewards of Truth that shall overtake the Elect. Hence too those, whom we see to have suffered for the sake of the Truth, we style in the Greek tongue, 'Martyrs,' i.e. witnesses. And the Lord says by John in the Angel's voice, *Even in those days, wherein Antipas was my faithful witness, who was slain among you*. Now the Lord 'renews His witnesses against us' when He multiplies the lives of the Elect to confront our wickedness, for the purpose of convicting and of instructing us. And so His 'witnesses are renewed against us,' in that all things that they do are opposed to the ends and aims of our wickedness. Hence too the word of Truth is called 'an adversary,' where it is said by the voice of the Mediator in the Gospel, *Agree with thine adversary quickly, whiles thou art in the way with him*. [Matt. 5, 25] And the sons of perdition in their persecutions say concerning that same Redeemer, *And He is clean contrary to our doings*; and soon afterwards, *For His life is not like other men's*. [Wisd. 2, 12. 15] Thus the Lord 'renews His witnesses against us,' in that the good things which we neglect to do ourselves, He shows us to be done by others to our upbraiding, that we who are not inflamed by precepts, may at least be stirred up by examples, and that in longing after righteousness, our mind may account nothing to be difficult to itself, that it sees to be done perfectly by others; and it is very commonly brought to pass, that while we behold the good actions of another man's life, we are more anxiously afraid of the deficiencies of our own, and it is made appear the plainer by what a weight of judgment we are afterwards assailed, in proportion as we are now widely at variance with the ways of the good. *Historical*

90. Hence after the renewal of the witnesses has been mentioned it is thereupon fitly added, *And multipliest Thy wrath upon me*. God's wrath is said to be 'multiplied upon us,' in proportion as it is shown to be manifold, since by the very lives and labours of the good we are instructed, if, whilst we have time, we will not amend our ways now, what a terrible visitation shall be dealt us hereafter. For we see the Elect of God at one and the same time leading godly lives and undergoing numberless sore hardships. And therefore we collect from hence with what rigour the strict Judge will There smite those whom He condemns, if he so torments here below those whom He loves; as Peter witnesses, who says, *For the time is come that judgment must begin at the house of God, and if it first begin at us, what shall the end be of them that obey not the Gospel of God?* [1 Peter 4, 17] Therefore Almighty God, when He 'renews His witnesses' against us, 'multiplies His wrath,' in that in proportion as He sets before our eyes the life of the good, He shows with what severity He will smite obduracy in the commission of sin at the Judgment. Now whereas He multiplies His gifts to those alone that follow Him, He shows that He has already forsaken those that go on in sloth. Thus when we see good things in others, it is very necessary to mix exultation with the dread that we feel, and dread with our exultation, that both charity may rejoice for the proficiencies of other men, and conscience tremble for its own frailties. But when we are gladdened with the proficiency of a brother, when we calculate the severity of the interior Judge against us for our mere slothfulness by itself, what is there left but that the mind turn back to search into itself, and that whatever it meets with in itself, that is blameworthy, whatever that is bad, it should chastise? Hence it is fitly subjoined, *Pains fight in me*. For upon considering the witnesses of God, 'pains fight in us,' in that whilst we behold their deeds, that command our admiration, our own life, which by comparison with theirs is displeasing in our eyes, we visit with serious self-chastening, that whatever pollution our deeds may have caused in us, our tears may wash clean, and if the guilt of taking pleasure therein still somewhat defiles us, the chastening of a sorrowful heart may cleanse away the stain. Therefore because blessed Job has his eye fixed on the life of the fathers of old time, he ascertains more exactly what he ought to bewail in himself. And by the preceptorship of extraordinary sorrow, whilst he bewails his own case, he instructs us to lamentation, that in proportion as we

perceive excellencies in other men, we may anxiously fear for our own offences in the sight of the strict Judge. It goes on,

Ver. 19. Wherefore then hast Thou brought me forth out of the womb. Oh that I had been consumed, and no eye had seen me.

lx. 91. Which same sentiment he had already uttered in his first speech, saying, *Why died I not from the womb?* [Job 3, 11] and whilst he subjoins that which he adds here, *I should have been as though I had not been, I should have been carried from the womb to the grave*; he adds in other words, but no other sense, saying, *Or as a hidden untimely birth I had not been, as infants which never saw light*. [Book IV, §48 &c.] But forasmuch as we have made out these particulars very much at length above, to avoid wearying the reader we forbear to unfold points already explained. It goes on,

Ver. 20. Will not the small number of my days be finished in a short time?

lxi. 92. He shows himself to live with good heed and circumspection, who, in considering the shortness of the present life does not look to the furtherance but to the ending of it, so as to gather from the end, that all is nought that delights while it is passing. For hence it is said by Solomon, *But if a man live many years and rejoice in them all, yet let him remember the time of darkness, and the days that shall be many; and when they come, the past shall be convinced of vanity*. [Eccles. 11, 8] Hence again it is written, *Whatsoever thou takest in hand, remember thine end, and thou shalt never do amiss*. [Ecclus. 7, 36] Therefore when sin tempts the mind, it is requisite that the soul should regard the shortness of its gratification, lest iniquity hurry it on to a living death, when it is plain that a mortal life is quickly speeding to an end. But often the eye of our contemplation is bewildered, while our pain is heightened by thickening scourges. It is good to bewail the exile of the present life, yet for mere anguish alone the mind cannot take account of the ills of its blind state. Hence he directly adds,

And let me go, that I may bewail my sorrow a little.

lxii. 93. For as moderate distress gives vent to tears, so excessive sorrow checks them, since that grief itself is as it were made void of grief, which by swallowing up the mind of the person afflicted, takes away the sense of grief. Therefore the holy man shrinks from being stricken more than he is equal to bear, saying, *And let me go, that I may bewail my sorrow a little.* As if it were in plain words, 'Qualify the strokes of Thy scourging, that, my pains being made moderate, in weeping I may have power to estimate the miseries I endure.' Which same nevertheless may likewise be understood in another sense. For oftentimes the sinner is so bound by the chains of his wickedness, that he bears indeed the burthen of his sins, and knows not that he is bearing it. Often if he does know with what an amount of guilt he is burthened, he strives to break loose and cannot, so as to hunt it down in himself with free spirit and full conversion. Thus he is unable to 'bewail his sorrow,' for at once he sees the guilt of his sinful state, and by reason of the weight of earthly business, is not at liberty to bewail it. He is unable to 'bewail his sorrow,' who strives indeed to resist evil habits, yet is weighed down by the still increasing desires of the flesh. The presence of this sorrow had inflicted anguish upon the spirit of the Prophet, when he said, *My sorrow is continually before me; for I will declare my iniquity, I will be sorry for my sin*; [Ps. 38, 17. 18.] but the bands of his sin being loosed, he knew that he was 'let go,' who gave vent to his exultation, saying, *Thou hast loosed my bonds, I will offer to Thee the sacrifice of thanksgiving.* [Ps. 116, 16. 17.]

94. Therefore God then 'lets us go' to bewail our sorrow, when He both shows us the evil things that we have done, and helps us to bewail the same, when we know them; He sets our transgressions before our eyes, and with the pitying hand of grace unlooses the bands of the heart, that our soul may lift itself up to liberty for the work of repentance, and loosed from the fetters of the flesh, may with free spirit stretch out towards its Maker the footsteps of love. For it very commonly happens that we the same persons blame our course of life, and yet readily do the very thing that we justly condemn in ourselves. The spirit lifts us up to righteousness, the flesh holds us back to habit; the soul struggles against self-love, but quickly overcome with delight is made captive. Thus it is well said, *Let me go that I may bewail my sorrow a little.* For except we be 'let go' in mercy from the guilt of sin, with which we are tied and bound, we cannot lament that which we grieve for in ourselves being set against ourselves. But the woe of our guiltiness is then really bewailed,

when that dark retribution of the place below is fore-reckoned with lively apprehension. Hence it is fitly added,

Ver. 21. Before I go whence I shall not return, even to a land of darkness, and covered with the shadow of death.

lxiii. 95. For what is denoted by 'the land of darkness' saving the dreary caverns of Tartarus, which are covered by the shadow of eternal death, in that it keeps all the damned for evermore severed from the light of life. Neither is the place below improperly called a land. For all they that have been made captive by it, are held fast and firm. As it is written; *One generation passeth away, and another generation cometh, but the earth abideth for ever.* [Eccl. 1, 4] Thus the dungeons of hell are rightly designated 'a land of darkness,' for all, whom they receive doomed to punishment, they torment with no transient infliction or phantasm of the imagination, but keep in the substantial vengeance of everlasting damnation. Yet they are sometimes denoted by the title of 'a lake,' as the Prophet bears witness, when he says, *They have borne their shame with them that go down into the lake.* [Ezek. 32, 24. 25] Thus hell is both called 'a land,' because it holds stedfastly all that it takes in, and 'a lake,' because it swallows up those whom it has once received, ever tossing and quaking in weltering floods of torment; but the holy man, whether in his own voice or in the voice of mankind, beseeches that he may be 'let go' before he departs, not because he that bewails his sin is to 'go to the land of darkness,' but because everyone that neglects to bewail it doth assuredly go thither, according as the creditor says to his debtor, 'Pay thy debt, before thou art put in bonds for the debt;' whereas he is not put in bonds, if he delays not to pay all that he owes. In which place too it is rightly added, *Whence I shall not return*, in that His pity in sparing never any more sets them free, whom His justice in judging once assigns their doom in the places of punishment, which same places are yet more minutely described, where it is said,

Ver. 22. A land of misery and darkness.

lxiv. 96. 'Misery' has relation to pain, 'darkness' relates to blindness. That land then which holds all those that are banished the presence of the strict Judge, is entitled 'a land of misery and darkness,' for pain without torments those, whom blindness darkens within, severed from the true Light. Not but that 'the land of misery and darkness' may be understood in another sense also. For this land too, in which we are born, is indeed 'a land of misery,' but not 'of darkness,' in that we here suffer the many ills of our corrupt condition, yet whilst we are in it, we are still brought back to the light through the grace of conversion; as Truth counsels us, Who says, *Walk while ye have the light, lest darkness come upon you*. [John 12, 35] But that land is 'a land of misery and darkness' together, for everyone, that has gone down to suffer the woes thereof, never any further returns to the light; for the describing of which same it is further added,

Where is the shadow of death, without any order.

lxv.

97. As external death divides the flesh from the soul, so internal death severs the soul from God. Thus the 'shadow of death' is the darkness of separation, in that every one of the damned, whilst he is consumed with everlasting fire, is in darkness to the internal light. Now it is the nature of fire to give out both light and a property of consuming from itself, but the fire that is the avenger of past sins has a consuming property but no light. It is hence that 'Truth' says to the lost, *Depart from Me, ye cursed, into everlasting fire, prepared for the devil and his angels*. [Mat. 25, 41] And representing in one individual the whole body of them all, He says, *Bind him hand and foot, and take him away, and cast him into outer darkness*. [Mat. 22, 1] Accordingly, if the fire that torments the lost could have had light, he that is cast off would never be said to 'be cast into darkness.' Hence too the Psalmist hath it; *Fire hath fallen upon them, and they have not seen the sun*. [Ps. 58, 8. Vulg.] For 'fire falls' upon the ungodly, but 'the sun is not seen' on the fire falling; for as the flame of hell devours them, it blinds them to the vision of the true Light, that at the same time both the pain of consuming fire should torment them without, and the infliction of blindness darken them within, so that they, who have done wrong against their Maker both in body and in heart, may at one and the same time be punished in body and in heart, and that they may be made to feel pangs in both ways, who, whilst they lived here, ministered to their depraved gratifications in both. Whence it is well said by the Prophet, *Which are gone down to hell with their weapons of war*. [Ezek. 32, 37] For the arms of sinners are the members of the body, by means of which they execute the wrong desires they conceive. Hence it is said rightly by

Paul, *Neither yield ye your members as instruments if unrighteousness unto sin*. [Rom. 6, 19] And so to 'go down into hell with the weapons of war' is together with those same members, with which they fulfilled the gratifications of self-indulgence, to undergo the torrents of eternal condemnation, that at that time woe may every way swallow them up, who being now subjected to their gratifications, every way fight against His justice, Who judgeth justly.

98. But that is very wonderful that is said, *without order*, since Almighty God, Who punishes evil things well, never permits even the torments to be 'without order;' because [read '*quia*'] the very punishments that proceed from the scales of justice, cannot in any way be inflicted 'without order.' For how is it that there is no order in His punishment, since according to the measure of his guilt is likewise the recompense of vengeance which pursues everyone of the damned. For hence it is written, *But mighty men, shall be mightily tormented, and stronger torment shall come upon the stronger ones*. [Wisd. 6, 6. 8.] Hence it is uttered in the sentence of Babylon, *How much she hath glorified herself, and lived deliciously, so much torment and sorrow give her*. [Rev. 18, 7] If then the infliction is marked out according to the measure of the sin, it is undeniably true that there is order preserved in the punishments, and except the acts of desert did distribute His aggregate of torment, the Judge that shall come would never declare that He will say to the reapers, *Gather ye together first the tares, and bind them in bundles to burn them*. [Mat. 13, 30] For if there were no order observed in dealing punishment, why are the tares that are to be burnt bound in bundles? But doubtless to bind up the bundles for the burning, is to unite like to like of those that are destined to be given over to everlasting fire, that all whom a like sin pollutes, an equal punishment may bind in one, and that they who were defiled by iniquity in no degree dissimilar, may suffer by torments not dissimilar either, that condemnation may dash to the earth together those whom pride uplifted together, and that all, whom ambition made to swell in no unlike proportion, no unlike proportion of suffering may wring hard, and a like flame of punishment torment those whom a like flame of sin kindled in the fire of lust. For as in the house of our Father there are 'many mansions' [John 14, 2] according to the diversities in virtue, so a difference in guilt subjects the damned to a difference of punishment in the fires of hell, which hell, though it be one and the same for all, by no means burns all men in

one and the same sort. For as we are all reached by one sun, yet we do not all glow beneath it in one class; for it is according to the kind of the body that the burthen of the heat too is felt, in the same way there is to the damned, but one hell that torments all, yet not one that consumes all men in one kind of manner, for what on the one side an unequal degree of healthiness in bodies occasions, that same on the other an unequal case of merit produces. How then is it said that there is 'no order' in the punishments, wherein without doubt every man is tormented after the measure of his sin?

99. But after the holy man brought in the shadow of death he adds what great disorder there is in the souls of the damned, since the very punishments, which come well ordered by justice, are doubtless far from well ordered in the heart of those undergoing death. For as we have said above, whilst every one of the damned is consumed with flames without, he is devoured by the fire of blindness within, and being in the midst of woe, he is confounded both within and without; so that he is worse tormented by his own confusion. Thus to rejected souls there will be 'no order' in their punishment, because their very confusion of mind torments most cruelly in their death; which same His equity in judging appoints by His wonderful power, that a punishment as it were 'without order' may confound the soul. Or, verily, order is said to be wanting to His punishments, in that when things arise for their punishment, their proper character is not preserved to them. Whence the words are forthwith introduced;

And everlasting horror dwells.

100. In the torments of this life fear has pain, pain has no **lxvi.**
fear, in that pain never torments the mind, when it has already begun to suffer what it feared. But hell both 'the shadow of death' darkens and 'everlasting horror inhabits;' in that they all, that are given over to its fires, both in their punishments undergo pain, and, in the pressure of pain coming upon them, they are ever stricken with fear, so that they both suffer what they dread, and unceasingly dread What they are suffering. For it is written concerning them, *For their worm shall not die, neither their fire be quenched*. [Is. 66, 24] Here the flame that burns gives light; There, as we have shown by the words of the Psalmist, the fire that torments veils the light. Here fear is gone so soon as the thing that was feared has begun to be

suffered; There pain rends at the same time that fear pinches. Thus in a horrible manner there will then be to the damned pain along with terror, a flame together with dimness. Then, then, alas! the weight of heavenly equity must be felt by the damned, that they who whilst they lived were not afraid to be at variance with the Will of the Creator, may one day in their destruction find their very torments at variance with their own properties, that in proportion as they are at strife with themselves, their torments may be increased, and as they issue in diverse lines may be felt in many ways. And these punishments doth torture those that are plunged therein beyond their powers, and at the same time preserve them alive, extinguishing in them the forces of life, that the end may so afflict the life, that torment may ever live without end, in that it is both hastening after an end through torments, and failing holds on without end. Therefore there is done upon the wretches death without death, an end without ending, failing without failing; in that both death lives, and the end is ever beginning, and the failing is unable to fail. Therefore whereas death at the same time slays and does not extinguish, pain torments but does not banish fear, the flame burns but does not dispel the darkness, for all that is gathered from a knowledge of the present life, the punishments are without order, in that they do not retain their own character through all particulars.

101. Though there the fire both gives no light for comfort, yet, that it may torment the more, it does give light for a purpose. For the damned shall see, by the flame lighting them, all their followers along with themselves in torment, for the love of whom they transgressed, that whereas they had loved the life of such in a carnal manner against the precepts of the Creator, the destruction of those very persons may also afflict them for the increase of their condemnation. Which doubtless we gather from the testimony of the Gospel, wherein, as 'Truth' declares, that rich man, whose lot it was to descend into the torments of eternal fire, is described as remembering his five brethren, in that he asked of Abraham that he would send to them for their instruction, lest a like punishment should torment them coming thither at some future time. Therefore it is plain without doubt that he who remembers his absent kindred to the increase of his pain might a little while after even see them present to his eyes to the augmentation of his punishment. But what wonder is it if he beholds the damned also burnt along with himself, who to the in-

crease of his woe saw that Lazarus whom he has scorned in the bosom of Abraham. He, therefore, to whom the very Elect Saint appeared, that his pangs might, be added to, why are we not to believe that he might behold in punishment those, whom he had loved in opposition to God? From which it is collected, that those whom the sons of perdition now love with inordinate affection, by a marvellous disposition of judgment, they will then see their fellows in torment; that the carnal tie, which was preferred to their Maker, may increase the pangs of their own punishment, being cursed before their eyes by a like retribution. Thus the fire that torments in darkness must be supposed to preserve light for torture. And if we cannot prove this from testimonies by the expression of the very thing, then it remains that we show it from the reverse.

102. For the Three Children of the Hebrew People, when the fire of the furnace was kindled by command of the king of Chaldaea, were cast into it with hands and feet tied. Yet when that king commiserating them sought them in the fire of the furnace, he saw them walking about with untouched garments. Where it is plain to infer, that by the wonderful dispensation of our Creator, the property of fire, being modified into an opposite power, at the same time never touched their garments, and yet burnt their chains, and for those holy men the flame was both cooled for the infliction of torment, and burnt out for the service of unbinding. And so as fire knows how to burn to the Elect in consolation, and yet knows not how to burn in punishment, so in the reverse case, at the same time that the flame of hell yields no light to the damned in the grace of consolation, it does yield light in punishment, that the fire of punishment may both glow with no brightness to the eyes of the damned, and for the increase of their pain may show how the objects of their affection are tormented. And what wonder is it if we suppose that hell fire contains at the same time the infliction of darkness and of light, when we know by experience that the flame of torches too burns and is dark. The devouring flame then consumes those, whom carnal gratification now pollutes. The gaping and immeasurable gulf of hell swallows up Then all whom vainglory exalts now, and they who by any sinful practice fulfilled here below the will of the crafty counsellor, then being cast off are brought to torments along with their leader.

THE SECOND PART.

103. And though there is a great difference between the nature of men and angels, yet those are involved in one and the same punishment, who are bound by one and the same guilt in sin. Which is well and shortly conveyed by the Prophet, when he says, *Asshur is there and all his company: his graves are about him.* [Ezek. 32, 22] For who is set forth by the title of Asshur, the proud king, saving that old enemy who fell by pride, who for that he draws numbers into sin, descends with all his multitude into the dungeons of hell. Now 'graves' are a shelter for the dead. And what other suffered a bitterer death than he, who, in setting his Creator at nought, forsook life? And when human hearts admit him in this state of death, assuredly they become his graves. Now 'his graves are about him,' in that all in whose souls he now buries himself by their affections, hereafter he joins to himself by torments. And whereas the lost now admit evil spirits within themselves by committing unlawful deeds, then the graves will burn together with the dead. *Moral*

104. See how we are informed, what punishment is in store for the damned, and, by Holy Writ instructing us, have no reason to question, how great may be the fire in damnation, how great the darkness in that fire, how great the terror in that darkness. But what does it advantage us to foreknow these things, if it is not our lot to escape them? Therefore with the whole bent of our mind, we must make it our business, that when the opportunity of being at liberty is ours, by application to living well, we escape the avenging torments of evil doers. For it is hence said by Solomon, *Whatsoever thy hand findeth to do, do it with thy might; for there is no work, nor device, nor knowledge, nor wisdom, in the grave, whither thou goest.* [Eccles. 9, 10] Hence Isaiah says, *Seek ye the Lord while He may be found, call ye upon Him while He is near.* [Is. 55, 6] Hence Paul says, *Behold now is the accepted time; behold now is the day of salvation.* [2 Cor. 6, 2] Hence he says again, *Whilst we have opportunity, let us do good unto all men.* [Gal. 6, 10]

105. But very often the soul girds itself up to walk in the way of uprightness, shakes off sloth, and is so transported into heavenly realms in affection, that it well nigh seems that there is nothing of it left here below; and yet when it is brought back to take account of the flesh, without which the course of the present life can never be accomplished, this keeps it weighed down below, as if it had not as yet reached aught of things above. When the words of the heavenly

oracle are heard, the soul is uplifted into love of the heavenly land; but when the occupation of the present life rises up anew, it is buried under the heap of earthly cares, and the seed of the hope above comes to nothing in the soil of the heart, because the thorn of care below grows rank. Which same thorn 'Truth' uproots with the hand of holy exhortation by Himself, saying, *Take therefore no thought for the morrow.* [Matt. 6, 34] And in opposition to this, it is said by Paul, *Make not provision for the flesh to fulfil the lusts thereof.* [Rom. 13, 14] But in, these words of the Captain and the soldier we see that the soul is then pierced thereby with a mortal wound, when a balance of measure is not kept therein.

106. For whilst we still live in mortal flesh, concern for the flesh is not wholly cut away from us; but it is regulated so that it should serve the mind as discretion dictates. For whereas 'Truth' forbids us to be anxious for the morrow, He does not deny us to take thought in a certain way for the present things, which He does forbid us to extend to the time that succeeds. And truly while Paul will not let provision be made for the flesh in the lusts thereof, most certainly he does permit it to be made in things of necessity. Thus the care of the flesh must be restrained under the discreet guidance of a complete control, that it may always obey and never rule, that it may not as a mistress bring the soul under its power, but being subjected to the dominion of the mind, may like a handmaid wait in attendance, that it may come when bidden, and when repressed dart off at a beck of the heart; that it may scarcely show itself in the rear of holy thought, and never present itself to one front to front when full of right thoughts. Which is well conveyed to us in the account contained in the sacred Lesson, when Abraham is related to have met the three Angels. [Gen. 18, 2. 9. &c.] For he met them by himself, as they were coming, without the door of the tent, but Sarah stood behind the door; for the Man and the master as it were of the spiritual house, i.e. our understanding, ought, in the acknowledgment of the Trinity, to issue out of the close chamber of the flesh, and, as it were, to go forth out of the door of his dwelling-place below; but let care of the flesh, as a woman, not show herself out of doors, and let her be ashamed to display herself ostentatiously, that being as it were behind the back of the husband, under the discreet guidance of the Spirit, busied with necessary things alone, she may learn never to go wantonly uncovered, but to be regulated by modesty. But often-

times, when she is charged never to presume on herself, but to resign herself wholly to undoubting hope in God, she turns away her ear, and disbelieves that, her exertions ceasing, the means of life can be forthcoming to her. And hence this same Sarah, upon hearing the promises of God, laughs, and for laughing is chidden, and still, so soon as she is chidden, she is made a fruitful mother. And she who in the vigour of youth had no power to conceive, when broken by the years of age, conceived in a withered womb; in that when care of the flesh has ceased to entertain confidence in self, by promise from God it receives against hope that which from human reasoning it doubted its ever obtaining. Hence he that is begotten is well called Isaac, i.e. 'laughing,' in that when it conceives sureness of hope in the Highest, what else does our mind give birth to but joy? Therefore we must take heed lest care of the flesh either transgress the limits of necessity, or in that which it discharges with moderation, presume on itself. For oftentimes the mind is betrayed to account that to be necessary, which it desires for pleasure, so that it reckons all that takes its fancy to be 'the useful' that we owe to life. And often because the effect follows the forecasting, the mind is lifted up in self-confidence. And when that is in its hand which is lacking to the rest, it exults in secret thought for the greatness of its foresight, and is so much the further removed from real foresight, in proportion as it is ignorant of the exaltation that it is feeling. Therefore we ought to bethink ourselves, with a heedful earnestness of vigilance, whether of what we execute in deed or what we revolve in heart, lest either earthly care, to the incumbrance of the mind, be multiplied without, or at least lest the spirit be lifted up within for its control thereof; that whilst we dread the judgment of God with temporal heed, we may escape the woes of 'everlasting horror.'

BOOK X.

The whole of the eleventh chapter of the Book of Job, and the five first verses of the twelfth, being made out, he closes the Second Part of this work.

1. As often as a mighty wrestler is gone down into the arena of the lists, those who prove no match for him in strength by turns present themselves for the working of his overthrow, and as fast as one is overcome another is directly raised up against him, and, he being subdued, another takes his place, that they may sooner or later find his strength in wrestling more yielding, in that his repeated victory by itself wears it out, so that as each fresh opponent comes to the encounter, he who cannot be overcome by the nature of their powers, may at least be got the better of by the changing of the persons. Thus, then, in this theatre of men and Angels, blessed Job approved himself a mighty wrestler, and how he prevailed against the charges of his adversaries, he shows by his continuance in unabated force; to whom first Eliphaz presents himself, and next Bildad, and finally Zophar puts himself forward in their place in the overthrow of him, and these lift up themselves with all their might to deal him blows, yet never reach so far as to strike the height of that well-fenced breast. For their very words plainly imply that they deal their blows upon the air, in that as they do not rebuke the holy man aright, the words of smiting being uttered in empty air are lost; and this is clearly shown, whereas the answer of Zophar the Naamathite begins with insult, in that he says, i.

Chap. xi. 2. Should not he that talketh much hear in his turn? and should a man full of words be justified?

2. It is the practice of the impertinent ever to answer by the opposite what is said aright, lest, if they assent to the things asserted, they should seem inferior. And to these the words of the righteous, however small in number they have been heard, are 'much,' in that as they cut their evil habits to the quick, they fall heavy upon the hearing, whence that is even wrested to a crime, which by a right declaration is pronounced against crimes. For the very person, who had delivered strong sentences on grounds of truth, Zophar rebukes and calls full of words, in that, whereas wisdom reprimands sins by the mouth of the righteous, it sounds like superfluity of talkativeness to the ears of the foolish. For froward men account nothing right, but what they themselves think, and they ii.

reckon the words of the righteous idle in the degree that they find them differing from their own notions. Nor yet did Zophar deliver a fallacious sentiment, 'that a man full of words could never be justified,' in that so long as anyone lets himself out in words, the gravity of silence being gone, he parts with the safe keeping of the soul. For hence it is written, *And the work of righteousness, silence.* [Is. 32, 17] Hence Solomon says, *He that hath no rule over his own spirit in talking, is like a city that is broken down, and without walls.* [Prov. 25, 28] Hence he says again, *In the multitude of words there wanteth not sin.* [Prov. 10, 19] Hence the Psalmist bears witness, saying, *Let not a man full of words be established upon the earth*; *but the worth of a true sentence is lost, when it is not delivered under the keeping of discretion.* [Ps. 140, 11. Vulg.] Thus it is a certain truth, that 'a man full of words cannot be justified,' but a good thing is not well said, because there is no heed taken to whom it is spoken. For a true sentence against the wicked, if it is aimed at the virtue of the good, loses its own virtue, and bounds back with blunted point, in proportion as that is strong which it hits. But that the wicked cannot hear good words with patience, and that wherein they neglect the amending of their life, they brace themselves up to words of rejoinder, Zophar plainly instructs us, in that he subjoins;

Ver. 3. Should men hold their peace at thee only? and when thou mockest at others, shall no man confute thee?

iii. 3. The uninstructed mind, as we have said, is sorely galled by the sentences of truth, and reckons silence to be a punishment; it takes all that is said aright to be the disgrace of mocking at itself. For when a true voice addresses itself to the ears of bad men, guilt stings the recollection, and in the rebuking of evil practices, in proportion as the mind is touched with consciousness within, it is stirred up to eagerness in gainsaying without; it cannot bear the voice, in that, being touched in the wound of its guilt it is put to pain, and by that which is delivered against the wicked generally, it imagines that it is itself attacked in a special manner; and what it inwardly remembers itself to have done, it blushes to hear the sound of without. Whence it presently prepares itself for a defence, that it may cover the shame of its guilt by words of froward gainsaying. For as the righteous, touching certain things which have been done unrighteously by them, account the voice of rebuke to be the service of charity so the froward reckon it to be the insult of mockery. The one sort immediately prostrate themselves to show obedience, the other are lifted up to show the madness of self-defence. The one sort take the helping hand of correction as the upholding of their life, by means of which whilst the sin of the present life is corrected, the wrath of the Judge that is to come is abated; the other, when they find themselves assailed by rebuke, see therein the sword of smiting, in that whilst sin is unclothed by the voice of chiding, the conceit of present glory is spoilt. Hence 'Truth' says by Solomon in commendation of the righteous man, *Give instruction to a wise man, and he will hasten to receive it* [Prov. 9, 9]; hence he makes nothing of the obstinacy of the wicked, saying, *He that reproveth a scorner getteth to himself wrong* [ver. 7]. For it generally happens that when they cannot defend the evils that are reproved in them, they are rendered worse from a feeling of shame, and carry themselves so high in their defence of themselves, that they rake out bad points to urge against the life of the reprover, and so they do not account themselves guilty, if they fasten guilty deeds upon the heads of others also. And when they are unable to find true ones, they feign them, that they may also themselves have things they may seem to rebuke with no inferior degree of justice. Hence Zophar, for that it stung him to be as it were mocked at by reproof, forthwith subjoins with lying lips,

Ver. 4. For Thou hast said, My speech is pure, and I am clean in Thine eyes.

4. Whoso remembers the words of blessed Job, knows how falsely this charge is fastened upon his voice. For how could he call himself pure, who says, *If I justify myself, mine own mouth shall condemn me* [Job 9, 20]; but there is this in the wickedness of the unrighteous, that, while it refuses to bewail real evil things in itself it invents them in others, for it makes use of it as a solace of evil doing, if the life of the reprover can be also stained with false accusations. But we must know that for the most part the wicked wish what is good so far as the lips, in order that they may show that that is bad which we have at present, and as if from the good will they bear others, they pray for favourable circumstances, in order that they may appear full of kindly affection. Whence too Zophar forthwith subjoins, saying, **iv.**

THE SECOND PART.

But oh that God would speak with thee, and open His lips unto thee!

v. 5. For man by himself speaks to himself when in all that he thinks he is not withdrawn by the Spirit of the Divine Being from the sense of carnal wisdom; when the flesh puts forth a sense, and inviting the mind as it were to the understanding of it, sends it forth abroad. And hence 'Truth' says to Peter, who was still full of earthly notions, *For thou savourest not the things that be of God, but the things that be of men*. [Mark 8, 33] Yet, when he made a good confession, the words are spoken, *Flesh and blood hath not revealed it unto thee, but My Father which is in Heaven*. [Mat. 16, 17] Now what do we understand by 'the lips' of God saving His judgments? For when the lips are closed the voice is kept in, and the meaning of the person keeping silence is not known; but when, the lips being opened, speech is put forth, the mind of the person speaking is found out. So 'God opens His lips' when He, manifests His will to men by open visitations. For He as it were speaks with open mouth, when the veil of interior Providence being drawn aside, He declines to conceal what is His will. For as it were with closed lips He forbear to indicate His meaning to us, when by the secresy of His judgments He conceals wherefore He does anything. Zophar therefore, in order that he might reprove blessed Job on the grounds of a carnal understanding, and show what kindness of disposition he himself was of, wishes good things for him, which even when they are there present he does not know to be so, saying, *But oh that God would speak with thee, and open His lips with thee*. As if he were to say in plain words, 'I feel for thy uninstructedness more than for thy chastening, in that I know thee to be endued with the wisdom of the flesh alone, and void of the Spirit of Truth. For didst thou discern the secret judgments of God, thou wouldest not give utterance to such daring sentences against Him.' And because when Almighty God raises us to take a view of His judgments, He forthwith puts to flight the mists of the ignorance that is in us, what instruction comes to us by His lips being opened, he forthwith shows by adding in the words,

Ver. 6. And that He would show thee the secrets of wisdom, and that her law is manifold.

vi. 6. The public works of Supreme Wisdom are when Almighty God rules those whom He creates, brings to an end the good things which He begins, and aids by His inspiration those whom He illumines with the light of His visitation. For it is plain to the eyes of all men, that those whom He created of His free bounty, He provides for with lovingkindness. And when He vouchsafes spiritual gifts, He Himself brings to perfection what He has Himself begun in the bounteousness of His lovingkindness. But the secret works of Supreme Wisdom are, when God forsakes those whom He has created; when the good things, which He had begun in us by preventing us, He never brings to completion by going on; when He enlightens us with the brightness of His illuminating grace, and yet by permitting temptation of the flesh, smites us with the mists of blindness; when the good gifts which He bestowed, He cares not to preserve to us; when He at the same time prompts the desires of our soul towards Himself, and yet by a secret judgment presses us with the incompetency of our weak nature.

7. Which same secrets of His Wisdom, but few have strength to investigate, and no man has strength to find out; in that it is most surely just that that which is ordained not unjustly above us, and concerning us, by immortal Wisdom, should be bidden from us while yet in a mortal state. But to contemplate these same secrets of His Wisdom is in some sort already to behold the power of His incomprehensible nature, in that though we fail in the actual investigation of His secret counsels, yet by that very failure we more thoroughly learn Whom we should fear. Paul had strained to reach these secrets of that wisdom, when he said, *O the depth of the riches both of the wisdom and knowledge of God! How unsearchable are His Judgments, and His ways past finding out! For who hath known the mind of the Lord? Or who hath been His counsellor?* [Rom. 11, 33] He, in a part above, turning faint even with the mere search, and yet through faintness advancing to the knowledge of his own weakness, says beforehand the words, *Nay but O man, who art thou that repliest against God? Shall the thing formed say to Him that formed it, Why hast Thou made me thus?* [Rom. 9, 20] He, then, that being unable to attain to the secrets of God, returned back to the recognition of his own weakness, and by thus falling short, recalled himself to the instructing of himself, in not finding out the secrets of wisdom, so to say, he did find them out. For when his strength failed him for the investigation of the counsels of the most High, he learned how to entertain fear with greater humility, and the man whom his own weakness kept back

from the interior knowledge, humility did more thoroughly unite thereto. Thus Zophar, who is both instructed by the pursuit of knowledge, and uninstructed by the effrontery of highswoln speech, because he has no weight himself, wishes for a better man that thing which he has, saying, *But oh that God would speak with thee, and open His lips unto thee; that He might show thee the secrets of wisdom.* And by wishing he also shows off that wisdom wherewith he reckons himself to be equipped above his friend, when he thereupon adds, *And that her law is manifold.* What should the 'law' of God be here taken to mean, saving charity, whereby we ever read in the inward parts after what manner the precepts of life should be maintained in outward action? For concerning this Law it is delivered by the voice of 'Truth,' *This is My commandment, that ye love one another.* [John 15, 12] Concerning it Paul says, *Love is the fulfilling of the law.* [Rom. 13, 10] Concerning it he says again, *Bear ye one another's burthens, and so fulfill the law of Christ.* [Gal. 6, 2] For what can the Law of Christ be more fitly understood to mean than charity, which we then truly fulfil when we bear the burthens of our brethren from the principle of love?

Moral

8. But this same Law is called 'manifold;' in that charity, full of eager solicitude, dilates into all deeds of virtue. It sets out indeed with but two precepts, but it reaches out into a countless number. For the beginning of this Law is, the love of God, and the love of our neighbour. But the love of God is distinguished by a triple division. For we are bidden to love our Maker 'with all our heart' and 'with all our soul' and 'with all our might.' Wherein we are to take note that when the Sacred Word lays down the precept that God should be loved, it not only tells us with what, but also instructs us with how much, in that it subjoins, 'with all;' so that indeed he that desires to please God perfectly, must leave to himself nothing of himself. And the love of our neighbour is carried down into two precepts, since on the one hand it is said by a certain righteous man, *Do that to no man which thou hatest.* [Tob. 4, 15] And on the other 'Truth' says by Himself, *Therefore all things whatsoever ye would that men should do to you, do ye even so to them.* [Mat. 7, 12] By which two precepts of both Testaments, by the one an evil disposition is restrained, and by the other a good disposition charged upon us, that every man not doing the ill which he would not wish to suf-

fer, should cease from the working of injuries, and again that rendering the good which he desires to be done to him, he exert himself for the service of his neighbour in kindness of heart. But while these same two are thought on with heedful regard, the heart is made to open itself wide in innumerable offices of virtue, lest whether for the admitting of things which it ought not, the mind being agitated be heated by passions; or for the setting forth of whatsoever it ought, being undone by indolence, it may be rendered inactive. For when it guards against doing to another what it would not on any account itself undergo at the hands of another, it looks about itself on every side with a heedful eye, lest pride lift it up, and while cutting down set up the soul even to contempt of our neighbour; lest coveting mangle the thought of the heart, and while stretching it wide to desire the things of another, straitly confine it; lest lust pollute the heart, and corrupt it, thus become the slave of its passions, in forbidden courses; lest anger increase, and inflame it even to giving vent to insult; lest envy gnaw it, and lest jealous of the successes of others it consume itself with its own torch; lest loquacity drive on the tongue beyond all bounds of moderation, and draw it out even to the extent of license in slander; lest bad feeling stir up hatred, and set on the lips even to let loose the dart of cursing. Again, when it thinks how it may do to another what it looks for at the hands of another for itself, it considers how it may return good things for evil, and better things for good; how to exhibit towards the impertinent the meekness of longsuffering; how to render the kindness of good will to them that pine with the plague of malice, how to join the contentious with the bands of peace, how to train up the peaceable to the longing desire of true Peace; how to supply necessary things to those that are in need; how to show to those that be gone astray the path of righteousness; how to soothe the distressed by words and by sympathy; how to quench by rebuke those that burn in the desires of the world; how by reasoning to soften down the threats of the powerful, how to lighten the bands of the oppressed by all the means that he is master of; how to oppose patience to those that offer resistance without; how to set forth to those that are full of pride within a lesson of discipline together with patience; how, with reference to the misdeeds of those under our charge, mildness may temper zeal, so that it never relax from earnestness for the rule of right; how zeal may be so kindled for revenge, that yet by kindling thus it never transgress the bounds of pity; how to stir the unthankful to love by benefits; how to preserve in love all that are thankful by services; how to pass by in silence the misdoings of our neighbour, when he has no power to correct them; how when they may be amended by speaking to dread silence as consent to them; how to submit to what he passes by in silence, yet so that none of the poison of annoyance bury itself in his spirit; how to exhibit the service of good will to the malicious, yet not so as to depart from the claims of righteousness from kindness; how to render all things to his neighbours that he is master of, yet in thus rendering them not to be swelled with pride; in the good deeds which he sets forth to shrink from the precipice of pride, yet so as not to slacken in the exercise of doing good; so to lavish the things which he possesses as to take thought how great is the bounteousness of his Rewarder, lest in bestowing earthly things he think of his poverty more than need be, and in the offering of the gift a sad look obscure the light of cheerfulness.

9. Therefore the Law of God is rightly called manifold, in this respect, that whereas it is one and the same principle of charity, if it has taken full possession of the mind, it kindles her in manifold ways to innumerable works. The diverseness whereof we shall set forth in brief if we go through and enumerate her excellencies in each of the Saints severally. Thus she in Abel both presented chosen gifts to God, and without resistance submitted to the brother's sword; Enoch she both taught to live in a spiritual way among men, and even in the body carried him away from men to a life above. Noah she exhibited the only one pleasing to God when all were disregarded, and she exercised him on the building of the ark with application to a long labour, and she preserved him the survivor of the world by the practice of religious works. In Shem and Japhet she humbly felt shame at the father's nakedness, and with a cloak thrown over their shoulders hid that which she looked not on. She, for that she lifted the right hand of Abraham for the death of his son in the yielding of obedience, made him the father of a numberless offspring of the Gentiles. She, because she ever kept the mind of Isaac in purity, when his eyes were now dim with age, opened it wide to see events that should come to pass long after. She constrained Jacob at the same time to bewail from the core of his heart the good child taken from him, and to bear with composure the presence of the wicked

ones. She instructed Joseph, when sold by his brethren, both to endure servitude with unbroken freedom of spirit, and not to lord it afterwards over those brethren with a high mind. She, when the people erred, at once prostrated Moses in prayer, even to the beseeching for death, and lifted him up in eagerness of indignant feeling even to the extent of slaying the people; so that he should both offer himself to die in behalf of the perishing multitude, and in the stead of the Lord in His indignation straightway let loose his rage against them when they sinned. She lifted the arm of Phinees in revenge of the guilty souls, that he should pierce them as they lay with the sword he had seized, and that by being wroth he might appease the wrath of the Lord. She instructed Jesus the spy, so that he both first vindicated the truth by his word against his false countrymen, and afterwards asserted it with his sword against foreign enemies. She both rendered Samuel lowly in authority, and kept him unimpaired in his low estate, who, in that he loved the People that persecuted him, became himself a witness to himself that he loved not the height from whence he was thrust down. David before the wicked king she at once urged with humility to take flight, and filled with pitifulness to grant pardon; who at once in fearing fled from his persecutor, as his lord, and yet, when he had the power of smiting him, did not acknowledge him as an enemy she both uplifted Nathan against the king on his sinning in the authoritativeness of a free rebuke, and, when there was no guilt resting on the king, humbly prostrated him in making request. She in Isaiah blushed not for nakedness of the flesh in the work of preaching, and the fleshly covering withdrawn, she penetrated into heavenly mysteries. [Is. 20, 2] She, for that she taught Elijah to live spiritually with the earnestness of a fervent soul, carried him off even in the body also to enter into life. She, in that she taught Elisha to love his master with a single affection, filled him with a double portion of his master's spirit. Through her Jeremiah withstood that the people should not go down into Egypt, and yet by cherishing them even when they were disobedient he even himself went down where he forbad the going down. She, in that she first raised Ezekiel from all earthly objects of desire, afterwards suspended him in the air by a lock of his head. She in the case of Daniel, for that she refrained his appetite from the royal dainties, closed for him the very mouths of the hungry lions. She, in the Three Children, for that she quenched the flames of evil inclinations in them whilst in a condition of peace, in the season of affliction abated the very flames in the furnace. She in Peter both stoutly withstood the threats of frowning rulers, and in the setting aside of the rite of circumcision, she heard the words of inferiors with humility. She, in Paul, both meekly bore the violence of persecutors, and yet in the matter of circumcision boldly rebuked the notion of one by great inequality his superior. 'Manifold' then is this Law of God, which undergoing no change accords with the several particulars of events, and being susceptible of no variation yet blends itself with varying occasions.

10. The multiplicity of which same law, Paul rightly counts up, in the words, *Charity suffereth long, and is kind, envieth not, vaunteth not itself; is not puffed up, doth not behave itself unseemly, seeketh not her own, is not easily provoked, thinketh no evil, rejoiceth not in iniquity, but rejoiceth in the truth.* [1 Cor. 13, 4. 5. 6.] For charity 'suffereth long,' in that she bears with composure the ills that are brought upon her. She 'is kind,' in that she renders good for evil with a bounteous hand. She 'envieth not,' in that from her coveting nought in the present life, she thinketh not to envy earthly successes. She 'is not puffed up,' in that whereas she eagerly desires the recompense of the interior reward, she does not lift herself up on the score of exterior good things. She 'doth not behave herself unseemly,' in that in proportion as she spreads herself out in the love of God and our neighbour alone, whatever is at variance with the rule of right is unknown to her. She is not covetous, in that as she is warmly busied within with her own concerns, she never at all covets what belongs to others, 'She seeketh not her own,' in that all that she holds here by a transitory tenure, she disregards as though it were another's, in that she knows well that nothing is her own but what shall stay with her. She 'is not easily provoked,' in that even when prompted by wrongs she never stimulates herself to any motions of self avenging, whilst for her great labours she looks hereafter for greater rewards. She 'thinketh no evil,' in that basing the soul in the love of purity, while she plucks up all hatred by the roots, she cannot harbour in the mind aught that pollutes. She 'rejoiceth not in iniquity,' in that as she yearns towards all men with love alone, she does not triumph even in the ruin of those that are against her, but she 'rejoiceth in the truth,' in that loving others as herself, by that which she beholds right in others she is filled with joy as if for the growth of her own

proficiency. 'Manifold,' then, is this 'Law of God,' which by the defence of its instructiveness is proof against the dart of every sin which assaults the soul for its destruction, so that whereas our old enemy besets us with manifold encompassing, she may in many ways rid us of him. Which Law if we consider with heedful attention, we are made to know how greatly we sin each day against our Maker. And if we thoroughly consider our sins, then assuredly we bear afflictions with composure, nor is anyone precipitated into impatience by pain, when conscience gives itself up by its own sentence. Hence Zophar, knowing what it was that he said, but not knowing to whom he said it, after he had premised the words, *That He would show thee the secrets of wisdom, and that her Law is manifold*, forthwith adds,

And that thou mightest know that God exacteth of thee less than thine iniquity deserveth.

Historical **vii.**

11. For, as we have said, the pain of the stroke is mitigated, when the sin is acknowledged; for everyone too bears the knife of the leach the more patiently, in proportion as he sees what he cuts to be gangrened. He therefore that comprehends the manifold character of the Law, reflects how much too little all is that he is suffering; for from this, that the weight of the sin is acknowledged, the pain of the affliction is made less.

12. But herein we must know that it was not without great iniquity that Zophar reproached the righteous man even to the charging him with iniquity. And thus Truth with justice reproves their boldness, but mercifully restores them to favour; for with the merciful Judge a fault never goes without pardon, when it is done through the heat of zealous feeling in the love of Him. For this oftentimes happens to great and admirable teachers, that in proportion as they are inflamed with the depth of charity, they exceed the due measure of correction, and that the tongue utters somewhat that it never ought, because love inflames the heart to the degree that it ought. But the word of offered affront is the more readily spared, in proportion as it is considered from what root it comes, whence the Lord rightly commanded by Moses, saying, *As when a man goeth into the wood with his neighbour merely to hew wood, and the wood of the axe flieth from his hand, and the head slippeth from the helve, and lighteth upon his neighbour that he die, he shall flee unto one of these cities and live: lest perchance the kinsman of him whose blood hath been shed pursue the slayer while his heart*

is hot, and overtake him, and slay him. [Deut. 19, 5. 6.] For we 'go to the wood with a friend,' whensoever we betake ourselves with a neighbour to take a view of our transgressions, and we 'merely hew wood,' when with pious purpose we cut away the evil doings of offenders; but the 'axe flieth from his hand,' when rebuke carries itself into severity beyond what ought to be, and the 'head slippeth from the helve,' when the speech goes off too hard from the act of correcting, and it 'lighteth upon a neighbour, that he die,' in that the offered insult kills its hearer as to the spirit of love. For the mind of the person reproved is instantly hurried into hate, if unmeasured censure condemn it beyond what ought to be. But he that heweth wood carelessly, and kills a neighbour, must take refuge in three cities, that he may live unharmed in one of them, in that if betaking himself to the lamentations of repentance, he be hidden in the unity of the Sacrament under hope faith and charity, he is not held guilty of the manslaughter that has been done; and when the 'kinsman of the slain' has found him he slayeth him not, in that, when the strict Judge comes, Who has united Himself to us by fellowship with our own nature, He doubtless never exacts retribution for guilt of sin from him, whom faith hope and charity hide beneath the shelter of His pardoning grace. Quickly then is that sin done away which is not committed of the set aim of malice. And hence, Zophar both calls him iniquitous, whom a sentence from above had extolled, and yet he is not rejected and shut out from pardon, in that he is prompted to words of contumely by zeal in the love of God, Who, for that he does not know the merits of blessed Job, further added in ill instructed mockery, saying,

Ver. 7. Canst thou find out the footsteps of God? Canst thou find out the Almighty unto perfection?

viii. 13. What does he call 'the footsteps of God,' saving the lovingkindness of His visitation? by which same we are stimulated to advance forward to things above, when we are influenced by the inspiration of His Spirit, and being carried without the narrow compass of the flesh, by love we see and own the likeness of our Maker presented to our contemplation that we may follow it. For when the love of the spiritual Land kindles the heart, He as it were gives knowledge of a way to persons that follow it, and a sort of footstep of God as He goes is imprinted upon the heart laid under it, that the way of life may be kept by the same in right goings of the thoughts. For Him, Whom we do not as yet see, it only remains for us to trace out by the footsteps of His love, that at length the mind may find Him, to the reaching the likeness contemplation gives of Him, Whom now as it were, following Him in the rear, it searches out by holy desires. The Psalmist was well skilled to follow these footsteps of our Creator, when he said, *My soul followeth hard after Thee*. [Ps. 63, 8] Whom too he busied himself that he might find even to attaining the vision of His loftiness, when he said, *My soul thirsteth for God, for the living God: when shall I come and appear before the face of God?* [Ps. 42, 2] For then Almighty God is found out by clear conception, when the corruption of our mortality being once for all trodden under our feet, He is seen by us that are taken up into heaven in the brightness of His Divine Nature. But at this present time, the grace of the Spirit which is poured into our hearts lifts the soul from carnal aims, and elevates it into a contempt for transitory things, and the mind looks down upon all that it coveted below, and is kindled to objects of desire above, and by the force of her contemplation she is carried out of the flesh, while by the weight of her corruption she is still held fast in the flesh; she strives to obtain sight of the splendour of uncircumscribed Light, and has not power; for the soul, being burthened with infirmity, both never wins admittance, and yet loves when repelled. For our Creator already exhibits concerning Himself something whereby love may be excited, but He withdraws the appearance of His vision from those so loving. Therefore we all go on seeing only His footsteps, in that only in the tokens of His gifts we follow Him, Whom as yet we see not. Which same 'footsteps' cannot be comprehended, in that it is all unknown, when, where, and by what ways the gifts of His Spirit come, as 'Truth' bears record, saying, *The wind bloweth where it listeth, and ye cannot tell whence it cometh, and whither it goeth*. [John 3, 8] Now in the height of the rewarding the Almighty may be found out in the appearance [*per speciem*] afforded to contemplation, yet He can never be found out to perfection. For though sooner or later we see Him in His brightness, yet we do not perfectly behold His Essence. For the mind whether of Angels or men, whilst it gazes toward the uncircumscribed Light shrinks into little by this alone, viz. that it is a created being; and by its advancement indeed it is made to stretch above its own reach, yet not even when spread wide can it compass the splendours of Him, Who at once in transcending, in supporting, and in filling, encloses all things. Hence it is yet further added,

Ver. 8, 9. He is higher than heaven, what canst thou do? Deeper than hell, what canst thou know? His measure is longer than the earth, and broader than the sea.

ix. 14. In that God is set forth as 'higher than heaven,' 'deeper than hell,' 'longer than the earth,' and 'broader than the sea,' this must be understood in a spiritual sense, inasmuch as it is impious to conceive anything concerning Him after the proportions of body. Now He is 'higher than heaven,' in that He transcends all things by the Incomprehensibility of His spiritual Nature. He is 'deeper than hell,' in that in transcending He sustains beneath. He is 'longer than the earth,' in that He exceeds the measure of created being by the everlasting continuance of His Eternity. He is 'broader than the sea,' in that He so possesses the waves of temporal things in ruling them, that in confining He encompasses them beneath the every way prevailing presence of His Power. Though it is possible that by the designation of 'Heaven' the Angels may be denoted, and by the term 'hell,' the demons, while by the 'earth' the righteous, and by the 'sea' sinners are understood. Thus He is 'higher than the heaven,' in that the very Elect Spirits themselves do not perfectly penetrate the vision of His infinite loftiness? He is 'deeper than hell,' in that He judges and condemns the craft of evil spirits with far more searching exactness than they had ever thought, He is 'longer than the earth,' in that He surpasses our long-suffering by the patience of Divine long-suffering, which both bears with us in our sins, and welcomes us when we are turned from them to the rewards of His recompensing. He is 'wider than the sea,' in that he every where enters into the doings of sinners by the presence of His retributive power, so that even when He is not seen present by His appearance, He is felt present by His judgment.

15. Yet all the particulars may be referred to man alone, so *Moral* that he is Himself 'heaven,' when now in desire he is attached to things above; himself 'hell,' when he lies grovelling in things below, confounded by the mists of his temptations; himself 'earth,' in that he is made to abound in good works through the fertility of a stedfast hope; himself 'the sea,' for that on some occasions he is

shaken with alarm, and agitated by the breath of his feebleness. But God is 'higher than heaven,' in that we are subdued by the mightiness of His power, even when we are lifted above our own selves. He is 'deeper than hell,' in that He goes deeper in judging than the very human mind looks into its own self in the midst of temptations, He is 'longer than the earth,' in that those fruits of our life which He gives at the end, our very hope at the present time comprehends not at all. He is 'wider than the sea,' in that the human mind being tossed to and fro throws out many fancies concerning the things that are coming, but when it now begins to see the things that it had made estimate of, it owns itself to have been too stinted in its reckoning. Therefore He is made 'higher than heaven,' since our contemplation itself fails toward Him. Hence the Psalmist too had set his heart on high, yet he felt that he had not yet reached unto Him, saying, *Thy knowledge is too wonderful for me, it is mighty, I cannot attain unto it*. [Ps. 139, 6] He knew One deeper than hell, who when sifting his own heart, yet dreading His more searching judgment, said, *For I know nothing by myself, yet am I not hereby justified: but He that judgeth me is the Lord*. [1 Cor. 4, 4] He saw One 'longer than the earth,' when he was brought to reflect that the wishes of man's heart were too little for him, saying, *Now unto Him that is able to do exceeding abundantly above all that we ask or think*. [Eph. 3, 20] He had beheld One 'broader than the sea,' who considered whilst he feared that the human mind may never know the immeasurableness of His severity, however it may toss and fret in enquiring after it, saying, *Who knoweth the power of Thine anger, and for fear can tell Thy wrath?* [Ps. 90, 11] Whose Power the inimitable teacher rightly gives us the knowledge of, when he briefly says, *That ye may be able to comprehend with all Saints what is the breadth, and length, and depth, and height*. [Eph. 3, 18] For God has 'breadth,' in that He extends His love even to gathering in the very persecutors. He has 'length,' in that He leads us onwards by bearing with us in long-suffering to the country of life. He has 'loftiness,' in that He far transcends the understanding of the very beings themselves that have been admitted into the heavenly assemblage. He has 'depth,' in that upon the damned below He displays the visitation of His severity in an incomprehensible manner. And these same four attributes He exercises towards each one of us, that are placed in this life, in that by loving, He manifests His 'breadth;' by suffering, His 'length;' by surpassing not only our understanding, but even our very wishes, His 'height;' and His 'depth,' by judging with strictness the hidden and unlawful motions of the thoughts. Now His height and depth how unsearchable it is no man knows saving he, who has begun either by contemplation to be carried up on high, or in resisting the hidden motions of the heart to be troubled by the urgency of temptation. And hence the words are spoken to blessed Job, *He is higher than heaven what canst thou do? deeper than hell, whence canst thou know?* As if it were said to him in open contempt, 'His depth and excellency when mayest thou ever discover, who are not taught either to be lifted up on high by virtue, or to deal severely with thyself in temptations. It goes on,

Ver. 10. If He overturn all things, or shut them up together, then who shall gainsay Him? Or who can say to Him, Why doest Thou so?

x. 16. The Lord 'overturns heaven,' when by His terrible and secret ordering He pulls down the height of man's contemptations. He 'subverts hell,' when He allows the soul of any affrighted under its temptations to fall even into worse extremes. He 'overturns the earth,' when He cuts off the fruitfulness of good works by adversities pouring in. He 'overturns the sea,' when He confounds the fluctuations of our wavering spirit, by the rise of a sudden panic. For the heart, disquieted by its own uncertainty, fears horribly for this alone, that she goes thus wavering; and it is as if the sea were overturned, when our very trembling towards God is itself confounded on the terribleness of His judgment being thought on. Whereas therefore we have described in brief, in what sort heaven and hell, earth and sea, are overturned, now the somewhat more difficult task awaits us, to show how these may be 'shut up together.'

17. For it very often happens that the spirit already lifts the mind on high, yet that the flesh assails it with pressing temptations; and when the soul is led forward to the contemplation of heavenly things, it is struck back by the images of unlawful practice being presented. For the sting of the flesh suddenly wounds him, whom holy contemplation was bearing away beyond the flesh. Therefore heaven and hell are shut up together, when one and the same mind is at once enlightened by the uplifting of contemplation, and bedimmed by the pressure of temptation, so that both by straining forward it

sees what it should desire, and through being bowed down be in thought subject to that which it should blush for. For light springs from heaven, but hell is held of darkness. Heaven and hell then are brought into one, when the soul which already sees the light of the land above, also sustains the darkness of secret temptation coming from the warfare of the flesh. Yea, Paul had already gone up to the height of the third heaven, already learnt the secrets of Paradise, and yet being still subject to the assaults of the flesh, he groaned, saying, *But I see another law in my members warring against the law of my mind, and bringing me into captivity to the law of sin which is in my members.* [Rom. 7, 23] How then was it with the heart of this illustrious Preacher, saving that God had 'shut up together' heaven and hell, in that he had both already obtained the light of the interior vision, and yet continued to suffer darkness from the flesh? Above himself he had seen what to seek after with joy, in himself he perceived what to bewail with fear. The light of the heavenly land had already shed abroad its rays, yet the dimness of temptation embarrassed the soul. Therefore he underwent hell together with heaven, in that assurance set him erect in his enlightenment, and lamentation laid him low in his temptation.

18. And it often happens that faith is now vigorous in the soul, and yet in some slight point it is wasted with uncertainty, so that both being well-assured, it lifts itself up from visible objects, and at the same time being unassured it disquiets itself in certain points. For very often it lifts itself to seek after the things of eternity, and being driven by the incitements of thoughts that arise, it is set at strife with its very own self. Therefore the 'earth and sea are shut up together,' when one and the same mind is both established by the certainty of rooted faith, and yet is influenced by the breath of doubt, through some slight fickleness of unbelief. Did not he experience that 'earth and sea were shut up together' in his breast, who both hoping through faith and wavering through faithlessness, cried, *Lord, I believe, help Thou mine unbelief?* [Mark 9, 23] How is it then that at the same time he declares that he believes, and begs to have the unbelief in him helped, saving that he had found out that earth and sea were shut up together in his thoughts, who both being assured had already begun to implore through faith, and being unassured still endured the waves of faithlessness from unbelief.

THE SECOND PART.

19. And this is allowed by secret providence to be brought about, that when the soul has now begun to arise to uprightness, it should be assailed by the remnant of its wickedness, in order that this very assault may either exercise it if it resist, or if it be beguiled by enjoyment may break it down. Therefore it is well said here, *If He overturn all things, or shut them up together, who shalt gainsay Him? Or who can say to Him, Why doest Thou so?* For God's decree can neither lose anything by opposition, nor be ascertained by enquiry, when He either withdraws the good graces which He had vouchsafed, or not entirely withdrawing them, lets them be shaken by the assault of evil inclinations. For oftentimes the heart is lifted up in highmindedness when it is established strongly in virtue by instances of joyful success, but when our Creator beholds the motions of presumption lurking in the heart, He forsakes man for the showing him to himself, that his soul thus forsaken may discover what she is, in that she wrongly exulted in herself in a feeling of security. Hence whereas it is said that 'all is overturned and shut up together,' he therefore adds,

Ver. 11. For He knoweth the vanity of men; when He seeth wickedness also, doth He not consider it?

xi. 20. As if he were subjoining in explaining the things premised, saying, 'Because He sees that by suffering them evil habits gain growth, by judging He brings to nought His gifts.' Now the right order is observed in the account, in that vanity is first described to be known, and afterwards iniquity to be considered. For all iniquity is vanity, but not all vanity, iniquity. For we do vain things as often as we give heed to what is transitory. Whence too that is said to vanish, which is suddenly withdrawn from the eyes of the beholder. Hence the Psalmist says, *Every man living is altogether vanity*. [Ps. 39, 5] For herein, that by living he is only tending to destruction, he is rightly called 'vanity' indeed; but by no means lightly called 'iniquity' too. For though it is in punishment of sin that he comes to nought, yet this particular circumstance is not itself sin, that he passes swiftly from life. Thus all things are vain that pass by. Whence too the words are spoken by Solomon, *All is vanity*. [Eccles. 1, 2]

Historical

21. But 'iniquity' is fitly brought in immediately after 'vanity.' For whilst we are led onwards through some things transitory, we

are to our hurt tied fast to some of them, and when the soul does not hold its seat of unchangeableness, running out from itself it goes headlong into evil ways. From vanity then that mind sinks into iniquity, which from being familiar with things mutable, whilst it is ever being hurried from one sort to another, is defiled by sins springing up. It is possible too that 'vanity' may be taken for sin, and that by the title of 'iniquity' weightier guilt may be designated; for if vanity were not sometimes sin, the Psalmist would not have said, *Though man walketh in the image of God, surely he is disquieted in vain: he heapeth up riches, and knoweth not who shall gather them.* [Ps. 29, 6. Vulg.] For though we preserve the image of the Trinity in our natural constitution, yet being disturbed by the vain motions of self-indulgence, we go wrong in our practice; so that in ever-alternating forms lust agitates, fear breaks down, joy beguiles, grief oppresses. Therefore from vanity, as we have also said above, we are led to iniquity, when first we let ourselves out in light misdemeanors, so that habit making all things light, we are not at all afraid to commit even heavier ones too afterwards. For while the tongue neglects to regulate idle words, being caught by the custom of engrained carelessness, it fearlessly gives a loose to mischievous ones. Whilst we give ourselves to gluttony we are straightway betrayed into the madness of an unsteady mind, and when the mind shrinks from overcoming the gratification of the flesh, it very often plunges even into the whirlpool of unbelief. Hence Paul, looking at the mischiefs that befel the Israelitish people, in order to keep off from his hearers threatened ills, was justly mindful to relate in order what took place, saying, *Neither be ye idolaters, as were some of them; as it is written, The people sat down to eat and drink, and rose up to play*. [1 Cor. 10, 7. Ex. 32, 6] For eating and drink set them on to play, and play drew them into idolatry; for if the offence of vanity is not restrained with care, the unheeding mind is swiftly swallowed up by iniquity, as Solomon testifies, who says, *He that despiseth small things falleth little by little*. For if we neglect to take heed to little things, being insensibly led away, we perpetrate even greater things with a bold face; and it is to be observed, that it is not said that iniquity is 'seen,' but that it is 'considered.' For we look more earnestly at those things which we consider. Thus God 'knoweth the vanity of men, and considereth their iniquity,' in that He leaves not even their minor offences unpunished, and prepares Himself with greater earnestness to smite their worse ones. Therefore whereas men set out with lighter misdeeds, and go on to those of a graver order, vanity overcasts while iniquity blinds the mind, which same mind, so soon as it has parted with the light, presently lifts itself so much the higher in swoln pride, in proportion as being taken in the snares of iniquity, it withdraws further from the truth. Hence also he fitly sets forth whereunto vanity forces men joined with iniquity, in that he forthwith adds,

Ver. 12. For the vain man is exalted in pride.

xii. 22. For it is the end of vanity, whereas it mangles the heart by sin, to render it bold by the offence, so that, forgetful of its guiltiness, the soul which feels no sorrow to have lost its innocency, blinded by a righteous retribution, should at the same time part with humility also; and it very often happens, that, enslaving itself to unlawful desires, it rids itself of the yoke of the fear of the Lord; and as if henceforth at liberty for the commission of wickedness, it strives to put in execution all that self-indulgence prompts. Hence when the vain man is said to be exalted in pride, therefore it is brought in,

And thinketh himself free born like a wild ass's colt.

xiii. 23. For by 'a wild ass's colt' is set forth every kind of wild animals, which being left free to the motions of nature, are not held by the reins of persons ruling them. For the fields leave animals in a state of liberty both to roam where they list, and to rest when they are wearied; and though man is immeasurably superior to insensate beasts, yet that is very often not allowed to man, which is granted to brute creatures. For those animals, which are never kept for any other end, assuredly never have their movements held in under the bands of discipline; but man, who is being brought to a life hereafter, must of necessity be held in all his movements under the controlling hand of discipline, and like a tame animal render service, bound with reins, and live restricted by eternal appointments. He then that seeks to put in practice in unrestrained liberty all the things that he has a desire for, what else is this but that he longs to be like the wild ass's colt, that the reins of discipline may not hold him in, but that he may boldly run at large through the forest of desires?

24. But oftentimes Divine mercy breaks by the encounter of sudden adversity those, whom it sees going into the unruliness of lawless freedom, that being crushed they may learn with what damnable

exaltation they had been swoln, that being now tamed by the experience of the scourge, they may like tame animals yield the mind's neck to the reins of the commandments, and go along the ways of the present life at the ruler's beck. With these reins he knew well that he was bound, who said, *I am as a beast before Thee, and I am continually with Thee*. [Ps. 72, 22] Whence too that raging persecutor, when he was brought away from the field of unbelieving self-indulgence to the house of faith, being pricked by the spurs of his ruler, heard the words, *It is hard for thee to kick against the pricks*. [Acts 9, 5] It remains then, if we would not henceforth be like the wild ass's colt, that in all that we desire we first look out for the token of the interior appointment, so that our mind in all that it strives at may be held in by the bridle of the Supreme control, and may fulfil its wishes the more effectually to the obtaining of life, by the very same act, whereby even against its will it treads under foot the aims and objects of its own life. Zophar delivered many forcible sayings, but he is not conscious that he is addressing them to a better than himself; whence he still further subjoins in words of upbraiding,

Ver. 13. Thou hast set firm thine heart, and stretched out thine hands towards Him.

xiv.

25. The heart is not here said to be 'set firm' by virtue but by insensibility, for every soul that submits itself to the consideration of the interior severity, is directly softened by the fear thereof; and the shaft of divine dread enters into him, in that he carries weak bowels through humility. But he that is hardened by obstinacy in insensibility, as it were sets his heart firm, that the darts of heavenly fear may not pierce it. Whence the Lord says mercifully to some by the Prophet, *And I will take away the stony heart out of you, and I will give you a heart of flesh*. [Ezek. 36, 26] For He 'takes away the stony heart,' when He removes from us the hardness of pride. And He 'gives us a heart of flesh,' when He thereupon changes that same hardness into sensibility. Now by 'hands' as we have often taught are denoted works. To stretch out the hands to God, then, with sin, is to pride ourselves upon the excellency of our works to the prejudice of the grace of the Giver. For he that, speaking in the presence of the Eternal Judge, ascribes to himself the good that he does, stretches out his hands to God in a spirit of pride. It is in this way truly that the lost ever let themselves loose against the Elect, and so

heretics against Catholics; that when they are unable to abuse their doings, they set themselves to blame the good for pride in those doings, that those, whom they cannot upbraid for weak points in practice, they may charge with the guilt of high-mindedness. And hence the good things which are done outwardly, they now no longer reckon to be good, in that they are set forth as it were in the prosecution of swelling conceit. And these oftentimes with swelling thoughts rebuke lowly deeds, and know not that they are dealing blows against themselves by their words. But whereas Zophar had hitherto chidden the righteous man with reproof, now, as giving him lessons of instruction, he subjoins,

Ver. 13, 14, 15. If the iniquity which is in thine hand thou put far from thee, and wickedness dwell not in thy tabernacle, then shalt thou lift up thy face without spot, yea thou shalt be stedfast, and shalt not fear.

26. Every sin is either committed in thought alone, or it is done in thought and deed together. Therefore 'iniquity in the hand' is offence in deed; but 'wickedness in the tabernacle,' is iniquity in the heart; for our heart is not unfitly called a tabernacle, wherein we are buried within ourselves, when we do not show ourselves outwardly in act. Zophar therefore, in that he was the friend of a righteous person, knows what he should say, but in that he reproached a righteous person, bearing the likeness of heretics, he does not know how rightly to deliver even the things which he knows. But let us, treading under our feet all that is delivered by him in pride of spirit, reflect how true his words are, if they had but been spoken in a right manner. For first he bids that 'iniquity' be removed from the 'hand,' and afterwards that 'wickedness' be cut off from the 'tabernacle;' for whosoever has already cut away from himself all wicked deeds without, must of necessity in returning to himself probe himself discreetly in the purpose of his heart, lest sin, which he no longer has in act, still hold out in thought. Hence too it is well said by Solomon, *Prepare thy work without, and diligently work thy field, that afterwards thou mayest build thine house*. [Prov. 24, 27] For what is it when the 'work is prepared,' to 'till the field diligently without,' saving when the briars of iniquity have been plucked up, to train our practice to bearing fruits of recompense? And after the tilling of the field, what else is it to return to the building of our house, than that we very often learn from good deeds the perfect purity of life which

we should build up in our thoughts. For almost all good deeds come from the thoughts, but there be some fine points of thought which have their birth in action; for as the deed is derived from the mind, so on the other hand the mind is instructed by the deed; for the soul taking the first beginnings of divine love dictates the good things which should be done, but after the deeds so dictated have begun to be fulfilled, being practised by its own actions, it learns how little it saw when it began to dictate good deeds. Thus the 'field is tilled without, that the house may afterwards be built;' for very often we gain from outward practice what an extreme nicety of righteousness we should keep in our hearts; and Zophar was well minded to observe this order, in that he spake first of 'iniquity being put away from the hands,' and afterwards 'wickedness from the tabernacle;' for the mind can never be completely set upright in thought when it still goes astray in deed.

Moral 27. Now if we thoroughly wipe away these two, we then directly 'lift our face without spot' to God. For the soul is the inner face of man, by which same we are known, that we may be regarded with love by our Maker. Now it is to lift up this same face, to raise the soul in [al. 'to'] God by appliance to the exercises of prayer. But there is a spot that pollutes the uplifted face, when consciousness of its own guilt accuses the mind intent; for it is forthwith dashed from all confidence of hope, if when busied in prayer it be stung with recollection of sin not yet subdued. For it distrusts its being able to obtain what it longs for, in that it bears in mind its still refusing to do what it has heard from God. Hence it is said by John, *Beloved, if our heart condemn us not, then have we confidence toward God; and whatsoever we ask we shall receive of Him*. [1 John 3, 21. 22.] Hence Solomon says, *He that turneth away his ear from hearing the law, even his prayer shall be abomination*. [Prov. 28, 9] For our heart blames us in offering up our prayers, when it calls to mind that it is set in opposition to the precepts of Him, whom it implores, and the prayer becomes abomination, when there is a 'turning away' from the control of the law; in that verily it is meet that a man should be a stranger to the favours of Him, to Whose bidding he will not be subject.

28. Wherein there is this salutary remedy, if when the soul reproaches itself upon the remembrance of sin, it first bewail that in prayer, wherein it has gone wrong, that whereas the stain of offences

is washed away by tears, in offering up our prayers the face of the heart may be viewed unspotted by our Maker. But we must be over and above on our guard, that the soul do not again fall away headlong to that, which it is overjoyed that it was washed away by tears; but whilst the sin that is deplored is again committed, those very lamentings be made light of in the eyes of the righteous Judge. For we should call to mind what is said, *Do not repeat a word of thy prayer*; [Ecclus. 7, 14] by which same saying the wise man in no sort forbids us to beseech pardon oftentimes, but to repeat our sins. As if it were expressed in plain words; 'When thou hast bewailed thy misdoings, never again do anything for thee to bewail again in prayer.'

XV. 29. Therefore that 'the face may be lifted up in prayer without spot,' it behoves that before the seasons of prayer everything that can possibly be reproved in the act of prayer be heedfully looked into, and that the mind when it stays from prayer as well should hasten to show itself such, as it desires to appear to the Judge in the very season itself of prayer. For we often harbour some impure or forbidden thoughts in the mind, when we are disengaged from our prayers. And when the mind has lifted itself up to the exercises of prayer, being made to recoil, it is subject to images of the things whereby before it was burthened of free will whilst unemployed. And the soul is now as it were without ability to lift up the face to God, in that the mind being blotted within, it blushes at the stains of polluted thought. Oftentimes we are ready to busy ourselves with the concerns of the world, and when after such things we apply ourselves to the business of prayer, the mind cannot lift itself to heavenly things, in that the load of earthly solicitude has sunk it down below, and the face is not shown pure in prayer, in that it is stained by the mire of grovelling imagination.

30. However, sometimes we rid the heart of every encumbrance, and set ourselves against the forbidden motions thereof, even at such time as we are disengaged from prayer, yet because we ourselves commit sins but seldom, we are the more backward in letting go the offences of others, and in proportion as our mind the more anxiously dreads to sin, the more unsparingly it abhors the injuries done to itself by another; whence it is brought to pass that a man is found slow to grant pardon, in the same degree that by going on advancing, he has become heedful against the commission of sin. And as he

fears himself to transgress against another, he claims to punish the more severely the transgression that is done against himself. But what can be discovered worse than this spot of bitterness [*doloris*], which in the sight of the Judge does not stain charity, but kills it outright? For every sin stains the life of the soul, but bitterness maintained against our neighbour slays it; for it is fixed in the soul like a sword, and the very hidden parts of the bowels are gored by the point thereof; and if it be not first drawn out of the pierced heart, no whit of divine aid is won in prayer. For the medicines of health cannot be applied to the wounded limbs, unless the iron be first withdrawn from the wound. Hence it is that 'Truth' says by Itself, *If ye forgive not men their trespasses, neither will your Father Which is in Heaven forgive you your trespasses*. [Matt. 6, 15.] Hence He enjoins, saying, *And when ye stand praying, forgive, if ye have ought against any*. [Mark 11, 25] Hence He says again, *Give, and it shall be given unto you; forgive, and ye shall be forgiven*. [Luke 6, 38] Hence to the form of petition, He affixed the condition of pity; saying, *Forgive us our trespasses, as we forgive them that trespass against us*: [Matt. 6, 12] that truly the good which we beg from God being pierced with compunction, we first do with our neighbour, being altered by conversion. Therefore we then truly 'lift our face without spot,' when we neither commit forbidden misdeeds, nor retain those which have been committed against ourselves from jealous regard for self; for in the hour of prayer our soul is overwhelmed with sore dismay, if either its practice still continue to pollute it, or bitterness kept for the injuring of another lay charge against it; which two when anyone has cleansed away, he forthwith arises free to the things which are subjoined, *Yea, thou shalt be stedfast, and shalt not fear*, in that doubtless he fears the Judge the less, the more stedfast he stands in good deeds. For he gets the mastery of fears, who retains possession of stedfastness, in that whilst he anxiously busies himself to do what our Creator tenderly enjoins, he bethinks himself in security of that which He threatens with terribleness.

31. Moreover it should be known, that there are some good deeds wherein we persevere unwearied, and again, there are some from which we are continually giving over and falling away, and we are restored to these, not without great endeavours at intervals of time; for in the active life the mind is stablished without failing, but from the contemplative, being overcome by the load of its infirmity,

it faints away. For the first endures the more stedfastly in proportion as it opens itself to things about it for our neighbour's weal; the latter falls away the more swiftly, in proportion as passing beyond the barriers of the flesh, it endeavours to soar up above itself. The first directs its way through level places, and therefore plants the foot of practice more strongly; but the other, as it aims at heights above itself, the sooner descends wearied to itself. Which is well and briefly conveyed by Ezekiel, when he relates the motions of the living creatures which he had seen, saying, *They turned not when they went*; and soon after he subjoins in addition, *And the living creatures went and returned*. [Ez. 1, 9. 14.] For sometimes the holy 'living creatures go and return not,' and sometimes they 'go and return forthwith;' for when the minds of the Elect, through the grace of an active life being vouchsafed them, abandon the paths of error, they never return to the evil courses of the world which they have forsaken; but when through the gaze of contemplation they are led to stay themselves from this same active life, they 'go and return,' in that hereby, that they are never able to continue for long in contemplation, they again let themselves out in action, that by busying themselves in such things as are immediately near them, they may recruit their strength, and may be enabled by contemplation again to soar above themselves. But while this practice of contemplation is in due method resumed at intervals of time, we hold on assuredly without failing all its entireness; for though the mind being overcome by the weight of its infirmity fall short, yet being restored again by continual efforts it lays hold thereof. Nor should it be said to have lost its firmness in that, which, though it be ever failing in, it is ever pursuing, even when it has lost the same. It proceeds;

Ver. 16. Thou shalt also forget thy misery, and no more remember it, as waters that pass away.

xvi. 32. The mind feels the ills of the present life the more severely, in proportion as it neglects to take account of the good that comes after; and as it will not consider the rewards that are in store, it reckons all to be grievous that it undergoes; and hence the blinded imagination murmurs against the stroke of the scourge, and that is taken for an immeasurable woe, which by the days flowing on in their course is daily being brought to an end. But if a man once raise himself to things eternal, and fix the eye of the soul upon those objects which remain without undergoing change, he sees that here below all whatsoever runs to an end is almost nothing at all. He is subject to the adversities of the present life, but he bethinks himself that all that passes away is as nought. For the more vigorously he makes his way into the interior joys, he is the less sensible of pains without. Whence Zophar, not being afraid with bold-faced hardihood to instruct one better than himself, exhorts to righteousness, and shows how little chastening appears in the eyes of the righteous man. As if it were in plain words; 'If thou hast a taste of the joy which remains within, all that gives pain without forthwith becomes light.' Now he does well in likening the miseries of the present life to 'waters that pass away,' for passing calamity never overwhelms the mind of the Elect with the force of a shock, yet it does tinge it with the touch of sorrow. For it drops indeed with the bleeding of the wound, though it is not dashed from the certainty of its salvation. But it often happens that not only stripes inflict bruises, but that in the mind of each one of the righteous the temptings of evil spirits come in force, so that he is grieved by the stroke without, and is in some sort chilled within by temptation. Yet grace never forsakes him, which same the more severely it smites us in the dealings of Providence, so much the more does it watch over us in pity; for when it has begun to grow dark through temptation, the inward light kindles itself again. Whence too it is added;

Ver. 17. And the noonday splendour shall rise to thee at eventide.

Historical 33. For 'the noonday splendour at eventide' is the renewing of virtue in the season of temptation, that the soul should be reinvigorated by the sudden heat of charity, which but now was full of fear, that the light of grace had sunk to it; which Zophar further unfolds with more exactness, when he subjoins, **xvii.**

Ver. 18. And when thou thinkest thyself consumed, thou shalt arise like the morning star.

34. For it often comes to pass that so many temptations beset our path, that the very multitude of them almost inclines us to the downfall of desperation. Hence for the most part, when the mind is turned to weariness, it scarce takes account even of the hurts that its virtue sustains, and notwithstanding that it is **xviii.**

wholly filled with pain, it is as if it were now dislocated from the sense of pain, and were unable to reckon up with what a tumult of thoughts it is overrun. It sees itself momentarily on the point of falling headlong, and grief itself withstands it worse, that it should not lay hold of the arms of resistance. Mists encompass the eyes, wherever turned about, and whereas darkness ever obstructs the sight, the sad soul sees nought else than darkness; but with the merciful Judge it often happens that this very sadness, which even weighs down the effect of prayer, intercedes for us the more piercingly. For then our Creator sees the blackness of our sorrow, and pours back again the rays of the light withdrawn, so that the mind being immediately braced up by His gifts becomes full of vigour, which same a little before contending evil propensities kept down under the heel of pride. At once it shakes off the load of torpor, and bursts with the light of contemplation after the darkness of its troubled state. At once that is raised to the joy of advancement, which amidst temptations was well nigh driven by despair to a sorer fall. Without a conflict of the heart it looks down upon present things, without let of misgiving it trusts in the retribution to come. Therefore when the righteous man 'thinks himself consumed, he arises like the morning star,' in that so soon as he has begun to be benighted with the blackness of temptations, he is restored anew to the light of grace, and he in himself manifests the day of righteousness, who the moment before, on the point to fall, dreaded the night of guiltiness. Now the life of the righteous is rightly compared to the 'morning star.' For the morning star, being precursor of the sun, proclaims the day. And what does the innocency of the Saints proclaim to us, saving the brightness of the Judge, That cometh after? For in our admiration of them we see what we are to account of the Majesty of the true Light. We do not yet behold the power of our Redeemer, but we admire His goodness in the characters of His Elect. Therefore in that the life of the good presents to our eyes on the consideration of it the force of Truth, the 'morning star' arises bright to us heralding the sun.

35. But be it known that all that we have made out, proceeding upon the opposition of spiritual temptations, may without hindrance be interpreted by external ills, for holy men, because they love the things above from the bottom of their heart, encounter hardships in things below; but at the end they find the light of joy, which in the span of this passing life they care not to have. Whence it is said on

this occasion by Zophar, *And the noonday splendour shall arise to thee at eventide*. For the sinner's light in the daytime is dimness at eventide, in that he is buoyed up with good fortune in the present life, but is swallowed up by the darkness of calamity at the end; but to the righteous man the noonday splendour ariseth at eventide, in that he knows what exceeding brightness is in store for him when he has already begun to set. Hence it is written; *Whoso feareth the Lord, it shall go well with him at the last*. [Ecclus. 1, 13] Hence it is declared by the Psalmist; *When He giveth His beloved sleep, this is* [*hoec est,* V. *ecce*] *the heritage of the Lord*. [Ps. 127, 2. 3.] He, while he is still set in the strife of this present life as well, 'when he thinketh himself consumed, ariseth like the morning star;' because whilst falling outwardly he is renewed inwardly. And the more that he encounters crosses without, the more richly he gleams with the light of his virtues within, as Paul testifies, who says, *Though our outward man perish, yet the inward man is renewed day by day. For our light affliction which is but for a moment worketh for us a far more exceeding and eternal weight of glory*. [2 Cor. 4, 16] And it ought to be observed, that he never says, 'when thou art consumed,' but, 'when thou thinkest thyself consumed,' in that both that which we see is doubtful, and that which we hope for certain. Whence too the same Paul did not know, but thought, that he was consumed, who even when falling headlong into sufferings and tribulations, shone bright like the morning star, saying, *As dying, and, behold, we live; as sorrowful, yet alway rejoicing; as poor, yet making many rich*. [3 Cor. 6, 9. 10.] And we should know that the worse plight the mind of the good is reduced to for the love of the truth, the more sure and certain its hope of the rewards of eternity. Whence too it is justly added;

Ver. 18, And thou shalt have confidence, because hope is set before thee,

xix.

36. For hope lifts itself the more firmly rooted in God, in proportion as a man has suffered harder things for His sake, since the joy of the recompensing is never gathered in eternity, which is not first sown here below in religious sorrowing. Hence the Psalmist says, *They went forth and wept as they went, bearing precious seed, but they shall doubtless come again with rejoicing, bringing their sheaves with them*. [Ps. 126, 6] Hence Paul says, *If we be dead with Him, we shall also live with Him; if we suffer, we shall also reign with Him*. [2 Tim. 2, 11. 12.] Hence he warns his disciples, saying, *And that we*

must through much tribulation enter into the kingdom of God. [Acts 14, 22] Hence the Angel, showing the glory of the Saints to John, says, *These are they that came out of great tribulation, and have washed their robes, and made them white in the blood of the Lamb.* [Rev. 7, 14] Therefore because we now sow in tribulation that we may afterwards reap the fruit of joy, the heart is strengthened with the larger measure of confidence in proportion as it is pressed with the heavier weight of affliction for the Truth's sake. Whence it is therefore fitly added,

Yea, being dug to the bottom [V. *defossus*], *thou shalt rest secure.*

XX. 37. For just as present security begets toil to the wicked, so present toil begets perpetual security to the good. Hence he already knew that it was his 'to rest secure after he had been dug to the bottom,' who said, *For I am now ready to be offered, and the time of my departure is at hand. I have fought a good fight, I have finished my course: I have kept the faith Henceforth there is laid up for me a crown of righteousness, which the Lord, the righteous Judge, shall give me at that day.* [2 Tim. 4, 6. 8.] For as he had striven without giving over against transitory ills, doubtless he reckoned without misgiving on enduring joys.

38. Not but that the expression, 'been dug to the bottom,' may be understood in another sense also: for oftentimes being busied with transitory matters, we neglect to consider in what great things we go wrong; but if the eye of reflection being brought in, the pile of earthly thoughts be discharged from the recesses of the heart, what lay hid from sight within is disclosed to view; whence holy men never cease to explore the secret hiding places of their souls; minutely searching themselves, they throw off the cares of earthly things, and their thoughts being thoroughly dug up from the bottom [*effossis*], when they find that they are not cankered in any wise by the guilt of sin, they rest secure in themselves as upon the bed of the heart. For they desire to be hid apart from the courses of this world. They are always thinking on their own concerns, and when they are not at all tied by the harness of government, they decline to pass judgment on what concerns others. Therefore 'having been dug to the bottom they rest secure,' in that whilst with wakeful eye they dive into their inmost recesses, they withdraw themselves from the toilsome burthens of this world under the disengagement of repose. And hence it is yet further added,

Ver. 19. Also thou shalt lie down, and there shall be none to make thee afraid.

xxi.

39. Whosoever seeks present glory doubtless dreads contempt. He, who is ever agape after gain, is ever surely in fear of loss. For that object, the receiving of which is medicine to him, the loss thereof is his wounding, and as he is rivetted under fetters to things mutable and destined to perish, so he lies grovelling beneath, far apart from the stronghold of security. But, on the other hand, whoever is rooted in the desire of eternity alone, is neither uplifted by good fortune nor shaken by adverse fortune; whilst he has nought in the world which he desires, there is nought which he dreads from the world. For it is hence that Solomon says, *It shall not grieve the just whatsoever shall happen unto him.* [Prov. 12, 21] Hence he says again, *The righteous as a bold lion shall be without alarm.* [Prov. 28, 1] Therefore it is rightly said here; *Also thou shalt lie down, and none shall make thee afraid*, in that everyone the more completely casts away from himself the fear that cometh from the world, the more thoroughly he overcomes in himself the lust of the world. Did not Paul lie down and rest in heart without fear, when he said, *For I am persuaded, that neither death, nor life, nor angels, nor principalities, nor powers, nor things present, nor things to come, nor strength* [So Vulg.], *nor height, nor depth, nor any other creature shall be able to separate us from the love of God which is in Christ Jesus our Lord.* [Rom. 8, 39] The force of which same love is commended by the true voice of the Holy Church, where it is said in the Song of songs, *For love is strong as death.* [Cant. 8, 6] For love is compared to the force of death, in that that soul which it has once taken possession of, it wholly kills to the delightfulness of the world, and sets it up the stronger in authority, that it renders it indifferent towards objects of terror. But herein it is to be known, that when bad men deliver right sentiments, it is very hard for them not to let themselves out upon that, which they are going after in secret within. Hence Zophar forthwith adds;

Yea, many shall make suit unto thee.

xxii.

40. For the righteous do not keep themselves in the narrow paths of innocency with this view, that they may be implored by others, but whether heretics or any that be perverse, all of them, in that they live with an appearance of innocency among

men, have the desire to show themselves as intercessors in behalf of men, and when in talk they convey holy truths, what they themselves are hankering after, they promise to others as something great; and whilst they tell of heavenly things, they soon show by their pledges what their hearts are bent on. But lest by long continuing to promise earthly things, they may be made appear what they are, they quickly return to words of uprightness. Whence it is immediately added;

But the eyes if the wicked shall fail and refuge shall perish from them.

xxiii. 41. That by the designation of 'eyes' the energy of the intention is set forth to us, 'Truth' testifies in the Gospel, saying, *If thine eye shall be single, thy whole body shall be full of light.* [Matt. 6, 22] Forasmuch as if a pure intention have preceded our action, howsoever it may seem otherwise to men, yet to the eyes of our interior Judge, the body of the deed that follows after is presented pure. Therefore the 'eyes' of the wicked are the intentions of carnal desires in them, and these fail for this reason, that they are careless of their eternal interests, and are ever looking for transitory advantages alone. For they aim to get themselves an earthly name, they wish above all things to grow and increase in temporal goods, they are daily advancing with the tide of transient things to the goal of death; but they think not to take account of the things of mortality upon the principles of their mortal nature. The life of the flesh is failing minute by minute, and yet the desire of the flesh is growing; property gotten is snatched off by an instant end, yet the eagerness in getting is not ended the more; but when death withdraws the wicked, then indeed their desires are ended with their life. And the eyes of these fail them through the Avenging of the Most High, for that they would not fail here by their own determination to earthly gratification. These same eyes of such persons the Psalmist had seen closed to their former enjoyment, when he said, *In that day all their thoughts perish*. [Ps. 146, 4] For they meet at once with eternal woes they had never thought on, and on a sudden lose the temporal goods, they had long while held and dealt with. And for these 'all refuge shall perish,' in that their iniquity finds not where to hide itself from the visitation of the searching Judge. For now, when the wicked undergo some slight mishaps or evil chances, they find a hiding-place for refuge, in that they forthwith have recourse to the enjoyment of earthly objects of desire. For that poverty torment them not, they beguile the spirit with riches. Or lest the contempt of their neighbours sink them, they exalt themselves with titles. If the body is cloyed with satiety, it is pampered with the variety of viands set before it. If the mind is weighed down by any impulse to sadness, it is immediately relieved by the beguilements of sportiveness being introduced. Here therefore they have as many places of refuge as they make for themselves entertainments of delight; but one time 'refuge shall perish from them,' in that their soul, when all these are gone, sees only itself and the Judge. Then the pleasure is withdrawn, but the guilt of pleasure is preserved; and ere long the miserable wretches learn by their perishing that they were perishable things they had possession of. Yet these as long as they live in the body never cease to seek after things of a nature to do them harm. Whence it is still further added,

And their hope shall be the abomination of the soul.

xxiv.

42. What does the sinner hope for here in all his thoughts saving to surpass others in power, to go beyond all men in the abundance of his stores, to bow down his rivals in lording it over them, to display himself as an object of admiration to his followers, to gratify anger at will, to make himself known as kind and gracious when he is commended, whatever the appetite longs for to offer to it, to acquiesce in all that pleasure dictates by the fulfilling of the thing? Well then is their hope said to be 'the abomination of the soul,' for the very same objects which carnal men go after, all spiritual persons abominate, according to the sentence of righteousness. For that which sinners account pleasure, the righteous, surely, hold for pain. Therefore the hope of the wicked is the abomination of the soul, for the spirit is wasted while the body is at ease. For as the flesh is sustained by soft treatment, so is the soul by hard dealing; soothing appliances cherish the first, harsh methods exercise the last. The one is fed with enjoyment, the last thrives on bitterness. And as hardships wound the flesh, so softness kills the spirit, as things laborious kill the one, so things delightful destroy the other. Therefore the hope of carnal men is said to be the abomination of the soul; in that the spirit perishes for ever by the same means whereby the flesh lives pleasantly for a while.

THE SECOND PART.

43. Now Zophar would have said this aright, if blessed Job had not proclaimed it all more fully even by living accordingly. But whereas he sets himself to give an holier man admonition concerning the way of living, and to instruct one more skilled than himself with the tutorage of wisdom, he by his own act makes the weight of his words light, in that by letting in indiscreetness he undoes all that he says; in that he is pouring on the liquid element of knowledge into a full vessel. For the treasures of knowledge are possessed by the indiscreet just as treasures of corporal substance are often in the possession of fools. For some that are sustained by a full measure of earthly goods at times give largely even to those that have, that they may themselves seem to have them in fuller measure than all men. So the wicked, since they are imbued with truth, speak in some respects right even to those that are more light than they are, not that they may instruct others that hear them, but that they may make it appear with what a fund of instruction they are furnished. For they hold that they excel all men in wisdom, therefore they imagine that there is nothing that they can say to any man beyond the measure of their greatness. Thus all the wicked, thus all heretics are not afraid to instruct their betters with a high tone, in that they look upon all as inferior to themselves. But Holy Church recalls everyone that is high minded from the height of his self esteem, and fashions him anew by the hand of discretion in the jointing of equality. Whence blessed Job, who is a member of the same Holy Church, seeing that the mind of his friend was swoln and big in words of instruction which he delivered, thereupon answered, saying,

Chap. xii. 2. No doubt but ye are the only men, and wisdom shall die with you.

XXV. 44. Whosoever reckons himself to excel all men in the faculty of reason, what else does such a man but exult that he is the 'only Man?' And it often happens that when the mind is borne on high through pride, it is uplifted in contempt of all men, and in admiration of self. For self-applause springs up in the imagination, and folly is itself its own flatterer for singularity of wisdom. It ponders all that it has heard, and considers the words that it utters; and it admires its own, and scoffs at those of others. He then, who thinks that he only is wise, what else is this but that he believes that that same 'wisdom dies with him?' For what he denies to be with others, ascribing to himself alone, he doth, in truth, confine within the period of his brief span. But we are to consider what exact discretion the holy man employs, in order that the arrogance of his friends in the fulness of pride might be brought within bounds, in that he adds forthwith,

Ver.3. But I have understanding as well as you; I am not inferior to you.

45. For who is ignorant how greatly the practice and the knowledge of blessed Job excels the knowledge that his friends have? Now in order to correct their pride, he asserts that he is 'not inferior' to them, and lest he should transgress the limits of his own humility, he keeps to himself that he is superior to them; not by setting himself above, but by equalling himself to them, he points out what they should learn concerning themselves, who are far unlike to him; that whereas that wisdom which is high is voluntarily bowed down, the knowledge which lies grovelling may never erect itself against the nature of its powers, and he does well that he immediately recalls these to a sense of their equal condition, reflecting that they are swoln to excess as if for singularity in greatness, when he afterwards proceeds, **xxvi.**

Yea, who knoweth not such things as these that ye know?

46. As though he said in plain words; 'Since what ye say is known to all men, wherefore are ye puffed up by the knowledge contained in your sayings, as of singular merit?' Therefore whereas in bringing back the pride of the self-conceited to a common level of equality, he has reproved with a full correction, he now breaks out into statements of instruction; that his friends having been humbled first might learn the weightiness of Truth, and how reverently they should hear it. It proceeds, **xxvii.**

Ver. 4. He that is mocked of his neighbour as I am, calleth upon God, and He answereth him.

47. Oftentimes the frail mind, when it is welcomed by the breath of human regard on the score of good actions, runs out into outward delights, so that it lays aside what it inwardly desires, and willingly lies all loosely in that which it gives ear to without. So that it does not so much delight to become as to be **xxviii.**

called blessed; and whereas it gapes after the words of applause, it gives over what it had begun to be; and so it is severed from God by the same means by which it appeared to be commendable in God. But sometimes it presses forward in good practice with a constant heart, and yet is pushed hard by the scoffs of men; it does admirable deeds, and gets only abuse; and he that might have been made to go forth without by commendations, being repulsed by insults, returns back again into himself; and stablishes himself the more firmly in God, that he findeth no place without when he may rest in peace: for all his hope is fixed in his Creator. And amidst scoffs and revilings, the interior Witness is alone implored. And his soul in his distress becomes God's neighbour, in proportion as he is a stranger to the favour of man's esteem. He forthwith pours himself out in prayer, and being pressed without, he is refined with a more perfect purity to penetrate into all within. Therefore it is well said at this time, *He that is mocked of his neighbour as I am, will call upon God, and He will hear him*. For whilst the wicked reproach the soul of the good, they are showing them Whom to seek as the Witness of their actions. And while their soul in compunction braces itself in prayer, it is united within itself to the hearing of the Most High, by the same act whereby it is severed from the applause of man without itself. But we ought to note how thoughtfully the words are inserted, *as I am*. For there be some men whom both the scoffings of their fellow-creatures sink to the ground, and yet they are not such as to be heard by the ears of God. For when mocking issues against sin, surely no virtuous merit is begotten in that mocking. For the priests of Baal, when they called upon him with clamorous voices, were mocked by Elijah, when he said, *Cry aloud; for he is a god either he is talking, or he is staying on a journey*. [1 Kings 18, 27] But this mocking was conducive to the service of virtue, in that it came by the deserts of sin. So that it is advisedly said now, *He that is mocked of his friend, as I am, calleth upon God, and He heareth him*. For the mockery of his fellow-creatures makes Him God's neighbour, whom innocency of life keeps a stranger to his fellow-creatures' wickednesses. It proceeds,

For the upright man's simplicity is laughed to scorn.

xxix. 48. It is the wisdom of this world to overlay the heart with inventions, to veil the sense with words; things that are false to show for true, what is true to make *Historical* out fallacious. This is the wisdom that is acquired by the young by practice. This is learnt at a price by children, they that are acquainted with it are filled with pride, despising other men; they that know nothing of it, being subdued and browbeaten, admire it in others; for this same duplicity of wickedness, being glossed over by a name, is their joy and delight, so long as frowardness of mind goes by the title of urbanity. She dictates to her followers to seek the high places of honour, to triumph in attaining the vain acquisition of temporal glory; to return manifold the mischiefs that others bring upon us; when the means are with us, to give way to no man's opposition; when the opportunity of power is lacking, all whatsoever he cannot accomplish in wickedness to represent in the guise of peaceable good nature. But on the other hand it is the wisdom of the righteous, to pretend nothing in show, to discover the meaning by words; to love the truth as it is, to eschew falsehood; to set forth good deeds for nought, to bear evil more gladly than to do it; to seek no revenging of a wrong, to account opprobrium for the Truth's sake to be a gain. But this simplicity of the righteous is 'laughed to scorn,' in that the goodness of purity is taken for folly with the wise men of this world. For doubtless everything that is done from innocency is accounted foolish by them, and whatever truth sanctions in practice sounds weak to carnal wisdom. For what seems worse folly to the world than to show the mind by the words, to feign nothing by crafty contrivance, to return no abuse for wrong, to pray for them that speak evil of us, to seek after poverty, to forsake our possessions, not to resist him that is robbing us, to offer the other cheek to one that strikes us? Whence that illustrious Wise one of God speaks well to the lovers of this world, *We shall sacrifice the abomination of the Egyptians to the Lord our God* [Exod. 8, 26]. For the Egyptians loathe to eat the flesh of sheep, but that which the Egyptians loathe, the Israelites offer up to God; for that singleness of conscience, which the unrighteous one and all scorn as a thing most mean and abject, the righteous turn into a sacrifice of virtue, and the just in their worshipping sacrifice purity and mildness to God, which the sons of perdition in abomination thereof account weakness. Which same simplicity of the righteous man is briefly yet adequately expressed, in that the words are forthwith introduced;

Ver. 5. A lamp despised in the thought of the rich.

THE SECOND PART.

XXX. 49. What is denoted in this place by the title of the 'rich,' but the highmindedness of the proud, who have no respect for the judge that shall come, while they are swollen with proud thoughts within themselves? For there are some that by a fortune are not lifted up in pride, but elevated thereby through works of mercy. And there are some who, while they see that they overflow with earthly resources, do not look for the true riches of God, and have no affection to the eternal land, for they think that this is enough for them, that they are set up with temporal goods. The fortune then Is not in fault, but the feeling. For all things that God created are good, but he who uses good things amiss, assuredly brings it about that as it were through gluttonness of greedy appetite, he perishes by the bread whereby he ought to live. The beggar Lazarus attained to rest, but torments racked the proud rich one. And yet Abraham was rich, who held Lazarus in his bosom. Yet holding commune with his Maker, he says, *I have taken upon me to speak unto the Lord, which am but dust and ashes!* [Gen. 18, 27] How then did he know to set a value on riches, who accounted himself to be *dust and ashes*? or how could his possessions even exalt him, who entertained such poor notions about himself who was the owner of them?

50. Yet again there are some, to whom earthly property is not vouchsafed, and yet they are set up in their own eyes, in height of swollen pride. At the same time that there is no fortune at all to uplift these to the display of power, yet the frowardness of their ways assigns them a place among the lost children of riches. All, then, that love of the life to come does not fill with abasement, the sacred word here calls rich. For in the avenging of Judgment, there is no difference to them whether they be swollen with gods, or only in disposition. These, when they see the life of the simple sort in this world to be lowly and abased, forthwith scoff at them with proud scornings; for they mark that that is wholly wanting to them without, which they pant after themselves with their best endeavours. Therefore they look down upon them as fools, who are without those things, by the having or merely loving of which they themselves in truth are perishing; and they take those for dead, whom they observe in no sort to live with themselves after the flesh. For he that dies from the desires of this world, is of course held by earthly minds to be utterly dead. Which is well represented by the miracle of our Redeemer when He frees a man from an unclean spirit,

concerning which same it is written: *And the spirit cried and rent him sore, and came out of him, and he was as one dead; insomuch that many said, he is dead. But Jesus took him by the hand, and lifted him up, and he arose*: [Mark 9, 26. 27.] for he looks like one dead that is set free from the power of an evil spirit. For whosoever has already got the better of earthly desires, makes the life of carnal conversation extinct in himself; and he seems dead to the world, in that he lacks the wicked one that possessed him, who urged him by impure desires; and many call him dead, in that they who know not how to live spiritually, look upon him who does not follow carnal good to be wholly lifeless.

51. But because the very scoffers at the simple ones are themselves too enrolled under the name of Christians, being overruled by reverence for religion, they are ashamed to make a display of the sin of open scoffing. Whence it happens that full of pride in themselves, and in silence, they scoff at those whom they take to be utterly mean and abject from their simplicity. Therefore it is well expressed, *A lamp is despised in the thought of the rich*; for all the proud, whereas they are unskilled to estimate the blessings to come, as we have said above, account him almost as nothing whom they do not see to be possessed of that which they are devoted to. For it often happens that each one of the Elect, who is being conducted to eternal bliss, is overwhelmed here with unintermitted calamity, there is no plentifulness of stores that buoys him up, no lustre from titles that makes him conspicuous, no crowd of followers falls to his lot, no pomp of raiment makes him a figure in the eyes of men, but he is regarded as an object of contempt by all men, and accounted unworthy of the regard of this world. Yet in the eyes of the hidden Judge he is bright with virtues, and full of lustre from the merits of his life; he dreads to be honoured, he never shrinks from being despised, he disciplines the body by continence, he is fattened by love alone in the soul, he ever sets his mind to bear with patience, and standing erect on the ground of righteousness, he exults in the insults he receives, he compassionates the distressed from his heart, he rejoices in the successes of the good as in his own, he carefully ruminates the provender of the sacred word in his heart, and when examined he is unskilled to give a double answer; 'a lamp' because he is bright within, 'despised' because he is not luminous without. Inwardly he glows with the flame of charity, without he shines with no gloriousness of

luster. Therefore he shines and is despised, who, while he glows with virtue, is accounted vile. Hence it is that his own father looked down upon holy David, when he refused to present him to the eyes of the Prophet Samuel, He, when he had brought out seven sons to receive the grace of anointing, being questioned by the Prophet whether he had gone through the whole number of his children, answered with despair enough, *There remaineth yet a little boy that keepeth the sheep*; and when he was brought forward and chosen, he heard the words, *Man looketh in the face, but the Lord searcheth the heart*. [1 Sam. 16, 10. &c.] Thus David was a lamp by his innocency, but yet a lamp greatly despised, in that he gave no light to those that regard the outside appearance. But be it known that every righteous man is either without temporal glory, or if he has it, he breaks it beneath himself, that he may freely rise on high above his own honour, lest overcome by enjoyment he be brought down beneath it. It is hence that that illustrious Preacher lowered the glory of his Apostleship before the eyes of men, saying, *We have not used this power, when we might have been burthensome as the Apostles of Christ, but we made ourselves little children among you*. [1 Thess. 2, 6. 7.] But the swelling of the neck still remained in the heart of the hearers of that same person, when they said, *For his letters say they are weighty and powerful, but his bodily presence is weak, and his speech contemptible*. [2 Cor. 10, 10] For him who they knew could say such things they determined could not live in common with themselves, and when they both saw him lowly in his mode of life and high in his tone of speech, their pride drove them on, that him whose writings had made him to be feared, his words in presence should make an object of little account. What then was Paul, saving 'a lamp despised in the thought of the rich,' who by the same act whereby he set forth a lesson of humility, got the affronts of highmindedness from ill-instructed disciples. For in a dreadful way, the sickness of those so filled with pride was increased by the same means, whereby it ought to have subsided; while the proud mind of carnal persons rejected, as if it were worthy of scorn that which their master set forth as deserving of imitation. Was not he 'a lamp despised,' who when he shone forth with so many virtues, underwent such adverse treatment at the hands of his persecutors? He discharges his mission in chains, and his bonds are made known in all the palace, he is beaten with rods, he is beset with numberless dangers from his own race and from the Gentiles; at Lystra he is battered with stones, he is dragged by the feet without the city, in that he is taken for dead. But to what point is this 'lamp despised?' Up to what point is it held contemptible? Does it never at any point unveil its lustre? Does it never show, with what excess of brightness it glows? It does show clearly. For when it is said that the 'lamp is despised in the thought of the rich,' it is therefore added,

Prepared for an appointed time.

xxxi.

52. For the 'appointed time' for 'the despised lamp' is the predestined Day of final Judgment, wherein it is shown how each one of the righteous, who is now contemned, shines bright in greatness of power. For then they come as judges with God, who now are judged unjustly for God's sake. Then their Light shines over so much the wider space, the more cruelly the persecutor's hand confines and fetters them now. Then it will be made clear to the eyes of the wicked, that they were supported by heavenly power, who forsook all earthly things of their free will. Whence Truth says to His own Elect; *Ye which have followed Me, in the Regeneration when the Son of Man shall sit in the throne of His glory, ye also shall sit upon twelve thrones, judging the twelve tribes of Israel.* [Mat. 19, 28] Not that the court of the interior Assize will have no more than twelve judges, but, surely, that by the number twelve the amount of the whole is described; for whosoever being urged by the incitement of divine love, has forsaken all that he possessed here, shall doubtless attain there to the height of judicial power; that he may then come as judge in company with the Judge, who now by consideration of the Judgment chastens himself with voluntary poverty. For hence it is that it is said by Solomon concerning the spouse of Holy Church, *Her husband is known in the gates, when he sitteth among the elders of the land.* [Prov. 31, 23] Hence Isaiah says, *The Lord will come to judgment, with the elders of His people.* [Is. 3, 14] Hence Truth proclaims these same Elders now no longer servants but friends. *Henceforth I call you not servants, but I have called you friends.* [John 15, 15] And the Psalmist regarding these same says, *Honourable also are thy friends unto me, O God.* [Ps. 139, 17] And whilst he beheld their loftiness of mind, and how they trod down with the heel of the foot the glory of the world, he thereupon added, *How stablished is their rule!* And that we might not think that they be few, who we learn thus advance even to the summit of such high perfection, he thereupon added, *If I should count*

them, they are more in number than the sand. For as many persons, then, as now wittingly abase themselves for the love of the Truth, so many lamps shall then blaze forth in the Judgment. Therefore let it be justly said, *A lamp despised in the thought of the rich, prepared for the appointed time*; for the soul of every righteous man is despised as abject, when in passing through life he is without glory; but he is beheld as an object to admire, when he shines from on high.

Allegorical

53. Amid these things it is good to lift the eye of the mind to the paths of our Redeemer, and to proceed step by step from the members to the head. For He did Himself prove truly 'a lamp' to us, Who by dying upon the Cross for our redemption, poured light through the wood into our benighted minds. John had attained to see that we are lightened by this Lamp, when he said, *That was the true Light, which lighteth every man that cometh into the world*. [John 1, 9] Yet he saw it 'despised in the thought of the rich,' when he soon after brought in, *He came unto His own, and His own received Him not*. [ver. 11] Herod desired to examine into the flames of this Lamp, when he longed to see the miracles of that One, as it is written, *For he was desirous to see Him of a long season, because he had heard many things of Him, and he hoped to have seen some miracles done by Him*. [Luke 23, 8] But this Lamp did not shine forth before his eyes with a single ray of light, in that to him, who sought Him not from piety but from curiosity, He exhibited nothing wonderful concerning Himself. For our Redeemer when He was questioned held His peace, when He was looked for, He scorned to show forth His miracles, and keeping Himself to Himself in secret, those whom He found looking for outward things He left in their ingratitude without, rather choosing to be openly despised by those who were led by pride, than to be commended with empty voice by those that did not believe. And hence this 'Lamp' is straightway 'despised,' according to what is there added, *And Herod with his men of war set Him at nought, and mocked Him, and arrayed Him in a gorgeous robe*. [Luke 23, 11]

54. Yet the 'despised lamp,' which is subject to scoffings on earth, flashes judgment from heaven. Hence it is justly added here, *prepared for an appointed season*. Concerning which same season He says by the Psalmist, *When I shall receive the time, I will judge uprightly*. [Ps. 75, 2] Hence in the Gospel 'Truth' declareth, saying, *My time is not yet come*. [John 7, 6] Hence Peter says, *Whom the heaven must re-*

ceive until the times of the restitution of all things. [Acts 3, 21] Therefore the 'Lamp' which is now 'despised' is 'prepared' for its coming 'at the appointed season.' For He by Himself judgeth sin on the last Day, Who now bears with the scoffs of sinners, and then He brings out severity the more rigorously, the more mildly He now spreads low His patience in calling sinners. For he that awaits long while for some to be converted, if they be not converted, torments them without revoke. Which same truth he conveys by the Prophet in few words, saying, *I have long time holden my peace, I have been still and refrained myself; now will I cry like a travailing woman*. [Is. 42, 14] For as we have already before said, a woman in travail with pain gives forth that which she bore for long in her inner parts, He then that for long time held his peace, 'crieth like a travailing woman,' in that the Judge that shall come, who for long bore with the deeds of men without taking vengeance, sooner or later brings to light with hotness of examination, as if with pain of mind, the sentence of direful visiting which He kept within. Therefore let none despise this Lamp, when it is out of sight, lest He burn up His despisers when He shineth from heaven. For to whomsoever He does not now burn to give pardon, He shall then assuredly burn to award punishment. Therefore because by grace from above we are vouchsafed the season of our calling, whilst there is still the room left, let us by altering our ways for the better flee from the wrath of Him, Who is every where present. For him alone that visitation fails to find, whom correction keeps in hiding.

55. Let it suffice for us by the Lord's bounty to have now run through these particulars in two volumes [*corporibus*]. For because we cannot embrace in a brief exposition the following parts of the sacred book, drawn out in the stream of mysteries, we must of necessity reserve them for other sheets, that the reader may return the more ardent to the task of reading, in proportion as he has breathing given him by the interruption of what is read.

THE SECOND PART.

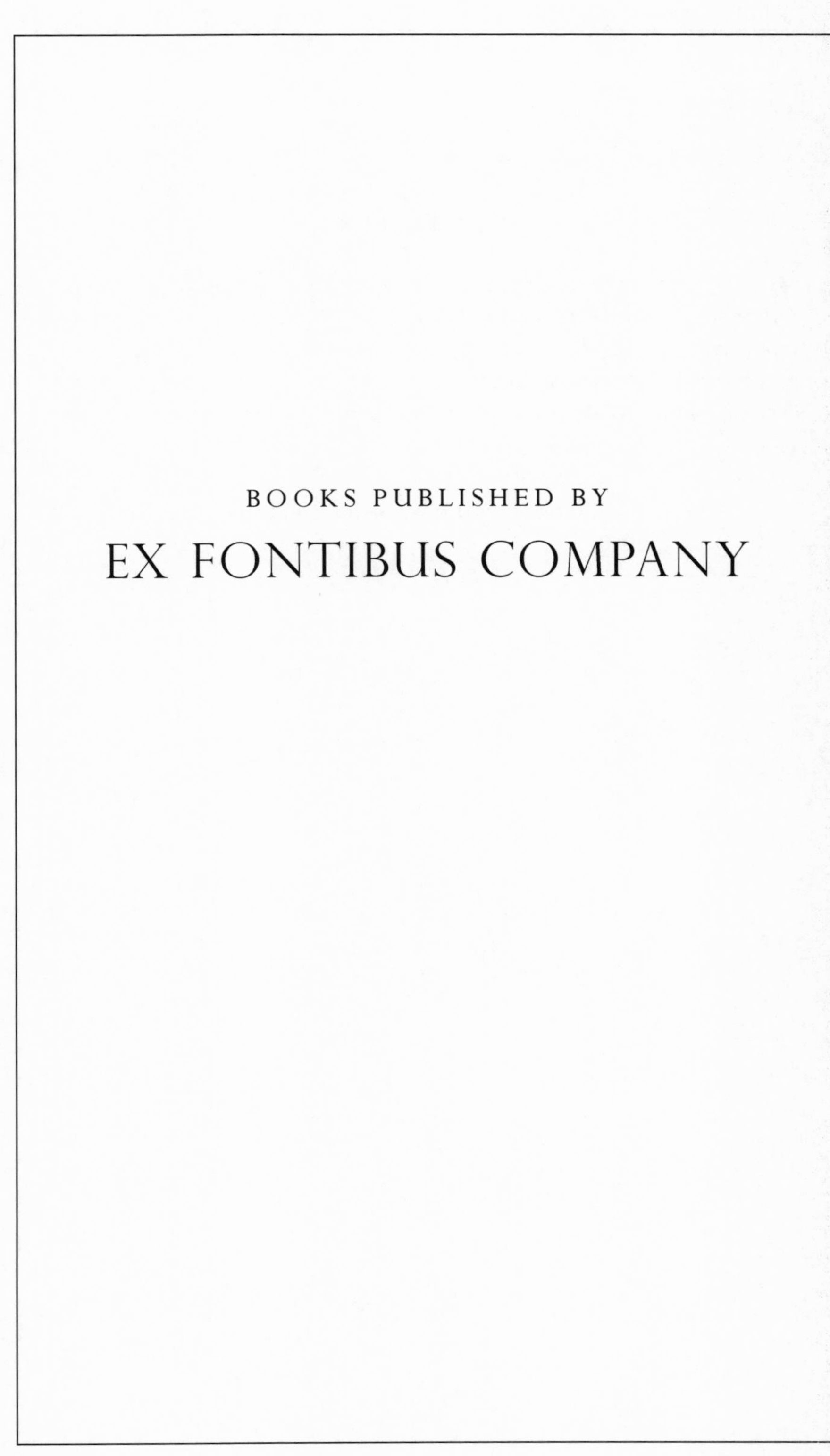

BOOKS PUBLISHED BY

EX FONTIBUS COMPANY

CONTENTS

CATALOGUE LISTING AS OF JULY 19, 2015

BOOKS PUBLISHED BY

EX FONTIBUS COMPANY

http://www.exfontibus.com
contact@exfontibus.com
http://www.facebook.com/exfont
exfontibuscompany@gmail.com

Our books are sold on our own website, at Amazon.com, & through other retailers

Get the latest news on our page!

SACRED TEXTS—SCRIPTURE, LITURGICAL TEXTS, AND PRAYER

Biblia Sacra—The Holy Bible in Latin and English [3 vols.]

A beautiful parallel Latin/English edition of the Bible of the medieval Catholic Church, using the Latin of the Clementine Vulgate and the English of Douay-Rheims Challoner Revision. **Vol. 1** includes the Pentateuch (Genesis, Exodus, Leviticus, Numbers, Deuteronomy) and the Historical Books (Joshua, Judges, Ruth, Samuel/Kings, Paralipomenon/Chronicles, Ezra/Nehemiah, Tobit, Judith, Esther). **Vol. 2** contains Job, Psalms, Proverbs, Ecclesiastes, the Song of Songs, Wisdom, Ecclesiasticus (Ben-Sirah), Isaiah, Jeremiah, Lamentations, Baruch, Ezechiel, Daniel, Hosea, Joel, Amos, Obadiah, Jonah, Micah, Nahum, Habakkuk, Zephaniah, Haggai, Zechariah, Malachi, Machabees. **Vol. 3** contains the entirety of the New Testament.

The New Testament and Psalms in Latin and English

An elegant smaller volume containing only the New Testament and the Psalms.

Kyriale Romanum

Gregorian chant has long transmitted the mystery and majesty of the Catholic liturgical tradition. Newly republished, the Kyriale Romanum of 1961, preserves between its covers an invaluable patrimony of ancient and medieval chants for the Ordinary of the Mass that can be used with both the extraordinary (1962) and the ordinary (post-1970) forms of the Roman Missal. It collects from the Graduale the most frequently-used chant settings throughout the liturgical year, with eighteen mass settings, six credos, and numerous settings for feasts and holy days, including the solemn procession on the feast of Corpus Christi. This beautiful and affordably-priced volume is of great value to all who wish to encounter this venerable musical tradition of the Roman Rite.

The Prayerbook of Ælfwine of Hyde

Decades before the Norman conquest of England in A.D. 1066, a Benedictine monk at Hyde Abbey named assembled a small prayer book from the tradition of early Saxon Christianity. That monk, who later became Abbot of Hyde, passed to his heavenly reward but fifteen years before the influx of Norman culture from France would reshape the prayer and liturgical tradition of English Christianity. The prayers that are preserved in his book bear witness to the zeal and vigor of early English Christianity, with a poetry that stirs the soul over ten centuries since first they were prayed.

THEOLOGY—PATRISTIC AND MEDIEVAL*

ST. IRENÆUS OF LYONS

Against Heresies and Other Writings

The complete text of *Against the Heresies*, with fragments of other writings. Available nowhere else as a standalone volume. Bishop St. Irenaeus of Lyons wrote his *Against Heresies* ca. A.D. 180 to preserve the Christian rule of faith against the Gnostic heresy. To vindicate the Incarnation against the Gnostics, he described and attacked their principal doctrine: the evil origin of the natural world. Affirming the unity of Old and New Testaments, the goodness of the Creator and the created world, and finally the mystery of divinization whereby human beings are elevated into the divine life, the saint produced an outstanding example of early Christian biblical theology. For the early Fathers, doctrines were taught to safeguard the confession of God's saving love revealed through His Incarnation as Jesus Christ. Of such work there is no better example than Irenaeus, disciple of Polycarp, disciple of John the Evangelist.

ORIGEN OF ALEXANDRIA

Against Celsus (Contra Celsum)

This is Origen's great apologetical work, undertaken in answer to the attack on Christianity by the pagan philosopher Celsus. The text that Origen composed to

* Chronological listing.

refute Celsus's self-styled Λόγος ἀληθής (*True Discourse*) consists of eight books, and belongs to the latest years of his life. It has always been regarded as the great apologetic work of antiquity; and no one can peruse it without being struck by the multifarious reading, wonderful acuteness, and rare subtlety of mind that it displays. It is a great work that well deserves the notice of the students of Apologetics and of Early Christianity in general.

ST. AMBROSE OF MILAN

Theological and Dogmatic Works (Fathers of the Church vol. 44)

These works present the thought of St. Ambrose, the bishop whose preaching first renewed St. Augustine's interest in Christianity. Included in this volume are several of Ambrose's works on the chief doctrines of the faith: "The Mysteries," "The Holy Spirit," "The Sacrament of the Incarnation of Our Lord," and "The Sacraments," including his famous teaching on the transformation of bread and wine into the Body and Blood of Christ.

ST. BASIL OF CÆSAREA

Ascetical Works (Fathers of the Church vol. 9)

Saint Basil the Great writes concerning the spiritual life, the discipline of the passions by which the soul rises to union with God.

ST. JOHN CASSIAN

On the Incarnation of the Lord, Against Nestorius

Near the end of his writing career, Cassian the monk was commissioned by an archdeacon—the future Pope Leo the Great—to write a reply to the Christological positions of Nestorius, who saw in Christ two subjects, that of the Word and that of the man Jesus. Cassian's foray into ecclesiastical controversy, a cannonade of arguments from the Scriptures and the early Fathers, offers a blusteringly-effective representation of the general Christological views of East and West. Unsurprisingly, for one such as Cassian who was so concerned with the heights of Christian sanctity, it places special emphasis on the distinction between Christ's divinity and the indwelling of the Word in the saints—for the full divinity of Christ is what indeed makes it possible for *Christ* to be said to dwell within those saints who tread the heights of union with God. What he lacks in the precision of an Athanasius or a Maximus the Confessor, Cassian more than makes up for in the passion of his argumentation.

ST. GREGORY THE GREAT

Dialogues [Forthcoming]

In the series of dialogues that he patiently holds with his deacon Peter, St. Gregory describes a vision of sacred stability in an unstable world; this stability is to be found in the saint's life, lived in the love of Christ and anchored in the power of God. Through tales of miracles and examples of charity, including a famous dialogue on heaven, hell, purgatory, and the power of the Mass, Gregory illustrates the guiding hand of providence in the life of the saint and in the divine power manifest in that saint's deeds and words. Through these stories he aims to teach his readers to offer themselves on the "altar of the heart" as a living sacrifice of love in union with the sacrifice of Christ on the Cross.

Moralia in Job (Morals on the Book of Job) [3 vols.]

Pope Gregory the Great (r. 590–604) wrote his *Moralia*, or moral homilies on Job, one of his greatest works, before his accession to the See of Peter. Seeking a life of contemplation, Gregory had retired to a house on Rome's Caelian Hill, forming the monastic community of St. Andrew's. Shortly thereafter, however, he was sent obediently but unhappily to Constantinople as papal nuncio (*apocrisarius*) at the court of the Byzantine emperor. There too he gathered a small community to whom he delivered his famed homilies on Job. For Gregory, Job is a figure of Christ, who suffered innocently—not for his sins but for the increase of his merits and the salvation of others by love. These homilies span Christian doctrine, from Creation to final Judgment, from the height of angelic hierarchies to the innermost depths of the human soul. Confident that the Holy Spirit has not idly chosen the words of Scripture, Gregory finds a depth of allegory out of which he draws a brilliant picture of Christ, whose humanity must mark our own and whose Cross is our path to eternal rest. A beautiful meditation on suffering, on the path from fear to love, and on the healing and glorification of the individual soul which, as a member of Christ's body, comes to participate in the life of the holy Trinity. When Gregory was elected bishop of Rome just a few years later, he would continue to draw on and to develop the teaching herein, to guide the spiritual lives of his flock amidst the terror-filled final dissolution of the Western Empire. The teaching of the *Moralia* became a source for the doctors of the middle ages, including Hugh of St. Victor, St. Thomas Aquinas, St. Bonaventure, and many others. Western Christianity today owes an incalculable debt to the homilies that Gregory preached to his small circle of ascetics so many years ago.

ST. JOHN OF DAMASCUS

Writings

St. John Damascene, among the greatest of the Eastern fathers during the patristic age, produced his work *The Fount of Knowledge* as a summary of Christian philosophy and theology. It is one of the most important works of the Greek patristic age. Included are "The Philosophical Chapters," "On Heresies," and the justly-famous "Exact Exposition of the Orthodox Faith"—a veritable *Summa* of the doctrine of the Eastern fathers. Now available in an attractive and affordable edition.

ST. CATHERINE OF GENOA

The Treatise on Purgatory

St. Catherine of Genoa's treatise gives her teaching on the repentant soul's purification by the fire of God's divine love. A beautiful meditation on both the love of God and Christian perseverance.

THEOLOGY—MODERN*

JEAN DANIÉLOU, S.J.

From Shadows to Reality: Studies in the Biblical Typology of the Fathers

From the first centuries of its existence, the Church has interpreted the historical events recounted in the Old Testament as being "types" or "figures" of the events of the New Testament and of the sacraments instituted by Jesus Christ. Jean Cardinal Daniélou, one of the foremost Catholic scholars of the twentieth century, and a theologian especially concerned with the relationship between history and the Christian revelation, examines in this book the typological interpretation of the Fathers of the Church and their contemporaries during the first three centuries of the Christian era. Among examples he discusses are the crossing of the Jordan by the Israelites as a type of baptism, Rahab as a type of the Church, and the fall of Jericho as a figure of the end of the world. The complex interpretations of Adam, the flood, and the sacrifice and marriage of Isaac are also described in full and commented on. The work is divided into five books entitled "Adam in Paradise," "Noah and the Flood," "The Sacrifice of Isaac," "Moses and the Exodus," and "The Cycle of Joshua". Each book is divided into chapters discussing the various types and the interpretations of Irenaeus, Clement, Gregory of Nyssa and their contemporaries, including Philo.

---

* Alphabetical listing.

RÉGINALD GARRIGOU-LAGRANGE

Reality: A Synthesis of Thomistic Thought

Dominican Réginald Garrigou-Lagrange was one of the most prominent thomistic neoscholastic theologians of the early and mid-twentieth century. This volume is his attempt to summarize a philosophical and theological worldview of thomism: Interpreting the teaching of St. Thomas Aquinas and his successors, reality is seen in light of the central doctrines of the Trinity, of Creation, and of the Incarnation of the Son as Jesus Christ, in Whom humankind is drawn into the intimacy of the inner life of the Triune God. Fr. Garrigou-Lagrange argues on behalf of 24 thomistic theses, which he presents as a lens through which to view salvation, the Sacraments, the Mother of the Redeemer, and the spiritual life whereby the divine image is restored in the soul. This work, which has been out of print for decades, is of interest to any who wish to enhance their understanding of the recent Catholic theological tradition through an acquaintance with this major and often controversial figure.

The One God: A Commentary on the First Part of St. Thomas' Theological Summa

Taking up a commentary on the first part of the *Summa*, Father Garrigou-Lagrange discusses not only the attributes of the one God who revealed Himself to Moses, but treats also of the very basis for this discussion in the first place—the nature of *sacra doctrina* ("holy teaching" or "sacred doctrine") and the pursuit of theology as a "science" (a body of knowledge) that has God Himself for its object and ultimate goal. To comment, therefore, on the first part of the *Summa* is to comment not only on God but also on the theological pursuit to which St. Thomas gave himself—a pursuit that has as its goal the beatific vision of God. In discussing the place of St. Thomas amidst patristic, medieval, and modern theologians, Garrigou-Lagrange argues in behalf both of the sanctifying end of theology and the synthetic genius of St. Thomas who, he says, summed up the preceding tradition and left a deposit of reflection on God that can scarcely be surpassed.

The Trinity and God the Creator: A Commentary on St. Thomas' Theological Summa, I^a, qq. 27-119

Father Garrigou-Lagrange here reflects on the triune God who created the heavens and the earth, and who is the object of that contemplative vision of God to which all human beings are called and which is their ultimate sanctification. In his characteristically-ordered style, Garrigou-Lagrange offers his interpretation of St. Thomas by expounding, explaining, and comparing the teaching of the angelic doctor to that of preceding and subsequent theologians. In particular, Garrigou-Lagrange depicts St. Thomas as fulfilling the foundation laid by St. Augustine: the persons must be treated in distinction but not in separation, for it is only in their mutual relations that they can be known as persons. He also lays special emphasis on the call of all humans to contemplative holiness. The exposition of the Trinity is a beginning of the journey of contemplation by which a man or woman enters the life of God to be reformed according to the likeness of the Trinity in whose image he or she was first created, body and soul.

Beatitude: A Commentary on St. Thomas' Theological Summa, I^a II^æ, qq. 1-54

The central theme of *Beatitude* is the human journey back to God, our Creator. For moral theology is a discipline concerned not merely with the avoidance of sin but also with the cultivation of virtue, with growth in likeness to God. The book has two major parts: First, it considers humankind's ultimate goal: to possess God and to share in His life; secondly, the means by which humans can reach this destination. These means are human acts, those over which a human being has deliberate control. Therefore, this volume covers St. Thomas's treatises on the End of Man, Human Acts, the Passions, and Habit. Or, you may consider it a short commentary on how to live in God's life in this life so as to inherit the vision of him forever in the next. For moral theology is not cold and empty speculation, but a systematic description of what it means to imitate God. There was a time when many moral textbooks leaned heavily on casuistry and laid no systematic doctrinal foundation for their moral discussions and solutions. Such is not the case in this volume. Human acts are the road to humankind's supernatural goal. Any discipline of inquiry must proceed from principles, from causes. As a consequence, moral theology must not be divorced from the study of the passions, habits, grace, virtue, and the gifts of the Holy Spirit. As an introduction for the interested reader, "Beatitude" raises Thomistic moral theology to a new life.

Grace: A Commentary on the Summa theologica of St. Thomas, I^a II^æ, qq. 109–114

Father Garrigou-Lagrange synthesizes and develops the teaching of St. Thomas on the deifying life of grace by a creative engagement with the Carmelite theology of St. John of the Cross. He distinguishes the various modes and movements of grace in the spiritual life from conversion to entrance into glory.

Christ the Savior: A Commentary on the Third Part of St. Thomas' Theological Summa

Father Garrigou-Lagrange engages the teaching of St. Thomas on the divine Incarnation by which was wrought the salvation of humankind. Hence he treats the motive of the Incarnation, the hypostatic union, and its effects. He discusses at length such difficult problems as the reconciliation of freedom with absolute impeccability in Christ, the intrinsically infinite value of His merits and satisfaction, His predestination with reference to ours, inasmuch as He is the first of the predestined, and the reconciliation, during the Passion, of the presence of extreme sorrow with supreme happiness experienced by our Lord in the summit of His soul. With reference to the Passion, everything is reduced to the principle of the plenitude of grace. This plenitude, on the one hand, was the cause in the summit of our Lord's soul of the beatific vision and, on the other hand, it was the cause of His most ardent love as priest and victim, so that He willed to be overwhelmed with grief, and die on the cross a most perfect holocaust. In all, Father Garrigou-Lagrange would manifest the unity of Christ inasmuch as He is one personal Being, although He has two really distinct and infinitely different natures. Hence the Person of Christ constitutes the one and only principle of all His theandric operations. At the end of the book is given a compendium on Mariology.

The Love of God and the Cross of Jesus (2 vols.)

Here, Father Garrigou-Lagrange describes the Christian interior life in light of the love of God and the mystery of the Cross. Guided by St. Thomas and of St. John of the Cross, he expounds what lies deepest in the interior life of the Lord Jesus Christ and what consequently must be appropriated most deeply in the life of every Christian who would imitate Him. For it is only by the royal road of the Cross that the Christian soul truly enters into supernatural contemplation of the mysteries of faith and lives lovingly and deeply by them.

JOHN HENRY NEWMAN

Callista: A Tale of the Third Century

Callista, a young and beautiful Greek girl, has just arrived with her brother in North African Carthage. Though she is a gifted young woman, she is unhappy with her life. Wooed by a troubled and lovesick young man named Agellius, Callista is drawn into his own struggle between a newfound Christian faith and the traditional pagan beliefs of his mother, a witch. After a terrible plague of locusts, a popular rage breaks out into persecution against the Christians and both Agellius and Callista must face for themselves the question of what indeed is the truth.

Written by Newman after his reception into the Catholic Church, this novel of the early Church is surely a bright light in a flourishing nineteenth century genre that produced few classics and many mediocrities. Indeed, Charles Kingsley, whose later attacks prompted Newman's own *Apologia Pro Vita Sua*, had essayed an earlier effort at early Church fiction with the novel *Hypatia*. To Kingley's dismay, Newman's *Callista* had been received as the better work. *Callista* is rich in prose and vivid in its imagining of Christian life in the early Church. [ISBN 1470133229]

Oxford University Sermons

Newman's fifteen sermons on faith and reason, sanctity, and the development of doctrine; preached before the University of Oxford between A.D. 1826 and 1843 by John Henry Newman. [ISBN 1453781463]

EDWARD DENNIS O'CONNOR, C.S.C.

The Dogma of the Immaculate Conception [Forthcoming]

A history of the dogma of the immaculate conception, given in a series of scholarly papers published half a century after the dogma's promulgation. Long out of print but useful to the novice and the specialist alike, this volume takes the long view of Church history and tradition, showing a doctrine's development in action.

MATTHIAS SCHEEBEN

Mariology (complete in one volume)

Writing in the nineteenth century, Matthias Scheeben forged a new creative synthesis of the teaching of the Fathers and of the scholastics. Scheeben's work had a decisive influence on later Catholic theologians such as Hans Urs von Balthasar. His primary theme is the nuptial union of God and the created order through the Incarnation, a marriage of heaven and earth that begins in the conception of Christ in the womb of the virgin Mary. Mary, therefore, is the temple in which God and humankind are reconciled. This and all that flows from it and preceded it by way of preparation is the subject-matter of his work Mariology. He draws together the teaching on the Incarnation, on deification, on the Marian dogmas, sacramental theology, and ecclesiology in a truly beautiful work. Originally published in two volumes, the entire work is gathered here in a single volume for the first time. It has been out of print for decades, now made available once more.

DOM JOHN CHAPMAN

Studies on the Early Papacy

Dom John Chapman, fourth abbot of Downside Abbey a renowned scholar of the early Church. Taking up the question of the papacy in the first centuries of Christianity, he eschews selective apologetics in favor of a reasoned study of textual sources in the context of historical events. By these he illustrates the position of the bishop of Rome in the early Church through the prominent and authoritative role taken by or expected of him at pivotal moments of early Christian history. So doing, this volume offers much substance to those who wish to understand better the question of papal prerogatives. Chapman argues in favor of the Catholic claims based on his reading of the history, but does so with such care as a historian that his work has received high approval even from such an eminence as the famed Anglican historian Henry Chadwick who, in his own book on the history of the early Church, saw fit to recommend Chapman's work to readers interested in the question. There have been many successors to Chapman but few, if any, have engaged precisely with the matters that he discusses with such detail and clarity. His book, therefore, remains an important voice in the modern conversation.

S. HERBERT SCOTT

The Eastern Churches and the Papacy [Forthcoming]

A detailed and critical survey of a complex subject, authored for a Research Doctorate degree at the University of Oxford in the 1920s. Asking the question of Rome's claimed primacy and of the degree to which such claims may have been acknowledged by Eastern churches, the author often reaches conclusions favorable to a claimed primacy of early, even of the very earliest, date. "I believe," he writes, "that the evidence of the second and first centuries, such as it is, will be found identical in character—Rome will be seen claiming authority, and expecting or demanding obedience—and for the same reasons; that the bishop is the successor of St. Peter, the chief of the apostles, the leader appointed by Christ." This thesis, invoking as it does the witness of the Eastern churches, raises questions sometimes not entertained in our day and, while more recent research has added to the information at our disposal, still usefully and pointedly brings the reader's focus rather to matters that the more irenic ecumenism of the present day sometimes glosses over. The book is published with a bibliography and an index.

EMILY HICKEY

Our Catholic Heritage in English Literature of the First Millennium

(Originally entitled *Our Catholic Heritage in Pre-Conquest English Literature*). Ms. Hickey's reflections sweep us into a magical world of ancient epic, poetry, and allegory--by the verses of Cædmon and Bede; in stories of the Phoenix, the Cross, and King Alfred; in old runes and lost loves--in all of which one again and again discovers that Christ has been the narrative's subject all along. She writes: "This little book makes no claim to be a history of pre-Conquest British Literature. It is an attempt to increase Catholics' interest in this part of the 'inheritance of their fathers.' It is not a formal course, but a sort of talk, as it were, about beautiful things said and sung in old days: things which to have learned to love is to have incurred a great and living debt. I have tried to clothe them in the nearest approach I could find to their original speech, with the humblest acknowledgement that nothing matches that speech itself. If this little book in any way fulfils the wishes of those who have asked me for some thoughts on English Literature, I shall be glad indeed."

LITERATURE—GREAT BOOKS AND THE "GOOD BOOKS"

Ex Fontibus Company is proud to present reprints of some difficult-to-find literary texts, such as Alexander Pope's translation of the *Iliad* and the *Odyssey*. However, our offerings are not limited to only the great books. We have also chosen to reprint some that are merely "good" books—yet not for that unworthy of our attention. Indeed, in his book *The Death of Christian Culture*, Dr. John Senior (1923–1999), founder of the once famed Integrated Humanities Program at the University of Kansas, offered a list of 1,0000 "good books" that prepare one to read the "great books." Among the "good" he includes such volumes as the Tarzan novels by Edgar Rice Burroughs:

> Taking all that was best in the Greco-Roman world into itself, Western tradition has given us the thousand good books as preparation for the great ones. . . . For us today, the [useful] cutoff point is World War I, before which cars and the electric light had not yet come to dominate our lives and the experience of nature had not been distorted by speed and the destruction of shadows....[These books are] part of the ordinary cultural matter essential for an English-speaking person to grow in.

Ex Fontibus offers the following—both good books and great—as points of entry into that heritage.

ROBERT HUGH BENSON

Lord of the World

> Interesting it must be to all to whom the deepest convictions of a man's heart are of moment. And in the artistic balance and taste of Father Benson's literary power every reader will find delight.
>
> —*The New York Times*

> Mr. Benson sees the world, . . . generations hence, free at last from all minor quarrels, and ranged against itself in two camps, Humanitarianism for those who believe in no divinity but that of man, Catholicism for those who believe in no divinity but that of God.
>
> —*The London Times*

> "The book as art is beautiful, delicately balanced, deeply inspired, intelligently executed.
>
> —*Putnam's*

One of Pope Francis's favorite novels, Benson's 1907 apocalyptic tale of the Antichrist is one of the first modern dystopias. Humanism has eliminated world conflict but practices a subtle barbarism upon the human mind. Religion is either suppressed or ignored. The Catholic Church, confined to ghettos, occupies an increasingly perilous position in the public square. The populace turns toward euthanasia as the solution to bodily pain and spiritual crisis. Meanwhile, a mysterious figure of apparent hope, Julian Felsenburgh, rises to become the head of a single world government. The plot follows a priest, Father Percy Franklin, who finds himself caught up in the final and increasingly open struggle between Antichrist and Christ. *Completely re-typeset with Latin phrases translated in footnotes.* [ISBN 978-1507790502]

ROBERT HUGH BENSON

The Dawn of All

Benson's alternative to *Lord of the World*, this later novel vividly imagines the final peace of the world in the triumph of Christianity and the re-establishment of the Church at the center of daily life. A mysterious priest who cannot remember his own name, nor even anything of the past, must make his way as a Monsignor in a world undergoing a dramatic transformation in preparation for the return of Christ. The world itself becomes an image of the priest's soul. Benson himself writes: "In a former book, called *Lord of the World*, I attempted to sketch the kind of developments a hundred years hence which, I thought, might reasonably be expected if the present lines of what is called "modern thought" were only prolonged far enough; and I was informed repeatedly that the effect of the book was exceedingly depressing and discouraging to optimistic Christians. In the present book I am attempting — also in parable form — not in the least to withdraw anything that I said in the former, but to follow up the other lines instead, and to sketch — again in parable — the kind of developments about sixty years hence which, I think, may reasonably be expected should the opposite process begin, and ancient thought (which has stood the test of centuries, and is, in a very remarkable manner, being "rediscovered" by persons even more modern than modernists) be prolonged instead." As always, the story is rendered with suitable dramatic tension and—as is characteristic of Benson—a spiritual conflict of individual souls that matches the large-scale conflicts in the wider world. *Completely re-typeset with Latin phrases translated in footnotes.* [ISBN 978-1515075172]

CHARLOTTE BRONTË

Jane Eyre

Jane Eyre (originally *Jane Eyre: An Autobiography*) was published in 1847 under the pen name "Currer Bell." The novel follows the emotions and experiences of its title character, including her growth to adulthood and her love for Mr. Rochester, the byronic master of fictitious Thornfield Hall. In its internalization of the action — the focus is on the gradual unfolding of Jane's moral and spiritual sensibility and all the events are colored by a heightened intensity that was previously the domain of poetry — Jane Eyre revolutionized the art of fiction. Charlotte Brontë has been called the 'first historian of the private consciousness' and the literary ancestor of writers like Joyce and Proust. The novel both reflects and heralds the literary movements of its day, containing elements of social criticism, with a strong sense of morality at its core, an individualistic protagonist, and explorations of class, romantic attraction, religion, and the social position of women.

EDGAR RICE BURROUGHS

The Tarzan Novels, Vol. 1 (Books 1–6)

The Tarzan novels initiate the young person or the adult into the thrilling and sometimes terrifying world of nature, a world that (we might add) religious formation ought not abstract us from, but immerse us in with eyes that see something of the eternal Beauty reflected even in the fallen temporal. Welcome to the "primeval forest." This omnibus collection presents the first six complete novels of the thrilling adventures of Tarzan of the Apes. Son of an English Lord, raised by the savage apes that killed his father, found again by a civilization that he would never quite come to call his own, he was at home in the primeval forest in which he was reared. Swinging through the treetops, bane of lions, tamer of elephants, terror of cannibals, finder of lost cities, and beloved of the American woman Jane Porter, this knight of the forest, never trained in chivalry, was known to the outside world as John Clayton, Lord Greystoke—but to himself and the denizens of the jungle in which he grew up, he would be forever Tarzan, King of the Apes. Included in this volume: *Tarzan of the Apes*; *The Return of Tarzan*; *The Son of Tarzan*; *The Beasts of Tarzan*; *Tarzan and the Jewels of Opar*; *Jungle Tales of Tarzan*. A new introduction gives the history of Burroughs' novels and addresses certain points that later writers have rightfully questioned. [ISBN 9781512370720]

The Tarzan Novels, Vol. 2 (Books 7–9)

This omnibus collection, second in a series, presents the seventh, eight, and ninth novels of Edgar Rice Burroughs' enthralling Tarzan of the Apes. In *Tarzan the Untamed*, World War I disrupts the peaceful life of Tarzan with his wife Jane on their East African estate. Taking up once more the way of the savage ape-man, Tarzan vows vengeance against the German soldiers that he believes to have murdered his wife. His adventures take him through and across a deadly desert, fighting enemies all the way. In *Tarzan the Terrible*, Tarzan finds himself in the mysterious country of Paul-ul-don, an evolutionary island in the African jungle interior. Here dinosaur descendants and intelligent tailed ape-men live amidst fabulous lost cities. In *Tarzan and the Golden Lion*, our hero rebuilds his life in Africa, only to be abducted and held prisoner in the lost city of Opar, whose priestess would have him as her mate. Trekking through the legendary Valley of Diamonds, Tarzan finds himself followed by a mysterious man—who is Tarzan's own double! From his stirring descriptions of the jungle itself to his adept conjuring of scenes of action and mystery, Burroughs does not fail to deliver the thrilling narratives that have made Tarzan so very famous. [ISBN 9781514120699]

JAMES FENIMORE COOPER

The Complete Leatherstocking Tales (2 volumes)

Cooper's epic historical romances of frontier and Indian life in the early American days created a unique form of American literature. In two volumes five novels are collected, following the order of the stories' internal chronology (rather than historical publication order).

Volume I—*The Deerslayer*; *The Last of the Mohicans*.

Volume II—*The Pathfinder*; *The Pioneers*; *The Prairie*.

HOMER

The Iliad, translated by Alexander Pope

> The thing that best distinguishes this from all other translations of Homer is that it alone equals the original in its ceaseless pour of verbal music. . . . Pope worked miracles in highlighting the play of vowels through his lines. . . . Every word is weighted, with a pressure of mind behind it. This is a poem you can live your way into, over the years, since it yields more at every encounter.
>
> —"On Reading Pope's Homer," *The NewYork Times*, 6/1/1997

> Many consider [this translation] the greatest English Iliad, and one of the greatest translations of any work into English. It manages to convey not only the stateliness and grandeur of Homer's lines, but their speed and wit and vividness.
>
> —Daniel Mendelsohn, "Englishing the Iliad: Grading Four Rival Translations," *The New Yorker* Blog, 11/1/2011

> For Homer to take his place among our classics it must be the case that a rendering could exercise the same spell over the collective ear as English-language poets. You could not memorize Fagles, or Lattimore—or Hobbes, a few phrases apart—while Pope, even at his least Homeric, is memorable. . . . Pope is not superseded.
>
> —David Ricks, Kings College, London, *Classics Ireland*, vol. 4, 1997

When Alexander Pope's majestic translation of Homer's Iliad appeared between 1715 and 1720, it was acclaimed by Samuel Johnson as "a performance which no age or nation could hope to equal." Pope himself was only 25 years old. While other translations have since claimed distinction in this or that respect, Pope's translation remains unrivaled in its melodious beauty. This is the Iliad that has formed generations of British and American culture through a beauteous poetics that lends itself to easy recollection. With a clean and crisp text illustrated by the inimitable line drawings of Flaxman, this edition finally gives to audiences a fitting rendering of this monument of English verse which captures uniquely the song of Homer himself.

The Odyssey, translated by Alexander Pope

The tale of Odysseus's return from the war at Troy, seeking Ithaca his home and Penelope his wife. Along the way he encounters the murderous Cyclops, the treacherous Circe, and the nymphs, gods, and goddesses who variously assist and impede his homeward journey. Many are his travails and dramatic his final homecoming wherein he joins battle with Penelope's erstwhile suitors. As with the Iliad, Pope, who had two collaborators on this project, renders Homer into a muscular and euphonious English poetry worthy of reading aloud. This volume is likewise illustrated by Flaxman.

Printed in Great Britain
by Amazon.co.uk, Ltd.,
Marston Gate.